Grace, Faith, and Holiness

GRACE, FAITH, AND HOLINESS

A Wesleyan Systematic Theology

by

H. Ray Dunning

Beacon Hill Press of Kansas City
Kansas City, Missouri

Abbreviations used in this work:
CT—Christian Theology
StS—Standard Sermons

10 9 8 7 6 5 4 3 2 1

Contents

Foreword   6

Preface   9

Acknowledgments   18

A Note to the Reader   20

PART I **Prolegomena**   21
- 1 The Nature and Scope of Theology   23
- 2 Sources of Theology: The Bible   55
- 3 Sources of Theology: Tradition, Reason, and Experience   77

PART II **Our Knowledge of God**   95
- 4 Revelation: Its Meaning and Necessity   97
- 5 Revelation: A Wesleyan Approach   140

PART III **The Doctrines of God the Sovereign**   181
- 6 The Nature and Attributes of God   183
- 7 The Trinity   208
- 8 God the Creator   234

PART IV **The Doctrines of God the Savior**   273
- 9 Man the Sinner   275
- 10 The Person of the Savior   302
- 11 The Work of the Savior   332
- 12 A Wesleyan View of the Atonement   362

PART V **The Doctrines of God the Spirit**   395
- 13 The Christian Experience of the Holy Spirit   397
- 14 The Work of the Holy Spirit   429
- 15 Sanctification: Renewal in the Image of God   478
- 16 The Communion of Saints   505
- 17 The Means of Grace   539

Appendix 1—Speculative Eschatology   569

Appendix 2—Hermeneutics   590

Bibliography (Works Cited)   629

Indexes   649

Foreword

Critics sometimes taunt that "the Church is on its last legs." While this is intended as a negative comment, it is an accurate statement of fact. The Church is required in every generation to transmit the gospel with which she is entrusted, the spiritual vitality she has experienced, the transforming grace she has received, the power of worship she has enjoyed, and the theological understanding she has inherited.

The Church, of course, belongs to Christ, and He has promised, "I will build my Church" (Matt. 16:18, Weymouth). He only can bring forgiveness to penitent sinners, new life to those who are dead in trespasses and sin, heart cleansing to those who are fully yielded to His will, and empowering to all who seek to serve in His name. Yet the Church by means of evangelism, stewardship, worship, and instruction can be an instrument for extending the kingdom of God.

Theological understanding and insight are necessary for faithful discipleship and effective service. The faith of the church must be known and continuously articulated in contemporary contexts. This volume seeks to accomplish this aim. For half a century Dr. H. Orton Wiley's monumental three-volume systematic theology, titled *Christian Theology,* has served the church and the broader Wesleyan/Arminian community. It will continue to do so. This current systematic theological expression takes into account more recent developments in Christian thought and biblical knowledge and strengthens the holiness witness.

The data from which the church constructs her theological understanding are the Scriptures properly interpreted. Christian history and experience have enriched and refined the church's formulations under the guidance and direction of the Spirit. The resulting corpus of doctrinal affirmations must be constantly checked by clear biblical teachings.

It is imperative that these theological expressions be stated in the language and thought forms of every new generation if the life of the church is to be nurtured and sustained. While Christian truths remain constant, their mode of presentation varies, and the means for comprehending them must be current in order to be relevant.

This is a major task of any theological work of the church.

With this in mind the Book Committee serving Nazarene Publishing House, with the approval of the Board of General Superintendents, commissioned Dr. H. Ray Dunning to produce a systematic theology in the Wesleyan tradition that is true to the doctrinal standards of the Church of the Nazarene and at the same time is aware of, and dialogues with, contemporary thought theologically, philosophically, psychologically, and culturally.

Dr. Dunning is well prepared for this weighty assignment. He is a longtime Nazarene, a loyal churchman, an elder in the church, a former pastor, a preacher of the Word, an author, and trained in theological studies. A graduate of Nazarene Theological Seminary, he received his Ph.D. degree in religion from Vanderbilt University with a major in theology and minor in philosophy. For over 20 years he has honed his theological skills while teaching in the religion and philosophy division of Trevecca Nazarene College, where he currently serves as professor and head of the Department of Philosophy. The spiritual quality of his life complements his theological expertise.

The Church of the Nazarene is committed to the declaration of the life of holiness and the doctrine and experience of entire sanctification in preaching, teaching, and daily living. To this end this volume has been prayerfully prepared. Oversight has been given to the project by an advisory committee, each member of which is qualified for this assignment by specialized training, years of study and service in the church, as well as Christian commitment.

In a work of this magnitude not every affirmation will solicit full agreement from all readers. But the fundamental declarations of faith are biblically and doctrinally sound and consistent with the Wesleyan tradition. Dr. Phineas F. Bresee's words serve us well at this point: "In essentials unity, in nonessentials liberty, and in all things charity."

It is with great joy that we commend *Grace, Faith, and Holiness* to informed readers, with prayers that it will bring praise to Him who has freely given His Son for our salvation and has sent forth His Spirit to lead us into all truth.

BOARD OF GENERAL SUPERINTENDENTS

Eugene L. Stowe
Charles H. Strickland
William M. Greathouse
Jerald D. Johnson
John A. Knight
Raymond W. Hurn

Preface

Theology is the attempt to provide a rational formulation of our Christian beliefs. Unfortunately, many sincere Christians feel that it is a luxury that we can easily do without. However, far from being a luxury, theology is an unavoidable task from which no one, clergy or lay, is exempt. As soon as one moves beyond reciting the words of Scripture, he is involved in doing theology. Actually, the choice of a translation of the Bible is a reflection of some theologizing, since any translation involves an interpretation. No language can be literally rendered into another. The selection of which passage to read or the order in which the texts are read all reflect a minimal amount of theological judgment. It is never a question of theology or no theology, but rather a question of good theology or poor, adequate or inadequate. Faced with this inevitableness, we are only exercising good sense in putting forth every effort to engage the task responsibly.

Doing theology is as important to the life of the church as it is unavoidable. The church is, we hope, more than an institution. Thus its decisions should be made on the basis of theological understanding rather than on pragmatic grounds or in terms of prevailing secular values. The pronouncements of the church through its ministry should be as theologically sound as possible. The minister who declares, "This may not be good theology, but I'm going to say it anyway," is betraying the biblical injunction to preach sound doctrine.

Without the guidance of theology, religion can degenerate into a "warm, fuzzy feeling" without definable content or moral implication. The church's business is proclamation, and apart from the constant dialogue between pulpit and lectern, that proclamation can lose its distinctiveness and essential character. Hence the task of theology is to be the business of the whole church, not simply a few scholars who are kept safely insulated from the life of the real world.

One major objection to theology is that it appears to many to

9

be an obfuscation of the simple gospel. To the uninitiated the technical jargon used by theologians merely obscures the message for the average person. The fallacy of this kind of reasoning is illustrated in a story told by R. C. Sproul about a meeting between a theologian and an astronomer. The astronomer said to the theologian: "I don't understand why you theologians fuss so much about predestination and supralapsarianism, about communicable and uncommunicable attributes of God, of imputed and infused grace and the like; to me Christianity is simple; it's the Golden Rule, 'Do unto others as you would have them do unto you.'" The theologian replied, "I think I see what you mean. I get lost in all your talk about exploding novae, expanding universes, theories of entropy, and astronomical perturbations. For me, astronomy is simple: It's 'Twinkle, twinkle, little star.'"[1]

Jack Rogers provides us with an unusually perceptive insight regarding the nature of Scripture and its relation to the untrained searcher for truth. He suggests that there are two levels of material in the Bible. The first level is the central, saving message of the gospel. That level is open to all who can read or will listen to the simple story of God's good creation, man's sinful fall, and Christ's gracious life, death, and resurrection for our salvation. The approach to that simple, central message is through faith. However, around that center there is a supporting material that is more difficult to interpret and subject to varied interpretations. This material needs to be approached with the aid of trained biblical scholars and exegetes.[2]

Conservative Christians often raise serious questions at the point of restating one's theology. An understanding of the nature of theology as spelled out in the first chapter of this work should dispel the misconception that informs this concern. The dynamic character of history, the fluid nature of language, the shifting cultural scene, as well as the development of the philosophical enterprise all make it mandatory that each generation shall attempt to come to terms with the contemporary significance of its faith. As Karl Barth says, "In the science of dogmatics the church draws up its reckoning in accordance with the state of its knowledge at dif-

---

1. "Right Now Counts Forever," in *The Necessity of Systematic Theology*, ed. John Jefferson Davis (Grand Rapids: Baker Book House, 1980), 16-17.
2. *Confessions of a Conservative Evangelical* (Philadelphia: Westminster Press, 1974), 62.

ferent times,"[3] and in recent years a whole theological renaissance has occurred, moving the world into a new theological era. In addition the method herein proposed is considerably different from the way systematic theology has been pursued in the Wesleyan tradition. Efforts identified as this theological genre have usually been in the form of compendia.

For the previous 45 years, the dominant theological work in the denominational context out of which this work emerges was the three-volume *Christian Theology* of H. Orton Wiley. He has been a point of reference for the theologians of the Church of the Nazarene as well as other Wesleyans in a way that no other work will ever be able to match. But he himself implicitly built into the theological program of the church the need for a continued pursuit of truth. He implied this conclusion when, in his preface, he explained why he was 20 years completing his assignment: "I was constantly discovering new truth."[4]

Furthermore he explained that his purpose was "to review the field of theology." But, as noted above, the last 45 years have been filled with vigorous theological activity of which the theologians of the church must take account in a responsible way.

Theology is a dialogue. The Christian faith encompasses many traditions; this effort to comprehend the true faith must proceed with the theologian in dialogue not only with his own tradition but with others as well. The fact is that probably every denomination reflects several different traditions that agree on certain central commitments, but there is usually also diversity at several significant points.[5] To refuse to hear what others have to say is not merely snobbish but obscurantist. And as W. T. Purkiser wrote in an editorial in the *Herald of Holiness,* speaking to this issue, "Obscurantism is not orthodoxy."[6] One may quote from a thinker without necessarily agreeing with all he has to say. In this light, we will be engaging as dialogue partners men like Karl Barth, Reinhold Niebuhr, Paul Tillich, Helmut Thielicke, G. C. Berkouwer, and nu-

---

3. *Dogmatics in Outline,* trans. G. T. Thomson (London: SCM Press, 1960), 11.

4. (Kansas City: Beacon Hill Press, 1940-43), 1:3. Since we shall be in interaction with Wiley's pronouncements throughout the work, we shall note most references in the body of the text abbreviated as *CT* rather than in footnotes.

5. A careful study of Timothy L. Smith, *Called unto Holiness,* vol. 1 (Kansas City: Nazarene Publishing House, 1962), will clearly footnote the distinctive characteristics of various traditions within the Church of the Nazarene.

6. Aug. 12, 1964, 11-12.

merous other more recent representatives of a century that probably had (or has) more competent scholars in the theological sciences than any like period in history. He who is committed to the One who declared, "I am the truth" (John 14:6, NEB), has no reason to keep himself from embracing truth wherever it is found. Only in following this procedure can one avoid becoming theologically ingrown and possibly allowing his theological presuppositions to become prejudices with the resulting loss of viability or credibility.

In a time when so many people in the Wesleyan movement are reading and being influenced by popular religious writings that reflect divergences from some of the basic theological commitments of the holiness movement, there is a desperate need to provide this segment of Christianity with a systematic treatment of its theological perspective. To that end this work is dedicated.

A few words may appropriately be said about the title chosen for this theology. It is Wesleyan by intention and design. Mr. Wesley argued that there were three fundamental doctrines that can be seen as informing the *ordo salutis* that is the focus of all his theological work. These are (1) original sin, (2) justification by faith, and (3) sanctification.[7] The all-pervasiveness of original sin that infects the whole of human existence is countered by the all-pervasiveness of prevenient grace—hence *grace*. The basis of one's relation to God that is the essence of salvation is justification by faith alone and not of works—hence *faith*. And the divinely intentioned outcome of God's saving work is sanctification. Justification is the root of religion and holiness is the fruit, "religion itself"—hence *holiness*. Grace, faith, and holiness encompass the whole scope of the Wesleyan *ordo salutis* and thus the total sweep of Wesleyan theology. It should be seen that all three elements inform this work at every point.

The organization of a systematic theology is a theological question. We have chosen to adopt the traditional Trinitarian structure, not only because it has a long history of acceptability but also because it seems theologically sound—given our understanding of the nature of theology (see chap. 1)—to structure the various doc-

---

7. *Explanatory Notes upon the New Testament* (London: Epworth Press, 1954), on Rom. 12:6; *The Works of John Wesley*, 3rd ed., 14 vols. (London: Wesleyan Methodist Book Room, 1872; reprint, Kansas City: Beacon Hill Press of Kansas City, 1978), 6:509; 7:284, 313; et al.

trines according to the mode of God's self-manifestation to which they are most appropriately related. The placement of particular doctrines is also a matter of theological judgment, and it will doubtless be impossible to please every theologian on every point. We will seek to give ample justification at points thought to be debatable.

A special comment needs to be made regarding two doctrines: eschatology and the doctrine of man. The traditional method of handling the doctrine of last things is to tack it onto the end as little more than an appendix. Developments in both biblical theology and systematics have demonstrated that eschatology is not an addendum to theology but a truth that weaves its way through the warp and woof of the whole system; almost every major doctrine has an eschatological aspect. In responding to this understanding, we will avoid a separate section on biblical (nonspeculative) eschatology and highlight the eschatological dimension throughout the system. This too may involve some decisions that will not satisfy everyone. The holiness movement has traditionally veered away from speculative eschatology, but that is a different matter from the foregoing point. The Articles of Faith of the Church of the Nazarene contain no hint of commitment to speculative ideas regarding the last things. Consonant with this very Wesleyan temperament, we will restrict our discussion of speculative eschatology to an appendix and make no claim for it as having any normative character. It will largely be descriptive but informed by critical (and personal) judgments. The ambiguity of this approach seems theologically and biblically justifiable.

We will deal with the crucial Christian view of man in much the same way as eschatology. If we are doing theology, it is inappropriate to develop an anthropology other than "theological anthropology." But the Christian view of man is an essential component of certain doctrines such as revelation, sin, and salvation. It will be elaborated extensively in connection with these.

A systematic theology, as our discussion of methodology will elaborate, must make use of philosophical models as the vehicle of expression. Since these come and go in the sense that certain models become outmoded when they are replaced by more adequate ones, the responsible systematic theologian must utilize the most adequate contemporary philosophical conceptual tools available to him. In attempting to manifest responsibility in this regard, I have adopted the relational model of ontology in contrast to substantial modes of thought. The latter is a carryover from Aristotle's metaphysics, which distinguished between substance (that which underlies or supports qualities) and accident. Hence the old metaphysics assumed that a substance was a "self-identical and enduring entity that does not itself change but that possesses changing properties, or attributes. It is independent—it is that which stands alone. It is self-subsistent."[8] Thus it was natural, for example, for Descartes to conclude from his self-awareness of thinking that he must be "a thing that thinks." The reason why this mode of thought persists with such tenacity is because it seems so congenial to common sense, and the language we use is so filled with substantial thinking. As Bertrand Russell puts it, " 'Substance,' in a word, is a metaphysical mistake, due to transference to the world-structure of the structure of sentences composed of a subject and a predicate."[9]

But as W. T. Jones points out, "Any attempt to interpret reality substantially runs into hopeless dilemmas. For instance, is there one substance or several? Either answer is unsatisfactory. If there is but one substance, it is impossible to account for the experienced diversity. If there are many substances, it seems impossible that they can be related in any significant way."[10]

Furthermore it is impossible to account for *real* change using the conceptual model of substance. The meaning of the term inevitably makes change to be only accidental and thus ultimately inconsequential.

With the rise of modern philosophy and its orientation to experience, it became apparent (re Hume and Kant) that substance was not an object of experience, and thus it fell under suspicion if not outright rejection. Many philosophers came to believe that the function served by the concept of substance was better served by the concept of relation. The self, for instance, is "self-consciousness" in the context of a relation to the not-self. "Self and object are

8. W. T. Jones, *Kant and the 19th Century* (New York: Harcourt Brace Jovanovich, 1975), 111.
9. *A History of Western Philosophy* (New York: Simon and Schuster, a Clarion Book, 1967), 202.
10. *The 20th Century to Wittgenstein and Sartre* (New York: Harcourt Brace Jovanovich, 1975), 46.

not distinct, unchanging entities that face each other across a metaphysical and epistemological chasm; self and object are structures that arise within experience. There is no object without self, and there is no self without object."[11]

The terms *relation, relational,* and *relationship,* when used in an ontological sense as they will be in this work, are ambiguous terms, however, and are in need of clarification. In the language of contemporary logic there are "internal relations" and "external relations."[12] In the former, such relations are inseparable from the essence of a thing. If properties that partake of the character of *internal* relations are absent, the thing is no longer what it was, it becomes something else. In the case of *external* relations, such properties are accidental to the thing's being what it is. A good example of this is two bricks lying side by side. If one is removed, the other remains a brick. Its presence is not essential to the other brick being a brick. In our discussion in the text we are assuming that man's essence is constituted by his relation to God, that is, an internal relation. If this is but an external relation, man is still a man in independence of God, and his religious character is only accidental to his being, which the history of Christian thought has generally denied, except in a few extreme cases. The ambiguity of the terms appears, theologically, in discussions of justification and sanctification. Justification is a change of relation in the external sense (the person is not changed by the relation), whereas sanctification involves a change of relation in the internal sense (the person is really changed by this relation). While the same language is used, the significance is quite different. If the distinction between external and internal relations is not observed, it is easy enough to conclude that relational ontology is Pelagian and makes no place for a real sanctification, whereas in fact it does so in a philosophically sound way using more contemporary modes of thought.

As we have earlier noted, language tends to sound substantial. This is especially true when metaphors are used, and such metaphors abound in Scripture. It is a "category mistake," however, to interpret these figures of speech in a literalistic/substantial way. A

11. Ibid., 113.
12. See Richard Rorty, "Relation, Internal and External," in *Encyclopedia of Philosophy,* ed. Paul Edwards (New York: Macmillan Co. and Free Press, 1967), vols. 7—8.

careful reading of biblical modes of expression betrays an irreducibly relational way of thinking. In explaining why Martin Luther abandoned the substantial modes of thought of Catholic theology, Douglas John Hall argues that the most "plausible explanation" as to why he had been "moved in a fundamental way by the relational character of the whole Biblical testimony" was because "intuitively . . . he grasped the fact that the primary categories of Hebraic-Christian belief are *all* relational."[13]

As later theology came to see (cf. chap. 7 on the Trinity), the Trinitarian designations are relational terms: Father, Son, and Spirit (often Spirit *of*) are all to be understood as reflecting internal relations within the Godhead. Great theological terms referring to the divine-human relation are always seen in this way: for example, Lord, disciple, covenant, grace, atonement, love, election, faith, sin, justification, hope, judgment, and so on. It is interesting that the use of the term *carnal*, widely employed in the holiness movement, is always adjectival in the New Testament. Thus *carnality* as a noun depicting a substance is carefully avoided in favor of *carnal* as describing acts, people, dispositions—a relation to be avoided.

In the light of the philosophical distinctions observed above between internal and external relation, W. T. Purkiser writes, "In a true theism, any relation between God and human persons—an 'I-thou' relationship—is an 'internal relation': e.g., the branches in the Vine, the members in the Body. It is precisely that relation of the branches in the Vine and the members to the Body that makes them what they are, that gives them their distinctive moral/spiritual character. Change that relationship and the character changes, as happens in the change from estrangement to reconciliation. How can anyone suppose that reconciliation with God does not radically alter the person reconciled?"[14]

Some writers in the holiness movement use the term *substance* with a connotation different from the classical philosophical usage. In their understanding, substance means basically the "essence" of something, for example, the "substance" of the argument, and hence does not carry any idea of "thingness." For this reason, it can be argued that the contrast between the substantial view and the

---

13. *Imaging God* (Grand Rapids: Wm. B. Eerdmans Publishing Co., 1986), 99.
14. Personal letter, Oct. 2, 1986. I am indebted to Dr. Purkiser for help and support in articulating this understanding of my theological model.

relational view is a false dichotomy.[15] However, since this is an adapted use and not the standard one, the term conjures up all the static images when it is heard without the accompanying qualifications. Therefore I feel that we must abandon the terminology in order to fully clear ourselves from the implications it carries to the modern reader.

---

15. See Richard S. Taylor, *Exploring Christian Holiness,* vol. 3, *The Theological Formulation* (Kansas City: Beacon Hill Press of Kansas City, 1985). The adapted use of the term in that volume was explained to me by the author in private conversation.

Acknowledgments

It now remains to give expression of appreciation to a few of those who have been of special help to me in this massive project. First, I want to publicly acknowledge the generosity of Trevecca Nazarene College, whose administration has been extremely supportive by providing me with a congenial environment and released time to pursue what would have been an otherwise impossible undertaking. I am deeply indebted to Dr. W. M. Greathouse, who has been my theological dialogue partner for many years as well as mentor and friend. He has provided invaluable assistance in working through sensitive issues and helping me see where I have not adequately covered the bases. His ability to couple the hectic life of a general superintendent with the constant study requisite to theological integrity continues to amaze me.

My colleagues in the Department of Religion and Philosophy at Trevecca have been a great source of encouragement and help. Dr. Hal A. Cauthron has assisted me in the area of biblical languages where my own competence is minimal, as well as in the field of biblical theology. Dr. Craig Keen, whose theological training was in a different orientation, has sharpened my statements by his observations. Dr. Don Dunnington and Mr. Joe Bowers have tried to keep my feet on the ground with practical concerns. The friendship and peer support of these men have been a continuing source of strength.

My thanks to the committee appointed by the church for their reading of the manuscript and comments: Drs. John A. Knight, W. T. Purkiser, A. Elwood Sanner, and Richard S. Taylor. These men have vigorously interacted with the manuscript. Our discussions have resulted in a much stronger and clearer statement than would have otherwise been the case, though they are not to be held responsible for its contents.

A number of my peers teaching in Nazarene educational institutions have read segments of the manuscript pertaining to their own area of specialization and provided constructive suggestions.

After all, they are the ones who will make the most use of the book if it is to be a significant contribution to the church. They must feel that it is worth exposing to their students. Some outside the holiness movement have also shown considerable interest in what is happening here. I trust that this work will expand the Wesleyan perspective into the wider theological world, which so often in recent years has shown an interest in it.

To the Book Committee of the Church of the Nazarene for their confidence in handing me this assignment, and to the Nazarene Publishing House for having been so supportive, I am very greatly indebted.

A word of appreciation is overdue to my wife and family, who have suffered long in my involvement in this process. Oftentimes, even when I have been present in body, my mind was so involved in theological reflection that I was "far, far away."

Most of all, I cannot repay the God who found me and led me to become a part of His kingdom.

A Note to the Reader

Doing theology in the present situation requires that a theologian identify openly the methodology that he is using in arriving at the substantive contents of his theology. Hence any contemporary theology sets forth a prolegomena for this purpose. Such a section is essential for the student of technical theology. The reader who only has an interest in the content of the Christian faith without giving attention to the process by which the writer arrived at his conclusions may, without irreparable damage, go directly to part III of this theology and begin his reading with the Doctrines of God the Sovereign.

PART I

Prolegomena

The Nature
and Scope
of Theology

In this chapter we propose to lay out some preliminary definitions and methodological considerations. The intention is to make clear at the outset precisely what it is we are about. Such a programmatic statement is intended to provide the guidelines that will be followed in every part of the work. It will let the reader know what to expect about method and presuppositions and at the same time provide him with a logical framework within which to engage in critical dialogue with the arguments insofar as he may perceive them to stray from the limitations herein set forth.[1]

What Is Theology?

At the most elementary level, the linguistic meaning of *theology* is "logos of theos," words about God. Marianne Micks has refined

---

1. It is the theological assumption of the writer that theology is a dialogic enterprise that is to be carried on in the context of the church. It is not an autonomous discipline where the theologian does his work in independence of the community of faith; neither is it heteronomous in the sense that certain authoritative theologians or ecclesiastics impose their ideas upon that community. Any official consensus must be the result of this dialogic process if it is to have viability.

this simple statement somewhat by defining theology as "disciplined thinking about God."[2] There may be noncognitive awareness and noncognitive emotion and perhaps religious experiences that transcend words, but when a cognitive dimension is present, as is the case with theology, thinking involves categories and concepts that are symbolized by words. At the very least, no communication of cognitive content is possible without words.[3] Zen Buddhism rejects the validity of words altogether and hence seeks only to transmit the experience of satori, which is beyond words. The communication of this experience from teacher to pupil is like transferring the flame from one candle to another. But the incarnational character of the Christian faith results in a different conception of both God and communication. As with any use of language, precision and adequacy require careful attention to the linguistic symbols used to assure that they represent the reality as accurately as possible within the limitations of human language. In this light one may define the nature of theology as the study and refinement of words about God and man before God (coram Deo). The emphasis here is upon the subject of theological language: God and related concepts.

Sometimes a distinction is made between the broader and narrower uses of the term, the latter referring to the doctrine of God as a specific aspect of theology. This presumes that there are aspects of theology in the broader sense that do not relate to God —but that suggests a contradiction in terms. A proposition that does not have a God-reference can lay no claim to being a theological statement. Thus the discipline is more strictly defined, or limited, than is often realized.

This understanding excludes certain kinds of talk that are not exclusively "God-talk." It excludes history qua history, science qua science, psychology qua psychology, and so on. History may be a proper subject of theological discourse insofar as it is discussed as

---

2. Introduction to Theology (New York: Seabury Press, 1967), xii.

3. There is strong evidence to support the idea that thinking is impossible without words. Gordon Kaufman, Systematic Theology (New York: Charles Scribner's Sons, 1968), suggests that all learning is vocabulary study: "It begins with words and meanings that in some sense we know and understand; it develops through processes in which we learn to criticize those meanings which we had taken for granted, and through which they become broadened and deepened as we explore levels and depths we had not previously apprehended; it grows as we come to relate these simple and more primitive notions to new and more complex words and meanings which we had not known before." 3-4.

the arena of divine activity. Science may be included insofar as one is speaking about the world as the creative activity of God. Or psychology insofar as we speak of man's nature in relation to his Creator.

This restriction implies that, as a theologian, one cannot in that capacity prejudice the result of historical research in the name of theology. The theologian cannot tell a scientist what the outcome of his experiments must be. He cannot, except insofar as it has theological overtones, influence the findings in any discipline unless it is done on the basis of the canons of truth indigenous to that discipline. This limitation is furthermore an implicit assumption about the nature of revelation that shall be explored further on.

As noted, theology involves not only words about God but also words about man in relation to God. This understanding was particularly stressed in the theological work of Martin Luther and John Calvin, the Protestant Reformers, who in their writings insist that there is a double subject in theology: God and man. Neither one can be known in and of himself except in relation to the other.[4] This suggests that a nontheological analysis of human reality can never be completely adequate from a theological perspective, because the psychologist or the anthropologist or the sociologist can never deal with man in his fallen nature unless he introduces the man's relation to God, that is, unless he becomes a theologian.[5]

This carefully restricted character of theology may be illustrated with a reference to the central belief of the Christian faith: the resurrection of Christ. "Jesus arose from the dead" is not, strictly speaking, a theological statement. It is a historical proposition that is subject to the methods of historical criticism. Insofar as any historical event can be, it is amenable to verification or falsification. That is not to say that it is not relevant to theology, but within itself it is not properly a theological assertion. It is interesting that the New Testament itself is normally careful to make plain that its unique claim is that "God raised Jesus from the dead," and that is a theological proposition.[6]

---

4. This has significant implications for the nature of our knowledge of God, which will be explored in Part II of this work.

5. Cf. John Calvin, *Institutes of the Christian Religion*, trans. Henry Beveridge (London: James Clarke and Co., 1949), vol. I, sec. I, art. I (hereafter I.I.I).

6. Cf. Acts 2:24; 3:15; 10:40; Rom. 4:25; 10:9; Eph. 1:20. While there are other ways of saying it, the emphasis upon the Resurrection being the activity of God is always central and clear.

Take Gen. 1:1 for an additional example. It is not so much a cosmological statement regarding the beginning of the world as it is a theological affirmation that "in the beginning, God created the world." This understanding furthermore highlights the fact that the Bible is a theological book from beginning to end. Later we will see that this is the hermeneutical clue to a proper exegesis of the biblical text.[7]

As they have been defined here, theological propositions are incapable of *empirical* verification or falsification.[8] This disconcerting truth has been brought to light forcefully by the contemporary discipline of linguistic philosophy. By its analysis of language and its uses, this approach to philosophical work has forced us to be more careful with our sometimes careless use of language and come to terms with the way theological language actually functions. One does not need to necessarily agree with the conclusions of some linguistic philosophers about religious language to recognize that their basic contention about the nature of language is largely sound. Thus theological propositions, dealing as they do with ultimate meanings, are not subject to the normal methods of scientific validation.[9]

However, there is a sense in which certain theological propositions are capable of falsification, not in and of themselves, but insofar as they involve interpretations of historical happenings. That is, if it can be demonstrated conclusively that a significant revelatory event, for example, the Resurrection, never occurred, that would count decisively against the validity of the theological meaning of that event as embodied in theological judgments.[10] The

---

7. W. T. Purkiser, Richard S. Taylor, and Willard H. Taylor, in *God, Man, and Salvation* (Kansas City: Beacon Hill Press of Kansas City, 1977), say: "Debate between 'science' and 'the Bible' often loses sight of the fact that the interest in the Scriptures is theological, not cosmological." 60.

8. John Hick has proposed an eschatological verification of a quasi-empirical nature, but this does not alter the situation with regard to present verification.

9. This does not mean that theological statements are nonsense or that there is no possibility of disagreement on religious matters. Even A. J. Ayer, *Language, Truth, and Logic* (New York: Dover Publications, n.d.), allows for the possibility of this, given certain conditions—see below on "The Norm of Systematic Theology."

10. In speaking of Paul's vision on the Damascus Road, I. Howard Marshall distinguished between the historical and the theological dimensions of the account. The former is "in principle open to historical study," but "it is not possible to prove by historical methods whether or not this vision was in fact what he says it was, namely a real appearance of the risen Lord Jesus." He concludes, however, that "if it could be proved historically that Paul never made the journey in question and never saw a vision of any

position suggested here stands midway between two extreme views. One is the thought of persons such as Rudolf Bultmann, who think that the only crucial thing is the faith embodied in the interpretation of a supposed historical event.[11] On the other extreme is the fundamentalistic tendency to believe that to have established the historicity of a revelatory event is to have proven its theological truth.[12] In the first case, it makes no significant difference whether Jesus ever lived. The second approach fails to recognize the essential nature of theology and its object and therefore reflects a rationalistic theory of knowledge or else reduces theology to history. The truth lies between these two poles. It makes all the difference in the world whether there was a Resurrection. However, to demonstrate by historiography that there was a Resurrection is not to necessarily validate the basic theological truth at stake, namely, that God was at work in the event.

---

kind, then the theological question would automatically be answered in the negative. Paul did not see the risen Lord." *Biblical Inspiration* (Grand Rapids: Wm. B. Eerdmans Publishing Co., 1982), 58-59.

11. Cf. Rudolf Bultmann, et al., *Kerygma and Myth,* ed. Hans Werner Bartsch (New York: Harper and Bros., Publishers, 1961), 41-42.

12. Fundamentalism is a multifaceted term and therefore may have a rather wide denotation. In this and subsequent uses of it, we are referring generally to the historical movement that emerged in the late 19th and early 20th centuries (and that is represented contemporaneously by some evangelical scholars) and specifically to that aspect of it that is informed by the philosophical presuppositions of Scottish realism (common sense philosophy) as developed by Thomas Reid and promoted by the "Princeton theology." Thus we are not suggesting any negative connotations regarding the so-called fundamentals to which this movement committed itself. At least the earlier formulations of the fundamentals would be generally acceptable to Wesleyans, although not all the Calvinistic elaborations of them would be consistent with Wesleyan thought. The summary statements of Jack Rogers and Donald K. McKim will reflect a brief survey of this philosophical aspect of fundamentalism: "Thomas Reid founded a school of Scottish common sense philosophy that sought to answer Hume while remaining solely empirical in method. Reid assumed a simple Aristotelian realism and accepted as normative Bacon's naive method of scientific induction. Reid claimed that the mind directly encountered objects in nature. His assurance that this was so was provided by an intuitive judgment of the mind. Scottish realism dominated the academic philosophy taught in American colleges during their first half-century. It was brought to Princeton by John Witherspoon in 1768 when he became president of the College of New Jersey. Witherspoon's Scottish realism laid the foundations for the theories of biblical interpretation developed in the late nineteenth and early twentieth centuries at Princeton Seminary." *The Authority and Interpretation of the Bible* (San Francisco: Harper and Row, 1979), 248. See also George M. Marsden, *Fundamentalism and American Culture* (New York: Oxford University Press, 1980), especially chap. 13; Ernest R. Sandeen, *The Roots of Fundamentalism* (Chicago: University of Chicago Press, 1970), chap. 5; S. A. Grave, "Reid, Thomas," in *Encyclopedia of Philosophy,* vol. 7. ed. Paul Edwards (New York: Macmillan Co. and Free Press, 1967); idem, *The Scottish Philosophy of Common Sense* (Oxford: Clarendon Press, 1960).

This does, nonetheless, raise certain questions that preoccupy much of contemporary theology. What is the precise relation between history and theological truth? What is there about a historical event that marks it as revelatory? Why are there certain events claimed by biblical writers as being especially revelatory although others may not be revelatory in a special sense? What is the principle of distinction between sacred history and secular history? Or most summarily, what is the relation between revelation and history?

How we may answer these questions is not crucial to these preliminary issues here under discussion. We are simply seeking to make clear the meaning of the discipline of theology. If we are to do theology in a rational manner, we must be aware of what we are about. The first principle we affirm, then, is this simple but strictly defined understanding of what theology is. Its proper subject matter is God and other subjects insofar as they are God-related. It will now be the responsibility of the writer to keep within the bounds laid down and the responsibility of the reader who will enter into dialogue with him to assume the same guidelines, or else the conversation that is theology cannot be fruitfully carried on. This must particularly be kept in mind whenever subjects are explored that lie near the boundary between theology and other disciplines.

At this point, we need to attempt to distinguish between theology and philosophy of religion. This is a difficult task for two reasons: (1) philosophy of religion is a discipline that has been understood and pursued in a multiplicity of ways;[13] and (2) the distinction must be made chiefly in some other way than in terms of subject matter because, like theology, philosophy of religion talks directly about God (or at least the idea of God) as part of its proper subject matter, along with many other theological claims.

The definition of philosophy of religion by Vergilius Ferm points to some pertinent insights: "An inquiry into the general subject of religion from the philosophical point of view, i.e., an inquiry employing the accepted tools of critical analysis and evaluation

---

13. We would use it in a more modern sense rather than in the way it has been used in the past as a prolegomena to theology, i.e., as the testing of theological claims in the light of philosophical criteria.

without a predisposition to defend or reject the claims of any particular religion."[14]

This suggests that while the theologian operates within what Paul Tillich calls the "theological circle," giving expression to a particular faith to which he is committed, the philosopher, by contrast, is committed only to free inquiry so far as any particular religion is concerned. He analyzes theological claims regarding the nature of ultimate reality, the basis of religious knowledge, and such other issues in terms of their relation to philosophical adequacy. This grows out of the philosopher's attempt to think comprehensively. Such an effort brings to bear the critical tools of philosophical inquiry upon the particular questions addressed in theological work.

On the surface, this appears to suggest that the distinction between the two areas is simply in terms of objectivity and subjectivity. That idea needs to be qualified. The philosopher may be relatively objective regarding the religious claims he is examining, but all philosophical analysis operates in terms of a perspective that the philosopher feels is "crucially significant for meaning."[15] Every philosopher of religion then functions in terms of a criterion of truth or perspective as to what constitutes valid knowledge or a meaningful proposition or justifiable claims about religious objects of faith. In that sense, he is as subjectively biased as the committed theologian.[16]

---

14. "Philosophy of Religion," in *Encyclopedia of Religion*, ed. Vergilius Ferm (New York: Philosophical Library, 1945).

15. Edward T. Ramsdell, *The Christian Perspective* (New York: Abingdon-Cokesbury Press, 1950), has explored the idea of the "point of view" that is present in every discipline and shows that it is absent from none; and furthermore that differences "among us as rational men are differences in what we believe to be crucially significant." 19. Langdon B. Gilkey adds: "Inescapably all philosophy, secular or Christian, has an 'existential' source. Every philosophical inquiry must make certain assumptions before it can begin at all. First of all, the inquirer must assume at the onset that certain kinds of experiences are valid clues to the reality, whatever it may be, which he seeks to understand; otherwise his mind has no significant material upon which it can work." *Maker of Heaven and Earth* (Garden City, N.Y.: Doubleday and Co., 1959), 134.

16. In his otherwise excellent discussion, this seems to be a severe weakness of Tillich's characterization of philosophy as distinct from theology. He defines philosophy as being committed to no particular perspective. *Systematic Theology*, 3 vols. in 1 (Chicago: University of Chicago Press, 1967), 1:22 ff. Cf. the criticism by George F. Thomas: "But Tillich begs the question as to the relation between philosophy and theology when he asserts that the philosopher seeks the truth only in 'the whole of reality,' 'the universal logos of being,' and never looks for it in any particular place. For there is nothing to prevent a philosopher from finding the key to the nature of reality in a concrete man-

A theologian may function as a philosopher of religion and in some sense is obliged to do so. As he seeks to test his own claims, he may (and should) examine them in the light of rational criteria. But his faith is ultimately based not upon rational conclusions but upon existential wholeness.[17] However, in full honesty, he may find himself called upon to modify some of the particulars of his theological views when he finds they cannot withstand such rational tests as he may feel (as a philosopher) are valid.[18]

Theology must also be distinguished from religion, although there is not a complete diastasis between them. Religion is primarily existential, and theology is primarily intellectual, but the intellectual is not absent from the religious experience, or vice versa.

---

ifestation, a particular part of reality. Indeed, every creative philosopher must take as his starting point some part or aspect of reality which seems to him to provide the clue to an understanding of reality as a whole. He begins with a 'vision of reality' in which this part or aspect appears as dominant, and then works out his philosophy under the guidance of his vision." "The Method and Structure of Tillich's Theology," in *The Theology of Paul Tillich*, ed. Charles W. Kegley and Robert W. Bretall (New York: Macmillan Co., 1964), 101.

17. A Christian who is also a philosopher may offer philosophical arguments to support his intellectual commitment to the Christian faith; however, these are never the only reasons he is a Christian, if they even enter into the question at all. The spiritual biography of very few Christians would reflect an intellectual conversion as the primary dynamic of religious experience. Rather a reorientation of the whole person around a new focus for life is generally if not universally the result of such a refocusing being efficacious for all dimensions of existence; one finds the inward transforming power of the gospel giving meaning and purpose to life in every relationship. This is the intent of the idea of "existential wholeness." The use of the term *existential* in this work is intended to convey the ideas of personal, inwardness, wholeness, and life-transforming in a far more profound way than the term *experiential* suggests (*experimental* in American usage is completely astray from the meaning, although in British usage it is very close). In no sense does it involve a commitment to any particular version of existentialism as a philosophy nor to the parody of various existentialisms that makes the term a synonym for mere subjectivity. In the sense in which we are using it, all religious teachers from Jesus and Paul to John Wesley along with all who are committed to more than external religion may be classified as existentialists. In discussing "The Redemptive Character of the Knowledge of God," the authors of *God, Man, and Salvation* affirm the argument of William L. Bradley, that religious knowledge is based "neither upon first principles nor upon sense perception" but is "personal in nature," yielding "the type of information that one receives from another person." (See my own discussion of the nature of personal knowledge below.) This kind of knowledge, they go on to elaborate, "cannot be tested as one tests a scientific hypothesis or a fact of recent history. But it is not necessarily contrary to other forms of knowledge. Many times it coincides with logical analysis and scientific investigation. Nevertheless, its *basic verification* lies in the encounter itself. *This is existential knowledge.* It comes in the unique effects of an encounter with another in the very throes of one's own existence." 210-11, italics added.

18. The role of philosophy in the theological enterprise will be discussed more fully in chapter 3.

J. B. Chapman defined Christianity as (1) a creed to be believed, (2) a life to be lived, and (3) an experience to be enjoyed.[19] Religion includes an emotional, a volitional, and an intellectual element.

It is not that religion necessarily involves "right thinking," but it does involve some intellectual content, else it could not be identified as religious as distinct from, say, an aesthetic experience. As John Wesley observed:

> Whatsoever the generality of people may think, it is certain that opinion is not religion: No, not right opinion; assent to one, or to ten thousand truths. There is a wide difference between them: Even right opinion is as distant from religion as the east is from the west. Persons may be quite right in their opinions, and yet have no religion at all; and, on the other hand, persons may be truly religious, who hold many wrong opinions.[20]

Fortunately for thousands of persons, this is true. Good religion is not to be equated with right thinking. However, it is a non sequitur to conclude from this that right thinking is unimportant. It is in fact because religion includes an intellectual element that unavoidably informs the other dimensions that good theology is important.

Jack Rogers suggests a clear and helpful distinction between theology and faith:

> Theology is not faith. Faith is a trustful commitment of the whole person to Christ. Theology is our careful, orderly

---

19. *A Christian: What It Means to Be One*, rev. ed. (Kansas City: Beacon Hill Press of Kansas City, 1967), 7, 11, 15.

20. "Sermon on the Trinity," *Works* 6:199. In order to properly appreciate Wesley's emphasis, the historical circumstances to which he was addressing himself should be kept in mind. During the 18th century there were two extreme positions regarding how Christian truth was validated: On the one hand was deism, with "enthusiasm" standing at the opposite end of the spectrum. Deism developed "rational religion," which held that reason was completely adequate to apprehend all truth, so that there was no need for revelation, and conversely no truth could be allowed that was not amenable to the cult of reasonableness. "Enthusiasm" (what today would be called fanaticism) denied any need for external revelation, since all truth was given internally by the "inner light." Orthodoxy stood between both, denying enthusiasm and affirming in opposition to deism that God had given an objective revelation of true propositions, and true religion consisted in affirming these truths. Thus orthodoxy was actually at one with deism in being rationalistic. Wesley rejected all three of these options prevalent in his century and insisted that true religion was inward, but not apart from an objective revelation found in Scripture. A further qualification should also be made. With regard to fundamental doctrines (the Trinity, divinity of Christ, the Atonement, et al.) Wesley distinguished between the fact and the explanation. He insisted on the fact but admitted that the complete explanation eluded him. As John Deschner says with regard to his Christology, "Wesley's willingness to think and let think does not extend to the 'facts' of the Trinity, of the divinity of Christ, of the atonement." *Wesley's Christology: An Interpretation* (Dallas: Southern Methodist University Press, 1960), 14.

thought about the revelation in Scripture of the God in whom we have faith. Theology and faith go together. You can't really have one without the other. But each has its distinctive role. Faith is primary. Theology is the necessary next step.[21]

It is a debated question about whether understanding precedes experience or vice versa. Classical liberalism tended to make religion prior, but it seems closer to the truth to recognize that one's preunderstanding influences to some extent his existential encounter with the Divine. This has some psychological support, since certain psychologists argue that expressive behavior is influenced by one's expectations about one's experience, rather than by the experience itself.[22] Later in our study we shall have occasion to note how this truth may help explain some very difficult problems in the Bible, including throwing valuable light upon the developing idea of the Holy Spirit as it emerges in the Scripture. The most adequate way to answer the question is to say that religion is ontologically prior, although theology (whatever its degree of adequacy) is psychologically (or epistemologically) prior but ontologically secondary.

Theology is a neutral term in the sense that it may be Muslim, Jewish, or otherwise. Our study, however, focuses on *Christian* theology. This does not necessarily mean that other theologies relate to a different God, since we believe in only one God. What it does imply is that it is a study of the God whose character has been decisively defined by His act in Jesus Christ. We also would affirm with Martin Luther that there is *no other* God than the Father of our Lord. What distinguishes Christian theology from other theologies is its source of wisdom.

This truth must be taken seriously, since it is this theocentric focus with a Christonormative character that guards the unity of the discipline we are pursuing. No theological understandings can be allowed to intrude themselves into this theology that are inconsistent with the revelation in Christ. Any candidate for inclusion must be critically judged by this criterion.

---

21. *Confessions*, 60.
22. E.g., Gordon Allport, *Becoming* (New Haven, Conn.: Yale University Press, 1955). "There is endless diversity among [religious people] in the degree to which religion plays a part in their lives, and in the forms and relative maturity of their religious outlook. It could not be otherwise, for religious becoming is influenced by our temperament and training, and is subject to arrest as well as growth." 96.

What Is Systematic Theology?

Systematic theology is a specific discipline with its own unique characteristics and should be distinguished from certain other areas of theological study. One of these is biblical theology. Biblical theology is the task of explicating in its own terms the theology that comes to expression in the biblical text. Quite often the term is applied to a theology that is ostensibly biblical in character, but this is to use the term adjectivally rather than nominally.[23]

Biblical theology as a discipline is a relatively recent phenomenon, but its roots lie deep in the Protestant Reformation. "Only among the followers of the Reformation could the concept 'biblical theology' have been coined at all" (Ebeling). The Reformers' insistence upon the principle of *sola scriptura* made its development a necessity. So long as biblical authority was subservient to that of tradition, as in Catholicism, biblical studies were of secondary importance; but when the Scripture became the primary court of appeal, the picture changed. However, it was 100 years before the term was actually coined and used in the title of a book,[24] and even longer before it emerged as an independent discipline.

In its earliest forms, biblical theology was conceived as the employment of proof texts taken indiscriminately from both Testaments to support the traditional systems of doctrine of early Protestant orthodoxy. The work that stands at the point of transition between the old dogmatic interest in the proof-text method and the science of biblical theology that was aborning was the four-volume work by B. T. Zachariae (1771-75). He deliberately abandoned the method of studying isolated proof texts in favor of an attempt to study the teaching of the Bible as a whole. In the arrangement of the material for such a project, he insisted that one follow a plan derived from the nature of the Bible and not one based upon a "method of theological classification used elsewhere in systems and compendiums." Previously, so-called biblical theologies had used the classifications of systematic theology, most usually the threefold theology-anthropology-soteriology organization.

But this was only a halfway house, because the center of interest was still in the theological system that Zachariae hoped to pu-

---

23. Cf. Gerhard Ebeling, "The Meaning of Biblical Theology," in *Word and Faith* (Philadelphia: Fortress Press, 1963), 81-86.
24. A German work by Wolfgang Jacob Christmann in 1629.

rify rather than in the Bible for its own sake. The man whose name is associated with the full liberation of biblical theology from dogmatics and its establishment as a purely historical discipline was Johann Philipp Gabler (1753-1826). Although he never really wrote a biblical theology, his inaugural lecture at the University of Altdorf on March 30, 1787, was the decisive proclamation. His famous declaration reads:

> Biblical theology possesses a historical character, transmitting what the sacred writers thought about divine matters; dogmatic theology, on the contrary, possesses a didactic character, teaching what a particular theologian philosophizes about divine matters according to his ability, time, age, place, sect or school, and other similar things.

He proposed an inductive, historical, and descriptive approach to biblical theology that would sharply distinguish between it and dogmatic theology, which, although based upon materials drawn from biblical theology, also makes use of philosophy and of ideas that arose in the later development of the Christian church. This proposal gave direction to biblical theology for the future.

The goal of a strictly historical biblical theology was first realized by G. L. Baur (1740-1806). He is also credited with being the first to publish an Old Testament theology (1796). So with him, biblical theology is separated into Old and New Testament theology.

Unfortunately most of the early work in biblical theology had been done from rationalistic presuppositions and then later under the influence of the philosophy of G. W. F. Hegel. Consequently there was a conservative reaction exemplified by the famous work of E. W. Hengstenberg, *Christology of the Old Testament* (1829-35). His reaction denied the validity of the historical-critical approach to the Bible and made little distinction between the Testaments. He rejects any real idea of progress in relation to the Old Testament prophecies and almost ignores any consideration of their original reference.

Many other conservative scholars were more balanced than Hengstenberg. The most significant example was G. F. Oehler, who published a massive *Theology of the Old Testament*, which was translated into both French and English. It is out of this milieu that the "salvation history school" *(Heilsgeschichte)* began, exemplified especially by J. C. K. von Hofmann. In this view the Bible is regarded primarily not as a collection of proof texts or a repository of doctrine but as a witness to God's activity in history.

At this stage, Old Testament theology virtually disappeared, being ousted from the scholarly scene by the "history of religion" approach *(Religionsgeschichte)*, which dealt with the history of Israel's religion rather than theology. The year 1878 marks the triumph of this approach with the publication of *Prolegomena to the History of Israel,* by Julius Wellhausen.

For over 40 years biblical theology was eclipsed by the *Religionsgeschichte* approach. In the decades following World War I several factors brought about a renaissance of biblical theology. R. C. Dentan suggests three major ones: (1) a general loss of faith in evolutionary naturalism; (2) a reaction against the conviction that historical truth can be attained by pure scientific objectivity, or that such objectivity is indeed attainable; and (3) the trend of a return to the idea of revelation in dialectical (neoorthodox) theology.[25] The Golden Age of biblical theology began in the 1930s and continues into the present.

It was thus only quite recently that biblical theology was recognized as a historical discipline that interprets what the text meant, and explicates the theology that comes to expression in the biblical text in terms of the rubrics found within Scripture itself, rather than importing the categories from systematic theology.[26]

Systematic theology must also be distinguished from historical theology, which is chiefly the study of the history of Christian thought or Christian tradition. Like biblical theology, it is a descriptive discipline except that it traces the development of theological thought throughout the centuries since the close of the New Testament canon. This history is a complex phenomenon with many different and variegated traditions woven into the main strand of

25. *Preface to Old Testament Theology* (New York: Seabury Press, 1963), 59.

26. The position I am advocating is the one that was given definitive expression by Krister Stendahl in his article "Biblical Theology," in *Interpreter's Dictionary of the Bible,* ed. George Buttrick (New York: Abingdon Press, 1962), 1:418-32, and in "Method in the Study of Biblical Theology," in *The Bible in Modern Scholarship,* ed. J. Philip Hyatt (Nashville: Abingdon Press, 1965). This view is also accepted by George Eldon Ladd, *A Theology of the New Testament* (Grand Rapids: Wm. B. Eerdmans Publishing Co., 1974), and John Bright, *The Authority of the Old Testament* (Grand Rapids: Baker Book House, Twin Books, 1975), 114-15. In agreement with these scholars I would hold that biblical theology is essentially descriptive, "an inductive, descriptive discipline, synthetic in approach, which on the basis of a grammatico-historical study of the Biblical text seeks to set forth in its own terms and in its structural unity the theology expressed in the Bible" (Bright). A full discussion of the various options and a criticism of this method may be found in Gerhard Hasel, *Old Testament Theology: Basic Issues in the Current Debate* (Grand Rapids: Wm. B. Eerdmans Publishing Co., 1972).

Christian thinking. It would also encompass the heretical movements and the crystallization of certain theological debates into
creeds or symbols.

Although historical theology is an important source for systematic theology, as will be discussed later, it is not to be considered
normative in any final sense. On this point it is markedly different
from biblical theology. Under certain conditions, however, when a
particular tradition sanctifies and absolutizes its own history, it
may be treated as normative; but the "Protestant principle" (Tillich)
forbids absolutizing any human authority, whether a particular
biblical interpretation or a denominational creed. God himself is
alone the Absolute.

Although systematic theology draws upon these disciplines, it
is to be distinguished carefully from them. Let us now seek to
define the discipline that we are pursuing. One definition builds
explicitly upon the understanding of theology emphasized in the
last section: "Systematic theology is a constructive analysis of the
structure and terminology of the Christian language."[27]

The following statement goes beyond this one in comprehensiveness and represents a more adequate understanding: "Systematic theology concerns those beliefs (of God and cognate beliefs) in
ordered elucidation and in their relation to contemporary thought
and life—'contemporary' in each age, the task of theology falling to
be done continually as the intellectual outlook and even the meanings of words undergo change."[28] This more complete statement
sets forth two elements that are basic to systematic theology.

We will look first at the element of *contemporaneity*. This implies that systematic theology is different from the two previously
discussed theological disciplines in that it is not uniquely a historical approach. Rather its task is to bring the Christian faith into
contact with the modern or contemporary situation.

This implies that systematic theology is a constructive undertaking and not merely the uncritical rehearsal of tradition. Its function is to interpret Christian beliefs holistically in faithfulness to
both the tradition and the present generation. This aspect of theology is what calls for every generation to theologize for itself, to say

---

27. Kaufman, *Systematic Theology*, 11.
28. John Line, "Systematic Theology," in *Encyclopedia of Religion*, ed. Vergilius Ferm
(New York: Philosophical Library, 1945).

what the faith means in and to its own historical situation. It is also one reason why the theological task can never be finished.

This characteristic poses somewhat of a dilemma, since it suggests that systematic theology must operate between two poles. There is the pole of the situation and the pole of what we may call the historical norm or tradition. Theologians tend to gravitate toward one or the other of these poles. But what systematic theology properly does is stand in dynamic tension between the two. If one succumbs to the pressure in either direction, the result is a perversion. If one moves toward the pole of the situation with the aim of becoming relevant and loses contact with the historical norm, he simply becomes relative. When this occurs it is usually the result of a subtle process.[29] If on the other hand, one develops a fixation with a particular historical expression of the norm and loses contact with the situation, he becomes irrelevant and even obscurantist.[30] He tends, in Helmut Thielicke's felicitous phrase, to guard the ashes rather than tend the flame.[31] To use terms loosely at this point, the first danger is the potential pitfall of the liberal, while the conservative usually tends toward the second. Both are inadequate answers to the theological task, and this task cannot be avoided through failure of nerve.

Thielicke speaks of this same tension, using the terms "actualization" and "accommodation." His point is that the Word of God must address men where they are. It must become actualized in the present situation. Using categories made prominent by Arnold Toynbee, he suggests that a new historical situation poses a challenge to which theology must make a response. This is to say that

---

29. In tracing the shift away from John Wesley's thought in a liberalizing direction by his theological successors, Robert Chiles says: "The loss of theological truth through willful distortion or deliberate desertion is comparatively rare; it does not reflect intellectual obtuseness or spiritual perversity as much as it does the committed effort of the theologian to speak a language meaningful for his day, enhancing thereby the impact of the spiritual tradition out of which he works." *Theological Transition in American Methodism: 1790-1925* (New York: Abingdon Press, 1965), 13.

30. This perversion always takes place when some historically conditioned formulation of the Christian faith is crystallized and held onto as the final statement as in the case of fundamentalism's fixation with 17th-century Protestant orthodoxy or any theologian of the holiness movement sanctifying the 19th-century formulations. In these cases they fall victim to the situation described by Alexander Schweitzer: "Once the fathers confessed their faith; today many Christians are concerned only to believe their confessions." Quoted in Helmut Thielicke, *The Evangelical Faith* (Grand Rapids: Wm. B. Eerdmans Publishing Co., 1974), 1:54.

31. Ibid.

theology is seeking to answer the questions that are being asked in a given age and bring the Word of God to bear on the ethos of that generation. This is what Thielicke means by "actualization," a bringing of the Word to bear on the present scene: "Actualization always consists in a new interpretation of truth, in its readdressing, as it were. The truth itself remains intact. It means that the hearer is summoned and called 'under the truth' in his own name and situation."

"Accommodation" occurs when the question or the questioner becomes the norm for truth. It brings the truth under me. He gives as an illustration of this, the "German Christians" of Hitler's Third Reich who "were trying to make Christianity a specific, made-to-measure religion which would exert no pressure and cause no offence. Here the contemporary did indeed make himself the measure of all things, including the truth, according to his own understanding of himself."[32]

But there is also danger (although of a different kind) in remaining in the middle of the road and keeping a proper balance between these two poles. One is then vulnerable to attack from both sides. The liberal accuses this position of being fundamentalist, and the fundamentalist accuses it of being liberal. Consistent Wesleyan theology with its indigenous tendency toward a *via media* is precisely fitted to occupy this mediating position, but this is a precarious position that places pressures upon the theologian who seeks to maintain it by having to guard himself on two fronts. The result is that authentic Wesleyan theology has too often succumbed to the pressures and escaped to the safety of one or the other of the extremes and thus lost its distinctive character.

The second characteristic of systematic theology is embodied in the words of the definition that speak of "ordered elucidation." This is what is specifically implied by the term *systematic* and can be referred to as *coherence.* It is significantly more than an "orderly arrangement of doctrines, or groupings of the doctrines according to some particular perspective." It is not even a logical arrangement of theological propositions believed to be found in the Scripture. It is much more profound than the working out of an intellectual jigsaw puzzle, a way of ordering the pieces that are given us in a disordered fashion. Actually, the Bible does not basically contain theological propositions. Although "many statements in the Bible

---

32. Ibid., 26-27.

do, in fact, represent first order theological affirmations . . . the Bible itself is not theology."[33]

Much more adequate is the statement of Gustav Aulen:

> When systematic theology seeks to investigate the meaning of the Christian faith, it does not deal merely with a multitude of disparate doctrines which, as in the so-called "loci theology," appears as unrelated statements. There is rather an inner organic homogeneity in everything that constitutes the object of systematic theology.[34]

There is an interrelatedness that characterizes every particular doctrine so that every doctrine requires every other doctrine. No matter where you begin, you would come logically to every other aspect of the system; in fact, they would all be required for a complete expression of the system. They coexist without any contradiction. What one believes about creation influences the doctrine of the Incarnation; what one believes about these directly influences his doctrine of man. Contradictions are acceptable in an eclectic approach, but not in a coherent, systematic theology. All the pieces must fit together.

These two characteristics taken together point to another important feature of systematic theology that we will call *comprehensiveness*. By this we intend to suggest, not that it deals with every conceivable problem or issue, but that it is concerned with a larger picture than that encompassed by soteriological interests; although, as we shall see, in a Wesleyan theology this is the ultimate point of focus and final arbiter of adequacy and validity. It is also concerned to develop and clarify the ontological and epistemological aspects of the Christian faith. Unless one is willing to settle for the medieval notion of a twofold truth, Christian theology presupposes a worldview of cosmic proportions.[35]

This is to take the position, contrary to Pascal's famous statement, that the God of the philosophers is the God of Abraham, Isaac, and Jacob. There is a considerable difference between the language of religion and the language of philosophy. One is existential or personal, and the other is abstract. Nonetheless, it is the

---

33. Purkiser, Taylor, and Taylor, *God, Man, and Salvation*, 19, 18.

34. *The Faith of the Christian Church*, trans. Eric H. Wahlstrom (Philadelphia: Fortress Press, 1960), 6.

35. Paul Tillich, *Biblical Religion and the Search for Ultimate Reality* (Chicago: University of Chicago Press, 1963), demonstrates how the personalistic character of biblical faith drives toward ontological explanation.

same reality about which they speak, and therefore the two realms of discourse should not contradict each other.

This means that theology is a philosophical task, as well as an exegetical and historical one.[36] There are those who have reservations about this, especially about the ontological analyses it involves. One objection given is that an ontological description of God is static and impersonal, whereas God is dynamic and personal, and thus the religious understanding is perverted. This is true if certain ontologies, for example, the Platonic or Aristotelian, are imposed upon the theologian. However, the fallacy here is assuming that one needs to necessarily import a foreign ontology rather than develop a view of reality that both arises out of and is congenial to biblical faith. In fact, the claim of revelation entails such a development.[37]

The earliest stages of the theological enterprise demonstrate the truth of these claims. The dogmatic struggles of the fathers were really attempts at an adequate systematic theology. There were several efforts, the first one being that proposed by the Gnostics. But the ontological structure of their system proved inadequate as a vehicle by which to set the Christian faith in a larger setting. Its basic premise was a metaphysical dualism based on ethical considerations. This dualism of matter and spirit led to an

---

36. This partly presupposes an understanding of philosophy such as is suggested by Matthew Arnold's definition: "Philosophy is the attempt to see life steadily and see it whole." Referred to in Abraham Kaplan, *In Pursuit of Wisdom* (Beverly Hills, Calif.: Glencoe Press, 1977), 16.

37. Concluding a discussion of the question, "What the idea of Creation is about," in *Maker of Heaven and Earth,* Gilkey says: "Although it [doctrine of creation] does not set out directly to answer metaphysical questions, nevertheless it cannot avoid entering the metaphysical arena. As we have noted, if God is the Creator of all, and if our finite life does depend for its existence on His power and will, then this affirmation involves an indirect answer to two metaphysical questions: What does it mean to be, and what is the ultimate reality through which things are? Thus the idea of creation inevitably challenges metaphysical conceptions of reality which are antithetical to its own primary intent, and inevitably generates a particular point of view about nature and about historical existence, which can become systematized into a 'Christian philosophy.' Although the idea of creation is directly 'about' God and his relation to the meaning and destiny of man's life, indirectly it is 'about' the metaphysical questions of reality and its nature." 42. In one of the finer sections of his *CT,* Wiley argues this same position. After demonstrating the necessity for theology developing both the philosophical and the religious conceptions of God, he points to the confluence of the two in the following statement: "The Christian conception of God is a conviction that the ultimate Personality of religion and the Absolute of philosophy find their highest expression in Jesus Christ; and that in His Person and work we have the deepest possible insight into the nature and purpose of God." 1:221.

understanding of salvation as escape from the flesh, which was counter to the basic Christian commitment.[38]

The attempt to create a larger intellectual setting for Christianity succeeded only when it was developed in the light of the Old Testament conception of God. This explains, in part, why the struggle for the Old Testament in the early days was such a crucial issue. Had Christianity declared its complete independence of the Jewish faith, instead of affirming a relation of fulfillment, it would have developed in a completely different direction theologically.[39] That fact highlights the crucial significance of the Old Testament in the theological task.[40]

The demands of the task of systematic theology are staggering. In the final analysis only God can be a completely competent systematic theologian. Human beings, living under the conditions of existence, must content themselves with partial perspectives, and most scholars have preoccupied themselves with essays on particular topics. Because of the immensity of the material involved, the one who attempts such a comprehensive endeavor must of necessity rely on the researches of his colleagues in those specialized areas that impinge on the discipline. The best he can hope to do is to get a firm grasp of the perspective from which the systematic theology is to be done, and using logical insight, incorporate the results insofar as they coincide with the adopted perspective.

Herein lies the significance of Gordon Kaufman's statement:

> It is important to distinguish between the perspective that informs a systematic theology and the detailed analysis of theological doctrines. A theologian's perspective affects the way he frames questions as well as the answers he gives to them; it shapes his fundamental judgments regarding what is theologically important as well as his way of resolving issues; it works at every level of his thinking. . . . His perspective is, in short, the most important determinant of his thinking, though often it remains concealed and unknown, even to the theologian himself.[41]

---

38. Cf. A. C. McGiffert, Jr., *The God of the Early Christians* (New York: Charles Scribner's Sons, 1924), 100 ff., for a detailed description of the struggles in this process.

39. We see here an illustration of the organic connection between the ontological and the soteriological.

40. H. Cunliffe-Jones, *The Authority of the Biblical Revelation* (London: James Clarke and Co., 1945), 52, makes the point that taken apart from the Old Testament, the story of Jesus Christ is much more easily assimilated to a non-Christian philosophy.

41. *Systematic Theology,* ix.

Or as Paul Tillich says of systematic theology, "It is the perspective that is crucial."[42]

On the surface, this sounds like a purely deductive method. But in practice, each part of the whole exercises its judgment upon the adequacy of the total point of view and may create an alteration in the perspective. The adequacy of the perspective will thus be continuously tested in this way, so that the inductive method is at work throughout. Actually, the point of view that informs the entire work should be the result of a lengthy inductive study. Rather than beginning with a perspective picked out of thin air and forcing each doctrine to conform, the perspective emerges out of specific study and experiences and then flows back into the particulars.

Furthermore, we must agree with Gustav Aulen in his contention that these characteristics of systematic theology do not imply that it is a rationally completed system.[43] By this he means that the unity of theology is not that it is a "closed system of reasoning but rather a unity characterized by an inner tension." That is, while there are no logical contradictions involved, there are paradoxical elements involved that cannot be reduced by rational compromise. This paradoxical element is present because it is the living God with which theology has to do and not a finite object.[44]

Nonetheless, it still implies that systematic theology is a rational enterprise. The critical approach of the philosopher is essential to producing this kind of result. It is for this reason that H. Orton Wiley lists philosophy among the required disciplines for doing theology (CT 1:30). We may identify three types of rationality that must be at work, all dependent on philosophical reasoning.

1. *Semantic rationality.* This has to do with words and involves "the demand that all connotations of a word should consciously be related to each other and centered around a controlling meaning." Terms should be used with consistent meanings, and the communicator should not equivocate in his arguments. This does not imply a wooden artificiality, since in different contexts words may legitimately bear different nuances of meaning. It only insists on semantic coherence that avoids logical equivocation.

---

42. *Systematic Theology* 1:159.
43. *Faith of the Christian Church*, 6-7.
44. See chap. 4 re "Revelation and Transcendence," where the precise nature and necessity of paradox will be discussed.

2. *Logical rationality.* Theology is not expected to accept a senseless combination of words, that is, genuine nonsense. John Wesley believed the Christian faith may be suprarational but not irrational; therefore reason must examine proposed beliefs for antirational elements. Thus he wrote: "It is a fundamental principle with us that to renounce reason is to renounce religion, that religion and reason go hand in hand, and that all irrational religion is false religion."[45] It does allow paradox, as noted above, but paradox is not logical contradiction; it "represents a movement of reality which transcends finite reason but does not shatter it." The confusion arises when these paradoxes are brought down to the level of genuine logical contradictions and people are asked to sacrifice reason in order to accept senseless combinations of words as divine wisdom.

3. *Methodological rationality.* This implies that the theology follows a definite way of deriving and stating its propositions. It entails that the writer set forth the method he proposes to use and follow it at every point.[46] It is this that we are attempting to do in the first part of this work.

The Norm of Systematic Theology

Our previous discussion implies that for systematic theology to become a reality there must be a norm (or control belief) that informs the way in which each aspect of the system is formulated. As Tillich correctly points out, "Sources and medium can produce a theological system only if their use is guided by a norm."[47] This is the same thing as saying that there is a perspective from which the total theology is developed. If there is consistency and coherence throughout, this perspective must be implemented at every point.

How is this norm derived? What is its source? Again, Prof. Tillich rightly suggests that it arises out of the spiritual life of the

---

45. *Letters of the Reverend John Wesley,* ed. John Telford, 8 vols. (London: Epworth Press, 1931), 5:364. Cf. John Allan Knight, "The Theology of John Fletcher" (Ph.D. diss., Vanderbilt University, 1966).

46. I am indebted to Paul Tillich for this discussion of rationality. Cf. *Systematic Theology* 1:53, 59.

47. Ibid., 47. The reliance on Tillich in this chapter is formal and not material. Not only does he provide what is possibly the clearest statement among contemporary sources of what constitutes a systematic theology, but he embodies it in a superior fashion in his architectonic system. This does not entail buying into the content of his work, however.

church as it encounters the Christian message; or stated differently, it emerges from the experience of the church in its encounter with the Bible in terms of its (the church's) sensed need.

A review of the history of theology will demonstrate the validity of this analysis. At different points in the life of the church, various norms have emerged out of the spiritual encounter between the ethos of the age and the biblical message. This means the selection of a norm is not an arbitrary decision. It comes forth out of the experience and in a sense impinges itself upon the consciousness of the church. In a word it lays hold of the community of faith.

In the first era of Christian theological history, commonly called the patristic period, the norm arose out of the sensed need that prevailed in that cultural milieu, namely, that man's greatest need is immortality to overcome his greatest enemy, death. The gift of God is life, and because it is spoken of so prominently in the Johannine literature, this biblical material served as a major resource of theological raw material. Theologians like Athanasius and Irenaeus developed their thought in terms of these motifs.[48]

Beginning with Augustine's thought, and apparently triggered by the trauma caused by the decline and fall of the Roman Empire, theology began to deal with the problem of guilt. The cultural situation was such as to create a sense of alienation that Augustine's own experience embodied, and he developed a full-orbed theology in terms of it. As a result, he introduced the writings of Paul into the mainstream of theological work, since they utilized the categories most appropriate to this dominant emphasis.

With the Protestant Reformation, the norm of "justification by faith" became prominent, owing to Luther's encounter with the biblical message within the matrix of his own experience. One major reason his protests created such widespread reaction was because his was but a reflection of the experience of multitudes. The Catholic system had produced a program of so-called salvation that created great anxiety. Thus Protestant theology was developed in the light of the great central truth by which Luther found freedom from this sense of anxiety. Luther even went so far as to pass judgment upon certain scriptures that he did not feel

---

48. Athanasius' major work, *De Incarnatione Verbi Dei* (The incarnation of the Word of God) (London: Religious Tract Society, n.d.), is a classic expression of the theory of redemption that grew out of this situation.

adequately supported faith alone as the means of salvation. This went a bit too far, but the point is that there was a norm that provided the possibility of systematic theology as a principle around which to organize biblical teaching, and in the light of which the biblical material was read and interpreted.

It might be objected at this point that the Bible as a whole should be considered the Norm. This is a most important question and needs to be addressed. Historically, it is true that the Bible in its entirety has never been the Norm of systematic theology (in practice, at least). But that does not preclude the possibility that it ought to be. Why, then, do we not take this route?

First, it needs to be said that it is not because the Bible itself has no unity (norm). We must grant that there is much diversity. The diversity is so great that many have argued that there are only biblical theologies, no biblical theology. But we are committed to the conviction that in spite of the real diversity, there is a coherence about the message of the total Scripture that makes it one book. It is one major task of biblical theology to attempt to identify this center and demonstrate how the various strands of biblical material implement this motif.[49]

However, to identify the unifying norm of the Bible, or each Testament taken separately, is to remain within the thought forms and concepts of the historical situation(s) out of which the material arose. The task of systematic theology being to translate this into contemporary conceptual models, it must have a vehicle by which to bridge the hermeneutical gap between then and now. Theoretically, one may attempt to simply recite biblical passages, but practically, no one lives by this principle. As Helmut Thielicke says: "Even rigid fundamentalists are trying to be more elastic at least in the techniques of homiletical presentation to the contemporary world."[50]

Maurice Wiles highlights the need for this aspect of the interpretive work of theology in these words:

> The Biblical writers share various cultural assumptions and characteristics of the ancient world which are alien to almost any [contemporary] world view.... Some form of interpretation is called for, and once again the criteria for that interpretative task are not provided by the Bible itself. Theology

---

49. Cf. Hasel, *Old Testament Theology*, chap. 4, for a discussion of the search for a center for Old Testament theology by contemporary scholars.

50. *Evangelical Faith* 1:29.

must involve something more than simply study of the ancient documents. One has only to recall the immensely varied and erratic views propounded by different sects all claiming to base themselves solely on the teaching of the Bible to recognize how important it is that "something more" be brought out fully into the open as an explicit element of critical theological work.[51]

In addition to this reason, one needs a principle of selectivity because no one takes the whole Scripture as equally significant regardless of claims to the contrary. J. Philip Hyatt points out— perhaps with tongue in cheek—that everyone has a canon within the canon. "It can be determined by looking through his Bible to see which passages or books are well-worn from reading and study, and which pages are still clean."[52]

Early on, the Church had to come to terms with the facts that the Bible needs to be interpreted and that it was susceptible to different interpretations, even interpretations contrary to the faith of the Christian Church in its mainstream expression. It was out of this disturbing reality that the creeds first arose, and later the hierarchy was identified as the official interpreters of the faith. One might suggest that if the Bible were approached with total objectivity or with a completely open mind, the true interpretation would emerge out of the encounter. Unfortunately it is impossible to verify this because either one is a situation that has never existed and will never exist. There is no such thing as complete objectivity, and all men approach the Scripture with some degree of pre-understanding. The problem is to avoid allowing this preunderstanding to so control the interpretation that the truth is perverted.

This leaves us with the necessity of providing an adequate norm to guide our use of the biblical material. Granted, as we have already suggested, this norm should arise out of the Scripture itself as we allow it to address us in our existential situation, and no norm should be adopted that runs into unresolvable contradiction with biblical theology at any point.

The norm that is self-consciously adopted in this theology is that which comes into being out of the encounter of people in the holiness movement with the biblical message. By name it is designated as Wesleyan. By adopting the name of a historical personage, we are not thereby saying that this is a historical study. We are not

51. *What Is Theology?* (New York: Oxford University Press, 1976), 5-6.
52. *The Heritage of Biblical Faith* (St. Louis: Bethany Press, 1964), 280-81.

intending to reproduce the theology of John Wesley in the 18th century. That is a perfectly worthwhile endeavor, but to make the work of Wesley the final word is to fall into the same trap discussed earlier in this chapter. What it is saying is that the spiritual impulses that originated with the founder of Methodism both resulted from and produced a particular theological insight or perspective; and these spiritual impulses are still live options among many persons in the segment of Christianity of which this work is a part. It is our purpose to attempt to identify what this perspective is and use it as the norm to develop a systematic theology for the latter part of the 20th century, thereby making it a true systematic theology in terms of the traits outlined in the previous section. The practical consequence of this is that the norm may be used to criticize and correct Wesley himself when he espouses formulations contrary to his own central theological commitment.

It needs to be added that this in no way suggests sectarianism or exclusivism. It does not preclude dialogue with other traditions within the Body of Christ. It certainly does not exclude these other perspectives in a bigoted way. It does affirm, within the larger Christian tradition, that a central biblical emphasis has chosen some to be special witnesses to itself. It is hoped that thereby some contribution can be made to the total Christian experience.

We propose that this norm is justification by faith/sanctification by faith[53] seen in the context of prevenient grace.[54] Martin

53. These should be understood as shorthand formulas for justification/sanctification by grace through faith. Faith, as Luther repeatedly argued, is not a "good work" meriting salvation, but the simple act of accepting God's gracious offer of reconciliation and cleansing. There is considerable discussion among Wesleyan scholars concerning the meaning of justification. We have opted to retain it at this point because it has been such a central term in soteriological discussion throughout the history of Christian thought, and our supporting quotations from John Wesley use this language as well. However, later on we shall argue that the primary metaphor in biblical thought for describing the restored relationship between God and man is "reconciliation," and that all other metaphors (including justification) must be interpreted in that light and not be allowed to lead soteriological discussions into nonpersonal categories, as justification tends to do with its legal connotations. The student who wishes to critically analyze this proposed norm should read and examine it in the light of this subsequent discussion, which may be found in chap. 12 on the Atonement.

54. Albert Outler, in a paper on "The Place of Wesley in the Christian Tradition," read at the celebration of the commencement of the publication of the Oxford Edition of The Works of John Wesley (1974), substantially agrees with this estimate. He sees the genius of Wesley to be the persistent holding together of "faith alone" and "holy living" and resisting all polarizations toward one or the other. He says: "It is in terms of his success and failure in this attempt . . . that we may speak of Wesley's place in the Christian tradition." 16. These two emphasize a via media between Western (Latin) Christendom

Luther is credited with rediscovering the truth of justification by faith in the 16th century; but because of his preoccupation with the problem of works righteousness, he did not provide a solid footing for sanctification in his theology. Neither Luther nor Calvin were able to have a viable doctrine of sanctification because of their commitment to the Augustinian view of predestination and election.[55] Wesley did not waver one iota in his commitment to the full Reformation teaching on justification by faith, but through his rejection of the Calvinistic doctrine of decrees, he was able to provide for a vital doctrine of sanctification. It is at this point that George Croft Cell's observation is appropriate. He interpreted Wesley's view as a synthesis of the Protestant ethic of grace and the Catholic ethic of holiness.[56]

These two doctrines of justification and sanctification may be visualized as two foci of an ellipse.[57] If either one is thought of as the center of a circle, the result is pervertive. When justification is placed at the center, the tendency is toward antinomianism; when sanctification is placed at the center, the tendency is toward legal-

---

and Eastern (Greek) Christendom, the first emphasizing "forensic images, metaphors from the law courts (Roman and medieval)"; the second has been "fascinated by visions of ontological 'participation in God.'" It has been my opinion for some time that Wesley has not been adequately interpreted by many of his followers, in part because they have considered him as if he stood exclusively in the Latin tradition and ignored the influence of Eastern Christianity upon his thinking. This should have been obvious when we remember that, as a good Anglican, he was much interested in the patristic (Greek) fathers.

In another essay, presented at the same meeting, Michael H. Hurley stressed the theological significance of Wesley's concept of prevenient grace. It has been my feeling here, too, that this theological category is the clue to unlocking what many doctrines and methodological considerations would look like from a distinctly Wesleyan perspective. *The Place of Wesley in the Christian Tradition,* ed. Kenneth E. Rowe (Metuchen, N.J.: Scarecrow Press, 1976).

55. See Mildred Bangs Wynkoop, *The Foundations of Wesleyan-Arminian Theology* (Kansas City: Beacon Hill Press of Kansas City, 1967).

56. *The Rediscovery of John Wesley* (New York: Henry Holt and Co., 1935).

57. This visualization is intended to reflect a normative relationship, not necessarily historical; but William Ragsdale Cannon, *The Theology of John Wesley* (New York: Abingdon Press, 1946), interprets Wesley's doctrine of justification in this same relation to sanctification, and Wesley himself reflects the balanced relationship in words from his sermon "On God's Vineyard" (*Works* 7:205): "It is, then, a great blessing given to this people, that as they do not think or speak of justification so as to supersede sanctification, so neither do they think or speak of sanctification so as to supersede justification. They take care to keep each in its own place, laying equal stress on one and the other. They know God has joined these together, and it is not for man to put them asunder: Therefore they maintain, with equal zeal and diligence, the doctrine of free, full, present justification, on the one hand, and of entire sanctification both of heart and life, on the other; being as tenacious of inward holiness as any Mystic, and of outward, as any Pharisee."

ism or moralism.[58] Like Paul, Wesley sought to maintain a proper balance as embodied in Paul's formula that Wesley adopted as his own motto: "faith working by love," derived from Gal. 5:6.

To place these concepts at the heart of the perspective is to highlight the centrality of soteriology in Wesleyan theology. The task of theologizing is not to develop an edifice of thought that is self-consistent but nothing more than an abstract, ivory-tower system. The saving or redemptive work of God is the burning focus of all theological work. Every doctrine must ultimately be brought to bear upon this point.[59]

Wesley only avoided the morass of Calvinism by a "hair's breadth," to use his own words. But that "hair" was enough to stand as a continental divide so that the two theologies (perspectives) lie miles apart in their fully developed expressions. The truth that holds them but a hair's breadth apart at the point of the watershed is the doctrine of *prevenient grace*. It could even be argued that this teaching was the most far-reaching and pervasive aspect of Wesley's thought.

As we will see, prevenient grace is the key to unlock many theological problems; and following its implications to their logical conclusion reveals that Wesleyan theology has a distinctive approach to numerous issues that is neither fundamentalist nor liberal.

Traditionally, Wesleyans have developed the idea of prevenient grace exclusively in terms of soteriological considerations, and ultimately, as we have noted, it must focus there. But Wesley himself treated it in a broader way, and we are proposing in this analysis to use it as an ontological as well as an epistemological principle of interpretation. In this way it becomes the most pervasive aspect of our suggested norm and will be the crucial element in several doctrines, including the doctrine of revelation. Fur-

---

58. It is a standard criticism that the majority of the so-called apostolic fathers (e.g., Clement of Rome, *Didache, The Shepherd of Hermas, Epistle of Barnabas*) are moralistic or legalistic in their understanding of the Christian life, stressing the new religion as a new law. A careful reading of these ancient documents reveals that this is a correct analysis and that it is true because the doctrine of justification by faith is noticeably absent from their writing. Their stress on the holy life would be sound if it were placed within the context of justification. Clement struggles with a tension between justification and sanctification, but the others have all but completely capitulated to the moralistic understanding.

59. Not every theological system agrees with this. E.g., dispensationalism sets salvation aside as secondary and declares "the glory of God" to be the most important. Cf. Charles C. Ryrie, *Dispensationalism Today* (Chicago: Moody Press, 1965).

thermore, prevenient grace needs to be placed in the same structure as is present in other Wesleyan doctrines. Each has both an
objective and a subjective aspect. Again, this is usually explicated
in relation to a narrowly soteriological concern, but it is so distinctively Wesleyan that it may profitably be applied to all doctrines, though they have not all been elucidated in this way by
much popular Wesleyan theology.

The earliest attempt at a Wesleyan systematic theology was
doubtless the work of John Fletcher.[60] Although by today's standards it lacks much of the required character of such a work, it has
great significance for us by using the idea of prevenient grace as its
foundation stone and controlling motif.[61]

At this point we must further refine our proposed norm by
giving it more precise definition. Mr. Wesley explicitly grounded
prevenient grace in Christology. Not only did he teach that grace is
freely bestowed upon all men for the sake of Christ, removing the
guilt of original sin, but knowledge of God is also interpreted as the
consequence of the grace of Christ. A Wesleyan theology will be
uniquely Christological in emphasis: justification, sanctification,
and prevenient grace in all its many ramifications must be interpreted from this standpoint. As the work of the Holy Spirit and
preventing grace are virtually synonymous concepts, the work of
the Spirit is seen by Wesley as Christological in nature. As John
Deschner says: "Much attention has been given to the power of the
Holy Spirit in Wesley's doctrine of sanctification. It needs to be
more clearly recognized that the sanctifying Spirit is the Spirit of
the victorious as well as the suffering Christ."[62] The Christological
grounding of every doctrine will be shown to be the all-encompassing character of the norm to be used in this systematic theology.[63]

---

60. So John A. Knight, "Fletcher," 189 n. 43.

61. Ibid., 178. The doctrine is spelled out epistemologically in terms of Fletcher's
own language of "dispensations."

62. *Wesley's Christology*, 116.

63. Ibid., 92; Lycurgus M. Starkey, Jr., *The Work of the Holy Spirit* (Nashville: Abingdon Press, 1962), 41; Charles Allen Rogers, "The Concept of Prevenient Grace in the
Theology of John Wesley" (Ph.D. diss., Duke University, 1967). See also Wesley's *Works*
6:223; 7:187 ff., 373-74; 8:277-78; *Standard Sermons*, ed. Edward H. Sugden, 2 vols.
(London: Epworth Press, 1961; hereafter abbreviated as StS), 1:118; 2:43, 445. Deschner
argues that Christology is the presupposition of Wesley's theology and comments: "The
author's conviction is that an explicit examination of Wesley's great presupposition can
lead to clarification and even correction of preaching in the present-day Wesleyan tradition."

One more point needs to be made in explicating the importance of a norm: It provides the basis for meaningful discussion within a given context. It is the opinion of this writer that there is the possibility of conversation across perspectival lines, but its value lies largely in discussing the relative adequacy of diverging perspectives. Although it may not be possible to prove one perspective to be right and the other wrong in any scientific sense, it is certainly possible to show one to be more consistent with the pertinent facts and more adequate in terms of total coherence than another. But once within a perspective, it is a matter of much greater concreteness to discuss the logical consistency of a particular position in relation to the perspective chosen.

A. J. Ayer, in *Language, Truth, and Logic,* one of the earliest and most devastating attacks of linguistic philosophy on statements of value (which include theological propositions), argues that since such statements are nonempirical in nature, they are not significant for meaning; they are merely expressions of emotion. He goes even further, on this basis, to argue that it is impossible to really dispute over such matters, since they cannot be adjudicated on empirical grounds. In this context, however, he does allow for the possibility of genuine argument if "some system of values is presupposed."[64] If there can be an agreement on a context, or point of reference, meaningful debate can occur. Although we do not need to necessarily concur with all of Ayer's views (he himself later admits that the issues were more complex than he first allowed), we still can recognize the value of a norm (perspective) as a setting for dialogue.

In a similar fashion Wiley argues that theology is a science. Calling attention to the basic empirical principle elucidated so consistently and radically by David Hume, he points out that science (meaning the natural sciences) is based on faith rather than knowledge. "It assumes such metaphysical truths as space and time, substance and attributes, cause and effect, and also assumes the trustworthiness of the mind in its investigations" (CT 1:61). There is a correlation between theology and the natural sciences in the sense that both, by an act of faith, accept a perspective that cannot be proven and carry on their respective enterprises within the circle defined by their perspective. This correspondence, however, goes only as far as the initial step of faith. Beyond that point there is a

---

64. P. 111.

considerable difference in both method and verification. Nonetheless, it is the importance of the norm that is recognized as being the crucial element in systematic theology.

If we take this approach seriously, it means that theological systems are similar to scientific hypotheses: They are experimental models. The failure to recognize that fact explains why history is replete with overly dogmatic scientists as well as overly dogmatic theologians. Jack Rogers has some wise words about this way of understanding the theological task:

> A scientist builds models of reality. A model is not the same as the real thing. But it helps us to understand reality. A model takes the essential pieces of the real thing and scales them down so that we can understand them. We speak of God by analogies, models from life. We say God is our Father. We mean that we see in his acts some of the best characteristics of certain fathers we know. When we forget that we are making models and speaking by analogies we run the risk of idolatry. Idolatry consists in worshipping the created model rather than pointing to the creator it represents. We must not get too attached to our thought forms, or fine distinctions of language, our cultural packaging.[65]

The great scientist is humble in the face of his data. So is the theologian. He recognizes that his theology is secondary to his faith. While his faith is not negotiable,[66] he is open to learn from anyone who is engaged in the same pursuit of understanding.

A Note on Legitimacy

Not every theologian would agree that systematic theology is a legitimate enterprise. Karl Barth, doubtless the most influential theologian in this century, spoke out against it. He insisted that the theologian cannot operate in terms of a key concept (norm) because he is in no position to make such a selection. The whole Bible is theoretically to be the norm of theological work.

He speaks of a critic who observes that "for the moment only the angels in heaven will know where the way of his *Church Dogmatics* will lead," and Barth fully agreed. What he proposed to do was approach each doctrine anew and "listen as unreservedly as

---

65. *Confessions*, 59.
66. If "faith" is misunderstood as intellectual rather than existential here, this distinction is nonsense. But we have in mind the primary biblical meaning as trust in a person rather than believing a proposition.

possible to the witness of scripture."[67] Unlike the systematic theologian, he thought, in following this approach, one cannot predict in terms of a central commitment what each new doctrine will look like. This implies that the theologian is unpredictable and free even to contradict himself if that is what he hears in the Scripture.

Two observations on this contention need to be made: (1) Barth really developed a systematic theology in the light of a controlling principle, and (2) the assumption is to be seriously questioned that the Scripture will yield contradictory positions to the open hearer (an option that we have previously called into question).

In seeking to justify the legitimacy of systematic theology, Wiley quotes approvingly the words of Charles Hodge:

> Such, evidently, is the will of God. He does not teach men astronomy nor chemistry, but gives them facts out of which these sciences are constructed. Neither does He teach us systematic theology, but He gives us in the Bible the truth which, properly understood and arranged, constitute[s] the science of theology. As the facts of nature are all related and determined by physical laws, so the facts of the Bible are all related and determined by the nature of God and His creatures, and as He wills that men should study His works and discover their wonderful organic relation and harmonious combination, so it is His will that we should study His Word, and learn that, like the stars, its truths are not isolated points, but systems, cycles, and epicycles, in unending harmony and grandeur. Besides all this, although the Scriptures do not contain a system of theology as a whole, we have in the Epistles of the New Testament, portions of the system wrought out to our hands. These are our authority and guide.[68]

This analogy with science suggests some interesting implications regarding the possibility of different norms for systematic theology. In dealing with the phenomenon of light, scientists have come up with two different theories, both of which make sense out of, and adequately explain, the facts. This points to a distinction between knowledge and opinion, which has been recognized by theologians from earliest times and was particularly stressed by John Wesley. Theology partakes of the character of opinion. Faith

---

67. *Church Dogmatics*, ed. G. W. Bromiley and T. F. Torrance (Edinburgh: T. and T. Clark, 1957), vol. 4, pt. 1, p. xi (hereafter 4.1.xi).

68. *CT* 1:54. It must be noted, however, in honesty, that Hodge's understanding of theology and the Bible is antithetical to the understanding of theology developed in this chapter.

more nearly corresponds to the category of knowledge, according to the biblical point of view. It occurs primarily if not exclusively in personal relations. It is this to which Wiley is pointing in his justly famous statement that "truth in its ultimate nature is personal. Our Lord made this clear when He said, *I am the truth.* He knocks at the door of men's hearts—not as a proposition to be apprehended, but as a Person to be received and loved" (*CT* 1:38). That distinction draws our minds once again to the importance of an existentially efficacious norm, requiring a whole-person response.

Wiley offers some further suggestions in defense of systematic theology: (1) the constitution of the human mind; (2) the development of Christian character in the sense that structured truth is more easily assimilated. In support of this he points out that the "uniform testimony of the Church is that the strongest Christians in every age are those who have a firm grasp upon the great fundamentals of the Christian faith." And (3) the presentation of the truth. This is the reverse side of the previous point. The communication of the truth is dependent upon its being grasped as an organic whole (*CT* 1:54-55). We feel that the task of systematic theology is not only a legitimate undertaking but a necessary one.

Sources of Theology: The Bible

God has not chosen to communicate a system of dogma encompassing finished statements concerning the whole scope of Christian truth, needing but to be memorized. He comes to man as the redeeming Presence and Divine Actor on the stage of history. The various vehicles that mediate knowledge of this activity and its implications for human life furnish the human intellect with the raw materials out of which men may construct doctrinal systems. It is to these media that we make reference when we speak about sources for theological work.

Traditionally the various sources of theology have been divided into two major groups: (1) the authoritative Source, which is the Bible; and (2) subsidiary sources, which include experience, creeds and confessions, philosophy, and nature. There is wisdom in such a classification, because the Scripture is the primary Source for theologizing. However, we would slightly modify the selection of secondary sources, eliminating nature, since contemporary developments in theology and philosophy have rendered this too problematic to serve as a theological source. Furthermore, from the biblical perspective, nature was never a source of knowledge of the character of God, although certain expressions of nature have validly served as illustrations of aspects of God's power and wisdom.[1]

The question of sources raises the question of authority, both with regard to the nature of the authority to be ascribed to the sources and the relative degree of authority among themselves. The second issue will be addressed during the total discussion. Regarding the first matter, it can be summarily stated that all sources carry only derivative authority, by which we mean that they are authoritative to the degree that they adequately bear witness to the primary revelation, which carries final authority. From the Christian perspective, this is the Christ-event and, in the light of it, the salvation-events of the Old Testament, of which it is the fulfillment. As Wiley so well puts it: "Christ was Himself the full and perfect revelation of the Father—the effulgence of His glory and the express or exact image of His Person. His testimony is the spirit of prophecy—the last word of all objective revelation" (CT 1:137); and again: "Christ the Personal Word was Himself the full and final revelation of the Father. He alone is the true Revealer" (138-39).

The following discussion presupposes many of the substantive conclusions developed in chapter 5, but logical order leads us to discuss the methodological matters first, although it must be admitted that the content of the theology informs the method. One really does his theological work first and then identifies the method that emerges out of the work. However, method is logically first and not a part of the theology as such, although it is implicit there. The major conclusion to which we are referring is the idea of revelation, which interprets God's self-disclosure as occurring primarily through interpreted events and always in a timeful way. This way of putting it does not exhaust the full meaning of revelation, as subsequent discussion will make clear. It does point to a major aspect of it, one that has become common coin in contemporary theological studies.

Like all historical events, those that biblical faith considers to be revelatory have two sides: (1) facticity and (2) meaning. The factual or objective side of the event is in principle subject to scientific verification or falsification according to the accepted meth-

---

1. It is noteworthy that religions that derive their understanding of God from nature hold a view radically different from the biblical idea of God, e.g., the Canaanites. Of Psalm 19, a classic creation psalm, Bernhard Anderson says: "It is important to notice here the Psalmist does not say that God is revealed in nature; rather the heavens are *witnesses* to his glory." *Creation Versus Chaos* (New York: Association Press, 1967), 90.

ods of historiography. However, the bare fact alone does not make history. These events must be interpreted in terms of their significance in relation to preceding events, contemporary happenings, and future consequences. It is their placement in this complex of contexts that gives meaning to them and turns them from statistical-type chronicles to history. Even the ambiguity that is resident in the word *history* conveys this twofold connotation: *History* may mean the course of events, or it may mean the recording of those events in a patterned narrative.

The interpretation of those events is a program that is carried out in terms of a point of view, or perspective. Every historical event is susceptible to more than one interpretation, and this is especially true when the theological dimension is injected into the interpretation.

Obviously one's knowledge of history is dependent upon one of two sources: (1) being an eyewitness of what took place, or (2) reports of such eyewitnesses. It is not necessarily true that the eyewitnesses are the most competent interpreters of history. However, if the event gives evidence of bearing within itself the clue to its own meaning, it would increase the likelihood that the primary participants would have experienced the most direct access to its proper significance. If an event becomes revelatory when it is experienced as an act of salvation (or judgment), then only a participant who by faith actualized the saving (or judgmental) value in his own personal (or corporate) experience could qualify to pass on the significance of such an event that in the passing on may become similarly revelatory for the one who hears (or reads). Hence, only believers author biblical documents, and usually in the context of the community of believers.

These considerations give rise to the priority of the Scriptures as a source of theology, since they contain both the primary record and faithful interpretation of the salvation history. This is why Wiley says: "The first subject in any discussion of the Christian revelation must of necessity be the Christian Book since here alone are to be found its documentary records" (*CT* 1:138).

Contemporary scholarship has achieved a high degree of unanimity in speaking about the Bible as "the Book of the Acts of God."[2] Although there are a few dissenting voices about the exclu-

2. Cf. W. T. Purkiser, ed., *Exploring Our Christian Faith*, rev. ed. (Kansas City: Beacon Hill Press of Kansas City, 1978), 54.

siveness of this way of viewing the Bible, scarcely anyone will question the historical nature of biblical revelation.[3] Thus the "Bible . . . is the basic source of systematic theology because it is the original document about the events on which the Christian Church is founded."[4]

Every evangelical, conservative Christian theologian accepts the authority of the Bible. The question to be discussed relates to the nature and shape of that authority. These are important matters, but as we shall argue later, they are not finally the most decisive issues regarding the Bible. Consequently we will not here enter into this question in elaborate detail, since this has been done many times, but attempt to briefly reflect a distinctively Wesleyan position.

Prevenient Grace and Biblical Authority

In dealing with the question of biblical authority, too many writers fail to come to terms with the nature of authority, and thus considerable ambiguity is present when claims are made for the authority of Scripture. We need to explore in a relatively simple manner some important distinctions involved in this question.

All authority at the human level is derived authority and is both penultimately and ultimately rooted in power. The power that is the basis of authority is not necessarily physical but may be moral or academic or possibly could take other forms as well. One of the most popular paradigms of authority is the policeman, and it serves well to illustrate some crucial aspects of the authority question. His badge or uniform is the symbol of his authority, which is derived from the government he represents. That is, as an individual or a person he has no inherent authority (or power) to stop traffic or make an arrest. An arrest is qualitatively different from physical coercion. The authority to do so derives from the government that commissioned him, and from the Christian perspective the government's authority ultimately derives from God

---

3. Among those who have questioned the consensus are James Barr, *Old and New in Interpretation* (New York: Harper and Row, Publishers, 1966); Langdon B. Gilkey, "Cosmology, Ontology, and the Travail of Biblical Language," *Journal of Religion*, July 1961, 194-205.

4. Tillich, *Systematic Theology* 1:35.

(Rom. 13:1-7). It is possible that governments may become so anti-Christ (e.g., Hitler's Third Reich) that one may legitimately deny them the right to appeal to divine authorization. In this case such government must depend upon the imposition of its will by the use of raw force. Conversely, when the fear of God wanes among the populace, there also seems to be an increase in anarchy with an increased need for government control.

This fact points to a further dimension of authority: Apart from being coerced by sheer physical force, one must make a personal (perhaps moral) decision to acknowledge any and all authorities and submit to their requirements. It is impossible to identify all the possible motives that precipitate such decisions. It may be fear, reverence, love, or some other, or a combination of several. Regardless of what the particular motive or motives of the decision to submit may be, it is ultimately personal in nature. The law-abiding citizen has made a personal decision to acknowledge and obey the authority of his government, whereas the criminal has made a decision to ignore and reject such authority, choosing thereby to submit to some other authority, probably of the individual self or else a counterculture. What determines each decision? It cannot be exclusively in the objective character of laws or the government; otherwise there would be no rejections of authority. Is it a matter of heredity or genetic structure or other factors beyond the control of the decision-making person? If so, there is no possibility of *moral* accountability, only legal. It must finally be acknowledged as a mystery that finds its locus in the hidden depths of personality.

The principles that inform this simple illustration apply directly to the issue of authority in the theological sphere as well. From the Christian perspective, authority is vested in God because He is Ultimate Reality, and all existents are dependent upon His creativity. Our knowledge of God is mediated to us through various media, the most authoritative of which is the Scripture. The Scripture, like the policeman, does not bear its authority within itself but roots in a prior source. Likewise, the acceptance of the authority of Scripture is not the result of coercion but is personal in nature.

A major question to be raised in any discussion of biblical authority concerns the basis for one's acceptance of the Scripture as authoritative or the nature of its existential authority. If it is received on the basis of some other authority, such as the church, then the church becomes a more ultimate authority than the Scripture. In order to avoid this dilemma, theologians have traditionally made efforts to establish an objective basis for this authority within the Scripture itself. This involves the formulation of rational grounds that were deemed sufficient to convince the mind to submit to the Bible as the Word of God.

One such proposal suggests the rationality of accepting the Bible's testimony to its own authenticity. Apart from the difficulty of establishing that the Bible makes any holistic self-references, this approach logically entails the conclusion that the argument would have validity only within the context of a prior acceptance of biblical authority on some other grounds and within itself would relieve the argument of any apologetic significance. If it is set forward as a front-line rationale, it provides no principle for limiting its application to the Hebrew-Christian Scriptures. The Book of Mormon also claims itself to be the Word of God. It thus is self-defeating and becomes a classic example of the logical fallacy of begging the question.[5]

One of the most prominent arguments among evangelicals—and also used by some Wesleyans—has been to base the Bible's authority on its inerrancy. The proponents of inerrancy have two major points that need to be noticed in order to understand the logic of their position. First, the conclusion is usually deduced from the doctrine of God. The premise is that the infallible God of Truth would not and could not direct His human instruments to write anything that is false, even in its minutest detail.[6] The reasoning thus moves from God to the Scriptures and precludes the possibility of error prior to examining the text itself.

The second part of the argument asserts that such inerrancy is confined to the original autographs, none of which have survived.[7]

---

5. John Miley, whose *Systematic Theology* was for several years the official text of the course of study for ministers of the Church of the Nazarene, makes the following comment on this argument: "If we should attempt to prove the inspiration of the Scriptures from their own statements, and then, that they are a divine revelation because inspired, our argument would move in a circle, and hence bring no logical result. Such is a rather common fallacy, one far more harmful than helpful to the truth." (New York: Eaton and Mains, 1894), 2:487.

6. See W. Ralph Thompson, "Facing Objections Raised Against Biblical Inerrancy," *Wesleyan Theological Journal* 3, no. I (Spring 1968): 21-29.

7. This argument originated in the 19th century with the Princeton theology formulated by A. A. Hodge and B. B. Warfield. "It was Hodge who first formalized the concept of autographs as the basis for infallibility of Scriptures." R. Larry Shelton, "John Wesley's

This, too, precludes the possibility of the discovery of error and therefore puts the claim itself beyond either empirical validation or falsification. It remains an a priori theological judgment that defers to some authority for its viability other than the Scripture itself, namely, the one who declares the autographs to be inerrant. John Wesley himself can be cited to support this idea, which often argues a kind of domino theory, as Wesley's statement reflects: "Now, if there be any mistakes in the Bible, there may as well be a thousand. If there is one falsehood in that book, it did not come from the God of truth."[8]

Other evangelicals—including many Wesleyans—equally committed to the final authority of Scripture for faith and life, do not find it efficacious to appeal to an errorless Bible in the above fashion. A. M. Hills, revered holiness scholar and author of once-popular *Fundamental Christian Theology,* takes great pains to avoid this approach. Incorporating quotes from others, he writes:

> It is truly said that "the man who binds up the cause of Christianity with the literal accuracy of the Bible is no friend of Christianity; for with the rejection of that theory, too often comes the rejection of the Bible itself, and faith is shattered." Those who maintain that we must accept every statement of Scripture, or none of it, should consider that no doctrine more surely makes skeptics. "It seems," says Dr. Stearns, "a very good and pious thing to assert that the Bible is absolutely without error. But nothing is good or pious that is contrary to fact."[9]

Clark H. Pinnock, an established evangelical scholar contemporary with this writing, argues as follows:

> To say that unless every point can be established, the entire edifice will come crashing down seems to indicate the fortress mentality of an orthodoxy in decline. When the awareness of God speaking powerfully through Scripture begins to subside, it is necessary to cling to rationalistic arguments in order to defend the Bible, and Scholastic orthodoxy is born. It is certainly difficult to understand why God, if he deemed errorlessness epistemologically so crucial, did not take greater care to pre-

---

Approach to Scripture in Historical Perspective," *Wesleyan Theological Journal* 16, no. 1 (Spring 1981): 38. See also Shelton's footnotes.

8. *The Journal of John Wesley, A.M.,* ed. Nehemiah Curnock, 8 vols. (London: Epworth Press, 1949), 6:117. Of this and similar comments, Shelton says: "These kinds of expressions relate primarily to his verbal dictation tendencies in inspiration, and are not used to establish an inerrantist basis for authority. His epistemology is different from that of Fundamentalism which bases biblical authority on an assumption of the nature of the external text of the autographs." "John Wesley's Approach," 38.

9. 2 vols. (Pasadena, Calif.: C. J. Kinne, 1931), 1:134.

serve the text errorless, and how it is that the errant Bibles Christian have always had to use have been so effective for millennia.[10]

The classical approach to the question of the existential authority of Scripture has pointed to a factor that transcends rational arguments as the ultimate court of appeal, finding such rationalistic defenses less than compelling. Speaking of such defensive efforts, John Calvin says:

> In vain were the authority of Scripture fortified by argument, or supported by the consent of the Church, or confirmed by any other helps, if unaccompanied by an assurance higher and stronger than human judgment can find. Till this better foundation has been laid, the authority of Scripture remains in suspense. . . . For the truth is vindicated in opposition to every doubt, when, unsupported by foreign aid, it has its sole sufficiency in itself.[11]

Wiley, addressing the same type of effort to defend the Bible rationalistically, says:

> It depended upon logic rather than life. Spiritual men and women—those filled with the Holy Spirit, are not unduly concerned with either higher or lower criticism. They do not rest merely in the letter which must be defended by argument. They have a broader and more substantial basis for their faith. It rests in their risen Lord, the glorified Christ (CT 1:143).

These theologians are appealing to the position known as the *testimonium internum Spiritus Sancti*—the internal testimony of the Holy Spirit. This has been identified as the Reformation teaching and is subscribed to by Martin Luther and John Wesley. In a thorough and wide-ranging study of these issues, Larry Shelton says:

> The primary basis for the authority of Scripture and the authenticating factor of its inspiredness (for Wesley) is the "internal testimony of the Holy Spirit." He says, "Then a Christian can in no wise doubt of his being a child of God. Of the former

---

10. "Three Views of Biblical Authority," in *Biblical Authority*, ed. Jack Rogers (Waco, Tex.: Word Books, Publisher, 1977), 65-66. Bruce Vawter emphasizes the same point, making an important distinction: "Textual criticism had not revealed to the church that it no longer possessed the word: What it had revealed was that the church could not always be certain of the *verbal* purity of the *text* through which it possessed the word. That is what was, or should have been, fatal to any theory of strictly verbal inspiration. . . . If God has really 'dictated' a text—however literally the anthropomorphism might be taken—then surely the text and its verbal exactness—and not simply the word mediated thereby—would have been the object of a continuing concern." *Biblical Inspiration* (Philadelphia: Westminster Press, 1972), 65.

11. *Institutes* 1.8.1.

proposition he has as full assurance as he has that the Scriptures are of God." . . . Thus, the authenticating basis for scriptural authority becomes for Wesley an element in his use of experience as a basis for authority.[12]

Wiley lends his full support to this position (*CT* 1:35-37 et al.). Even the Westminster Confession acknowledges the work of the Spirit in authenticating the authority of Scripture. After listing the various external characteristics that impress our minds, it reads: "Yet, notwithstanding, our full persuasion and assurance of the infallible truth, and divine authority thereof, is from the inward work of the Holy Spirit, bearing witness by and with the word in our hearts."[13]

Why does not the work of the Spirit convince all men to accept and submit to the authority of Scripture? Can it be concluded that His work in this regard is selective? Here we may draw a parallel to the Wesleyan doctrine of prevenient grace and in fact assert that the doctrine of the *testimonium internum Spiritus Sancti* is but a special case of prevenient grace. It is extended to all men equally; in this case, to all who have been exposed to the contents of the Scripture. The reason some respond is a mystery, hidden not in the secret counsels of God, but in the equally impenetrable mysteries of human personality.

Richard S. Taylor points implicitly to the priority of the issue of existential authority to all other questions of authority in his closing words to his *Biblical Authority and Christian Faith*: "If the concept of biblical authority is going to be helpful to us, we must resolve our own personal authority problem." And he furthermore suggests the nearest theoretical solution to which we may come for the problem raised in the preceding paragraph: "As long as there is within us hostility toward God as the supreme Authority, there is bound to be resistance toward all lesser authorities. But this is a sin problem, not an intellectual problem."[14] This is a reflection of the solution to the matter of His own authority in relation to the Jews by the Johannine Christ.

In addition to the type of authority we have labeled as *existential* (because it involves a personal decision that is life-transforming), there is another type of authority that must also be addressed in the context of the discussion of biblical authority. To this we

---

12. "John Wesley's Approach," 37.
13. Quoted in Marshall, *Biblical Inspiration*, 46-47.
14. (Kansas City: Beacon Hill Press of Kansas City, 1980), 93.

ascribe the term *cognitive,* because it relates to the cognitive content of Scripture. If the internal testimony of the Holy Spirit witnesses to the authenticity (divine authority) of the written Word, it does not do so apart from the content of the Scripture.

This point highlights the interdependence of the two types of authority. There is an inseparable connection, but it is very delicately balanced and must be kept from becoming imbalanced. Søren Kierkegaard, in his statement that "if the contemporary generation had left nothing behind them but these words: We have believed that in such and such a year God appeared among us in the humble figure of a servant, that he lived and taught in our community, and finally died, it would be more than enough . . . and the most voluminous account can in all eternity do nothing more," upsets the balance in one direction.[15] He who would equate religion with right thinking upsets it in the other.

A most important interpretative principle in understanding religious experience is that one's experience of God is informed by his understanding of both the object of knowledge and the nature of the divine-human encounter as well as the outcomes (emotional, ethical, etc.). John Fletcher's doctrine of dispensations, which describes facets of the knowledge of God, recognizes this fact. Each dispensation has both an external and an internal aspect. The former is cognitive and depends upon actual information or content concerning God that may be granted to man. The latter aspect is personal and relates to one's commitment to what has been revealed cognitively to him.[16]

This recognizes the validity of an experience of God apart from full grasp of all the theological implications of the Christian faith, but allows for growth in personal experience as one's knowledge increases: "But grow in the grace and knowledge of our Lord and Savior Jesus Christ" (2 Pet. 3:18). This principle applies to both individual and racial history.

The recognition of this cognitive dimension of authority raises an important question: What aspect of the cognitive content of the Bible is authoritative? This logically leads to the issue of the inspiration of Scripture, since the solution to this issue defines the parameters of the answer to the question. Thus we will explore this

---

15. *Philosophical Fragments,* trans. David F. Swenson (Oxford and New York: Oxford University Press, 1936), 87.
16. John A. Knight, "Fletcher," 8.

subject as a way of further elaborating the matter of cognitive authority.

The Inspiration of Scripture

There are three issues that emerge in connection with this much-discussed topic: (1) the fact of inspiration, (2) the mode of inspiration, and (3) the extent of inspiration.

The Fact of Inspiration

The idea of the "inspiredness" of Scripture is a biblical truth. Two passages (2 Tim. 3:16-17 and 2 Pet. 1:20-21) refer explicitly to it. However, it is somewhat anachronistic to use these passages to refer to the Bible as a whole, since they clearly have explicit reference only to the Old Testament Scriptures. Nonetheless, if one can derive a principle from these references, it would not be improper to extrapolate a theory of inspiration that may then be referred to the whole Hebrew-Christian Scriptures. The problem, however, is that we are given little more than a statement that the Scriptures are "God-breathed" (Amp., NIV), but scarcely a clue as to the method or extent or character of the inspiring activity of God. Yet these are the issues that have been debated in periods when the question of biblical authority was being challenged.

Perhaps some clue may be gained by exploring the possible source of the word *theopneustos* used in 2 Tim. 3:16 and translated in most versions "inspired." The term itself is derived from classical Greek, where it refers to an ecstatic experience where the person inspired is possessed to the point of having no consciousness or volition of his own. In such a state he may become the passive vehicle through whom oracles are pronounced. But all the evidence points to the fact that the term, derived from the world of ecstatic seizure, is used in the New Testament passage to point to an Old Testament concept, namely, the idea of the Spirit of God: The breath of God is seen as the source of life. Man, otherwise a corpse, became a "living being" when God breathed (inspired) into his nostrils the breath of life (Gen. 2:7).[17]

---

17. Vawter, *Biblical Inspiration*, 8-13, has given a careful analysis of the biblical evidence and concludes that "we have to do here with a linguistic syncretism. Although both the LXX and the NT made a studied effort to avoid the language of mantic experience (ecstatic seizure) in referring to the unique Judeo-Christian prophetic tradition, it was not possible to avoid it entirely, since it was the only language available." 9. John Burnaby, *Is*

Out of this context, it is quite possible that Paul was simply intending to convey the idea that God's Spirit breathed life into an otherwise dead text of the Old Testament, thus making it profitable for doctrine, reproof, correction, and instruction (KJV). John Wesley understood it this way and says in his *Notes* on this verse: "The Spirit of God not only once inspired those who wrote it, but continually inspires, supernaturally assists, those that read it with earnest prayer."[18] So 2 Tim. 3:16-17 has been translated: "Every inspired scripture has its use for teaching the truth and refuting error, or for reformation of manners and discipline in right living, so that the man who belongs to God may be efficient and equipped for good work of every kind" (NEB). The context clearly and unequivocally refers to the *use* to which Scripture may be put, not primarily to the production of it originally, though that is apparently assumed. It thus at least includes the existential aspect of authority previously discussed.

---

the Bible Inspired? (London: Duckworth and Co., 1949), analyzes the biblical understanding of the nature of God as love and the distinctiveness of man as person to both demonstrate the inappropriateness of using the model of "Spirit possession" for explaining the phenomenon of "inspiration" and suggest a model based on this divine-human relationship: "The influence of the Holy Spirit upon the soul of man is . . . rightly to be understood by analogy with the influence of person upon person. Under that influence the soul is constrained, but constrained willingly. As it yields to the Spirit's influence, it is at the same time brought nearer to unity of personal life in itself, and drawn into union with God's world of persons and with God Himself. . . . But there remains, inviolate throughout, the distinction and the difference between Creator and creature." 80. Cf. also Alan Richardson, *The Bible in the Age of Science* (Philadelphia: Westminster Press, 1961), 75.

18. On the phrase "living oracles" in Acts 7:38, Wesley explains in his *Notes:* "These are termed *living,* because all 'the word of God,' applied by His Spirit, 'is living and powerful,' Heb. 4:12." Paul Bassett says on this subject: "Wesley doubts that the 'letter of Scripture' has value apart from the operations of the Spirit." "The Holiness Movement and the Protestant Principle," *Wesleyan Theological Journal* 18, no. 1 (Spring 1983): 14. A number of very reputable biblical scholars concur with this interpretation: Alan Richardson, in *Bible in Science,* writes: "The Greek text suggests that God has breathed into the 'dead' words of the Old Testament Scriptures the breath of life, as once he breathed into man's nostrils and man became a living soul. The AV translation has behind it a long history of misinterpretations, since Alexandrian and pagan notions of inspiration as a kind of divine *afflatus* had entered the church as early as the days of Justin Martyr in the middle of the second century. From these misconceptions the rise of modern historical criticism in the nineteenth century has set us free." 75. See also idem, *Christian Apologetics* (New York: Harper and Bros., Publishers, 1944), 202-5; R. P. C. Hanson, *Allegory and Event* (Richmond, Va.: John Knox Press, 1959), chap. 7. I. Howard Marshall argues that the total thrust of the passage relates to the purposes for which God inspired it and thus relates to "its adequacy for what God intends it to do." *Biblical Inspiration,* 53. Concurring are Perry B. Yoder, *Toward Understanding the Bible* (Newton, Kans.: Faith and Life Press, 1978), 69-70; Paul J. Achtemeier, *The Inspiration of Scripture* (Philadelphia: Westminster Press, 1980), 107-8.

The other side of the coin (what we have called the cognitive authority) is more clearly reflected in 2 Pet. 1:20-21. Here the author is concerned with prophecy. In the light of the larger context of the book, the issue seems to be the fulfillment of the prophetic Word, whether of the Old Testament in terms of Jesus' first advent, or Christian prophecy in terms of the Second Advent. The fact that the First Advent transcended the literal word of the prophet (see Appendix 2) meant that its fulfillment needed a verification, the anticipation of which Peter and his peers had actually received on the Mount of Transfiguration: "We have the prophetic word made more sure" (v. 19). By parallel, the Second Advent need not entail a fulfillment within the time frame demanded by many, since "one day is with the Lord as a thousand years, and a thousand years as one day" (3:8, KJV). The implication of this is that the prophets spoke more than they knew, that is, when fulfilled, the meaning transcended their historically conditioned situation. The only answer for this is that their message was not a "private interpretation" (1:20, KJV), but rather they were "borne along" (v. 21, Amp.) or "moved by the Holy Spirit."

Again, this does not convey any specific methodology beyond the mere affirmation that the Holy Spirit was at work in the production of the "prophetic word" as well as in the reading of it. If one accepts the authority of Scripture as an act of personal decision under the influence of the Holy Spirit (as discussed above), included is the *fact* that the Scripture makes some self-reference to its own inspired character. But this does not commit the Bible-believing Christian to any particular mode of inspiration. One's view of this point depends upon what he perceives to be theologically adequate and true to the data of Scripture. Unfortunately, many theories can sustain themselves only by refusing to take certain facts into account. Our discussion seriously seeks to avoid that pitfall.

The Mode of Inspiration

The various theories of the mode of inspiration may be visualized as different positions on a continuum, depending on the way the divine and human elements are related in producing the Sacred Book. In this sense there is a parallel, often noted, to the Christological debates, which reproduce the same pattern.[19] In

---

19. Marshall expresses reticence about using this analogy, having doubts that it really illuminates the issue: "The difference between the incarnation of the eternal Word in the

both cases, the difference between theories seems to be the result of the degree to which history is taken seriously. The extreme views (Docetism and Ebionism in Christological terms) are inadequate, but attaining a satisfactory theory has been extremely difficult. The final solution in both cases may be to settle for a paradoxical relation incapable of complete resolution in fully rational terms. This would be most nearly the authentic Wesleyan approach, since Mr. Wesley on such questions always insisted only on belief in the *fact* but not on theoretical explanations.

A survey of the different options will serve to demonstrate the difficulty of the problem and the probable necessity of settling for a paradoxical answer.[20] The closer one approaches the left of the continuum—the human end—the more the emphasis tends to be on continuity. The Bible is understood to be in the same category and susceptible to the same principles of interpretation as other

---

person of Jesus and the divine composition of Scripture through human authors are so considerable that it is perhaps wiser not to hang a doctrine of Scripture on conclusions drawn from an analogy." *Biblical Inspiration*, 44-45. We are not drawing conclusions here but simply illustrating similarities by the analogy.

20. Wiley says: "The rationalistic explanations emphasize unduly the human element, while the supranaturalistic theories minify [sic] it, maintaining that the sacred writers were so possessed by the Holy Spirit as to become passive instruments rather than active agents" and then proposes his "dynamical theory," which he claims is a "mediating theory and is advanced in an effort to explain and preserve in proper harmony, both the divine and human factors in the inspiration of the Scriptures." *CT* 1:173, 176. He further maintains that this balanced theory has been most generally accepted in the church. Cf. 173-77.

Origen, the earliest biblical scholar, held that the Bible was harmonious throughout and supernaturally perfect in every particular, but at the same time he was conscious of the human character of the Scripture. Cf. F. W. Farrar, *History of Interpretation* (Grand Rapids: Baker Book House, 1961), 190.

Augustine held the same balance in a somewhat curious fashion that revealed a leaning in the supranaturalistic direction. Scripture was a divine unity for Augustine. No discordancy of any kind was permitted to exist. But he had several ways of handling apparent disharmonies. He claimed variously that the manuscript was faulty, that the translation was wrong, or that the reader had not properly understood. When none of these seemed appropriate, he sometimes concluded that the Holy Spirit has "permitted" one of the Scripture writers to compose something at variance from what another biblical author had written. For Augustine, then, variances were meant to whet our spiritual appetite for understanding. But variant readings were not an ultimate problem for Augustine because the truth of Scripture resided ultimately in the thought of the biblical writers and not in their individual words. He commented, "In any man's words the thing which we ought narrowly to regard is only the writer's thought which was meant to be expressed, and to which the words ought to be subservient; and further that we should not suppose one to be giving an incorrect statement, if he happens to convey in different words what the person really meant whose words he fails to reproduce literally." Cited in A. D. R. Polman, *The Word of God According to St. Augustine* (Grand Rapids: Wm. B. Eerdmans Publishing Co., 1961), 49. Cf. also Vawter, *Biblical Inspiration*, 38-39.

literature. It does not require a special hermeneutic. Furthermore, this tendency stresses the historical character of the biblical documents both in terms of their origin and in emphasizing the historically conditioned character of their message. This gives the appearance of depreciating the divine aspect of the Scripture and explains, in part, the violent reaction of many conservative Christians to the rise of historical criticism in the 19th century.[21]

At the other end of the continuum, the tendency is to eliminate the human element. This view, in a simplistic form, emphasizes the supernatural aspect to such an extent that the personality of the writer is set aside. Wiley quotes a representative of this extreme position who says: "They [the biblical writers] neither spake nor wrote any word of their own, but uttered syllable by syllable as the Spirit put it into their mouths."[22] One would be hard put to find a representative of such a theory among contemporary scholarship, since virtually all modern scholars have opted for a historical (timeful) understanding of the Bible and agree that this is the proper mode of interpretation. However, certain evangelicals have been reticent to accept the full implications of this fact for the historically conditioned character of the biblical writings. To deny its emersion in history, however, is to upset the balance between the divine and human elements involved in its production.

Wiley, following John Miley and many other Methodist theologians, advances what he terms the *dynamical theory* as an attempt to mediate between the two extremes and hold in proper, if paradoxical, balance the divine and human factors in the inspiration of the Scriptures. On the basis of 2 Pet. 1:21 he insists that the locus of inspiration is the persons or the writers rather than the writings (CT 1:174). But he makes no effort to spell out the implications of this theory beyond merely asserting its mediating character.

In the modern period, the historical antecedent to this position seems to be William Sanday, whose Bampton Lectures of 1893 marked a significant advance in the debate over inspiration. Sanday's position is summarized by Alan Richardson as follows: "It is not the words of the Bible that are inspired but the writers of the

---

21. Cf. Alan Richardson, *Bible in Science*, chap. 2.
22. *CT* 1:173-74. Wiley offers three solid refutations of this position: "[1.] it denies the inspiration of persons and holds only to the inspiration of the writings; . . . [2. it] does not comport with all the facts; . . . [3.] it is out of harmony with the known manner in which God works in the human soul." 174-75.

scriptural books. God's action is personal, not mechanical; he seeks illumination to the minds of his servants, so that they think out the truth for themselves and make it their own."[23] With this interpretation, the mechanical or dictation theory of inspiration is rejected.

A fact that few seem to take into account is that the Bible is such a complex and variegated phenomenon that it is impossible to encompass it with a simple or single formula. There are not only numerous literary forms but also various types of material ranging from Wisdom literature to Temple records. Many contemporary treatments focus exclusively on the "acts of God" model of revelation. While this is clearly central to the biblical faith, recent scholarship has called attention to other dimensions than these events that effect deliverance or salvation. There is also the state of salvation, which likewise includes God's activity and about which the Bible speaks extensively in both Old and New Testaments. This facet of the biblical material has been subsumed under the rubric of "blessing."[24] It is also legitimate to see a "creation theology," which is centrally reflected in the Wisdom literature as well as elsewhere. How does one explain all this by any traditional theory?

Ultimately, as with the Christological questions, we must confess a paradoxical relation between the human word and the Divine Word that resists any completely satisfactory rational solution. Attempts to formulate such an explanation always seem to resolve the paradox into one truth or the other while tending to lose the one not agreed upon. (See discussions of paradox in chaps. 1 and 4.)

In setting forth his dynamical theory, H. Orton Wiley's abstinence from any attempt to explain the interpenetration of the divine and human elements is wise. However, his view does entail a particular form of exegesis that is very important for proper biblical interpretation. This implication needs exploring as background for the major thrust of this chapter that is yet to follow.

In transforming the locus of inspiration from the writings to the writers, the dynamical theory implies the historical character of biblical language. In this it is significantly different from dictation or mechanical modes of inspiration. In the latter, the words are

---

23. *Bible in Science*, 68. It is not here claimed that Wiley's position is the same as Sanday's, but we are simply pointing out the apparent historical moment when a significant advance was made in attempting to unravel the problem of inspiration.

24. See Claus Westermann, *Blessing in the Bible and the Church* (Philadelphia: Fortress Press, 1978).

given directly to the writers so that the words are God's and not man's. If the writers themselves are inspired, words are involved but in a different sense. Since thoughts are of necessity conceptualized in terms of language, or words (see discussion on relation between language and thought in chap. 1, n. 3), there is a real sense in which one may speak in this context of verbal inspiration.[25] However, the crucial difference is that the words are the words of men who have their own understanding of what the words that they use mean. That is, they are historically conditioned by the writer's intellectual, cultural, and societal milieu. They are even limited by his *factual* knowledge or lack of it. But none of this is essential to the authenticity of the thoughts. The issue becomes one of determining by careful exegetical methods the intention of the writer through analysis of his historical and linguistic context. The scrupulous attention biblical scholars give to the study of words is precisely to discover the original intention or understanding of the writer so as to accurately recover the truth that he was intending to convey and so determine what the text meant.

In a word, the dynamical theory of inspiration entails the grammatico-historical method of biblical interpretation. Conversely, the dictation theory leads almost inevitably to the allegorical method of interpretation and ultimately to the loss of meaning altogether.[26] If the meaning is controlled by the interpreter, as is unquestionably the case in any form of allegorical exegesis, rather than by the original writer, whose own understanding of his intention provides the objective criterion for meaning, there is no way of affirming one meaning to be more correct than another—thus no objective meaning.

The Extent of Inspiration

This topic brings us directly to the question of what we have termed the *cognitive* authority of the Bible. Some evangelicals hold that inspiration, and thus authority, extends to everything of which the Scripture writers speak, including chronology, reports of speeches, statistical data, and so on. This is logically a corollary of a dictation (or mechanical) theory of inspiration, since some of it

---

25. Having said this, we must still admit that the variegated character of the biblical material, as noted in the text, makes much of it resistant to this kind of model.

26. Hanson, *Allegory and Event*, chap. 7 on "Inspiration," which shows this to be the case with Origen.

assumes a level of knowledge not normally available to finite or historical individuals. Other evangelicals, equally as committed to the authority of Scripture, have held that its efficacy extends to those areas of truth pertaining to salvation, or more broadly to the theological content of Scripture.

The adjudication of the question largely hangs on how one interprets the significance of the term *plenary,* the traditional term used by evangelicals to qualify the idea of inspiration. The word itself means "full," but it is quite imprecise in and of itself, thus leaving itself open to varieties of understanding. The article of faith in the *Manual of the Church of the Nazarene* reads:

> We believe in the plenary inspiration of the Holy Scriptures, by which we understand the 66 books of the Old and New Testaments, given by divine inspiration, inerrantly revealing the will of God concerning us in all things *necessary to our salvation,* so that whatever is not contained therein is not to be enjoined as an article of faith. [italics mine]

While some Nazarenes interpret this to imply full authority in the broadest sense, as described above, other Nazarene sources allow a more restricted interpretation, defining it as extending to the whole canon; and in terms of the content of Scripture, to the soteriological aspects of the Bible, that is, it holds that the way of salvation set forth in Scripture is completely reliable and dependable.

One major contemporary document defines *plenary* as follows:

> By plenary inspiration we mean that the whole and every part has been brought into being under specific direction, and as a result of that inspiration these writings are "the final and authoritative Rule of Faith in the Church."[27]

This definition repeats, for all intents and purposes, Wiley's statement:

> By plenary inspiration, we mean that the whole and every part is divinely inspired. This does not necessarily presuppose the mechanical theory of inspiration, as some contend, or any particular method, only that the results of that inspiration give us the Holy Scriptures as the final and authoritative rule of faith in the Church (*CT* 1:184).

Wiley's qualifications make it plain that there is considerable room within this very broad statement for a significant variety of

---

27. Purkiser, Taylor, and Taylor, *God, Man, and Salvation,* 204.

interpretation, thus freeing Nazarene theologians to concur in general with the view of classical Protestant theology (see immediately below) that focuses upon the soteriological and/or the theological as the special dimension within the Scripture that bears the stamp of unique inspiration (authority). Colin Williams' interpretation of John Wesley implies that Mr. Wesley, too, relied upon the soteriological authority of Scripture: "By *homo unius libri* Wesley means a reliance upon the way of salvation given in the Scripture."[28]

In the final analysis, however, the decisive question does not relate to one's theory concerning the nature of biblical authority, but to the way one uses the Bible. Various cults, such as the Jehovah's Witnesses, the Mormons, Christadelphians, and Unitarian Pentecostals (Jesus Only), affirm belief in the inerrancy of Scripture. Evangelicals who have arrived at a fairly well established consensus on the theory of biblical authority and inspiration manifest significant divergences in their interpretation of Scripture.[29] This tells us that the practical issue at stake in the whole discussion about the Bible is *hermeneutical*. Thus our most definitive task is to develop a method of biblical interpretation that allows the Bible to speak for itself, and this will set free the self-authenticating message that is the essence of biblical authority. At the same time we will be coming to terms with the way the Bible should be used as a source of theology. To these issues we now speak briefly.

Rightly Dividing the Word of Truth

H. Cunliffe-Jones, in a programmatic volume issued in 1945, called for Christian scholars to develop a method of interpreting the Scripture that took adequate account of both the historical and the theological study of the Bible. He was writing at a time when the historical study of the Bible had all but completely preoccupied the attention of scholars for many years, and the theological had been suppressed in what he called "the letter without the spirit." In the earlier days of the Christian era, the theological (allegorical) had dominated, but the historical dimension of Scripture had not been recognized: "the spirit without the letter." The validity of the historical study of the Bible must be recognized, he argued, "because the Incarnational principle is at the heart of Chris-

---

28. *John Wesley's Theology Today* (New York: Abingdon Press, 1960), 25.
29. Robert K. Johnson, *Evangelicals at an Impasse* (Atlanta: John Knox Press, 1979).

tianity, and we do not honour the great Revelation to which the Bible bears witness by not taking seriously the humbler details of the origin and compilation of the witness."[30]

But this must be joined with the theological for the Scripture to become contemporary. Cunliffe-Jones further suggests that the clue to achieving this goal is understanding the New Testament interpretation of the Old Testament, "because this, though it can be the object of a strictly scientific study, is of central importance for a theological exposition of the Bible as the witness to the Christian revelation."[31] This latter point is an unusually acute insight with which we fully concur, because here we can see the New Testament principle of biblical interpretation at work. It will also further illustrate the proper relation between the existential and cognitive types of authority. In summary, the way the New Testament interprets the Old may give us a key to the proper interpretation of the whole Bible from the Bible's own perspective.[32]

This issue has exercised the best minds of the church from the beginning. The problem first appears on the pages of the New Testament, where the followers of Jesus struggle with His identity. They had become convinced by divine revelation that He was the Messiah of Israel's hope (Matt. 16:16), but they were perplexed over the lack of correspondence between the contours of that hope as they understood it and the image of Jesus that His life and ministry projected. The way in which the New Testament writers ultimately came to relate Jesus to the Old Testament was very subtle and seemed at times to do violence to the Old Testament texts. They clearly were not appropriating them in some artificial or literal sense.

The church through the ages since has wrestled with the issue in terms of a hermeneutic of prophecy. At every critical point, Christian thinkers recognized that to demand a literal correspondence between prophecy and fulfillment was to either exclude the Old Testament from the Christian Scriptures or deny any relation between Jesus of Nazareth and the Hebrew faith. Both were unacceptable. The earliest efforts resorted to an allegorical use of

---

30. *Authority*, 26.
31. Ibid., 10.
32. An extended survey of this topic is found in Appendix 2. There the biblical material is carefully analyzed and critical historical periods are surveyed to see how both Bible and tradition would address this question. The discussion that follows in the text is built upon the findings in that research.

Scripture with all its inherent problems, but it was appealed to again and again as a way of solving the dilemma.

In modern times, the emergence of the historical study of Scripture made the allegorical approach both impossible and irresponsible. But this method only intensified the difficulty, as it made the traditional appeal to prophecy as an apologetic for the faith highly problematic. Such appeals had depended on allegorizing the Old Testament text. Scholars searched intently for the key to unlock the mystery.

Appropriating the studies of several competent scholars, this writer has come to the position that the key to unlock the enigma is a theological hermeneutic. In a word, the New Testament claim may be explained as declaring that the theology that informed the Old Testament passages was filled full (fulfilled) of Christian content by the person and work of Jesus and the new Israel, the Church.

If we extrapolate a general hermeneutic from this, we may affirm that it is the theological content of Scripture that is its authoritative dimension, and the most critical step in biblical interpretation is bringing to expression the theological structure that informs the text. There are no nontheological texts in the Bible. Oftentimes large blocks of material (especially in the Old Testament) are needed to bring a single theological point to word, and one should not necessarily be preoccupied with a kind of exegetical myopia that seeks to squeeze some revelatory significance out of every verse. This is what led to allegorizing in the first place. A parable is a literary case in point illustrating this principle.

Oftentimes the theological understanding is expressed in highly provincial ways, as when Paul addresses the issue of eating meat offered to idols in 1 Corinthians 8. It certainly lies closer to the surface in some texts than others and oftentimes is synonymous with the literal word, so that minimal exegetical excavation is required.

Part of the preparation for the task of theological exegesis is gaining a grasp of the structure of biblical theology in its coherent unity (see chap. 1 on the discipline of biblical theology). It should then be a relatively simple step to determine the degree to which that theology comes to expression in a specific passage. Since certain passages give fuller and more complete expression of the informing theology than others, some are more valuable than others although all texts are valid, since all are informed by some theological understanding, however minimal.

The truth of this claim is reinforced when one compares the cultic activities of Israel with those of her neighbors. Often they have much in common. What then constitutes the distinctive feature of Israel's cult? Have they simply appropriated a pagan practice such as sacrifice? The answer is in the theology that informs the cultic practice. The time of the ceremony during the year, the ceremony itself, the form it takes, and other features may be no different, but the theological significance is radically transformed. This was the case when an original agricultural festival was transformed into the celebration of a historical, saving event, such as occurred with the Feast of Pentecost.

In discussing the way in which archaeology has cast light upon "Israel's profound indebtedness to the ritual and mythology of its neighbors," Bernhard Anderson writes concerning the parallels between Israelite and Canaanite worship, rituals, and so on: "Israel did not say a flat No of repudiation to the advanced culture into which it entered but rather said No and Yes. Faith in Yahweh, the God of Israel, demanded turning from other 'gods,' and consequently, challenging the theological presuppositions of the religions of the environment."[33] Hence it was in the context of the existing culture that revelation occurred, a divinely given understanding of the rationale for the observance of these cultic activities. Since the theological is the divinely revealed dimension of these practices, it is this that carries the distinctiveness and that has enduring significance even though the ceremonials may become merely a matter of antiquarian interest to the New Testament believer.

In using the Bible as a source of theology, the systematic theologian must first proceed with the work of theological exegesis and then utilize his findings to give direction to his work in constructing an organic, homogeneous system of theology while oftentimes employing nonbiblical categories in order to address the contemporary situation. This is the normative source by which all other sources of theology must be evaluated and tested.

---

33. *Out of the Depths* (Philadelphia: Westminster Press, 1983), 40.

3

Sources of Theology: Tradition, Reason, and Experience

Following John Wesley, Wesleyan theology has always built its doctrinal work upon four foundation stones commonly referred to as the Wesleyan quadrilateral. In addition to the Scripture, they are tradition, reason, and experience. These are not of equal authority, however. In fact, properly understood, the three auxiliary sources directly support the priority of biblical authority. This should become clear in the following exposition.

Tradition

Tradition is difficult to define and often carries with it certain unfavorable connotations. We must attempt to come to a clear apprehension of its theological nature in order to properly understand its function. It is derived from the Greek word *paradosis,* which suggests that which is delivered, and the Latin word *traditio,* signifying that which is passed on. A survey of the way tradition has functioned in the Hebrew-Christian faith reveals that both of these dimensions are important to include in the definition.

Correctly defining tradition requires being reminded of the nature of revelation as briefly outlined in the last chapter. It occurs chiefly (although not exclusively, as we noted) through historical events that must be interpreted. Thus both the accounts of the events (fact) and their interpretation (meaning) must be passed on, and since the event and its interpretation are inseparable, we are suggesting that the complex that is defined as tradition be referred to in its preliminary stage as the event/interpretation that is passed on.

From Oral to Written Tradition

When tradition is understood in this way, it becomes clear that the Scriptures, both old and new, are "fixated" tradition (H. Berkhof). Long before the tradition dealing with God's self-disclosure and promises to Abraham, Isaac, and Jacob were written down, recorded by Moses, they were transmitted from generation to generation in the form of oral tradition.

The same was obviously true with the New Testament revelation in and through Jesus Christ. Those to whom the original revelation was vouchsafed (eyewitnesses) transmitted it to others in the form that the early fathers termed the *apostolic tradition.* In time this was embodied in documents that later became Scripture. The process of collecting the authoritative documents was accelerated by the canon of Marcion, which reflected a tradition different from that held by the classical Christian faith.[1]

Prior to its fixation in Scripture, this apostolic tradition was passed on in different forms. At least four can be identified with some certainty: (1) catechetical instruction, which may be reflected in the kerygma (C. H. Dodd) of the Early Church, embodied in sample sermons in Acts. Paul makes reference explicitly to this sort of thing in 1 Cor. 15:1-3: "Moreover, brethren, I declare unto you the gospel which I preached unto you, which also ye have re-

---

1. The understanding of revelation as historical, implicit in this discussion, has profound implications for the question of the canon. If the test of canonicity is the matter of inspiration exclusively, one cannot a priori exclude the possibility of further inspired writings. Furthermore, if biblical faith was composed of abstract, timeless teachings regarding God, man, and ethics, that too would allow no reason in principle why the canon should ever be closed. "But the Bible's theology does not consist of timeless, abstract teachings. Rather, it is concerned with events, with the interpretation of events, and the meaning of life in the context of events: the events of a specific history in which, it is asserted, God acted for man's redemption. . . . The canon, therefore, must be closed: there can never be a primary witness to this history again." Bright, *Old Testament,* 159.

ceived, and wherein ye stand; by which also ye are saved, if ye keep in memory what I preached unto you, unless ye have believed in vain. For I delivered unto you first of all that which I also received, how that Christ died for our sins according to the scriptures" (KJV); (2) hymns, of which Phil. 2:6-11 and 1 Tim. 3:16 seem to be two; (3) liturgy; and (4) sacrament.

In the Corinthian correspondence Paul appears to be using the phrase "from the Lord" as a technical term to refer to a tradition stemming from Jesus himself. In 1 Corinthians 7, he finds himself called upon to supplement this tradition by one of his own, based on his apostolic authority, when the dominical tradition has no specific word for a new set of problems.

Tradition as Interpreted Text

When the oral tradition was transcribed into a written document, the nature of tradition shifted somewhat. Instead of being the transmission of the event/interpretation complex, it becomes an interpretive tradition in relation to the transcribed text. The presence of various traditions in Jesus' day testifies to the reality of this process. The law, for instance, was a given; but the necessity for its interpretation (how work is to be defined in connection with the fourth commandment, for instance) called forth varying schools of thought. In addition to the Pharisees and the Sadducees there were the rabbinic schools of Shammai and Hillel interpreting the law with different degrees of strictness. Jesus condemned the Judaism of His day for perverting the pure religion of the Old Testament with the traditions of the elders. This may not necessarily imply that all tradition is bad but rather that it may have a pervertive function.

Very early in the history of Christian thought, the church fathers spoke of the apostolic tradition as that which gives catholicity to the Christian church, the teachings held by the worldwide church. The emergence of this tradition of an authoritative interpretation of the written Scripture (New Testament) occurred in response to the threat of Gnosticism. The Gnostic teachers could appeal to Scripture to support their views, so that the issue became one of interpretation. Irenaeus, in particular, appealed to the apostolic tradition as the only authoritative interpretation. Any other fell outside the pale of authentic Christian teaching. The Gnostics' appeal to a supposed secret tradition forced Irenaeus to emphasize the superiority of the church's public tradition.

> The whole point of his teaching was, in fact, that Scripture and the Church's unwritten tradition are identical in content, both being vehicles of the revelation. If tradition is . . . a more trustworthy guide, this is not because it comprises truths other than those revealed in Scripture, but because the true tenor of the apostolic message is there unambiguously set out.[2]

In a detailed survey of the literature of the fourth century, J. N. D. Kelly shows that the idea of the apostolic tradition retained the priority of Scripture. Even though it was the interpretation that was at stake, the tradition was not understood as having any independent status. The "authority of the fathers consisted precisely in the fact that they had so faithfully and fully expounded the real intention of the Bible writers."[3]

Tradition as Creed

The creeds of the ecumenical (undivided) church may be viewed as the crystallization of Christian doctrine concerning certain doctrines for which the Scripture provides raw material but which are not addressed in any formal theological way. They are attempts to spell out the theological (oftentimes ontological) implications of the biblical message, or at least avoid such interpretations that do not truly embody biblical faith. Hence the classical creeds are an aspect of tradition that follows the same pattern present in the earlier years as being interpretations of the Bible. The most important creeds may be identified as the Apostles' Creed, the Nicene Creed, the Athanasian Creed (*Quicunque Vult*), and the Creed of Chalcedon.

The strength of these creeds is largely in their negative character. They arose out of controversy and were primarily formulated to reject certain heretical teachings, and thus their precision lies precisely at this point. However, in many instances they do provide a positive formulation of the doctrine under discussion and thus serve as pointers to what would constitute a valid interpretation. They are "signposts, pointing to dangers for the Christian message

---

2. J. N. D. Kelly, *Early Christian Doctrines* (San Francisco: Harper and Row, Publishers, 1978), 39. Note the implication of this statement for the necessity of a good hermeneutic.
3. Ibid., 49.

which once have been overcome by such decisions,"[4] plus indicating the theological commitments of the community of faith.

The controversy with Gnosticism, however, paved the way for
a later perversion of the function of tradition. Against the Gnostic
appeal to a secret tradition the fathers had appealed to the universal voice of the church. However, certain practices arose that could
not be defended on the interpretive principle (e.g., the seven sacraments, etc.), so the Catholic church in the late medieval period
turned to the earlier Gnostic position and claimed a separate oral
tradition delivered to the apostles, who in turn passed this on to
their successors. The apostolic succession guaranteed the validity
of the second—now separate—source of doctrine. Now there are
"two sources," the second being contained "in the unwritten tradition that the Apostles received from Christ himself or that were
handed on, as it were from hand to hand, from the Apostles under
the inspiration of the Holy Spirit, and so have come down to us."[5]
The First Vatican Council (1870) declared that the content of this
oral tradition can be infallibly determined only by the pope.

Martin Luther and the other Protestant Reformers rejected
this separate source of doctrine by the principle of *sola scriptura*.
On this basis Protestant theology likewise maintains the possibility
that the church fathers, the councils, and the creeds have fallen
into error, as firmly as the Roman church maintains just the opposite with its doctrine of papal infallibility.[6] However, this does
not preclude the positive contribution of tradition in its interpretive function.

Importance of Tradition

The importance of tradition at this point is reinforced by three
major considerations: (1) The Bible, even though recognized as the
documentary Authority for Christian theology, is in need of interpretation (see chap. 2). The experience of the Early Church in its
struggle with heresy verifies this. Furthermore the contemporary
hermeneutical problems of evangelical fundamentalism accen-
tuate it. (2) The impossibility of reading the Bible apart from some

---

4. Tillich, *Systematic Theology* 1:52.
5. Hendrikus Berkhof, *The Christian Faith*, trans. Sierd Woudstra (Grand Rapids:
Wm. B. Eerdmans Publishing Co., 1980), 98.
6. Wesley does not hesitate to point out that church councils not only "may err"
but "have erred." *Journal* 1:275 (Sept. 13, 1733); or *Works* 1:41.

preunderstanding of it (see chap. 1). Tillich expresses this truth poignantly and correctly:

> No one is able to leap over two thousand years of church history and become contemporaneous with the writers of the New Testament, except in the spiritual sense of accepting Jesus as the Christ. Every person who encounters a biblical text is guided in his religious understanding of it by the understanding of all previous generations.[7]

(3) The nature of Christian theology. As developed earlier, one of the essential characteristics of theology is to interpret the faith in contemporary terms. "What is involved is not merely a reproduction of the biblical message"; thus theology "cannot act as if there were a vacuum between Scriptures and our own day."[8] The history of this contemporizing task is called by Aulen "the living testimony of the church." Thus tradition is understood not as something separate from Scripture but the continuing task of reinterpreting the biblical message and may even be recognized as the continuing activity of the Holy Spirit (John 16:13-14). Thus understood, tradition "stands guard against irresponsible interpretations of the Bible" (Aulen).

This function would appear to have greater force in a situation where there is a single, undivided tradition of interpretation as the early fathers claimed. But in post-Reformation Protestantism, with the multiplicity of denominations reflecting a bewildering variety of traditions and all claiming the support of the Bible, what sort of validity does it have?

Within the basic Protestant commitment to the *sola scriptura* principle, where it is recognized that no tradition has an ultimately normative authority, the diversity of tradition does not necessarily need to lead to the abandonment of a self-conscious appeal to one's own tradition. Within certain limitations, it is doubtless the case that each tradition witnesses to some important aspect of the biblical message, and all together witness to the inexhaustible riches of its truth. This issue has become especially acute in contemporary theological scholarship, which has become concerned with the question of ecumenicity.

If the theologian recognizes his tradition to fall within the general parameters of the Christian faith—and the Wesleyan could

7. *Systematic Theology* 1:36.
8. Aulen, *Faith of the Christian Church*, 69.

suggest that these are drawn by the councils and creeds of the undivided church—he may without embarrassment draw upon the resources of that tradition to develop his own distinctive systematic theology. Therefore, as Tillich says, "The denominational tradition is a decisive source for the systematic theologian, however ecumenically he may use it."[9]

For the Wesleyan theologian this tradition would include, in addition to the ecumenical creeds—in reverse historical order—creedal statements of his own denomination, the 25 Articles of Faith of Methodism, and the 39 Articles of Faith of the Church of England. It also includes the theological work done in the Wesleyan movement but would not exclude good scholarly work done outside the tradition. Wesley's catholic spirit warrants this broad appeal.

The chief danger to any person or persons acknowledging his debt to tradition is the danger of sanctifying or canonizing any particular historical expression of the biblical faith. All interpretations or reinterpretations of the faith must repeatedly and as openly as possible be brought before the bar of the biblical Word and judged in the light of it as interpreted by the best biblical scholarship available.

Reason[10]

Looked at in his relation to the created world, the uniqueness of man is his powers of thought, hence the classical definition of man as a "rational animal." But man is also a "religious animal," and these two aspects of his essence (seen from two different perspectives) cannot be kept in separated compartments. Their relation is most overtly seen in the task of theologizing, since it is a rational enterprise brought to bear upon man's religious beliefs. The question to be explored here is the function of reason in this undertaking or as a source of theology. John Wesley, perhaps in part because he lived in the 18th century, the Age of Reason, gave considerable attention to the question and insisted that he who rejects reason rejects religion also.[11]

---

9. *Systematic Theology* 1:38.
10. A discussion of reason from a different perspective in relation to revelation can be found in the next chapter. This section is simply analyzing the use of man's capacity of ratiocination in developing a theology.
11. *Letters* 5:364.

The Limitations of Reason

We must first affirm that reason cannot function as an independent source for theology. We are here rejecting that approach to theology that was given classic expression by Thomas Aquinas and followed by most systematic theology from that time until the 19th century. Reason, in this methodology, was seen as providing a rational foundation or beginning point upon which a superstructure of revealed theology was constructed. This foundation included a section containing proofs for the existence of God. Having demonstrated the existence of God by rational argument, this natural theology gave way to revelation, which then elaborated the nature of God that could not be discovered by unaided human reason.

Since the time of David Hume and Immanuel Kant, it has been generally recognized that this approach is inadequate. Both Hume and Kant analyzed the epistemological capacities of the finite mind and found it to be limited to experience, so far as scientific knowledge is concerned. John Wesley argued the same point, saying "natural senses" are "altogether incapable of discerning objects of a spiritual kind."[12] Since God is not an object of empirical experience, natural theology is a contradiction in terms.

Furthermore, for reason to demonstrate the truths of Christianity, it must show them to be necessary truths. By definition, necessary truths are limited to propositions involving artificial constructs such as tautologies or mathematical formulas. However, reason may be able to show religious truths to be intelligible and thus contribute to understanding them. Although faith precedes understanding (Augustine), the movement from faith to understanding "saves the believer from acquiescing in a faith which is no more than acceptance of an unmediated and opaque authority."[13]

This does not preclude the possibility that reason does have some preliminary functions leading to faith. It is all but impossible to believe in something about which there is no understanding. If I were to ask you, "Do you believe that all wobblewings are wombats?" you would be unable to give an intelligible faith response. Augustine, the classic exponent of the *credo ut intelligam* principle, says: "If it is rational that faith precedes reason in the case of certain great matters that cannot be grasped, there cannot be the least

---

12. *Works* 8:13.
13. John E. Smith, *The Analogy of Experience* (New York: Harper and Row, Publishers, 1973), 8.

doubt that reason which persuades us of this precept—that faith precedes reason—itself precedes faith."[14] So while it is true that reason cannot function as an independent source of revelation, it does receive and grasp with some degree of comprehension that which is offered to faith.

An additional reason why reason cannot be an independent source of theology is the nature of revelation, which has already been touched on in the beginning of the chapter and elsewhere. If God makes himself known through historical events, such media are not open to reason to discover. This fact explains why men of the Enlightenment (18th century) sought to identify religious truth with eternal (timeless) truths of reason, and why they looked with disdain upon the Christian claim regarding historical revelation. Lessing's famous "ugly ditch" embodies this perspective: "Incidental truths of history can never become the proof of necessary truths of reason."

Unlike classical philosophy, which believed knowledge was possible only when it was of universals, Christian faith affirms that truth, ultimate Truth, comes to man via particulars, specific acts in history. "The [Logos] became flesh and dwelt among us" (John 1:14).

Function of Reason

On the positive side, reason has both a structuring and an interpretive function. Colin Williams summarizes John Wesley's view on this point in relation to the previous one:

> The importance of reason is not that it provides another source of revelation, but that it is a logical faculty enabling us to order the evidence of revelation; and that with tradition, it provides us with the necessary weapons for guarding against the dangers of the unbridled interpretation of Scripture.[15]

It is the structuring role of reason (philosophy) that Wiley emphasizes: "Its [philosophy's] claim as a subsidiary source of theology lies solely in the fact that it has the power of systematizing and rationalizing truth, so that it may be presented to the mind in proper form for assimilation."[16] In a word, this is logic.

---

14. Quoted ibid., 9.

15. *John Wesley's Theology Today*, 32.

16. *CT* 1:49. Interestingly he does not keep to this principle but proceeds to use philosophy in more substantive ways. It is inevitable that this should occur.

The importance of logic to Wesley is apparent throughout his works. He uses it to present his own reasoned arguments. He advocates it as an indispensable discipline in ministerial training, second only to the study of the Bible. The last volume of his *Works* includes a logic textbook. The chief importance, it appears, is in its interpretive function. Reason serves to guard against the unbridled and illogical private interpretation of the Scripture. Thus the Wesleyan understanding of the use of reason supports the principle of *sola scriptura* and points to the importance of proper exegesis.

In addition to its structuring and interpretive functions, reason (philosophy being the conceptual product of reason) provides the conceptual vehicles with which theological ideas are expressed.[17]

This does not necessarily mean that a theologian needs to be committed to a particular systematic philosophy, although this has been done many times. Augustine made extensive use of Neoplatonism, and Thomas Aquinas utilized the philosophy of Aristotle as a basis for his famous medieval synthesis. A number of contemporary theologians have attempted to appropriate the process philosophy of Alfred North Whitehead as a vehicle to express the Christian faith conceptually. And several have attempted to do the same with Martin Heidegger's thought or other versions of existential philosophy. One of the major problems here would be finding a comprehensive philosophy that would adequately explain all the facets of reality. Since such a philosophy strives for rational coherence, and (1) the finite mind finds it almost impossible to be sufficiently all-encompassing for the task, and (2) reality is so complex as to resist total rational formulation, such a philosophy is almost a chimera. For these reasons the attempt to develop such a systematic philosophy has all but been abandoned in recent times. If such an accomplishment could be actualized, it would serve successfully as an adequate conceptual vehicle for the theoretical aspects of the Christian faith, since they would both be speaking about the same reality.

The very nature of systematic theology requires that philosophy be used, since it is philosophical language that provides the greatest precision of expression. Quite obviously to meet its requirements of contemporaneity (see chap. 1), it must use current

---

17. Cf. Tillich, *Ultimate Reality*.

philosophical language.[18] While Jesus warned against putting new wine in old bottles, it oftentimes becomes necessary and helpful to put old wine in new bottles.

Granted, there is always an imminent possibility of distortion; but despite this danger, no theologian ever has expressed or ever could express the Christian faith in a set of ideas wholly of biblical origin and entirely free of content derived from not only philosophy but also other forms of secular thought.[19]

History validates the soundness of this claim. All the creeds and confessions utilize prevailing philosophical concepts to attempt to address the particular issues under debate.[20] It may be that the theological use of language injects a dimension into it that transcends the purely philosophical content. Just how this is so remains to be seen in a subsequent discussion of religious language.

Experience

In the Anglican tradition into which John Wesley was born, theologians customarily appealed to the threefold source of Scripture, reason, and tradition.[21] To these Wesley added experience, a reflection, many feel, of his pietistic associations. He was not alone in this, however, since others have likewise referred to experience as an important ingredient in theological work. Liberal theology, following Friedrich Schleiermacher, elevated experience to a primary role, all but making it the definitive source of theology. In reaction

---

18. This is one reason why the work of theology is never completed. The theologian is constantly in search of more adequate forms of expression; and with increasing precision of thought and expression regarding theology-related issues, he avails himself of the new terminology and categories to more adequately fulfill his role of clarifying faith's language about God.

19. In commenting on this danger of distortion that has led some to attempt to reject the use of philosophy altogether, Anthony C. Thiselton, *The Two Horizons* (Grand Rapids: Wm. B. Eerdmans Publishing Co., 1980), says, "Many of the standard criticisms brought against Bultmann, for example, turn out to be not arguments against his use of philosophy, but arguments against the use of a particular philosophy, such as that of Heidegger or Neo-Kantianism." 9.

20. Aulen implicitly recognizes this point in a comment about the Chalcedonian Creed: "The significance of the formula is not to be sought in the terminology used, such as the ancient conception of substance, etc., but rather in the rejections of the two extremes." *Faith of the Christian Church*, 74.

21. John Dillenberger and Claude Welch, *Protestant Christianity* (New York: Charles Scribner's Sons, 1954), 74.

to this overemphasis, many contemporary theologians have rejected experience as having any part whatsoever in the theological task.

The Meaning of Experience

The first problem to be faced in attempting to find a legitimate role for experience is determining the meaning of the term. It is very difficult to define. In particular, a special understanding of experience stemming from classical British empiricism has dominated much of modern thinking, so that this particular meaning has all but become synonymous with the concept of experience.

The British empiricists (Locke, Berkeley, and Hume) restricted experience to the domain of sense and thus distinguished it from reason or thought. Experience was limited to the data that could be transmitted to the mind by way of the five senses. All ideas could be traced to some such impression (Hume), and thus there were no ideas that found their source in any other stimulus. The corollary to this theory concerning the source of ideas was that the ideas in the mind were private mental images that could not necessarily be traced to an objective reality outside the mind. Obviously, if this understanding of experience is maintained, there can be no valid experience of a supersensuous reality such as God.

However, this limited concept is quite inadequate as a definition of experience that is much more adequately seen as a multidimensional encounter between a concrete person and whatever there is to be encountered, embracing a variety of levels of experience, including the moral, aesthetic, scientific, and religious dimensions.[22]

Using this richer definition, we may suggest a more positive role of experience. When Wiley speaks of it as a "source" of theology, he wishes to limit it to a specific type of experience: "We do not mean . . . merely human experience of the unregenerate; but Christian experience, in the sense of an impartation of spiritual life through the truth as vitalized by the Holy Spirit" (CT 1:38). He clearly assumes the broader view of experience and refers to one facet of it.

This calls for a more precise delineation of this facet of experience. What characterizes a religious experience? Two elements may be identified: (1) The awareness of an Other impinging upon one's

---

22. John Smith, *Analogy*, 33.

consciousness. This is what Rudolf Otto calls the "numinous" or sense of the holy. (2) It involves a basic orientation or reorientation of one's life and being. The account of the prophet Isaiah in his Temple experience (Isaiah 6) and Paul's Damascus Road encounter exhibit both elements. In a distinctly Christian religious experience, the content of the experience would be informed by the character and work of Christ.

Experience as a Medium of Revelation

It is much more appropriate to speak of experience as medium rather than a source. That is in fact the way Wesley understood it. Colin Williams is pointing in this direction in his comment about Wesley's view of authority: "Experience therefore is the appropriation of authority, not the source of authority."[23]

All Christian doctrines originally emerged out of experience in the sense that they were given in or to someone's experience. The nature of revelation requires this: If revelation occurs at all, there is both a giving side and a receiving side. If a communication, whatever its nature, is made but not received, no revelation occurs. It is much like the conundrum about the tree falling in the uninhabited forest. One can argue continually about the objectivity of the falling tree, but unless a person with auditory capabilities was present to experience the sound, there is no significance to the claim that a sound was made. Thus, as Tillich says so precisely,

> The event on which Christianity is based is not derived from experience; it is given in history. Experience is not the source from which the contents of systematic theology are taken but the medium through which they are existentially received.[24]

A survey of the revelatory events of the Bible, however many one claims there to be,[25] will demonstrate that they were all events that were experienced by human beings. This, in part, explains why no listing of the mighty acts of God in the Scripture or elsewhere includes the creation. It may have been the mightiest demonstration of divine power of all, but there were no human beings present to experience it as revelatory.

---

23. *John Wesley's Theology Today*, 33.
24. *Systematic Theology* 1:42.
25. G. Ernest Wright and Reginald H. Fuller, *The Book of the Acts of God* (Garden City, N.Y.: Doubleday and Co., Anchor Books, 1960), 9, say there are five. Purkiser et al., *Exploring Our Christian Faith*, 55, identify seven.

In *Creeds in the Making,* Alan Richardson highlights the fact that all early Christian doctrines originated in some form of experience. Early Christians, for instance, experienced God in a threefold way: They encountered Him as always and everywhere (Father); as there and then (in Jesus Christ); and as here and now (Holy Spirit). This experience is what gave rise to the doctrine of the Trinity. The believing contemporaries of Jesus experienced Him as a man among men but likewise met God in Him in some mysterious way. Their attempt to explain this paradoxical experience was the source of the Christological controversies of the early centuries.

Experience as a Confirming Source

Subsequent to the formalizing of early Christian experience in the Scriptures,[26] experience continues to function as a medium in the sense of a confirmatory source. It is in this sense that Wiley's limitation of experience becomes crucial. If a certain epistemological claim is made and a person wishes to verify it for himself, he may do so by meeting the necessary condition for having the cognitive experience. At the elementary level this involves opening his eyes and placing himself in the physical position to see the phenomenon in question. In like manner, certain theological claims are made in the Scripture, or may be interpreted as made, and one may confirm such claims by meeting the requisite spiritual conditions to see for himself. "O taste and see that the Lord is good!" (Ps. 34:8).

As long as verification is understood in terms of the narrow view of experience bequeathed to us by the British empiricists, only scientific propositions can be seen as objectively verifiable through repeated experiment. But theological claims are obviously not amenable to this narrow understanding of experimental verification. However, with the broader and more adequate understanding with which we are working, verification can be accepted as occurring within the life process itself—an experiential verification. "The verifying experiences of a non-experimental character are truer to life, though less exact and definite. By far, the largest part of all cognitive verification is experiential."[27]

That John Wesley understood this to be the function of experi-

---

26. This is not proposed as a complete explanation of the nature of the Scriptures.
27. Tillich, *Systematic Theology* 1:102.

ence is reflected in a response to a question in his *Plain Account of Christian Perfection*:

> If I were convinced that none in England had attained what has been so clearly and strongly preached by such a number of preachers, in so many places, and for so long a time, I should be clearly convinced that we had all mistaken the meaning of those Scriptures; and, therefore, for the time to come, I too must teach that "sin will remain till death."[28]

It was Luther's (and Calvin's to a less-obvious degree) attempt to validate the teaching of the Catholic church about salvation that led to the Reformation. Thus it could be legitimately stated that this great upheaval grew out of Luther's experience. It was not first a debate over the proper interpretation of biblical texts and authorities, but it was first the discovery that the merit system could not resolve the problem of guilt.

> Neither Luther nor Calvin could find within themselves an experience of divine acceptance through institutional absolution. Something else was required, something that could at once transcend the system-mediated grace and gain entrance to their own lives.[29]

The same could be said about Augustine's quest as recorded in his *Confessions*. While there was an intellectual element involved in his search that led him from one philosophy to another, it was the element of existential efficacy that caused him to abandon them all until he found the solution to his moral problem in the transforming grace of Christ.

Augustine, Luther, and Calvin all placed themselves under the guidance of the systems that offered solutions to their felt needs. But when the results were not forthcoming, they looked for more adequate solutions. One could identify Wesley's "heart-warming" experience at Aldersgate as the same sort of verification. He had sought in vain for acceptance, but now it came at the moment of faith. Thus it became a watershed in his life.

A significant qualification now needs to be entered. The confirmatory value of experience is hedged about by the community. Private experience is not sufficient, in and of itself, to validate

---

28. *Plain Account of Christian Perfection as Believed and Taught by the Reverend Mr. John Wesley from the Year 1725 to the Year 1777* (London: Wesleyan Conference Office, 1872; reprint, Kansas City: Beacon Hill Press of Kansas City, 1966), 67.

29. John Smith, *Analogy*, 27.

theological truth. In the case of Martin Luther, the overwhelming response his message received testified to the fact that he was not alone in having tried the penitential system and found it wanting.

In deciding psychological normalcy, the difference between hallucinations and real seeing is determined by the public character of the vision. Likewise, individual experiences in only a limited sense serve as the confirmation of religious belief. The biblical emphasis upon the community or "body" is a barrier to individualistic perversions that often occur. This is doubtless one of the considerations that led Paul to emphasize the public character of Jesus' resurrection appearances (cf. 1 Corinthians 15).

Experience may also serve as the means to understanding. Whatever has no point of contact with our experience means absolutely nothing to us. Understanding involves being able to relate to what is already known. Thus what is accepted in faith is understood in terms of analogies from our experience.

This provides a clue to the meaning of religious language.[30] Historically, the suggestion has been repeatedly made that language about God is analogical in nature. If what is said about Him is to involve any meaningful content, we must be able to relate it to some facet of our finite experience. If there is no correlation between God's love and human love, we do not have any comprehension of what it may mean. However, it transcends (but not infinitely) human love, so that while we are not saying exactly the same thing about both, there is a proportional relation that is the ground of understanding.

However, we must proceed one step further in delineating a distinctly Wesleyan view of experience and note that in certain limited ways, experience does serve as a source for theologizing. Wesley derived his understanding of the substance (content) of his distinctive doctrine of Christian perfection from the Scripture, but his understanding of the structure (circumstance) of the experience he derived from experience itself, since he did not find a clear-cut structural pattern in the Bible.[31] This in part accounts for his undogmatic character when dealing with such issues. He found, from experience, that he could talk about how God customarily dealt

---

30. A fuller discussion of this topic is found in the next chapter.
31. Rob L. Staples, "Sanctification and Selfhood," *Wesleyan Theological Journal* 7, no. 1 (Spring 1972): 3-16.

with people but not how He *must* deal with them. In the *Plain Account,* he refers to his quest for deeper understanding: "By viewing it in every point of light, and comparing it again and again with the word of God on the one hand, and the experience of the children of God on the other, we saw farther into the nature and properties of Christian perfection."[32]

Word and Spirit

Since the topic of experience refers, in theological terms, to the work of the Holy Spirit, we need to take note of the relationship between the Word and the Spirit here. This relation becomes an issue in connection with groups who lay emphasis upon the continuing activity of the Spirit, especially with regard to revelation. Oftentimes a valid emphasis becomes perverted, as was the case with some segments of the radical Reformation groups. The "Zwickau prophets," who came to Wittenberg insisting that God had spoken to them directly through His Spirit and that the Bible was unnecessary, were one of the most extreme instances. Oftentimes this kind of claim results in ethical deviation, at other times in doctrinal perversion.[33]

Both Luther and Calvin correctly insisted that the work of the Spirit (experience) was always checked and given guidance by the Word. The Spirit works in and through the Scripture but never contrary to it. His leadership is always within the parameters of the revelation of God in Jesus Christ.

Although John Wesley was often accused of enthusiasm (fanaticism) in precisely this area, he remained firmly within the Reformation tradition. He repeatedly asserted the Scriptures to be the final authority and always hedged about his teachings concerning the work of the Spirit in the believer with biblical criteria, so as to avoid the charge so falsely made against him. The relation of the Spirit and the Word in Wesley's thought is summarized well by Lycurgus Starkey: "The Spirit-guide, though he may act independent of the reading or hearing of scripture, will always be in accordance with the rule of scripture. The Spirit is tested by the scripture to see whether it be of God."[34]

---

32. P. 37.
33. Dillenberger and Welch, *Protestant Christianity,* 58 ff.
34. *Work of the Holy Spirit,* 90.

Summary

The primary purpose of the preceding discussion of the sources of theology is to provide an insight into the working methodology of this theology. Put in a brief summary form, it would look something like this: At every point the first consideration is the scriptural teaching. Thus each topic will normally begin with an exegetical section in an effort to identify as accurately as possible the theology that comes to expression in the relevant biblical passages. This will be further developed by referring to the historical interpretation in selected classical expressions, especially where the topics have been addressed in the ecumenical creeds (tradition).

In relation to each doctrine, a distinctive effort will be made to identify the way in which a Wesleyan formulation would influence the shape of the doctrine. This perspective will serve a controlling function but only as a principle of interpretation and always subject to correction by the insights derived from biblical theology.

The philosophical dimensions of each doctrine cannot be avoided. Therefore, we will endeavor to explore the significance of specific philosophical categories in terms of their adequacy to elucidate the doctrine under consideration from a contemporary point of view. This will at times involve the criticism of certain traditional philosophical forms that have been used in the past, or even in the present, but that turn out to be unsatisfactory vehicles to carry the freight of biblical theology.

The final aim is to provide as adequate a statement as possible of a uniquely Wesleyan form of the major Christian doctrines.

PART II

Our Knowledge
of God

Revelation: Its Meaning and Necessity

The Christian faith understands itself to be a response to a divine self-disclosure. It claims that God has made himself known in a preliminary way in a history recorded in the sacred writings known as the Old Testament and in a final and decisive way in the person and work of Jesus of Nazareth. Revelation, the doctrine of this divine self-disclosure, is the central methodological category of Christian theology.

Traditional liberal approaches to theology began with the phenomenon of religion as a uniquely human experience. From an analysis of the universality of religion and the common characteristics of its various manifestations, the argument moved to the contention that Christianity was the highest form of religion.[1]

Following the leadership of Karl Barth, the Swiss theologian,

---

1. Cf. William Adams Brown, *Christian Theology in Outline* (Edinburgh: T. and T. Clark, 1912); and William Newton Clarke, *An Outline of Christian Theology* (New York: Charles Scribner's Sons, 1922). Clarke says, "Theology is preceded by religion, as botany by the life of plants. Religion is the reality of which theology is the study. . . . Christianity is a religion . . . appealing to the same elements in human nature as the others, but appealing with a fulness of truth and power peculiar to itself." 3.

contemporary theology has generally agreed in rejecting this approach and in rightly reinstating revelation as primary from the Christian point of view. Defining religion as man's quest for God, Barth denied that Christianity was a religion. Its uniqueness, he argued, is in its claim that God has taken the initiative and disclosed himself.

There are three major reasons why it is necessary for God to make himself known, or why, conversely, man's knowledge of God cannot depend upon a discovery relying wholly upon human initiative: (1) the transcendence of God with its corollary of human finitude; (2) the nature of God as personal;[2] and (3) the fallenness of man.[3] This chapter will address these three themes under the headings: (1) Revelation and Transcendence; (2) Revelation and Knowledge; and (3) Revelation and Reason.

The idea of revelation has always held a central place in theological work; however, the idea has not been uniformly understood. There is a history of revelation in the same sense that there is a history of theology. Partly in terms of responding to the situation in the cultural and intellectual milieu of the times, theologians have formulated in various ways their understanding of how revelation occurs. New discoveries, along with deeper insight into the faith itself, have caused the abandonment of certain inadequate explanations and subsequent attempts to provide for more adequate ways of talking about it.[4] The method of this chapter is to

2. This reflects a special mode of transcendence. John Macmurray states the point succinctly: "All knowledge of persons is by revelation. My knowledge of you depends not merely on what I do, but upon what you do; and if you refuse to reveal yourself to me, I cannot know you, however much I may wish to do so. If in your relations with me, you consistently 'put on an act' or 'play a role,' you hide yourself from me. I can never know you as you really are. In that case, generalization from the observed facts will be positively misleading. . . . a being who can pretend to be what he is not, to think what he does not think, and to feel what he does not feel, cannot be known by generalization from his observed behavior, but only as he genuinely reveals himself." *Persons in Relation* (London: Faber and Faber, 1961), 169.

3. In addressing this point, John Calvin says: "Vain, therefore, is the light afforded us in the formation of the world to illustrate the glory of its Author, which, though its rays be diffused all around us, is insufficient to conduct us into the right way. Some sparks, indeed, are kindled, but smothered before they have emitted any great degree of light. Wherefore the Apostle . . . says: 'By faith we understand that the worlds were framed by the word of God;' thus intimating, that the invisible Deity was represented by such visible objects, yet that we have no eyes to discern him, unless they be illuminated through faith by an internal revelation of God." *Institutes* 1.5.14.

4. The term *adequacy* is used in the same technical sense as defined by John Macmurray in relation to philosophy: "The adequacy of a philosophy depends upon its range; upon the extent to which it succeeds in holding together the various aspects of human experience." *The Self as Agent* (London: Faber and Faber, 1966), 39.

explore the various elements that enter into an understanding of the doctrine of revelation from a historical perspective. This will involve raising the philosophical issues and illustrating them as well as elucidating them from the history of revelation theory within the above-outlined structure. This task will be carried out against the background of the perspective of biblical theology insofar as the biblical material addresses the issues under investigation. Thus each section will open with an attempt to give careful exegetical attention to the text of Scripture. This will serve the dual purpose of acquainting the reader with both the history of revelation theory and the issues that must be addressed in formulating an adequate Wesleyan statement.[5]

Three preliminary matters need to be reinforced, although already mentioned implicitly. First, while the problem of revelation is often treated as part of a prolegomena, it should be noted that it properly belongs under the doctrine of God. Although it is an issue that addresses epistemological considerations, it is—or should be —recognized that knowledge is correlated with the known. Since God is the Known in revelational discussion, the discussion cannot proceed with any success apart from taking account of the Subject of the inquiry, namely the Ultimate Reality that religion designates as God. It is for this reason that this chapter will explore, at least in a preliminary way, a number of aspects of the doctrine of God.

If revelation is treated as mere prolegomena, the doctrine is either informed surreptitiously by the doctrine of God or else formulated in terms of categories or criteria drawn from extra-theological sources, in which case one may not obtain a true picture of the phenomenon under investigation.

Second, it should be noted that there is no articulated doctrine of revelation in Scripture, at least not in the modern sense of that term. The biblical writers were far more concerned with the reality and demands of their encounter with God than with explaining in some theoretical way how it took place, much less with defending the possibility of its occurrence. This does not mean, however, that there are not certain clues concerning how such a phenomenon may be explained philosophically.

F. G. Downing has pointed out that certain key Hebrew words

---

5. An extraordinarily valuable resource for the historical aspect of this study is H. D. McDonald, *Theories of Revelation: An Historical Study 1700-1960* (Grand Rapids: Baker Book House, 1979).

that might be expected to be used to talk about revelation in contexts where revelation would logically be mentioned are in fact not used. These words are used in various other settings but not in the context of revealing God. The Old Testament writers "never use it [one of the key words] of God making possible a 'knowledge of himself,' nor of God 'revealing himself.' They do not build around it any concept of revelation."[6] But again, this does not preclude the possibility that a rather definite understanding of a divine self-disclosure takes place even though specific terms may not be used to describe it. Downing, in fact, points to the most appropriate way of addressing the issue when he suggests that the Scripture does not so much speak of God acting "revealingly" as "savingly." In other words, what God is doing can best be described by the term "salvation."[7] Later on, we shall be able to see that properly understood, "salvation" and "revelation" are virtually synonymous terms in biblical faith. He further calls attention to the important truth that such "salvific revealing" is envisioned in the New Testament as an eschatological reality (1 Cor. 13:12).

Third, the idea of revelation as a theoretical problem is of relatively modern vintage.[8] The history of Christian thought dem-

---

6. Downing concludes that the term "revelation" is far too intellectualistic to reflect what the biblical message is about. This is doubtless true if one interprets the doctrine of revelation in certain ways, but not if one adapts the term to the biblical perspective. James Barr makes the same suggestion, but his approach further shows the weakness of doing biblical studies by means of word analysis. Both of these men make critiques in terms of defining *revelation* as the "making clear" (without obscurity or ambiguity) of something that has not hitherto been known. To the first point Downing makes the powerful points that (1) no such clarity is claimed in the biblical material, and (2) if there had been such a revelation without ambiguity, there would not be the multiplicity of diverse understandings of it as is obviously the case. *Has Christianity a Revelation?* (Philadelphia: Westminster Press, 1964). Barr makes much the same criticism in these words: "This fact that so many diverse theologies have agreed in assigning a central place to revelation may have been a factor which has caused the intrinsic weakness of the revelation concept to remain obscure." *Old and New,* 87. With regard to the second criticism, he points out that "in the Bible, apart from some quite limited concessions, there is no stage at which God is not known." Ibid., 89. He further argues that it is precisely this problem that has created somewhat of an impasse between "revelational theologies" and biblical exegesis. 90-94.

The value of these criticisms is not that they lead, as the two critics have suggested, to the abandonment of the concept of revelation. We have already seen that their conclusions are based upon a previously agreed-upon definition of the term based on semantic considerations. Rather, their criticisms should point to a more adequate, that is, biblically based, understanding of what it means for God to show himself to man, arrived at inductively.

7. *Has Christianity a Revelation?* 13.

8. Cf. Barr, *Old and New,* 84. John McIntyre, *The Christian Doctrine of History* (Grand Rapids: Wm. B. Eerdmans Publishing Co., 1957), 2-3. James Barr, "Revelation," in

onstrates a pattern that corresponds to Arnold Toynbee's hypothesis that the history of civilizations reflects a "challenge-response" structure. As challenges presented themselves to Christian thinkers either from inside or outside the church, they addressed themselves to them. For example, the challenge of Marcion caused the church to address the question of the Old Testament; the challenge of Monarchianism called for a full-scale study of the Trinity; and so on. It seems that the challenge to authority that arose during the Enlightenment is what gave rise in the 18th century to a central preoccupation with the doctrine of revelation, and it gives evidence of exercising the mind of the church for some time to come.[9]

Revelation and Transcendence

Transcendence is a spatial metaphor denoting distance. When applied to God, it speaks of His separateness from the world. The term that stands in opposition to it is *immanence,* which suggests nearness or withinness. Both are philosophical rather than biblical words and generally are developed with metaphysical overtones. The biblical writers do not centrally occupy themselves with either metaphysical otherness or nearness. They tend to talk about God as the Holy Other rather than the Wholly Other. The Bible does have its own way of addressing the issue, however, as we will discuss here so as to provide background from biblical theology for our historical and systematic analysis.

Biblical Background

The biblical concept of "otherness" and its relation to the divine self-disclosure comes to expression in connection with the term "glory," which in the Old Testament is a translation of the word *kabod* and in the New Testament of *doxa.* The Old Testament use is crucial as groundwork, since its use results in a complete transformation of the meaning of *doxa* in the New from the classical Greek meaning of that term. *Kabod* originally meant "weight" and carries the connotation of something solid or heavy. It is often used of that which is impressive, such as wealth or honor (e.g., Ps.

Hastings Dictionary of the Bible, ed. James Hastings. Rev. ed. by Frederick C. Grant and H. H. Rowley (New York: Charles Scribner's Sons, 1963).

9. McDonald, *Theories of Revelation.*

49:16-20; Isa. 66:11-12). It also came to suggest the idea of "brightness" or "radiance."

When used in relation to God, *kabod* implies that which makes God impressive to man, the form of His self-manifestation. The "glory of God" is, in effect, the term used to express that which man can apprehend, originally by sight, of the presence of God on earth. It does not mean God in His essential nature, but the luminous manifestation of His person, His glorious revelation of himself. It is characteristically linked with seeing (Exod. 16:7; 33:18; Isa. 40:5) and appearing (Exod. 16:10; Deut. 5:24; Isa. 60:1). It may be recognized in creation (Pss. 19:1; 148:13; Isa. 6:3), but it expresses itself above all in salvation, that is, in God's great acts (Exod. 14:17-18; Ps. 96:3). "Sooner or later," says A. M. Ramsey, "the *kabod* appears in the Old Testament literature with the meaning of the character of Yahweh as revealed by His acts in history."[10]

The major sources that give expression to the "glory" as revelatory of God's presence are Exodus, Isaiah, and Ezekiel. In Exodus the glory is largely interpreted in cultic circumstances, appearing on Mount Sinai and hovering over the Tabernacle. In Ezekiel the element of brightness is added to the fundamental meaning.

The theological assumption that underlies the Old Testament *kabod* is the invisibility (transcendence) of Yahweh. The glory is the visible manifestation of the being of God. There were rare occasions when the glory was directly visible, but other times it was veiled by the cloud that was over the tent as the visible significance of Yahweh's presence; the Presence itself was veiled by it. A. M. Ramsey states it: "The glory is that union of sovereignty and righteousness which is the essence of the divine character."[11]

H. Orton Wiley described the glory as being similar to the reflection of the sun in a pool of water.[12] The sun itself is too

---

10. *The Glory of God and the Transfiguration of Christ* (London: Longmans, Green, and Co., 1949), 12. Cf. also G. Horton Davies, "Glory," in *Interpreter's Dictionary of the Bible,* ed. George A. Buttrick, 4 vols. New York: Abingdon Press, 1962), vol. 2; S. Aalen, "Glory, Honor," in *The New International Dictionary of New Testament Theology,* ed. Colin Brown, trans. from *Theologisches Begriffslexikon zum Neuen Testament,* 3 vols. (Grand Rapids: Zondervan Publishing House, 1975), vol. 2; Walter Betteridge, "Glory," in *International Standard Bible Encyclopedia,* ed. James Orr et al., 6 vols. (Grand Rapids: Wm. B. Eerdmans Publishing Co., 1949), vol. 2; Gerhard von Rad, "Doxa," in *Theological Dictionary of the New Testament,* ed. Gerhard Kittel, trans. and ed. Geoffrey W. Bromiley, 10 vols. (Grand Rapids: Wm. B. Eerdmans Publishing Co., 1964), vol. 2.

11. *Glory of God,* 13.

12. In a lecture at Trevecca Nazarene College, ca. 1947.

brilliant to be looked at by the naked eye, but its true nature may be seen by the image in the pool, its reflected "glory." Thus God is both seen and unseen. He does not reveal himself but does make himself known. If this sounds paradoxical, it is. Revelation cannot be defined from this point of view as "making clear," but rather as involving an ambiguity. We may say that there is a balance of transcendence and immanence, or that God is here represented as both hidden and revealed at one and the same time. The locus classicus for this truth is Exod. 33:18-23:

> Moses said, "I pray thee, show me thy glory." And he said, "I will make all my goodness pass before you, and will proclaim before you my name 'The Lord'; and I will be gracious to whom I will be gracious, and will show mercy on whom I will show mercy. But," he said, "you cannot see my face; for man shall not see me and live." And the Lord said, "Behold, there is a place by me where you shall stand upon the rock; and while my glory passes by I will put you in a cleft of the rock, and I will cover you with my hand until I have passed by; then I will take away my hand, and you shall see my back; but my face shall not be seen."

This incident is part of the aftermath of the golden calf apostasy when, with Moses' intercession, God promises His personal presence to go with the people in their journey to the Promised Land. But Moses, as the leader, wishes a deeper insight into the God who knows him "by name" (v. 12) and asks, "Show me thy glory." This is a prayer to see God as He is in himself. But Moses has requested something that is not possible to mortal man. In very anthropomorphic terms the profound theological truth is taught that while man can know something of the ways of God with man in his world, the ultimate mystery of God's nature is hidden from man. Using the vivid pictorial language of God's "face," His "hand," and His "back," the passage suggests that men may see only where God has passed by, and so know Him by His past doing and acts. God as He is in himself cannot be known or comprehended. As Rabbi Hirsch suggests, the intent of the statement may be worded: "Thou canst not see me working, but the traces of my work thou canst and thou shouldst see."

Note that it is God's "goodness" that passes before Moses. This is interpreted as His gracious attitude toward man: "I will be gracious to whom I will be gracious, and I will have compassion on whom I will have compassion" (v. 19, NEB, NKJV). It is in knowing the ways of God (and also His demands) that Moses knows God.

He is known in His dealings with man, in His moral character. The theological implications of this great passage point to the nature of revelation as occurring on the plane of history, and this "incarnate" disclosure is all that can be known of God.[13] The glory eventually came to be conceived as an element in the coming Messianic age and so became an eschatological concept. A typical expression of this is Isa. 60:1-3:

> Arise, shine; for your light has come,
>   and the glory of the Lord has risen upon you.
> For behold, darkness shall cover the earth,
>   and thick darkness the peoples;
> but the Lord will arise upon you,
>   and his glory will be seen upon you.
> And nations shall come to your light,
>   and kings to the brightness of your rising.

In the New Testament, the principle of the glory of God (and the term) is retained as the self-disclosure of God, but now its locus is in the person of Jesus Christ. In 2 Cor. 4:6 the glory *(doxa)* of God is given in the face of Jesus Christ, so that God's glory is incarnate in human form (cf. Phil. 4:19). As God's glory used to be manifest in Israel in the Tabernacling Presence (Rom. 9:4), so now it is manifest in Christ. Thus in the Transfiguration story, the cloud (cf. Mark 9:7) represents the cloud that overshadowed the "tent of meeting" when the glory of the Lord filled the Tabernacle (Exod. 40:34). In Hebrews, Christ reflects or is the Revelation or Effulgence of the divine glory (1:3).

The Fourth Gospel regards the entire life of Jesus as an embodiment of the glory of God (cf. John 1:14), although the glory is revealed only to believing disciples and not to the world. This truth highlights the twofold aspect of the glory of God found in the Old Testament, namely, an ambiguity of being both revealed and

---

13. This veiling of God as He is in himself does not contradict the statement in Exod. 24:10 that "they saw the God of Israel." All they saw was the "pavement of sapphire" that was "under his feet." Likewise all that Isaiah saw was the skirt of the royal garments that filled the vast Temple courtyard (Isa. 6:1). Cf. J. Philip Hyatt, *Exodus*, in *The New Century Bible*, Old Testament ed. Ronald E. Clements (Grand Rapids: Wm. B. Eerdmans Publishing Co., 1971); R. Alan Cole, *Exodus*, in *The Tyndale Old Testament Commentary* (Downers Grove, Ill.: InterVarsity Press, 1973); Samuel Raphael Hirsch, *The Pentateuch* (London: L. Honig and Sons, 1967); George A. F. Knight, *Theology as Narration* (Grand Rapids: Wm. B. Eerdmans Publishing Co., 1976).

veiled. Jesus is "God incognito." His deity is not necessarily apparent; it is possible to miss it or not recognize it.

"Glory" also has an eschatological dimension in the New Testament. It is a partly fulfilled reality and a future expectation into which we enter by degrees (2 Cor. 3:18; cf. Rom. 9:23; 2 Thess. 2:14). There are several passages that speak of the heavenly state in terms of "glory" (e.g., Rom. 5:2; 8:18; 2 Cor. 4:17; Col. 3:4). Alan Richardson summarizes the total outlook of the New Testament:

> The whole NT regards the incarnate Lord as the first installment, as it were, of the unveiling of the *doxa* in the latter days. . . . During his earthly life the *doxa* was indeed present, but eschatologically; it was veiled from men without faith. The incarnate Lord must enter into his *doxa* by suffering and death as Jesus himself had with such difficulty taught his disciples.[14]

The disclosure of the enigmatic name Yahweh to Moses further highlights the mystery that accompanies revelation in the Old Testament. The names of God are commonly considered to be manifestations of God's nature, but the central, personal name is both an unveiling and a veiling. Scholars have explored the significance of the Tetragrammaton without achieving full unanimity. Hebrew thought prohibits the interpretation of it as referring to God's eternal, unchanging nature; it is far more dynamic than that. The most likely translation is "I will be what I will be," suggesting that God's activity in salvation history will give evidence of His nature or character or purpose. Doubtless it points forward, in particular, to the mighty events of the Exodus.

Philosophical Dimensions

Since revelation is more of a philosophical problem than a biblical one, one's understanding of it is directly affected by his philosophical view of the transcendence of God. This is an inquiry that systematic theology cannot avoid since, as Wiley says, "In proportion as man's thought approaches maturity, the religious and philosophical conceptions of God tend to become more and more identified" (*CT* 1:220). The more radically distinct from the world, the more critical is the need for God to disclose himself. Conversely, if one's philosophical perspective tends toward an immanental understanding of the relation between God and the

---

14. *An Introduction to the Theology of the New Testament* (New York: Harper and Bros., Publishers, 1958), 65 ff. Cf. also L. H. Brockington, "Presence," in *A Theological Word Book of the Bible*, ed. Alan Richardson (New York: Macmillan Co., 1950).

world, the need for revelation is less critical. Hence, an adequate view of revelation will depend on how one conceptualizes the relation between God and the world. We will survey several historical examples to illustrate this correlation between one's view of the God-world relation and revelation.

The earliest theologians, commonly called the patristic fathers, worked in a period dominated by Hellenistic philosophy, especially that phase termed Middle Platonism. That particular approach to speculation was dualistic in stressing the distance between God and the world. While this had significant consequences when allowed to inform the doctrine of creation, it also was influential in shaping the philosopher's perception of how Ultimate Reality could be known, if at all. Those early Christian fathers who were pervasively influenced by this philosophy, such as Justin Martyr, Clement of Alexandria, and Origen, reflect this stress upon transcendence in both their cosmology and their statements about our knowledge of God. But both Irenaeus (more influenced by biblical thought) and Tertullian (who denied the value of philosophy) express this same sort of understanding as well, doubtless reflecting the pervasive influence of the prevailing philosophical ideas on the thinking of a person even when they are overtly rejected.

Hellenistic philosophy emerged as a religious expression of Platonism. It developed out of the previous period, which was centrally concerned with ethics. The reason for this transition in Hellenistic philosophy from the ethical to the religious perspective was the failure of the ethical philosophy to achieve its goals. Classical philosophy had had a threefold aim: to know, to be virtuous, and to be happy. None of them had been effectively realized, culminating in the failure of philosophical ethics. Thus there was a disposition to accept help from beyond the outstretched fingers of the wise man—this is religion.

One of its primary characteristics, if not the most distinctive one, was a dualism between God and the world that was basically ethical in nature. It was just this dualism, which opposed the earthly world of the perishable to a supersensuous world of the divine, that ultimately proved to be the right expression for that inner discord that ran through the entire life of the aging Greek and Roman world. It was because of the congeniality of Plato to this dualism that a religious development of Platonism is the fundamental character of this period.

The first expression of the new feeling of religion was Neo-Pythagoreanism. This is understandable, since the original impetus of Pythagoreanism was religious, being very closely associated with the mysteries. It had largely faded from view during the heydays of Plato and Aristotle but revived under the drive for a new religious orientation.

Others who give expression to the characteristic features of this period, including especially an emphasis on the divine transcendence, were Plutarch, Philo the Jew, and the Gnostics, with all of these culminating in the Neoplatonism of Plotinus. "Neo-Platonism is thus like the sea, to which the various contributing rivers are flowing and in which their waters are at length mingled."[15] The center of this philosophical development was Alexandria, Egypt; thus it is sometimes referred to as the Alexandrian philosophy.[16]

In emphasizing the transcendence of God, two concepts are present in the Alexandrian philosophy: (1) God is interpreted as "beyond being" and therefore unknowable. This is the case because He is the One who is above all differentiation and determination. Beginning with Philo, and radically expressed in Neoplatonism, it is emphasized that God is devoid of qualities. "Since God is exalted above all, it can be said of him only that he has none of the finite predicates known to human intelligence; no name names him."[17] This is a type of thought that came to be known as "negative theology" and found expression in many Christian thinkers. (2) Since the religious ethos of the period sought salvation by overcoming the chasm between the finite and the infinite, there was an emphasis on intermediate beings that provided the link between the two. "The dualism of God and world, as well as that of spirit and matter, is but the starting-point . . . and the presupposition of the Alexandrian philosophy: its goal is everywhere, theoretically as well as practically, to vanquish this dualism."[18]

Of special interest to Christian thought is the speculation of Philo, the Jew of Alexandria. His insistence on God's elevation above the world led to a conception of mediary beings to bridge

---

15. Frederick Copleston, A History of Philosophy (Garden City, N.Y.: Doubleday and Co., Image Books, 1962), vol. 1, pt. 2, 196.

16. Cf. Wilhelm Windelband, A History of Philosophy, 2 vols., Torchbook ed. (New York: Harper and Bros., Publishers, 1958), vol. 1.

17. Ibid., 237.

18. Ibid., 239.

the gulf between God himself and the material cosmos. The highest of these intermediary beings is the Logos or Nous who is the firstborn of God. Also, out of his Jewish heritage, he spoke of angels as well as "powers" as mediating beings. While God is unknowable in himself, according to Philo, the Logos is knowable. It was thus in terms of the Logos doctrine that the way is opened up to overcoming the radical dualism that made knowledge of God impossible. Various forms of the same idea were present in Plutarch, Gnosticism, and Neoplatonism. It thus becomes apparent in Hellenistic philosophy how knowledge of God is impossible because of a radical view of transcendence—except for or by a being from God who is less than God.

As suggested, these ideas exercised a significant influence upon the patristic fathers. Justin Martyr speaks of God as transcendent, changeless, and indescribable because He is *sui generis.* He cannot be in relation to the world, because He cannot change. If He is in relation to the changing world, He would be changing himself and therefore by definition not God. In explaining the scriptural references to God "coming down" among men, he says, "You must not imagine that the unbegotten God himself came down or went up anywhere. For the ineffable Father and Lord of all neither comes anywhere nor walks nor sleeps nor rises up."[19]

The consequence of this understanding of God's nature is that He is essentially unknowable. Justin makes this point quaintly by stating:

> The Father of all has no name given him, since he is unbegotten. For a being who has a name imposed on him has an elder to give him that name. "Father," and "God," "Creator," "Lord," "Master," are not names but appellations derived from his benefits and works ... the title "God" is not a name, but represents the idea ... of an inexpressible reality.[20]

Clement of Alexandria was also representative of the typical Hellenistic view of God. For Clement, He is the Absolute, the Source of all things, beyond the world and finitude and beyond understanding. Language is inadequate to describe Him. Such terms as *good* and *existing* are all applicable only to finite things. No category applies to Him because He is beyond being, number, and relation; thus He is not known in himself. In the *Stromateis* Cle-

---

19. *Dialogue with Trypho,* chap. 127.
20. *Apologia* 2.5.

ment says: "God is undemonstrable and therefore is not an object of knowledge."

Like Justin, Clement denies that human language is adequate to speak of God:

> For how can that be spoken of which is not genus, differentia, species, individual, number, accident, subject of accident? . . . Though we ascribe names, they are not to be taken in their strict meaning; when we call him One, Good, Mind, Existence, Father, God, Creator, Lord, we are not conferring a name on him. Being unable to do more, we use these appellations of honor in order that our thought may have something to rest on and not wander at random.[21]

Those fathers who were more influenced by biblical thought did not hold such a radical view of transcendence. While recognizing the otherness of God, they do not hold Him to be completely unknowable. Origen was a Hellenistic philosopher but was also an influential biblical scholar. He depicts God as the Source of being who transcends time and temporality, but He is not beyond all qualities. More like Plato than Hellenistic thought, Origen sees God as the perfection of all being, so there is the possibility of knowing God in some sense. God is incomprehensible in himself, but He is not irrational. Although we cannot fully understand the perfection of a spiritual being such as God, we shall know in eternity. Here and now He transcends our finite conceptions, but the conceptions we have are not inaccurate. Origen expresses it in these words: "Our mind cannot behold God as he is in himself, therefore it forms its conception of the Creator of the universe from the beauty of his works and the loveliness of his creatures"; and "there is a kinship between the human mind and God; for the mind is itself an image of God, and therefore can have some conception of the Divine nature, especially the more it is purified and removed from matter."

Irenaeus, even more influenced by Hebrew thought than Hellenistic, held that God is not inscrutable, not absolutely beyond our talking but nonetheless transcendent to His creation. Consequently we cannot understand Him because we are finite; however, He is rational, "wholly intelligible," understandable in himself. Irenaeus stresses the ethical characteristics of God in this connection rather than the metaphysical: "Through his love and

---

21. *Stromateis*, chap. 12.

infinite kindness God comes within the grasp of man's knowledge. But this knowledge is not in respect of his greatness or his true being; for no one has measured that or grasped it."[22]

Even Tertullian, the father least consciously influenced by Hellenistic philosophy, recognizes the unknowable dimensions of God's nature: "It is God's infinity which gives us the conception of the inconceivable God; for his overwhelming majesty presents him to man as at once known and unknown."[23] Like Justin Martyr, Tertullian holds that those references to God appearing in the sphere of human history must be interpreted allegorically. He asks: "How is it that the omnipotent, invisible God whom no man hath seen or can see, who inhabiteth light inaccessible, who dwelleth not in temples made with hands . . . should have walked at evening in the paradise seeking Adam [and similar appearances in the space/time realm]?" The answer is negative.

This rather uniform emphasis on transcendence with its corollary of God's unknowability led to a standard solution to the problem of overcoming the chasm between the unknowable God and the human understanding. Revelation was interpreted in terms of the Logos, a prevalent philosophical theme that gained scriptural support from the Fourth Gospel. The idea of the Logos, first used by the apologists, "soon became generally recognized as an essential part of Christian theology."[24] The term Logos has two meanings—reason and word, the indwelling and outgoing Logos —which especially fitted it to mediate between God in himself and God in His relation to the world and to men.

The Logos was interpreted as being the reason of God, which therefore embodies the nature of God. This Logos as universal reason becomes the means by which a universal knowledge of God is disseminated, especially to the Greek philosophers, and, as incarnate, the most definitive revelation of God in the world.[25]

The Logos becomes the principle of explanation for some of the Fathers as to how the eternal God could appear in time. Those

---

22. *Against Heresies* 3.24.1.

23. *Apology,* 17. It should be remembered that Tertullian, probably under the influence of Stoicism, argued that God is corporeal in nature, has a body. Thus denying the spirituality of God would reduce the distance between God and human understanding.

24. McGiffert, *God of the Early Christians,* 122.

25. The two aspects of the Logos were interpreted as two stages in the "life" of the Logos by some of the fathers. This has far-reaching significance for Christology, and we will look more closely at this aspect of the subject in a later section of the theology.

Old Testament passages that speak of God in human history are really referring to the Logos. In speaking of the Logos, Irenaeus says: "It is he himself who says to Moses, 'I have surely seen the affliction of my people in Egypt, and I have come down to rescue them.' From the beginning he was accustomed, as the Word of God, to descend and ascend for the salvation of those who were in distress."[26]

Reformation Perspectives

The Protestant Reformers, influenced decisively by the biblical perspective, laid stress upon both the hiddenness and the revealedness of God. One of the basic principles of Reformation theology is that "we do not know God as He is in himself, but only as He makes himself known."[27] Martin Luther elaborated this truth in terms of his distinction between the *theologia gloria* and the *theologia crucis*; or in terms of *Deus absconditus* and *Deus revelatus*.[28]

By the *theologia gloria* Luther meant the attempt to apprehend God in His naked transcendence or majesty. Such a knowledge, he argues, would not and could not save but would rather terrify and destroy. The *theologia crucis* is the veiled knowledge of God given us in Christ, particularly in the sufferings of the Cross. The noetic aspects of this are reflected in Luther's words: "God . . . does not manifest himself except through his works and word, because the meaning of these is understood in some measure. Whatever else belongs essentially to the Divinity cannot be grasped and understood."[29]

In order for finite man to "grasp" the Holy One, He must descend to present himself in veiled or covered form (*Deus velatus*). This is to say that God must embody himself. Of the Holy Spirit Luther writes: "The Holy Spirit is now truly present among us and

---

26. *Against Heresies* 4.12.4.
27. Wiley adopts this dictum as his own, affirming that "God . . . can be known to us only through a revelation of Himself." *CT* 1:218.
28. Luther's category of the "hidden God" has been interpreted in various ways in subsequent theology. It has been related to the doctrine of predestination and to scholastic voluntarism that emphasized God's arbitrary will. For a careful analysis of the history of Luther's interpretation on this point see John Dillenberger, *God Hidden and Revealed* (Philadelphia: Muhlenberg Press, 1953). The view adopted in this exposition generally concurs with that supported by Dillenberger.
29. Quoted in Paul Althaus, *The Theology of Martin Luther*, trans. Robert C. Schultz (Philadelphia: Fortress Press, 1966), 20.

works in us through the word and sacraments. He has covered himself with veils and clothing so that our weak, sick, and leprous nature might grasp him and know him."[30]

When Luther spoke of the hidden God, he was not suggesting that the God who was not known before Christ (hidden) had at that time become known (revealed). Rather the revelation of God in Christ carried with it the sense of hiddenness or mystery that is never absent from God's self-disclosure. In other words, revelation and hiddenness are correlative and inseparable concepts. In Luther's own expression, "This is clear, that he who does not know Christ, does not know the hidden God in his suffering."

Nonetheless, it is still Luther's contention that the essence of God is made known in the Cross *(theologia crucis).* By this he intends to suggest that the true character of God is made known but in a veiled form open only to faith. This is the basis for Gustav Aulen's insistence that faith's affirmation about God differs from any rational metaphysics. "God is exactly such as he is manifested in the act of Christ. There is no other God [Luther's phrase]. All other 'conceptions' of God are eliminated. As far as the Christian faith is concerned they are nothing but caricatures."[31] Luther expresses this in the 19th and 20th propositions of the Heidelberg Disputations: "Not that is legitimately called a theology which takes as true and understands God's unseeable essence through his works, but that is theology which grasps that God's essence has become visible and has been turned to the world, as expressed in suffering and the cross."[32]

Calvin agrees with Luther in recognizing that if man is to know God, God must accommodate himself to man's finite comprehension. In his comments on 1 Cor. 2:7 he says: "He accommodates himself to our capacity." The reason for this is that "the nature of God is spiritual, it is not allowable to imagine respecting him anything earthly or gross; nor does his immensity permit of his being confined to place."[33] Thus any attempt to define God by human concepts apart from His accommodation is futile. On Exod. 3:2 he remarks:

> It was necessary that he should assume a visible form, that he might be seen by Moses not as he was in his essence but as

30. Ibid., 21.
31. *Faith of the Christian Church*, 41.
32. Quoted in Dillenberger, *God Hidden and Revealed*, 148.
33. Commentary on Ezek. 3:4.

the infirmity of the human mind could comprehend. For thus we believe that God, as often as he appeared of old to the holy patriarchs, descended in some way from his loftiness, that he might reveal himself as far as was useful and as far as their comprehension would admit.

Calvin finds in the scholastic theology of the Roman church a speculation about God that is dissociated from revelation, and criticizes it as follows:

> All thought about God which does not proceed from the fact of Christ is a fathomless abyss which utterly engulfs our faculties. A clear example of this is furnished not only by Turks and Jews who under the name of God worship their fantasies but also by the Papists. The principle of their theological schools, that God in Himself is the object of faith, is generally known. Hence they philosophize at length and with much subtlety about the hidden majesty of God while overlooking the fact of Christ. But with what result? They get entangled in curious and delusive ideas, so that their error has no limits.[34]

Both Luther and Calvin vigorously resist all speculation about God beyond what is revealed. Each, with a great deal of seriousness, tells the same anecdote about anyone who would raise a question about what God was doing before He created the world. The answer: He was making hell for curious people. Far more crucial are those truths about God that affect us, specifically those relating to His attitude toward us. As Calvin says: "Cold and frivolous . . . are the speculations of those who employ themselves in disquisitions on the essence of God, when it would be more interesting to us to become acquainted with his character, and to know what is agreeable to his nature."[35]

Modern Adjustments in Transcendence and Immanence

In the years following the Reformation, various movements narrowed the gap between God and man, each in its own way. Deism, or rational religion, would accept only those religious beliefs that conformed to the canons of reason. This was tantamount to the rejection of revelation. Protestant scholasticism, in the name of revelation, likewise lost the sense of transcendence by laying brash claims to being able to conceptualize for belief all the truth of God. They "usually knew too much about the intricacies of the

---

34. Quoted in Wilhelm Niesel, *The Theology of Calvin*, trans. Harold Knight (Philadelphia: Westminster Press, 1956), 116.
35. *Institutes* 1.2.2.

working of God to permit genuine mystery or hiddenness as a part of their heritage. . . . They represented a self-constructed picture of the mind of God in rigid contrast to the mind of man."[36]

The 19th century has been characterized as the Age of Immanence. It was dominated philosophically by the thought of Spinoza and Hegel, and theologically by the work of Schleiermacher and Ritschl. The philosophical monism of both Spinoza and Hegel asserted continuity between the finite mind and the Infinite Mind. In the theologies of Schleiermacher and Ritschl, God is to be located in the religious experience. Schleiermacher declares:

> The usual conception of God as a single being outside of the world and behind the world is not essential to religion. . . . The true essence of religion is neither this idea nor any other, but the immediate consciousness of Deity as we find him in ourselves as well as in the world.[37]

In commenting upon the influence of the Age of Immanence on the idea of revelation, A. C. McGiffert says:

> As God is immanent in the life of man divine revelation comes from within, not from without. The religious man looks into his own experience for the disclosure of divine truth, and if he also turns to the pages of a sacred book, it is simply because it is a record of the religious experience of other men who have found God in their own souls and have learned from him there.[38]

This approach eliminates the need for any special revelation or agents of revelation since all nature and life is the place of God.

Studies of the Gifford Lectures up to 1920 reveal that immanence remained the dominant tone in England, and it continued so until the 1930s. However, there were developments in the 19th century that challenged the adequacy of immanency and laid the groundwork for a change of climate in the 20th century that returned to an emphasis on the transcendence of God and thus on the decisiveness of revelation.

The prophetic voice crying in the wilderness was the Danish theologian/philosopher Søren Kierkegaard. Stressing the infinite qualitative distinction between time and eternity, he called for a view of religious truth that required a leap of faith, since eternal

---

36. Dillenberger, *God Hidden and Revealed*, xvii.
37. Quoted in Edward Farley, *The Transcendence of God* (Philadelphia: Westminster Press, 1960), 17.
38. *The Rise of Modern Religious Ideas* (New York: Macmillan Co., 1915), 214.

truth was not easily approached by reason as an apparent truth. The shape of his polemic was an attack upon the idealism of Hegel. This idealism "obliterates the infinite qualitative difference between God and man, loses sight of the inevitable paradox of the Incarnation, and ends in . . . the ludicrous identification of the thought of the philosopher with the mind of God."[39]

The emphases of Kierkegaard flowered in the neoorthodox theologies of Karl Barth and Emil Brunner. In the introduction to his "bell-ringing" commentary on Romans (Der Romerbrief) Barth declared that if he had a "system it is limited to a recognition of what Kierkegaard called the 'infinite qualitative distinction' between time and eternity." It is thus that contemporary theology has been led back to a central emphasis on the idea of revelation.

Transcendence and Immanence—Maintaining a Balance

This brief survey has demonstrated somewhat of a pendulum swing back and forth between emphasis on transcendence and immanence with the sense of the importance of revelation being influenced by which one is in the ascendancy. However, the biblical picture that was explored at the outset reflected a balanced view between the two, pointing us to a view of revelation that presents God as both hidden and revealed in the same moment. The chief theologians of the Reformation seemed to most clearly grasp this truth.

A proper doctrine of revelation will, then, maintain an insistence upon the mystery of God, or as it has often been termed, the abysmal nature of God.[40] It is to this dimension that Rudolf Otto pointed in his classic exposition of the "numinous" or "mysterium

---

39. Alasdair I. C. Heron, *A Century of Protestant Theology* (Philadelphia: Westminster Press, 1980), 50.

40. Using the term "the Unfathomable," Aulen elucidates the point this way: "It is important to note in what manner God appears as the Unfathomable. It does not mean simply that there are certain limits to revelation, and that beyond these limits there exists a hidden territory which would grow less and less in the measure that revelation increases. Nor does it mean merely that under these earthly circumstances there will remain questions which cannot be answered and riddles which cannot be solved; that the Christian faith cannot become a rational world view to which the divine government of the world would be transparently clear. It means rather that the nature of divine revelation appears to faith as an impenetrable mystery; a 'mystery disclosed' (Rom. 16:25-26), which yet remains a mystery. Since the very center of this revelation is divine love which gives itself in order to establish fellowship with sinners, that love itself appears inscrutable and impenetrable. Faith beholds the revealed God as the Unfathomable, the 'hidden' God." *Faith of the Christian Church*, 41-42.

tremendum" in *The Idea of the Holy.* [41] Here one must distinguish between a mystery and a problem. When a problem has been solved, the truth about it has been revealed, and the mystery disappears. With a mystery, however, the mysteriousness cannot be removed even when a revelation occurs. Paul Tillich adequately describes it in this way: "Revelation of that which is essentially and necessarily mysterious means the manifestation of something within the context of ordinary experience which transcends the ordinary context of experience." [42] Or as Karl Rahner puts it: "Revelation is not the bringing of what was once unknown into the region of what is known, perspicuous and manageable: it is the dawn and the approach of mystery as such." [43]

A God who is the Wholly Other, who is completely transcendent, would have no relation to man and thus would be both unknowable and irrelevant to us. On the contrary, if God were completely immanent, He would cease to be what we mean by God, even though He might be lucidly knowable. Christian thought must thus not allow itself to lose either aspect of its understanding of God.

This relation of tension points to the nature of revelation, if indeed a revelation of God is to occur at all. Since God in His "naked majesty" (Luther) transcends the realm of ordinary experience, He can be known only as He enters the world of experience. This implies that He cannot be discovered but must discover himself. It is the central Christian affirmation at this point that God has indeed descended into our realm by His saving acts in history, climaxing in the event in which the Divine took on the conditions of finite existence, "tabernacled among us" (John 1:14, Amp., ASV margin), and so became knowable and visible to us.

> Thus the gulf between the Creator and the finite creature has been bridged by revelation, and the absolute mystery of that transcendent source from which we come has been illumined to our spirits and made partially intelligible to our minds. To Christians, therefore, the transcendence of God implies and requires the revelatory acts of God, and for this reason, Christian theology rightly feels that all that it can validly say about the transcendent God must be based upon and guided by God's revelation of Himself. [44]

---

41. Otto refers to numinous as nonrational, by which he means that it is nonconceptual but not unknowable.

42. *Systematic Theology* 1:109.

43. *Theological Investigations* (Baltimore: Helicon Press, 1966), 4:330.

44. Gilkey, *Maker of Heaven and Earth*, 93.

The hiddenness of God in His self-disclosure dictates that theological language must be understood in a special way. One cannot speak of the transcendent Reality in the same way that he speaks of finite objects such as tables and chairs. Immanuel Kant called our attention to this fact in his critical analysis of the powers of the human mind and suggested the term *transcendental* to refer to realities that we are able to think (such as God, the self, and the cosmos) but that cannot be described in terms of the categories of the mind that refer only to phenomenal reality, the sensible manifold that presents itself to the senses. These realities correspond to no object of our experience but rather are transcendental ideas.

Religious Language

This leads us necessarily to a discussion of the nature of religious language, or in contemporary jargon, "God talk." This is not a new problem by any means but has been brought into the center of theological discussion by relatively recent developments in philosophy. Here too it will profit us considerably to survey the various suggestions that theologians have made in past centuries, culminating with a brief analysis of some of the issues in terms of recent developments.

Before beginning this survey, we will note the basic consideration that the transcendent nature of God requires that many theological assertions about God must be paradoxical in nature. Rationalists decry *paradox* as being an appeal to irrationality, but the Christian doctrine of God affirms a suprarational dimension, not an irrational one, to our knowledge of the Ultimate. As Thomas Aquinas said, "Only the divine intellect is in its capacity equal to its substance [essence], and therefore . . . understands fully what it is, including all its intelligible attributes."[45]

Some have suggested that a more appropriate term is *antinomy* rather than paradox. This is a term used by Kant to express the resistance of transcendental ideas (see above) to complete rational formulation. The reason given is that antinomy suggests an irreducible quality, whereas paradox is only so in a limited sense. While it is unclear as to whether we can assume from Scripture that all paradoxes will ultimately be resolved to our understanding or whether our finitude for all eternity will render divine paradoxes forever beyond our total comprehension, we will continue to

45. *Summa Contra Gentiles* 1.4.

use the traditional term, since it is more common and adequately carries the intention of the discussion from our present point of view.

Paradox means "contrary to expectations, to common opinion, to what seems to be." It must be distinguished from a logical contradiction. The distinction between a paradox and a contradiction relates to the degree of complexity of the subject of which the assertions are made. A contradiction occurs when two opposing or different things are stated about a specified reality when this reality is insufficiently diverse to support within itself discordant predicates.

If, for example, we assert that John Smith is both old and young, we are involved in a contradiction if we are intending both predicates to refer to chronological age. But if we are suggesting that he is old in body while young in spirit, there is no contradiction but only an apparent one—a paradox. John Smith is a sufficiently complex reality to bear such opposing predicates, and sufficiently available to our investigation so that we have access to the unifying center of the paradox.

The simplicity of this illustration and many others, such as Jesus' paradoxical dictum that "whoever would save his life will lose it" (Matt. 16:25; Mark 8:35; Luke 9:24), depends on the accessibility of the object of paradoxical assertions. That is, we are dealing with a finite reality whose unity is not beyond the grasp of our understanding. If, on the other hand, the "hidden unity of these experienced characteristics is beyond our grasp, when, in other words, we meet something individual, unique, or transcendent, and therefore not to be completely analyzed by our minds," it is not within our capacity to resolve in clear explanation the apparently conflicting characteristics; that is, paradox is necessarily used.[46]

The question could legitimately be raised: If we cannot gain access to the hidden unity of the object, how are we indeed able to determine the difference between paradox and contradiction? The response to this reveals an insight into the nature of our knowledge of God. It is the result of personal encounter in which we have a self-disclosed experience of the qualities involved, yet when they are translated into the objectifying propositions of ordinary lan-

---

46. Cf. Gilkey, *Maker of Heaven and Earth*, 275-76. I am indebted to this source for these basic insights about paradox and the illustration of it.

guage, there is an apparent falsification; but it is the only way in which experience can be articulated in an adequate way. It is likely that the apparent contradiction between human freedom and divine foreknowledge is an example of this phenomenon.

As Donald M. Baillie puts it, "God can be known only in a direct personal relationship, an 'I-and-Thou' intercourse, in which He addresses us and we respond to Him. . . . He eludes all our words and categories. We cannot objectify or conceptualize Him."[47]

Langdon Gilkey explains the issue succinctly:

> It is not at all strange that this unusual way of speaking of the unusual should be commonly found in religious language about deity. For in all high religions the divine is unique, transcendent, and so beyond our clear comprehension. Thus talk about Him, or It, cannot be the usual consistent, clear, matter-of-fact sort of description which we use with familiar objects. It is more like talking about the mysterious depths of other persons, whom we know in part and yet do not know. In talking about God at all, we must assume He is like what we know in experience—lest He be quite ineffable and irrelevant; and yet we must indicate as well His transcendent strangeness and unlikeness—lest He cease to be God. Thus whatever we say of Him must be affirmed and denied at the same time. Moreover, we cannot hope to penetrate with our concepts to the mysterious essence of God, to discover how this likeness and unlikeness are resolved, for the ultimate cannot be put into a class of things which we can clearly measure, or adequately define. In the encounter of faith we do stand before Him; but in our theological language we can never grasp the inmost unity of His nature and being. Thus paradoxes are the only way of speaking about God: we affirm and deny things about Him, affirming something of God so we shall not be silent, and yet at the same time denying it so we shall not make of Him an ordinary object.[48]

This analysis is in complete accord with the biblical picture of God's self-disclosure as discussed earlier in this section.

Proposed Uses of Religious Language

From the beginning of theologizing, thinkers have recognized the problem of speaking about God. Historically, there have been three major ways of addressing the issue: the way of negation (*via*

---

47. *God Was in Christ* (London: Faber and Faber, 1961), 108-9.
48. *Maker of Heaven and Earth*, 276-77.

negativa), the way of ascribing positive perfection to God, and the way of analogy, which is a combination of the first two.[49]

The way of negation proposes to speak about God by denying to Him all finite qualities: He is not this, not that. Many of the terms commonly used of God are actually negative designations, such as *infinite,* meaning not finite. The most serious criticism of this approach points out that when it is carried to its logical conclusion, one ends in silence. However, it could be argued that some advance is made toward an adequate conception of God when we clear the ground of inadequate concepts. The more radical one's view of transcendence is, the more one thinks it impossible to speak of God in positive terms, and therefore the more dominant the way of negation may become.

The *via negativa* appears in the history of Christian thought as early as Origen. It is mentioned by Augustine and comes to its most extensive expression during the Middle Ages in the anonymous work attributed to the first-century Dionysius the Areopagite. It also finds a significant place in the writing of Nicholas of Cusa titled *On Learned Ignorance.*

The way of ascribing perfections to God takes positive qualities, usually drawn from our being human, and applies them to God in an absolute way. God is thus seen as being all good, or perfectly loving, and so on.

The way of analogy combines the way of negation with positive ascriptions of characteristics to God. It recognizes that God is both like and unlike the attributes ascribed to Him. Thus it simultaneously affirms and denies. Analogy, like the *via negativa,* is found in the writings of Origen and Augustine but comes to its classic expression in the work of Thomas Aquinas, who bases the possibility of language about God on the ontological assumption that there is a relationship between the being of God and the being of man, hence the analogy of being *(analogia entis).*

Thomas suggests three types of language: (1) univocal, which

---

49. Note that in recent times considerable use has been made in the scholarly world of the term *myth.* There has been much controversy about its meaning with various scholars using it in different senses. But since the term conveys discordant overtones suggesting unreality to many people, it is the better part of wisdom to avoid using it here, since in its most proper use it does not suggest any dimensions of the problem not covered by the less-colored language we are employing. Perhaps the best working definition of it for contemporary thinkers is "a way of talking about the God who transcends history in the dramatic terms of an active agent in history."

means literally "one voice." Univocal language is applied in exactly the same way to each referent. Such is not the way we use language about God; for when, for example, we speak of God as Father, we do not mean literally or precisely what we mean when we speak of a human father. This would be nonsense. (2) Equivocal, meaning "with different voice," so that terms are used of different referents in a completely unrelated way. If language about God was equivocal, when we speak of Him as Father the term would have absolutely nothing in common with what we mean when we refer to a man as a father, and thus nothing would be communicated. (3) Analogical language suggests that there is some commonality, so that while there is a similarity between calling God and man father, there is also a dissimilarity.

Karl Barth has sharply criticized the *analogia entis* on the basis that it does not take seriously the "infinite qualitative" distance between the being of man and the being of God. He proposed instead an *analogia fides*, which suggests that the primary analogue is God, of whom we have knowledge by revelation, with man being the secondary analogue. "It is therefore not that there is first of all human fatherhood and then a so-called divine Fatherhood, but just the reverse: true and proper fatherhood resides in God, and from this Fatherhood of God, what we know as fatherhood among us men is derived. The divine Fatherhood is the primal source of all natural fatherhood."[50]

Perhaps the most adequate proposal in contemporary theology for an understanding of religious language is that of Paul Tillich, who develops the idea of "symbol." This concept stands at the center of his theological doctrine of knowledge and is posited as a very serious recognition of the infinity of the divine, the transcendence of God.[51]

A symbol, in Tillich's thought, must be distinguished from a sign, which is artificial. In this connection he insists that one should never say "merely" or "only" a symbol. A religious symbol points beyond itself to Ultimate Reality and participates in the reality to which it points. This is clearly a specialized use of the com-

---

50. *Dogmatics in Outline*, 43.
51. As a result of criticism that unless there were at least one nonsymbolic statement, symbolic language would be impossible, Prof. Tillich concedes that there is one, which he identifies as "God is being itself." "Reply to Interpretation and Criticism," in *The Theology of Paul Tillich*, ed. Charles W. Kegley and Robert W. Bretall (New York: Macmillan Co., 1964).

mon concept of symbol and presupposes a particular ontology of the type first articulated by Plato. A symbol can be both linguistic (a word or words) and nonlinguistic (e.g., the flag or the crucifix).

The function of a symbol is to "open up levels of reality which otherwise are closed to us." This suggests that it becomes a medium through which the reality encounters us and by means of which we confront it. Thus a symbol also unlocks dimensions and elements of our soul that correspond to the dimensions and elements of the reality symbolized. That symbols cannot be created or replaced intentionally further points to the fact that it is in experience that our understanding of God comes to expression in linguistic and/or nonlinguistic symbol.

As noted above, the religious symbol points to Ultimate Reality. "The intention of every religious symbol is to point to that which transcends finitude. Nothing finite, no part of the universe of finite relations can be the referent of religious symbols, and therefore, no inductive method can reach it."[52]

This view safeguards the holiness of God and at the same time prohibits the elevation of finite reality to the level of ultimacy. To think of language as standing in the same relation to God as it stands to objects such as tables and chairs is to lapse into linguistic idolatry. This fact requires that the theological task be pursued with great humility and in a worshipful attitude. Another way of saying the same thing is that religious symbols transcend their nonsymbolic meaning.

The practical outworking of this symbolic view of religious language is that certain symbols may die when they cease to reflect the experience of those who use them. In religious communions, symbols that were alive and vital to the founding fathers sometimes lose their efficaciousness in the second and third generations when the original religious experience has grown dim. While the language may be retained, it can become hollow and meaningless. Tillich speaks of these as "nonauthentic" symbols, those "which have lost their experiential basis, but which are still used for reasons of tradition or because of their aesthetic value."[53]

---

52. "The Meaning and Justification of Religious Belief," in *Religious Experience and Truth*, ed. Sidney Hook (New York: New York University Press, 1961), 6.
53. Ibid., 20.

Revelation and Knowledge

The category of knowledge is also a corollary of the concept of revelation. The two concepts inform each other when used in a theological context. However one conceives revelation determines his understanding of what it means to know God. At the same time one's concept of knowledge influences his view of the nature of revelation. This correlative character of knowledge and revelation requires that these two ideas be consistently interpreted.

In addressing this issue, we will begin by exploring the biblical concept of knowledge, since the Scripture is the definitive or normative Source for our interpretation. We will then seek to discover parallels in nonbiblical thought; and finally we will draw some conclusions concerning the way in which these concepts affect our understanding of revelation.

It is important in the ensuing discussion to recognize the distinction between knowing God and knowing about God. The interplay between these two essential aspects of religious knowledge is delicate and difficult to maintain. The analysis below attempts to keep them separate so as not to confuse the two to the degree that one is collapsed into the other. If the dimension of "knowing about" is lost, the result is a mysticism that rejects any cognitive revelation; whereas if the element of "knowing God" is not retained, the result is a rationalism that reduces God to a finite object, or an intellectualism that makes religion a matter of gnosis. The reader should keep this balance in mind and remember that he is working with two ideas discussed somewhat seriatim, both of which are requisite to a balanced understanding.

Biblical View of Knowledge

We would not expect to find any theoretical discussions of epistemology in the Bible. Neither would the use of "knowledge" in a mundane sense concern us here. The way in which the biblical writers speak of the "knowledge of God" is alone relevant to our purpose, and we must derive our understanding from their actual use. There is abundant material in the Old Testament, since "knowledge of God" is the primary way of describing man's right relation to God. It is used in much the same way as "faith" in the New Testament.

The origin of man's knowledge of God is in God's self-disclosure, and this self-revelation is usually connected with some historical event. This truth is often reflected in the formula, "And you [or, they] shall know that I am the Lord [Yahweh]," found 54 times in Ezekiel and numerous times elsewhere (cf. Exod. 6:7; Deut. 4:32-39). Thus knowledge of God originates in experience either directly or as a result of the testimonies of those who have been privy to the revelatory acts (cf. Exod. 10:1-2; 18:8-11).

This knowledge of God derived from His self-disclosure is not theoretical or abstract in nature but, like the general character of knowledge in Hebrew thought, means more than the awareness of an item and its nature. It "implies also the awareness of the specific relationship in which the individual stands with that object, or of the significance the object has for him."[54] Thus "knowledge of God in the Old Testament is not concerned with the speculative question of the being of God, but in the God who, working in grace and judgment, has turned to man. To know him means to enter into the personal relationship which he himself makes possible."[55] Interpreted in this way, knowledge of God implies also knowledge of the self that stands in relation to God (cf. Ps. 51:3).

We may term this kind of knowledge "existential." Its nature is reflected in the use of the word "know" to describe the sexual act between husband and wife, the most intimate of relationships. Another example is the "knowledge" of good and evil that resulted from the act of disobedience in the Garden of Eden. This is knowledge by acquaintance or experience as a result of having actually disobeyed the Creator's command. Knowledge of God therefore entails more than intellectual awareness, though some elements of this are doubtless included; it involves personal acquaintance. "It is experience of the reality of God, not merely knowledge of propositions concerning God."[56]

This kind of knowledge manifests itself by a certain behavior, and conversely, the absence of such behavior is the sure sign that such knowledge is absent. Frequently this aspect of knowledge is seen in the description of the object of "to know" as "God's ways"

---

54. Otto A. Piper, "Knowledge," in *Interpreter's Dictionary of the Bible*, ed. George A. Buttrick, 4 vols. (New York: Abingdon Press, 1962), vol. 3.

55. E. D. Schmitz, "Knowledge," in *The New International Dictionary of New Testament Theology*, ed. Colin Brown, trans. from *Theologisches Begriffslexikon zum Neuen Testament*, 3 vols. (Grand Rapids: Zondervan Publishing House, 1975), vol. 3.

56. Piper, "Knowledge."

or "precepts" (cf. Pss. 25:4, 12; 119). The Book of Hosea is the locus classicus of this idea (cf. 4:1-2; 6:6).

The same perspective chiefly informs the New Testament understanding of knowledge, especially in the Fourth Gospel. "According to John," says Piper, "knowledge does not lead to a gradual merger of the knower's mind with that of God, but rather to a harmony of their wills in which God remains distinctly the authority to be recognized."

The same personal dimension informs the extensive use of "knowledge" by Paul. Actually, for him, it is more important to be "known by God," which is tantamount to being elected (Gal. 4:9; cf. 1 Cor. 8:3). "It is clear that Paul's polemics [against false views of knowledge] remain essentially within the limits of the O.T. concept of knowledge. At the same time he amplifies and works out this concept Christologically."[57]

According to Piper, there is in the Old Testament the awareness that "to know a person is more difficult than to know a thing; because a person must disclose his will in order to be adequately known" (cf. Prov. 25:3). This theoretical distinction is not presented as an abstract principle, but it does lie at the very root of the biblical knowledge of God. If to know Him is to be intimately acquainted with Him and to demonstrate this by obedience to His will, personal knowledge by self-disclosure is of the very essence of such knowledge.

Alan Richardson's summary captures the heart of the matter:

> Thus, knowledge in the biblical sense of the word is not theoretical contemplation but an entering into subjective relations as between person and person—relations of trust, obedience, respect, worship, love, fear and so on. It is knowledge in the sense of our knowledge of other persons rather than our knowledge of objects, "existential" rather than "scientific" knowledge. I cannot know a person with whom I refuse to enter into personal relations (or vice versa). To disobey God is to refuse to enter into the relation which he has so graciously made possible and hence is to remain ignorant of him.[58]

It becomes clear, then, that the distinctive nature of knowledge in biblical theology is existential. Since this is a technical term bearing several possible connotations, we need to define the way

---

57. Schmitz, "Knowledge."
58. *Theology*, 40-41.

we are using it here. We mean by this kind of knowledge, knowledge that determines the existence of the knower.[59]

Very early in the development of Christian thought a different view of knowledge (scientific) began to impinge upon Christian understanding. This view was associated with the teaching known as Gnosticism and created a significant threat to the distinctly biblical view of salvation by faith (trust). It came to mature expression in the second century but appeared in incipient form in the first century and was opposed by some of the New Testament Epistles (cf. 1 Corinthians and 1 John as well as Colossians and 1 Timothy).

There were several schools of Gnostics with vast systems of great complexity and imagination. The common element seems to be the belief that salvation from the world comes by knowledge rather than by faith. It operated within the framework of the popular science of the day, which identified the planets as "heavenly determiners of human destiny." These planets were fixed in orbit around the earth and stood as barriers to the soul in its flight from the earth-body to the immortal home beyond the stars. In order to reach this eternal destiny, these dangers must be traversed. The Christian version of Gnosticism said that "the Christ-Redeemer came to earth to bring men *Gnosis* or knowledge of the passwords (usually foreign gibberish or nonsense syllables) by which the soul could deceive and escape the unfriendly planets."[60] In addition to projecting an unsatisfactory understanding of the Incarnation, it offered a salvation by means other than faith and taught that theoretical knowledge was vouchsafed to only a select few rather than being offered freely to all men.

Two Types of Knowledge

We now look at the contrast between the two types of knowledge that have emerged in the process of our discussion: existential and scientific. The former involves a relatedness to the object of cognition, while the latter strives for objectivity or detachment.

---

59. Cf. Eric Frank, *Philosophical Understanding and Religious Truth* (London: Oxford University Press, 1963), 100: "Mathematics has cognitive truth in the highest sense. Here our thoughts literally correspond to their objects, since we produce them by thinking them. But mathematics has no existential truth because its objects do not refer to anything beyond themselves. On the other hand, ideas of religious imagination do not claim to be literally adequate to their object. But they have certainly existential truth because they express uniquely man's total determination by a Being beyond himself."

60. See Alan Richardson, *Creeds in the Making* (London: Macmillan and Co., 1969), 39.

Both of these are ideals that are unrealizable in pure form. Scientific knowledge seeks to change its object into a thing by removing all subjective qualities from the cognitive relation. However, as Michael Polyani demonstrates in an extensively illustrated study, all science involves a personal dimension that cannot be eliminated. Even in the most abstract science, there are subjective elements.[61]

The more impersonal the object of cognition (e.g., a rock), the more the cognitive relation tends toward detachment or objectivity; the more personal, the more it tends toward union with its objective or toward subjectivity. Conversely, when cognition of personal reality is pushed toward the pole of detachment, the consequence is increasing distortion and results in a dehumanizing of both subject and object.

One of the most influential efforts in modern theology to come to terms with the issues of personal knowledge is that of Martin Buber, a Jewish scholar. Buber proposes that the distinctly human form of relationship is the "I-Thou" (Ich-Du) relation. There is a twofold implication of this nomenclature. First, his use of the second person singular pronoun (Du in German) highlights the intimacy of the relation, as it does in French also. One uses not the singular but the plural when speaking to strangers or casual acquaintances not within one's intimate circle. Second, it calls attention by contrast to what Buber calls the "I-it" relation.

The "I-it" relation is the objectifying "thing knowledge" that may obtain between a person and a stone. While it may be possible to have an "I-Thou" relation with a stone, the "I-it" always dominates. Also, though one may relate to another person in "I-it" fashion by describing his observable qualities, such as the color of his eyes, his hair, and so on, this falls far short of really knowing that person. That possibility only occurs in an "I-Thou" situation.

The dominant element in the response to the "I-Thou" encounter is trust rather than assent, which dominates in response to truths such as are contemplated in the "I-it" relation. However, as we shall see later, the two responses cannot be so neatly separated or compartmentalized. Nonetheless, Buber's insights have significantly influenced many contemporary theologians.

The Christian theologian who has most centrally appropri-

61. *Personal Knowledge* (Chicago: University of Chicago Press, 1962).

ated these categories is Emil Brunner.[62] Both Buber and Brunner set the personalistic understanding of revelation in contrast to propositional revelation, which elicits a response of assent rather than "obedience-in-trust" (Brunner). In fact, most of modern theology has concurred with the famous words of Archbishop William Temple: "What is offered to man's apprehension in any specific Revelation is not truth concerning God but the living God Himself."[63]

John Baillie's analysis explains this reorientation of the understanding of revelation: "The deepest difficulty felt about the equation of revelation with communicated truth, is that it offers us something less than personal encounter and personal communion."[64]

John Wesley took much the same stance toward the rational religion of his day when it equated right religion with right thinking (see above). And Wiley seconds this emphasis when he says: "Truth in its ultimate nature is personal. Our Lord made this clear when He said, *I am the truth*. He knocks at the door of men's hearts—not as a proposition to be apprehended, but as a Person to be received and loved" (CT 1:38).

Buber and Brunner both distinguish the encounter with God from analogous encounters with other persons by asserting that the divine-human encounter is completely free of "I-it" elements. While these elements are inevitably present in human relations, the transcendence and ineffable nature of God eliminates these objectifying aspects. Thus revelation as personal, they say, is noncognitive in its nature.

However, Ronald Hepburn, in a penetrating critique of this logic of encounter, criticizes the claim to an absence of "I-it" elements, since some aspect of these elements is essential to a genuine encounter. Otherwise there is no criterion for differentiating it from a purely subjective experience. His words that follow illuminate the question:

> On the occasions when I sit opposite a friend and observe his gestures and expression, I am neither looking at these as at so many objects, nor in the belief that his entire personal being consists in such overt actions (behaviorism), nor am I looking "through" these to the hidden personality, as I might look

---

62. *Revelation and Reason*, trans. Olive Wyon (Philadelphia: Westminster Press, 1946); and *Truth as Encounter* (Philadelphia: Westminster Press, 1964).

63. *Nature, Man, and God* (London: Macmillan and Co., 1935), 322.

64. *The Idea of Revelation in Recent Thought* (New York: Columbia University Press, 1965), 39.

through the glass of a window, concerned only with the view beyond. His behavior is not being taken as a "window" into his immaterial, ghostly "mind." I admit that his inner life, like mine, is more than gestures, speech, smiles; but I doubt if we know what we are saying when we declare that personality and knowledge of personality are possible without these; I doubt if anything recognizably personal can be left over, once we have mentally stripped all such behavior away.[65]

Since it is the bodily aspect of human-to-human relation that provides the most obvious basis for objectification and thus the "I-it" dimension of the relation, it is easy to understand why Buber and Brunner wish to eliminate all such aspects from the "I-Thou" encounter with God. It would appear impossible for "I-it" elements to be present in a relation with a wholly incorporeal reality not locatable in a specific space or time. However, critiques of the encounter theories are doubtless correct in noting that no such "I-Thou" relation, with all that entails, is possible apart from the presence of at least a minimal element of the "I-it" aspect. For instance, it would not seem to be faith but foolhardiness to trust one's total existence into the hands of one who has not demonstrated himself to be a person of integrity. Given the condition of God's incorporeality, it would appear that such elements are only possible when or if God objectifies himself in a body, in an incarnation. That is precisely what the Christian faith claims has happened in the person of Jesus of Nazareth, and earlier in theophanies and/or occurrences that are admittedly, from the Christian perspective, less than adequate representations of God's nature.

The absence of this incarnational principle explains the vague and highly abstract way in which deity is described in most Eastern non-Christian religions, for example, Hinduism and its so-called descriptions of Brahman as "not this" or "not that." The uniqueness of Zen Buddhism is in its teaching that meditation leads to insight, but it denies the possibility of conceptualization (words) and seeks to point beyond that to experience itself. This is an intuitive experience called *satori*, which is a mystical union transcending language.[66]

Revelational Knowledge

This qualification will provide us with a clue to help untangle the issues regarding the relation between existential and scientific

---

65. *Christianity and Paradox* (New York: Pegasus Press, 1968), 36.
66. Huston Smith, *The Religions of Man* (New York: Harper and Row, Publishers, 1965), 145, 149-50.

130 GRACE, FAITH, AND HOLINESS

knowledge. If Jesus Christ, as the incarnation of the Divine, is the Locus of revelation, the way in which persons responded to Him as revelation should enable us to sort out the matter. The Fourth Gospel provides a particularly fruitful study here.

All the observable data were available to both the Jews and the "disciple whom Jesus loved." Yet the responses were radically different. Jesus himself emphasized this contrast by calling attention to the Jews' refusal to believe in Him. Apparently the difference was in their unwillingness to relate to Him in a personal encounter. This suggests that the decisive aspects of Jesus' person were nonempirical, although there were empirical pointers (signs) to them. This would imply that the knowledge about Jesus referred to theological factors; that is, the "I-it" elements were not objectifiable in the same sense that "primary and secondary qualities" (Locke) are. Thus, even though there are objectifiable aspects to one's knowledge of who Christ is, these are given in and with the personal encounter and are inseparable from it.

Here we see that a radical distinction between "I-it" and "I-Thou" relations is unjustifiable when they function within the theological circle. It further implies that only those who reveal themselves to Him know who He is. John Macmurray, in his very significant analysis of the nature of personhood, makes this point: "One can only really know one's friends, and oneself through one's friends, in a mutuality of self-revelation. This self-revelation is, of course, primarily practical, and only secondarily a matter of talk. We sometimes call it 'giving oneself away,' and contrast it with 'keeping oneself to oneself.'" He goes on to explain:

> Now because of this, such knowledge of another person as we can achieve depends upon our emotional disposition toward him. In formal terms . . . a negative personal relation between persons makes knowledge of the other and of oneself impossible. For mutual dislike and hostility inhibits self-revelation. Of course, I still form an "idea" of my enemy; and I shall take my representation of him to be the truth. But this will necessarily be an illusion. I shall know him as he appears to be, but not as he really is; and the knowledge will be "unreal." My knowledge of another person is a function of my love for him, and in proportion as my knowledge is a function of my fear of him, it is illusory or unreal.[67]

---

67. *Persons in Relation*, 170.

Arthur F. Holmes makes a distinction between "metaphysical objectivity" and "epistemological subjectivity," which is a philosophical way of speaking about the issues raised in this discussion of existential and scientific knowledge. He incisively notes:

> This distinction pays dividends. Some rationalists are concerned that any admission of subjectivity is a denial of metaphysical as well as epistemological objectivity, but that patently is not the case and does not logically follow. My knowledge of what is independently real may well be subjectively influenced and may involve me passionately, but that does not affect its metaphysical status. Metaphysical objectivity and epistemological subjectivity are quite compatible with each other and come ready-mixed all the time. Fears to the contrary were unfounded.[68]

All this suggests that we have tended to posit a false dichotomy between objective and subjective in the realm of religion because we have conceptualized knowledge in terms of "thing-knowledge." Perhaps we have furthermore falsely conceptualized the knower by conceiving him as a thinker rather than an agent, and thus we have too radically separated the realms of thought and action.[69] This diastasis seems to have stemmed from what William Temple called René Descartes's faux pas.[70]

This more philosophically adequate explanation of personal knowledge coincides much more closely with the view of knowledge that we found to be distinctive of biblical theology. It takes into account both the nature of the object known and the nature of the epistemological occurrence.

A further implication of this is that while there may be knowledge of revealed truth (about God) in the same way that there may be external knowledge of other persons, knowledge of God in the existential sense occurs only in a correlation of self-giving to the divine self-disclosure. In this latter sense, that which is distinctive of the Old Testament view of knowledge comes to light: Revelation and salvation are synonymous. To experience revelation is to be saved. In summarizing his analysis of "knowledge" in the Old Testament, W. T. Purkiser says: "Essentially, the knowledge of God for the Hebrew constitutes his personal redemption."[71]

---

68. *Contours of a World View* (Grand Rapids: Wm. B. Eerdmans Publishing Co., 1983), 148.
69. Cf. Macmurray, *Self as Agent;* and Stuart Hampshire, *Thought and Action* (New York: Viking Press, 1960).
70. *Nature, Man, and God,* lecture 3.
71. *God, Man, and Salvation,* 46.

We are now in a position to ascertain more adequately the relative functions of trust and assent in the divine-human relation. Gustav Aulen's analysis reflects a balanced relation. He points to the danger of defining faith as trust unless it is understood that it has "reference to the theocentric God-relationship"; that is, the relationship is determined from God's side. Defining faith as assent also is dangerous if it is interpreted intellectualistically and made primary. "In the measure that fellowship with God is understood as an unqualified assent to that revelation in which faith is rooted, this definition also gives expression to an essential element of faith."[72] Thus both are essential to proper knowledge of God.

Revelation and Reason

We have suggested that there are three theological facts that make divine revelation necessary if there is to be a proper knowledge of God. The last of these is the reality of man's fallenness. More so than either the transcendence of God or the nature of personal knowledge, this is a theological judgment. The fact that man is estranged from his essential created nature cannot be verified by psychology or anthropology but must itself be acknowledged as revealed. This does not preclude, however, the possibility that the empirical disciplines whose subject is man may provide pointers to a problem that the theological idea of fallenness explains.

Reason and Fallenness

The topic of reason may emerge in relation to several issues within the larger province encompassed by the doctrine of revelation. For instance, the relation of human understanding and God's transcendence called for a discussion of reason and its limitations compared with the transcendent reality. Traditionally, this has been the chief focus of discussions by theologians of the question of faith and reason. What we are suggesting here is another dimension of the problem. In the light of the doctrine of original sin, which holds that man's reason and understanding were warped and impaired in the Fall, our question is: Why does this perversion of man's rational capacities make necessary a revelatory activity initiated by God?

---

72. *Faith of the Christian Church,* 22-23.

As we shall seek to demonstrate in the next chapter, fallen man is not completely ignorant of God. We believe that the conditioned character of man's existence arouses in his consciousness at least a vague awareness of an unconditioned aspect of reality over against him. Certain experiences of nature doubtless stimulate or trigger an awareness of a Ground of Being to account for the origin of all this. Even Immanuel Kant acknowledged that the presence of design raised a sense of reverence in the mind of the observer that came very close to constituting an argument for God's existence. However these experiences be explained, in the context of Wesleyan theology it is never as reason's unaided discovery of God but rather as reason's recognition of the Eternal Presence that impinges upon all human consciousness.

John Wesley acknowledged that there is this sense of the existence of God, but he refused to give it the status of a natural theology. Rather he considered it to be "existentially irrelevant," since it had no real content and cannot answer the really important question: "What kind of God?"[73]

The crucial question concerns what man does with this primordial awareness. Paul's vivid descriptions of the perversions of the Gentile world in Romans 1—3 picture perfectly the result of fallen man's typical response to general revelation (what we mean by this term will be fully explained in the next chapter).

> For the wrath of God is revealed from heaven against all ungodliness and wickedness of men who by their wickedness suppress the truth. For what can be known about God is plain to them, because God has shown it to them. Ever since the creation of the world his invisible nature, namely, his eternal power and deity, has been clearly perceived in the things that have been made. So they are without excuse; for although they knew God they did not honor him as God or give thanks to him, but they became futile in their thinking and their senseless minds were darkened. Claiming to be wise, they became fools, and exchanged the glory of the immortal God for images resembling mortal man or birds or animals or reptiles (1:18-23).

Augustine gives a classic expression to the perversion of a general knowledge of God by fallen reason or, more specifically in his case, the perverse will. Because the condition of man is fallen, he loves himself, and that perverted love results in his turning his back upon the Truth.

---

73. Williams, *John Wesley's Theology Today*, 31.

When this will [love] is directed toward the creatures, the inclination toward God and, therefore, the awareness of God diminish. They decline in proportion to the liveliness of a man's concupiscence toward the world of the senses. The immoderate love of the things of sense is derivative, however, and rests upon a foundation defection, namely, self-love or pride.[74]

Even the Platonists, whose insights Augustine estimates highly, fall short of true knowledge. Even though they rationally discover foregleams of the Trinity, they do not recognize the truth of the Christian doctrine. That waits for the submission of the will (faith) to the historical revelation of the Mediator. In a beautiful passage in his *Confessions,* Augustine describes the profound insights of the Platonists regarding the disincarnate logos; but because they know nothing of the incarnate logos (special revelation), their visions are like visions of a distant Eden with no means of access. Only in the humble confession of God's way in Christ can the way be found there.

For it is one thing, from the mountain's wooded summit to see the land of peace, and not to find the way thither . . . and another to keep to the way that leads thither, guarded by the host of the heavenly general, where they rob not who have deserted the heavenly army, which they shun as torture.[75]

In his own experience, Augustine found the perversion of the will to be a hindrance to knowing God. After having seen the Truth from afar, he says:

But I was not able to fix my gaze thereon; and my infirmity being beaten back, I was thrown again on my accustomed habits, carrying along with me naught but a loving memory thereof, and an appetite for what I had, as it were, smelt the odor of, but was not yet able to eat.[76]

For John Calvin, all persons had an inborn knowledge of God. However, that innate knowledge was suppressed by sinful humans, leaving them responsible for their condition. He noted that because of this, God gave "another and better help" properly to direct us to God the Creator. The purpose of this revelation of His Word was so God could "become known unto salvation."[77] The

74. Robert Cushman, "Faith and Reason," in *A Companion to the Study of St. Augustine,* ed. Roy W. Battenhouse (New York: Oxford University Press, 1956), 304.
75. *Confessions,* translation from *Basic Writings of St. Augustine,* ed. Whitney J. Oates, 2 vols. (New York: Random House Publishers, 1948), bk. 7, chap. 21 (hereafter 7.21).
76. Ibid. 7.17.
77. *Institutes* 1.6.1.

means of this revelation was Scripture, which functioned like "spectacles gathering up the otherwise confused knowledge of God in our minds," which "having dispersed our dullness, clearly shows us the true God."[78]

Here we have expressed one form of Calvin's doctrine of accommodation. All knowledge of God is the result of His accommodation of himself to the human condition, first to man's finitude but also to his sinfulness. To the latter, God accommodated himself in a special or historical revelation in the mediatorial work of His Son:

> For there are two distinct powers which belong to the Son of God: the first, which is manifest in the architecture of the world and the order of nature; and the second, by which he renews and restores fallen nature. As he is the eternal Word of God, by him the world was made, by his power all things continue to possess the life which they once received; man was endued with an unique gift of understanding, yet he still sees and understands, so that what he naturally possesses from the grace of the Son of God is not entirely destroyed. But since by his stupidity and perverseness he darkens the light which still dwells in him, it remains that a new office be undertaken by the Son of God, the office of Mediator, to renew by the spirit of regeneration man, who had been ruined.[79]

Calvin believes that the revelation of God in all forms was clear and comprehensible. "It was the noetic effect of sin, not the inadequacy of revelation, that causes errors of understanding."[80] It was for this reason that His gracious accommodation to human sinfulness was connected with the work of redemption.

The Results of Fallen Reason

The fallenness of human reason provides the basis for what legitimacy there is in the so-called illusionistic critiques of religion. The most influential modern version of these critiques can be traced back in part to the influence of Ludwig Feuerbach (1804-72) whose book *The Essence of Christianity* (1841) was one of the most devastating attacks upon Christianity ever conceived and the inspiration for subsequent attacks.

In substance, Feuerbach reduced theology to anthropology.

---

78. Ibid.
79. Commentary on John 1:5.
80. Edward A. Dowey, Jr., *The Knowledge of God in Calvin's Theology* (New York: Columbia University Press, n.d.), 179.

His analysis of the situation was that religious belief or experience may be interpreted as man's effort to objectify some wish. Thus what men worship are nothing but *wunschwesen* ("wish beings"), or personified wishes. What the human mind does, says Feuerbach, is to take all the positive and good qualities of man, abstract them from their embodiment in human form, and objectify them by projecting them upon a cosmic screen. The human qualities, raised to an infinite degree, are what is worshiped; and thus theology (words about God) becomes anthropology (words about man), and religious adoration is really self-worship. With the good qualities of human life abstracted and projected as God, man is left with no goodness of his own—thus the doctrine of original sin.

Feuerbach's own summary goes like this:

> When religion—consciousness of God—is designated as the self-consciousness of man, this is not to be understood as affirming that the religious man is directly aware of this identity; for, on the contrary, ignorance of it is fundamental to the peculiar nature of religion. To preclude this misconception, it is better to say, religion is man's earliest and also indirect form of self-knowledge, as in the history of the race, so also in that of the individual. Man first of all sees his nature as if *out* of himself, before he finds it in himself. His own nature is in the first instance contemplated by him as that of another being. . . . Hence the historical progress of religion consists in this: that what by an earlier religion was regarded as objective, is now recognized as subjective; that is, what was formerly contemplated and worshipped as God is now perceived to be something *human*. [81]

The point of all this is for man to provide himself with a means of having his desires fulfilled. As Elton Trueblood summarizes Feuerbach's view of miracle:

> Miracle is the very heart of faith, for, though natural modes of dealing with human wishes and needs are satisfactory, miracle "satisfied the wishes of man in a way corresponding to the nature of wishes—in the most desirable way." We love a miracle because in it we get what we wish right away—without any tiresome waiting. [82]

Karl Marx and Friedrich Engels were influenced by Feuerbach when their ideas that resulted in the philosophy of dialectical ma-

---

81. *The Essence of Christianity*, trans. George Eliot, Torchbooks/Cloister Library (New York: Harper and Bros., Publishers, 1957), 13.
82. David Elton Trueblood, *Philosophy of Religion* (New York: Harper and Bros., Publishers, 1957), 179.

terialism were taking shape. The "wish fulfillment" theme was developed in sociological terms.

Marxist philosophy combines the concept of dialectic as the pattern of historical development with a crass materialism that reduces all reality to economic factors. The dialectical movement (thesis-antithesis-synthesis) is characterized by a struggle between classes, the "haves" versus the "have-nots." In the present stage, it is the bourgeoisie (capitalist) and the proletariat (working class) that are the principals in the struggle. The capitalists are depriving the workers of what is rightfully due them (alienation), and thus the plutocrats become richer and richer while the laborers become more and more deprived. The function of religion in this setting is to keep the oppressed classes of society happy in their penury by offering them "pie in the sky by and by." This is the context of Marx's famous dictum that "religion . . . is the opium of the people." One of the most obvious examples of such exploitation and religious justification for it was the institution of slavery in pre-Civil War America, where efforts were made to keep the slave content with his bondage by the wonderful visions of heaven expressed in the composition of spirituals.

The nature of religion as an ideology renders it incapable of social criticism. There it functions (like in jurisprudence and morality) as a reflection of the economic substructure. Religion, by nature, is a custodian of the status quo—and particularly used by the owner to sustain his exploitation of the worker.

Sigmund Freud, father of modern psychoanalytic psychology, developed the Feuerbachian thesis in psychological terms. Freud finds the origin of religion in man's attempt to cope with the problems of life. Out of childhood experiences of a father figure who provided a sense of security, man posits a fatherlike divine being to help him cope with life. Thus religion is an *illusion*, by which he means a belief based on wish. Freud's analysis is well represented by the title of his famous critique: *The Future of an Illusion*.

Religion, Freud hypothesized, involves the creation of a divine Father whose providential rule provides the security we need to reduce the anxiety created by the dangers of life. Thus God is the projection of the infantile experience of an earthly father. Other religious beliefs function in the same illusionistic way to address inner needs. Thus they arise as a means of wish fulfillment.

As suggested, all these critiques have a measure of truth in them. They fairly, if not fully, describe the nature of religion if it were the product of fallen human reason. In fact, an analysis of idolatrous worship as it appears in the Old Testament shows it to be chiefly a catering to the desires, oftentimes the most base desires, of man. It is a way of providing religious sanction for sensuality. This perversion highlights the need for revelation.

But biblical faith stands as a thundering contradiction to the views of religion criticized by these analysts. One need only think of Amos in controversy with Amaziah over the religious approvals of economic injustice in Bethel, or Isaiah's "Woe is me" when he encountered the Holy One of Israel in the Temple, to know that God does not come to satisfy man's egocentric desires but to sit in judgment upon them, not to authenticate the status quo but to call for its alteration so as to implement justice in human relations. Elton Trueblood drives a final nail in the coffin of such illusionistic critiques with these scathing words:

> The blunt truth is that the upholders of the doctrine of *Wunschwesen*, from Feuerbach to Freud and beyond, do not know what they are talking about. They have spun a theory without bothering to check the evidence, most of which is never seen in clinics or laboratories. That there have been men whose alleged religious experiences have been highly comforting, wholly in line with their desires, none doubts, but to assert that this has been the universal experience or even the characteristic one is to reveal gross ignorance. If this dogma were true, we should expect all prayer to be self-seeking; instead, we find the recognition of a demand for the most rigorous self-denial and self-sacrifice. Those who have claimed to know God best have found that He demands things almost impossible to perform. How, on the hypothesis of *Wunschwesen*, did the notion of the *Cross* ever enter the world? Pascal seems to be addressing men of our time when he says, "Let them at least learn what is the religion they attack, before attacking it."[83]

It is not always the case, obviously, that non-Christian forms of religion are either grossly idolatrous or cater to the immoral tendencies of human depravity. The great religions often reflect high moral standards of conduct sometimes approximating Christian ethical codes; for example, Confucius' negative version of the Golden Rule, called the Silver Rule: "What you do not want done to yourself, do not do to others."

However, it is almost universally the situation that in non-

---

83. Ibid., 188.

Christian versions of religion, the fallenness of human reason manifests itself in a self-help approach to salvation. This tendency is an expression of the flesh as Paul spells it out in his polemic against works righteousness in Galatians. Man, in his pride, finds it outside the parameters of reasonableness to accept the Christian doctrine of grace. Since this issue will be explored in some depth in the next chapter, we will defer further elaboration at this point.

One additional observation needs to be made. Unfortunately, not all religion that goes under the name of Christian is free from the perversions of fallen reason. Many in the church still live on the assumption of salvation by works. Furthermore, many in Christendom operate on the premise that Christianity is a means of achieving health, wealth, and success. Certain cults are based on this misapprehension. It is even possible to advocate Christianity for its experiential benefits as a primary consideration. While there are psychological issues difficult to untangle in this question, the motive for Christian devotion is the glory of God, not His benefits to us.

In such cases of perverted Christian faith, the cause is doubtless the overriding of the revelation of God in Christ with the insights of reasonableness without an awareness that this is being done. Paul put it succinctly: "Let no one deceive himself. If any one among you thinks that he is wise in this age, let him become a fool that he may become wise. For the wisdom of this world is folly with God" (1 Cor. 3:18-19).

Summary

We have explored three theological facts about God and man that make revelation necessary if there is to be a true knowledge of God. This does not argue that revelation has occurred; that is a faith assumption that lies at the basis of the Christian faith. Rather the discussion calls attention to the reality that man's knowledge of God, if it is true, cannot be the result of merely human discovery. It furthermore provides pointers to the way in which revelation will occur if and when it occurs. These clues will be picked up and incorporated as we attempt to develop a Wesleyan understanding of the phenomenon of the divine self-disclosure in the next chapter.

Revelation: A Wesleyan Approach

One of the major factors in the complex of views that constitutes one's theory of revelation is his doctrine of man. Is man essentially "in the truth" or "out of the truth"? This is a question that is both philosophical and theological. The philosophical aspect includes both epistemological and ontological considerations. The theological dimension may be highlighted by capitalizing the term *Truth,* with the implication that God and Truth are synonymous in this context. How one answers this question will decide many issues involved in identifying the nature of revelation.

We must note in a preliminary way the technical significance of the term *essential.* We are using it in the special philosophical sense as referring to that which makes something what it is, and without which it would be something else.[1] It is in contrast to the term *accidental,* which refers to qualities that may or may not be

---

1. Cf. Plato's *Euthyphro* for the first development of the concept of essence in a philosophical work. It is there seen as synonymous with a connotative definition (genus and difference), which Socrates is credited with inventing.

present but do not contribute to a thing's "isness." Essence may be described as referring to something's "whatness."

Our question implies that there are logically only two possible alternatives involved. If the concept of essential is taken seriously, one either is or is not in essential relation to the Truth.

Man and Truth: Historical Survey

What we propose to do is to use paradigms, both philosophical and theological, to illustrate the way in which these two possibilities have been in interface throughout the history of thought. To identify a particular position is not necessarily to say that every aspect of it is acceptable, but only to illustrate how it falls into one camp or the other on this crucial question. Finally, by developing some distinctively Wesleyan doctrines relevant to the issue (especially the doctrine of man), we will attempt to show which way Wesleyan theology might answer the question and what would be the precise contours and implications of such a position. In sum, it is an extension of the question of immanence and transcendence in relation to the knowledge of God as discussed in the preceding chapter.

One of the clearest juxtaposing of the two possible answers to the question, cast in philosophical terms but with theological overtones, is found in Søren Kierkegaard's *Philosophical Fragments.* Socrates is used as the foil for the view that man is essentially in the truth; Kierkegaard wishes to demonstrate the greater viability of the position that man is essentially in error.

The question with which Socrates is concerned is "How far does the Truth admit of being learned?" Kierkegaard describes the situation as follows:

> In so far as the Truth is conceived as something to be learned, its non-existence is evidently presupposed, so that in proposing to learn it one makes it the object of an enquiry. Here we are confronted with the difficulty to which Socrates calls attention in the Meno and there characterizes as a "pugnacious proposition:" one cannot seek for what he knows, and it seems equally impossible for him to seek for what he does not know. For what a man knows he cannot seek, since he knows it; and what he does not know he cannot seek, since he does not even know for what to seek.[2]

---

2. *A Kierkegaard Anthology,* ed. Robert Bretall (New York: Modern Library, 1946), 155.

Or to put the ambiguity in another way: One cannot know that he does not know something if he does not already know it. This paradox is worked out by Socrates in terms of the doctrine of reminiscence or recollection. Man in his preincarnate existence knew the Truth, but in his present existence that knowledge is retained at a subconscious level, needing only to be stimulated to the level of conscious awareness. Socrates, as a teacher, saw his task to be intellectual midwifery, to help bring the Truth to birth that was present in the student in a forgotten form. As a teacher he did not impart information as if writing upon a blank tablet but rather elicited the hidden knowledge from his pupil. The dialogues of Plato, in which Socrates plays a prominent role, portray this understanding in both structure and content. The dialogue method itself embodies this point of view in the way in which it reflects the process of bringing to knowledge. Oftentimes the principals in the dialogue find themselves both knowing and not knowing at one and the same time. Even though the existential condition of man's present limitation prohibits clear and precise comprehension of the Truth, man is aware that he does not know with the kind of clarity he desires and therefore demonstrates that he is essentially in the Truth.

Kierkegaard, in proposing the alternative position, is seeking to establish the decisive significance of the historical moment, particularly the historical Incarnation. He feels that the Socratic view undercuts the decisiveness of it. His concern is, at the same time, to counter G. E. Lessing's depreciation of history in favor of "eternal truths of reason." He formulates the question: "Is an historical point of departure possible for an eternal consciousness; how can such a point of departure have any other than a mere historical interest; is it possible to base an eternal happiness upon historical knowledge?"

If Socrates is right, thinks Kierkegaard, the Teacher is dispensable and can be forgotten as soon as the Truth within has been discovered; therefore in order to give the Teacher greater significance, Kierkegaard wishes to affirm that the "learner is in a state of error." In this situation, the Teacher becomes more than the occasion for learning: "Now if the learner is to acquire the Truth, the Teacher must bring it to him; and not only so, but he must also give him the condition necessary for understanding it." That is, being "in error," the learner does not have the capacity to receive the Truth, to recognize that he does not have the Truth, or even to recognize the Truth when it is given to him. The Teacher must create the capacity at the same time that he communicates the Truth. Let us keep this stipulation in mind, for we shall encounter it again in an influential 20th-century dress.

These same two options are developed in a different way in an essay titled "Two Types of Philosophy of Religion," by Paul Tillich. He identifies two ways of approaching God, which he refers to as "the way of overcoming estrangement" and "the way of meeting a stranger." In the first, when a man finds God, he finds himself because there is a kinship between man and God, although they are estranged existentially. In the second, the relation between man and God is accidental because "essentially they do not belong to each other."

Tillich refers to these two approaches as (1) the ontological type of philosophy of religion and (2) the cosmological. The first is represented in the history of Christian thought by Augustine and his successors, including the Franciscans, Alexander of Hales, and Bonaventura. In this way, knowledge of God is prior and immediate.

The cosmological is represented by Thomas Aquinas, whose view, Tillich contends, is a dissolution of the Augustinian approach. Under the influence of Aristotelian epistemology, Thomas begins with empirical knowledge and moves to the knowledge of God by inference. Knowledge of God is mediate rather than immediate. The Augustinian approach makes atheism impossible, he argues, because it is the awareness of God that makes possible the question of God; in the Thomistic approach, since the inference is not necessary, atheism is inevitable.

Like Socrates, Augustine was intrigued by the capacity of the mind to apprehend necessary truths, ideas that could not be derived from empirical experience. This involves the presupposition that the mind has been informed by Truth a priori. "The memory also contains the innumerable principles and laws of numbers and dimensions. None of these can have been conveyed to it by means of the bodily senses, because they cannot be seen, heard, smelled, tasted, or touched."[3] When asking himself about the source of these and other such ideas, he takes recourse to memory. Concerning the basic categories of

> whether a thing is, what it is, and of what sort it is . . . I retain
> images of the sounds of which these words are composed. I

---

3. *Confessions* 10.12.

know that these sounds have passed through the air and now
are no more. But the facts which they represent have not
reached me through any of my bodily senses. I could not see
them at all except in my mind, and it is not their images that I
store in my memory but the facts themselves. But they must
themselves tell me, if they can, by what means they entered my
mind.[4]

On the common empirical understanding, nothing can be in
the memory that is not first in the senses. But when Augustine
examines these "changeless, invariable ideas," he finds that he simply discovered them within; they were not learned. However, they
are so deeply hidden in the recesses of the memory that they can
only be elicited by external stimuli.

> Then whereabouts in my mind were they? How was it that
> I recognized them when they were mentioned and agreed that
> they were true? It must have been that they were already in my
> memory, hidden away in its deeper recesses, in so remote a part
> of it that I might not have been able to think of them at all, if
> some other person had not brought them to the fore by teach-
> ing me about them.[5]

In attempting to explain this phenomenon, Socrates was able
to suggest the myth of the immortality of the soul so that in its
preincarnate state it lived in the realm of eternal ideas and brought
this knowledge with it into existence. Augustine could not accept
this conclusion because of his Christian presuppositions, thus he
took recourse to the immediate activity of God, the Divine Light,
the disincarnate Logos who functioned as the immediate Illuminator of the mind. "All the certainties of the sciences are like
those things which are brought to light by the sun, that they may
be seen, the earth, for instance, and the things upon it; while God
is Himself the Illuminator."[6]

For Augustine, all significant knowledge is revealed knowledge. This informing of the intellect by the divine activity is grace,
so that no man is devoid of "epistemological grace."

> Great then are the powers of the natural reason as illu-
> minated by the disincarnate Son, the eternal Word of God. To
> be sure, since there is a continuous divine illumination of the
> mind, the *ratio* is not in Augustine's thought ever "unaided" in
> its learning of God.[7]

4. Ibid., 10.
5. Ibid.
6. *Soliloquies* 1.12.
7. Cushman, "Faith and Reason," 295.

What is true of eternal ideas is also true of the knowledge of God. This knowledge is not learned but found within, in memory. "If I now find thee not in my memory, then am I unmindful of thee; and how shall I find thee, if I do not remember thee?"[8] This explains his statement that he desires to know two things: God and his own soul. It is through knowledge of the second that he comes to knowledge of the first.

Clearly, we are here dealing with an unusual understanding of memory, and therefore we must seek to comprehend this somewhat odd use. Why did Augustine choose to use the image of memory to convey his view of the relation of the mind to Truth, or of the soul to God? First, he was impressed with the power of memory to retain knowledge of that which has passed from present experience. He refers to the parable of the lost coin in Luke 15 as a signal example of this capacity. When the coin was lost, the woman would not have searched for it if she did not remember it; and when she found it, she would not have recognized it as the one lost if it was not remembered. Thus the coin, "though lost to the sight, was retained in the memory."[9]

Second, he was doubtless fascinated by the ability of memory to call back to the level of conscious awareness that which had apparently been forgotten.

> Something of this sort happens when we see or think of a person whom we know, but cannot remember his name and try to recall it. If any other name but his occurs to us, we do not apply it to him because we do not normally associate that name with him. So we reject all names until we think of the one which corresponds accurately with our normal mental picture of the man. But how can we think of his name unless we bring it out from the memory? For even if we recognize it because someone else prompts us, it is still by our own memory that we do so, because we do not accept it as a fresh piece of knowledge but agree that it is the right name, since we can now remember it.[10]

This theory presupposes the widely accepted theory that whatever is truly known is never really forgotten, although it may slip below the level of consciousness. It may be recalled by the proper stimulation, even by an act of one's own will. Thus all cognition is recognition.

---

8. *Confessions* 10.17.
9. Ibid., 18.
10. Ibid., 19.

This is Augustine's answer to the enigma posed by Socrates concerning how one can search for a truth that he does not know, or be aware that he does not know something without already knowing it. The concept of memory as above outlined makes it possible for something to both be known and not known at one and the same time. God is the Object of the questing soul of man because God is known by men, even though He has been forgotten. He explores this mystery in the *Confessions,* book 10, chapters 20—25:

> How, then, do I look for you, O Lord? For when I look for you, who are my God, I am looking for a life of blessed happiness. I shall look for you, so that my soul may live. For it is my soul that gives life to my body, and it is you who gives life to my soul. How, then, am I to search for this blessed life? For I do not possess it until I can rightly say, "This is all that I want. Happiness is here." Am I to seek it in memory, as though I had forgotten it but still remembered that I had forgotten it? Or am I to seek it through the desire to get to know it as if it were something unknown to me, either because I have never known it or because I have forgotten it so completely that I do not even remember having forgotten it? Surely happiness is what everyone wants, so much so that there can be none who do not want it. But if they desire it so much, where did they learn what it was? If they have learnt to love it, where did they see it? . . . It must, then, be known to all, and there can be no doubt that if it were possible to put the question in a common language and ask all men whether they wished to be happy, all would reply that they did. But this could only happen if happiness itself, that is, the state which the word signifies, were to be found somewhere in their memories *(chap. 20).* [11]

The fact that God is retained in the memory is the basis for the universal desire for beatitude. Even though one may not know that his desire for happiness is really a desire for God, nonetheless knowledge of happiness is tantamount to knowledge of God; therefore because of this primordial knowledge men are characterized by a longing for God. This is the theoretical rationale for the famous statement upon which Augustine builds his *Confessions*: "Thou hast formed us for thyself, and our hearts are restless till they find rest in Thee." In a word, we have here Augustine's epistemological construction of the doctrine of prevenient grace.

How do men then come to recognize Truth? Or why do all men not acknowledge the Truth that is within? The answer is that

---

11. Ibid., 20.

men, in their perverseness, are unwilling to face the consequences of such acknowledgment. To acknowledge the Truth is to acknowledge oneself in relation to the Truth. There must be mutual self-disclosure, but men are too often unwilling to accept the resultant exposure.

> Therefore they hate the truth for the sake of that thing which they love instead of the truth. They love truth when she shines on them, and hate her when she rebukes them. For because they are not willing to be deceived, and wish to deceive, they love her when she reveals herself, and hate her when she reveals them.[12]

This means, for Augustine, that knowledge hangs on the movement of the will: "I believe in order to know." He noted that Socrates taught that God can only be known by a purified mind. He extended this to explain that right knowledge is dependent upon right love, and right love is the result of an act of will.

> In the case of God, as in the instance of all other cognition, full knowledge waits upon desire or love. It is appetition, love, or will which turns diffused awareness into true cognition. The crucial words of Augustine are these: "the bringing forth of the mind is preceded by some desire, by which through seeking and finding what we wish to know, the offspring, viz., knowledge, itself is born!" . . . With reference to God, as to anything else, this means that man's universal awareness of God cannot pass to knowledge without *appetitus* or desire or consent of the will.[13]

A crucial question in all this—one that Kierkegaard raised in the face of Socratic thought—concerns the role of the historical revelation in Christ. Clearly Augustine develops his whole Christian philosophy upon the assumption that the Eternal Logos has become incarnate in the person of Jesus Christ. But is Kierkegaard correct in saying that this a prioristic interpretation of knowledge makes the Teacher of only temporary interest and dispensable as soon as he has led the pupil to the knowledge of the Truth? The clue to Augustine's answer is found in his volitional epistemology, especially as it relates to knowledge of God. The will is in bondage to self-love, and thus the knowledge of God awaits the breaking of this bondage. "Real cognition of God is at the same time dissolution of the bondage of the will to self-love."[14]

---

12. Ibid., 23.
13. Cf. Cushman, "Faith and Reason," 299-303.
14. Ibid., 305.

Augustine found this problem of the incapacitated will through his own experience, which he describes in the terms we are now exploring:

> I was astonished that although I now loved you and not some phantom in your place, I did not persist in enjoyment of my God. Your beauty drew me to you, but soon I was dragged away from you by my own weight and in dismay I plunged again into the things of this world. The weight I carried was the habit of the flesh. But your memory remained with me and I had no doubt at all that you were the one to whom I should cling, only I was not yet able to cling to you.[15]

He also found in his own experience that the solution to the problem of the will was the Mediator. He states it clearly in the following passage:

> And I sought a way of acquiring strength sufficient to enjoy Thee; but I found it not until I embraced that Mediator between God and man, the man Christ Jesus, who is over all, God blessed for ever, calling unto me, and saying, I am the way, the truth, and the life, and mingling that food which I was unable to receive with our flesh.[16]

Robert Cushman explains both Augustine's view and its relation to classical philosophy in a succinct statement:

> History becomes the medium of revelation and instrumental to the fulfillment of knowledge. Time and change become, by the incarnation, the vehicle of the Eternal; whereas, in Platonism, the temporal tended to bind *nous* in ignorance. Augustine has at length, through reflection upon the Incarnation, succeeded in showing what Plato wrestled to make plausible, namely, how, from the knowledge of the particulars, the mind could mount up to the intuition of divine Reality. It is because, in a singular instance, the universal unfolds itself without deficiency in the particular.[17]

And the relation between the general and the special revelation is further shown:

> Not even the Word made flesh could induce faith and love to God had not the eternal Word already visited the reason of man. Of this visitation the heart retains vestiges. Were it not so, the eternal could not be discerned in the historical—wounding man's pride. Neither could the historical recall the heart to the eternal.[18]

---

15. *Confessions* 7.17.
16. Ibid., 18. Note the significance of this statement for the necessity of God becoming immanent within history as a prerequisite for saving knowledge of Him.
17. "Faith and Reason," 307.
18. Ibid., 309.

The perspective of Thomas Aquinas stands in a contrary relation to that of Augustine. The context within which the contrast between them may be best seen is that of the doctrine of nature and grace. For Augustine, as a result of the Fall, nature is totally corrupt and perverted, but nonetheless all of nature is graced.[19] For Thomas, there is a much more optimistic understanding of nature.

Aquinas's ideas may be conceptualized as a two-story building, the whole representing the unity of truth. The bottom floor will stand for nature, while the top floor stands for grace. At the creation of man, the total building was intact. Following Irenaeus's faulty exegesis of Gen. 1:26, Thomas identified the top floor with the "likeness" and the bottom with the "image" of God. In the Fall, the top floor was taken away, while the bottom remained generally undisturbed. This dichotomy sees grace to be a *donum superadditum* imposed upon a good nature. The image of God is spelled out chiefly in terms of reason. Thus man's rational capacities are unimpeded in their proper function in the quest for truth.

In the realm of nature (reason) the epistemology of Aristotle became normative. In Aristotelian empiricism, "nothing exists in the intellect unless it is first in the senses." Therefore all knowledge begins, for Thomas, with experience, and such knowledge as one has of nonempirical reality is by inference. He moves from the individual to the universal, and not vice versa as Augustine, following Platonism, had done. Or, as Gordon Leff describes it: "We can best describe St. Thomas' outlook by saying that, whereas all Christian thinkers before him had sought to explain the effect by the cause, he started with the effect: that is, instead of trying to explain God in His own transcendent terms, he began with what could be known from His creatures."[20]

Using this methodology, Thomas built up a whole system of natural theology that provided a prolegomena to revealed theology. Natural reason, by its own unaided power, could demonstrate that God existed but must be supplemented by revelation to know about the nature of God, especially such truths as that He is Trinitarian in nature. The relation between nature and grace is complementary. "It was necessary for man's salvation that there should be a doctrine revealed by God, besides the philosophical disci-

---

19. It does not seem necessary for our purposes here to work out the relation between this and his view of predestination.
20. *Medieval Thought* (Chicago: Quadrangle Books, 1959), 214.

plines investigated by human reason. First, because man is directed to God as to an end that surpasses the grasp of his reason."[21]

It is important to note that the object of both reason and faith is truths. There are certain truths offered to the intellect by revelation that may also be discovered by reason, but all are presented to the mind for assent. Thus faith is defined as the assent of the mind to truths presented by a sufficient authority. These truths are to be found in the Scripture.

The contrast between Augustine and Aquinas may be seen by comparing their respective interpretations of Rom. 1:20, a pivotal verse for both men: "For since the creation of the world His invisible attributes are clearly seen, being understood by the things that are made, even His eternal power and Godhead" (NKJV).

Augustine denies that a knowledge of God may be gained through a direct observation of the external world. Rather "they only understand it who compare that voice received from without with the truth within."[22] From the knowledge of God resident in the soul (memory) the observer of nature is able to recognize God in the world. Knowledge of God is not inferential but a priori, or immediate. It is because the Logos is present within that God's handiwork in nature can be discovered.

This text is also a chief source for Thomas's natural theology. On the basis of it he argues that the existence of God can be demonstrated by inferring cause from effect. He denies that God can be known directly, that is, we cannot argue from "what is prior absolutely" to what is derivative. On the empirical principle, this approach is precluded. Conversely, "when an effect is better known to us than its cause, from the effect we proceed to the knowledge of the cause."[23] Knowledge of God is thus inferential and a posteriori, or mediated.

Man and Truth: the Imago Dei

The theological solution to the issue posed by these two ways of interpreting man's relation to the Truth is one's doctrine of the *imago Dei.* That man was created in the image of God is a clear biblical teaching. What that means in its original constitution and

---

21. *Summa Theologica*, part I, ques. I, art. I (hereafter I.I.I).
22. *Confessions* 10.6.
23. *Summa Theologica* I.I.I.

how it relates to man in his present condition is largely a matter of theological construction based upon exegetical inference.

When we turn to the biblical material, we find an ambiguous representation. After the account of the Fall, the Old Testament suggests rather clearly that man is still a creature in God's image. Following the Deluge, God's command prohibiting murder is based upon the fact that "in the image of God made he man" (Gen. 9:6, KJV). But in the New Testament, the total process of salvation is seen to be the restoring of man to the image of God (cf. 2 Cor. 3:18 et al.), which assumes that man has fallen away from it. The Bible itself does not address this apparent contradiction but leaves it (not consciously, of course) for subsequent theological reflection. The best solution appears to be that both claims must be taken seriously and to acknowledge the paradoxical situation that man has both lost and retained the *imago* at one and the same time, in his present state.

A survey of the history of Christian thinking concerning man discloses that there is a long history of attempting to define the *imago* in a dual sense.[24] One of the earliest stems from Irenaeus, who, in this respect, became the fountainhead of the Roman Catholic tradition. Failing to understand the nature of Hebrew parallelism, Irenaeus interpreted Gen. 1:26 to imply two different realities: the image and the likeness. The latter is "man's relation to the supernatural and his responsive obedience to and reflection of God's revealed will."[25] It was the "likeness" that man lost in the Fall, whereas the "image" was not affected (see above). "This part [likeness] of man's original nature Catholic thought designates by the phrase *donum superadditum,* indicating that these supernaturally added gifts are not, like reason, of the unalterable substance of human nature."[26]

The image is interpreted as man's rational capacity to apprehend the first principles of philosophy, even including the ability to demonstrate the rational necessity of certain theological ideas. This is the aspect retained after the Fall.

---

24. Cf. G. C. Berkouwer, *Man: The Image of God* (Grand Rapids: Wm. B. Eerdmans Publishing Co., 1962). In chap. 2 he surveys the extensive attempts by Reformed theologians and others to distinguish between the broader (or wider) and narrower aspects of the *imago.*

25. Paul Ramsey, *Basic Christian Ethics* (New York: Charles Scribner's Sons, 1950), 260.

26. Ibid.

Martin Luther, with a surer sense of biblical exegesis, rejected this artificial distinction.[27] However, traditionally, Protestant theology has attempted to maintain the same double connotation by speaking about the moral image and the natural image. The latter is "a picture of His own immortality; a spiritual being indued with understanding, freedom of will, and various affections" (Wesley). The former is a reflection of the moral attributes of God such as love, justice, mercy, and truth. In the Fall, the moral image was lost and the natural was impaired. Wiley makes the same distinction but centrally identifies the natural image with *reason.*

A famous attempt to retain the dual emphasis of the Scripture was made by Emil Brunner in an early controversy with Karl Barth.[28] In an effort to establish a "point of contact" for God's revelation in the *humanum* of man, Brunner suggested that there is a formal image and a material image. The formal refers to that capacity of the human spirit that produces culture and involves reason, imagination, will, sensitivity to values, and so on. This formal image is the basis for a "Christian natural theology" and is summarized as a "capacity for words," which is the point of contact since man is a man and not a cat. He elaborates this distinction, less polemically, in terms of "responsibility" (response-ability) in his later *Dogmatics.*[29]

Brunner contended, with validity, it seems, from a Wesleyan perspective, that such a human condition is a necessary precondition for "the ability to sin," and it (this human condition) furthermore "continues in the state of sin." If man is not a responsible person, the whole idea of sin becomes meaningless, and it makes no sense to refer to man as a sinner. "This quid of personality," he argues, "constitutes the *humanum* of every man, also that of the sinner."

Barth responded with an angry "Nein." He decisively disagreed with Brunner and rejected the idea of any point of contact (*Anknupfungspunkt*) between the Christian gospel and human na-

---

27. There is an ambivalence in Luther since he, at times, argued both for a total loss of the *iustitia originalis* and therefore of the *imago* and for the survival of the "relic" of the *imago.*

28. Emil Brunner and Karl Barth, *Natural Theology,* ed. John Baillie (London: Geoffrey Bles, Centenary Press, 1946). The summary of the debate that follows is taken from this volume.

29. Emil Brunner, *The Christian Doctrine of Creation and Redemption,* trans. Olive Wyon (Philadelphia: Westminster Press, 1952), 55-61.

ture. The basis of his rejection was his commitment to the premise that there is no knowledge of God whatsoever apart from that given in the Jesus of history. This restriction is placed within a larger context of belief that there is no knowledge of God apart from revelation, that is, there is no natural theology or natural knowledge of God. Within this setting, the sole source of revelation is Jesus Christ. As Barth says, "Only the man who knows about Jesus Christ knows anything at all about revelation."

The image of God, in which man was created, was totally effaced by the Fall; not a trace has been left behind. Thus there is no possibility of a remnant of the *imago* being a point of contact. Also, Brunner's attempt to retain an uneffaced "formal" image is rejected by Barth since (1) it is impossible to have form without content, and (2) even Brunner admits that man has lost freedom of will and thus contributes nothing whatsoever to his salvation—it is all of grace.

What occurs in the moment of revelation (salvation), said Barth, is a wholly new act of creation. "Man, it is true, still remains human—'he is still man and not cat,' as he [Barth] quaintly expresses it; but his humanity has been so totally corrupted by sin that no more than a cat is he able to hear God's voice until, through faith in Christ, the image and similitude of God are created in him afresh."[30]

This means that Barth takes not only seriously, but quite literally, the words of Paul in 2 Cor. 5:17. The "new creation . . . in Christ" is the production of something totally different and altogether new as fully as the initial act of creating the world brought something new into being. It is actually a creation out of nothing. This says that the relationship between the preconversion and the postconversion man is one of complete discontinuity.

So far as revelation is concerned, since there is nothing within man to which the gospel may appeal, the capacity to receive the revelation of God is given in and with the revelation itself. That is, it creates its own point of contact. Within the context of Barth's Calvinistic tradition this is perfectly acceptable and provides the logical rationale for predestination. If no human response is possible, and if the work of salvation (revelation) is so totally monergistic, only those to whom God chooses to reveal himself may be

---

30. John Baillie, *Our Knowledge of God* (New York: Charles Scribner's Sons, 1959), 20.

saved. It is because Barth shies away from this selectiveness that he has been accused of universalism because, on his theory, those are the only two logical options—except, of course, the unlikely conclusion that no one will be saved. Barth's conclusions, as will be noted subsequently, were modified in the quieter mood of the *Church Dogmatics.*

What can be made of these discussions? It is plain that there are weaknesses and strengths in each of the expositions surveyed in this sketch. How shall we separate the chaff from the wheat and distill a satisfactory synthesis? It is the contention of this chapter that Wesleyan theology provides the theological categories with which to accomplish this task. But first we must delve more deeply into the question of the *imago Dei.*

Traditionally, efforts have been made to define the meaning of the *imago* by seeking to identify that in man which differentiates him from the rest of creation. That involves defining it from below. Under the influence of Greek thought this differentia has been classically identified as reason, freedom, and/or personality. When defined from below, it can be affirmed that man's essential form includes freedom, rationality, the capacity for self-transcendence and immortality. All these are created characteristics that differentiate him from the lower orders of creation. These qualities do indeed provide the irreducible requirements necessary for man to stand in a relation to God, but within themselves they do not constitute that capacity. That is a God-given possibility, since all these "ontic" qualities may conceivably be present without any essential orientation toward the Divine. G. C. Berkouwer, following Luther, makes the incisive observation that "if the image of God should lie in such ontic qualities, then Satan himself would exhibit the image of God."[31] Aristotle's definition of man as "a rational animal" has been pervasively influential at this point. It was doubtless this approach that was the origin of the term *natural image.* There are two difficulties with this way of addressing the question: (1) It defines the *imago* from below rather than from above, which results in a false perspective. It is not a question of how man differs from other beings, but a question of how he stands in relation to his Creator. (2) It suggests that the *imago* is some quality or faculty or characteristic that man possesses in himself, an aspect of his substantial

---

31. Berkouwer, *Man,* 56.

form. This aspect is then identified with the same quality in God. This theory can be criticized

> for its proneness to blur the distinction between man and God. Seeking to provide a barrier against a naturalistic rejection of man to the dead level of physical or animal nature, these views fall into the error of exalting man to the level of the divine. They assert discontinuity between man and nature in such a fashion as to overlook or understate the discontinuity between man and God. . . . Thus man is thought to be consubstantial with God; whereas, according to the biblical view, man was made of the same substance as the dust of the earth, consubstantial with all other living beings (nephesh) whose breath is in their nostrils.[32]

G. C. Berkouwer comments on this way of interpreting the wider image:

> It is regrettable that the valid emphasis in the dogma of the image of God in the wider sense has often taken on the form of an analysis of the ontic structure of man, e.g., as defined by person, reason and freedom. For it is undeniable that Scripture does not support such an interpretation. Scripture is concerned with man in his relation to God, in which he can never be seen as man-in-himself, and surely not with man's "essence" described as self or person.[33]

This statement points to a much more adequate way of interpreting the *imago*, that is, in terms of a relationship within which man stands, and one with which the preponderance of contemporary theologians agree.[34] This approach may best be understood through the analogy of a mirror. When we stand in front of the mirror, in proper relation to it, our image is reflected therein. Analogically, when man is in proper relation to God, His image is reflected in human life. The chief strength of this interpretation is that it avoids the naturalism of the substantial view and provides a genuinely theological explanation. The mirror itself is not the image; the mirror images. God's image is in the mirror. The image of God consists in man's position before God, or rather the image of God is reflected in man because of his position before Him. Like all illustrations, it has its limitations and must not be pressed to "walk

---

32. Paul Ramsey, *Christian Ethics*, 252.

33. Berkouwer, *Man*, 59-60.

34. See explanation in the Preface of the philosophical and theological significance of the relational concept. See Hall, *Imaging God*, chap. 3, for an illuminating discussion of the two models of the image of God that exactly parallels our discussion and with the same conclusion.

on all fours." Thus the proper way of speaking is not to speak of the image of God in man but of man in the image of God.

According to Paul Ramsey, "in the course of Christian thought, most of the decisive and distinctive Christian interpretations of man have been of this sort. Those of St. Augustine, Søren Kierkegaard and Karl Barth may be cited as examples; and back of them, that of St. Paul."[35]

T. F. Torrance argues that Calvin, too, shares this perspective, holding that the *imago* is not a natural possession but a spiritual one. Calvin, says Torrance, always thinks of the *imago* in terms of a mirror that reflects God when man is in the proper posture. An important stipulation upon which Calvin insists is that it is fundamentally God who does the beholding of the image. Since the image is to be understood spiritually, the soul is the seat of the image, but "he does not mean that the *imago dei* is the soul, or any natural property of the soul, but that the soul is the mirror which reflects in it or ought to reflect in it the image of God." The soul reflects the image "by way of spiritual ornaments or endowments such as wisdom, virtue, justice, truth, and holiness."[36]

In his *Dogmatics*, while retaining the language of a "formal" and "material" image (see above), Emil Brunner declares that "in both instances the fact that man has been made in the image of God is conceived not as a self-existing substance but as a relation. And this is the most important point to grasp. Responsibility (the essence of the 'formal' image) is a relation; it is not a substance."[37]

Karl Barth, too, in his *Church Dogmatics*, came to the position that man's being, man's nature, is to stand in grace. Man is not essentially a "rational animal"; his essence is to be an object of God's grace. This essence is indeed covered and hidden by sin, but how can something that has its basis in God's grace be wholly destroyed? There is and remains a "continuum, an essence unchanged and unchangeable by sin."[38] Barth goes on:

> Is it not astonishing that again and again expositors have ignored the definitive explanation given by the text itself, and instead of reflecting on it pursued all kinds of arbitrarily invent-

---

35. *Christian Ethics*, 255.
36. *Calvin's Doctrine of Man* (London: Lutterworth Press, 1952), 35-82.
37. *Creation and Redemption*, 59.
38. 3.2.43-50, 54-55. Brunner, in his *Dogmatics*, rejoices that Barth has now changed and admits this structural concept of the *imago*, so the issue of the early controversy is now settled—in Brunner's favor. *Creation and Redemption*, 44-45.

ed interpretations of the *imago dei*? . . . Could anything be more obvious than to conclude from this clear indication that the image and likeness of the being created by God signifies existence in confrontation [relation] . . . Is it that expositors were too tied to an anthropology which expected the description of a being in the divine likeness to take the form of a full description of the being of man, its structure, disposition, capacities, etc., and found it impossible to think that it could consist only in this differentiation and relationship?[39]

In any complete sense, only pre-Fall Adam and Jesus Christ reflect the glory or image of God. Those who are made new in Christ reflect the image in a more limited sense and look forward to an eschatological perfecting while at the same time progressively seeking to more perfectly embody the image of Christ. But what shall we say about those humans who do not fall into any of these categories? This brings us around once again to the question of man's relation to God or Truth in his fallen condition.

Interpreting the *imago Dei* as relationship, and rejecting the idea that it involves some aspect of man's substantial form (such as reason), seems to open the door to the position apparently taken by the early Barth in his reply to Brunner that there remains nothing to which the gospel can appeal. However, we must not forget that the biblical picture of man presents him in a dual role, as both having lost and retained the image at one and the same time. Is it then possible to sustain a position that speaks of fallen man as standing in a relation to God that is a perpetual relation, not lost through the original sin, or if lost, restored by an act of sovereign grace? At this point we must now turn to an analysis of the distinctively Wesleyan doctrine of prevenient grace.

Prevenient Grace and the Image of God

Wesley used the term "natural man" to describe the human condition apart from grace (not to be confused with the same term used by Paul in 1 Corinthians 2). He paints a dark picture of such a creature. Pertinent to our question in this discussion, he denies that such a man has any knowledge of God, nor could he ever attain to any such knowledge. In his sermon on "Original Sin" he hypothe-

---

39. *Church Dogmatics* 3.1.195. We will explore more deeply the implications of this profound suggestion in our discussion of sin.

sizes that if two infants were brought up from the womb without being instructed in any religion, they would have no religion at all and no more knowledge of God than wild beasts. In this description, however, he makes two stipulations: (1) parenthetically he notes an exception, "unless the grace of God interposed"; and (2) that this result would occur apart "from the influences of God's Spirit."

In his sermon "On Working Out Our Own Salvation" he cashes in on these stipulations:

> For allowing that all the souls of men are dead in sin by *nature*, this excuses none, seeing there is no man that is in a state of mere nature; there is no man, unless he has quenched the Spirit, that is wholly void of the grace of God. No man living is entirely destitute of what is vulgarly called *natural conscience*. But this is not natural: It is more properly termed *preventing grace*. [40]

This grace that goes before is universal in its extent and is the source of all good in man, and of feelings of right and wrong that are the result of the activity of conscience. Furthermore, in reference to John 1:9 he says: "Everyone has some measure of that light, some faint glimmering ray, which sooner or later, more or less, enlightens every man that cometh into the world." The end result of universal prevenient grace is that "no man sins because he has not grace, but because he does not use the grace which he hath."

In his "systematic" discussion of the law, Wesley says that the law, as an embodiment of the mind of God, was coeval with man's nature but was "well nigh effaced" by the Fall. "And yet God did not despise the work of His own hands; but, being reconciled to man through the Son of His love, He, in some measure, reinscribed the law on the heart of the dark, sinful creature."[41] John Deschner comments on this passage, "This may be taken as an important element in Wesley's understanding of prevenient grace."[42]

What we are suggesting here is that prevenient grace is simply another way of talking about that aspect of the *imago Dei* as a relationship within which man perpetually stands, while at the same time recognizing that this grace is not, in and of itself, saving grace, even though it may become so if properly responded to. Rather, what we are saying is that of all earthly creatures, only

---

40. *Works* 6:512.
41. *StS* 2:43.
42. *Wesley's Christology*, 100.

human beings are, in Mr. Wesley's words, "capable of God," and this is not a natural but a gracious capacity.

Prevenient grace is a post-Fall category and thus potentially redemptive in the literal sense of the word ("to buy back"). But to infer that the human relation to God in the pre-Fall state (about which we know very little historically) was qualitatively different is to misunderstand the gracious nature of creation. Nature and grace cannot be artificially separated even in Eden, as Thomism does. Karl Barth correctly emphasizes the absence of any independent nature that the creation has apart from the gift of grace by the Creator:

> It [the creation] has no attributes, no conditions of existence, no substantial or accidental predicates of any kind, in virtue of which it can or may or must be alien to the Founder of this covenant. It has no ground on which it can deal with Him on an equal footing.[43]

The original filial relationship was broken by the first sin, but the ground for the possibility of that relation was preserved or restored by the gracious love of the Creator so that it can be renewed without an ontological creation of a new, qualitatively different being.

The long-standing question of nature and grace thus takes on unique contours from the Wesleyan perspective. Unlike the Thomistic solution, it does not hold to a good human nature that needs but to be supplemented by grace to complete man's full, twofold telos. Nature is not good but radically fallen, perverted, corrupt, devoid of any redeeming qualities before God. Furthermore, grace is not restricted to a segment of man's life, that part that has to do with the supernatural virtues. The distinctiveness of the Wesleyan view is that nature is so graced that the natural man is but a logical abstraction. This grace extends to the whole of human existence.

In terms of the metaphor of the mirror, this means that even though man in sin no longer maintains the posture enabling him to reflect the image of God, the mirror retains—by grace—the capacity to once again reflect that image. The metaphor should not be misunderstood. It is not intended to leave the idea that there is something within man (the mirror) that is a part of his substantial form, and certainly not a "relic" of the *imago*. We intend nothing more than a pictorial way of describing a relationship of grace.

---

43. *Church Dogmatics* 3.1.96. See also his discussion ibid., 194-95.

The implications of this for the theological definition of man are significant. Instead of identifying some quality such as reason, freedom, or personality, which distinguishes him from the brute creation, or attempting to find some "divine spark" within that blurs the distinction between man and God, it defines the essence of man as "man in relation to God." In other words, when prevenient grace is interpreted as an ontological principle, it is grace that constitutes the humanity of man. The very being of man qua man is his essential standing in grace. This clearly retains the Creator-creature relationship with all that that entails.

This position is in full accord with the statement of John Baillie that "the truth is that there is in man no *nature* apart from *revelation.* Human nature is constituted by the self-disclosure to this poor dust of the Spirit of the living God." He goes on to make the pertinent observation that this is the reason why humanism, when divorced from living religion, has more and more tended to collapse into mere nihilism.[44]

Prof. Baillie cites several statements from Emil Brunner that reflect substantially the same view of human nature: "Man has spirit only in that he is addressed by God . . . Therefore the human self is nothing which exists in its own right, no property of man, but a relation to a divine Thou." Also, "the essential being of man as man . . . is identical with his relation to God."[45]

Karl Barth, using his method of deriving anthropology from Christology, sees an analogy between the relation of Father and Son (thus a relation within the being of God) and the relation between God and humanity. Thus he rejects the *analogia entis* (analogy of being) by which certain naturalistic qualities were ascribed to man as being the *imago* and affirms instead an *analogia relationis* (analogy of relation). This is an ontological concept that determines the essential nature of man.[46]

Another way of saying the same thing is that man is "essentially good but existentially estranged." If this were not the case, in conversion man would cease to be a man, since that which is essentially evil cannot become good without ceasing to be what it was and becoming something else. There is, in other words, a rela-

---

44. *Knowledge of God,* 42-43.
45. Cited from Brunner's work titled *God and Man.* See John Baillie, *Knowledge of God,* 42.
46. *Church Dogmatics* 3.2.220 ff.

tionship of continuity between the man whose personhood is constituted by prevenient grace and the man who has by faith responded to this grace and allowed it to become saving grace that overcomes the existential estrangement.[47]

John Burnaby points to a further, epistemological dimension of this matter. He declares that "to assert that man is totally corrupt, that there is no longer any free response to the Spirit which is the Life of God manifesting itself as love," is contrary to experience.

> If this dogma were true, the work of redemption would be strictly impossible. For the redeeming activity of God is not like the original creation, a making of something "out of nothing" . . . We must needs believe that the capacity to recognize and bow down in adoration of goodness exists in all men; for it is to this capacity that the Spirit ever makes his appeal.[48]

An additional and ultimately decisive argument for this position is the Incarnation. No real incarnation could have occurred where God became man if man were not "essentially good."[49]

Prevenient Grace and General Revelation

Systematically, the Wesleyan understanding agrees wholeheartedly with the emphasis of most postliberal theology that there is no knowledge of God apart from revelation. Prevenient grace, understood as an epistemological principle, asserts that God has in fact made himself known to every man. There is a disagreement, however, with those who assert that God is known only in connection with the historical Jesus (at least in an external sense). In traditional language, prevenient grace is the foundation for a valid doctrine of general revelation. This is not to be construed as a natural revelation, which is a contradiction in terms. Furthermore, it is clearly in opposition to the traditional approach, which believes that man,

---

47. Cf. T. L. Kantonen, *The Theology of Evangelism* (Philadelphia: Muhlenberg Press, 1954), 37, who says: "If the essence of human nature were sin, then man would be unsalvable, for God does not save sin. The truth is that sinful man is unsaved but salvable." Donald G. Bloesch, using the "Essential/existential" categories, vigorously affirms the goodness of man on the same grounds. *Essentials of Evangelical Theology*, 2 vols. (San Francisco: Harper and Row, Publishers, 1978), 1:95.

48. *Is the Bible Inspired?* 82.

49. Kantonen, *Evangelism*, 37.

by his unaided reason, can come to some knowledge of God. It merely asserts with Scripture that God has not left himself without a witness to any man (Acts 14:17).

This claim immediately raises a problem that must be addressed. There are passages in the Bible that move in a universalizing direction, such as John 1:9: "That was the true Light, which lighteth every man that cometh into the world" (KJV). There are also passages that move in a particularizing direction, such as Acts 4:12: "Neither is there salvation in any other: for there is none other name under heaven given among men, whereby we must be saved" (KJV). Is one left only with the option of choosing one or the other, or is there a way of relating the two in a creative tension by taking them both seriously? Our suggestion is that they can be reconciled by recognizing that the God who makes himself known in a general revelation is the same God who makes himself known in the special revelation in Jesus Christ. Or, to use the phrase of Martin Luther, there is no other God than the Father of our Lord Jesus Christ. The same thing is intended when we take seriously the claim of Jesus that He is the Way, the Truth, and the Life. If He is the Truth, wherever men encounter Truth, they encounter Christ.[50]

In the history of Christian thought, there have been two traditions representing these two movements that have coexisted, usually in tension with each other. On the one hand there are those, represented in the early centuries by the Alexandrians (Clement and Origen) and Justin Martyr, who see a continuity between Christianity and culture and philosophy. On the other hand there have been those like Tertullian who insisted on discontinuity and asked skeptically, "What has Athens to do with Jerusalem?" and preferred to believe "because it is absurd." The Wesleyan position,

---

50. John A. Knight comments on this point: "Through the doctrine of prevenient grace, assuming man's proper use of it, Wesley was enabled to maintain the absolute character of the claims of Christ and the church, and also the validity of the non-Christian's knowledge." "Fletcher," 117. Commenting on the universalizing passage found in Mal. 1:11, Stephen Winward says: "The truth that men may be worshipping 'the only true God' even when they do not know his name . . . should not be regarded as a contradiction of the complementary truth that worship is acceptable to God only through Jesus Christ. For 'all that is noble in the non-Christian systems of thought, or conduct, or worship is the work of Christ upon them and within them;' (Wm. Temple, *Readings in St. John's Gospel,* 10) and the worship of men, whether offered B.C. or A.D., is acceptable to God only in view of the sacrifice of Christ the Savior of the world." *A Guide to the Prophets* (Atlanta: John Knox Press, 1976), 223.

consistently understood, stands in the former tradition without denying some validity to the latter. All Truth is the result of prevenient grace.

In classical theological terminology, this interpretation holds that God is first in the *ordo cognoscendi* (order of knowing) as well as the *ordo essendi* (order of being or essential order). This is the consequence of holding, in accord with the Augustinian tradition, that God is the Ground of all knowledge as well as the Ground of all being. Knowledge of God, like the being of God, is not derived from knowledge of other things. This is the reverse of the traditional cosmological theistic proofs, which begin with empirical knowledge of the world, or some aspect of it, and infer God's existence from this prior knowledge. The doctrine of prevenient grace as a principle of knowledge affirms that one's experience of the world raises the question of God because one is already aware of an impinging presence. Knowledge of God is not secondary and inferential, but primary and direct.[51] The words of Paul Tillich capture this perspective:

> Arguments for the existence of God presuppose the loss of the certainty of God. That which I have to prove by argument has no immediate reality for me. Its reality is mediated for me by some other reality about which I cannot be in doubt, so that this other reality is nearer to me than the reality of God. For the more closely things are connected with our interior existence, the less they are open to doubt. And nothing can be nearer to us than that which is at times farthest away from us, namely God. A God who has been proved is neither near enough to us nor far enough away from us. He is not far enough, because of the very attempt we have made to prove Him. He is not near enough, because nearer things are presupposed by which the knowledge of Him is mediated. Hence this ostensibly demonstrated subject is not really God.[52]

In the previous chapter we noted that one of the necessities for revelation was based upon the fact that knowledge of God is like knowledge of other persons. Taking this as a clue, we may now

---

51. It is well known that John Wesley himself subscribed to the empirical epistemology of John Locke and in this vein gave some credence to arguments for the existence of God. What we are suggesting here is that this commitment is inconsistent with Mr. Wesley's own *theological* perspective, but he should not be faulted for this. Neither should he be slavishly followed into this epistemology that is contrary to the whole tenor of his theological teaching. His way of avoiding the unsatisfactory conclusion of his Lockean epistemology is to posit a second set of senses. This is, of course, a very unsatisfactory out.

52. Quoted in John Baillie, *Knowledge of God*, 177.

notice further how there is an analogy between knowledge of God and knowledge of other minds. In this area of epistemology, there are two major approaches corresponding to the two types of understanding concerning our knowledge of God: inferential and immediate or direct.

Thomas Aquinas is a classic example of the inferential approach, which is the logical corollary of an empirical epistemology. Direct knowledge of the self, the other's as well as one's own, is not possible. One simply observes behavior of a certain type from which an inference is made that there is a mind or self. David Hume, taking the empirical principle down the path to its logical conclusion found it impossible to understand how the self could be an object of experience, and thus he lost it completely. As John Cook Wilson incisively summarized Hume's analysis:

> The very presupposition of experience is condemned by the test of that experience to be non-existent, simply because we can't be aware of ourselves as objects of sensuous experience. Yet that we are conscious of ourselves—though, of course, not in the way of such experience—is the most absolutely certain thing of all.[53]

With this, Wilson points to the second way of apprehending: immediately and intuitively. In his essay titled "Rational Grounds of Belief in God," which John Baillie evaluated as "one of the most important theological documents of our time," Wilson makes the following statement:

> If we think of the existence of our friends; it is the direct knowledge which we want; merely inferential knowledge seems a poor affair. To most men it would be as surprising as unwelcome to hear it could not be directly known whether there were such existences as their friends, and that it was only a matter of (probable) empirical argument and inference from facts which are directly known. And even if we convince ourselves on reflection that this is really the case, our actions prove that we have a confidence in the existence of our friends which can't be derived from an empirical argument (which can never be certain), for a man will risk his life for his friend. We don't want merely inferred friends. Could we possibly be satisfied with an inferred God?[54]

By careful and cogent reasoning, Wilson demonstrates that

53. *Statement and Inference*, ed. A. S. L. Farquharson, 2 vols. (Oxford: Clarendon Press, 1969), 2:857.
54. Ibid., 853.

one does not believe either in God or the self or the external world[55] as a result of rational argument. Furthermore, rational argument is not utilized or attempted because one feels that such beliefs are irrational. Rather the arguments arise out of a conviction of the reality of the self, God, and the world that antedates such philosophical reasoning and is ultimately unaffected by it. "The true business of philosophy [in these areas] seems to be to bring the belief [in such existences] to a consciousness of itself."[56]

In addition, Wilson demonstrates philosophically by the use of several examples that "even in the acts of knowing and perceiving there may be something really existing and operating in our minds of which we may not be explicitly aware."[57] Thus our knowledge of God does not wait upon the validation of His existence by argument but in a real sense is simply a manifestation of the ground of the possibility of argument. "The fact, then, that people have tried to find a proof of God's existence is so far compatible with His direct presence in their consciousness; and the fact that they think, or some think, they certainly have no direct experience or knowledge of God is compatible with the same hypothesis."[58]

This philosophical discussion shows how both knowledge of the self and, by parallel, the knowledge of God are prior considerations and become the very basis of the question about them. Even atheism is a reflection of an awareness of God; otherwise the question of His existence would never be raised so as to be denied. It is a knowledge that is both known and unknown in the paradoxical relation we have earlier discussed. Philosophy leads to the

---

55. These were the three problematics of modern philosophy in its beginning. Cf. the work of Descartes and Kant.

56. Wilson, *Statement and Inference* 2:851. H. H. Farmer, *The World and God* (London: Fontana Library, 1963), argues for the immediacy of *personal* knowledge: "There can be no question that the awareness has in actual experience what Tennant calls 'psychical immediacy,' that is to say, it is not at the moment of its occurrence the result of a process of mental construction or inference; rather it has an intuitive and intrinsic certainty which neither requires, nor admits of, any attestation other than its own self-evidence." 21 ff.

57. Wilson, *Statement and Inference* 2:856.

58. Ibid., 858. John Fletcher explicitly adopts this position as he explicates the task of the "enlightened pastor" in relation to his doctrine of dispensations: "He preaches the dispensation of the Son to those who, like Socrates and Plato, are longing for a Divine instructer [sic], as well as to those who, like Simeon, Nicodemus, and Cornelius, are waiting for the consolation of Israel. He leads them either from the law of Moses, or from the law of nature, to the Gospel of Christ." *The Works of John Fletcher,* 4 vols. (Salem, Ohio: Schmul Publishers, 1974), 3:177.

same conclusion to which an epistemological construction of the doctrine of prevenient grace leads.

This interpretation of the *imago Dei* and use of prevenient grace as a clue to the nature of general revelation has implications for the relation of Christianity to non-Christian religions. Unlike those theories that insist on radical discontinuity and call for a missionary theology that takes a negative stance toward everything in other religions, the Wesleyan approach is to recognize that whatever truth may be found in other religions is the result of the activity of prevenient grace in its revelatory function. The missionary can gratefully accept such truth and use it as a point of contact to demonstrate the fulfillment of those glimmers of truth by the fuller revelation in Christ. After all, Judaism is a non-Christian religion; and if Christianity is seen centrally to be a fulfillment of its truth as found in the Old Testament, to a lesser degree it could also be validly claimed that other religions also find their fulfillment in Him who is the Apex of all revelatory activity.

Such a consideration leads on to the question of the nature of such general revelation. First, it does not provide a basis for a philosophical prolegomena of truths that need but to be supplemented by further information via special revelation. Rather it impinges upon the human consciousness as an "awareness" or a "mysterium tremendum" (Otto), or a sense of an infinite dimension filtering through finite experience. It is this aspect of the uniquely human experience that manifests itself in the universal phenomenon of religion. In primitive or primal religions it takes the form of mana or spiritism, where the forces of nature, whether personal or impersonal, are invested with power over human fortunes or destiny. Anthropologists tend to be almost exclusively preoccupied with this level of religious awareness, doubtless because it is the purest form of the natural expression of the religious sense unperverted by technological culture. It also seems to be the case that conversion from this primitive level to Christianity is the easiest of all transitions to make. The so-called higher religions are simply sophisticated expressions of this same eros.[59]

---

59. The classical (philosophical) description of *eros* that becomes the paradigm for its theological use is found in Plato's *Symposium:* In an ode to love (eros) Socrates describes him as the child of poverty or need and Plenty or Resource. Thus he stands midway between having and not having and longs for fullness because of his kinship to Plenty. Out of his poverty he experiences need and is fulfilled or happy when united with his parent, Resource. The pattern of being aware of a lack because of being already in possession of should be noted here.

Is it possible to identify any specific character of this general revelation? Perhaps the insight of Martin Luther provides a fruitful avenue of investigation. Luther suggests that the universal divine sense leads to the knowledge of the law but not to the gospel. A survey of the way of salvation taught by the major world religions tends to verify this insight. Knowledge of the law would imply a sense of obligation, of coming short, with the solution to the problem being good works, overcoming the sense of alienation by self-effort. The four types of Yoga in Hinduism, Buddhism's Eightfold Path to Enlightenment, as well as the rigorous disciplines of Zen Buddhism all clearly manifest the pattern of salvation by good works, merit, achievement, and so on. The nearest to a concept of grace is found in Pure Land Buddhism. This comes very close to the New Testament concept of grace, but the object of hope is false from a Christian perspective (see Huston Smith, *Religions of Man*).

Wesley seems to concur with Luther's opinion by virtue of the fact that he lays such stress upon conscience as the work of prevenient grace. He insists that conscience is not a natural faculty, except in the sense that it is found in all men, but a supernatural endowment. He even equates conscience with the work of the Son of God as "the true light, which enlighteneth every man that cometh into the world." It is furthermore related to the work of the Spirit of God. The universality of conscience along with the nature of its work creates a sense of the law.[60]

Immanuel Kant also argued for the universality of a moral consciousness, a sense of ought. His arguments provide some support, from the philosophical side, of the hypothesis that general revelation manifests itself in terms of the moral law within. Kant, of course, founded his claims in reason; but that is not necessarily in contradiction to the view we are exploring, even if true or adequate, since Wesley, too, relates reason and conscience and holds that reason in its ontological function is a gift of prevenient grace.[61]

If this interpretation is correct, what can be said concerning

---

60. Wesley defines conscience as "that faculty whereby we are at once conscious of our own thoughts, words and actions; and of their merit or demerit, of their being good or bad; and consequently, deserving either praise or censure." *Works* 7:186 ff. Cf. Harald Lindström, *Wesley and Sanctification: A Study in the Doctrine of Salvation* (Wilmore, Ky.: Francis Asbury Publishing Co., n.d.), 48-49.

61. This is to distinguish conscience as a function of reason from technical reason, or "reasoning." Cf. Tillich, *Systematic Theology*, vol. I, for an analysis of these two types of reason.

the function of general revelation in relation to salvation? There are those who take the position that it serves only as the occasion for God's universal condemnation of the human race. It is the basis of justice's declaration of all men as guilty before God. It is true that this is the main thrust of Paul's discussion in Romans 1; but that does not preclude the possibility that additional conclusions may be drawn from the evidence, based on the nature of God, and Paul does seem to draw one of those conclusions in Rom. 2:14: "For when the Gentiles, which have not the law [the revealed law of Moses], do by nature the things contained in the law, these, having not the law, are a law unto themselves" (KJV).

A full-orbed concept of justice would open the door to the possibility that what is the basis of condemnation would also be the basis for approbation. Mr. Wesley, in his sermon "On Faith," appears to draw this conclusion. He refers to "a small degree of light [that] is given to those that are under the heathen dispensation,"[62] and goes on to talk about the small measure of faith that is vouchsafed to those who have such minimal light. He refers to such faith as the "faith of a servant," which, while inferior to the "faith of a son," is nonetheless saving faith and should not be despised but led to the fuller stage when it is recognized that salvation is by faith. This reflects Wesley's own experience, when as an Oxford fellow he sought acceptance by God on the basis of law and later came to claim this stage of his pilgrimage as involving the "faith of a servant." The clear implication is that if, by conscience (general revelation), the unbeliever is led to a knowledge of the law and by such knowledge responds in obedience, he may be saved.

John Fletcher, upon whose work Wesley depended in this discussion, developed this position fully in his doctrine of dispensations. This doctrine posits the existence of three dispensations that refer to degrees of knowledge of God: that of the Father, of the Son, and of the Spirit. It is the first that chiefly concerns us here. Fletcher refers to this dispensation variously as "the natural law," "the remains of the Creator's image in the human heart," "the secret grace of the Redeemer which is more or less operative in every man," "Gentilism," or "Judaism."

He supports and describes the dispensation of the Father scripturally by reference to those passages that speak of the universal knowledge of all men: Acts 17:26-27; Titus 2:11; 1 Tim. 4:10;

---

62. *Works* 7:195.

Acts 10:34-35; Heb. 11:6; Mic. 6:8. Although inadequate and falling far short of the full revelation of God as is found in the dispensation of the Spirit (not a period of time so much as a relationship based on an advanced understanding), this revelation is sufficient unto salvation if God is just. Otherwise impartial justice would have required that God had seen to it that there had been only one dispensation of grace and all men given full knowledge. Although all men do not have access to the same degree of truth, "nevertheless, it is equally certain that every man, in what period of time and in what peculiar circumstances soever he found himself placed, has received sufficient light to discover, as well as sufficient power to perform what God has been pleased to require at his hands."[63]

It is this construction of Wesley's doctrine of prevenient grace that is the developed implication of the teaching and is not contrary to Wesley's own mature understanding. John A. Knight has argued that Wesley's development of his understanding of justification by faith in relation to works is the expression of an implicit "theology of history" that he did not fully carry through.[64] Although his basic aim remained the same, the documents reveal a progression of thought and expression in his understanding of the relation between the two. In his earlier writings Wesley denied that good works can be done unto justification, and he asserted that faith is the sole condition of justification. Slowly, however, he came to see that good works can be done prior to conversion, and even spoke of repentance and obedience to God as conditions of salvation. These conflicting assertions can best be explained, claimed Knight, by the latent "theology of history" that in time came to pervade Mr. Wesley's thought. At first he thought only in terms of Christian faith—thus he held that works cannot bring justification.

63. Fletcher, *Works* 3:170-79. Richard S. Taylor spells out the same perspective in an essay on "A Theology of Missions": "Should a South American Indian or African Hottentot or *anyone* respond to this inner agitation of his conscience, and in sincere repentance reach out for God and His goodness, and continue in that frame of mind until death, he would be saved. He would have thus embarked on the pursuit of that holiness 'without which no man shall see the Lord' (Heb. 12:14), even though ignorant of where to find it. Since we believe that the mercy of God, through the atoning work of Christ, provides for the salvation of infants, and also regenerate believers who have not yet received light on entire sanctification, it is not unreasonable to grant the same mercy to the repentant heathen." *Ministering to the Millions* (Kansas City: Nazarene Publishing House, 1971), 30. See Taylor's further discussion in *Exploring Christian Holiness* 3:121-22.

64. By "theology of history" is meant an interpretation from the Christian perspective of the pre-Christian and non-Christian eras and individuals of world history.

Gradually his perspective broadened to include non-Christian believers, for example, Cornelius, who had never heard the gospel.
He saw that God would accept them on the basis of their degree of
faith and obedience to what light they had. In this sense their
works were good, although they preceded justification by faith in
the Christian sense.[65]

Thus it was fully in accord with Wesley's later views that
Fletcher could say:

> Such is the faith by which those Jews, Mohammedans and
> Pagans, whose hearts are principled with humility, candor, and
> the fear of God, have been, and still continue to be, saved in
> every part of the world. For the Father of mercies, who know-
> eth whereof we are made, will no more absolutely condemn
> such worshippers, on account of the extraordinary respect they
> have discovered for Moses, Mohammed, and Confucius, than
> he will finally reject some pious Christians, for the sake of that
> excessive veneration which they manifest for particular saints
> and reformers.[66]

However much this concept of prevenient grace as general
revelation vindicates the justice of God, takes account of such
knowledge of truth as there may be outside the Christian faith, and
theoretically provides for the possibility of salvation not limited to
the accidents of birth (place and time), it is still incomplete in both
its subjective and objective aspects. It does not provide a true picture of God's relation to fallen man, and it does not lead in any
significant way to salvation. Thus general revelation points beyond
itself and drives toward special revelation. This is the point of John
Fletcher when he describes the dispensation of the Father leading
to the dispensation of the Son and that in turn leading to that of
the Spirit. Wherever the Christian worker finds his hearer, he
needs to recognize the dispensation in which he is found and attempt to direct him with instruction to the highest level of Christian experience. Here, once again, we encounter the crucial truth
that experience is the result of knowledge or understanding. However one experiences God is dependent upon his level of apprehension of the measure of the Divine that is available to him. With
these foundation stones in place, we can now move on to the idea
of special revelation.

65. "Fletcher," 170-74.
66. *Works* 3:176-77.

Special Revelation

Our discussion of general revelation has suggested already the substance of special revelation. If general revelation leads one only to knowledge of the law, then special revelation must carry us on to the gospel. Both Luther and Calvin insist that the most crucial issue in our knowledge of God is His disposition toward us rather than knowledge of His existence. It is this disposition that is basic to true saving knowledge. Luther says:

> All men have the general knowledge, namely that there is a God, that he created heaven and earth, that he is just, that he punisheth the wicked. But what God thinketh of us, what he will give or what he will do, to the end that we may be delivered from sin and death, and be saved (which is the true knowledge of God indeed), this they know not.[67]

If this true knowledge is indeed the substance of the special revelatory activity of God, it will furthermore provide a clue to the proper understanding of the mode of revelation. It seems logical that these two should be self-consciously developed as correlative concepts.

Our first task, then, is addressing the question of the substance or content of special revelation, or what is the same thing, defining the gospel. An appropriate place to begin the inquiry is with the "sermon" with which Jesus opened His ministry in the synagogue at Nazareth. His text was drawn from Isa. 61:1-2: "The Spirit of the Lord is upon Me, because He has anointed Me to preach the gospel to the poor. He has sent Me to heal the brokenhearted, to preach deliverance to the captives" (NKJV). Upon reading the text, He announced: "This day is this scripture fulfilled in your ears" (KJV; Luke 4:18, 21).

In the original setting of the text, the prophet is proclaiming "good tidings" to Jerusalem, that her time of captivity is over. For some 70 years Judah had suffered under the great Babylonian Captivity. Now the circumstances had changed on the international scene; Babylon had succumbed to the Persians under Cyrus the Great, and the door had been opened for the devastating separation from the homeland to be brought to an end. From the theological perspective of the prophet, all of this was the result of the

---

67. *Commentary on Galatians*, 318-19. Quoted in *A Compend of Luther's Theology*, ed. Hugh T. Kerr (Philadelphia: Westminster Press, 1974), 24.

activity of God, and thus he was heralding the good news (the meaning of "gospel") that God was doing something resulting in salvation (meaning "freedom," as in connection with the Exodus. See Exod. 14:30).

Jesus' use of this text for His inaugural sermon was fitting because He was here announcing that God was once more about to perform a mighty act that would be good news to those in captivity. Throughout His ministry He performed acts of healing, exorcisms, and other miracles to demonstrate that this power was being released in the world to effect the deliverance.

A decisive step in further explicating the meaning of "gospel" is taken by Paul in Rom. 1:16: "For I am not ashamed of the gospel of Christ, for it is the power of God to salvation for everyone who believes" (NKJV). He has in mind the same general meaning as in Jesus' announcement, but now, for him, the gospel has become Jesus Christ. It is not the gospel Christ taught, but the good news about Him. This is his point when he says to the Corinthians: "I determined not to know anything among you except Jesus Christ and Him crucified" (1 Cor. 2:2, NKJV).

The gospel is thus the good news that God has acted in history in Jesus Christ, and that act is the guarantee of deliverance from captivity. It is not a body of abstract teaching involving a doctrine to be believed so much as it is an announcement that God has done something in history, and what He has done is His last and decisive act. H. Richard Niebuhr summarizes this nicely:

> The preaching of the early Christian church was not an argument for the existence of God nor an admonition to follow the dictates of some common human conscience, unhistorical and super-social in character. It was primarily a simple recital of the great events connected with the historical appearance of Jesus Christ and a confession of what had happened to the community of disciples.[68]

Martin Luther, whose lead we are partially following in identifying the heart of the Christian revelation with the content of the gospel, recognizes substantially the same content and summarized it as follows: "The Gospel, then, is nothing but the preaching about Christ, Son of God and of David, true God and man, who by His death and resurrection has overcome all men's sin, and death and hell, for us who believe in Him."[69]

---

68. *The Meaning of Revelation* (New York: Macmillan Co., 1962), 43.
69. From "Preface to the New Testament," quoted in *Compend*, 9.

Luther further defines the nature of the gospel in his commentary on Peter and Jude. It "means nothing but a proclamation and heralding of the grace and mercy of God through Jesus Christ, . . . it does not bid us do works whereby we may become righteous, but proclaims to us the grace of God, bestowed freely, and apart from any merit of our own."[70] He points to an additional implication of the gospel in discussing the Bible and the Word of God: "The word is the Gospel of God concerning His Son, who was made flesh, suffered, rose from the dead, and was glorified through the *Spirit who sanctifies*" (italics added).[71] We shall call attention to this emphasis later.

When we turn to the Old Testament, we do not find a contradictory revelation but rather a preparatory one that doubtless did not make sufficiently clear the way of God's dealings with man, and the recipients of the revelation soon perverted the "gospel" of the earlier revelation into legalism. A careful reading of the central event of the Old Testament—the Exodus—will disclose that it was an explicit act of grace of the nature of gospel. God came to a weak, enslaved people and without any preparation or worthiness on their part effected a mighty deliverance that brought them into being as a people. The law did not precede but followed this saving act as a "response to grace."[72] When the law and sacrifices became the means of gaining acceptance with God, the gracious basis of Old Testament faith was obscured and all but lost.

At this point we are able to perceive how the content of the revelation clarifies the mode of revelation. It did not, at the first and primary level, involve the communication of abstract truths to the intellect, but the intervening activity of God in history effecting salvation. Consequently, we can assuredly affirm with the majority

---

70. Ibid.

71. From *Treatise on Christian Liberty*, quoted in *Compend*, 11.

72. John Bright, *The Kingdom of God* (New York: Abingdon Press, 1953), 28-29. Walter Brueggemann, *Tradition for Crisis: A Study in Hosea* (Atlanta: John Knox Press, 1968), in discussing what he calls the historical and legal traditions, says of them: "The historical traditions bear witness to the graciousness of Yahweh toward Israel, and the legal traditions manifest Yahweh's claim upon Israel. It is this healthy and dynamic interrelation between historical and legal tradition, between God's graciousness and his claim, which is at the center of Israel's faith in every new circumstance. The delicate relation of God's graciousness and God's claim is the most problematic for the community of faith. Without the first, the community becomes paralyzed in moralism and legalism. . . . Without the second, the community becomes complacent and undisciplined." 21.

of modern interpreters that God's self-disclosure occurs in His mighty acts that comprise a *Heilsgeschichte.*[73]

We need now to explore further the content of the gospel by looking at the proclamation (kerygma) of the Early Church, what the pioneering scholar C. H. Dodd identified as the substructure of New Testament theology.[74] By analyzing the preaching of the Early Church, including Paul's, Dodd was able to isolate six items that made up the central proclamation of the apostolic message. These are: (1) the age of fulfillment has dawned; (2) this has occurred through the ministry, death, and resurrection of Jesus; (3) Jesus has been exalted to God's right hand; (4) the Holy Spirit has been given; (5) the Crucified One will return in glory; and (6) finally an appeal for repentance, the offer of forgiveness, and the Holy Spirit.[75]

This fuller elaboration of the content of the gospel provides us with some significant insights. The first clue to an important inclusion in the gospel revelation is found in the first of the six affirmations and repeated in some others: the age to come has dawned in fulfillment of the Old Testament scriptures. In fact, this opens up the really new element in the gospel.

The language of the ages (the present age and the age to come) was derived from Jewish apocalyptic and becomes the central motif of New Testament theology.[76] One of the major characteristics of the anticipated age to come, though by no means the only one, was that it would be an age of the Spirit. The most obvious expression of this prophetic hope is found in Joel 2:28-32, which envisions a universal outpouring of the prophetic spirit in fulfillment of Moses' magnanimous expression in Num. 11:29. However, a more profound, yet less explicit, expression of this phase of the hope for a

---

73. Cf. Purkiser, *Exploring Our Christian Faith,* 54-56.

74. *The Apostolic Preaching* (New York: Harper and Bros., Publishers, 1962).

75. That Dodd in his initial work interpreted this kerygma exclusively in terms of "realized eschatology" does not invalidate the substance of the preaching. He simply misinterpreted his own evidence. Elsewhere, in *Gospel and Law* (New York: Columbia University Press, 1951), he reflected a different view, as the following words indicate: "In view of the facts, the church accepted a revision of its early expectations. The result of all this was a certain tension which can be discerned in almost all parts of the New Testament: the Kingdom of God will come; it has come: Christ has come; Christ will come." 28.

76. Cf. Ladd, *Theology;* and Herman N. Ridderbos, *Paul: An Outline of His Theology,* trans. John Richard de Witt (Grand Rapids: Wm. B. Eerdmans Publishing Co., 1975).

new day is found in Jeremiah and Ezekiel. Jeremiah, perplexed over the continual idolatry of his people (cf. Jeremiah 2), agonized over the reason for it and discovered that it was because the old covenant did not make explicit provision for a real change in the human heart (sanctification); and, inspired by the Lord, he looked forward to a day when God would establish a new covenant, unlike the old one, where God would write the law in their hearts (31:31-34). Ezekiel echoes this hope in Ezek. 36:27: "And I will put my spirit within you, and cause you to walk in my statutes and be careful to observe my ordinances."

The kerygma thus highlights, not only that God has acted in Jesus Christ to make crystal clear that grace is the proper basis of one's reconciliation to God but also that in the same act He provides for the sanctification of the heart. With this we see that the core of the gospel revelation is the core of the perspective of Wesleyan theology (see chap. 1). It all comes to focus in soteriology with this twin emphasis.

C. H. Dodd, however, further calls attention to an additional body of biblical material that he refers to as the *didache* (teaching) and that includes doctrinal and ethical teaching. How are we to understand the relation of the *didache* to the kerygma, and does this not call for a modification or addition to the understanding of the mode of revelation?

Clearly we are dealing with beliefs that are derived from the primary revelatory acts and thus in some sense secondary to them. Furthermore, the central revelation calls for a certain response that Paul refers to in Phil. 1:27 as living according to the gospel: "Only let your manner of life be worthy of the gospel of Christ." In a word, the acceptance of the saving message calls for a special ethical life informed by that message. The act of God in Christ provides insight into theological truth and a basis for value judgments that inform conduct.

In the light of this, we would propose that special revelation involves two moments: the first occurs in the existential experience of the saving act of God, an experiential involvement that makes a particular event revelatory (the Exodus, for instance, was experienced by Pharaoh but not as saving, although it is logically possible that it could have been revelatory for him as judgment; the Roman soldiers, of all people, most directly experienced the Resurrection, but there is no evidence that it was revelatory for them);[77] the second moment involves the Spirit's guidance in the process of inferring the theological and ethical implications of the saving event(s), and inscripturating these interpretations and inferences, so that in a derivative sense the Bible becomes a part of revelation. Since both of these inferences are historically conditioned by virtue of the timefulness of the interpreter (which is inescapable), they are often expressed in terms colored by particular circumstances but always informed by sound theology; therefore they must be utilized in terms of the interpretive process referred to in chapter 2 and explored in depth in Appendix 2.

We may identify a further aspect of revelatory truth that is not directly revealed. This wisdom to which we refer pertains to the cosmic (or philosophical) implications of the gospel. This involves a further process of inference for which no special inspiration is claimed but doubtless is an activity reserved for those with advanced training—the theologian who seeks to spell out the ontological and epistemological implications of the "simple gospel."[78]

It is only to this dimension of truth that Archbishop William Temple's famous remark properly applies: "There is no such thing as revealed truth. . . . There are truths of revelation, that is to say, propositions which express the results of correct thinking concerning revelation; but they are not themselves directly revealed."[79] One can even identify the explication of these truths as the task of

---

77. This is substantially the point of Alan Richardson: "The biblical revelation was originally received existentially, and it must be received in every subsequent age of the church also existentially—by those who are themselves seeking to find and to teach the will of God in the actual historical situation which confronts them in their own day. It is in this way that the Christian knowledge of God comes into being—in the first or in the twentieth century." *Apologetics,* 152. Many interpreters who recognize that revelation through events also requires an interpreter tend to explain it in an intellectualist direction by emphasizing the illumination of the mind of the interpreter. What we are suggesting does not exclude the mind but includes more. To recognize a historical event as an act of God, it must be (1) saving in nature and (2) experienced as such by the participant-observer. Only in this way does revelation (all revelation is saving) occur at all. This close correlation of salvation and revelation is in accord with the basic thrust of biblical faith. Note the discussion of revelation and knowledge in previous chapter.

78. This same interpretation of theological work is stated by Laurence W. Wood in *Pentecostal Grace* (Wilmore, Ky.: Francis Asbury Publishing Co., 1980), 26: "There is an ontological structure implicit in the functional categories in Scripture. Without this implied ontology there would be no theologizing at all—no Christology, soteriology, ecclesiology, or eschatology. In this respect, one may define theological reflection as making explicit the structure which is implied in the biblical experience of God."

79. *Nature, Man, and God,* 317.

systematic theology. Historically, the formulation of dogma by the Early Church falls into this category. No doctrine of the Trinity, explanation of the relation of the divine and human aspects of Jesus, or other such areas are found in the New Testament, but only the raw materials out of which the theologian seeks to develop Christian wisdom. The unfortunate part of it is that certain groups have crystallized particular historical formulations of this level of theological work and failed to perceive them for what they are, thus reacting to attempts to provide more adequate ontological explanations as attacks upon revealed truths. One strength of John Wesley was his capacity to recognize such distinctions and avoid dogmatism where none was appropriately called for. Compare his sermon "On the Trinity" and chapter 1 of this book.

Thus the full scope of special revelation may be conceptualized as a series of three concentric circles, with the saving significance decreasing as the circles stand further away from the heart of the gospel, which is the redemptive act of God in history: "God was in Christ, reconciling the world unto himself" (2 Cor. 5:19, KJV).

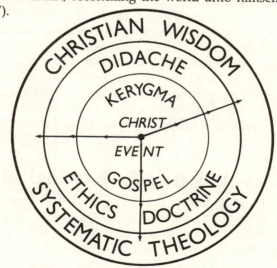

NATURE OF THEOLOGY

General revelation, the intuitive awareness of the Infinite ("The Beyond that is Within"—Underhill), is not enough. However, special revelation does not grow out of general revelation; it is not the logical outcome of a universal knowledge of God. Alan Richardson describes the relation this way: "Special revelation is no mere addition to general revelation, as revealed knowledge was formerly thought to be an addition to natural knowledge; it is rather the means by which the truths given in general revelation can be adequately apprehended and known to be truth."[80] Or, to use Calvin's happy metaphor, it provides the spectacles to enable men to correctly read the book of nature.

General revelation, if left to itself, seems almost universally to lead to a religion of works, or self-salvation. Humanistically produced religion would exalt the category of strength, might, power. This is why "Christ crucified" is a stumbling block (1 Cor. 1:18-25). Who would devise a religion based on weakness, exemplified by a Servant who serves as the paradigm for true power?

Thus revelation in terms of the gospel opens up God's way of salvation in contrast to all humanly devised ways. It involves the entrance of the transcendent God into history, thus making His attitude (or disposition) toward man abundantly clear while not making clear His essential nature (as He is in himself). Faith response to these events brings one into a personal encounter with God and strikes a deathblow to the essence of sin (independence from God), which resists the divine way of salvation, and involves acceptance of a free gift of forgiveness apart from all deserving. All the qualifications prescribed in our previous analysis are thus fulfilled, and the way is now opened for our discussion of Christian wisdom, the process of inferring the fuller implications of the basic revelation.

Revelation as Eschatological

Throughout our discussion of revelation, we have noted the impossibility of defining revelation as "making clear," since the transcendence of God forbids the possibility of eliminating the element of mystery. Paradox is an essential aspect of putting the self-disclosure of God into words. While there is the reality of the existential encounter and the certainty of God's disposition toward us in the gospel, it remains true that we always "see through a glass, darkly" (1 Cor. 13:12, KJV).

---

80. *Apologetics*, 134.

Paul, however, points to the "beatific vision," which shall be "face to face." Thus the "already" of revelation is balanced by the "not yet." While it would be presumptuous to make concrete assertions about the nature of this eschatological encounter, it seems safe to assume that in some way much of the mystery that surrounds our finite knowledge of God will be dispelled.

It was one of the central convictions of the early believers that the glory of God (His self-revelation accommodated to human limitation; see chap. 4), which had appeared in transience on the face of Moses, representing the old covenant, had appeared in a more permanent and final way in the person of Christ (2 Cor. 4:6; 5:1-18). However, this glory was still veiled because of man's finitude. This glory shone forth in a brilliant outflashing at the Transfiguration, and this disclosure was sufficient until the day dawn and the daystar of the unveiled Parousia glory arise (2 Pet. 1:16-19). Thus the "glory," which is the biblical way of referring to the transcendent One's self-accommodation to man's knowledge, is likewise eschatological in the New Testament context.

This "yet to be" aspect of our knowledge of God correlates with the future dimension of salvation. As noted earlier, revelation properly understood involves salvation, since to know God in the biblical sense is to be saved. Thus final salvation doubless entails also a more profound level of knowing. Therefore revelation partakes of the same dual character as other aspects of the new age. It involves a present actuality and a future consummation.

PART **III**

The Doctrines
of God
the Sovereign

The Nature
and Attributes
of God

According to our definition of theology, the whole of the subject is concerned with the doctrine of God. However, this doctrine must still be treated in a specialized way. We have already discussed several facets of theology in this special sense in connection with the analysis of our knowledge of God, but there are many other truths commonly subsumed under the rubric of the doctrine of the Father, or God the Sovereign.

The Central Importance
of the Doctrine

Bishop J. S. Whale tells the well-known story of the young curate who once called upon William Stubbs, bishop of Oxford, to ask him for advice about preaching. The great man was silent for a moment and then replied: "Preach about God; and preach about 20 minutes." This correctly identifies not only the substance of Christian preaching but also the central tenet of Christian doctrine. The traditional way of making this point is to affirm that the doctrine of God is first in the *ordo essendi* of doctrines. All other truths ultimately root in a sound understanding of the Divine Being. It is as H. F. Rall puts it: "God is not one of our religious beliefs; he is *the* belief. He is not one doctrine; he is the heart of all doctrine."[1]

All the ancient and modern heresies alike stem from a faulty understanding of God.[2] Each of the Christological heresies results from a nonbiblical view of the divine nature. Faulty atonement theories fall short at this point as well. Many teachings that, from the Wesleyan perspective, are unacceptable are often logical corollaries of a doctrine of God that is at variance with the Wesleyan view. For example, the Calvinistic doctrines of election and predestination are more logical inferences from a particular understanding of the divine nature than the result of exegesis of biblical passages. We have already seen (chap. 4) the crucial significance of one's understanding of the divine nature in relation to the question of divine revelation.

Despite its cruciality, no doctrine has experienced more difficulty in the hands of theologians and philosophers during the past few decades. Developments in theology, philosophy, and culture have made belief in God problematic for many. The storm of controversy that arose over the publication of Bishop John A. T. Robinson's *Honest to God* in 1963 was symptomatic of these developments, all of which may be summarized as secularism. The most extreme expression of it was in the so-called Death of God theology, with several attempts made out of this milieu to formulate an "atheistic Christianity."

It is interesting that much of this phenomenon came as an aftermath of the work of Karl Barth, whose emphasis on radical transcendence seemed to lay the groundwork for the denial of God.[3] The following paragraph from John Macquarrie shows how Barth's position, when the balance Barth sought to achieve is seen in an imbalanced way, could logically lead to this kind of conclusion:

---

1. *The Meaning of God* (Nashville: Abingdon-Cokesbury Press, 1925), 6-7.
2. Cf. Alan Richardson, *Creeds in the Making*.
3. But see *Church Dogmatics* 2.1.313-14, where Barth says: "It is just the absoluteness of God properly understood which can signify not only His freedom to transcend all that is other than Himself, but also His freedom to be immanent within it, and at such a depth of immanence as simply does not exist in the fellowship between other beings." However, it should be noted that this is an immanence of communion, but not "within the fabric of history."

Barth's criticism of religion is simply a consequence of his Christocentrism. If God has made himself known exclusively in Jesus Christ and the Biblical tradition, then there can be no truth in the non-Christian religions, and "religion" must be defined, however tendentious or arbitrary the definition may appear to be, as man's attempt to grasp God. This in turn is interpreted along the lines of Feuerbach to mean that the "religious" conceptions of God are simply idols projected by our own minds. Of course, Barth makes an exception for God, the Father of Jesus Christ. This God is the God of revelation, not of religion. But the time would surely come when people would ask: "Well, why make this exception?"[4]

We have earlier surveyed the pendulum-like movement in the history of Christian thought between immanence and transcendence. The immanental emphasis of liberalism was reacted to and replaced by the stress on transcendence by the neoorthodox movement. Both had adverse effects on the doctrine of God and point to the necessity of formulating a theology that maintains a balanced relationship between the two.

T. F. Torrance refers to the distinction of Duns Scotus between *theologia in se* (the knowledge that God has of himself) and *theologia nostia* (knowledge of God as is mediated to us within the bounds and conditions of our life in this world) and comments:

> Restricted and circumstantial as it is, and refracted as it is through the damaging effect of sin upon our relation with God, it is nevertheless grounded in God himself, who infinitely transcends what we can conceive of him within the limits of our creaturely minds. If our theology were not interpenetrated at least in some real measure by God's knowledge of himself, it could not be real knowledge of God; nor could it be genuinely our theology if it were not concerned with knowledge granted to us within the bounds of our finite order of existence and thought.[5]

In a word, if we would speak meaningfully about *God,* we must speak in terms of transcendence; conversely, if we are to speak meaningfully about God, we must speak in immanental terms.

According to Peter C. Craigie, this is precisely the way in which the Old Testament conceives the divine self-disclosure: "The primary affirmation concerning God in the Old Testament is that

4. *God and Secularity,* vol. 3 of *New Directions in Theology Today* (Philadelphia: Westminster Press, 1967), 41.
5. *Reality and Evangelical Theology* (Philadelphia: Westminster Press, 1982), 22.

although he is transcendent, the living experience of the immanent God is to be found within the fabric of human history."[6]

Raising these issues leads to a consideration of two ways of thinking about God. One has been referred to as the "immobilist" view, while the other is designated the "out-going."[7] We surveyed the way in which these two understandings relate to our knowledge of God in an earlier discussion of that topic, and we saw the dangers of an exclusivist interpretation of God in terms of either one view or the other. Another way of addressing the same question is in terms of time and eternity. If "eternity" is understood as timelessness, there is no possibility of an interrelation between the two. In that case there would be an "infinite, qualitative distinction between time and eternity" (Kierkegaard/Barth).

But in the Hebrew view, eternity is not timelessness but unending time.[8] The view that eternity is timelessness is usually identified with Greek thought, but while this is generally true, it is not universally the case. Plato's Form of the Good (which is not God, in his philosophy) and Aristotle's Unmoved Mover provide the classical examples here. The balance in biblical thought allowing the "immanence of the transcendent" (William Temple's phrase) creates the possibility of genuine knowledge of God, and that is reflected most clearly in the Old Testament. Thus we now turn to

The Biblical Background

Wiley makes the point that it is impossible to define God, since to do so sets limits upon Him (*CT* 1:217). This principle adequately appropriates the actual practice of biblical thought as is apparent in the Old Testament, since it makes no effort to provide an abstract, formal definition of God. The nearest approach to a definition is found in the words, "I am Yahweh thy God, who brought thee out of the land of Egypt" (Exod. 20:2, cf. ASV). In other words, the God of Israel is identified as the Agent in a historical event that informs the existence and destiny of Israel.

Otto J. Baab concurs by emphasizing a different aspect of the

---

6. *The Problem of War in the Old Testament* (Grand Rapids: Wm. B. Eerdmans Publishing Co., 1978), 39.

7. A. Boyce Gibson, "The Two Ideas of God," *Philosophy of Religion*, ed. John E. Smith (New York: Macmillan Co., 1965), 61-68.

8. Ladd, *Theology*, 47.

same point: "Perhaps the most typical word for identifying the God of the Old Testament is the word 'living.' . . . This signifies the God who acts in history, who performs mighty deeds of deliverance, and who manifests his power among men."[9] This truth is poignantly presented in Jer. 10:10, where the context draws a contrast between the living God who speaks and acts, and idols who do neither: "But the Lord is the true God; he is the living God and the everlasting King." The term is used at least 60 times in a formal oath, connected with the personal name of the Hebrew God (Yahweh). (Cf. Judg. 8:19; Ruth 3:13; 1 Sam. 19:6; 20:21.)

Therefore God, in the Old Testament, is not simply an idea but an experienced reality acting in and through human life. In fact, the Hebrew language is ill equipped to reflect other than dynamic modes of thought. Norman Snaith notes: "The Hebrew does not say that Jehovah *is,* or that Jehovah *exists,* but that He *does.* Properly speaking, the Hebrew verb *hayah* does not mean 'to be,' so much as 'to come to be.' Hebrew has no real verb of 'being,' but one of 'becoming.'"[10] God is not confined and cannot be confined to a verbal definition or an abstract concept but is the living God who delivers Israel.

In addition to "living" as a biblical appellation, "holiness" is also attached to the God of the Old Testament. The Hebrew word *qodesh,* translated as "holiness," is derived from a root meaning "apart" or "separateness." It is "holiness" that conveys the idea of transcendence, whereas "living," or the "acting God," implies immanence.

Holiness is that essential character of Deity that places God in a completely exclusive category and sharply distinguishes Him from the human and the naturalistic. Isaiah 6 gives us an insight into the biblical understanding of the nature of the holiness of God. It did not take the form of sheer, paralyzing power but was revealed for redemptive purposes. It provided genuine self-

9. *The Theology of the Old Testament* (New York: Abingdon Press, 1949), 24-25. "Strictly speaking, the Bible does not present a doctrine of God but a way of thinking about God. . . . As a matter of fact, they were not interested in exploring the nature of God. The very thought of attempting to describe what God is in himself would have seemed to them impious (Dt. 29:29). All that their statements imply as to the essential nature of God—and, to be sure, it is a great deal—is that the capacity for personal relations with man is included in the nature of Deity." Millar Burrows, *Outline of Biblical Theology* (Philadelphia: Westminster Press, 1956), 63.
10. *The Distinctive Ideas of the Old Testament* (London: Epworth Press, 1944), 48.

knowledge based upon God's own nature and will. Isaiah's ethical and personal reaction could "hardly have occurred had the holiness involved in the divine nature appeared simply as undifferentiated, super-natural power."[11]

The holiness of God is the theological basis for the Old Testament's affirmations about the jealousy of God. Many have objected to the ascription of this characteristic to God on the basis that it is an unworthy anthropopathism (applying human emotions to God). But this criticism fails to recognize that there are two possible meanings to the symbol. First, it may refer to a feeling of envy, for example, of someone else's accomplishments; and second, it may refer to the intention to maintain one's rights to the exclusion of others' (cf. Num. 11:29; 2 Sam. 21:2). It is clearly the second sense that the Bible has in mind when it declares that He is God and will not share His glory with anyone else. His holiness gives God the right to claim undivided or unshared love and worship.

This emphasis on exclusiveness distinguishes the worship of Yahweh from the "tolerance and easy balance of opposing forces characteristic of polytheism."[12] In a pantheon of gods, no individual deity may claim exclusive rights; but Yahweh can demand: "Thou shalt have no other gods besides me" (Exod. 20:3, ASV margin).

In the practical outworking of Israel's national life this principle called for an exclusive relation with Yahweh as it concerned alliances with the great empires of the ancient Near East. To depend upon such treaties would imply that God was not strong enough to protect her. That was the theological basis for the great prophets' (e.g., Isaiah) opposition to making treaties for purposes of national security with Egypt, Assyria, or other nations.

Joshua 24 provides a vivid example of the truth of Yahweh's demand for exclusive worship. In response to Joshua's challenge to serve the Lord, the people make an affirmative reply. But Joshua responds with a rejection of their commitment: "You cannot serve the Lord; for he is a holy God; he is a jealous God" (v. 19). The context makes it clear that they had agreed to serve Yahweh *alongside* their other deities. But Joshua pointed out the impossibility of

---

11. Baab, *Theology*, 37.
12. G. E. Wright, *The Old Testament Against Its Environment* (Chicago: Henry Regnery Co., 1950), 38.

such a shared allegiance and insisted that to serve Him would entail putting away all other gods (cf. v. 23).

The holiness of God also stands as a barrier to any approach to God by the unholy. In certain difficult passages of the Old Testament, there appears an irrational element that seems primarily related to the idea of ceremonial impurity (e.g., 2 Samuel 6). But the ethical understanding prevails in much Old Testament thought, especially among the classical prophets. This theme appears in the worship literature, where the necessity of purity is confessed as essential to standing in the presence of the Holy One (Psalm 24). The reverse side of the emphasis highlights the judgmental consequences to those who do not acknowledge God's rightful demands upon their lives. Both sides are seen in Isa. 33:14-16: "The sinners in Zion are afraid; trembling has seized the godless: 'Who among us can dwell with the devouring fire? Who among us can dwell with everlasting burnings?' He who walks righteously and speaks uprightly . . . will dwell on the heights."

Another central emphasis of Old Testament theology is the unity of God: There is one God. The golden text of the Hebrew faith affirms: "Hear, O Israel: The Lord our God is one Lord" (Deut. 6:4; the Shema). In philosophical language, this implies monotheism.

Old Testament scholars have debated the question of whether the Hebrew faith was monotheistic from the beginning or if this understanding emerged after a period of development. The old *Religionsgeschichte* school (cf. chap. 1) interpreted it as the result of an evolutionary process. Another school of thought represented by W. F. Albright, John Bright, and G. Ernest Wright argues that Moses was a monotheist, and thus it was the genius of Israel's faith from the earliest days to believe in one God. The issue partly hangs on critical questions about the dating of certain Old Testament documents. The soundest view seems to be that the central core of Hebrew theology was monotheistic from the earliest times. Some qualifications have to be made, however. The popular mind was clearly henotheistic (belief in many gods but the worship of one god) until the time of the Babylonian Captivity. No other conclusion is possible in the light of the continued turning away from Yahweh to the worship of other gods by the Hebrews as recorded in the historical literature. But popular conceptions of the people do not invalidate the central conception of God as One as the normative Old Testament faith.

These three major theological affirmations—that God is living, holy, and One—provide the biblical basis for the claim that the transcendent One (holy) is at the same time the immanent One (living) because He is One. While there are paradoxical elements thus injected into our understanding of God, biblical faith experiences both as essential to its object. It is this conviction that informed the decision of the Early Church to oppose Marcion's dualism and embody that rejection in the Apostles' Creed: "I believe in God the Father Almighty, Maker of heaven and earth."

Augustine gave classical expression to the paradoxical movement of our understanding raised by the biblical picture of God when experienced in human life:

> You, my God, are supreme, utmost in goodness, mightiest and all-powerful, most merciful and most just. You are the most hidden from us and yet the most present amongst us, the most beautiful and yet the most strong, ever enduring and yet we cannot comprehend you. You are unchangeable and yet you change all things. You are never new, never old, and yet all things have new life from you. You are the unseen power that brings decline upon the proud. You are ever active, yet always at rest. You gather all things to yourself, though you suffer no need. [13]

The question then arises: What is the character, or nature, of this one God to whom the Old Testament bears witness? For the decisive Christian answer to this question, we turn to the New Testament, where we see the character of God portrayed in the person and teaching of Jesus and elaborated in the Epistles. Here we learn that the central Christian affirmation about this one God is that His "name and nature is love" (Wesley).

Jesus' teaching about God stands in greater contrast to first-century Judaism than to the Old Testament, but in contrast to both He makes God's nature as love His central emphasis. Dale Moody rightly declares, "As holiness is the starting point, so love is the high point in the Biblical unfolding of the nature of God."[14]

Many scholars agree that the one new characteristic of God that is introduced by Jesus is the Fatherhood of God. But even this is not entirely new, since the idea appears in the Old Testament (cf. Hosea). However, the full depths of its meaning are not brought to

---

13. *Confessions* I.4.
14. *The Word of Truth: A Summary of Christian Doctrine Based on Biblical Revelation* (Grand Rapids: Wm. B. Eerdmans Publishing Co., 1981), 104.

light there. The significance of this symbol must be derived from its use in Jesus' day and not from contemporary implications, since these may be quite different. In Jesus' day it was a man's world. The father in those days was the absolute power in the household. He was the patriarch who dispensed love and justice. Thus when Jesus used the word "Father," His hearers understood Him to be speaking of at least two aspects of God's nature: that God is both just and loving.[15]

Love thus becomes the unifying focus that brings together in creative tension the paradoxical elements in our experience of God. All the affirmations of the Christian faith about God are clustered around the central idea of God's *agapē*. The Johannine statement stands as definitive: "God is love *[agapē]*" (1 John 4:8).[16] The basis for this claim is that the character of God is decisively defined by Jesus Christ and His work.

The Wrath of God

When God's essential nature is seen to be love *(agapē),* it immediately sets up a tension in our conception of God. Love appears to exclude the wrath of God, but the latter is an unavoidable aspect of the biblical revelation. Is God divided against himself? Biblical faith cannot allow that conclusion. Thus we need to look in another direction. Martin Luther suggests the classical way to address this apparent tension by speaking of love (gospel) as the proper work of God, while wrath (law) is His foreign work. Thus wrath is the "dark side of love" or the "back of God's hand" (Barth). It is love's opposition to evil (Aulen). The tendency among some has been to separate love and wrath and allow one to exclude the other in principle, if not in expression. Donald G. Bloesch identifies this as one reason "why Evangelicalism fell into partial eclipse in the early twentieth century: Among the doctrinal distortions that the older Evangelicalism promoted, in one form or another, were . . . the separation of God's love from his wrath."[17]

C. H. Dodd's exegetical work has called attention to an impor-

---

15. William A. Spurrier, *Guide to the Christian Faith* (New York: Charles Scribner's Sons, 1952), 91.

16. On his *Notes* on 1 John 4:8, Wesley says that God's love is "His darling, His reigning attribute, the attribute that sheds an amiable glory on all His other perfections."

17. *Essentials of Evangelical Theology* 1:2-3.

tant aspect of the biblical witness. He has noted in his commentary on Romans that Paul never uses the verb "to be angry" with God as Subject. Other attitudes are so used, for example, "God loves us" (cf. 2 Thess. 2:16; Eph. 2:4) and "God is faithful" (1 Cor. 1:9; 10:13; cf. 1 Thess. 5:24); but God is never made the Subject of "to be angry." He concludes from this evidence that "wrath is not to be understood as a feeling or attitude of God toward us (as love and mercy should properly be) but rather as some process or effect of human sin; mercy is not the effect of human goodness but is inherent in the character of God."[18]

Although G. E. Ladd registers some disagreement with Dodd's suggestion that the wrath of God is impersonal, he basically agrees with his interpretation of the evidence.

> The New Testament concept of the wrath of God is not to be understood as equivalent to the anger of pagan deities, which could be turned to good will by suitable offerings. . . . In Paul, the wrath of God is not an emotion telling how God feels, it tells us rather how he acts toward sin—and sinners.[19]

Martin Luther quite clearly identifies the "wrath of God" as our experience of God's love in a state of disobedience. *Coram Deo* (before God) when faith is absent, the presence of God creates fear, as in the case of Adam and Eve hiding from the Lord in the garden following their act of disobedience.

H. Orton Wiley affirms the emphasis we are suggesting here and states: "The Christian position generally, is that wrath is but the obverse side of love and necessary to the perfection of the Divine Personality, or even to love itself" (*CT* 1:385).

Holiness, Love, and Attribution

In the light of the claim that the essential nature of God is holy love, we may now address the traditional question of the attributes of God. This discussion needs to first take account of the way the holiness of God informs the attempt to ascribe attributes to God. There are three theories that have been offered by theologians: (1) holiness is one attribute among others; (2) holiness is the sum total of all the attributes; or (3) holiness is the background for all the attributes. Our earlier analysis of the meaning of holiness quickly

18. *The Epistle of Paul to the Romans* (London: Collier, 1959), 47-50.
19. *Theology*, 407.

eliminates the first of these options. To adopt the second would evacuate the holiness of God of any decisive significance. Therefore the third option is the most theologically helpful.

It is imperative, in interpreting holiness as the background of the attributes, to recognize that the root meaning of holiness as "separateness" is understood in biblical theology as "otherness" rather than "remoteness." Thus the spatial metaphor of transcendence is transmuted into a religious category rather than a merely metaphysical one. This truth is embodied in the words of Isaiah the prophet as he proclaims the futility of Judah's dependence upon Egyptian help in a revolt against Assyria rather than trusting God: "Woe to them that go down to Egypt for help; and stay on horses, and trust in chariots, because they are many; and in horsemen, because they are very strong; but they look not unto the Holy One of Israel, neither seek the Lord! . . . Now the Egyptians are men, and not God; and their horses flesh, and not spirit" (Isa. 31:1, 3, KJV).

Maintaining this religious significance of the holiness of God is imperative to avoid obliterating the distinction between the human and the divine. "It guarantees that every affirmation about God retains its purely religious character,"[20] in contrast to a metaphysical character. It furthermore guards against misinterpreting sin in a moralistic direction and thus losing its distinctly religious character. This occurs as the result of a too-quick-and-easy ethicizing of the concept of holiness.

> Holiness is not primarily a moral attribute, as if it meant merely the perfect goodness of some superbeing with a white beard. Rather it refers to that absolute "otherness" which distinguishes the divine from all that is creaturely, and so characterized every aspect of God. Holiness is the word that refers to the *divine* aspect of any attribute asserted of deity, the quality which makes any attribute essentially different in God than in other things, the quality that raises anything, be it power or love or anger, to the *nth* degree when it is applied to God.[21]

Maintaining the religious character of holiness also "stands as a sentinel against all eudaemonistic and anthropocentric interpretations of religion."[22] If God's godness is retained by a proper understanding of holiness, religion cannot be seen as serving hu-

20. Aulen, *Faith of the Christian Church*, 104.
21. Gilkey, *Maker of Heaven and Earth*, 89.
22. Aulen, *Faith of the Christian Church*, 105.

man selfish interests and being primarily a means to human happiness. God cannot be domesticated to such ends.

God's otherness prohibits interpreting His character and nature in complete continuity with human categories. Such categories, when ascribed to God, are always more than the same qualities when they are attributed to finite reality (see discussion of religious language in chap. 4), but they are not in radical discontinuity either. The holiness of God serves as the barrier to reducing theology to anthropology.

This truth suggests that holiness both defines and warns against idolatry. Linguistic idolatry "arises when some image or concept of God gets absolutized, for no idea of God can be equal to the ineffable mystery of the reality."[23] Other forms of idolatry occur when finite objects, even if seen to be mediating the holiness of God, are elevated to a position of ultimate significance.

In this light, it becomes apparent that all attributes used of God will have to be prefaced by the qualification of God's holiness. We have noted above that the unique character of God in Christian theology is love. But love is susceptible to being reduced to human sentimentality. Therefore, even the central declaration of Christian faith about God must be qualified as "holy love."[24]

With "love" qualified in this way, we may now turn to the analysis of the nature of God from this perspective and finally observe how the traditional way of attribution takes shape when the theological concept of God as "holy love" serves as a control rather than some version of Greek ontology, as has too often been the case in the history of Christian theology.

The term that the writers of the New Testament chose to use to refer to the kind of love that God is, is *agapē*. Perhaps one of the values of this choice was its openness to new content. It had not been widely used in the ancient world and was open to being informed with God's kind of love. All other forms of love (represented by *eros, philia, storgē*) were to some degree motivated by the object loved. That which was loved contributed something to the one who loved. Thus love generally was based upon some form of need in the lover and a corresponding attractiveness in the object or person loved that at least offered the possibility of meeting that

---

23. Macquarrie, *God and Secularity*, 111.
24. Compare the discussion of G. E. Ladd on this qualification in relation to justification. *Theology*, 445.

need. By contrast, God's *agapē* was not generated by the potentiality of its object to meet a need in God. It arose out of the fullness of the Divine Being. It is disinterested love, concern for the well-being of the object, in no way based on the worth of the object. "We love Him because He first loved us" (1 John 4:19, NKJV). "God commendeth his love toward us, in that, while we were yet sinners, Christ died for us" (Rom. 5:8, KJV).

Love becomes the dynamic of God's self-disclosure. He is not discovered by human insight but comes to us out of His own initiative. On the basis of this aspect of God's nature, faith affirms that while God cannot reveal to us His full glory, because in our finitude we would be destroyed by its brightness, His character is faithfully made known, so that He is not in himself other than He reveals himself to be in relation to our understanding. In this sense holiness is qualified by love as much as His love is qualified by His holiness.

Love and Passivity

Identifying the decisive character of God as *agapē* speaks directly to the ancient discussion over God's passivity. Under the influence of Greek thought the early fathers shrank from the idea that God could suffer, and they dubbed one of the early Christological heresies, Patripassianism. To show that a particular interpretation led logically to the conclusion that God would suffer was sufficient to condemn it.

This fear of taking seriously the idea of love with its full implications was reflected in the Thirty-nine Articles of the Church of England, which defined God as "without . . . passions." This article was adopted into the Twenty-five Articles of Methodism, but in 1786 the Methodist bishops omitted the word "passions."[25] Did this reflect a firmer grasp of a more biblical concept of God? As Geddes MacGregor puts it: "To love is to suffer, and therefore to say that love is essential to the Being of God is to say that in one way or another suffering is essential to his nature."[26] We will later be able to see how crucial this fact is in developing the doctrine of the Atonement.

---

25. Wiley, *CT* 1:218.
26. *He Who Lets Us Be* (New York: Seabury Press, 1975), 4.

Love and Will

An important consideration for Wesleyan theology is the relation of God's love to His will. This is not unrelated to the question debated in the Middle Ages between the intellectualists and the voluntarists. In fact, it is an aspect of that larger debate.

That whole discussion involved the rather questionable procedure of projecting human psychological distinctions upon the cosmic screen of the Divine Reality. At the human level, it is a valid question to consider whether the primary motivation of behavior is the will or the intellect. Does one act volitionally based upon the dictates of knowledge, or is the will incapable of choosing what it knows to be good apart from a divine healing, as Augustine had insisted (cf. his treatise *On the Spirit and the Letter*)?

When the discussion was transferred to God, the issue became: Is an act good because God wills it, or does He will it because it is good? Which is prior, His will or His nature? The voluntarists affirmed the former, the intellectualists the latter. Mr. Wesley, with one deft stroke, pointed out the futility of the whole debate:

> It seems, then, that the whole difficulty arises from considering God's will as distinct from God: otherwise it vanishes away. For none can doubt but God is the cause of the law of God. But the will of God is God Himself. It is God considered as willing thus or thus. Consequently, to say that the will of God, or that God Himself, is the cause of the law, is one and the same thing.[27]

Nonetheless, the traditional way of putting the matter serves to highlight a significant theological perspective when the question of God's love is cast in these terms. Is love a manifestation of His nature or His will? The Calvinist sees it to be an expression of His will; Wesleyan theology, a manifestation of His nature.[28]

The position that love is an expression of God's will comports well with the teaching of particular predestination. It can affirm without qualms as literally true such declarations as "Jacob have I loved, but Esau have I hated" (Rom. 9:13, KJV). No theological problem is posed, because God can freely extend His love to, or withhold it from, anyone He chooses.

The Wesleyan holds that God's love is a manifestation of His nature, and consequently it is universal rather than selective. He

---

27. *StS* 2:50.
28. J. Glenn Gould, *The Precious Blood of Christ* (Kansas City: Beacon Hill Press, 1959), 71.

extends His "arm" in mercy and reconciliation to all without discrimination. None is excluded, for this would involve a violation of God's own nature. God, being who He is, "loves each one of us as if there were only one of us to love" (Augustine). It is this aspect of the doctrine of God that provides the theological grounding for the Wesleyan doctrine of prevenient grace. That this love is "holy love" guards this fundamental truth against a perversion into actual rather than potential universalism.

The conclusion of this whole discussion is that both holiness and love stand apart as other than mere attributes of God. Together they provide the fundamental presuppositions in the light of which all attribution must be made. When taken seriously, they would entail some modification of the traditional way of developing the attributes of God, which has been more often informed by Greek rationalism than biblical faith.

Wiley, in discussing the unifying character of God that provides harmony among the attributes, says: "If God is Father, holy love must be supreme and central. Indeed, love is so central, that the other attributes of personality may be regarded as love energizing in certain directions. . . . Holy love must occupy the central place in our knowledge of God."[29]

The Problem of Attribution

Before pursuing the analysis of particular attributes, something should be said about the whole concept of attribution as it relates to the Divine Reality. Wiley argues that the attributes are not rationalistically apprehended but are the result of "analyzing the personal knowledge of God which has been revealed to us in Christ through the Spirit." This means that personal knowledge is prior, primary, and unitary, as is our knowledge of other persons. Or, in his words, "it is our personal knowledge of God that makes possible a true knowledge of His attributes, and not a mere rationalistic summing up of the attributes that gives us our knowledge of God" (CT 1:323-24).

If, as Wiley argues, this personal (existential) knowledge is the experiencing of God as love, then logically all the particular attributes should be interpreted as expressions of love. This will clearly

---

29. CT 1:324. Cf. also 367: "We may with perfect propriety say, therefore, that the nature of God consists in holy love, but in this statement we neither identify nor confuse the terms."

give them a radically different cast from the rationalistic interpretations found in much traditional theology.

An additional comment seems in order concerning the philosophical underpinning of any discussion of the attributes of God.
The way much theology of the precontemporary period handled
this matter was in terms of the ancient and venerable, but now
philosophically outmoded, concept of substance. Technically the
term *substance* suggested an underlying substratum of that which
sustained attributes. It appeared possible to some to describe the
qualities of this underlying substance that existed apart from the
attributes that it sustained. Even though it seems reasonable to
common sense, contemporary philosophical modes of thought
have moved away from the category of substantiality (see discussion in the Preface). The result has been that philosophical
models, involving more dynamic concepts, have moved closer to
biblical thought than was true when the heritage of classical Greek
thought prevailed. As a consequence of this shift in philosophical
perspective, contemporary theism has tended to the genuinely religious significance of the attributes of God as the Source of all
beings.[30]

Classification of the Attributes

In general, the biblical understanding of God's holiness calls into
question the traditional distinction between the so-called natural
and moral attributes of God. Bishop Aulen insists that while such
a division may be serviceable for a rationally constructed idea of
God (rational metaphysics), it "is entirely inappropriate to a Christian conception of God."[31] In fact, the so-called natural attributes
are also termed by some as metaphysical.

The explanation of the two categories of attributes by Wiley
and Culbertson serve adequately to describe the meaning of the
designations as well as to highlight their inadequacy:

> The natural attributes are those which are essential to His
> nature, and which do not involve the exercise of His will. . . .
> The moral attributes are qualities of His character, and involve
> the exercise of His will. . . . The weakness of this classification
> is the fact that it gathers in one group the relative attributes of

---

30. Cf. Macquarrie, *God and Secularity*, 118-19.
31. *Faith of the Christian Church*, 104.

God in His relation to creation and those which apply to Him apart from His relation to the world.[32]

It has already been established that we cannot know God as He is in himself but only as He makes himself known (*CT* 1:217-18). Thus, even if the psychologizing distinction between His nature and will is allowed, it is apparent that to speak of natural attributes in the above fashion is logically contradictory. By disallowing such a distinction of psychological functions within God, the basis for the distinction disappears. We are then required to interpret the so-called natural or metaphysical attributes in terms of God's nature as holy love. To do so casts them in a different mode and turns them into truly religious categories.

Sovereignty and Love

The metaphysical attributes are often understood as expressions of the sovereignty of God and introduce the question of God's power. If the nature of God is revealed as love, a tension is immediately created. The history of Christian thought records numerous attempts to resolve the problem rationalistically, with one pole usually suppressing the other. The nominalist theology of Scotus and Occam, which made the will of God undefinable, capricious, and despotic, obscured love in favor of power. Marcion, in rejecting the Creator God of the Old Testament in favor of the God of love of the New, dissolved the tension in an equally unsatisfactory way.

The problem is intensified when it is viewed in terms of the problem of evil. From the time of Epicurus, the poles of love and power have been posed as horns of a dilemma with which faith struggles. Various proposals for a "finite" God have given up the claim of power in order to retain God's character of love (e.g., Edgar Sheffield Brightman and Edwin Lewis). Others have sought in various ways to deny the reality of evil as a way of avoiding the dilemma.

A doctrine of creation that avoids absolute idealism and affirms the reality of created being inevitably raises problems for the idea of absolute sovereignty. Nels F. S. Ferré puts this dilemma as follows: "If God is power, and if there is any power beside Him, He cannot be all-powerful. If, on the contrary, there is no power out-

---

32. H. Orton Wiley and Paul T. Culbertson, *Introduction to Christian Theology* (Kansas City: Beacon Hill Press, 1946), 89.

side Him at all, we have no reality in history or in nature; and Christian theology is an illusion."[33]

Numerous contemporary theologians have sought to work through the issues by identifying God's sovereignty with the sovereignty of love. Karl Barth writes:

> This power, God, is the power of His free love in Jesus Christ, activated and revealed in him. . . . God's power is not a characterless power; and therefore all those childish questions, whether God can bring it about that twice two equals five, and the like, are pointless, because behind these questions stands an abstract concept of "ability."

He further calls attention to the fact that the Apostles' Creed joins the terms "Father" and "Almighty," the one defining the other, thus qualifying the concept of power by the character of "fatherhood" with all that it entails (see above).[34]

Gustav Aulen affirms the same commitment in the face of attempts to separate power and love. In contradiction to such a division, he says, "Christian faith maintains that divine power is nothing else than the power of love. The power of God is not some obscure and inert fatum [fate or destiny] or a capricious and indefinable will to power, but only and exclusively the power of love."[35]

Ferré demonstrates how interpreting sovereignty as love skirts the dilemma created by a realistic doctrine of creation:

> Suppose, then, that we define power in terms of love. Power is the capacity of love to effect its end. Power is operability. Power is the control and persistence of purpose or force, including the capacity for survival value. Then when God shares His power, He gives of Himself without the limiting of Himself. The nature of love is to bestow freedom on its object.[36]

Aseity. This term is derived from the Latin *a se*, which means "from itself," and is used to suggest that God is the source of His own being. There is no reality beyond Him to which He owes His being, but He is "Being itself." When this is reinterpreted to be the aseity of love, it tells us that God's love is spontaneous. This implies that its cause is contained within itself, not in anything else. It is

33. *The Christian Understanding of God* (Westport, Conn.: Greenwood Press, 1979), 99.
34. *Dogmatics in Outline*, 49.
35. *Faith of the Christian Church*, 123.
36. *Christian Understanding of God*, 101; cf. MacGregor, *He Who Lets Us Be*. Ferré's own theology tends to betray this principle since he sees God, as love, ultimately overriding all human rebellion, i.e., granting universal salvation.

not called forth by external causes but breaks forth by itself. Thus it becomes simply another expression for the idea of the "prevenient grace of God." God's love is always prevenient. Its cause is not outside God, but in God himself and in His nature. To the question, why does God love? there is only one proper answer: because that is the way God acts, and thus that is the way God is. This perfectly exemplifies the meaning of the term *agapē* used by the New Testament writers to set forth the nature of God.

Eternity. In metaphysical categories, this proposed attribute was intended to convey the idea of timelessness in relation to time. This raises the issue of God's relation to time in terms of the question: "Is time real to God?" While the question needs to be addressed in another connection (foreknowledge), we may simply observe here that the biblical picture of God seems rather clearly to suggest that time is indeed real to God. It thus alleviates the dilemma raised by such metaphysical interpretations if we affirm that eternity is the sovereignty of God's love in relation to time. That is to say, "God's love is not transient and changing as is everything that belongs to time."[37]

Omnipotence. Perhaps this is the most all-encompassing of the so-called metaphysical attributes and the one that it seems most religious to ascribe to God. But careful reflection reveals that to apply this idea without qualification drives one into certain ridiculous questions that are meaningless, such as "Can God create a stone so large that He cannot roll it away?" Such questions are based on a conception of the will of God as entirely capricious. In a word, the attribute of omnipotence raises the question of the possibilities of God. The Scripture affirms, for instance, that it is "impossible for God to lie" (Heb. 6:18, KJV; cf. Titus 1:2; 2 Tim. 2:13). Why not? Because it is contrary to His faithfulness.[38]

If God's essential nature is love, then the question of God's possibilities is a question of the possibilities of divine love. God does and wills nothing else than that wherein divine love realizes itself. God can do anything that love can do.

Omnipresence. This subquality of omnipotence likewise leads to perplexing dilemmas when it is interpreted in a meta-

---

37. Aulen, *Faith of the Christian Church*, 127.
38. Anselm, in the 11th century, raised this objection to the ascription of raw power to God. *Cur Deus Homo.* I.xii.

physical mode. If God is equally present everywhere, then He is just as much in the heart of the sinner as the saint. Or prayers that invoke the presence of God are so many meaningless words.

But if God's omnipresence is understood from the point of view of the sovereignty of divine love, these anomalies disappear. It is not a question of whether God fills every space. It means that there is no place closed to the sovereign power of God as holy love.

When the Psalmist exclaimed (139:7-10), "Whither shall I go from thy Spirit? Or whither shall I flee from thy presence? If I ascend to heaven, thou art there! If I make my bed in Sheol, thou art there! If I take the wings of the morning and dwell in the uttermost parts of the sea, even there thy hand shall lead me, and thy right hand shall hold me," he was making a religious assertion of the inescapable presence of God, not proposing some ontological theory. He had become aware that God is present wherever His love realizes itself in grace and judgment.

Omniscience. Numerous problems emerge in this further aspect of omnipotence, that is, the assertion of God's omnipotence in the realm of knowledge. But from the point of view we are exploring, it becomes something entirely different than the abstract idea of His foreknowledge. Rather, it expresses the unerring certainty of God's judgment: "He *knows me.*" His is the all-seeing eye of love that sees everything in a crystal-clear light. Every attempt to hide something from this all-seeing eye is doomed to failure.

Immutability. Changelessness is an attribute traditionally referred to God by both popular piety and classical theology. Biblical support for this quality presents us with an ambiguous picture, however. There is a strong movement in the positive direction; for example, "For I the Lord do not change" (Mal. 3:6). But there are balancing tendencies in the other direction. God is frequently pictured as changing His mind in response to human repentance or other behavior, that is, as dynamic in character. Identifying God's essential nature as holy love provides a way of holding on to both of these scriptural emphases. God's love, His intention for good, never changes, although His response is an interaction with human freedom. Perhaps an even more satisfactory way of describing this attribute is in terms of faithfulness, the faithfulness of love to promises made.[39]

---

39. Cf. a good development of this point in *God, Man, and Salvation,* 155.

God as Personal. Few characteristics ascribed to God have been more vigorously discussed than this one. Much of the debate revolves around the contemporary meaning of the term and whether or not God should appropriately be called a person. This language emerged rather late in the history of Christian theology as applied to God. It was early used of the Persons of the Trinity but not of God himself. The idea seems to be present first in Augustine's Trinitarian doctrine. The chief objection to its use on the part of many theologians is that it implies, in modern use, a limitation that does not seem appropriate to impose upon God as Ultimate Reality. Therefore, it seems sounder to refer to God as personal, that is, as capable of personal relations involving volition and freedom. The biblical picture of God certainly supports this character. Furthermore, if God's nature is love, then it is the very nature of love to establish personal relations.

Paul Tillich provides a strong ontological argument to retain the symbol of "personal" to refer to God. If God is the Ground of Being (Tillich's distinctive appellation for God), then He certainly must be the Ground of the personal and cannot be less than personal himself. He is the "ontological power of personality." He argues the same point from the standpoint of his definition of religion as "ultimate concern": "The symbol 'personal God' is absolutely fundamental because an existential relation is a person-to-person relation. Man cannot be ultimately concerned about anything that is less than personal."[40]

H. H. Farmer argues for the personal nature of God from the biblical evidence:

> Every category, phrase, doctrine, movement of thought [of the New Testament], presupposes and implies the possibility . . . of a personal relationship to a personal God. "God is love and he that abideth in love abideth in God and God abideth in him." "If God so loved us, we ought also to love one another." These statements can have no straightforward meaning if God be not thought of as in some sense personal, constituting with men an ultimate order of personal relations.[41]

The personal dimension of God's nature is fundamental to a proper understanding of many other theological doctrines. If God is conceived in impersonal terms as in the case of many philosoph-

---

40. *Systematic Theology* 1:244. See our discussion of the significance of this understanding of God for the doctrine of revelation in chap. 4.
41. *World and God*, 9.

ical constructs (e.g., Aristotle, Neoplatonism), it becomes impossible to satisfactorily formulate many Christian commitments in the resultant categories. Especially in connection with many implications of the doctrine of creation, we shall see how crucial this issue is. We have already seen (chap. 4) how essential it is to the doctrine of revelation. If God be not personal, vital religion is an impossibility—unless, of course, it is mere autosuggestion. The experience of generations who have encountered a disturbing reality beyond themselves testifies against this. We must now turn to the more explicitly personal characteristics of this personal God.

Biblical Attributes

We have chosen to speak of biblical attributes rather than moral attributes in order to emphasize the nature of the biblical revelation. God is presented in biblical revelation in relation to man rather than as He is in himself or in terms of any rationalistic metaphysics. It is this type of attribution to which dogmaticians have traditionally given the term *moral*. We include here the qualities: righteousness, mercy, truth. The fascinating thing here is that God's acts in history define the meanings of these attributes, and they often turn out to be quite different from the typical Greek connotation of the terms.

An additional uniqueness of these qualities is that they are to be reproduced in the lives of the people of God. This is why some theologians refer to them as the "communicable" attributes. In fact, they come to inform the ethical content of the holiness of God so that they provide a partial definition of what it means to be a "holy people." The development of this understanding of holiness in the Old Testament was most centrally proclaimed by the eighth-century prophets.

Truth. The Hebrew word *emeth,* translated as "truth," is used to describe the character of God's acts. It means that God is not arbitrary or capricious but can be trusted. The word connotes that which is firm, reliable, or trustworthy. Thus God is absolutely true in this sense of being worthy of confidence. He is faithful to His promises.

> The God of *emeth* (II Chron. 15:3; Jer. 10:10) is not the God who is guardian of some abstract entity called "truth" or one who belongs to the realm of eternal truth as over against the

realm of appearance; he is the God who can be trusted, who is able to act, and whose care for his people is true.[42]

This means that there is an ethical element in truth by contrast to the dominant Greek or intellectualistic view. Here truth is the correspondence of an idea or word to its reality. For the rationalist, knowledge of the truth would then be a mental activity, whereas for the biblical understanding it involves obedience in faith. Faith is the proper response to faithfulness.

The Fourth Gospel makes central use of this concept, and the author's use of it "does not indicate so much an intellectual apprehension of theological truth as a full personal apprehension of the saving presence of God that has come to men in Jesus."[43]

Righteousness. This attribute of God provides the basis for the consistent appeal in the Scripture for righteousness among men. As the character of God, it is understood from His acts in history, and originally His righteousness was manifested in the deliverance from Egyptian slavery. Thus the primary meaning is salvific. It refers to God's disposition to "put things right" and thus is nearly equivalent to *justice*. In particular, God showed this righteousness by coming in saving power to those who were needy and helpless. When Pharaoh says to Moses and Aaron (Exod. 9:27) that "the Lord is righteous, and I and my people are wicked" (KJV), he is not using the words in a truly ethical sense. He means that God has proved himself to be the stronger, and Pharaoh and his people the weaker—that is, God has won the victory in the contest of the plagues.[44]

This meaning becomes normative for the Old Testament concept of righteousness. "The original Hebrew words [tsedeq, tsedaqah], therefore, include the idea of God's vindication of the helpless, with the result that already in the Old Testament (Ps. 112:19; Dan. 4:27), they are closely connected with 'showing mercy to the poor.'"[45]

This meaning is reflected throughout the Old Testament in its concern for social justice and especially for those who are dispossessed: "the sojourner, the fatherless, and the widow" (Deut. 14:29;

42. Ladd, *Theology*, 265.
43. Ibid., 268.
44. Norman H. Snaith, "Righteousness," in *A Theological Word Book of the Bible*, ed. Alan Richardson (New York: Macmillan Co., 1950).
45. Ibid.

16:11, 14; et al.). It is seen also in the New Testament in the Book of James, where the writer defines pure religion as visiting "the fatherless and widows in their affliction" (1:27, KJV).

The apostle Paul makes use of the idea of the righteousness of God to refer to His justifying activity toward those who were undeserving, thus preserving the essentially salvific connotation of the idea from the Old Testament. Augustine did the history of Christian thought a great disservice when (in *On the Spirit and the Letter*) he interpreted it to mean the righteousness (ethical) that God bestows upon believers, which then becomes the basis on which God accepts them. In doing so, though explicitly intending to extol the merits of grace, he actually laid the foundation for later Catholic developments that interpreted salvation in terms of works righteousness. One of Martin Luther's contributions was the restoring of the biblical understanding that God's righteousness was His free bestowal of mercy upon the believing sinner who is justified (put right) by faith alone.

In reviewing his pilgrimage, Luther makes the following comment on his great discovery:

> At last, by the mercy of God, meditating day and night, I gave heed to the context of the words, namely, "In it the righteousness of God is revealed, as it is written, 'He who through faith is righteous shall live.'" There I began to understand that the righteousness of God is that by which the righteous lives by a gift of God, namely by faith. And this is the meaning: the righteousness of God is revealed by the gospel, namely, the passive righteousness with which merciful God justifies us by faith, as it is written, "He who through faith is righteous shall live." Here I felt that I was altogether born again and had entered paradise itself through open gates. There a totally other face of the entire Scripture showed itself to me.[46]

Mercy. In the Old Testament, this English word is chiefly a translation of the word *chesed*, one of the truly pregnant terms in the Hebrew theological vocabulary. It is variously rendered in the English versions as "loving-kindness," "steadfast love," or merely "mercy." It is a covenant word and refers to faithfulness to covenant commitments. In this sense it stands close to the idea of *truth*.

The *chesed* of God is seen in contrast to the faithlessness of

---

46. Preface to Latin Writings, from *Martin Luther* (selections), ed. John Dillenberger (Garden City, N.Y.: Doubleday and Co., 1961).

Israel. He has given His word and committed himself, and He has not failed in standing by His word. All that He has promised has been fulfilled. Israel, to the contrary, has broken her promises and turned aside to other lovers. The Book of Hosea is probably the most vivid exposition of these truths.

In speaking of the paradox that appears when one considers the attributes of love and omnipotence in tandem, John Macquarrie says: "The fundamental paradox finds expression in the Christian symbol of the cross, where power and suffering, exaltation and humiliation, are presented together."[47] Once H. Orton Wiley addressed the question: What would happen if all the attributes of God were brought into play at one time? The answer: The cross of Christ. And he quoted Ps. 85:10: "Mercy and truth are met together; righteousness and peace have kissed each other" (KJV).[48]

47. *God and Secularity,* 127.
48. In a lecture at Trevecca Nazarene College, ca. 1947.

CHAPTER

7

The Trinity

The Christian understanding of God includes the belief that there is a threefoldness in the divine nature. In fact, it has been argued that the Christian understanding of God is the belief in the Trinity.[1] This commitment stands between a stark unitarian belief on the one hand and a polytheism on the other, although the difficulty of formulating the doctrine in rational terms has often resulted in its collapse into one or the other of these perversions. But the classical Christian position is firmly committed to a monotheism that manifests itself in a Trinitarian mode of being.

The Trinitarian question is largely one of dogmatic development. Certain elements in the Old Testament may be seen in retrospect to be consistent with a Trinitarian understanding of God, but it is anachronistic to speak of the Trinity in the Old Testament.[2] The New Testament provides the data but does not explic-

---

1. See Norman Pittenger, *The Divine Triunity* (Philadelphia: United Church Press, 1977), 97-99.

2. Cf. Purkiser, Taylor, and Taylor, *God, Man, and Salvation*, 239 ff.; Edmund J. Fortman, *The Triune God* (Philadelphia: Westminster Press, 1972), 3-33. The words of Bernard Lonergan are fitting here: "Too many students have been misled into believing that, by some kind of mysterious intuition, they can see at once in Scripture something which emerged originally only with the passage of time and with great labor; something which many resisted and many denied; something which it took great minds to grasp, and which only gradually received acceptance in the Church." Quoted by Conn O'Donovan in translator's preface of Bernard Lonergan, *The Way to Nicea* (Philadelphia: Westminster Press, 1976), xi.

itly state a doctrine of the Trinity.[3] It does make it necessary to develop such a doctrine, however, because of the clear claims for the deity of the Son.[4] Because of this, the doctrine has been the subject of discussion in theological inquiry from a fairly early time.[5]

Is there a distinctive Wesleyan approach to the question? Not if we think about a particular philosophical formulation. However, Mr. Wesley himself provides us with some suggestions in his sermon "On the Trinity" that could help us identify a uniquely Wesleyan stance with regard to the subject. If we follow his lead, we will find ourselves taking a different tack from the usual evangelical approach.

Wesley hints at three important qualifications on this topic. First, he refuses to insist on anyone adopting a particular "explication" of the doctrine, although he acknowledges that the best he knows is the Athanasian Creed *(Quicunque Vult)*. His reticence is obviously based upon the recognition of the point just made that we are dealing with dogmatic formulations and not explicit biblical teaching. He will not impose, as absolutely essential to Christian faith, the use of terms such as *Trinity* or *Person*, because they are not found in the Scripture. While he has no difficulty in using them himself, he says, "If any man has any scruple concerning them, who shall constrain him to use them? I cannot."

This stance would suggest, not that Wesley would have no interest in ontological discussions, but that they must always be recognized as opinions that cannot be sanctified with divine authority. Such an attitude reflects a position about creedal statements to which Paul Tillich gives the designation the "Protestant Principle."[6] Thus a Wesleyan theology would examine with open

3. Bernard Lonergan draws a brief but illuminating contrast between the biblical data and the doctrinal formulations that emerged later: "Dogmatic development contains two distinct elements, which are also two kinds of transition. The first of these transitions is from one literary genre to another: the scriptures are addressed to the whole person, whereas the councils aim only at enlightening the intellect. The second transition pertains to the order of truth: where scripture presents a multitude of truths, a conciliar pronouncement expresses one single truth, which is related to the many truths of scripture as a kind of principle or foundation." *Way to Nicea,* 1-2.

4. J. S. Whale writes: "You cannot escape some . . . trinitarian formulation if you take the witness of the New Testament seriously." *Christian Doctrine* (London: Cambridge University Press, 1960), 91.

5. Cf. Fortman, *Triune God,* for a thorough and detailed survey of the history of Trinitarian doctrinal discussion from the beginning to the 20th century.

6. Cf. *Dynamics of Faith* (New York: Harper and Row, Publishers, 1957), 29.

mind any ontological proposal, not rejecting it out of hand because of the philosophical milieu out of which it emerges, but never committing itself unequivocally to any. He would, nevertheless, have grounds for rejecting any proposed explication that was not true to the biblical witness. This was, in fact, the strength of the early creeds: Their power is in their rejection of deviations rather than in their positive formulations.

Second, and closely related to the first, Mr. Wesley insists on a recognition of the distinction between the substance of the doctrine and philosophical explications of it. In terms of this distinction one may put the first emphasis differently: The Christian faith is committed to the substance but not to the explication of the substance. An important fact about the nature of theology emerges at this point. The conceptual tools of theological work are derived from philosophy. When one goes beyond biblical language and formulations (and to some extent even when he doesn't), he unavoidably must use the language of philosophy.[7] Efforts at precision in statement drives the theologian to choose the most accurate tool available to him, but always with the recognition that it is both temporally conditioned and somewhat inadequate to the subject. Augustine probably speaks for all those theologians who recognize the profundity of the subject: "Yet, when the question is asked, What three? human language labors altogether under great poverty of speech. The answer, however, is given, three 'persons,' not that it might be (completely) spoken, but that it might not be left (wholly) unspoken."[8]

Wesley puts this distinction another way by referring to the fact and the manner. It is the fact that has been revealed, but the manner has not. It is the former that we are called upon to believe. Consequently we are not asked to believe what we cannot comprehend. (This doubtless reflects Wesley's belief, which he shared with his 18th-century contemporaries, that faith and reason are completely compatible. Cf. his *Earnest Appeal to Men of Reason and Religion.*) He says: "The Bible barely requires you to believe such facts, not the manner of them. Now the mystery does not lie in the *fact* but altogether in the *manner.*"

One may object that it is impossible to distinguish between the substance and the explication. However, Wesley's third empha-

7. Cf. Tillich, *Ultimate Reality.*
8. *On the Trinity* 5.9.10.

sis addresses this matter and brings us to what is perhaps the most distinctive aspect of a uniquely Wesleyan approach. The substance is not ontological but soteriological. Since the word *fundamental* is too ambiguous, he is reticent to declare which are "fundamental" truths, but he does hold that the doctrine of the Father, Son, and Spirit is one that we must know because it has "a close connexion with vital religion." He says further that there is no wisdom in rejecting what God has revealed (the fact), "especially when we consider that what God has been pleased to reveal upon this head, is far from being a point of indifference, is a truth of the last importance. It enters into the very heart of Christianity: *It lies at the root of all vital religion*" (italics added).

In our discussion of the norm for a Wesleyan theology in the Prolegomena, we noted the central position of soteriology as that which brings all Christian doctrines into focus. This analysis further reinforces the validity of that position. Ultimately, Wesleyan theology asks about the saving significance of every Christian doctrine and resists bringing purely speculative questions into the arena of fundamental theology.

The *Manual of the Church of the Nazarene* is informed by this same perspective. The "Agreed Statement of Belief" is prefaced by the stipulation that "we . . . require only such avowals of belief as are essential to Christian experience" (par. 25). This is not saying that believing such doctrinal assertions as are listed will make one a Christian, but rather that such truths must be the case if Christian experience is to be a reality. The first such avowal says: "We believe in one God—the Father, Son, and Holy Spirit" (25.1).

This brings us back once again to the ontological questions and points to the fact that, although we must hold particular explications with a tentative grip, there are ontological dimensions to the subject to which we can and must give legitimate attention. Bishop Whale highlights it this way: "If Jesus really is the Word of God Incarnate, the problems of soteriology ultimately involve insoluble problems of the Trinity and the Incarnation which no theologian worth his salt has ever minimized or neglected."[9]

Hence we propose in this chapter to attempt to survey the major dimensions of the Trinitarian discussion, both historical and contemporary, with the intention of pointing out the soteriological

---

9. *Christian Doctrine*, 91.

substance of those discussions and conclusions where they appear. This cannot be exhaustive because of time and space limitations but will seek to be representative. However, such a survey cannot avoid touching on the philosophical/ontological aspects of the question.

On the Way to Nicea

The period from the close of the New Testament to the Council of Nicea in A.D. 325 may be called the decisive period of the Trinitarian doctrinal development. The question upon which debate focused was the relation of the Logos (who became incarnate in Jesus of Nazareth) to God.[10] Though the discussion had Christological overtones, it was fundamentally a Trinitarian question. With the establishment of the full deity of Christ, the Trinitarian settlement was virtually assured. At a synod called by Athanasius at Alexandria in A.D. 362, the church in the East came to see that what was true of the Son must be also true of the Spirit. The consubstantiality of the Spirit as well as the Son was recognized by the ecumenical Council of Constantinople in 381. With these conclusions, explicit Trinitarianism was complete.[11]

There were three basic commitments of the Early Church that entered into the discussion. They existed in tension with each other, and in fact, they appeared to be mutually exclusive.[12] First there was monotheism, which derived both from the Hebrew faith and the dominant Hellenistic philosophy. "The doctrine of one God, the Father and Creator, formed the background and indisputable premise of the Church's faith."[13]

The second component was its faith in the deity of Christ as witnessed to in the New Testament. Third was their experience that God is Spirit, "immanent in the whole creation as the Hebrews had known him to be, but now newly experienced and understood as the Holy Spirit of the God and Father of the Lord Jesus Christ."[14]

In the process of attempting to produce adequate doctrinal

---

10. "It should be borne in mind that the construction of the doctrine of the Trinity in its theological form did not so much grow out of a consideration of the three Persons, as from a belief in the deity of the Son." CT 1:407.

11. Kelly, *Doctrines*, 263; Whale, *Christian Doctrine*, 110.

12. Whale, *Christian Doctrine*, 101-10.

13. Kelly, *Doctrines*, 87.

14. Whale, *Christian Doctrine*, 108; see note 13 above.

formulations that would do justice to all these commitments, the Church resisted three basic Trinitarian deviations: Sabellianism (Modalism), Subordinationism, and Tritheism.[15] It was, in fact, these deviations that drove the Church toward adequate dogmatic formulations. As Wiley says: "During the apostolic and sub-apostolic period, the doctrine of the Trinity was held in an undogmatic form. There was no scientific or technical expression of it, nor was there any necessity, until heresies arose which demanded exact and guarded statements" (CT 1:405).

Tritheism

This term refers to an interpretation that regards the Father, Son, and Spirit as "three gods" and emphasizes the distinction of Persons in such a way as to obscure the unity of God. It is the commitment to monotheism that guards against such a dissolution.

In early attempts to explain the threeness of God, it was almost inevitable that forms of expression should be used that would be interpreted by at least some as breaking down the "Monarchy." This was the case with Origen's effort to account for the threefold life of God. He chose the term *hypostasis* to identify the Three and used it to mean "individual subsistence" or "individual existent." In attempting to counter Modalism (see below), a teaching that did not distinguish the Three, he sought to draw the distinctions more clearly. Thus there is a strongly pluralistic strain in his Trinitarianism. "The Three, on his analogies, are eternally and really distinct; They are separate hypostases or even, in his crude-sounding language, 'things.'"[16]

It is not surprising that Pope Dionysius was disturbed over what he took to be tritheism and spoke in a public letter against those who preach "three gods since they divide the sacred unity into three different hypostases completely separate from one another."[17] This encounter highlights some important considerations in the development of the Trinitarian understanding, not the least of which is that the theologians of the East stressed the divine plurality, while those in the West emphasized the divine unity.

---

15. Fortman, *Triune God*, 61.
16. Kelly, *Doctrines*, 129-31.
17. Fortman, *Triune God*, 58-59; Kelly, *Doctrines*, 134.

Modalism

A popular and widespread teaching, apparently dominant in the West because of its emphasis on the divine unity, was Modalistic Monarchianism. This interpretation denied any real distinction between God and Christ. It affirmed that Father, Son, and Spirit are merely modes or successive phases of the one God.

The man whose name has been traditionally attached to this view is Sabellius because he gave it its most philosophical expression. He attempted to avoid some of the crudities of earlier, more naive Modalism:

> Sabellius, we are told, regarded the Godhead as a Monad . . . which expressed itself in three operations. He used the analogy of the sun, a single object which radiates warmth and light; the Father was, as it were, the form or essence, and the Son and the Spirit His modes of self-expression. Thus the one Godhead regarded as Creator and Law-giver was Father; for redemption It was projected like the ray of the Sun, and was then withdrawn; then, thirdly, the same Godhead operated as Spirit to inspire and bestow grace.[18]

Another fascinating development out of Modalism came from its apparent logical corollary that it was the Father who suffers on the Cross, dies, and is buried. While there are logical conundrums that may be devised out of this, the repugnant factor to most people was the implication of the suffering God. Thus Cyprian nicknamed the teaching Patripassianism. This makes clear the influence upon early Christianity of a Hellenistic view of Ultimate Reality. Today, with a more biblical understanding, many contemporary theologians gladly embrace the "heresy" of Patripassianism in its implication that God enters empathetically into the human situation, not in its ontological implications.[19]

Subordinationism

In various and sundry forms, this deviation was the most pervasive and widespread of all the pre-Nicene abortive attempts to

---

18. Kelly, *Doctrines*, 122.

19. "The notion that God the Father can suffer is incompatible with any Christian theology that is thoroughly entrenched in a metaphysical system developed in the Platonic tradition; but apart from one element in that tradition there would seem to be no particular objection to it. Those who look to the Bible as their warrant of orthodoxy will note that God is called Father not only because he is Creator but also because the characteristics of a good human father aptly symbolize him." MacGregor, *He Who Lets Us Be*, 51.

explain the relation between the Father and the Son. The apex of its expression that led to its rejection by the Council of Nicea (325) and subsequently by the Councils of Constantinople (381) and Chalcedon (451) was Arianism, but there were several pre-Arian forms that aroused less crisic reactions but that nonetheless were rejected implicitly by the Nicene "settlement."[20]

Dynamic Monarchianism (Adoptionism), though not the earliest, was a popular version of subordinationism that did not exert significant influence upon doctrinal development. It is here that the "monotheistic" commitment of early Christianity obviously created tensions for a Trinitarian understanding.[21] God is understood as the *Monarch* (Tertullian's term) who chose the "mere man," Jesus of Nazareth, as the vehicle of redemption. Its more famous exponent was one Paul of Samosata. We may classify this as a "mundane subordinationism" to distinguish it from later forms; the unique relation between the Father and the Son began in this "mundane" realm of existence.

Behind this solution lay a less-than-Christian doctrine of God. Adoptionism could not conceive of a God who could take the initiative in human salvation, but must wait for a "good man" to come along. Thus the Church rejected it because it brings God in during the process and not at the beginning of the redemptive work. While it could be intellectually satisfying to certain rational presuppositions, it was soteriologically unacceptable.

> Adoptionism does not know of a God who loves sufficiently to take the initiative in world-salvation. It falls short of the Christian doctrine of God in that it does not tell us of a God who was so loving, so interested in the affairs of men, that he conceived a plan for human salvation ... The Christian doctrine of the Person of Christ is in reality a doctrine of God's nature and love.[22]

The *Apologists* (Justin Martyr et al. in the second century) were the first to try to frame an intellectual solution to the question of

---

20. The subsequent controversies, both political and theological, along with the reiterated rejection by the two later councils mentioned above show that the Creed of Nicea was not a "settlement" except in principle.

21. J. N. D. Kelly argues that the concern of the original adoptionists were more influenced by "current philosophical rationalism" than concern to "salvage the Bible dogma that God is One." Thus we have put the term *monotheistic* in quotes to show an adapted sense. The outcome is not affected by the milieu out of which the concern arose. *Doctrines*, 115-16.

22. Richardson, *Creeds in the Making*, 47. Cf. our discussion of God's nature as love in chap. 6.

the relation of Christ to God the Father. They, too, were committed to strict monotheism and attempted to utilize the Logos concept to provide an answer to the question.[23] In doing so, they developed what has been termed the "two-stage theory of the Logos," which was widely held prior to Nicea and culminated in the Arian version that triggered the great controversy.[24] Their presuppositions led them to a "premundane subordinationism" (see above).

The apologists made explicit use of the technical Stoic distinction between the immanent Word and the expressed Word. They buttressed or illustrated this by reference to Old Testament theophanies. The Logos was first immanent within God and then became distinct from Him in much the same sense that human reason is immanent within a man but becomes expressed when a word is spoken. The immanent Word became the expressed Word for purposes of creation, revelation, and redemption. The problematic in this picture is whether the generation occurred at some point before creation or was from all eternity.[25]

These philosophical categories made it possible for the apologists to maintain the preexistence of the Logos as the Father's intelligence or rational thought. He becomes distinct without diminishing the Father, so the Godhead is not divided in such a way as to have two semideities. They used a number of illustrations to demonstrate this point; for example, the sun emits light, which is of the same nature, but the sun is not diminished by the generation of the light. The Logos has preexistence and is of the nature of Deity, so is worthy of worship.

One key question that emerges with the apologists concerns whether the Logos is generated by an act of the Father's will or as an expression of His nature. The apologists themselves seem to

---

23. Kelly, *Doctrines,* 95-101; Fortman, *Triune God,* 44-51.

24. Cf. our discussion of the apologists' view of God and the function of the Logos in relation to the question of divine revelation in chap. 4.

25. There are some ambiguities in Justin that have resulted in differences of opinion about the extent of his subordinationism. J. N. D. Kelly takes the view that it was not critical, based on his belief that Justin taught an eternal generation of the Son. This is questionable, and Fortman is probably sound in his observation: "Was Justin then a subordinationist? He was not a subordinationist in the full Arian sense of the term, for he regarded the Logos-Son not as a thing made, a creature, but as God born of the Father. But if, as is quite probable, the Logos for him was not a divine person from eternity but only became one when He was generated as Son of God shortly before creation in order to be the Father's instrument of creation and revelation, then to this extent the Logos-Son was subordinate to God both as to His person, which was not eternal, and to His office, which was instrumental." *Triune God,* 46.

uniformly attribute it to the will. This actually militates against an essential Trinity and later comes under discussion by Athanasius in his anti-Arian polemics.

An important contribution to the development of Trinitarian dogma was made by Origen, who introduced the famous phrase "the Eternal Generation of the Son." This formulation reflected a measure of subordinationism, since it recognized that the being of the Son is derived from the being of the Father, but clearly the Son is not a created being. The term "generation" was used to avoid the idea that the Son was a creature. That it was an eternal generation cleared up any ambiguity that may have been present in the apologists and attributes not only preexistence to the Logos but also distinct and separate existence, while seeking to maintain His full deity. The contributions of Origen, remarks Wiley, are "of such importance that they mark an epoch in the history of Trinitarianism" (CT 1:413).

Origen's "eternal generation" has two meanings: First, the generation has no beginning. "There is never a time when the Son was not the Son. . . . there was not a time when He was not" (Wis. 7.25). Second, it has no ending but is continuous: "The Father did not generate the Son and dismiss Him after He was generated, but He is always generating Him" (Hom. 9.4 in Jer.).[26]

But while Origen made a distinct forward thrust, he "ended up by making the Son and the Holy Spirit not precisely creatures but 'diminished gods,' inferior to the Father who alone was God in the strict sense."[27] Because of this he became a source of authority for both Arians and anti-Arians in the controversy to which we now turn.

Arianism

Arius begins with a "pagan view of God as unknowable, impassible, unchangeable and unreachable" and so could not conceive of the incarnation of such a being.[28] Thus, like the apologists,

---

26. Quoted in Fortman, Triune God, 55. This also points to a clear emphasis on an essential or immanent Trinity, not just as manifested in the "economy." "This is one of his most important contributions to Greek theology and stems directly from his belief in the eternal generation of the Son." Ibid., 58.

27. Ibid., 68. Cf. Wiley, CT 1:413-14. Cf. Kelly, Doctrines, 130: "One must be careful, however, not to attribute to Origen any doctrine of consubstantiality between Father and Son. . . . Origen always represents the union of Father and Son, . . . as one of love, will and action."

28. Alan Richardson, Creeds in the Making, 52.

he envisioned that it could only be the Logos who could be incarnate; but unlike the apologists, Arius declared Him to be a creature, affirming that "there was when he was not."[29]

The conclusion of the Arian premise is that to worship Christ would be to worship a creature and thus idolatry. To support his position, Arius appealed to the several scriptural passages that point to a submission of Christ to the Father and interpreted them in his own subordinationist sense. He also appealed to the subordinationist strain in the teaching of Origen. Here we encounter the full flower of the subordinationist motif that we have been tracing. Thus it is, as Wiley says, that "Arianism proper was the most formidable enemy encountered in the development of the Trinitarian doctrine" (CT 1:414). Bishop Whale declares, "Carlyle hit the nail precisely on the head when he wrote, 'If Arianism had won, Christianity would have dwindled into a legend.'"[30]

The most celebrated opponent of Arianism was Athanasius, who "is to a large extent responsible for the survival of Catholic Christianity, at any rate in the East, at a time when the Arian triumph had seemed complete."[31]

Athanasius' opposition to Arianism was activated in large part by a soteriological concern, and so we now come to a point that merges with the central concern of Wesleyanism. Athanasius shared with his contemporaries the belief that the central human predicament was the meaninglessness created by the constant threat of nonbeing illustrated so vividly by death. Thus salvation was seen in terms of immortality, or life. Since immortality is the "exclusive" possession of Divinity, salvation waited upon man's divination. In these terms, the Incarnation provided hope for salvation if that which was incarnate was fully God. If not, there was no redemption possible. Thus, literally, it was a life-or-death matter to Athanasius whether the Son who became incarnate was a creature or uncreated God. If He is a mere creature (as Arius

---

29. His view of God as absolutely transcendent, including timelessness, precluded his formula from saying, "There was a time when he was not," because *time* only began with the creation. That this is logically self-refuting is plain enough, but to be historically accurate, Arius's views must be faithfully presented. Cf. quote from Arius in Wiley, CT 1:415: "before time."

30. *Christian Doctrine*, 105.

31. Alan Richardson, *Creeds in the Making*, 54.

said), then He cannot redeem mankind but stands in need of redemption himself.[32]

Against Arius's position that the Son is produced by an act of the Father's will, Athanasius went against a long tradition and declares that He is generated by nature. "He [God] is truly Father of the Son by nature and not by will."[33] Wiley assumes the Athanasian position in his discussion of the Trinity and holds that the Trinity is a necessity of nature. This would give a strong support to an "essential" Trinity in contrast to a merely "economic" Trinity. A later Catholic council, however, repudiated both the ideas of necessity and voluntarism.[34]

The Nicene Settlement

In general, it could be said that the fathers in the pre-Nicene period were concerned to preserve the unity of God. This was natural in the face of threats from paganism and Gnosticism. Thus they "showed little disposition to explore the eternal relations of the Three, much less to construct a conceptual and linguistic apparatus capable of expressing them."[35] The outcome was that many of them formulated the Trinitarian theology in some form of subordinationism. The Council of Nicea came to terms with this issue and decided decisively against any form of subordination of the Son. It explicitly rejected the Arian solution that Jesus was a "second" God and declared that He is "very God of very God."

The key word around which the debate focused was *homoousia*. The Lord Jesus Christ was affirmed as "of one substance" (homoousion) with the Father. What the term connoted to the Nicene bishops is not altogether clear. It was resisted by more than one group. Conservatives were reticent because it was not scriptural and was a new term. The Arians knew that if it were adopted, it would be totally inconsistent with their position.

There are two possibilities for its meaning. It had for some time meant "of generically the same substance." It could also have meant "numerically the same substance." Some interpreters have

32. See Athanasius' classic treatise, *De Incarnatione*, for an extended and exciting discussion of the Incarnation from the perspective of this "realist theory of redemption."
33. Quoted in Fortman, *Triune God*, 73.
34. "The 11th Council of Toledo in Spain declared that 'God the Father must be believed to have generated neither by will nor by necessity." Ibid.
35. Kelly, *Doctrines*, 109.

argued that the bishops intended the first.[36] Later Catholic theologians have defended the second, even though this meaning would have run the danger of smelling like Sabellianism. Bernard Lonergan explains the issue this way:

> The theological ambiguity will clearly appear if we compare Peter and Paul, on the one hand, and on the other, the Father and the Son. Peter and Paul are consubstantial; the Father and the Son are consubstantial. But Peter and Paul are consubstantial, not because they have numerically the same individual substance—for indeed they have not—but because the individual substance of Peter and the really distinct individual substance of Paul both belong to the same species: Peter and Paul are two particular instances of the species, man. The Father and the Son are also consubstantial, but the analogy with Peter and Paul breaks down because unlike the consubstantial Peter and Paul, who are two men, the consubstantial Father and Son are one and the same God: there is numerically only the one God, who is, nonetheless, truly Father and truly Son.[37]

The practical and, from the Wesleyan perspective, the most significant result is suggestively described by Richardson in these words:

> Its significance lies in the fact that it denies the old Greek or Gnostic conception of God as remote, transcendent, uninterested and unknowable; for it affirms that God's essence is that of Jesus, and that the presence and substance of God are realisable and knowable through Jesus in his character of love. It affirms that God is not unknowable, but is revealed in his very nature of love in Jesus Christ. The God incarnate in Jesus cannot be the distant, unfriendly Supreme Being of pagan philosophy or modern Humanism.[38]

Augustine and the Cappadocians

The Nicene settlement had addressed the question of the deity of Christ. While, as we noted, this was an essentially Trinitarian question, that issue was not at the forefront of the discussion. The establishment of Trinitarian orthodoxy had yet to be made. This was done somewhat differently in the East (Greek church) than in

---

36. Ibid., 233-37.
37. *Way to Nicea*, 88-89. Wiley gives his interpretation that the meaning is "not only generically . . . but numerically" the same substance. Cf. *CT* I:423-25.
38. *Creeds in the Making*, 57-58.

the West (Latin church). The most influential theologians in the East are known as the Cappadocian fathers (Basil the Great, Gregory of Nazianzus, and Gregory of Nyssa). In the West, it was Augustine of Hippo who gave shape to the Trinitarian understanding.

The Cappadocians addressed the questions bequeathed to them by Athanasius. Although he had fought vigorously and with great success for the consubstantiality *(homoousia)* of the Father, Son, and Holy Spirit, he did not formulate a technical vocabulary to express his commitments. Neither did he speak to the problem of how God can be at the same time objectively One and Three. Attempting to answer these questions was the major contribution made by the Cappadocians.

The terms they chose to express their understanding were *ousia* and *hypostasis.* The Council of Nicea had equated the two, but Basil insisted on a distinction, and the formula that was accepted was *mia ousia, treis hypostaseis* (one substance and three hypostases).

Hypostasis had been used by Origen to refer to the Father, Son, and Holy Spirit; but, as seen earlier, he had interpreted the Son and Spirit in a subordinationist way as "diminished gods." The Cappadocians rejected this subordinationism. But the use of this term laid them open to the charge of tritheism, since hypostasis implied an individual being. They sought to explain the unity of the *hypostases* by identifying the *ousia* with a universal and the *hypostasis* with a particular. In much the same way that Peter, James, and John (individual *hypostasieis*) share in the common substance *(ousia)* of manness, so each of the divine hypostases is the *ousia* or essence of the Godhead.

The Cappadocians recognized the inadequacy of this analogy and rejected its tritheistic implications by firmly insisting upon the unity of the Godhead. The distinction of hypostases in no way rends the oneness of nature asunder. There are differences among scholars as to whether they interpreted the "one ousia" as numerically one or a unity of nature (see this discussion in previous section).

A much more satisfactory way of explaining the distinction between *ousia* and *hypostasis* was their explanation that the one Godhead exists simultaneously in three "modes of being." Basil refers to the Holy Spirit as "a mode of the ineffable existence" (*De*

Sp. s.46). Gregory of Nyssa speaks of both the Son and the Spirit in terms of "modes of existence."[39]

To the question of how God could be objectively at the same time One and Three, they spoke of the distinction of the *hypostases* in terms of their origin and mutual relation. While carefully avoiding subordinationism, they taught that the Father is the Source or principle of the Godhead. In a sense, the Father causes the other two Beings, because He imparts His being to them. Each divine hypostasis is distinct in terms of the property that uniquely belongs to Him, and the properties are relational, that is, have to do with the relation each sustains to the other hypostases in the *ousia.* Basil sees these distinctive properties to be "fatherhood, sonship, and sanctification" and comments that "the Father precedes the Son according to the relation of causes to the things which proceed from them" and adds that "it is clear to one thinking over the names *father* and *son,* that when they are said alone, they indicate only a mutual relation."[40] In a word, the divine names do not imply a multiplication of the divine substance but signify only mutual relations.

One problem that emerges from the conceptualization of the Father as the Source of the being of the other two hypostases is the relative status and relation of the Son and the Spirit. If the Son and the Spirit are both generated, there would seem to be two Sons, with the Second Person not being the "only begotten Son." The Cappadocians tried to avoid this dilemma by referring to the Son as the "generation of the Father's image" and the Spirit as the "breath of the Father." Gregory of Nyssa provided the definitive answer. For him, the Spirit is out of God and is of Christ; He proceeds out of the Father and receives from the Son; He cannot be separated from the Word. He uses the analogy of a torch imparting its light first to another torch and then through it to a third in order to illustrate the relation of the three Persons. Kelly comments: "After him [Gregory] the regular teaching of the Eastern church is that the procession of the Holy Spirit is 'out of the Father through the Son.'"[41]

The Cappadocians stressed the unity of the Godhead by em-

---

39. Fortman, *Triune God,* 81; Kelly, *Doctrines,* 264; William G. Rusch, ed. and trans., *The Trinitarian Controversy* (Philadelphia: Fortress Press, 1980), 24.

40. Quoted in Fortman, *Triune God,* 80-81.

41. *Doctrines,* 263.

phasizing that the activities peculiar to each hypostasis are the work of the one *ousia*. The Father never acts independently of the Son, nor the Son of the Spirit. None of the Persons possesses a separate operation of His own, but one individual energy passes through all Three. Gregory of Nyssa writes:

> If we observe a single activity of Father, Son and Holy Spirit, in no respect different in the case of any, we are obliged to infer unity of nature from the identity of activity, for Father, Son and Holy Spirit cooperate in sanctifying, quickening, consoling and so on.[42]

In concluding this survey, we must add that the Cappadocians embody the Eastern tendency to emphasize the threeness of the Trinity. They begin with the three Persons and attempt to explain the unity. Thus the problem is posed in a particular way, and the issue is to avoid tritheism. One of their major contributions was showing that God was not One and Three in the same sense, and in doing so they blunted the rationalistic critiques of the Trinitarian faith.

When we turn to the West, and Augustine as the apex of its Trinitarian development, we encounter a somewhat different flavor. Augustine begins with the unity of God and then attempts to explain how one God can be in three hypostases. It follows that Father, Son, and Spirit cannot be conceptualized as three separate individuals in the same way as three human beings who belong to one genus. Rather, each of the divine Persons, from the point of view of substance, is identical with the other or with the divine substance itself. All the Persons of the Trinity are involved in all divine operations.

Following the lead of the Cappadocians, Augustine distinguishes the Persons in terms of their mutual relations within the Godhead but without any trace of subordinationism. He is reluctantly willing to adopt the term *Person* to distinguish the Catholic faith from Modalism. Father, Son, and Spirit are thus relations in the sense that whatever each of them is, He is in relation to one or both of the others. This position avoids the philosophical pitfalls implicit in using the category of substance. Kelly's comment on this should be illuminating:

> To modern people, unless schooled in technical philosophy, the notion of relations (e.g. "above", "to the right of",

---

42. Cf. ibid., 266-67.

"greater than") as having a real subsistence sounds strange, although they are usually prepared to concede their objectivity, i.e. that they exist in their own right independent of the observer.[43]

In distinguishing between the Son and the Spirit, Augustine says:

> The Son is from the Father, the Spirit also is from the Father. But the former is begotten, the latter proceeds. So the former is Son of the Father from Whom He is begotten, but the latter is the Spirit of both since He proceeds from both. . . . The Father is the author of the Spirit's procession because He begot such a Son, and in begetting Him made Him also the source from which the Spirit proceeds.[44]

In his effort to explain how the one undivided God could sustain a threefoldness without being divided, Augustine worked on the premise that since man is made in the image of God, there should be a reflection of the divine life in the individual person. The central analogy that he draws is from the mind's activity as directed upon itself or upon God. It can take the form of mind, its knowledge of itself, and its love of itself; or memory, understanding, and will; or the mind remembering, knowing, and loving God himself. Each of these illuminate the inner divine life but dimly and inadequately. He says: "The image of the Trinity is one Person, but the Supreme Trinity itself is three Persons."

The Athanasian Creed

The intense theological work of the early centuries reached its consummation and culmination in the West in the *Quicunque Vult*, mistakenly called the Athanasian Creed. It, in turn, is built upon the work of Augustine. The creed has theological significance for both Trinity and Incarnation, but we will reproduce here only that portion that relates to the topic at hand:

1. Whosoever will be saved, before all things it is necessary that he hold the Catholic Faith.
2. Which Faith, except every one do keep whole and undefiled, without doubt he shall perish everlastingly.
3. And the Catholic Faith is this, that we worship one God in Trinity, and Trinity in Unity.

---

43. Ibid., 272-73.
44. Quoted ibid., 276.

4. Neither confounding the Persons, nor dividing the Substance.

5. For there is one Person of the Father, another of the Son, and another of the Holy Ghost.

6. But the Godhead of the Father, of the Son, and of the Holy Ghost is all one, the glory equal, the majesty coeternal.

7. Such as the Father is, such is the Son, and such is the Holy Ghost.

8. The Father uncreate, the Son uncreate, and the Holy Ghost uncreate.

9. The Father incomprehensible, the Son incomprehensible, and the Holy Ghost incomprehensible.

10. The Father eternal, the Son eternal, and the Holy Ghost eternal.

11. And yet there are not three eternals, but one eternal.

12. And also there are not three incomprehensibles, nor three uncreated, but one uncreated and one incomprehensible.

13. So likewise the Father is Almighty, the Son Almighty, and the Holy Ghost Almighty.

14. And yet there are not three Almighties, but one Almighty.

15. So the Father is God, the Son is God, and the Holy Ghost is God.

16. And yet there are not three Gods, but one God.

17. So likewise the Father is Lord, the Son is Lord, and the Holy Ghost is Lord.

18. And yet there are not three Lords, but one Lord.

19. For like as we are compelled by Christian verity to acknowledge every person by himself to be God and Lord.

20. So we are forbidden by the Catholic Religion to say there be three Gods, or three Lords.

21. The Father is made of none, neither created nor begotten.

22. The Son is of the Father alone, not made, nor created, but begotten.

23. The Holy Ghost is of the Father, and of the Son, neither made, nor created, nor begotten, but proceeding.

24. So there is one Father, not three Fathers; one Son, not three Sons; one Holy Ghost, not three Holy Ghosts.

25. And in this Trinity none is afore or after another; none is greater or less than another.

26. But the whole three Persons are coeternal together and coequal.

27. So that in all things, as is aforesaid, the Unity in Trinity, and the Trinity in Unity is to be worshipped.

28. He, therefore, that will be saved must thus think of the Trinity.

At the outset of the creed we encounter a stated connection between the belief in the Trinity and salvation. Edmund J. Fortman says that it is not suggesting that the "Catholic faith" is merely an intellectual assent but rather that it involves the "worship of one God in Trinity, and Trinity in Unity." If this is indeed its intention, it concurs with John Wesley's approach noted at the beginning of this chapter. Of this creedal statement Wesley says, "I am far from saying, he who does not assent to this 'shall without doubt perish everlastingly.' For the sake of that and another clause, I, for some time, scrupled subscribing to that creed."[45]

The formulations are very careful to exclude all the deviations from the faith that we have surveyed: subordinationism, especially in its Arian form; tritheism; and Modalism. It is thoroughgoingly Augustinian in its emphasis on the unity of the divine substance, all attributes of God being applicable to each Person of the Trinity but not thereby dividing the divine nature. Its summary formula in verse 4 provides the guidelines for all subsequent Trinitarian speculation while at the same time identifying the fallacy of each earlier "heresy": "neither confounding the Persons, nor dividing the Substance."

The language of the creed calls for special attention. No doubt the reader will already have recognized that the Trinitarian discussions were marked by considerable terminological confusion. Not only were there two languages (Latin and Greek) in the picture, but particular terms in one language could have different meanings depending upon the philosophical context from which they were taken. There was a great deal of misunderstanding as various persons used terms such as *ousia, persona, prosopon, substantia,* and *hypostasia.* It is not strange that, as H. A. Wolfson says: "Whatever term one happened to use he could be suspected of some heretical doctrine."[46]

The two key words in the creed are "substance" and "Person." Both convey ideas to our modern ears quite different from what the fathers intended. Substance seems to connote solidity, but it basically implies "nature" or "essence." Augustine much preferred "essence" to "substance," because "substance" seems independent of its attributes, and that is not the case with God.

---

45. *Works* 6:200.
46. *The Philosophy of the Church Fathers* (Cambridge: Harvard University Press, 1964), 1:334. This source contains a thorough analysis of the terms used in the debates.

"Person" is the term that has occasioned the most reticence among modern theologians. This term has come to mean an individual center of consciousness or personality. Rather, in its original use it was much less concrete and in no way dissolved the unity of God as does the term if understood in its contemporary sense. Virtually all theological writers concur with the words of Gustav Aulen: "If we were to explain to the men of the ancient church what we mean by person and personality, the ancient church fathers would no doubt deny us the right to use this trinitarian formula according to *our* concept of person; they would brand us as tritheistic heretics."[47]

H. Orton Wiley recognizes this problem and denies that the theological use of the term has the modern meaning in mind (*CT* 1:419). This suggests that we may continue to use the traditional term but recognize that it has a very special, adapted meaning. To do this puts us in the position of using esoteric language, and so from this point on it is usually shown the first time in quotes. Most theologians today have opted for the terminology of "modes of being" to refer to the threefoldness in God but explicitly deny its Sabellian meaning. This language, we have found, has a venerable history.[48]

In the final analysis, we will find ourselves unable to formulate in a fully consistent and satisfactory way these two movements in the Divine Reality. The mystery of God will finally elude rational formulation. Cyril Richardson is doubtless correct when he says:

> There is no way to overcome the paradox that we must think of God *both* as one and as a society. Logically we cannot do both; yet we must say both. . . . There simply is no way in human thought to compose the paradox. Every solution, however ingenious, hides the paradox in one form or another. Is it not better to admit the paradox, to confess we have reached the limits of human thought, and to acknowledge that, to guard Christian truths, we must say [apparently] self-contradictory things?[49]

It is interesting and not without significance that each of the two basic approaches to the Trinity we have previously noted

47. *Faith of the Christian Church,* 227.
48. If the student masters the material covered in this chapter up to this point, he should have a sufficiently adequate frame of reference to read with reasonable comprehension most contemporary discussions of Trinitarian issues.
49. *The Doctrine of the Trinity* (New York: Abingdon Press, 1958), 95. Compare our discussion of paradox in chap. I. It applies perfectly in this case. This does not entail accepting Richardson's conclusions in his enlightening book.

(Cappadocian and Augustinian) can be accused of falling into or at least closely approaching a classical heresy. The construction that begins with threeness barely avoids tritheism if at all, while the Augustinian orientation to oneness with the subsequent attempt to explain the threeness always runs the danger of Modalism.

Essential or Economic Trinity

Wiley observes: "The twofold idea of the 'essential Trinity' and the 'economic Trinity' must be held in firm grasp, if there is to be any proper view of this fundamental doctrine of Christianity" (*CT* 1:422). The *Manual of the Church of the Nazarene*, in Article I of the Articles of Faith, affirms its belief in an essential Trinity. This issue needs further discussion in terms of contemporary thought.

The economic understanding speaks of the Father, Son, and Holy Spirit not in themselves but as manifested in creation, redemption, and sanctification successively. The immanent view of the Trinity holds that these functional distinctions reveal real, ontological, and eternal distinctions in the Godhead.

Historically this issue has been debated largely in terms of Sabellianism vs. orthodoxy (see above). The former denied any distinctions within God but affirmed that there were simply three successive manifestations of one undivided God in His management of mundane affairs as reflected in creation, redemption, and sanctification.

Orthodoxy rejected this interpretation. Consequently much of subsequent theological debate on the subject revolved around speculative metaphysics that attempted to explain the threefold structure of the inner divine life. However, many of the early fathers attempted to recognize both aspects. Irenaeus, for example, taught that in His intrinsic being, God is the Father of all things, ineffably one, and yet containing in himself from all eternity His Word (Son) and His Wisdom (Spirit). In revelation, these immanent realities are extrapolated or manifested. Thus he claimed that "by the very essence and nature of His being there is but one God," while at the same time "according to the economy of our redemption there are both Father and Son." He is followed in this emphasis by Hippolytus and Tertullian.[50]

---

50. Kelly, *Doctrines*, 104-12.

Martin Luther, with his antimetaphysical bias, had little time for the subtleties of the schoolmen (scholasticism). His principle that we cannot know God as He is in himself but only as He reveals himself would seem to preclude speculation about the immanent Trinity. Nonetheless, he asserts repeatedly that the Christian faith is captured in the Trinitarian formula of the creeds, but he bases it upon revelation rather than philosophical speculation. Like Wesley after him, Luther also identifies the Trinity with vital Christian experience, tying it to creation, redemption, and sanctification. Calvin, thanks to Michael Servetus, gave considerable support to the idea of an immanent Trinity, although his theological methodology made it somewhat incongruous.[51]

Developments in philosophy, symbolized centrally by the critical philosophy of Immanuel Kant, have made theologians from the 18th century on reticent to address the issues raised by the idea of an immanent Trinity. Hence, most have been content to attempt to point to the theological significance of the doctrine of the Trinity without entering into the intricacies of metaphysical analysis.[52]

However, several recent analyses have provided powerful supports for an essentially Modalistic interpretation of the divine life. They have called attention to the fact that the early patristic discussions functioned in terms of a view of the Divine Being that was more Hellenistic than biblical and so distinguished between the Father and the Son in terms of Ground and Expression or Absolute and Relatedness. The Father is the symbol of the Divine Ground who is beyond—the Absolute—and the Son is His Relatedness to the world, in creation and redemption. These critiques have argued that such a distinction should be understood as a paradoxical tension within God and does not necessarily require two distinct hypostases. Thus, in substance, Father and Son are basically expressions of our experience of the paradoxical nature of God.[53]

---

51. Cf. Fortman, *Triune God*, 239-42; Aulen, *Faith of the Christian Church*, 229. I am indebted to the researches of Dr. Craig Keen for a more positive evaluation of Luther's Trinitarian concerns than the above sources allow.

52. Cf. Kaufman, *Systematic Theology*, 100-102; Aulen, *Faith of the Christian Church*, 225-30.

53. Cyril Richardson, *Doctrine of the Trinity*, has a sustained and thoughtful analysis of the various forms of Trinitarian construction and shows that all have at least some dimensions of this Absolute-Relatedness dichotomy that serves as a principle of differentiation within the Godhead. MacGregor, *He Who Lets Us Be*, discusses the issue, arguing its incongruity with the basic biblical affirmation that "God is love."

No less a theologian than Karl Barth has declared himself as holding to an essential Trinity, and his influence has been extensive among 20th-century thinkers. He speaks about three modes of being that are essential and not simply manifestations of the divine life, even though he derives the Trinitarian structure from an analysis of revelation.[54]

Geddes MacGregor gives a simple statement of Barth's position here:

> If I claimed to know nothing of God [as He is in himself] yet made affirmations about how he appears to me, anything I said about God would be merely a description of my own psyche. If we claim to know anything of God, we are claiming to know that the symbols under which we know him do point in some way or other to his essential nature; they are not merely descriptions of his manifestations.[55]

Following the emphasis of Barth that God has truly revealed himself "and not just something of himself," T. F. Torrance comments:

> It is as our knowing God passes from what is called the "economic Trinity" to the "ontological Trinity" that we have *theologia* in the supreme and proper sense, knowledge of God on the free ground of his own Being, knowledge of him in which our knowing is controlled and shaped by relations eternally immanent in God.[56]

Although not using the traditional language of "economic" and "essential," several contemporary theologians have actually defended an essential Trinity, using the methods of "existential ontology." This approach understands God as Being and, from the place where Being appears most significantly, that is, in human beings (*Dasein* in the jargon of philosopher Martin Heidegger), have extrapolated a theory about the structure of Reality as Being-Itself. They find, through this method, that God as Being reflects a Trinitarian structure. Paul Tillich is perhaps the most prominent of these with John Macquarrie further developing Tillich's insights along this line. Tillich says: "It is impossible to develop a doctrine of the living God and of the creation without distinguishing the

---

54. *Church Dogmatics* I.1; see Bloesch, *Essentials of Evangelical Theology* I:35, who follows Barth explicitly.

55. *He Who Lets Us Be*, 52.

56. *Reality and Evangelical Theology*, 24. See this principle of divine revelation as derived from the nature of God as revealed and the implied balance between immanence and transcendence in chap. 6 on the doctrine of God.

'ground' and the 'form' in God, the principle of abyss and the principle of self-manifestation in God."[57]

Following a long tradition beginning with Augustine, Tillich sees the Third "Person" emerging in the divine life as the principle of unity binding the Father and Son together. Just as spirit is the unifying principle in human experience (existential), so the Spirit is the unifying principle of Being (ontological). So the Spirit has necessary and separate function and reality. He says of the early struggle that resulted in the establishing of the full Deity of the third "hypostasis":

> The motive for it was . . . Christological. The divine Spirit who created and determined Jesus as the Christ is not the spirit of the man Jesus, and the divine Spirit who creates and directs the church is not the spirit of a sociological group. And the Spirit who grasps and transforms the individual person is not an expression of his spiritual life. The divine Spirit is God himself as Spirit in the Christ and through him in the church and the Christian.[58]

We may concur in principle with the claims of Barth and others. Thus with a grounding of the economic Trinity in an ontological Trinity, we may now safely turn to the significance of the doctrine and reflect the distinctive Wesleyan concern for the practical implications of it. In this context, we may draw upon those sources that emphasize the economic Trinity without committing ourselves to mere Modalism or subjective appropriation only but rely upon the veracity of the biblical revelation as to the fact without delaying any further with the manner.

Theologically, the doctrine of the Trinity safeguards the doctrine of God from falling into either pantheism or deism. The latter is an exclusive emphasis on transcendence, while the former results from a too-exclusive emphasis on immanence. It was the Arian view of transcendence that led to the denial of the full deity of the incarnate One. But to affirm the consubstantiality of the Father and the Son avoids this pitfall and affirms that God has indeed involved himself in His creation. The Spirit as God's presence in and with His creation, especially His new creation, also guards against a deistic withdrawal. The Father, as the Ground of

---

57. *Systematic Theology* 3:288.
58. Ibid., 289; cf. also John Macquarrie, *Principles of Christian Theology* (New York: Charles Scribner's Sons, 1966), 174-85.

Being of the Son and the Spirit, guards against pantheism by affirming the otherness of God.

John Macquarrie recognizes this point when he says: "The Christian could not go along with a stark monotheism in which God is utterly transcendent and sovereign, and still less with a pantheism in which God is entirely and universally immanent"; for as Aulen notes, "All so-called unitarian interpretations tend to inevitably become pantheistic or deistic and impoverish the content and vividness of faith in God."[59]

Turning now to Mr. Wesley himself, we note the significance he attaches to the Trinitarian fact of Scripture. First, it is the basis for honoring the Son, that is, worship. In the Arian controversy this was a critical point. If, as Arius thought, the Son was a creature, it was inappropriate to worship Him. But the Catholic faith insisted that the proper worship of the Second Person was itself an indication of His deity.

In soteriological terms, the Trinity is involved in the sense that, thinking of the Father as Him to whom we are reconciled, it is the basis of our acceptance with God (the Son) and the basis of the witness of the Spirit. Wesley concludes: "Therefore, I do not see how it is possible for any to have vital religion who denies that the Three are One."[60]

Wiley stated the redemptive implication of the Trinity in a slightly different way: "God the Father sent His Son into the world to redeem us; God the Son became incarnate in order to save us; and the Holy Spirit applies the redemptive work to our souls" (CT 1:394).

This way of putting it calls for a reminder that the orthodox understanding of the Trinity guards against either pitting one Person of the Trinity against another or dividing up the activity so as to make it a seriatim activity in the work of salvation. The indivisibility of God's activity was guaranteed by the traditional doctrine of *perichoresis* (Greek) or *circumincession* (Latin), according to which the three Persons of the Godhead are in no sense independent but in fact coinhere in each other. This refers to both the coinherence of the Persons and the works. The latter is spelled out in the doctrine of the *opera Trinitatis ad extra sunt indivisa* (indivisibility of the outward works of the Trinity).

---

59. Macquarrie, *Principles*, 175; Aulen, *Faith of the Christian Church*, 229.
60. *Works* 6:205.

This aspect of the doctrine of God has important implications for our subsequent study of the doctrines of atonement and sanctification. It guards against seeing the work of salvation as the work of the Son over against the Father and guarantees that it be fully the work of God (Father, Son, and Spirit). It furthermore guards against identifying the work of sanctification with the Spirit in some exclusivistic way so as to not include the Son and the Father such as in popular, but misguided, piety: "receiving the Son in initial salvation but receiving the Holy Spirit in sanctification."[61]

A further Trinitarian barrier to these misconceptions is found in the vigorously debated question of the *filioque*, or procession of the Spirit from the Son. In 1054 the Eastern and Western churches divided over the issue, with the Western churches affirming and Eastern denying that the Spirit proceeds from both the Father and the Son. To modern ears, this appears so insignificant a subtlety as to have been merely a pretext, but it really has practical implication, especially for the doctrine of sanctification. The Spirit proceeding from the Son assures us that the work of the Spirit in the life of the believer, imparting to him the benefits of the salvation provided through the Son, shall both partake of and produce the character of the Son, who in turn perfectly reproduces (because of the *homoousia*) the character of the Father.

Speaking of these deviations from Trinitarian orthodoxy in faulty interpretation of the work of salvation, Aulen incisively comments: "In comparison with this danger of dividing the conception of God into a tritheism [in relation to salvation], the numerous abstract speculations about the 'immanent' Trinity and the mutual relation of the three persons are relatively harmless."[62]

The words of the Gloria Patri appropriately express the attitude of worship that the truth of the Trinity should elicit:

Glory be to the Father, and to the Son, and to the Holy Ghost;

as it was in the beginning, is now, and ever shall be, world without end. Amen.

---

61. Bishop Whale quotes Sydney Cave's account: "In the unthinking piety of the Church, the 'persons' of the Godhead have been so distinguished that it is possible to read in a revivalist magazine of prayers for a sick child being offered in vain to God the Father, and to God the Son, although, when offered to God the Holy Spirit the child immediately was healed." *Christian Doctrine*, 113.
62. *Faith of the Christian Church*, 228.

8

God the Creator

One of the important implications of the doctrine of the Trinity is that we cannot speak of creation exclusively in terms of one Person of the Trinity. The biblical witness testifies that the Father, Son, and Spirit were all involved in the creation act/process (Col. 1:16-17; John 1:3; Gen. 1:2; 1 Cor. 8:6; Ps. 104:30). Thus when we speak of God the Creator, we speak of the total Godhead.[1]

In theology strictly understood (see chap. 1), we must speak not of cosmology or pseudoscience but of God and of the implications for man in relation to God. Or more specifically, we speak about the relation of God and the world. To put the matter differently, we are concerned with the theological implication of the truth that God is the Creator.[2]

There are few doctrines that have more wide-ranging implications for life and belief. It touches on ontological questions; it

---

1. "When we hear of the divine *fiat* of creation, as in Genesis, we tend to think of the Father; if there is actual carrying out of the *fiat*, we think of the Son, the creative *Logos;* and when we hear of the renewal of the earth we think of the Spirit of God, the Lord and Lifegiver . . . If the perichoretic [from *perichoresis*, meaning interpermeation of the 'Persons'] is taken seriously, as I strongly believe it should be, what can such distinctions mean? If the works of the Trinity *ad extra* are indivisible, what is predicated of one *persona*, one *hypostasis*, must surely be predicated of all." MacGregor, *He Who Lets Us Be,* 50-51.

2. See Aulen, *Faith of the Christian Church,* 156-57: "It has been very common to confuse the affirmations of faith about creation with cosmological theories, or to interpret these affirmations as a theory of the origin of the universe. . . . Even if such a theory of origins could be theoretically demonstrated, which is impossible, this whole conception is completely meaningless to faith, since it has no religious character."

provides a basis for ethical understanding and the foundation for human social institutions; it relates to providence, miracle, and prayer. In education, it bears on the whole question of the relation between faith and learning and joins inseparably the phenomenon of a Christian liberal arts education.[3] It brings ecology within the purview of Christian theology and opens the door to a sacramental view of nature. Thus it reaches far beyond mere cosmological considerations and issues dealing with the relation between science and religion. This question is more appropriately in the domain of philosophy of religion than theology proper. Langdon Gilkey can go so far as to say: "The idea that God is the Creator of all things is the indispensable foundation on which the other beliefs of the Christian faith are based."[4]

Theological Analysis of Gen. 1:1—2:4a[5]

It is unfortunate that this passage has so often been used to create a struggle between science and revelation. Such a conflict is the result of failing to recognize the nature of the account. "While the account of creation in the Bible is not mythological [see below], neither is it intended to be cosmological or scientific."[6] Emil Brunner suggests an appropriate analogy that demonstrates how the two ways of explanation (scientific and theological) can never truly collide if each recognizes its own methodological contexts:

> How can we combine the chemical analysis of a painted canvas with the aesthetic judgment of this canvas as a work of art? Obviously the two are mutually exclusive, because the two subjects are on different planes. Where the chemist only sees

3. See Arthur F. Holmes, *The Idea of a Christian College* (Grand Rapids: Wm. B. Eerdmans Publishing Co., 1975).

4. *Maker of Heaven and Earth*, 15. Arthur Holmes, in developing the considerations necessary for a worldview, says: "The God-creation theme thus differentiates Christian theism from other world-views and is crucial to thinking Christianly about anything at all." *Contours*, 58.

5. The student would do well to review Appendix 2, since it provides the methodological underpinning for this exercise. It can serve as an example of the "theological exegesis" propounded formally in that discussion. Gerhard von Rad says of this unit of Scripture: "These sentences cannot be easily overinterpreted theologically! Indeed, to us the danger appears greater that the expositor will fall short of discovering the concentrated doctrinal content." *Genesis* (Philadelphia: Westminster Press, 1961), 46.

6. *God, Man, and Salvation*, 56.

the various elements of a chemical mixture, the artist sees a significant whole, an expression of mind and spirit.[7]

H. Orton Wiley, in his discussion of the creation narratives, remains firmly within these contextual limitations. He refers to the account as an "inspired Psalm," designating it as the "Hymn of Creation" or "Poem of the Dawn." Being of the nature of poetry, it cannot be treated as a technical scientific treatise, although we must emphasize, as Wiley does, that it is historical in nature.[8]

We must be very careful to understand what is meant when we say that an account is historical, though poetical. In order to see the significance of this distinction we must first differentiate poetic symbolism from myth. Myth, in ancient religions, was taken from the realm of nature where rituals celebrated repeatable phenomena such as the cyclical recurrence of the seasons.[9] The creation story is not mythical, in that it was a once-for-all event and not a repeated event; thus it is historical. We would not speak of the recurring seasons as historical in this context. Karl Barth has suggested the term *saga* to describe such narratives:

> It is assuredly a basic error to speak of creation myths. . . . A myth has to do with the mighty problem that at all times propounds itself to man and therefore is timeless, the problem of life and death, of sleep and wakening, of birth and dying, of morning and evening, of day and night and so on. These are the themes of myth. . . . If we are to give the biblical narrative a name or put it in a category, then let it be that of saga.[10]

To say that the Genesis account is historical is to say something quite different from such interpretations as the following:

> The Christian doctrine of creation is a symbolic assertion, not that the world was made by the Great Artificer as a carpenter makes a box, but that man in all his felt finitude comes from God and goes to God; he is not surrounded by a sheer abyss of nothingness. . . . Creation out of nothing is not to be understood as an historical event but as a description of existence.[11]

---

7. *Creation and Redemption*, 39-40.
8. *CT* 1:449 ff.
9. This is only one of many uses of the term *myth* in contemporary theology. For a brief survey of other ways of interpreting it, see Eric Dinkler, "Myth," in *Handbook of Christian Theology*, ed. Marvin Halverson and Arthur A. Cohen, Meridian Books (Cleveland: World Publishing Co., 1958), 238-43; Van A. Harvey, "Myth," in *A Handbook of Theological Terms* (New York: Macmillan Co., 1964), 155-56.
10. *Dogmatics in Outline*, 51.
11. Whale, *Christian Doctrine*, 13, 30.

The doctrine of creation is not the story of an event which took place "once upon a time." It is the basic description of the relation between God and the World. . . . The doctrine of creation does not describe an event. It points to the situation of creatureliness and to its correlate, the divine creativity.[12]

We must respond with a no and a yes to these statements. Our view is that the historical dimension (an event) must not be rejected but that the dimension that points to the human situation must be affirmed. It is certainly the case that the creation accounts provide an insight into man's existential situation, but that does not preclude the possibility of their historicity. Although the historical dimension of the account lies outside our experience and therefore is inaccessible to us, it is nonetheless historical in nature.

Against this background, we propose to focus on the theological exegesis of the biblical narratives of creation. The purely theological dimensions are most clearly seen when they are set in contrast to the Babylonian creation epic that antedates them.[13] The cosmology is essentially the same but the theology is significantly different. These records have "done more than anything else to confirm the real divine inspiration"[14] of the Bible, which we have seen in chapter 2 to be found in the theology that informs the text.

In the Babylonian text, the universe as the ancients knew it was described as coming into existence out of conflict among the gods. Bel, the supreme god of Babylon, vanquished Tiamat, cut her body in two, and with one half of it made a firmament supporting the upper waters in the sky; the other half became the "waters below." The parallels to Genesis are obvious. But the inspired account attributes the origin of the universe to one God and thus is monotheistic. There is neither previously existing divine nor inert stuff out of which the universe was formed. It is ethical and monotheistic rather than immoral and polytheistic.[15]

The structure of the account of the process of creation in Genesis 1 is clearly set forth to emphasize the theological truth that the

---

12. Tillich, *Systematic Theology* 1:252-53.
13. This document was discovered in 1872 by George Smith on some clay tablets that contained accounts of the creation and the Flood from the religious standpoint of the Babylonians.
14. "Genesis and the Babylonian Inscriptions," in *A Commentary on the Holy Bible,* ed. J. R. Dummelow (New York: Macmillan Co., 1936), xxxii.
15. See Bernhard W. Anderson, *Creation Versus Chaos;* Alexander Heidel, *The Babylonian Genesis* (Chicago: University of Chicago Press, 1951).

Sabbath principle is grounded in the creative activity of God. It ultimately makes little difference, for this point, whether the Hebrew *yom* (day) is interpreted literally as a 24-hour period or as epochs of time of indefinite duration. The point is that the seventh day is a day of rest. The very nature of the universe supports the principle, and thus to ignore it in practice is to flirt with the chaos that was driven back by the divine fiat. The shift of the day of worship from the seventh to the first day of the week does not invalidate this but is based upon the principle of "a day of rest," and the day itself in Christian observance is grounded in the "new creation" rather than the "old creation."[16]

Another institution is also seen as being grounded in creation: monogamous marriage. This arrangement is not an artificial, sociological construct that can be violated without penalty. The structure of human persons is such that to fail to conform to this natural law is to wreak havoc with one's created nature. Not only is monogamous marriage "good" because of God's fiat, but it is fulfilling of personhood.[17]

To make such a claim is to argue that marriage is not essentially legal or artificial, but natural. This has far-reaching implications for social ethics and political issues when interpreted from a Christian perspective.[18]

The Goodness of Creation

One of the central features of the creation narrative is the Creator's judgment that it is "good." What is the significance of this

---

16. Wiley argues extensively for the view that "day" is not to be taken literally. This position is doubtless the result of efforts to reconcile the primitive cosmology with modern science. Interestingly enough, Wright and Fuller take the view that the original intention of the writer was seven 24-hour days. This would, they think, more strongly reinforce the theological point about the Sabbath. *Acts of God,* 50.

17. This does not, of course, mean that single persons are condemned to live unfulfilled lives. There are obviously exceptions to this rule, but the Scripture seems to suggest that it is because of a special dispensation (1 Cor. 7:7-9). One should also bear in mind that the intrusion of sin into the created world skewed the natural situation in numerous ways but did not destroy essential human nature, which is structured by the creative act and maintained by prevenient grace.

18. "Regarding marriage, again, the religious view that it is an institution ordained by God has been largely superseded by the contractual view that marriage is an entirely human arrangement, a social convention, one that we devised and can revise, and that only a legal contract holds a couple to it. As Paul Ramsey points out, this has profound significance regarding sex, abortion, adoption, sterilization, and so forth, for if a marriage is simply a conventional contract, and if the contract specifies nothing in these regards, then marriage has no ethical implications for them at all." Holmes, *Contours,* 29.

evaluation? First, it is God's judgment and not that of the creation; therefore it cannot be primarily that it is good for the created beings, although we cannot a priori say that that is excluded. It does preclude the judgment being originally derived from finite experience. Only God has the perspective, as Creator, to pass the judgment.

The Hebrew word translated "good" may also mean "beautiful," but its significance in this passage transcends this meaning. However, it may be included in a secondary sense as a description of the awesomeness and orderliness of the created world. Basically, "good" is a purpose word, and therefore the Creator pronounced His handiwork good because it perfectly fulfilled the purpose that He had in mind. While we are not given a clear clue in the Genesis account as to what that purpose might be, Ps. 148:1-6 may provide us one indicator:

> O praise the Lord.
> Praise the Lord out of heaven;
>   praise him in the heights.
> Praise him, all his angels;
>   praise him, all his host.
> Praise him, sun and moon;
>   praise him, all you shining stars;
>   praise him, heaven of heavens.
> and you waters above the heaven.
> Let them all praise the name of the Lord,
>   for he spoke the word and they were created;
>   he established them for ever and ever
> by an ordinance which shall never pass away.
>   (NEB)

The purpose of creation is apparently understood by the Psalmist to be the praise and glory of God, and it is this purpose that it was properly structured to fulfill. Thus the judgment that "it was very good" (Gen. 1:31) tells us that there is purposefulness in created finitude. This faith provides the context in terms of which man properly experiences or may experience the goodness of creation.

We may gain further light on the purpose and goodness of creation by now turning to the New Testament, where the Logos or Christ is posited as the Agent of creation (John 1; Ephesians 1; Colossians 1; and 1 Corinthians 8). Thus the character of the creative word is here defined by the character of Christ, and the purposive intention of God is illuminated thereby. Emil Brunner suggests that theology must begin with the New Testament rather than the Old Testament. We disagree with this procedure, since it implicitly calls into question the authority of the Old Testament.[19] Brunner's statement that "the Word by which Yahweh creates heaven and earth is a pure word of command which expresses His power, but it is not the Word which gives divine meaning to His creation"[20] heads down the road followed by Marcion. It implies a separation of the God of creation from the God of redemption. Although it is very true that the Creative Word is most fully understood when it is interpreted in the light of the Incarnate Word, they are one and the same.

Creatio ex Nihilo

W. T. Purkiser distinguishes two Hebrew words (*bara* and *asah*) in the Genesis account. One (*bara*) implies bringing into existence what had previously had no being, and the second (*asah*) implies the shaping or forming of material already existing.[21] From earliest times, Christian theology made this distinction by formulating the doctrine of creation as *creatio ex nihilo* (creation out of nothing).[22] This doctrine has numerous important implications.

God the Source. First, it tells us that God is the Source of all that is. It is difficult for the philosophically untrained person to think about "nothing" without treating it as "something." But "out of nothing" says that there was nothing beside God, nothing out of which the world was formed. This excludes all forms of dualism.

---

19. See Bright, *Old Testament,* where he argues that all approaches to the Old Testament that begin with the New Testament inevitably end with an unsatisfactory account of the Hebrew Bible. The only solution to this dilemma is to begin with the Old Testament itself and then move to the New for amplification or, as he puts it, to turn the B.C. word into an A.D. word.

20. *Creation and Redemption,* 13.

21. *God, Man, and Salvation,* 57. Von Rad concurs with this interpretation: "It is correct to say that the verb *bara,* 'create,' contains the idea both of complete effortlessness and *creatio ex nihilo." Genesis,* 47.

22. Brunner writes: "The explicit formulation of the idea of *creatio ex nihilo* appears for the first time in the literature of later Judaism, in the second Book of the Maccabees." *Creation and Redemption,* 11. The earliest occasion of its Christian use seems to be in Theophilus of Antioch. Cf. Jaroslav Pelikan, *The Emergence of the Catholic Tradition* (Chicago: University of Chicago Press, 1973), 36.

Man's way is always to shape something new out of previously existing material, but God brought His raw material into being.

The classic example of a dualistic view of creation is Plato's cosmology (actually he has three realities rather than two, but the principle is the same). In the *Timaeus,* the Demiurge takes the previously existing receptacle (space)[23] and shapes it according to the forms or eternal ideas into the present ordered universe. The forms are the principles of meaning, and the receptacle is the principle of recalcitrance that constantly resists the orderliness imposed upon it. Both provide limiting elements to God (the Demiurge), and so He is not the Ultimate. (The Ultimate Reality in Plato's thought is the Form of the Good, which became identified with God in later Christian thought.)

Several positive lessons may be derived from this truth of creation.

1. God was the sole Source of all existence. Though this statement is redundant, it is important to reemphasize. The Early Church was faced with a powerful threat to its faith on this point by Gnosticism. Basing their metaphysical speculations on the premise that matter was evil, the Gnostics attributed the creation to a lower god. It is well known how Marcion rejected the Old Testament with its Creator God because he could not reconcile creation with redemption. This is one reason why the Early Church was so inflexibly committed to retaining the Old Testament as authentic Scripture, and identifying the God of creation with the God of redemption to whom the New Testament bore witness, even though it posed serious hermeneutical problems for them. Irenaeus was perhaps the most powerful champion of the authenticity of the truth of creation versus the Gnostics in his *Against Heresies.*

2. Since all that is derives from God's will, nothing in existence can be intrinsically evil; not matter, or finite reality as we have already observed, and no other form of existence, either personal or impersonal.

This affirmation of faith raises serious questions concerning evil. From whence did it arise? Dualism has no problem with the

---

23. Cf. A. E. Taylor, *Plato: The Man and His Work* (Cleveland and New York: World Publishing Co., 1964), 456-57.

question because evil is easily attributed to a source other than God, often to a malevolent being. Under the influence of dualistic thought encountered in Babylon, Jewish thinkers began to speak dualistically, especially in the literary genre known as apocalyptic.[24] Thus from this milieu there appears on the pages of the New Testament the sinister character of Satan as the personal embodiment of evil. Preoccupation with the devil has led many modern Christians into a popular version of dualism that involves a denial of the doctrine of *ex nihilo*.

For such persons, reading the Old Testament can create a powerful culture shock. The Old Testament writers take their monotheism seriously and attribute everything to God, including evil (cf. 1 Sam. 16:14 ff.; 18:10; 19:9; 1 Kings 22:20-23). The Old Testament thus serves as an important theological underpinning for the New to help us avoid collapsing the dramatic ethical dualism found on its pages into a metaphysical dualism. Moral evil then must be accounted as a perversion of the good that God created.

In 1945, when the world had been forcibly impressed with the demonic dimension of human history by the rise of Hitler and the atrocities that accompanied it, forcing the rosy optimism that flourished in the 19th and early 20th centuries to reevaluate its presuppositions, William Robinson wrote a perceptive, theologically sound treatment of the question, which he titled *The Devil and God*. Rejecting dualism as a nonpossibility for Christian thought, he shows how this does not weaken a proper biblical belief in the reality of the devil. He argues that Jesus' temptation is the decisive passage and concludes: "The story of the Temptation clearly implies that Jesus was up against some sinister personal force at work in the world, and to refuse to accept this lands us in terrible difficulty with regard to the doctrine of the Incarnation."[25] Robinson

---

24. Cf. Leon Morris, *Apocalyptic* (Grand Rapids: Wm. B. Eerdmans Publishing Co., 1972). A fascinating illustration of this point is found in I Chron. 21:1, where this post-exilic history attributes to Satan the influencing of David to conduct a census, whereas the older account in 2 Sam. 24:1 attributes it to the Lord. William Robinson comments that "this is the one clear piece of evidence, in the *canonical* books, of that radical theological development which took place in Israel between the return from the Exile and rise of Christianity." *The Devil and God* (Nashville: Abingdon-Cokesbury Press, 1945), 56. The later Old Testament books speak about Satan, but there he is not depicted in quite the same sinister way as in the New Testament. It should be carefully noted that apocalyptic is a complex phenomenon. Insofar as canonical literature manifests apocalyptic characteristics, it is not ever dualistic.

25. P. 67.

refers to the fact, noted above, that early Old Testament writers attributed evil to God, as a primitive understanding. In other words, the New Testament presents the fully revealed view of the nature of moral evil.

The origin of the idea of Satan is not exceedingly difficult to identify, but his origin in reality is more complex. Some scriptures used to address this question are of questionable exegesis, while others do speak of fallen angels (Jude 6; 2 Pet. 2:4), and some more directly imply a satanic apostasy (John 8:44; 1 John 3:8). One must primarily resort to inferences from certain theological doctrines, notably that of creation as herein explored. Care in doing that, however, must be taken in order to avoid imaginative speculation. Furthermore one must recognize that much of popular imagery of the devil comes from noncanonical sources. Canonical sources are amazingly free from such descriptions.

Satan, as the embodiment of evil, must be seen as having dependent existence, or else *creatio ex nihilo* is compromised. He furthermore cannot be affirmed as having been created by God as an evil reality. Hence the only logical conclusion to which one can come is that Satan is a personal reality having a measure of freedom like Adam and Eve, who was good in the beginning but by some precreation choice rebelled against his Creator, as did the first pair, and thus perverted God's good creation. It is on this basis that the passages of Scripture referred to above are brought in, since they reflect such a pattern. It is therefore apparent that evil is personal in nature, concrete but not empirical, a perversion of good rather than having ultimate positive significance. In a word, the New Testament teaching is not contradictory to the Old Testament revelation upon which it is firmly erected.

3. In all creation there is nothing other than God worthy of man's worship. Everything else is finite and finally owes its own existence to God. Thus to place dependency in any aspect of the creation is to be guilty of idolatry. This precludes all forms of superstition from the consistent Christian life. It condemns as pagan any kind of belief in fate, such as astrology, where it is believed that man's destiny is somehow determined by the stars. God alone is worthy of the kind of dependence that is religious in nature. Herein lies the real significance of Friedrich Schleiermacher's defi-

nition of religion as "the feeling of absolute dependence."[26] Paul Tillich's definition of faith as ultimate concern is also a graphic description of a true understanding of the religious nature of human existence when the truth of creation is recognized.

The Status of Creation

The second major implication of the doctrine of creation as classically formulated is that creatures are dependent yet real and good. In philosophical jargon, it excludes pantheism where the distinction between God and His creation (if the term can even be used) is blurred.

It is not generally known that the full formula designed by theology to reflect the total implications of the doctrine reads: *creatio ex nihilo, non de Deo, sed ex nihilo* (creation out of nothing, not out of God, but out of nothing).[27] This avoids an interpretation of creation as emanation, where God's nature is projected into reality like the rays of the sun emanate from the source, as in Neoplatonism. In that imagery the distinction between infinite and finite reality is obscured.

In this view what is not God is neither real nor good. The result is that finite being is illusory, as the following analysis clearly shows:

> Now finite things as finite, that is as material, individual, partial, historical, or personal creatures are clearly in only a very small degree identical with God. For God, as the transcendent source of all, is the negation of all these characteristics of finitude. The divine Being who is above all and in all, clearly can be neither material, individual, personal nor temporal; as the principle of the unity of all things it tends inevitably to absorb, and so to remove these very characteristics that make things finite and diversified. If finite things *are* God, and if God transcends their finite characteristics, then inevitably the creature *as* finite becomes unreal. Only if finite things have an existence, so to speak, "of their own," separate and distinct from God, can they be said to be real as finite.[28]

The doctrine of creation *non de Deo* affirms, by contrast, that the world with all the finite beings within it are not a part of God

26. Basing his theology on the monistic, pantheistic philosophy of Spinoza, Schleiermacher's explicit understanding of this dependence is not fully Christian and certainly is not the consequence of the biblical doctrine of creation.

27. Augustine, *On Marriage and Concupiscence*, chap. 48.

28. Gilkey, *Maker of Heaven and Earth*, 60.

but possess real though dependent existence. Here Christianity stands apart from most, if not all, Eastern religions, which see all creaturely existence as more or less illusory manifestations of the real. Thus the way of salvation or enlightenment consists of meditation in order to penetrate to the depth of one's own being where the Divine is to be found. The following passage from the Hindu scriptures reflects this pantheistic identification of our own reality with that of the All or the Whole: "That which is the finest essence—this whole world has that as its soul. That is reality. That is Atman [soul]. That art thou, Svetaketu."[29] Final salvation in such a pantheistic worldview is always sought through an escape from space-time existence or the limitations of history.

But to assert that creatures are real does not suggest an independent status. The very fact that creation is out of nothing implies that their continued existence is dependent upon the sustaining power of God. If or when this is removed, the creature lapses back into nothing. Hence all creation lives on the knife-edge of nonexistence. It is this that explains a Christian existentialist understanding of anxiety, the threat of nonbeing of which only human creatures are aware. Paul underscored this point when he spoke to the Athenians about the Creator God: "In him we live and move and have our being" (Acts 17:28). Wesley echoes this understanding: "Man is a merely dependent being; . . . Dependence is woven into his very nature; so that, should God withdraw from him, he would sink into nothing" (*Works* 9:456).

It is clear from this that taking seriously the doctrine of creation will directly influence our understanding of the nature of salvation. The view that sees salvation as simply saving souls is inadequate. Salvation in the full biblical sense encompasses the whole man, reaching to his physical needs, his psychic needs, and his political needs. It is this dimension of biblical faith that William Temple had in mind when he made his classic statement that "Christianity is the most avowedly materialist of all the great religions."[30]

It is this commitment that makes the Incarnation fully comprehensible in principle and likewise depreciates any view that despises the body, making it ipso facto evil. Not only can the body be sanctified in this life, but finally the Christian hope entails the

29. Quoted from the Upanishads by Gilkey, ibid., 75 n. 8.
30. *Nature, Man, and God*, 478.

bodily resurrection, not disembodied existence. A careful survey of all reaching out for life beyond death in the Old Testament will reveal that nowhere is it conceived as a possibility in any other way than in the flesh.

We can now see that maintaining the reality of finite being maintains the reality of sin as a significant act against God. Men are not epiphenomena of the Divine Reality but real centers of effective action. Here is the Achilles' heel of Christian Science. Being a popular version of pantheism, it denies the reality of sin but declares it to be simply a wrong manner of thinking. The cure for sin as well as sickness is a proper evaluation of the status of such illusory concepts, says the Christian Science practitioner.

Furthermore, *creatio ex nihilo* implies that in becoming related to God, man does not slough off his creaturehood but remains finite. This is the ground of our humility (not humiliation) of which Paul spoke when he referred to the "treasure in earthen vessels" (2 Cor. 4:7).

A further implication of the truth that creatures have real existence and are essentially good is that sin is not in things but in the misuse of things. All the material creation and all the natural physical drives of the body are good in themselves. They may be perverted, satisfied in the wrong way, used in all sorts of twisted manners; but this is the result of the rebellious will of man who chooses to exercise his freedom to revolt against the purposes of his Creator.

Freedom and Purpose

The third major implication of *creatio ex nihilo* is that God creates in freedom and with purpose. God's freedom in relation to His creation means that man cannot discover the how and the why of the creation, since it lies outside his experience. Our scientific explanations occur within the context of finite relations, which are subject to our knowledge. But the relation between the Creator and the creation is not the same as the relation between one finite event (or person) and another.

The nearest we can come to an explanation is through the use of analogies, yet all analogies ultimately fall short because they are derived from common experience. The critiques of David Hume concerning all forms of the cosmological argument for the existence of God make this positive contribution to preserving the transcendence and freedom of God. William Paley, in the 18th century, had proposed the famous argument of the analogy between the watch and the human eye by which he felt that he had demonstrated the existence of a cosmic Designer of the universe. Hume replied simply that when we discover a watch, we infer a watchmaker because we have had experience of watchmakers making watches. But we have never had any experiences of a Divine Artificer creating a world out of nothing. Thus the analogy breaks down as proof. "The basic formula 'out of nothing' is in fact an explicit abandonment of any 'how' explanation."[31]

This formula likewise precludes a naturalistic discovery of the purpose of God in creation. Since purpose implies "person-ness," we are introduced to an additional dimension: To know the purposes and intentions of a person, we must receive a personal word of explanation from him. (See the discussion of this point as it pertains to "revelation" in chap. 4.) Pertinent to this point is the fact that the Hebrew perceived history rather than nature to be the primary source of revelation. God's personal purposes can be more readily discerned in His saving acts than in natural phenomena. Old Testament scholars are virtually unanimous in holding that the Hebrew chronology of belief was from God's activity in bringing Israel into being to God as Creator, that is, from history to nature and not vice versa.[32] As Langdon Gilkey puts it: "Knowledge of the 'purpose' of God in creation is derived from the experience of His love in the Covenant with Israel and in Christ."[33]

This illuminates the significance of Karl Barth's Christological interpretation of creation. Following Barth's lead, Gustav Aulen says:

> The content of its [creation's] significance and goal derives from the fact that the whole act of creation [beginning, process, and climax] is connected with Christ. . . . When Christ is connected in this way with creation as a whole, and his act of redemption illuminates it, the meaning and purpose of God's creative will becomes clear and unequivocal.[34]

---

31. Gilkey, *Maker of Heaven and Earth*, 65.
32. See Norman Young, *Creator, Creation, and Faith* (Philadelphia: Westminster Press, 1976), 40.
33. *Maker of Heaven and Earth*, 72.
34. *Faith of the Christian Church*, 157.

Creation, Life, and History

We have previously noted modern attempts to interpret the doctrine of creation exclusively in terms of what might be called its "existential" meaning. Against this we have affirmed that the Genesis narrative is also historical, but now we come to acknowledge the validity that resides in these claims. The narratives do have existential import, and this is centrally that the doctrine of creation is faith's assertion that finitude is not surrounded by a "sheer abyss of nothingness," or put positively, that life has meaning.

If the world, and especially man, is the product of blind fate or irrational forces or is the ground of its own explanation, the result is inevitably meaninglessness. But biblical faith declares that there is a transcendent Ground of finite existence and that this Ground is intelligent and purposeful.

Langdon Gilkey suggests that there are three factors necessary to a sense of meaning: (1) the hope of the ultimate fulfillment of our deepest needs, (2) a vision of an intelligent and purposive order of significance in which one's life can participate, and (3) some promise of inner health and unity.[35] Apart from these, there can but be cynicism and despair. We may summarize these as (1) a Ground of Hope, (2) a Ground of Coherence, and (3) a Ground of Wholeness. All these are affirmed in the doctrine of God the Creator.

Modern versions of nihilism are all consequents of the loss of faith in God. The French existentialist Jean-Paul Sartre's indictment of the meaning of life (see his novel *No Exit*) is the direct result of denying that there is a purpose to human existence, and that denial in turn results from a rejection of the existence of God. Unlike a paper knife whose maker presupposed a function for his product, and which he built into it, mankind is thrown into history with no preconceived purpose for being, no essence, and is left with the "dreadful freedom" of creating its own values and any meaning that life may have.[36]

What is true of individual life is also true of history. God as the transcendent, Creative Ground of history is faith's warrant that

---

35. *Maker of Heaven and Earth*, 153.
36. See his essay "Existentialism Is a Humanism." Many people mistakenly identify existentialism exclusively with this brand of atheistic existentialism. But there are other more positive versions, e.g., that of Kierkegaard.

history is not a series of fortuitous events without pattern or purpose. One of the most fascinating facts of history is that the Hebrews, almost alone of ancient peoples, produced a sense of history that is the heritage of the Western world. This is because they understood history to be linear in nature, originating in the creative will of Yahweh and directed by His providence toward an eschatological consummation in the kingdom of God.[37]

Almost, if not all, ancient peoples conceptualized history in some form of cyclical movement. If history moves in cycles, it is going nowhere; and history without a goal is history without a purpose and thus without meaning. So life within such a history partakes of the same characteristics.

One of the most mysterious, and least understood, books of the Old Testament is Ecclesiastes. Its heterodoxy puzzles many. But if it is envisioned as an attempt to show the futility of life from the perspective of a cyclical view of history, it becomes a scintillating apology for the biblical doctrine of faith in God the Creator.

"Vanity of vanities! All is vanity," is a perfect description of life in a history that is going nowhere, because if history simply repeats itself, "there is nothing new under the sun" (Eccles. 1:2, 9). Most cyclical views derived their understanding of God and history from nature (see the comments on the "chronological order" of Israel's faith above). This derivation can be clearly seen in verses 5-7, where the cyclical processes of nature provide the paradigm for history:

> The sun rises and the sun goes down,
> and hastens to the place where it rises.
> The wind blows to the south,
> and goes round to the north;
> round and round goes the wind,
> and on its circuits the wind returns.
> All streams run to the sea,
> but the sea is not full;
> to the place where the streams flow,
> there they flow again.

Augustine encountered this devastating view in his day with its consequent meaninglessness and vigorously opposed it on both

---

37. See Bernhard W. Anderson, *Creation Versus Chaos*, 26-33.

a creational and a Christological basis.[38] He points out the impossibility of meaningfulness and happiness (bliss) unless history leads to an eschaton: "For how can that be truly called blessed which has no assurance of being so eternally, and is either in ignorance of the truth, and blind to the misery that is approaching, or, knowing it, is in misery and fear?" In contrast to the deadening cyclical view of time, "if it [the soul] passes to bliss, and leaves miseries forever, then there happens in time a new thing which time shall not end."[39]

If history is real and linear, as the doctrine of creation validates, there is the possibility of freedom and purposefulness, creative action and change. All are essential for historical existence to have significance. Consequently, there is profound existential import to affirm: "I believe in God the Father Almighty, Maker of heaven and earth."

Creation and Evil

The most difficult problem for all forms of theistic faith is what has been called the problem of evil. We have bypassed several issues along the way as being most properly a subject of the discipline of philosophy of religion. Philosophy is indeed much preoccupied with this problem, but theology must also address it head-on because it is the most devastating challenge that religious faith must face. What we will do is seek to focus on the distinctly theological dimensions of the question, and at best we can only be suggestive.

The first step is one of definition. Evil, like good, is not to be defined from man's experience primarily. If this is done, it is too apt to be easily identified with absence of pleasure or conversely simply with pain or in other anthropocentric ways. Evil is the perversion of good. We have seen that good is a purpose or teleological idea. Thus evil is dysteleological or the perverting or thwarting of purpose—God's purpose. Avoiding a merely anthropocentric definition eliminates already some aspects of the question, but it does not solve it, for clearly there are many factors present in this finite world that oppose and thwart God's purposes. This is evil.

---

38. "Far be it, I say, from us to believe this. For once Christ died for our sins and, rising from the dead, He dieth no more." *City of God*, bk. 12, chap. 13; hereafter 12.13.
39. Ibid.

When the biblical writer rejected the polytheistic mythologies that informed the Babylonian cosmology, and "hordes of warring deities were made to give way to the one all-sovereign creator," the problem of evil was heightened and intensified.[40] So long as the world was attributed to multiple sources and they were not considered particularly ethical in nature, evil was relatively easy to explain.

Consequently, sensitive people have often resorted to dualistic explanations as a way out of this most excruciating dilemma for faith. But creation out of nothing, as we have seen, precludes this easy answer, and biblical faith will not allow it. Others have sought to evade the difficulty by denying the reality of evil. This way is not so much a head-in-the-sand approach as an attempt to explain evil as a necessary part of creation to make the picture complete. Just as the dark hues are necessary for a portrait, it holds that evil is necessary in the total picture of history. This has been the way out for theologies influenced by monistic philosophy. A much more serious and very helpful interpretation seeks to see evil as purposeful, as being pedagogical.[41] A modern version of this tradition has been suggested by Geddes MacGregor on the principle that "God is love" (1 John 4:8, 16) and that this entails a special way of relating to His creation. In granting us freedom, God recognizes that its full meaning cannot be achieved without struggle, and evil becomes the occasion for its actualization. The metaphysical presupposition, he says, of an impassible God

> lies at the root of our gravest difficulties with the concept of evil. We have rarely taken seriously enough the supreme biblical testimony about the character of God: God is love. The case I have been arguing, far from doing injury to the concept of divine omnipotence, exalts it as a kenotic almightiness. What then remains of the problem of evil turns into a question about the nature of freedom and the necessity of the struggle entailed in its development. The reality of that freedom and of that necessity in Nature confronts us daily. Nothing that we know in Nature seems to achieve its status without struggle. Development, whether of life or of mind, is a succession of prison-breaks.[42]

---

40. Norman Young, *Creator, Creation, and Faith*, 38.

41. Thomas Aquinas asserted that God permits evil for a greater good, and the history of Christian thought includes a tradition that holds that God intends by means of suffering to build faith and character into our lives. See Aquinas, *Summa Theologica* 1.48-49; John Hick, *Evil and the God of Love* (New York: Harper and Row, Publishers, 1966).

42. MacGregor, *He Who Lets Us Be*, 146.

We have not yet distinguished between moral evil (sin) and natural evil (sometimes called physical evil). We are obviously speaking about the latter, but a strong tradition has attributed natural evil to sin, so that man is himself responsible for everything in the world that is pervertive of God's purposes, including all disturbances in nature that cause human misery.[43] This was the theology that informed the "miserable comforters" of Job and was the understanding with which the book was struggling.

It is the case that many examples often given of evil, for example, war, must be attributed to sin. Man's rebellious will, his refusal to acknowledge the Lordship of his Creator, has far-reaching implications, and many forms of pain, suffering, and sickness can be traced directly or indirectly to human rebellion—far more than we have sometimes imagined. These forms of evil do not pose a serious intellectual problem for theistic faith because they do not call into question the power (assuming He has self-limited it by human freedom) or the love of God.[44]

We need further to identify those aspects of experience that we have sometimes called evil that are the inevitable consequences of finitude. Apart from being God, we cannot avoid pain, suffering, and death by virtue of being in this kind of world, that is, by being created. This does not seem to be a crucial indictment of the Creator. As H. H. Farmer puts it:

> Unless we are going to ask for a world so utterly different from the one in which we find ourselves alive that it is impossible to form any conception of it, it seems clear that life could not persist, nor could it develop, unless on the one hand it could suffer the discomfort of at least temporarily dissatisfied [sic] desire, and unless, on the other hand, it were set in a world sufficiently stable and regular in its behaviour to negate, even painfully, any desires which in effect presume it to be other than it is.[45]

---

43. Richard S. Taylor advocates a modified version of this view in *Exploring Christian Holiness* 3:20 ff.

44. Some have suggested that God might grant real freedom while at the same time eliminating the possibility of sinning, but this seems to be playing with words. H. H. Farmer says: "The fact of wickedness, from one point of view, does not constitute a problem for the religious mind, or indeed for mankind in general. It is bound up with the fact of freedom, without which anything in the nature of a truly personal relationship is unthinkable. Whatever may be the problems which the problem of freedom raises for philosophy, it raises none for the practical life and least of all for the religious man as he is aware of himself standing in a living relationship with God." *World and God*, 94.

45. Ibid., 90.

However, when we have pursued these limitations of the problem to the fullest extent, we are still left with evils for which we cannot find rational explanation within the limits of our finite sphere and which *appear* to call into question either the power or the love of God. Does the Bible offer us any kind of solution? Not if we are looking for a rational, neatly packaged explanation of a philosophical nature. In fact, it has been observed by some Jewish rabbis that the essence of the Jewish religion is wrestling with God, and the problem of evil is one issue about which the rabbis have sought to get a "hammerlock" on God, but without ever being able to throw Him. (Habakkuk is a classic example of such wrestling.) However, there are some clues in the Scripture that may suggest faith's way out of the dilemma.

The first of these is a hint that begins in the Genesis account of creation itself and traces its way in a subtle way throughout the Bible, coming into open view in the final vision of the Book of Revelation. There appears in Gen. 1:1-2 the adaptation of a "chaos," which is symbolized by the sea, or turbulent waters.[46] It is this that God overcomes in the ordering act/process of creation. As Gerhard von Rad says, it

> speaks not only of a reality that once existed in a preprimeval period but also of a possibility that always exists. Man has always suspected that behind all creation lies the abyss of formlessness; that all creation is always ready to sink into the abyss of the formless; that the chaos, therefore, signifies simply the threat to everything created.[47]

This complex of ideas seems to provide a symbolism of evil that has been rejected by God at the beginning but that stands as a constant threat to the good creation and even at times impinges itself upon God's world. The account of the Deluge may to some extent reflect the same imagery. The sinful rebellion of man opens up the doors to the watery chaos that all but engulfs the world, leading to the promise of preservation by God symbolized by the rainbow. It is altogether possible that the parting of the waters of the Red Sea conveyed the same idea to the Hebrew mind.

Throughout the Scriptures, the "sea" and "waters" on occasion symbolize evil, and on occasion faith takes comfort and hope in

---

46. There is a vast amount of literature on this subject beginning with Herman Gunkel's pioneering work, *Creation and Chaos,* published in 1895. See massive bibliography in Bernhard W. Anderson, *Creation Versus Chaos.*
47. *Genesis,* 48-49.

recalling God's initial parting the waters of chaos (cf. Psalms 74; 77; Isa. 51:9-11). The water miracles of Jesus could suggest the same creative power at work in the defeat of evil. Norman Young argues that Mark's intention in his accounts of the stilling of the storm (4:41) and of Jesus walking on the sea (6:51) is to call attention to the power of the new creation that was bringing the powers of evil into (further) subjugation.[48]

The final picture of ultimate victory over evil in the Book of Revelation presents us with the conquest in what, apart from this symbolism, could be an otherwise enigmatic comment: "I saw a new heaven and a new earth, for the first heaven and the first earth had vanished, and *there was no longer any sea*" (21:1, NEB, italics added). The result of "no more sea" (KJV) was the absence of all of those consequences of evil in the old creation: "He will wipe every tear from their eyes; there shall be an end to death, and to mourning and crying and pain" (v. 4, NEB).

This brief survey seems to suggest that evil is an excluded reality (i.e., it does not exist as a positive existence but as the absence of being, the "nothing" out of which all things were made; it is not a veiled dualism) that God holds back from its full force bursting upon and destroying His creation; and ultimately, when finitude is swallowed up in immortality, it will be totally overcome. By analogy we, too, are engaged in a struggle with evil, but with God we shall be able to overcome it both *en via* and in the eschaton. Thus it is suggested that the main issue with evil for biblical faith is not to understand it but to triumph over it.

This leads us to the next clue to the biblical understanding of the problem, which is the cross of Christ. The Cross may be interpreted as God's final word to the issue of suffering. The Old Testament struggles repeatedly with this problem and offers penultimate proposals that point toward the Cross. The Book of Job is the best known of these attempts. The striking thing about this theodicy is that the book introduces at least five proposed rational solutions to suffering, but its final word is found when Job transcends his predicament and comes to put implicit faith in God:

> Then Job answered the Lord:
> "I know that thou canst do all things,
> and that no purpose of thine can be thwarted.

---

48. *Creator, Creation, and Faith*, 73-74.

'Who is this that hides counsel without knowledge?'
Therefore I have uttered what I did not understand,
things too wonderful for me,
which I did not know.
'Hear, and I will speak;
I will question you, and you declare to me.'
I had heard of thee by the hearing of the ear,
but now my eye sees thee;
therefore I despise myself,
and repent in dust and ashes."

(42:1-5)

This is not a rational but a personal answer.

The high point of the Old Testament's effort to make sense out of suffering is found in the Suffering Servant passages in Isaiah 40—55, where the suffering of God's righteous servant is seen to be redemptive. It is but one short step to Calvary, where the Servant suffers and, in the moment of His most intense agony reflected in the cry of dereliction from the Cross, masters evil. Thus we see from this perspective, once again, that in Christian faith evil and suffering are presented to us, not as a problem to be solved, but as a challenge, as something to be overcome with redemptive consequences. William Robinson suggests that we see three things in the Cross: (1) We see, in the face of all contrary evidence, that God is love. (2) We see that God is righteous, that He is not indifferent to moral considerations. And (3) we see that this is no mere piece of information—"cold comfort for such distress as ours. Involved in it is the *action* of God."[49]

His conclusion is: "The centering of our perplexities at the Cross gives us a *faith* by which to live, something much better than a *gnosis* making every step of the way plain—which after all is a prescription for cowards and not for heroes."[50]

Nature and history create the problem of evil. The Cross points the way to the solution. And in the light of the Cross, the Christian way is a faithful walk, sometimes through the "deep waters" until there is "no more sea."

---

49. *Devil and God*, 82-83.
50. Ibid., 81.

Providence, Miracle, and Prayer

The question of the continued relation of God to His creation raises a number of issues crucial to theology and very practical in their orientation. It is one thing to speak of God bringing the world into being by divine fiat so that it has a beginning; it is quite another to speak about the status of that creation after the *ex nihilo* act. Has God established an independent set of laws by which the realm of nature operates so that He no longer intervenes (deism—radical transcendence)? Or can every so-called natural occurrence be attributed to immediate divine activity (primitivism)? The same issues can be raised in regard to the realm of history as the world of human reality, but other dimensions impinge themselves into the picture when human beings are involved, due to the fact of freedom. The more general term for this complex of questions is *Providence*.

Providence

Providence is a logical extension of the concept of creation. Unless we proceed to His providence, we have a partial concept of the meaning of the affirmation "that God is the Creator." No one seriously believes that the world was made by God who is not also persuaded that He takes care of His own works.

The term *providence* is derived from two Latin words *pro* and *videre*, meaning to look ahead, to foresee, and thus to plan in advance. It also means "to carry out a plan." In a word it suggests the idea of purpose or intention and guiding to the achievement of that purpose.

Theologically, the doctrine is usually divided into general providence, having to do with God's general oversight of the creation; and special (or personal) providence, having to do with individual life or specific acts of God.

General providence relates to the more or less ontological idea that God sustains the creation so that its continued existence is moment by moment dependent upon His activity. He upholds all things by the word of His power (Heb. 1:3; Acts 17:28). It may also be used to refer to His universal guidance of human history to its cosmic climax.

Special providence is always related, either directly or indirectly, to the affairs of men. In one sense, the whole Old Testament may be considered as a story of God's providential activity in relation to the people of Israel. There are times when God's purposes are seen to be working in and through but overriding the sin of man. Perhaps the most dramatic, self-conscious example of this is the case of Joseph, whose words in Gen. 45:7-8b capture the confidence that God is overruling man's evil intentions in order to accomplish His own long-range plans.

The pivotal passage in the New Testament is Rom. 8:28. One problem here is that the widely quoted King James Version has left it with a somewhat naturalistic flavor, but perhaps an even more pervertive factor is that the verse is too often appropriated out of its context, which essentially includes verse 29. It does not affirm that God is the immediate Source of every occurrence that affects the believer's life, but that God is able to bring good out of whatever happens. The meaning hangs on the significance of the term "good." This is a purpose word, as we have often seen, and verse 29 makes clear what the good is, what God purposes to produce in the lives of His people through the occurrences of life: that they may be "conformed to the image of his Son." If we identify good with pleasure, lack of discomfort, or other egocentric consequences, we shall ultimately be disappointed. But if in faith our response to life's adversities is proper, the result will be Christlikeness of character and attitude, and thus the good that God purposes will be achieved.

This analysis takes us to the fundamental fact that providence has an inescapably personal element. It is a truth that is seen through the eyes of faith. If one takes specific events in which he sees God at work and generalizes them into an abstract theory, he will end up with not the God of love but a monster. As H. H. Farmer so well puts it: Faith in providence means, "not a quasi-philosophical affirmation of an ultimate harmony in things, but a confidence that man's personal life is the concern of a wisdom and power higher than his own."[51]

One of the most critical issues with the doctrine of providence involves the relation of God's sovereignty to free will. A deterministic worldview, whether philosophical or theological, avoids the question but abandons any meaningful personal dimensions in God's relation to the world. If men are pawns that (not whom) the

---

51. *World and God,* 89.

Sovereign Chessmaster moves in a unilateral, even capricious, way, the personal character of the divine-human relation is effectively eliminated.

To take the other position is to acknowledge a limitation of the sovereignty of God that may be interpreted as self-imposed. Geddes MacGregor, in a sustained effort to draw out the systematic implications of the biblical declaration that God is love, says to this point:

> To say that the Biblical God is love is to say that his creation is an act, not of self-expansion but of self-limitation. For the Biblical God, being ontologically perfect himself as well as sovereign and independent of his creatures, could have nowhere to go by way of expansion . . . The only way he could go in his creative act would be a way of self-limitation, self-emptying, self-abnegation. That is what *agape* would entail.[52]

And yet, on the other hand, it could be argued that if God is love, it is not a limitation but an expansive expression to grant man full freedom, since love manifests itself in such an outgoing fashion. In either case, the outcome is the same, and the Wesleyan perspective affirms God's activity within the context of human freedom. This means that God does not determine one's choices, but He influences them. Man may submit his will to God for guidance, but this does not violate his freedom. God may even influence opposing wills but not by coercion. While this is a mystery beyond our capacity to fully comprehend, perhaps the nearest we can come to an explanation is to say that God uses the methods of persuasion. Ultimately the doctrine of providence is shrouded in a mystery that faith cannot penetrate so as to formulate a rational solution. However, this does not deter faith's confidence in the watchcare of the living God over His creation.

William Robinson puts his finger upon the core of the issue when he says:

> If we boldly rid our minds of metaphysical, bloodless concepts and think of God in personal terms, as the Bible invites us to do, and accept the view that both creation and redemption, in their differing degrees, involve the notion of self-limitation in God, then we shall not indeed be able fully to understand the mystery of the providence of God, but at least we shall not be starting from assumptions which prevent us from arriving at any kind of understanding whatever.[53]

---

52. *He Who Lets Us Be*, 19.
53. *Devil and God*, 116.

Miracle

The discussion of providence impinges directly on the question of miracle. The most crucial aspect of this highly debated topic is one's definition of miracle. The definition makes all the difference in the world whether one can or does believe in the possibility of miracle, although it is not, of course, the ultimately decisive matter. C. S. Lewis is certainly correct when he observes that "what we learn from experience depends on the kind of philosophy we bring to experience. It is therefore useless to appeal to experience before we have settled, as well as we can, the philosophical question."[54] It is for this reason, above all, that a contemporary theology would never think of using miracle as evidence for the proposition that revelation has occurred.[55]

The usual beginning place of a discussion of miracle is to raise the question of its relation to natural law. But this is to commit what Gilbert Ryle called in another connection, a "category mistake." This approach treats miracle as a scientific category, whereas it is primarily, if not exclusively, a theological category (see discussion of theology as it pertains to other disciplines in chap. 1). If it is not treated in this way, it becomes a pseudocategory so far as religious faith is concerned.

The etymology of the term provides a beginning point. It means "that which produces astonishment, or awe or wonder," or it may mean "that which causes one to marvel." This opens the door but does not yet distinguish the distinctive religious significance of miracle. For example, it does not differentiate miracle from magic, which would also produce "astonishment." One additional step is needed to give content to the astonishment. A miracle is that event (or nonevent) that creates in one a personal awareness of God.

Many events transcend our understanding and create a sense of mystery but do not generate an experience of ecstasy, that is, the response to God in obedient faith, praise, adoration, and thank-

---

54. *Miracles* (New York: Macmillan Co., 1947), 7.
55. This was standard procedure for premodern theologies. However, to do this often led to the logical fallacy of begging the question if the argument took the turn of using miracle to authenticate revelation and then claiming that the accounts of the miracles were valid because they were inspired. Interestingly, John Wesley, who lived in the heyday of such appeals, refused to share this apologetic and explicitly rejected the idea that miracles serve to prove basic theological claims. They are self-authenticating. See "The Principles of a Methodist Farther Explained," in *Works* 8:467-68.

260 □ GRACE, FAITH, AND HOLINESS

fulness that it is the purpose of biblical miracle to produce. This explains why Jesus refused to perform "signs and wonders" for those who wanted their wills coercively persuaded by spectacular events. Their preconceptions prohibited them, not from believing in miraculous happenings but from allowing such occurrences to lead them to the truth as it is in Jesus. It has been persuasively argued that the central message of Jesus' story of the rich man and Lazarus was the climactic line of Abraham in replying to Dives' request for Lazarus to be sent as an evangelist to his brothers: "They have Moses and the prophets . . . If they do not hear [them], neither will they be convinced if some one should rise from the dead" (Luke 16:29, 31).

With this basic understanding and proper category classification in mind, we can now proceed to speak to the question of the relation of miracle to other aspects of experience that we have of the world around us, that is, its relation to "natural law."

It should be first noted that natural law is a concept that would be foreign to the biblical writers. It is a relatively modern construct. Furthermore, natural law must not be thought of in any deterministic sense but simply as a descriptive generalization of the way phenomena usually behave. This within itself should create a guarded attitude toward judging religious miracle in the light of this criterion.

The most common and popular definition of miracle is "an interference with nature by supernatural power."[56] Seldom noticed are the disastrous consequences to which this restriction may lead. It can, as a matter of logic, lead to the impossibility of recognizing when a miracle does occur, since our finite understanding can never be sure that an ostensive miraculous event does indeed circumvent a natural law. But perhaps more obvious is the historical results. Not having seen such events that can be identified as genuine,[57] many modern conservative Christians have seriously taken the position that the day of miracles is past, their having been restricted to biblical times. Others, less conservative, have gone further and rationalized away the miracle stories in the Bible, based upon their present experience of scientific laws.

---

56. This is the definition with which C. S. Lewis opens his apologetic for miracles. *Miracles*, 10.

57. This statement is made in full cognizance of the fact that there are many religious charlatans who are miracle-mongers, exploiting the gullible and doing much harm—along with a modicum of good as a fallout, no doubt.

But this popular understanding is not the only interpretation, and there is a strong tradition that rejects this way of viewing it. Augustine expresses himself in favor of another construction: "For we say that all portents are contrary to nature; but they are not so. For how is that contrary to nature which happens by the will of God, since the will of so mighty a Creator is certainly the nature of each created thing? A portent, therefore, happens not contrary to nature, but contrary to what we know as nature."[58]

H. Orton Wiley concurs with this tradition, since he qualifies his definition of miracle with the phrase "beyond that of creaturely measure" (CT 1:150).

We have seen that many facets of the doctrine of God required a delicate balance between transcendence and immanence. Here we must walk the same path. Totally avoiding immanence would put God outside His creation in such a way that His direct activity would always involve an interruption of the natural order and thus eliminate many facets of what the man of faith recognizes as miracle. In taking an extreme immanental view, the real meaning of miracle is dissipated, and we would end up with the very unsatisfactory definition of Schleiermacher, who dogmatized, "Miracle is simply the religious name for event."[59]

To define miracle as we are suggesting means that it is virtually synonymous with revelation. All genuine miracles from the biblical perspective are revelatory, and all revelation is miraculous (in contrast to merely human discovery). Therefore there is a symmetrical relation between the concepts. Alan Richardson contends that both general and special revelation are by their very nature miraculous because they cannot be explained in terms of any known natural processes of human perceiving and apprehending, and it arouses in us in the highest degree the sense of wonder, awe, and humility.[60]

One does not necessarily need to restrict miracle to an event that appears to interrupt the normal processes of nature and/or history. It may be a purely patterned happening, the timing of which impinges upon our consciousness as God's activity. Thus like all other apprehensions of the Divine that we have studied,

---

58. *City of God* 21.8.
59. Friedrich Schleiermacher, *On Religion: Speeches to Its Cultured Despisers,* trans. John Oman (New York: Harper and Row, Publishers, 1958), 88.
60. *Apologetics,* 165.

there is entailed both a giving side (the event) and a receiving side (faith's apprehension of God at work) with the resultant religious response. In this context, Gordon Kaufman's definition is excellent: "Any event which one finds himself led to interpret by reference to God's act rather than finite acts or causes (though not necessarily denying that such finite agency is also involved) is a miracle."[61] We should emphasize that such events may transcend our understanding of natural law but need not necessarily do so.

Prayer

Prayer is related to both providence and miracle. To pray petitionary prayer is to appeal to God's providence. And as H. H. Farmer suggests in the following quotation, prayer and miracle are inseparable:

> Where then must we look for those experiences wherein the word miracle comes with a maximum of spontaneity and inevitability to the lips of the religious man? The answer is, in that relationship to God which we call prayer, especially as it arises out of a deep sense of need and takes the form of a believing petition.[62]

Not only is prayer the most difficult of Christian practices to theologize about, but G. Campbell Morgan correctly observes that "any discussion of the doctrine of prayer which does not issue in the practice of prayer is not only not helpful, it is dangerous."[63]

Prayer may take different forms: thanksgiving, praise, adoration, as well as petition or intercession. The former types, which primarily acknowledge the state of affairs ordained by God, create no theological problem. But petitionary prayer is the type that is difficult to provide theological rationale for, yet Farmer argues that this form is really the *essence* of prayer.[64]

There would be two possible ways of approaching the question, either of which revolves around the Creator-creature relationship. One could begin with the biblical concept of God and attempt to deduce the implications of this for prayer; or one could begin with the biblical pattern of prayer and seek to determine the implications of such a picture for the nature of God. In the context

---

61. *Systematic Theology*, 307.
62. *World and God*, 116.
63. *The Practice of Prayer* (Westwood, N.J.: Fleming H. Revell Co., 1960), 11.
64. *World and God*, 127-28.

of this chapter on "God the Creator" the logical approach would be the first.

Prayer is the natural reaction of one who feels deeply the sense of dependence that a proper understanding of finitude entails. It therefore assumes the quality of spontaneity. Thus at one level, petitionary prayer may be seen as the normal response of the person of faith—the acknowledgment that "every good endowment and every perfect gift is from above, coming down from the Father of lights with whom there is no variation or shadow due to change" (James 1:17). This explains why persons who do not pray normally (because they feel self-sufficient) often turn to prayer in times of difficulty as they come to the realization that here is an aspect of life over which they have no control.

But at another level, it takes the form of prayer whose intent is to effect a change in the state of affairs. Numerous objections have been raised to this: God already knows our needs and intends to supply them, so it is pointless to either inform Him or attempt to persuade Him to do so; or it could be said that such prayer is childish and even egocentric if its ends are eudaemonistic.

On the basis of these and other difficulties, many have felt that petition should be abandoned for another form of prayer that is less presumptuous about influencing God to change something. Prayer, rather, should be either a confession of resignation to the way things are, or a devotional method of bringing our own inner life into submission to the unchanging divine will.

We must avoid the "all or none" fallacy in addressing the question and recognize the value in these objections while not capitulating completely to their implications. Certainly prayer, even of petition and intercession, may properly function to enable us to align our own goals and desires with God's will.

It is also generally recognized that prayer has a powerful therapeutic value. Dr. Alexis Carrel, a Nobel prize winner in the field of medicine, is quoted as calling prayer "the most powerful form of energy that one can generate" and claiming that "its influence on the human mind and body is as demonstrable as that of secreting glands."[65]

It is the objective dimension of petition, however, that gives more difficulty. Yet the Bible and Christian experience is replete

---

65. Quoted in MacGregor, *He Who Lets Us Be,* 158.

with "mountain-moving" responses to prayer, and this, to faith, cannot be gainsaid. It may be granted that in many cases finite causes can be appealed to as entering into the outcome, but as in the case of miracle this does not invalidate faith's recognition that God has been providentially at work.

Ultimately the issue of prayer will remain a mystery. But so long as God is understood to be personal (not an impersonal Brahman or Aristotelian Unmoved Mover), the interaction of the wills of Creator and creature must be acknowledged as having possible dynamic results.

In the light of the biblical picture of God, we may with some degree of assurance make a few theological judgments regarding this relationship. First, prayer is not to be seen as a means of overcoming God's reluctance, and by some form of arm-twisting or unceasingly worrying the issue, pressuring God to do something that He is unwilling to do. God as a loving Father precludes such a parody.

How then does one explain Jesus' parables that call for importunity or persistence in pressing one's case with the Heavenly Father? We might suggest that such an extended period of petitioning may serve at least one major function. The prayer may, in process of seeking, move further away from purely selfish motives and purge his attitudes of eudaemonistic concerns. What he begins to pray for, as a means of his own relief, he may end up praying for, for the glory of God. Hendrikus Berkhof implicitly supports this suggestion with this insight:

> Even the most superstitious who came to Jesus, asking for bread or healing, he did not send away unanswered. On the contrary, in fellowship with him they learned to ask for more than they had begun with, and to ask differently: no longer only from the standpoint of their own needs, but much more from the perspective of God's purposes of which their cares were a part.[66]

Childish prayers, which envision God as a divine Santa Claus compiling lists of gifts for good children, may be inevitable at the outset of the Christian life. But in the process of maturation, while petition is not to be abandoned, it becomes more God-centered and less self-centered. Gustav Aulen's words capture this point well:

---

66. *Christian Faith*, 493.

The ultimate purpose of the prayer of militant faith is the realization of the loving will of God. This is the constitutive element in all militant prayer. Whatever the prayer of faith asks for, its ultimate goal points in this direction. Faith cannot and does not desire anything else than the realization of God's loving will. Therefore the prayer of all prayers is always "Thy will be done."[67]

All manipulations that have as their purpose the bending of the divine will to our will are unworthy of the Creator-creature relationship. Efforts to find formulas, patterns of prayer, or practices of prayer that will be pragmatically more effective in bringing results when simple petition in faith falls short are ultimately the result of a misconception of the nature of God and His relationship to finite persons.

This analysis leads us to the topic of faith. Prayer and faith are Siamese twins of the devotional life. To understand their connection will illuminate further the issue of prayer. Prayer in faith, the New Testament teaches, is the effective prayer. Faith is the human response to the revealed divine will. "Faith comes from what is heard, and what is heard comes by the preaching of Christ" (Rom. 10:17). Faith is not possible where God's promise or will has not been disclosed. I can have faith for only that which is according to His will.

The article of faith on divine healing in the *Manual of the Church of the Nazarene* reflects the biblical understanding: "We . . . urge our people to seek to offer the prayer of faith." It is not always possible. But where God's will is positive, we may be able to pray the "prayer of faith," and God will answer in the affirmative. But such a prayer is impossible when God wills otherwise. True faith submits to the loving will of the Father and always prays: "Thy will be done."

A word on fasting and prayer will perhaps further illuminate the question. Fasting is primarily an Old Testament activity and is symbolic of repentance. In this light, it is clearly understood as bringing oneself into conformity with the will of God, whether personally or nationally. The New Testament speaks only sparsely about fasting; and here either the Old Testament meaning is continued, or it may be interpreted as an aid to faith.[68]

---

67. *Faith of the Christian Church*, 356-57.
68. In his comments on Mark 9:29, Ralph Earle says: "This passage is one of several such in the New Testament where the earliest and best Greek manuscripts do not have

Fasting is never to be understood as an act of self-denial because the body and its appetites are evil (this, as we have seen, violates the whole doctrine of creation), or as a means of somehow eliciting the divine pity and persuading Him thereby. Rather, properly understood, fasting is a way of bringing oneself more intimately into union with the divine will so that, in a sense, it is an acted prayer seeking the mind of God.

Once again, we must find our best understanding between radical transcendence and thoroughgoing immanence. Prayer is neither a stoic acquiescence to the inevitable, even if seen as God's will, nor a desperate calling out to a withdrawn Deity who must be coaxed into relating himself to the world. It is walking "the narrow way between magic and mysticism."[69] True prayer is the interaction of personal covenant partners out of which consequences may take place that might not otherwise occur. Clearly the dynamics of this interaction and its outcome transcends any rational metaphysics and even eludes the pious theologian.

Creation as Eschatological

The overall pattern reflected in the Hebrew-Christian Scriptures can be described as a movement from the old creation to the new creation. This movement must be seen as analogical or typical, but not cyclic. It is not a return to the beginning, but a new creation occurring at the consummation of history.

Israel's appropriation of the prevailing symbolism of creation, as we saw earlier, broke decisively with the mythological representations found in the pagan religions. Everything was decisively historicized as it was picked up and used to inform the crucial events of Israel's history. The saving acts of God, especially the Exodus, were interpreted as the creative power of God manifesting itself in driving back the waters of chaos. Thus this historicizing itself entails an eschatological dimension.

Israelite prophets and poets appropriated the old chaos imagery in order to portray the continuing creative and re-

---

any reference to fasting. Examples are the parallel in Matthew 17:21, as well as Acts 10:30 and I Corinthians 7:5. It seems evident that the growing emphasis on asceticism in the early church led to the interpolation of 'fasting' in several places where it did not exist in the original Greek text." *The Gospel of Mark,* in *The Evangelical Commentary* (Grand Rapids: Zondervan Publishing House, 1957).

69. Hendrikus Berkhof, *Christian Faith,* 493.

demptive work of God. The struggle between Creator and chaos is one which goes on in the realm of history, and this historical struggle continues from the first day to the last day.[70]

To the beginning there corresponds an ending, to creation a completion, to the "very good" here the "perfect" yonder; they correspond, each to each; in the theology of the Old Testament creation is an eschatological conception.[71]

The eschatological dimension is found implicitly in the Psalms, but the point at which it becomes most explicit is in the prophecies of Isaiah 40—55. The prophet is addressing a people who have gone through a deep valley, all but eclipsing their faith in Yahweh, and his task is to rekindle their faith in their God. Apart from this renewal of confidence, his announcement that God is about to renew His redemptive activity in history would fall on unresponsive ears. In order to accomplish this goal, the prophet appeals to the Creation as a paradigm (see 40:21-23, 25-26). The idols who have challenged Yahweh's place in the hearts of His people are themselves entrapped within the confines of nature and history; Yahweh the Creator transcends both and thus is the Controller of history. Thus history is a continuation of the creative power of God.

Israel has now passed through the chaos of the Babylonian Captivity and has nearly been overcome, but the Creator God has held back the Deluge as He promised to Noah (Isa. 54:9-10). Now He is going to give them redemptive victory over the waters and bring into being a new creation. (See 48:6*b*-7; the word "created" is from the verb *bara* used in Genesis 1 of the creative fiat. See also 44:24-28 where the explicit language of creation overcoming chaos informs the announcement of Cyrus as God's instrument in the new Exodus.)

The heart of the prophet's message is that God is conquering the chaos of the Babylonian Captivity and making a path through the "sea" for the redeemed to pass through and return to Zion with "joy and gladness" (Isa. 35:10).

Prophecy in the Old Testament passed eventually into apocalyptic with its vision of a consummation that will become actual only beyond the boundaries of history. In the apocalyptic vision,

---

70. Bernhard W. Anderson, *Creation Versus Chaos*, 132.

71. Ludwig Kohler, *Old Testament Theology*, trans. A. S. Todd (Philadelphia: Westminster Press, 1953), 71.

the "chaos monster" who was overcome at the beginning will break loose from his fetters at the end time and rage against the Lord and His people. But then he will be decisively defeated once and for all. In "The Little Apocalypse," found in Isaiah 24—27, the defeat of the Leviathan who has intruded himself throughout the conflicts of history will be final:

"In that day the Lord with his hard and great and strong sword will punish Leviathan the fleeing serpent, Leviathan the twisting serpent, and he will slay the dragon that is in the sea" (27:1).

The culmination is a "new heavens and a new earth" wherein dwells righteousness (see Isa. 65:17; 66:22; 2 Pet. 3:13; Rev. 21:1). Edmund Jacob says:

> Eschatology is a return to the beginning, but with something which was absent at the first creation. This is why interest in the new creation goes hand in hand with the intensity of Israel's hope, which becomes the more eager as sin has increasingly turned the earth into a chaos. The new heavens and the new earth will not be essentially different from the first creation, but they will be freed from the forces of chaos which threatens its integrity and security.[72]

This cosmic dimension of biblical faith is captured in the summary words of Bernhard Anderson:

> Thus in apocalyptic the whole historical drama, from creation to consummation is viewed as a cosmic conflict between the divine and the demonic, creation and chaos, the kingdom of God and the kingdom of Satan. According to this view, the outcome of the conflict will be God's victorious annihilation of the powers which threaten his creation, including death which apocalyptic writers regarded as an enemy hostile to God. Seen in this perspective, the role of the Anointed One, the Messiah, would be not just to liberate men from the bondage of sin but to battle triumphantly against the formidable powers of chaos.[73]

The Christ who was the Instrument of creation in the beginning and who successfully combated the powers of chaos in the middle will because of that be *Christus Victor* at the end. "They [the powers of chaos] will make war on the Lamb [who was slain on

---

72. *Theology of the Old Testament* (New York: Harper and Row, Publishers, 1958), 142.
73. *Creation Versus Chaos*, 143.

the Cross], and the Lamb will conquer them, for he is Lord of lords and King of kings, and those with him are called and chosen and faithful" (Rev. 17:14).

Creation Ethics

Discussions of theological ethics (whether termed Old Testament, New Testament, biblical, or Christian) have traditionally not recognized a distinction between what can be called *creation* as distinct from *redemption* ethics. The latter has usually been the focus of attention. But it should be recognized that this ethical understanding applies uniquely to the people of God and only in a very awkward way to others. This truth in no sense invalidates the universal character of redemption ethics but simply recognizes its distinctive character.

Creation ethics assumes, on the basis of the doctrine of creation, that God has informed the created world with certain structures. These structures cannot be validly compared with scientific natural law for at least three reasons: (1) natural law is simply a description of the regular behavior of inert phenomena; (2) ethics can have meaning only in the context of freedom, hence is in no sense deterministic; (3) human experience cannot discover an inexorable creation law that cannot be violated or that functions in a rigid, inevitable way without exception.

It does assume that so far as human persons are concerned, there are certain behaviors (e.g., monogamous marriage, see above) that are most fulfilling, and that when these structures are violated, there is damage done to the human spirit.

There is a close correlation between this view and the conservative branch of the Wisdom literature of the Old Testament. This literature may be classified as a "theology of creation." As represented chiefly in the Proverbs, the wise men "sought for a unified structural principle in life. By generalizing from experience they propounded rules as indicators of this moral structure of life, and as guideposts on its way."[74] The religious wise man saw this principle "built into" the moral order by the Creator.

---

74. R. B. Y. Scott, *Proverbs, Ecclesiastes,* vol. 18 in *The Anchor Bible,* ed. William Foxwell Albright and David Noel Freedman (Garden City, N.Y.: Doubleday and Co., 1965), xvii.

Today this guidance would appear to relate chiefly to the secular field, but the Hebrew mind knew of no such distinction between sacred and secular.

It is most important to note that the ethical proverbs recommend (not command) certain behaviors because of the consequences in terms of self-interest. It is to the advantage of the person to follow this advice because undesirable results normally occur when it is ignored, and good results when it is heeded.

The skeptical branch of the Wisdom literature (notably Job and Ecclesiastes) wrestle with the problem of reconciling the general principles derived by the wise men with divergent facts of experience. Hence we observed the distinction from natural law referred to in point 3 above.

Perhaps the clearest expression of the skepticism of this literature is found in Eccles. 8:14: "But there are anomalies in life: there are just men to whom what happens should happen to the wicked, and there are wicked men to whom what happens should happen to the just" (*Anchor Bible* translation; see n. 74 above).

In Job, the problem becomes very acute because of its existential nature. The point is that the "structural principle" is not questioned, it is simply not understood. The struggle of Job is to attempt to see what God is doing, not call into question the fact that God somehow has informed the creation with His purposes. In a word, the difficulty in identifying the ethic of creation does not invalidate the wise man's faith that it exists.

Another illustration of this universal ethic is found in the prophecy of Amos. In a series of oracles against foreign nations (chaps. 1—2) the prophet condemns these people on the basis of their inhuman treatment of other human beings. In other words, there is a covenant of brotherhood to which all men, even outside the revealed law, are amenable. God will bring them into judgment when they violate it. The Hebrews themselves, by contrast, are condemned by Amos for specifically religious sins. This clearly implies that there is an ethic that applies to persons outside the covenant people. Its understanding and application is far less precise than the revealed law, but it is nonetheless present as a reality to be accounted for.

Men do not obey this ethic automatically because it is a matter of instinct or because of some inborn tendency. But their corporate and individual lives are more meaningful and happier if they conform to it. Conversely, corporate and individual life is maimed and scarred when this ethic is violated. The fallenness of man has no doubt created serious problems in clearly identifying the contents. But some light may be attained by analyzing the destructive and constructive facets of human existence.

PART IV

The Doctrines of God the Savior

Man the Sinner

To speak of God as Savior brings into the picture those doctrines traditionally associated with the Son, although we must avoid speaking of Christ as Savior in such a way as to set the Son over against the Father or so as to leave the impression that salvation is not the work of God. It also introduces the question of the object of God's saving love and work (man) and the reason why such saving work is needed (sin). We will first address the issue of sin.

One cannot properly speak of sin in isolation as an abstract concept. Sin does not exist independently of man. It is furthermore not to be regarded as some flawed or defective part of human nature. The Bible always speaks of man in his totality in this connection. So we must not so much speak about sin as about man as sinner. W. T. Purkiser states that sin "is best defined not as a thing, an entity or quantity having ontic status, but as the moral condition of a personal being," and further reinforces this position by these words: "It should be remembered that good and evil are personal terms. They are qualities and acts of persons, not abstractions having independent existence."[1]

The biblical sources use an almost bewildering variety of terms for the idea that is commonly subsumed under the one English word "sin." It is very difficult to organize these into any sys-

---

1. *God, Man, and Salvation*, 87, 120. He also suggests that the Old Testament understanding of sin is as a "distortion" and that the "evidence inclines in the direction of privative, *relational*, and dynamic categories" (italics added). 86.

tematic pattern. The first step to clarification seems to be to recognize the context in which they are used, and particularly the broadest one(s). In the Old Testament most are used as covenant terms. That is, they are best understood as referring to a phenomenon within the covenant relation. Sin constituted a violation of the covenant terms. The New Testament presents somewhat the same picture, especially when its comments on sin have the Old Testament as background.[2]

The other side of the coin is that for the Old Testament, the most poignant source for our understanding of man as sinner, Genesis 1—11, makes minimal use of the standard terminology. The pivotal passage in the New is Romans 1—3, where Paul is dealing with the whole world outside of Jesus Christ. However, he elsewhere, more than any other New Testament writer, addresses the question of the predicament of fallen man in special ways, but always in terms of man outside of Christ. Within this larger context, the focal point is Rom. 3:23: "All have sinned [hēmarton], and come short of the glory of God" (KJV). This refers to man's present state outside of Christ.

The key term in this verse, hamartanō, means literally "to miss the mark." While it is somewhat redundant, since it reiterates the significance of the word, the latter clause of the verse may be taken as a definition of sin. This opens the door to an understanding of what it essentially means for man to be a sinner. The term "glory" is a New Testament synonym for "image" (cf. 1 Cor. 11:7; 2 Cor. 3:18; et al.). Man was created to bear the likeness of God; ideally he is "the image and glory of God." This gives us the clue to the meaning of the present passage. "The glory of God" is the divine likeness, which man is intended to bear. Insofar as man departs from the likeness of God, he is sinful. To "come short of the glory of God is to sin. This definition, simple, broad, and profound, should be borne in mind whenever Paul has occasion to speak about sin."[3]

Gustav Aulen makes the point decisively:

---

2. A vivid example of both the inadequacy of attempting to build a doctrine of sin upon linguistic studies of the words involved and failure to take account of the context is C. Ryder Smith, *The Bible Doctrine of Sin* (London: Epworth Press, 1953). The result is a very unsatisfactory treatment that ends in defining sin as disobeying God. This is quite proper as a covenant concept; but, as Smith shows in his own logical development, it leads inevitably to a denial of the concept of original sin or sinfulness as a viable category.

3. Dodd, *Romans*.

The concept of the image of God cannot be demonstrated or established independently of faith; it is an affirmation *of faith* which becomes meaningful in and through the revelation of God and in the measure that man grasps what fellowship with God means. It emerges in and through the encounter with God's condemning and restoring love. It then becomes apparent that man's destiny is to live under God's dominion, that sin is that which separates man from that kind of life God intended him to live.[4]

This insight sends us directly to the Old Testament, where we may find the theological underpinning for a truly biblical understanding of sin as a missing the mark of the divine ideal, the *imago Dei.*

Original Righteousness and the *Imago Dei*

In a previous section we discussed the *imago* in terms of its dual implication in biblical faith and there attempted to demonstrate the viability of a relational interpretation and what this meant in terms of general and special revelation. There we looked at the relation in which man stands perpetually as a fallen being (prevenient grace) and spoke of man qua man being constituted by "confrontation" (Barth). Now we must look more specifically at the content involved when man stands in proper relation to his Creator so that we may understand its perversion, which is sin. The words of Wesley poignantly reflect this understanding of sin as a perversion of man's original condition of being rightly related to God: "And thus man was created looking directly to God, as his last end; but, falling into sin, he fell off from God, and turned into himself" (*Works* 9:456). The theological implication of the Genesis account(s) provides us with much of the scriptural resource for our systematic development.

In our earlier discussion, where we explored the thesis that the *humanum* of man is constituted by prevenient grace interpreted as "man in relation to God," our emphasis was upon the *imago* that was retained (or restored) after the Fall, the wider image. Now we are turning to the *imago* proper or man standing in right relation to his Creator, what has traditionally been referred to as the "moral

---

4. *Faith of the Christian Church,* 236-37.

image." It is this relationship, we want to say, that constitutes original righteousness, with original sin to be seen as the loss of this
pre-Fall relation.

Western theology generally, including specifically the Protestant Reformers, have interpreted the *imago* in the context of law,
and thus original righteousness was identified with legal righteousness.[5] It is here where we see Wesleyan theology being more
of an expression of Eastern thought with its emphasis upon sanctification as a real (ontological) change. The inability of much of
Western theology to maintain a viable doctrine of sanctification
rests to a great extent upon its penchant for legal categories,
whereas Wesleyan theology and Eastern theology in stressing ontological participation in God are able to provide a structure of
human nature that allows for a realistic sanctifying experience. In
a word, the ontology that we have adopted in this systematic theology, in contrast to a substantival view, makes possible a consistent development of a doctrine of sanctification, as will be more
fully shown later.

Original righteousness, then, is constituted by a fourfold freedom. The use of the concept of *freedom* in this context presupposes
the reality of freedom as the power to choose to be or remain in this
relation of *freedom*, but the two uses are not synonymous. When
one is speaking theologically rather than philosophically, both are
lost in the Fall, with freedom to choose to return to God restored
only by prevenient grace. Freedom, as we are using it here following Dietrich Bonhoeffer, is

> not something man has for himself but something he has for
> others. No man is free "as such," that is, in a vacuum, in the way
> that he may be musical, intelligent or blind as such. Freedom is
> not a quality of man, nor is it an ability, a capacity, a kind of
> being that somehow flares up in him. Anyone investigating
> man to discover freedom finds nothing of it. Why? because
> freedom is not a quality which can be revealed—it is not a pos-
> session, a presence, an object, nor is it a form for existence—but
> a relationship and nothing else. In truth, freedom is a rela-
> tionship between two persons. Being free means "being free for
> the other," because the other has bound me to him. Only in
> relationship with the other am I free.[6]

The original *imago* includes: (1) Freedom for God; (2) Freedom
for the Other; (3) Freedom from the Earth or World; and (4) Free-

---

5. Cf. Barth, *Church Dogmatics* 3.1.192.
6. *Creation and Fall* (New York: Macmillan Co., 1967), 37.

dom from Self-domination. The first three are explicitly spelled out symbolically in Genesis 1—11, and the fourth is implied quite clearly in the other three.

Freedom for God

The same idea can be conveyed by the term *openness*. It is symbolized by the time of communion with the Creator that Adam enjoyed in the "cool of the day" (Gen. 3:8). This highly anthropomorphic account is a profound theological presentation of an uninhibited tête-à-tête, since there was nothing in the relation to hide. It was informed by Truth, since no subterfuge was necessary: no turned-away head, no averted eyes, no double-talk, the yea was yea and the nay was nay (cf. Matt. 5:37; James 5:12, KJV).

This freedom of man for God was grounded in the freedom of God for man. With God it was *a se*, but with man it was a gift. There is with God not only an "I" but an "I-Thou" relation within the divine nature. With man, it is the I who is himself in relation to the Thou who is God. Thus the analogy of relation is, as Barth says, the "correspondence of the unlike."

Athanasius recognized the same meaning in the symbolism of the garden. He speaks of Adam as

> having in the beginning had his mind to Godward in a freedom unembarrassed by shame, and as associating with the holy ones in that contemplation of things perceived by the mind in the place where he was—the place which the holy Moses called in a figure a garden. So purity of soul is sufficient of itself to reflect God, as the Lord also says, "Blessed are the pure in heart, for they shall see God."[7]

H. Orton Wiley, following W. B. Pope, holds that the tree of life in the garden is symbolic of communion with God and suggests that it bears sacramental fruit. It bears a relation to the other trees in the garden, much as the bread of Communion bears to bread as the staff of life. It is sacramental in the sense that it gives meaning to the whole of life (*CT* 2:54-55).

Obedience is the condition for maintaining this openness. The forbidden fruit of the Genesis account symbolizes the point of testing. No genuine relation is possible unless it is freely chosen, and apart from the possibility of violating it, it cannot be affirmed.

---

7. Quoted in David Cairns, *The Image of God in Man* (New York: Philosophical Library, Xerox copied in 1978), 91.

Obedience, as the means of continuing the "I-Thou" relation, is not to be understood moralistically. The decision to obey or to not obey is more profoundly a decision to either maintain or violate a personal relation.

Freedom for the Other as Imago

One of the intriguing features of the Genesis creation narratives is the use of the plural form for Deity. Gen. 1:1 declares: "In the beginning *Elohim* [plural for the singular *El*] created the heavens and the earth." The plural pronouns become both pronounced and prolific when the writer comes to speak of the origin of human being. Up to that point the first narrative (1:1—2:4*a*) records, "Then God said," in connection with each day's creative activity with the originating fiat immediately following. But in 1:26 it is followed by an "in-house" consultation concerning this particular potentiality: "Let Us make man in Our image, according to Our likeness." The plural is then transferred to the proposed created being: "Let them have dominion." In the 27th verse, the creation of mankind is stressed to be in the form of "male and female," a plural creature (all NKJV). Certainly all other "animals" also had male and female species, but the structure clearly indicates that something special is implied by this characteristic of human being.

Karl Barth, in particular, has been influential in contemporary theology in calling attention to the crucial theological significance of the "male and female" factor in defining the *imago Dei.* Barth insists that this is the most definitive element in the account. It seems clearly the case that he is at least correct concerning the decisive significance of the point, and when joined with the other evidence in the passage, it seems almost unequivocal that man's creation in God's image involves a social dimension.[8]

Traditionally, biblical scholars have had difficulty with the plural forms used of God in these passages. Some have argued that it indicates the idea of a heavenly court where the Supreme Deity gathers His court of lesser beings around Him, and together they plan the strategy of the apex of the creative work. It is claimed that evidences of this idea may be found elsewhere in the Old Testament. Conservatives have many times suggested that here we have a foregleam of the Trinity. As long as this is not taken to be an

---

8. Cairns correctly observes on this point that "it is the personal element in this situation and not the sexual which is distinctive." *Image of God,* 175.

explicit teaching, it can be properly recognized as pointing to an important truth. The New Testament revelation of God's Trinitarian nature is here found to be not in conflict with Old Testament monotheism. More to the point of the Hebrew mind is the suggestion that the plural indicators reflect the fullness of being of Yahweh, which involves no compromise of monotheism but does support the theology of God as a social reality.[9]

Augustine was groping for a basic truth about man in his efforts to identify a Trinitarian structure within human nature on the assumption that the *imago* would entail the same ontological structure in man as revelation disclosed obtained in the divine nature. His basic error, however, was in seeking to confine the social structure within the individual.[10] The truth to which these biblical affirmations point is an interpersonal ontological structure. Modern understandings of the self have brought this more clearly to light, but it was a truth that the biblical mind grasped all along.[11]

As in the case of the basic divine-human relation, the person-to-person relation can be described as "openness." That is the significance of the phrase "freedom for." It is an "I-Thou" relationship that was marked by the absence of shame. The references in the second creation account (2:25) to the fact that "they were both naked . . . and were not ashamed" (KJV) symbolize this kind of openness. They were radically "free for" each other. The absence of lust, which has self-gratification (see discussion of freedom from self) as an element in its motivation, made such unashamed openness possible in this picture of almost naive unselfconsciousness.

Many of the fathers of the Church have toyed with the idea that somehow the body is included under the rubric of "image of God." This would not likely have been totally repugnant to the Hebrew mind, which did not "sharply distinguish between body and spirit as does Western thought, and the body for him was, so to speak, a sacrament of the spirit."[12] Under the influence of later thought about the spiritual nature of God, this view was aban-

---

9. This is not intended as a support for the "social Trinity" theories such as were advanced by certain British scholars like Leonard Hodgson. These theories do, however, point to a fundamental truth about God.

10. See criticisms of this way of identifying the image of God by Augustine in Cairns, *Image of God*, 93-99.

11. Karl Barth holds that man is in God's image because his relationship to the woman is like the harmonious confrontation between the Persons of the Trinity.

12. Cairns, *Image of God*, 23.

doned as unworthy. Contemporary Old Testament theologians Gerhard von Rad and Walther Eichrodt explicitly reject this as a possible interpretation. However, in his book *The Bible Doctrine of Man,* C. Ryder Smith claims that Gen. 1:26 refers to a physical resemblance between God and man. On this basis he argues that the image can be retained following the Fall. Using a method of word study that we have found to be less than adequate, he sought to show that the terms used in relation to the image, both in Hebrew and Greek, all refer to a visible form. He suggested that the Hebrews thought of God as having visible form, though not a material body, a view that simply fails to recognize the theological implications of a high anthropomorphism.[13]

In the context of the interpretation of the *imago* as relation to the other, it is possible to recognize a legitimate significance to the place of the body in the biblical understanding. We can agree with David Cairns that there are "physical overtones in the conception" as developed in the narratives. It would be different, however, from Cairns's argument that

> there would be a line of development through to the notion of the image in the New Testament, where transformation into the image involves also a new physical life, and where it is promised that the believer will be clothed also with a new spiritual body when the spiritual likeness is revealed in its glory.[14]

The symbolism that we are suggesting as indicating the openness of man for woman and vice versa as well as each human to the other revolves around the body. The body is the means by which one human being relates to the other.

This insight provides a solid theological basis for the admonitions regarding physical adornment found in 1 Pet. 3:3-5 and 1 Tim. 2:9-10. Clement of Alexandria spends a great deal of space admonishing against the decoration of the body with clothes, jewels, and cosmetics because it is basically an attempt to present a false picture of the self, thus not true openness of person to person. He comments:

> But if one withdraw the veil of the temple,—I mean the head-dress, the dye, the clothes, the gold, the paint, the cosmetics,—that is, the veil, with the view of finding within the true beauty, he will be disgusted, I know well. For he will not

---

13. (London: Epworth Press, 1951).
14. *Image of God,* 23.

meet the image of God dwelling within, as is meet, but instead
of it a fornicator and adulteress has occupied the shrine of the
soul. And the true beast will thus be detected—an ape smeared
with white paint.[15]

Freedom from the Earth as Image

Because of man's status in relation to God he is given "dominion" over the remainder of created reality. It is true, as many have
argued, that we cannot equate this dominion with the image of
God, but it seems clearly to be a subsidiary aspect of it. The earth
does not dominate man when the divine-human relation is in order, but it serves man. Adam's task of naming the animals symbolizes his dominion over them and their subservience to his ends.

The commission to "be fruitful and multiply; fill the earth and
subdue it; have dominion over the fish of the sea, over the birds of
the air, and over every living thing that moves on the earth" (Gen.
1:28, NKJV) is a cultural mandate. Culture implies a tilling, and
man's appointed role is to till God's creation, or cultivate it. The
clue to the boundaries of this mandate is "the glory of God," to
which unfallen man would be committed. It thus carries responsibility as well as privilege and implies ecological caretaking.

Freedom from Self as Image

Implicit in each of the other relationships is a focus upon God
and His glory so that the Lord is the dominant Partner in the
primary confrontation, and this dominance informs and so gives
character to the others. This is, however, a relationship that is not
impersonal, arbitrary, or forced but free. The logical consequence is
that the relation can be upset if the uncoerced partner (man) de-
cides to dissolve the situation of the Lordship of the Creator and
attempts to assume an equal partnership role or usurp the prerog-
atives of the Creator. This possibility was actualized in the Fall,
which basically takes the form of a revolt against heaven.

Man in Revolt

Our discussion to this point has focused on the relationship to God
that is original righteousness, and we saw how this relationship
could be violated by actual sin. To this aspect of sin we now turn,

15. *The Instructor,* Bk. 3, chap. 2.

and this will involve making further use of the theological implication of the biblical account of the Fall. But first, we must make some general observations concerning the nature of sin.

It is crucial to any discussion of sin to recognize that it is a religious category. It has meaning only in terms of one's relation to God. Any attempt to understand the nature of sin that ignores this will pervert the truth.[16]

The Psalmist clearly understood this truth, and in his classic confession articulated the religious dimension: "Against You, You only, have I sinned, and done this evil in Your sight—that You may be found just when You speak, and blameless when You judge" (Ps. 51:4, NKJV).

In the judicial sphere, or realm of criminal justice, we speak of crime but not of sin. In ethics we speak about good and evil, right and wrong, but not about sin. In psychology we speak about abnormalities and personality disorders but not about sin. The idea of sin is meaningful only in relation to God, and when it is removed from this realm, as Gustav Aulen correctly says, "it becomes weak and enfeebled."[17]

Not only must sin not be interpreted as an ethical concept (although there are ethical elements involved), but neither should it be interpreted as an ontological or metaphysical category. Interpreting the creation account as historical although symbolic, as Wiley does in a thoroughgoing fashion (CT 2:52 ff.), is necessary to safeguard the religious character of sin. If this is not the case, sin logically becomes equated with finitude and is thus inevitable in the human situation.

Contemporary theologians, aside from conservatives, are all but unanimous in rejecting the historicity of a "state of integrity" and thus are virtually unanimous in affirming the futility of claims to the possibility of freedom from sin in this life. Yet this possibility stands at the center of the Wesleyan witness to the biblical revelation. This point calls attention to the crucial nature of the discussion for Wesleyan theology.

An influential example of an ontological interpretation of the human situation is the position of Paul Tillich, whose interpretation reveals the results of approaching the issue in this way. He dis-

---

16. Cf. E. J. Bicknell, *The Christian Idea of Sin and Original Sin* (New York: Longmans, Green, and Co., 1923), ix.

17. *Faith of the Christian Church*, 232.

cusses the Fall as a transition from essence to existence. Under the conditions of existence man cannot actualize his essence; thus the Genesis description of man before the Fall is a myth that describes a state of what Tillich calls "dreaming innocence." This term refers to the idea that "the state of essential being is not an actual stage of human development which may be known directly or indirectly," but it nonetheless can be thought or "dreamed about." It points to a nonactualized potentiality, to something that precedes actual existence. But "it has no time; it precedes temporality, and it is suprahistorical."[18] The consequence of this view is the equation of finitude with sin because man stands in opposition to God as infinite and thus can never actualize his essence under the conditions of existence. This approach obscures the true nature of sin.

The theological structure of the account of the Fall is explicitly designed to make clear that sin is not the result of man's creaturehood or in any sense the result of forces or factors beyond his control. It is the consequence of the exercise of his God-given gift of freedom. There can be no meaningful sense in which man is free *for* God unless he can, by his volition, become free *from* God.

This truth is clearly seen when one compares the role of the serpent in Genesis with the same symbolism in the Babylonian Epic. The standard symbol for evil in the ancient world was the snake. It was only later that Christian theology identified it with Satan.[19] In the Epic the story of the "Fall" revolves around a man named Utnapishtim (the Babylonian Noah) who is seeking eternal life. He learns that it can be acquired through eating a certain herb that grows at the bottom of a deep pool of water. After having

---

18. *Systematic Theology* 2:31 ff. Classical philosophy, especially Plato and Plotinus, also equated being-in-time with sinfulness or separation from the Source of Being. Hence time is of the essence of man's predicament in these theories. Augustine took over much of Plotinus's interpretation and thus has been misunderstood as holding to an ontological view of sin. However, Augustine used the Christian doctrine of creation to modify the Neoplatonic scheme of emanation and thus made time the good creation of God. Man's being-in-time is related not to his sinfulness but to his separation from God in terms of rebellion and perverted love. Hence union with God, for Augustine, was not loss of historicity but a relation of love that retains man's timefulness, which is only the mark of his finitude. Cf. Hans Urs von Balthasar, *A Theological Anthropology* (New York: Sheed and Ward, 1967), chap. 1.

19. One significance of the identification of the serpent with Satan by Christian thought is to show that "sin existed in the universe before its origin in man" (Wiley) and that therefore "it does not follow inevitably from the situation in which he stands" (Niebuhr).

found the pool, Utnapishtim dives to the bottom, secures the plant, and rises to the surface. Exhausted by the deep dive, he lays down to recuperate. At this point the serpent sneaks up, steals the herb, and eats it itself, thus gaining eternal life.[20]

In the inspired account the serpent is the agent in the temptation but in no sense steals life from an unsuspecting victim. The first pair consider the options and make a conscious decision to violate the condition of their paradisaic existence. This does not suggest, of course, that they were fully aware of all the consequences of their act, but they knew and willfully decided against God. This fact points us to a further question.

The Essence of Sin

We have argued that sin is essentially a religious category, but further definition is necessary, since religion may be conceived in different ways. If religion is interpreted pharisaically in terms of law, sin is defined as the transgression of precepts, that is, moralistically. It is possible to conceive religion rationalistically, in which case sin tends to be seen as heresy in not believing certain doctrinal formulations. But we have insisted throughout that man's relation to God must be conceived personalistically. Thus sin is whatever violates that relationship and causes a separation between God and man. We have interpreted the divine-human relation as constituting the *imago Dei*, so in this context the words of Gustav Aulen are quite apropos: "From the point of view of sin the concept of the 'image of God' sets forth the lost destiny of man, and from the point of view of salvation it reveals the divine purpose in creation."[21]

There are four major categories that have been proposed as candidates to identify the essence of sin: (1) Unbelief, (2) Egocentricity or Pride (hubris), (3) Disobedience, and (4) Sensuality.

Sin as Unbelief. This proposal is misunderstood if unbelief is interpreted intellectualistically. In that case it would be both superficial and meaningless. But if we correctly define faith as trust and confidence in God, we can see the significance of Paul's assertion

---

20. The snake is also a standard symbol for unending time in the ancient world because of the idea that when it sheds its skin annually, it renews its life. Some calendars depicting a cyclical view of history have the round calender encircled by a snake with its tail in its mouth.

21. *Faith of the Christian Church*, 237.

that whatsoever is not of faith is sin (Rom. 14:23). Perhaps we should better designate unbelief as "unfaith."

John Wesley uses his logical acumen to underscore this point: "All truly *good works . . . follow after justification;* and they are therefore good and 'acceptable to God in Christ,' because they 'spring out of a true and living faith.' By a parity of reason, all *works done before justification are not good,* in the Christian sense, *forasmuch as they spring not of faith in Jesus Christ '. . .* yea rather, . . . they have the nature of sin.' "[22]

In the temptation in the garden, the element of not believing the truth of God's word, stimulated by the insinuations of the serpent, is present; but that is not the most profound element. What is more serious is the loss of the trust that includes acknowledgment of the Creator-creature relation. This results in rejecting God's Lordship, with the unavoidable outcome that some other lord is acknowledged, and that primarily is the self.

Egocentricity or Pride as Sin. If God does not have dominion in man's life, something else does, and this something else is his own ego. This is the state that Martin Luther defines as *incurvatus in se* (man curved in upon himself). Therefore unbelief and egocentricity are simply the same thing seen from different points of view.

Reinhold Niebuhr acutely analyzes the human situation to demonstrate how sin as pride emerges. Human existence is caught in the paradox of finiteness and freedom. These constitute both its limitation and its greatness. As finite, man is a creature, but in his freedom is the capacity to seek to transcend that creatureliness. Yet that is precisely where he goes astray. In the exercise of his freedom he refused to accept his creatureliness, or in the language of the biblical account, he sought to "become like God" (cf. Gen. 3:5). In a word, he exalted himself to the point of being his own god.[23]

Augustine is one of the classic proponents of the position that sin is to be identified as pride. In *The City of God* he defines sin in this way:

> What could begin this evil will but pride, that is the beginning of all sin? And what is pride but a perverse desire of height, in forsaking Him to whom the soul ought solely to

---

22. Sermon on "Justification by Faith," *StS* I:123-24.
23. *The Nature and Destiny of Man,* 2 vols. (London: Nisbet and Co., 1946), vol. I.

cleave, as the beginning thereof, to make the self seem the beginning. This is when it likes itself too well.[24]

When interpreted in these terms, it is apparent that sin has an element of self-deception. Although man may choose the way of sovereignty, it is always illusory, for he is always still a finite creature. It is thus correct to refer to the delusion of self-sovereignty.

This aspect of sin has also been correctly characterized as idolatry, since it involves the elevation of a created and dependent reality (the self) to the position that can only be properly held by the Creator, who alone has independent being. Self-idolatry is no less perverse than the worship of finite artifacts or deified natural forces or objects.

G. Eldon Ladd's summation of Paul's teaching touches centrally on this aspect of sin:

> The nature of sin can be seen from a study of the several words Paul uses, but the most profound theological word for sin is *asebeia*, translated "ungodliness" in Romans 1:18. The most fundamental sin of the Gentiles is their refusal to worship God as God; all wickedness (*adikia*) arises from the perversion of worship. The fundamental sin of the Jews who have the Law is "boasting," i.e. perverting the Law so that it becomes the basis of self-confidence that seeks glory before God and relies upon itself. Boasting is thus the antithesis of faith. For both Gentile and Jew, the root of sin is not found in acts of sinfulness but in a perverted, rebellious will. This is supported by Paul's view of man as "flesh"—man standing in rebellious opposition to God.[25]

Disobedience as Sin. John Wesley defined sin "properly so-called" as "a voluntary transgression of a known law." This definition has often been criticized by those not congenial to Wesley's perspective as being superficial and moralistic. This criticism is itself superficial since it fails to recognize the profound understanding that informs the definition. It is virtually a reproduction of the Johannine statement in 1 John 3:4 that "sin is lawlessness." The KJV has obscured the depths of this pronouncement by its improper translation, "Sin is the transgression of the law." This would indeed make sin both moralistic and atomistic and basically rob it of its distinctive religious dimension.

Lawlessness is an attitude, a mind-set, that declares one's free-

24. Bk. 12, chap. 13.
25. *Theology,* 405.

dom from legitimate constraints. It intends to break out in anarchic ways. It is to this inner rebellion that Wesley's definition really points. He is not defining sin in terms of sins or wrong deeds but in terms of the motivation that lies behind particular acts that express the inner rebelliousness.

Since rebelliousness is the antithesis of faith, we do not see sin as disobedience to be essentially different from sin as unbelief or egocentricity. The Scripture does define faith in terms of obedience (Rom. 1:5; 16:26; 1 Pet. 1:14); thus disobedience is a manifestation of unbelief involving the elevation of the self into the position that properly belongs to the Creator.

Sensuality as Sin. Here we encounter another possible deviation from the distinctively religious nature of sin. If the understanding of sin as disobedience tends toward Pelagianism, the understanding of sin as sensuality tends toward Gnosticism. Reinhold Niebuhr has pointed out that when influenced by Hellenistic thought, Christianity has always been tempted to regard sin as basically lust and sensuality.[26]

This can take several different forms including the metaphysical distinction between a physical (evil) and a spiritual (good) nature in man. Sin, or more properly evil, is identified with the body and its appetites, while the Spirit remains pure even though hindered by being imprisoned in a "house of clay." Salvation, on this model, involves escape from the flesh and flight to a purely disembodied existence. The problem is that this interpretation makes sin both inevitable, thus destroying its religious character, and partial, whereas the biblical view is that man in totality is under sin.

Sensuality, in the strictest sense, is seeking one's own gratification. This self-gratification brings it directly into connection with the basic sin of egocentricity. Since sexual lust is one of the most graphic instances of how egocentricity manifests itself in the form of self-gratification, it has been the preoccupation of Christian thinkers, and many have mistakenly identified sin with sexuality under the rubric of concupiscence.

Augustine is perhaps the most prominent example of this. Taking Paul's example of "covetousness" (Rom. 7:7-8) as being the epitome of sinfulness and coupling it with his own experience of

---

26. *Nature and Destiny of Man* 1:242-55.

an inordinate sex drive, Augustine developed an elaborate explanation of original sin as concupiscence epitomized by sexuality. This must be qualified, however, by noting that Augustine also taught a much sounder view of sin as perverted love. We will have occasion to examine this later.

Luther reacted against this tradition and, with a much surer sense of the biblical understanding of man and sin, redefined concupiscence as "self-love." Thus he brings sensuality into direct relation to the more fundamental nature of sin as egocentricity.

We may allow Reinhold Niebuhr's penetrating analysis to summarize this point:

> If we discount Hellenistic theology with its inclination to make sensuality the primary sin and to derive it from the natural inclinations of the physical life, we must arrive at the conclusion that Christian theology, in both its Augustinian and semi-Augustinian (Thomistic) forms, regards sensuality (even when it uses the words *concupiscentia* or *cupiditas* to denote sin in general) as a derivative of the more primal sin of self-love. Sensuality represents a further confusion consequent upon the original confusion of substituting the self for God as the centre of existence. Man, having lost the true centre of his life, is no longer able to maintain his own will as the centre of himself.[27]

Original Sin and Prevenient Grace

Original sin involves the loss of original righteousness; therefore it may be seen as the absence or perversion of the relationship in which man stood in the "state of integrity." However, we must emphasize that it is more than privative. There is a positive aspect in the sense that man in his natural state as it is now is corrupt in every aspect of his being. In classical theological language, he is "totally depraved." Both truths must be seriously considered in any estimate of man as sinner, as well as in seeking to evaluate the redemptive activity of God in human life.

Original Sin as Loss of Relation

In theologically analyzing Genesis 1—11, we see indications that all four relationships that constitute original righteousness

---

27. *Nature and Destiny of Man* 1:247. It should be noted here that Niebuhr interprets Augustine classically by attempting to show that his view of sin as concupiscence is derivative from his view of sin as pride, and thus they are organically connected.

(imago) were disrupted. When the time came for the evening tryst, Adam and Eve failed to keep the rendezvous because now through disobedience they were no longer open to the Lord God and so were afraid of His presence. Here is the first instance of man's experience of the wrath of God. Note that the Creator is coming to His creation in grace and love, but man's disobedience caused him to experience that love as wrath. With delightful simplicity, the biblical writer makes this point by leaving the impression that the Lord God knew nothing about the apostasy. This anthropomorphism is a profound testimony, not to God's naïveté and obliviousness to man's sin, but to His willingness to seek man's communion in spite of his waywardness. There is a sense in which we here have a foregleam of the atoning work of God, which culminated with the death of Christ. He is a seeking God.

God's first word to man after the Fall was a question: "Where are you?" (Gen. 3:9). This inquiry was not for His own benefit but for man's. In the words of Delitzsch, "God seeks him, not because he is lost from His knowledge, but from His communion."[28]

We saw that the garden is symbolic of that communion that marked the original divine-human relation. As a result of the rebellion of the first pair against the divine authority, they were expelled from the garden, or park. Of particular significance is the symbolism of the "flaming sword" that God placed at the gate of the garden to bar the way to the tree of life (Gen. 3:24). It is a symbol of both judgment and grace. It testifies to the fact that though man has broken the relation to God by his own volition, he cannot find his way back through his own initiative. The sword stands guard against all forms of works righteousness as a means to earn the favor of God. This relation can only be reestablished from God's side—and that is grace.

The disobedience also radically altered the interpersonal relation, so that man was no longer free for the other. This loss was symbolized by the covering of the body with fig leaves and the sense of shame that emerged (Gen. 3:10). Augustine, although mistakenly making sexuality the essence of original sin, highlighted the results of this apostasy by pointing to the shame that attaches to conception, so that while everyone knows its cause, it always occurs in the greatest possible secrecy.

---

28. Quoted by E. F. Kevan, "Genesis," in *New Bible Commentary*, ed. F. Davidson, 2nd ed. (Grand Rapids: Wm. B. Eerdmans Publishing Co., 1960).

A graphic illustration of the devastating consequences for community occurs in this presalvation history section of Genesis with the story of the Tower of Babel (11:1-9). The basis for community is a common language as a means of communication. Thus with the confusion of tongues there is a strangeness that intrudes itself into the human situation, which results in men taking separate directions. It is not accidental that the diversity of tongues is depicted as the result of man's broken relation to God. The building of the ziggurat is a symbol of self-exaltation that no longer acknowledges human creatureliness but now seeks to force its way back past the flaming sword by building a tower to heaven. This is not so much a cosmological spectacle of naïveté as a religious tragedy.

The further result entailed the loss of freedom from the earth. This is symbolized by the cursing of the ground with resulting "thorns and thistles" (Gen. 3:18). It was not work that came into being through the curse, but the resistance of the earth to man's efforts to cultivate it.

Dietrich Bonhoeffer's description of this loss is pungent:

> We . . . try to rule, but it is the same here as on Walpurgis Night. We think we are pushing and we are being pushed. We do not rule, we are ruled. The thing, the world, rules man. Man is a prisoner, a slave of the world, and his rule is illusion. Technology is the power with which the earth grips man and subdues him. And because we rule no more, we lose ground, and then the earth is no longer *our* earth, and then we become strangers on earth. We do not rule because we do not know the world as God's creation, and because we do not receive our dominion as God-given but grasp it for ourselves.[29]

We have observed the increasing sophistication of man in his conquest of the earth. He has wrested its secrets from it and created artifacts with seemingly limitless possibilities, but he has been unable to keep them under his control. His inventions seem to take on a life of their own and assert themselves in mastery over the creator. And the larger and more complex the inventions, the more destructive they seem to become to human well-being. It is not the monster of nuclear power, for example, that threatens human life. It is the man who discovered it who has no dominion over himself and so loses control of what many dreamed would be the solution to many human problems. Having revolted against his own Cre-

---

29. *Creation and Fall,* 38.

ator, man has lost the power to hold dominion over his own creation.

It now becomes clear how interwoven in all three of the other relations is the place of the self. Adam's rejection of the sovereignty of the Creator resulted in his consciously coming under the lordship of self. That, we saw earlier, was the essence of sin. Thus the divine judgment upon the first pair was that they have "become like one of us" (Gen. 3:22). Under the influence of the serpent they aspired to be like God, and they succeeded in becoming their own god.

The great tragedy of this is seen in Adam's being barred from the tree of life. The curse of death was upon him, yet he was still called to live. Except now he no longer has the grace of life but must live out of his own resources, and this resource is totally inadequate. A graphic picture of the lifelessness of life outside of grace is depicted in Jer. 17:5-8, when the prophet describes the wicked as a rootless bush blown hither and yon by the winds of life: "Cursed is the man who trusts in man and makes flesh his strength, whose heart departs from the Lord. For he shall be like a shrub in the desert, and shall not see when good comes, but shall inhabit the parched places in the wilderness, in a salt land which is not inhabited. [By contrast,] Blessed is the man who trusts in the Lord . . . For he shall be like a tree planted by the waters" (NKJV).

The intrusion of a perverted relation to self in relation to the other gave a specific character to human interaction. The openness symbolized by nakedness was now replaced by shame and resulted in hiding their bodies from each other. What now pollutes the relation is the motif of self-gratification. All men now tend to do as Augustine confessed he had done: "I polluted the spring of friendship with the lust of concupiscence." This is what we saw to be the significance of sensuality as a fundamental expression of sin. The sexual relation becomes the most obvious instance of the dominance of self-gratification in interpersonal relations. It is what, per se, makes sexual activity outside of marriage sinful. Since the marriage bond entails commitment to the other person, seeking the benefits of marriage outside that commitment cannot avoid the primary motivation of self-gratification.

It is true, as Martin Luther suggested when he spoke of the "rape of the wedding night," that marriage does not necessarily preclude the dominance of self-gratification within wedlock; and while this, too, is an essentially sinful expression, it does not justify extramarital sexual behavior. In a word, what happens is that the primordial "I-Thou" relation degenerates into an "I-it" relation. In terms of the Kantian categorical imperative, other persons are not treated as ends in themselves but as means to an end.

The significance of *agapē* as the distinctively biblical form of love emerges again at this point. Other forms of love, for example, *eros*, have as an essential aspect of their meaning the desire for what is loved because it contributes something to the lover. *Agapē*, by contrast, in its pure form seeks only the well-being of the loved. It is informed by no self-seeking. Arthur F. Holmes, developing the idea of personhood in a Christian perspective, says along this line:

> If I relate to my wife as to an object, I to it, then I dominate her and use and repress her, and remain closed to what she could be to herself. But if we relate to each other as persons, subject to subject with trust and openness and mutuality, then communication develops, as does friendship. This is egalitarian, equal persons equally respected and equally responsible. It evokes love, not the *eros* that desires for oneself, often selfishly, but the *agape* that gives of oneself in serving the other. Such relationships to other persons are the matrix where freedom and responsibility come alive. I become my brother's keeper, and he becomes mine.[30]

The exaltation of self to the control tower of life likewise perverts man's relation to nature or the earth. His original mandate was to cultivate the created world (culture) for the glory of God. The Fall twisted this around so that the task of tilling the earth (developing culture) became motivated by self-advantage. The practical results in terms of the "rape of the earth" are appalling. Exploitation, irresponsibility, and greed all paint a gloomy picture for the future of the environment, because men have sought to exploit the earth for their own pleasure in ways that far exceed his needs.[31]

Original Sin as Corruption of Nature

Genesis 1—11 further provides us with vivid examples of the positive perversion of human nature that resulted from the loss of the *imago*, or relation to God, with all the attendant aspects. Jeal-

---

30. *Contours*, 113.
31. See Robert E. Webber, *The Secular Saint* (Grand Rapids: Zondervan Publishing House, 1974), chap. 3.

ousy (an expression of egocentricity) sprang up like a weed and manifested its fruit in fratricide. Cain's murder of his brother was only the first in a long line of bloodletting. One reason the American Civil War has been looked upon with such morbid fascination is because it was a battle between brothers, and that seems so inconsistent with human nature. Yet at the deeper level all men are brothers, and all wars express this contradiction within human nature. That fact highlights the depth of depravity that expresses itself in cruel acts of violence. (Cf. Amos' condemnation of inhuman treatment of others in chaps. 1—2. This was addressed to people other than Israel and is generally interpreted to imply a covenant of brotherhood to which all men are accountable before God even without specific knowledge of the Sinai covenant.) The sequel to the first murder reveals graphically how this dastardly deed resulted from the loss of the relation to the other that formed the original constitution of man. Cain attempted to shun his God-given responsibility by his question: "Am I my brother's keeper?" (Gen. 4:9). The loss of a sense of "Thou-ness" made violence possible, and verbally denying the responsibility for the other person did not invalidate it.

That mysterious passage in Gen. 6:1-8, a prelude to the Flood and used as a justification for it, further illuminates the ugly abyss that was opened up in the human heart. The growth of civilization simply provided man with more subtle means of manifesting his inner perversity.

The profound perversity of the original sin that affects the human race and the nature of its manifestation (self-centeredness) raise a significant question. The greed and acquisitiveness that are the expressions of this self-centeredness would certainly result in self-destruction if unchecked. Why has this not happened? And furthermore, how does one account for the altruism and other similar expressions that are found so frequently among unredeemed humanity? Maybe the Christian evaluation of man is too pessimistic; perhaps there is remaining natural goodness after all. This suggestion has appeared from time to time, but the realities of history have always shattered its optimism.

Thomas Hobbes was not far from the truth when he diagnosed the human condition as a "war of all against all" and proposed that the only solution to the inevitable self-annihilation that would result was for the instinct of self-preservation in man to set up a social contract to control human aggressiveness. But if Hobbes was completely correct, then the only safe form of government was a totalitarian Leviathan (monster) to keep men in check by the sanction of force. Is there not a brighter picture?

Theologically, the classical Christian answer to the question of the control placed upon grasping greediness that keeps man from destroying himself is *grace*. John Calvin developed the idea of "common grace" to explain this idea. While it was not potentially saving, it was extended to all men and was the source of all goodness, aesthetic values, and so on, of natural man. Donald Bloesch, a contemporary Reformed theologian, gives excellent expression to the theme:

> It is . . . the common grace of God that accounts for sinful man's ability to arrive at a modicum of justice. Common grace is the grace of preservation by which man's rapacity is restrained. Indeed, if it were not for common grace, the world would fall into anarchy and disorder, but God preserves his created order out of his mercy so that people may hear the good news of redemption through Christ and turn to him and be delivered from their sins. Common grace . . . is responsible for the fragments of wisdom and truth that exist in the non-Christian religions and also in the moral codes of the great civilizations of pagan antiquity.[32]

The Wesleyan would extend the province of prevenient grace to cover the function Calvin attributed to common grace. Thus it is a theological judgment that the most devastating consequences of original sin upon the human race have been mitigated by the intervention of God to preserve His creation from self-destruction. Since grace is persuasive, however, rather than coercive, this unfortunately is no absolute guarantee against the blood-chilling possibility that the human race will finally destroy itself as the present threat of nuclear war attests.

Original Sin and Actual Sin

Our discussion of man as sinner up to this point should make it clear that sin is dual in nature: It is a state of being, and it is a manifestation of that state. It is somewhat misleading to use the shorthand form, "act and being," because the state of sinfulness

---

32. *Essentials of Evangelical Theology* 1:91. For Calvin's original statement see *Institutes* 2.3.3.

expresses itself in attitudes and motives as well as behaviors, and all of these fall under the rubric of actual sin.

Man's sinful state of being is his lost relation to God. This way of conceptualizing original sin makes it possible, when coupled with prevenient grace, to maintain the completeness of the Fall while at the same time maintaining the humanity of man. This theme was fully developed in our discussion of revelation as it impinges on the question of man's knowledge of God. The same principles elucidated there must be applied in this setting. The Protestant Reformers attempted to explain the human situation by arguing that a "relic" of the *imago* remained after the Fall. But as Brunner correctly criticizes this, it says both too much and too little. Too much, because it indicates that there remains in our nature an undamaged spot; and too little, because it forgets that even in our sin we bear witness to our original relationship to God.[33]

A modern version of this same approach (and subject to the same criticism) is expressed by Donald Bloesch:

> In our view the essential nature of man is good, since it is created by God, but his existential nature, his being in the world is corrupted. Man's humanity remains just as the eye remains after a poisonous insect sting destroys its sight, though it is now deprived of its luster and checked in its moral activity (Abraham Kuyper). True human nature as we find it in Jesus Christ is without sin, and therefore sin is rightly seen as a deviation from human nature. It signifies the unnature of man, the abnormal which has now become natural. The imago dei, the reflection of the being of God in man, is defaced, but it is not destroyed. Man is still responsible before God, though his freedom has been considerably impaired.[34]

It is the way of expressing this rather than the truth it is attempting to maintain that raises questions of theological adequacy. The Wesleyan position of prevenient grace provides a far more viable solution than the Reformed view of a relic of the *imago*. It identifies this grace with the "wider image" by means of which a relationship to God is restored that actually becomes the basis for man's continuing personhood, since personhood is constituted by relation.

Furthermore, defining man's being ontologically in terms of relation and speaking of original sin (state of being) relationally

---

33. *Man in Revolt: A Christian Anthropology*, trans. Olive Wyon (New York: Charles Scribner's Sons, 1939), 96.
34. *Essentials of Evangelical Theology* 1:95.

makes possible a viable doctrine of sanctification as "renewal in the image of God," which is John Wesley's central way of conceptualizing it. Substantial modes of describing man's state of being in sin makes entire sanctification difficult if not impossible to fit logically into a theological conceptuality.

Original Sin and Guilt

The question of guilt has been widely discussed among theologians in its connection with original sin. Does guilt attach to the descendants of Adam because of the progenitor's apostasy? One tradition has argued that all are born guilty because of Adam's transgression. This is at home in the Augustinian-Calvinistic stream of Christian thought and provides a logical basis for particular predestination. No ethical problem is entailed in affirming the eternal damnation of infants who are not among the elect, if they are born guilty, that is, culpable and deserving of punishment. This also becomes a logical basis for a doctrine of infant baptism understood as "washing away the guilt of original sin."[35]

Another tradition interprets guilt legalistically and denies the possiblity or questions the ethical fairness of imputing guilt where no possibility of accountable action is present. This view maintains that guilt can only be attached to actual sin. Thus it denies that guilt is in any way to be connected to original sin.

H. Orton Wiley makes a significant distinction between "personal blameworthiness as regards the commission of sin" (reatus culpoe) and "liability to penalty" (reatus poenoe). Actual sin, he says, includes both forms, whereas only the second attaches to original sin (CT 2:88). This distinction is recognized by Wesley, and in accord with it he does attach "guilt" to original sin when it is interpreted as penalty. Following Paul (Romans 5), Wesley identifies death as the penalty of sin (see Wesley's Notes on Rom. 5:13), and thus all men are born guilty of original sin, because all men die. But in no way does this involve culpability and thus susceptibility to eternal punishment.

Actual Sin as Expression of Being

The Scripture often points to the inward depravity of the human being as the source of the evils found in human life. Jesus is

---

35. Infant baptism does not necessarily need to be interpreted in this way, as we will show in a later discussion of the sacraments.

quite explicit on this relationship: "That which cometh out of the man, that defileth the man. For from within, out of the heart of man, proceed evil thoughts, adulteries, fornications, murders, thefts, covetousness, wickedness, deceit, lasciviousness, an evil eye, blasphemy, pride, foolishness: All these evil things come from within, and defile the man" (Mark 7:20-23, KJV).

The prophetic movement eventually came to realize, in the persons of Jeremiah and Ezekiel, that the great weakness of the old covenant lay in its lack of explicit provision for the being of sin. Actual sin had been prohibited. The early prophets had reiterated their condemnations of breaches of the law. But Jeremiah now saw that "the heart is deceitful above all things, and desperately wicked" (Jer. 17:9, KJV). Hence he, along with Ezekiel, pointed forward to a new covenant that would deal not only with transgressions of the law but also with the inner cause of these sins and address the issue of the heart where the "being" of sin resides. In a word, they anticipated a divine provision for both reconciliation and sanctification, a solution for both original sin and actual sin.

The Universality of Sin

The doctrine of original sin is theology's way of affirming the universality of sin. Someone has observed that this doctrine is the most empirically verifiable of all Christian doctrines. However, a number of questions emerge. One major problem concerns the issue of determinism. Does the doctrine affirm that all men *must* sin, or that they *do* sin? While it is paradoxical, Christian faith affirms that sin is both inevitable *and* volitional. This assertion stands against numerous attempts to dissolve the paradox rationalistically in either one direction or the other.

Pelagianism overcame the paradox by defining sin in a casuistic and atomistic way so as to effectively deny the doctrine of original sin. Each man is his own Adam, is born into the world in the same state of being as the first man, and commits the original sin himself. This means that he is free to sin or not to sin of his own volition. Grace, understood as divine enablement or healing, is not needed in this case. However, Pelagius did not overtly deny grace but defined it externally as the gift of freedom, the light of the law, the example of Christ, as well as the encouragement of a reward. Pelagius explained the universality of sin by the pervasiveness of bad examples. While he retained the reality (though greatly weakened) of actual sin, the truth of the inevitableness of sin, to which the doctrine of original sin points, is lost.

Interpretations of the human situation that equate sin with finiteness, or with some aspect of human nature that is essentially evil, dissolve the paradox in another direction by making it inevitable to the exclusion of the volitional. This is at home in deterministic schemas like extreme Calvinism.[36]

The historical interpretation of the Fall, which we have attempted to maintain, avoids the position of making sin endemic to the human situation. It maintains the position expressed by Wiley that "sin is but an accident of man's nature and not an essential element of his original being" (CT 2:95). But it raises the difficulty on the other hand of explaining why all men do sin, and we must avoid the trap of the rationalistic solution proposed above. This can possibly be done by simply affirming with Paul that empirically all the evidence points to the conclusion that "all have sinned, and come short of the glory of God" (Rom. 3:23, KJV).

Rationalistic efforts have been made to resolve the paradox by explaining the universality of sin in terms of theories of the transmission of sin. Some of these, such as the so-called genetic mode of transmission, are patently inadequate as being too physical, too tied to an unbiblical view of sin (the tendency to equate sexuality with sinfulness), and in the light of modern medicine's developing capacity to manipulate the genes, nonessentially related to grace as a cure. Other theories depend upon the currency of particular philosophical realisms. It is true that the Old Testament concept of "Corporate Personality" (H. Wheeler Robinson) provides a viable Weltanschauung to explain it, but developing that in contemporary philosophical terms provides some difficulty, although it is not insurmountable.

Theologically the doctrine of original sin underscores two fundamental truths. First, it refers to man as a whole. This is the true significance of the term total depravity. Before God (coram Deo), "the judgment that man is a sinner is a total judgment and there-

---

36. Both Calvin and Luther deny the possibility of freedom from sin in this life, but they are too soundly grounded in Scripture to attribute this to the body's being evil. Rather they simply do not share the "optimism of grace" that informed Wesley's confidence in the possibility of the triumph of grace over sin in this existence. They would affirm that all men *must* sin, but the Wesleyan would be nervous about going beyond saying that all men *do* sin.

fore" applies also "to the 'inner' and 'spiritual' in man."[37] It is this that is the foundation for the assertion of Augustine, reiterated by Luther and Wesley among others, that "the virtues of the heathen are but splendid vices." Man is wrong, all wrong, before God, and therefore everything he does is wrong. It is in this way that actual sin is always an expression of original sin.

Second, the doctrine of original sin is intended to view humanity as a whole. Here is where the relevance of the Hebrew concept of corporate personality enters the picture (see above). There is a solidarity in sin that takes in all the "sons of Adam's race." It may be that we can legitimately speak of a "mystical body of sin" comparable to the "mystical body of Christ" (Oswald Chambers). It is this solidarity of man in sin that brings to the fore the idea of the inevitability of sin.

Gustav Aulen's words provide an incisive summary of our whole discussion of man as sinner:

> When the idea of the original state and the fall is combined with Christian faith, the "original state" reveals to every man the destiny given him by God, and "the fall" declares that the solidary interrelationship of sin does not remove the character of sin as an act of will, or in other words, when sin becomes actual in our lives, we are engaged in destroying the destiny given us by God.[38]

Ultimately, we are more concerned with the divine answer to the sin problem and His provision for its healing than with a rationalistic answer to its source and origin. Thus we now turn to the saving work of God.

37. Aulen, *Faith of the Christian Church*, 239.
38. Ibid., 247.

CHAPTER

10

The Person
of the Savior

The subject of Christology brings us to one of the central motifs of
Wesleyan theology (see chap. 1). This in turn is organically related
to the primary focus of our norm, since Christological questions
always impinge upon soteriological concerns. It is also conversely
the case that questions of soteriology shape the Christological
questions. In fact, John Deschner points out that such Christological statements as are found in Wesley's writings are "largely
imbedded in or even concealed under soteriological material."[1]
Wolfhart Pannenberg argues that all Christologies are actually informed by soteriological concerns and seeks to demonstrate the
systematic relations in certain prominent theories.[2]

This orientation toward soteriology in Wesley is correlative
with an attitude toward Christology that we discovered to be also
present in his approach to the doctrine of the Trinity. He has little
interest in speculative theories but distinguishes between the "fact"
and the "manner" of the Incarnation. Of the manner, he can say, "I
know nothing about it . . . It is no more the object of my faith, than

---

1. *Wesley's Christology*, 5. He also suggests in his introduction that certain "defi-
ciencies" in Wesley's theological formulations, e.g., the penal satisfaction theory of the
Atonement, can be best modified or altered "on Christological grounds." 4.

2. *Jesus—God and Man*, trans. Lewis L. Wilkins and Duane A. Priebe (Philadelphia:
Westminster Press, 1977).

it is of my understanding."[3] But of the fact (that Christ is both divine and human) he speaks much more surely: "That Jesus is the Christ; that He is the Son of God; that He came in the flesh, is one undivided truth, and he that denies any part of this, in effect denies the whole."[4]

This would suggest that Wesley would be more interested in a functional Christology than in a speculative ontological one. This doubtless is in part because of the fact that the New Testament does not offer an explicit doctrine of the person of Christ, that is, does not explain how the two natures are related. But it is perhaps even more so because of his consistent interest in relating all doctrines to salvation. However, as we noted with the Trinity, even functional issues inevitably reflect ontological underpinning, although we may not have at hand the necessary conceptual categories to adequately formulate them.

It is our intention, in developing a Wesleyan systematic theology, to work under the limitation implied by this perspective. Consequently we will not discuss the various contemporary speculative efforts at Christological formulations but basically survey the classical Christological debates. This approach will unveil the central commitments of the classical Christian faith. In doing this, we will seek to focus attention on those aspects of the person of the Savior that impinge upon questions of reconciliation and sanctification.

Theological Significance of the Incarnation

The term *Incarnation* (literally en-flesh-ment), refers to the uniquely Christian belief that God has entered history in the form of a hu-

---

3. *Works* 6:204.
4. *Notes* on 1 John 2:22. Colin Williams comments on this point: "There can be no doubt that Wesley accepted the orthodox Christological formulations, but always his interest was in the saving significance of Christ. He showed a constant dislike for metaphysical speculations. To lead people aside into a discussion of doctrinal subtleties could easily produce an argumentative spirit, and whereas a true living knowledge of Christ produces increasing dependence upon him and fosters a spirit of love, speculative arguments concerning his person can result in division and bitterness (cf. *Letters* 4:159).

"Where the true living knowledge of Christ is actually at stake, however, Wesley was prepared to pursue the accuracies of doctrinal formulations." *John Wesley's Theology Today*, 91-92.

man person. "The Word became flesh and dwelt among us" (John 1:14) is one of the foundation stones with which the Christian faith stands or falls. It is the "focal point" of the "confession of faith in Christ" that identifies the substance of Christian doctrine.[5]

The affirmation that God has become immanent in a particular event in world history further includes the commitment that that event is normative for the whole of history. This belief is a scandal to the rationalist mind, but its purpose is not simply to create a stumbling block to belief, that is, its significance does not lie in its absurdity. There are fundamental truths that become problematic if there is no Incarnation; therefore, the fact of God's enfleshment in Jesus of Nazareth has profound theological meaning for certain basic tenets of Christian doctrine.

Revelation

We have discovered in our study of the idea of revelation (chap. 4) that unless God becomes immanent in some way ("accommodation," Calvin), there is no knowledge of Him at all. We furthermore noted that the distinctiveness of Christian theology, in contrast to other theologies, is its belief that God has decisively and finally made himself known in Jesus Christ. Thus the Incarnation stands as the pillar of confidence that God's true nature is adequately known through this historical event.

Gordon Kaufman's statement relates beautifully to this complex of ideas:

> God is the utterly self-suffcent being, the One incomparable to all others, absolutely unique, the ultimate limit of man and all other finite reality. How could we possibly come to know such a being? If God transcended us and our world absolutely and in all respects, we could never come to know anything about him at all—even that he is and that he is transcendent. Such a being could come to be and mean something for us only through entering into our world, thus becoming a possible object of our knowledge. God would have to take on the form, as it were, of something we could experience and understand, and make himself known to us in that way. This is precisely the Christian claim: God himself has come to man in the very person of a man.[6]

The Fourth Gospel emphasizes, as one of its major motifs, the thesis that God is fully made known by the Son. The Johannine

5. Aulen, *Faith of the Christian Church*, 185.
6. *Systematic Theology*, 168.

Christ says, "He who has seen me has seen the Father" (John 14:9). And John declared, "No one has ever seen God; the only Son, who is in the bosom of the Father, he has made him known" (1:18). Faith in God is at the same time faith in Christ, and vice versa. Aulen's summary captures this truth:

> The confession of faith in Christ is, therefore, not a statement about Christ, it is first and last an affirmation about that God who has revealed himself. If Christian faith affirms that Christ is of the same substance with the Father, it thereby makes a statement about the character of the Father's being. Then the real function of the confession of faith in Christ is to guard the content and purity of the Christian conception of God.[7]

Not only does the Incarnation reveal God, but also it reveals man. Athanasius, in the fourth century, saw this truth and described it in a fascinating way. He suggests that the Incarnation had for its purpose the restoring of man to the *imago Dei*. Men could not do this work of restoration for each other, for they are at best copies of the image, and marred ones at that. If a portrait has been effaced by a stain, says Athanasius, it has to be restored by the painter painting it over again from the original, who must come and sit for him a second time. So the Word had to come to earth, that the image might again be visible, and copied afresh in the nature of man.[8]

As contemporary theology consistently emphasizes, we do not have access to the man (Adam) at the beginning so as to derive an adequate picture of normative human being. Our knowledge of this reality is "from the middle" (Bonhoeffer). In Jesus Christ we perceive the full measure of manhood, undeformed by sin. He is not only what man means by God, but what God means by man.

John Wesley describes a remarkable comparison of Christ and the law. When he describes the origin and nature of the law, he uses language peculiarly appropriate to the Incarnation.[9] His point is that God's nature and will as it relates to human nature, destiny, and behavior is embodied in the law, which is thus a revelation of divine virtue and wisdom. Since the law was a less-than-adequate means of self-disclosure and was susceptible to legalistic perversion, God more perfectly embodied His will and nature as it

---

7. *Faith of the Christian Church*, 189.
8. *De Incarnatione*, chap. 14.
9. *StS* 2:45-47.

relates to man's destiny by the incarnation of His nature in Jesus Christ. Thus Christ is the express image of the divine nature, the *eikōn* of God (Col. 1:15; cf. Heb. 1:3). The relation between these two revelations is discussed by Paul in 2 Corinthians 3 in terms of "glory." The fading glory of the law (illustrated by the temporary glory that shone from Moses' countenance) was superseded by the permanent glory that shines (perpetually and undistortedly) from the face of Jesus Christ.

Redemption

The Western church, with its penchant for justification and legal modes of thought, has usually spoken of redemption almost exclusively in terms of the death of Christ. The Incarnation is interpreted as a necessity for redemption in this context, largely under the influence of Anselm's satisfaction theory of the Atonement. It was further emphasized by the penal satisfaction explanation, classically formulated by John Calvin. Here redemption is interpreted as resulting from the satisfaction of God's honor (Anselm) or justice (Calvin), and this satisfaction must be rendered by Jesus Christ as man, whose death meets the requirements of justice. Since redemption is the work of man, and only discontinuously the work of God, the Incarnation is necessary to provide the sacrifice. (This is the argument of Anselm's *Cur Deus homo?*) Thus it does not seem to have critical significance within itself for redemption.[10]

Eastern Christianity, on the other hand, with its greater preoccupation with sanctification, saw the Incarnation as significant for this aspect of redemption. In categories typically Wesleyan, we can speak of the Eastern emphasis in terms of restoration to the image

---

10. John Deschner argues that Wesley's adoption of the penal satisfaction theory creates one ground for his understanding of the necessity of the Incarnation, so that "God's justice and love are harmonized in the penal substitution of Christ on the cross for man's sin." *Wesley's Christology,* 19. However, he points out that this creates a tension within Wesley's thought, and he has difficulty relating this to his teaching about sanctification. This is only one aspect of what Deschner calls a two-sidedness in Wesley's theology, "a moralistic side" stemming from his pre-Aldersgate understanding, and "an evangelical side stemming from his conversion, which, it is here asserted, labors to convert his theology, but with only a partial transformation of its form." 77. I believe Deschner is correct in his analysis as well as in his assertion that the evangelical side "rules the intention of his theology." Ibid. This tension points to the incompatibility of a satisfaction theory of the Atonement with a viable doctrine of sanctification, as we will observe later, and thus shows how Wesley's uncritical use of satisfaction categories when referring to the work of Christ (such as "merit") are inconsistent with the major commitments of his theology and thus must be rejected in a systematic development of Wesleyan theology.

of God. In the quotation above from Athanasius, the Eastern stress on the importance of the Incarnation as modeling the *imago* can be seen. But even more crucial is the belief that the Incarnation potentially transforms human nature, making it possible for man to become godlike through union with Christ. The great recapitulation teaching of Irenaeus demonstrates how Jesus Christ effects a reversal of the Fall at each stage of human life. Thus "he [Christ] became what we are [man] that we may become what he is [divine]." The problems with the divination of human nature inherent in the realistic theory of redemption as formulated by Athanasius and Irenaeus do not invalidate the formal importance of the sanctifying significance of the Incarnation. David Cairns's conclusion supports this positive evaluation of the realist theories:

> The language of divinization is an attempt to do justice to a real change worked in human nature through union with Christ in His Church. But this union is a union of faith. It is real, and the fruits of the Spirit bear witness to it, but it never amounts to a fusion of the believer or the Church with the Lord. It is a singular union of persons with the Divine Person, whereby Christ's benefits pass to His disciples, while His Lordship remains unassailed, and the boundary between Creator and creature remains uncrossed. To describe this union is the real aim of Irenaeus, Clement and Athanasius.[11]

R. V. Sellers concurs with this estimate. He maintains that Athanasius' conception was moral and spiritual and not so much realistic as the language implies, meaning thereby that man can, "in Christ," enjoy perfect fellowship with God.[12]

The emphasis on Incarnation that we are here encouraging does not at all diminish the decisive significance of the death of Christ. It is calling for a more broadly based understanding of how the work of Christ relates to salvation. This will be explored more thoroughly in the following chapter.

Christology of the New Testament[13]

The Christology of the New Testament is an indispensable resource for the work of systematic theology. While the task of theol-

---

11. *Image of God*, 108-9.
12. *Two Ancient Christologies* (London: SPCK, 1954).
13. This is one of the most vexing subjects in the field of New Testament studies. It is impossible to even cover the vast amount of material that has been produced on the topic. Consequently, we shall simply set forth some of the major issues and conclusions

ogy goes beyond the descriptive task indigenous to biblical theology, it cannot develop categories and interpretations that violate the New Testament perspective if it takes the authority of Scripture seriously. But on the positive side, it seeks to set forth a contemporary formulation that is an extrapolation of the insights of the biblical writers.

The most common, as well as the most adequate, beginning point in exploring the New Testament's answer to the question of Christ is to examine the titles ascribed to Jesus in the Gospels. It is here that the understanding of the Earliest Church as to who Jesus was, as well as His own self-understanding, came centrally to expression. While we cannot examine all of those titles that may be isolated when the New Testament is searched with a fine-tooth comb, we will look at those that seem to have decisive significance and more broad-based use in the documents.

It is important to note, at the start, that the "Christological problem" of the New Testament was not the problem of His person and work. That way of addressing the issue emerged in the early centuries as the church sought to answer the questions of the relation of Christ to the Father and the relation of the divine and human natures in Christ. This was doubtless an inevitable development, but putting the question this way made it possible to separate Christ's person from His work, that is, Christology and soteriology could now become two separate considerations. The New Testament, however, hardly even speaks of the person of Christ without at the same time speaking of His work. The various New Testament answers to the question "Who is Christ?" incorporate both Christ's person and His work as indistinguishable realities.

---

that seem to this writer, who is not a technical New Testament scholar, to be reasonably sound. No doubt many, if not all, of the positions taken here will appear incredibly naive to at least some specialists. It will assume the reliability of the New Testament documents and that the Gospels faithfully reproduce the person and teachings of Jesus in substance and not the later faith of the early Christians that had gone through a process of evolutionary development. The theories on all these issues are a veritable thicket of varied points of view and interpretations. Trying to work one's way through this tangled undergrowth is a major task. The nontechnical student of the New Testament is often tempted to think that the need to produce some new interpretation overrides the quest for truth among technical scholars. A survey of some basic data bearing on the issues of New Testament Christology can be gleaned by reading the section in Appendix 2 dealing with the schematic of Jesus' ministry. The present discussion relies upon a relatively few primary studies that are chosen from among many for utilitarian reasons but also because their work generates the confidence of the writer in both their scholarship and their commitment to the authority and veracity of Scripture.

This implies that, as Richard Longenecker argues, all the titles ascribed to Jesus by the Earliest Church are understood as functional rather than ontological.[14]

In answering the question "Who is Jesus?" the earliest Christians had at their disposal certain concepts from their Jewish background that seemed to apply to Jesus. The Christological problem of the New Testament was therefore to answer such questions as: To what extent did Jesus fulfill these Jewish concepts? The outcome of approaching the question in this way led eventually to a meaning that transcended all these concepts taken separately or together. But our task here is to follow these attempts as they come to expression in the New Testament.

Two major critical questions emerge in such an investigation. First, we must determine if we are dealing with Jesus' own self-understanding in His recorded teachings or with the later theological understanding of the Christian community. We have encountered this issue at certain key points in this book, so we simply reiterate the conclusions affirmed in those places. While it is true that the Gospels reflect the later perspective and situation of the Early Church, we are nonetheless presented with a faithful picture of Jesus that we accept as reliable. Second, the decision must be made concerning the origin of the titles applied to Jesus. Did they come from a Hebraic or a Hellenistic milieu? In a few cases there is no real option involved, but where there is, it is highly significant which source is identified. In general in this discussion, we are assuming the position taken by many reliable scholars that the primary source is Hebraic, although some titles will have special contact with the Hellenistic world. Where there are crucial issues at stake, they will be noted.

The Messiah

Basic to the Christology of the earliest Jewish Christians was the conviction that Jesus was the Messiah. It was so basic, in fact, that the Greek word for Messiah (*Christos*) became associated with the person of Jesus as a proper name. This is really a rather strange phenomenon because (1) it was a very uncertain designation, a catchall term for a quite fluid concept in Judaism; (2) Jesus did not fulfill many of the basic aspects of the Messianic hope, especially

14. See Richard Longenecker, *The Christology of Early Jewish Christianity* (Naperville, Ill.: Alec R. Allenson, 1970).

in its contemporary form; and (3) Jesus seldom applied the term to himself. Despite these considerations, this was the term fixed on by the Church as most prominent. Therefore, the question to be addressed is, To what extent did the Christians take over the Jewish view, and in what way did they transform it? Or the same question could be formulated, and perhaps should be, in relation to Jesus' own self-understanding.

The place to begin is with the meaning of the term, or idea. Although as a technical designation the term "Messiah" is not found in the Old Testament, the idea is certainly present. (A possible exception is the mysterious and enigmatic reference in Dan. 9:25-26. However, scholarship is so fragmented in its interpretation and translation as to make its use highly problematic. Compare the comments in the *Abingdon Bible Commentary* with the diametrically opposite interpretation in the *New Bible Commentary*.) It was primarily a political concept (cf. Ezek. 37:21 ff.), since it involved a Davidic king ruling over a restored Israel. Apparently the primary hope for the future is not that of the Messianic king, since in many eschatological passages the picture is drawn of a Golden Age and a restored kingdom, but the description of the king is absent. The Messianic hope as we encounter it among the Jewish people of Jesus' day was chiefly a product of the postexilic period.

Some scholars have identified at least two strands of the Messianic hope, both of which are eschatological. The first is of a this-worldly, natural, political, and nationalistic ruler. This seems to be the substance of the popular view. T. W. Manson argues from the Psalms of Solomon that this is the way the "average godly and patriotic Jew" viewed the Lord's Anointed in the first century B.C.[15]

Others have suggested a second interpretation, which is of an other-worldly and transcendent Messiah who comes with miraculous workings of God. Sigmund Mowinckel describes these two views as follows:

> It appears that, as in the general future hope of later Judaism there were two tendencies, originally quite distinct, but now fused with each other, so the conception of the Messiah in later Judaism manifests the same double character. The one side is national, political, this-worldly, with particularistic tendencies, though universalistic when at its best. The other is super-terrestrial, other-worldly, rich in religious content and mytho-

---

15. *The Servant-Messiah* (Grand Rapids: Baker Book House, 1977), 23 ff.

logical concepts, universalistic, numinous, at home in the sphere of the "Holy" and the "wholly Other."[16]

John Wick Bowman has proposed a third strand, which he identifies as the true prophetic understanding and refers to it as the "Remnant-Messiah." We shall explore this suggestion more fully later in this section.

The first technical use of the term Messiah occurs as an instance of the first complex of ideas and involves a modification of the Old Testament material. This use of the term appears in the Psalms of Solomon, 17 and 18, which comes from the mid-first century B.C. Whereas, as we have seen, the Golden Age is the more significant idea in the prophetic literature, with the Messiah appearing in some places but not in others, the understanding of the Messiah here was as the agent of God to bring in the Kingdom. In the Old Testament he was an aspect of the Kingdom, but now he is the effective instrument who ushers it into reality by defeating the enemies of its establishment. And, of course, it is aways seen in terms of Jewish nationalism. While this development is not in gross contradiction to the major contours of the biblical hope, there was one major exception: Zech. 9:9 pictured the coming king as a peaceful ruler rather than a warlike figure who would exterminate Israel's enemies. This was the one passage with which Jesus explicitly identified himself at the Triumphal Entry. It most nearly reflected His own understanding of Messiahship.

There was also another modification of the Messianic expectation during the intertestamental period. In the Jewish apocalypses the idea arose that the Messiah would usher in a provisional kingdom. Yahweh himself would usher in the permanent one. Thus, in this view, the Messiah is the forerunner of Yahweh, resulting in the idea of a time between the times.[17]

Longenecker's summary will provide an adequate background statement for looking at the New Testament use of the title in relation to Jesus:

> While other elements vied for recognition, this political
> and nationalistic conception came to take the place of as-

---

16. *He That Cometh* (New York: Abingdon Press, n.d.), 281.

17. William Barclay argues that this concept of a provisional kingdom, which arose in the first century B.C., was the source of the idea of a 1000-year interim reign of Christ (millennium) found in the enigmatic 20th chapter of Revelation. *Daily Study Bible: The Revelation of John*, 2 vols. (Philadelphia: Westminster Press, 1960), vol. 2.

cendency in Jewish thought. And in Jesus' day, this son-of-David understanding of messiahship was dominant.[18]

Jesus and the Messianic Title

Jesus is the "melting pot" into which the ideas of Jewish Messianism flowed. It is the way in which He dealt with these conceptions that becomes crucial, especially if we take seriously, as we are doing, the historical Jesus and His own self-consciousness.

To begin with, we must take account of what William Wrede in 1901 referred to as the "messianic secret." Especially in Mark's Gospel, Jesus is presented as avoiding the title. He silenced demons who recognized Him as Messiah (1:23-25, 34; 3:11-12). He charged those He healed to tell no one (1:43-44; 5:43; 7:36). After the Transfiguration, He told His disciples not to tell what they had seen (9:9). How do we explain this?

Liberal scholars such as Rudolph Bultmann and Gunther Bornkamm say that it was because Jesus had no Messianic consciousness. More conservative scholars like Oscar Cullmann suggest that Jesus completely rejected the title because of its political overtones. There are several crucial passages that must be examined as evidence before a conclusion can be reached.

It is quite clear that Jesus rejected the political aspects of His mission in the Temptation in the wilderness. He refused to become the kind of messiah who could attract a following on such grounds. The encounter with Satan sets the pattern for His subsequent ministry and doubtless provides us with a pattern in terms of which we can evaluate later events.

There are four passages where Jesus' relation to the Messianic title is a critical issue:

Mark 14:61-62. In response to the high priest's question, "Are you the Christ, the Son of the Blessed?" Jesus answers in what appears to be an unequivocal way: "I am." But in Matthew's report, His answer is much more ambiguous: "You have said so." (This is supported by manuscript evidence, even though some newer translations read, "Yes.") It would seem that Matthew's purpose would have disposed him to take advantage of an unambiguous claim if it had actually occurred. Furthermore, in both places Jesus is reported as identifying himself with the Son of Man. The reac-

---

18. *Christology*, 66.

tion of the priests seems to more clearly support a claim to be the Son of Man than a claim to be Messiah. They charge Him with blasphemy, which would be more appropriate to the prevailing Son of Man concept in Judaism. If they had understood Him to be claiming to be Messiah, another type of response would have been more appropriately called for, since that did not entail any claims to "otherworldliness" (see discussion below on Son of Man). Oscar Cullmann, in a very esoteric argument, insists the Markan account is really an evasion rather than the straightforward response our translations suggest. He bases his argument on philological grounds involving a retranslating of the Greek back into the original Aramaic that Jesus spoke.

Mark 15:2 ff. In His encounter with Pilate, Jesus is faced with another direct question regarding His Kingship. But He responds in a similar ambiguous way by saying, "Thou sayest it" (KJV). Matthew reports the discussion in the same way. Thus there is clearly here an evasion of the Messianic terminology.

Mark 8:27 ff. Here Peter's great confession at Caesarea Philippi declares the disciples' conclusion that Jesus is the Messiah (Christ). Although this announcement is enthusiastically received by Jesus, as recorded in Matt. 16:17, He charges His disciples to tell no man and then proceeds to talk about the Son of Man and emphasizes the role of suffering, which is foreign to the Jewish concept of Messiah. That Peter confessed more than he understood is reflected in his negative reaction to Jesus' amplification of the Messianic mission as involving rejection and death. He was still using the Messianic terminology in the popular Jewish sense.

Why did Jesus evidently avoid the term when He had the opportunity to make clear-cut claims and at the same time warn His disciples about disseminating their conclusions? One conservative view is that the contexts of all these passages are understood as laden with nationalistic overtones, which is precisely what Jesus wished to avoid.

One additional passage in the Fourth Gospel needs attention. In **John 4** Jesus seems to directly announce himself as Messiah to the Samaritan woman. In response to her acknowledgment that her religious tradition includes the hope of a coming Messiah (v. 25), Jesus declares: "I who speak to you am he." Two considerations are relevant here. First, there are obviously no dangers of political uproar in the situation. Second, it is not insignificant that the Samaritan scripture included only the Pentateuch, which would have had only a "prophetic messiah" in its purview, not a political one. It is possible to identify the idea of a "prophet like Moses" of Deuteronomy 18 with the Samaritan hope. The very context of Jesus' conversation with the woman highlights this fact: Her response was, "Come, see a man, which told me all things that ever I did: is not this the Christ?" (v. 29, KJV). Thus this passage, too, seems to simply veer around the traditional Messianic view.

But there is one other consideration to which several scholars have called attention. Despite the fact that Jesus quite clearly refused to associate himself with the existing idea of a political messiah, even to the point of withdrawing from His followers when they attempted to force it upon Him (John 6:15), Jesus could hardly have claimed to be the fulfillment of Old Testament prophecy without at least implying that He was in some sense the Messiah of Israel's hope. The bare minimum must involve a continuity between the work of Jesus and the mission of the chosen people of Israel.

The answer proposed to this dilemma arises out of a Jewish pattern of thought discovered in the Dead Sea Scrolls. As Richard Longenecker puts it: "From the strictly theological point of view no man can be defined as a messiah before he has accomplished the task of the anointed." In the Jewish view, that is, the function and work must be accomplished first before the title may be rightfully claimed. This means that Jesus would be "messiah-designate" or "messiah elect" because of His forthcoming passion and resurrection.[19]

This analysis leads us to the conclusion that the function of the Messiah as Jesus reinterpreted it is intimately connected with suffering and in substance becomes the Suffering Servant. Thus the Messiah's work was not as the Jews had conceived it. In fact, the conjoining of the two ideas of Messiah and suffering created a serious stumbling block to Jewish belief because the two ideas had not been identified, at least not in their interpretation of the Scripture.[20]

---

19. Ibid., 73 ff.

20. H. H. Rowley, *The Meaning of Sacrifice in the Old Testament* (The John Rylands Library Bulletin, vol. 33, no. 1, [September 1950]), cites some writers who contest this statement but adds: "No solid evidence coming from a pre-Christian date can be produced in support of their position, and the evidence of the New Testament is firmly against it.

John Wick Bowman attempts to provide an alternate interpretation to the ones explored above. He takes his point of departure from the question raised by the radical reinterpretation of
the Old Testament prophecy involved in applying the Messianic
title to Jesus. What does this do to the question of divine revelation?
Was there, he asks, no true conception revealed by God in ages
past, recorded by God's inspired prophets, that found its fulfillment in Jesus as Messiah?

In response to these questions, Bowman argues that there was
another strand that Judaism had obscured through its nationalistic
perversions. He calls this strand "the prophetic heritage" and identifies it with the "divine revelation rightly conceived." This voice
had its own doctrine of the Messiah, which may be characterized
as universalistic because of its highly ethical and spiritual nature.
In support of this position he quotes C. F. Burney as saying: "We
can trace in the prophets the doctrine of a future religious universalism in which the nations are united to Israel by community in
the highest of interests. This develops side by side with the Messianic ideal, and is of a piece with it. The two ideas cannot, therefore,
be properly dissociated" (*Outlines of Old Testament Theology*,
99-100).

This universalism, which seems to be the key to his position,
was achieved through several steps. It began with the doctrine of
the remnant, which appears implicitly in Amos but comes to most
explicit expression in the teaching of Isaiah of Jerusalem. This limitation of the "people of God" to a faithful group within the nation
broke down the idea that Israel stood related to God *as a unity*. It
thus became clear that a man stood related to God on a personal
level. Membership in the remnant became a matter not of racial
ties but of moral choice. The necessary corollary of this individualism was the universalization of man's relation to God. "Take
away from a religion its national and racial basis," says Bowman,
"make of it a matter of an individual relationship achieved between God and man, and obviously the religion is well on its way
to becoming a universal faith."

The concept of the Messiah developed in conjunction with
these two concepts of the remnant and universalism, according to

---

For the Gospels show that whenever our Lord spoke of His mission in terms of suffering,
the disciples were completely bewildered and failed to understand what He meant. Hence
most scholars support the view which [is] expressed . . . above." 103-4 n. 4.

Bowman's interpretation. In the highest thought of the prophets, he argues, the remnant was conceived as joining forces with individuals from every race and nation who should come to worship the true God as a genuine portion of His people. The Messiah of the Remnant was clearly then an ethico-spiritual one, far removed from the nationalistic Messiah of the popular thought. Thus we have the true prophetic concept of the Remnant-Messiah.

Although this strand is not connected in the Old Testament with the Suffering Servant, the two are fused in the person of Jesus and proclaimed at the Baptism in the one ordination formula: Suffering Servant Messiah of the Remnant (Isa. 42:1 and Ps. 2:7). Bowman suggests that the correlation of the concepts is the foundation of New Testament theology and that we only feel the impact of it when we translate these Hebrew expressions into common Christian speech, which was largely molded by Greek thought forms, thought forms to which we are more accustomed. Translated into Greek concepts, the phrase Suffering Servant, Messiah of the Remnant becomes Crucified Savior, Lord of the Church. Bowman concludes: "It is that simple combination of phrases, indeed, that is responsible for the transformation of a religion. Apart they lay sterile within the prophetic literature. Brought into relation with one another, they formed together the living seed out of which the Christian faith was born."[21]

Jesus as Son of Man

The title Son of Man is uniquely a self-designation of Jesus. It belongs peculiarly to the Gospels, appearing only four times elsewhere, with three of these references being quotations from the Old Testament (Heb. 2:6; Rev. 1:13; 14:14; Acts 7:56). It is used exclusively of Jesus, and in the Gospels it is found without exception on His lips.

There are at least four possibilities of its origin and thus of what Jesus intended by its use. It has been shown that it was used by the rabbis as a circumlocution for "I." Jesus' use clearly transcended this rhetorical device. It could mean, as it frequently did in

---

21. *The Intention of Jesus* (Philadelphia: Westminster Press, 1943), 72, 82. This passage in the text summarizes Bowman's thesis, which is developed throughout the book. A further implication of these ideas for New Testament theology is that the Early Church should be properly interpreted as the fulfillment of the remnant concept of the Old Testament.

the Old Testament, simply man as the frail, transitory creature (Ps. 8:4-5). Some have suggested that it was derived from the religious language of the surrounding peoples where "Man" frequently meant "the original Man" or "Primordial Man" who would come to earth as Savior to lead humanity back to its original destiny. The generally accepted source, however, is Dan. 7:13. A further suggestion is that the "Son of Man" Christology from the Daniel passage is adumbrated by Jewish apocalyptic literature where the Son of Man is pictured as the preexistent, universal, heavenly Judge of the last days. Richard Longenecker, along with other scholars, has called attention to the fact that there is no evidence that the supposed source of these ideas (1 Enoch 37—71) is a pre-Christian document. The earliest evidence for its existence is in the fourth century A.D. Thus Longenecker concludes:

> The evidence to date is of such a nature as to make the employment of 1 Enoch 37—71 in reconstructing pre-Christian thought precarious indeed, and to suggest that the confidence with which these chapters are employed in current discussion as representing early Jewish apocalypticism is supported more by dogmatic assertion than critical judgment.[22]

The conclusion to this analysis is that while later usage of the title Son of Man did in fact carry the implication of His full manhood, on the lips of Jesus it referred exclusively to the Danielic Son of Man.

Why did Jesus so clearly opt for this title in distinction from the Messianic designation? An examination of the Gospel texts leads most scholars to the view that Jesus chose this title because it was least compromised with Jewish nationalism and warlike hopes. Furthermore, it is significant that in context, the title contains a suffering motif. C. F. D. Moule has illuminated this point:

> But the fact remains that in Dan. 7:21, 25, the specially aggressive "horn" on the beast's head "made war with the saints, and prevailed over them" and was destined to "wear out the saints of the Most High"; and it is precisely with these saints of the Most High that the Son of Man is identified. It is irrelevant that this interpretation of the Son of Man vision is a secondary interpretation (as at times asserted): all that concerns the present investigation is that it was in Dan. 7 as Jesus and his disciples knew it—and I know of no evidence to the contrary. But, if so, the Son of Man, in the only document known to have

---

22. *Christology,* 82 ff.

been available then, stands for a loyal, martyr-group who are brought to glory and vindicated through suffering.[23]

We can distinguish three types of uses by Jesus: (1) In some passages He refers to himself as Son of Man at the time of speaking (Mark 2:10, 28; 14:41). (2) In many passages He refers to His approaching sufferings and resurrection (Mark 8:31; 9:12; 10:45; cf. Luke 17:24-25). (3) There are other places that involve an eschatological use: He is the Judge to come (Mark 14:61-62; Matt. 25:31-46).

We may conclude that the use of the term Son of Man by Jesus had two connotations:

First, Jesus used this self-designation to mean precisely a Messiah who suffers according to the Scriptures, the distinctive feature about the Christian, as over against the Jewish, doctrine of the Messiah. This explains why Jesus preferred the title over the Messianic one. The latter term was filled with ready-made ideas that needed radical correction; therefore He set it aside and used a title into which He could pour a more scriptural content. In a word, He combined the Son of Man with the Servant of the Lord.

Second, there is the element of judgment embodied in the sayings about the Son of Man coming at the end of the age. This second meaning is the result of the first. It is precisely the Son of Man who suffers who will be the Agent of judgment in the end, and the basis of judgment will be the response to His mission as the Servant. Connected with this is the corporate dimension that many have found in the Danielic Son of Man. There is such a close affinity between the "saints" and the Son of Man who receives the Kingdom from the "Ancient of Days" that they are inseparably connected. Jesus picks up this idea also in such sayings as, "As you did it to one of the least of these my brethren, you did it to me" (Matt. 25:40).

Jesus as Lord

The earliest Christian confession seems to be "Jesus is Lord" (Rom. 10:9). That, along with the confession that "Jesus is the Christ [Messiah]" (John 20:31), expresses the deepest conviction of primitive Christian faith. The designation "Lord" embodies as no other the thought that Christ is exalted to God's right hand, glorified, and now intercedes before the Father. It declares that Jesus is

---

23. Quoted ibid., 87.

a living reality in the present. Thus the believer prays to Him, and the Church appeals to Him in worship and makes its prayers in His name. As Lord, Jesus is the exalted Head of the Church, which is His Body (Ignatius' Letter to the Ephesians, 1:23).

With this title, we are faced for the first time in our discussion with a decision regarding the origin of the term. The previous two were unequivocally derived from a Hebraic milieu. However, Lord (kyrios) was a common term in Hellenistic culture, and some have argued that it emerged from this source. In the Hellenistic context, the general meaning is "master" or "owner." In an address it was simply equivalent to "sir." This was its use in the address of the Samaritan woman to Jesus in John 4.

In its religious use, the title was ascribed to various deities. Paul refers to this meaning in 1 Cor. 8:5 ff. when he speaks of "many 'gods' and many 'lords.'" It was also used in a religious sense to designate the lordship of the Roman emperor. The confession was "Caesar is Lord." This formula became the bone of contention in the situation reflected in the Book of Revelation.

In the Hebrew understanding, however, Lord was the exalted designation for God himself and was used as a substitute name for the revered personal name, Yahweh. Thus it carried specific implications of the highest adoration and clearly meant Deity.

As the term came to be employed in early Christianity, it referred to the post-Easter, present work of Christ in His state of exaltation (cf. Acts 2:36). Although the term was used in the Gospels, the term does not have there the definitive significance that it takes on after the Resurrection (except possibly in Matt. 7:21-23). Our contention is that it is the Hebraic rather than the Hellenistic meaning that informs this early Christian use.

Thus the title Lord ascribed to Jesus points beyond His work to His person, although it is not radically separable from His work. The point is that after the completion of His mission, God has given to Christ His own unique authority (Rom. 1:3-4; cf. Heb. 1:1-3). In Jesus as Lord, God exercises His sovereignty. This means that Jesus is fully God.

As a consequence of this understanding, the New Testament can in principle apply to Jesus all the Old Testament passages that speak of God. This of course is not true of Jesus' own sayings, since when He quotes the Old Testament, the word kyrios refers to God. But in the New Testament letters, which reflect the Easter faith of the early believers, the writers commonly apply such Old Testament passages to Jesus. For instance, Isa. 45:23 is quoted in Phil. 2:10-11 as referring to Jesus. Ps. 102:25-27 is used in Heb. 1:10-12 in the same way. In the psalm, the reference is obviously to God the Father, the Creator. But as a result of the transfer of the title Lord to Jesus, the Hebrews writer does not hesitate to address Him with the words of the psalm and thus designate Him as the Creator.

A final consequence of calling Jesus "Lord" is that all titles of honor for God himself (except that of Father) may be transferred to Jesus. Lord is the "name which is above every name" (Phil. 2:9). No wonder the central confession was "Jesus is Lord."

An important conclusion to this analysis is that we can more clearly see the close correlation between the person and work of Christ in the New Testament. It is not to be inferred that after the Resurrection, Jesus became God in some ontological sense that He was not before the Resurrection. Rather, His work, and its validation by God's raising Him from the dead, declared His Lordship and demonstrated that because of His full implementation of the Servant mission He is recognized as Lord.

Jesus as Son of God

One additional title needs scrutiny, one that has occasioned considerable discussion with greatly varying conclusions. To speak of Jesus as Son of God raises numerous questions, but we shall simply restrict ourselves to the two major questions identified at the outset: Jesus' own self-awareness and the cultural context out of which it arose, whether Hebraism or Hellenism.

In Hellenic thought, Son of God was a prominent designation with considerable variety of meaning. It implied a very good man or a righteous man. A comparison of Mark 15:39 and Luke 23:47 makes it clear that this is the meaning that the Roman had in mind when he said of the Victim on the center cross, "This man was a son of God" (NEB).

In this milieu, the world was full of divine men who claimed to be sons of God and were actually worshiped as manifestations of deity (cf. Acts 8:10; 12:22; 14:11 ff.; 28:6). On the basis of the ancient belief that kings, philosophers, priests, and righteous men were offspring of God (see 17:28), the emperor was called the "Son of God." But these views are at the opposite pole from the biblical teaching of man as the creation of God. Alan Richardson correctly observes that

> it is exceedingly unlikely that any Christians, even Hellenistic ones, would have begun to call Jesus "the Son of God" because they had mistaken him for one of the Greek "sons of God" of the type of Simon Magus or Elymas, still less of the type of Caligula or Herod Agrippa (cf. Acts 12:22), or of the wandering Stoic philosophers.[24]

The title was used in Hebrew thought of angels (Gen. 6:2; Job 1:6; 38:7) and the king (2 Sam. 7:14; Pss. 2:7; 89:26 ff.). But its most definitive use seems to be in relation to Israel (Exod. 4:22; Hos. 11:1). In this context the idea of sonship conveys the thought of obedience (cf. Exod. 24:7). The Son of God is one who does the righteous will of the Father.

Jesus, according to the Gospel accounts, manifested a unique sense of sonship. He taught the Fatherhood of God for those who by repentance and faith enter His kingdom and accept the obedience of sons, but He seems to relate this to His own Sonship (cf. Matt. 11:25-27). Jesus addressed God as Abba, a most intimate term. He refers to "My Father" and "your Father," but not to "Our Father" so as to lump himself and His followers together; thus He reflects His special relation to God that men do not share.

In the light of the Old Testament understanding of sonship and obedience, it is apparent how significant it is to refer to Jesus as the New Israel.

> Jesus clearly conceived his Sonship as the perfect obedience of the Servant of the Lord. The reiterated "If thou art the Son of God" in the Temptation Story (Matt. 4:3, 6; Luke 4:3, 9 [ASV]) emphasizes the fact that the Sonship of Christ is the same thing as the obedience of the Servant. The very shape of the Gospel narrative brings out the meaning of Christ's Sonship as the obedience of the New Israel.[25]

In some passages "Messiah" and "Son of God" are brought together, implying that the latter was the logical implication of the former. However, an important qualification must now be made. Jesus' carrying out His mission was the consequence of His sense of filial relationship, not the reverse. He was the Son of God, and thus He fulfilled the will of God. Richard Longenecker makes the insightful point that with Jesus himself, "awareness of his own

---

24. *Theology*, 147-48.
25. Ibid., 150.

character preceded and gave insight into the nature of his mission," but for the disciples, "apprehension of his mission preceded and gave guidance into the nature of his person." That is, "the resurrection confirmed and manifested an existing reality."[26]

Thus we have the same pattern as with the title Lord. The completion of the mission of the Servant became the basis of the declaration of Jesus' Lordship and Sonship, but this did not involve the conveying of an ontological reality that did not previously exist. It simply brought it to light, thus reinforcing the close correlation between Person and work. The later use of the term Son of God conveyed specific convictions regarding His person (see especially Paul and Hebrews) and doubtless did become prominent in a Hellenistic context. But in its earliest use, it implied a functional significance only coming to designate divine nature as an epistemological consequence.

Development of Christology in the Church

What we find in the New Testament documents can best be described as the raw materials for a developed Christological doctrine. Early believers were content to simply affirm the dual declaration that Jesus was fully man and fully God but without attempting to articulate any rational explanation of this commitment. The history of this developing discussion is a long and exceedingly complex one, coming to a climax with the Chalcedonian Creed of A.D. 451 This creed is the culmination of a long period of controversy involving "imperial policy, ecclesiastical politics and doctrinal formulations."[27] Since this is not a history of doctrine, we will attempt to delineate only the major systematic considerations that were brought to focus in the creed and note some theological aspects of this ecumenical symbol.

From the beginning, the problem of Christology is how to define the relation between the divine and human in Christ. The Trinitarian discussions addressed in the Nicene Creed of 325 settled the full deity of the Logos (*homoousios* with the Father) and thus addressed one phase of the Christological problem. The

---

26. *Christology*, 96-97.
27. R. V. Sellers, *The Council of Chalcedon* (London: SPCK, 1961), xi.

Church steadfastly resisted all proposed solutions that compromised in any way either aspect of Jesus' person. Thus it early rejected the Ebionite heresy that "solved" the problem by denying the divinity altogether. This was a Jewish heresy resulting from the Jewish commitment to monotheism, and a consequent inability to affirm Godhead of Jesus. On the other side was Docetism, a complex teaching based on the presuppositions of Hellenistic philosophy, which rejected the humanity of Jesus, declaring Him to be a phantom. Human aspects of His person were merely appearances.

The classic stance of the earliest theologians is well represented by Ignatius of Antioch. He was martyred in 117, and his "letters reveal an almost apostolic sense of Jesus' person as a whole and have left a deep mark on later Christology."[28] Ignatius is profoundly influenced by Johannine thought (as was all of early Eastern Christianity) and like John asserts both the divinity and humanity of the Savior.

There are strong statements on His divinity, emphasizing that Jesus Christ is God. Such phrases as "Jesus Christ, our God," "the blood of God," and "the passion of my God" reflect as high a Christology as one can imagine. Yet he also emphasized His humanity so as to avoid Docetism. He specifically states in his Epistle to the Smyrnaeans: "He suffered truly as also He raised himself truly; not as certain unbelievers say, that He suffered in semblance, being themselves mere semblance." In fact, flesh, in Ignatius' view, belongs to Christ's nature permanently, even in heaven. The whole value of Christianity would perish with the denial that He came into a genuinely human life. To support his views, he appeals to Scripture and tradition and also argues in the light of his imprisonment: "If Christ did not suffer, why am I in chains?"

As H. R. Mackintosh says, for Ignatius "the union of these two sides, in a vitally indissociable union" is the hallmark of his Christology.[29] This early father said, "There is only one physician, of flesh and spirit, generate and ingenerate, God in man, true life in death, Son of Mary and Son of God, first passible and then impassible" (Ignatius' Epistle to the Ephesians, 7).

However, Ignatius makes no effort to provide a philosophical explanation as to how these two indispensable and inseparable

---

28. Hugh Ross Mackintosh, *The Doctrine of the Person of Christ* (New York: Charles Scribner's Sons, 1915), 130.
29. Ibid., 131.

attributes coexist in Jesus Christ. He merely utters the classic Christological paradoxes and leaves them for the church to solve: "He was man and God . . . born yet unbegotten . . . suffering yet eternal . . . death yet life . . . of Mary and yet of God . . . flesh and spiritual." As Mackintosh writes: "He rather glories in the paradoxes and antitheses of Christ's being."[30]

In subsequent discussions there were three major sources of theological interpretation. One source was the theology of the Church in the West, where the temperament was more juridical and dogmatic and less speculative than in the East. The other two sources originated in the East, where two patterns emerged, chiefly identified with the schools of Alexandria and Antioch. These three compose the basic positions that were brought together at the Council of Chalcedon.

The Western church, under the influence of Tertullian and Cyprian, became more and more legalistic in its interpretation of the Christian life. This temperament informed its doctrinal concerns as well. It was Tertullian, essentially a jurist, who provided the West with its terms for answering the Christological problem. He insisted on the existence of two natures in Christ, to which he preferred the term *substances.* He was the first to directly address the question of the relation between the two. He rejects the possibility that the Word was metamorphosed into flesh, since this would be to lose its distinctive quality that exists after the Incarnation. Neither is the result a third kind of being, *a tertium quid.* Both substances remain unaltered and unimpaired after the union. Thus the God-man is one person *(una persona)* in which are presented the two substances of Godhead and manhood. Tertullian's formula warns: Do not confuse the substances or divide the Person.

The Westerners furthermore make much use of the principle of the communication of properties *(communicatio idiomatum).* Thus the qualities of one substance may be communicated to the other so that it is proper to refer to the human nature attributes that properly belong to the divine and vice versa. This is their way of avoiding a dividing of the Person while insisting on the recognition of the full, undiminished, distinctive attributes of each nature.

In the East, the fourth century witnesses a vigorous debate between two major perspectives on the question of the relation of

---

30. Ibid., 130-31.

the two natures. One has been called the "Word-flesh" type and the other the "Word-man" type, and they have been designated respectively as Alexandrian and Antiochene from the ecclesiastical centers where the tendencies were dominant. (See Appendix 2 where it can be seen how these two schools demonstrated a significantly different and distinctive hermeneutical approach to Scripture.)

In the efforts of these schools to address the Christological question, they were in part distinguished by their use of divergent anthropologies. The "Word-flesh" type worked with a Platonic view that conceived man as a body animated by a soul or spirit that was essentially alien to it. It held to an ontological (in contrast to a functional) trichotomy with the spirit being the seat of volition or personality and thus the most distinctive rational part of the human individual.

The "Word-man" type utilized the Aristotelian concept of man as a psychophysical unity that did not conceive the human person as composed of separable parts. Man is more of a unitary being in this anthropology, which is actually closer to the Hebrew perspective.

It is meaningful that the "Word-flesh" type can be detected early in the left-wing Alexandrian teaching of Arius. Though best known for his teaching about the origin of the Logos, as a corollary to this, he taught that the Logos had united himself to a human body lacking a rational soul, himself taking the place of one.

The fourth-century controversies, however, were precipitated by the teachings of Apollinaris, who reproduced, for all intents and purposes, the Arian Christology. In this ingenious effort to explain the Christological union, he taught that the eternal Logos (thus different from Arius) assumed the place of the rational soul (spirit) in the person of Jesus. Thus the presupposition is that the divine Word was substituted for the normal human psychology in Christ. Apollinaris expressed it in this way: "The divine energy fulfills the role of the animating spirit and of the human mind." J. N. D. Kelly says that this means that "the Word was both the directive, intelligent principle in Jesus Christ, and also the vivifying principle of His flesh."[31] There is thus an organic, vital unity of the Person.

It is important to note the soteriological concerns of Apol-

---

31. *Doctrines*, 292.

linaris, which reflect the Alexandrian views so movingly expounded by Athanasius. The assumption of human nature by the Logos deified it and thus provided for salvation in the realistic mode (see above).

The response to this teaching was quick and decisive. It was easily seen that the resultant Person was not fully man, since the rational soul was divine and not human. Thus the valid soteriological concern was undercut, since "what was not assumed was not restored; it is what is united with God that is saved" (Gregory of Nazianzus). Perhaps the most telling criticism of all is that the picture drawn by Apollinaris is inconsistent with the Gospel picture of a fully human person.

The alternate perspective of the "Word-man" type was best represented in the fourth century by Theodore of Mopsuestia. In response to the dehumanizing tendency of the Alexandrian School, these thinkers sought to provide a picture of a thoroughly human life as per the Gospels. In a word, they brought back the historical Jesus.

In opposition to Arius and Apollinaris, Theodore affirmed the full humanity of Christ including a human rational soul. "He presupposes a human nature which is complete and independent, which undergoes real growth in knowledge and the discernment of good and evil as well as in physical development, and which has to struggle with temptation."[32]

It should now be clear that the Alexandrian tendencies were actuated by redemptive concerns, while the Antiochian theologians were dominated by an ethical concern. This difference becomes obvious in connection with the issue of temptation. On the premise of the former, the seat of volition being the Divine Logos, it was impossible for Jesus to have yielded to the temptations, which could only be a charade. But for the latter, the mutable human will of Jesus faced the real possibility of submitting to the suggestions of the tempter.[33]

---

32. Ibid., 304.

33. It is a fascinating fact that both of these ancient traditions have been represented in the theological history of the Church of the Nazarene. Two major theologians during the first 50 years of Nazarene history were H. Orton Wiley and Stephen S. White, each teaching at separate institutions and each exerting extensive influence over their students. Wiley clearly stood in the Alexandrian tradition. Assuming the position basically taken by Apollinaris, he argued for the impossibility of Jesus' sinning: "Sin is a matter of the person, and since Christ was the preexistent Logos, the Second Person of the adorable Trinity, He

The decisive period climaxing with the Council of Chalcedon in 451 began with the Nestorian controversy. Enthroned as patriarch of Constantinople in 428, Nestorius was early called upon to make a pronouncement concerning the appropriateness of the term *theotokos* (God-bearer; Mother of God) applied to the Virgin Mary, a term dear to the Alexandrians. Using intemperate language, he rejected it as "question-begging" and proposed *Christotokos* (Christ-bearer; Mother of Christ) as more adequate. Cyril of Alexandria, an unscrupulous and contentious bishop, used Nestorius's outbursts to accuse him of teaching "two Sons," thus dividing the person of Christ.[34] That Nestorius actually taught this is disputed by many contemporary scholars.[35]

---

was as such, not only free from sin but from the possibility of sin." *CT* 2:177. This conclusion was the result of his interpretation of the Christological union: "The union of the divine and human natures in Christ is a personal one—that is, the union lies in their abiding possession of a common Ego or inner Self, that of the eternal Logos." 180. An awareness of this tendency would also alert one to the consistent influence of the Alexandrian temperament upon Wiley in his penchant for allegorizing Scripture. (See his book of sermons, *God Has the Answer* [Kansas City: Beacon Hill Press, 1956].)

Stephen S. White, on the other hand, placed his feet solidly on Antiochian soil. In his popularly written booklet (he was not widely published) *Essential Christian Beliefs* (Kansas City: Beacon Hill Press, n.d.), he laid central emphasis on the limitation of Christ to full humanity. With regard to the issue of temptation, he wrote: "Jesus Christ as the Incarnate One, faced temptation as human beings face it, with the exception that there was no sin in His human nature. This made it possible for Him to be tempted in all points like as we are. Could the God-man have sinned? Of course He could have. Either this was the case or else His temptation was a farce. There can be no genuine temptation where there is no possibility of sin. . . . In the realm of moral acts there are no musts or cannots; there are only wills or will nots." 48. This writer remembers—and now understands more about it—sitting in White's theology class at Nazarene Theological Seminary and hearing the students of Wiley (who taught at Pasadena College) debate with him over the question of the possibility of Jesus yielding to temptation. It was a replica of the debate of the Early Church.

34. Alan Richardson says of Cyril, he "is not a lovable figure; his motives in attacking Nestorius are not above suspicion, since he wished to exalt the See of Alexandria at the expense of its great rival in the East, Constantinople. He desired to become the 'pope' of the Eastern Churches. Nor were his methods above reproach. But he was an astute and capable theologian, and he played an important part in the formulation of the Church's Christological doctrine." *Creeds in the Making*, 74-75.

35. Cf. Donald M. Baillie, *God Was in Christ*, 91 n. 1, for bibliography. There was a real terminological problem involved in the debate between the two sectors of the church. When Nestorius spoke of nature *(physis)*, he understood it to mean the "concrete character of a thing." By this he meant to convey, not that each nature was an actually subsistent entity, but that it was objectively real. Cyril, his opponent, spoke of the God-man as having one nature produced by a hypostatic union. This would suggest to Nestorius that the natures were confused, and this he deplored. Yet Nestorius's way of putting it suggested to Cyril the idea of two Persons artificially linked together, since for him the term *nature* meant a "concrete individual, or independent existent." In this sense nature approximated to, without being actually synonymous with, hypostasis.

In response to Nestorius's teaching that insisted that Jesus was fully a man and not the Logos assuming the flesh of a man, Cyril developed the doctrine of *anhypostasia* (impersonal humanity), that "there was no man Jesus existing independently of the Divine Logos: the human element in the Incarnation was simply human nature assumed by the Second Person of the Trinity."[36] This meant that Jesus was man but not a man. And therein lies the distinction between the "Word-flesh" type (Alexandrian) and the "Word-man" type (Antiochian) of Christology.

Even though the *anhypostasia* interpretation of the Incarnation has received widespread support and some contemporary scholars have opted for it, many criticisms can be leveled against it. D. M. Baillie points out that it is extremely difficult to distinguish it from Apollinarianism. But the basic critique of the *anhypostasia* is that it leaves us with a less than (or more than) human Christ. As R. C. Moberly said, "Human nature which is not personal is not human nature."[37]

By political manipulation, Cyril managed to get Nestorius condemned at the Council of Ephesus in 431. The delegates from Antioch were late in arriving, and the council was convened with Alexandrian delegates alone present. This made it simple for Cyril to secure his enemy's condemnation. The late-arriving delegates from Antioch formed their own council and returned the compliment to Cyril.

Following Cyril's death in 444, one of his professed followers by the name of Eutyches precipitated a further phase of the controversy. He was an elderly, muddleheaded monk who took an extreme Alexandrian stance and "fell into the pit which Cyril had barely managed to avoid,"[38] and taught that the human nature of Christ was transformed into a divine nature. There were two natures before the Incarnation, but only one afterward. Efforts to settle the debate resulted in violence, with the outcome that the emperor called a council to convene at Chalcedon to bring peace in the church.

---

36. Ibid., 86.
37. Quoted ibid., 92.
38. Alan Richardson, *Creeds in the Making*, 78. According to J. L. Neve, *History of Christian Thought*, 2 vols. (Philadelphia: Muhlenberg Press, 1946), 1:134, Cyril actually avoided this position only in words. He describes Cyril's position as follows: "Only before the union and *in abstracto* can we speak of two natures; after the incarnation and *in concreto* we can speak only of one divine-human nature [theanthropic]."

As we have attempted to suggest, the two major Eastern tendencies moved toward emphasizing either the deity (Alexandrian) or the humanity (Antiochian) of Christ to the loss of adequate emphasis on the other. Each emphasis was needed, but the dangers needed to be avoided. These two movements fed into the Chalcedonian considerations. The Western influence was heard in the form of a letter from Pope Leo, called Leo's Tome, in which he asserted the Western position of one person and two natures in Christ. "It does not enter at all upon the consideration of the problem which perplexed the Greeks, and the dogmatic simplicity of the pope is most strikingly revealed."[39]

The concern for the existence of the two natures by the Antiochenes and the preoccupation with the unity of the Person by the Alexandrians were preserved in the formula, however, and all were amalgamated into the creed, which rejected the classical heresies. It read as follows:

> Following, then, the holy fathers, we unite in teaching all men to confess the one and only Son, our Lord Jesus Christ. This selfsame one is perfect both in deity and also in humanness; this selfsame one is also actually God and actually man, with a rational soul[A] and a body. He is of the same reality as God as far as his deity is concerned[B] and of the same reality as we are ourselves as far as his human-ness is concerned;[C] thus like us in all respects, sin only excepted. Before time began he was begotten of the Father, in respect of his deity,[B] and now in these "last days," for us and on behalf of our salvation, the selfsame one was born of Mary the virgin, who is God-bearer (theotokos) in respect of his human-ness.[D]
>
> We also teach that we apprehend this one and only Christ —Son, Lord, only-begotten—in two natures, without transmuting one nature into the other,[C] without dividing them into two separate categories,[D] without contrasting them according to area or function. The distinctiveness of each nature is not nullified by the union.[C] Instead, the "properties" of each nature are conserved and both natures concur in one "person" and in one hypostasis. They are not divided or cut into two prosopa,[D] but are together the one and only and only-begotten Logos of God, the Lord Jesus Christ. Thus have the prophets of old testified; thus the Lord Jesus Christ himself taught us; thus the Symbol of the fathers has handed down to us.[40]

---

39. Reinhold Seeburg, *Textbook of the History of Doctrines*, trans. Charles E. Hay, 2 vols. in 1 (Grand Rapids: Baker Book House, 1964), 1:270.

40. Trans. Albert C. Outler, taken from *Creeds of the Churches*, ed. John H. Leith, rev. ed. (Atlanta: John Knox Press, 1977). Teachings specifically excluded are indicated in

The Great Paradox

The Chalcedonian settlement left subsequent Christian theologians with some clearly defined parameters. Its positive point, however, was not addressed in a final way, but the door was left open for further creative thought as new philosophical categories might become available. However, all efforts to this point have simply left us with a prevailing sense of mystery. When the mystery was erased, some boundary of the creed was violated. Consequently, many contemporary scholars have acknowledged that the Christological paradox remains such and must be recognized as such.[41]

Some, like Gustav Aulen, have argued that the real significance of the confession lies in its religious meaning rather than its metaphysical significance. The real intent of the fathers, he says, was not to sanctify a concept of philosophical substance that would make it now outmoded and passé. Rather "the question to which the confession of faith in Christ gives an answer is the question as to what kind of being God is, what his will is, and how he acts."[42] Scholastic efforts to move beyond this basic concern have merely fallen into the trap (using Aulen's terms) of either a "theophany Christology" (which denies His full humanity) or a "separation Christology" (which compromises His deity). In contrast to both perversions, the element of paradox is essential to religious faith because "God cannot be comprehended in any human words or in any of the categories of our finite thought."[43] This is so, "not because the divine reality is self-contradictory, but because when we 'objectify' it all our judgments are in some measure falsified, and the higher truth which reconciles them cannot be fully expressed in words, though it is experienced and lived in the 'I-and-Thou' relationship of faith towards God."[44]

Such paradoxes must be distinguished from contradiction. That can be done only when both affirmations of the paradox spring from the "immediate utterances of faith" (H. R. Mack-

---

the text by this writer as follows: [A]anti-Apollinarian; [B]anti-Arian; [C]anti-Eutychian; [D]anti-Nestorian.

41. See A. N. S. Lane, "Christology Beyond Chalcedon," in *Christ the Lord*, ed. H. H. Rowdon (Downers Grove, Ill.: InterVarsity Press, 1982).

42. See n. 7 above.

43. *God Was in Christ*, 108.

44. Ibid., 109.

intosh). This simply means that the disciples of Jesus, both then (directly) and now (indirectly through the Gospels), experienced Him as a fully human being, and yet at the same time in Him they encountered God. They experienced the mystery and proclaimed it even though they were not able to fully explain it.

The rationalist will doubtless be dissatisfied with this position; but the Wesleyan will recognize that his faith holds to the fact, while his intellect must often be held in abeyance about the manner of this central mystery of the Christian faith—the Incarnation. Yet, the Wesleyan insists, the fact must be maintained with steadfastness because, in agreement with the debaters of Chalcedon, he sees his salvation solidly based upon the reality of the person and work of the God-man.

11

The Work
of the Savior

When we come to this point in our study, in a true sense it can be said that we have arrived at the telos of all that has preceded, since in Wesleyan theology all doctrines are interpreted to have soteriological significance (see norm developed in chap. 1). Soteriology is grounded in the work of the Savior, and therefore, as Cell says of Wesley himself, the Atonement is the "burning focus of faith," "comprehensive of the whole meaning of the Gospel," "the whole of Christianity."[1]

In a letter to a correspondent, Wesley asserts, "Indeed, nothing in the Christian system is of greater consequence than the doctrine of the Atonement. It is properly the distinguishing point between Deism and Christianity."[2] However, despite its central role in his thinking, there is no special sermon or treatise among his writings on the subject, although references are sprinkled profusely throughout.[3]

As in the case of the doctrines of the Trinity and Incarnation,

---

1. Cell, *Rediscovery of John Wesley*, 297.
2. *Letters* 6:197-98.
3. "The Lord Our Righteousness" has been suggested as a possible exception to this widely recognized fact. But this sermon does not actually address the question of the Atonement so much as the issue of imparted and imputed righteousness, which is a closely related issue.

Wesley insisted on the fact of the Atonement but would not insist on an orthodox explanation.[4] On this point, Colin Williams says of Wesley's stance:

> It is true that we must speak of the benefits that derive from the Cross, and therefore it is right to say that the Abelardian view is inadequate. But since we are unable to comprehend how these benefits are secured by Christ's death, we cannot make a particular attempt to explain the mystery orthodox.[5]

The fact is that no ecumenically agreed-upon statement was formulated by the church on this doctrine. Thus one cannot speak of an orthodox doctrine of the Atonement in the same sense as we speak of orthodox doctrines of the Trinity and the person of Christ.

This Wesleyan perspective reminds us of Philipp Melanchthon's dictum that "to know Christ is to know His benefits," actually provides us with a criterion by which to evaluate any explanation of the work of Christ, and positively gives guidance for constructing a Wesleyan position. The benefits that Wesley sees flowing from the Atonement are always articulated as justification and sanctification (see norm). But, as he says in the sermon on "The Scripture Way of Salvation," in the broader sense salvation may be extended "to the entire work of God, from the first dawning of grace in the soul, till it is consummated in glory," and thus includes prevenient grace as well as final salvation. All these benefits are understood as provided by the work of Christ.

The Atonement is the objective ground for Wesley's "optimism of grace," which guarantees the availability of the sinner's acceptance with God and the possibility of the believer's perfection in love. It is the basis of God's work both for us and in us. It is also the source of prevenient grace, which is extended to all men everywhere as "the true light that enlightens every man . . . coming into the world" (John 1:9; universality). Thus any theory of the Atone-

---

4. In reference to a saying of Lord Huntingdon's about the Atonement, Wesley wrote: "It is true I can no more comprehend it than his lordship; perhaps I might say than the angels of God, than the highest *created* understanding. One's reason is here quickly bewildered; if we attempt to expatiate in this field we find 'no end' in 'wandering mazes lost,' but the question, the only question with me, I regard nothing else, is what saith the Scripture." *Letters* 2:297.

5. *John Wesley's Theology Today*, 76 n. 8. J. Ernest Rattenbury observes that "when the traditional doctrine, which [the Wesleys] inherited and believed in, was challenged they declined to speculate and fell back on the fact of the Atonement and their personal experience of its benefits. That fact was dynamic and central to all their preaching. It was sufficient in their evangelical appeal." *The Evangelical Doctrines of Charles Wesley's Hymns* (London: Epworth Press, 1941), 206.

ment that fails to include all these benefits is inadequate from a Wesleyan perspective.

The absence of a systematic treatise by Wesley on the Atonement is a serious weakness and creates a profound tension, since it results in his apparently adopting or at least using the formulations of some form of the satisfaction theory.[6] He was constantly having to fight against its implications. Had he developed a logical analysis of his own, he might have become aware that this view did not support, in fact was antithetical to, his major theological commitments. We have noted this point at numerous critical junctures in our development thus far and now need to pull this together.

Three reasons may be suggested as to why he followed this line of thinking, apart from the negative observation that he did not apparently do his own theologizing on this point. First, this was the position of the Thirty-nine Articles and the Homilies of the Church of England.[7] Wesley was convinced of the orthodoxy of his church and endeavored to avoid conflict with her authoritative teachings. At the conference in 1788, after a long conversation on the question of separation from the Church of England, "it was agreed: (1) That in a course of 50 years, we had neither premeditatively nor willingly varied from it in an article either of doctrine or discipline. (2) That we were not yet conscious of varying from it in any point of doctrine."[8]

A second reason may be Wesley's commitment to an objective Atonement. Certainly, the satisfaction theory is objective rather than subjective, since it involves a transaction between Jesus and God related to man's salvation that occurs apart from man's involvement. Since he may not have perceived a ready-to-hand alternative objective interpretation, this may have subconsciously appeared to him to be the only live option. We will see in our later discussion that there is a much more viable way of identifying an objective dimension of Christ's work that is more consistent with Wesleyan theology's large commitments, as well as with New Testament theology.

Renshaw suggests further that possibly the practical orientation of Wesley's theology explains the absence of a special trea-

---

6. See John Rutherford Renshaw, "The Atonement in the Theology of John and Charles Wesley" (Ph.D. diss., Boston University, 1965).

7. Cf. discussion by Lindström, *Wesley and Sanctification*, 60 ff.

8. *Journal* 7:422.

tise on Atonement. The whole burden of his concern, he says, "lay not in the realm of speculative or formally academic inquiry, but in the personal appropriation and practical application of the saving act of God in Christ in the lives of all who heard the message."[9]

Classical Theories

At this point we should note that there are basically three classical formulations of Atonement theory with some minor variations on these three basic forms. These have emerged in the history of Christian thought as the amplification of one or more New Testament motifs elaborated in terms of some cultural context. Thus William Spurrier can claim:

> If we take any of the interpretations of the Atonement out of their cultural context, if we take them literally, and as being complete authoritative descriptions for all time, we will both falsify them on the one hand, and make nonsense out of them on the other hand.[10]

We will briefly summarize the salient features of these three models as a basis for the systematic discussion[11] and call attention to some of the strengths and weaknesses of each.

Ransom Theory

The earliest one to be elaborated was apparently the ransom theory. The first statement of it seems to be found in Irenaeus.[12] It takes its point of departure from such statements as Jesus' words that "the Son of man came . . . to give his life a ransom for many" (Matt. 20:28; Mark 10:45, KJV). In answering the obvious questions arising from attempting to make this a full-blown explanation, it is declared that man is a captive of Satan, to whom God pays the ransom price of His Son. Later exponents use rather bizarre illustrations to show how God "deceives" the devil and by the Resurrection retrieves the ransom that had been demanded for man's freedom.

---

9. Renshaw, "Atonement," 69-70.

10. *Guide to the Christian Faith.*

11. A fuller, very adequate, and insightful analysis can be found in Gould, *Precious Blood of Christ.* See also Wiley, *CT,* vol. 2.

12. Irenaeus articulates another view that seems to be more central to his own theology and that is very congenial to Wesleyan thought. We will discuss his recapitulation theory later.

J. Glenn Gould explains that one reason for the popularity of this view lay in its power of homiletical appeal. It was an easy and acceptable view to preach. It appealed to the love of the dramatic in man's soul. The idea of a ransom paid to Satan, or a bargain entered into between God and the devil with the soul of Jesus the redeeming consideration, was easily grasped by the humblest and most illiterate listener to the Christian message.[13]

This theory is given less emphasis in Wesley than the other two traditional models, according to Williams and Lindström who speaks of it as "ancillary"; but Deschner finds it to be more pervasive.[14]

Satisfaction Theories

The classic statement of the satisfaction theory was developed by Anselm in the 11th century, partly in reaction to the grotesque expressions of the ransom theory and partly as a result of a different cultural setting that was influential in forming the prevailing understanding of God. However, its roots lie much further back in history. Both Tertullian (cf. *On Repentance,* 2; *Scorpeace,* 6) and Cyprian (*Treatises,* 8.5) suggest that good deeds accumulate merit in God's sight, but that bad deeds require satisfaction for expiation. Upon this basis the idea of penance as satisfaction was developed, and the possibility of the transfer of merit that exceeds the limits of obligation was advanced. However, it was not until Anselm that these notions were effectively integrated with the concept of the Atonement. "In Anselm, . . . the satisfaction rendered by Christ to the divine honor is the acquisition and offering of merit."[15]

Appearing during the age of chivalry, the idea of honor played a prominent role in Anselm's theory. God was conceptualized on the order of a feudal lord whose honor had been violated by man, whose sin was a failure to give Him His just respect. Thus God's honor must be satisfied, and so God sent His Son as the God-man in order that His death on the Cross could perform the function of a substitute satisfaction.

Using the emerging political and legal ideas of the 16th century, John Calvin produced a modified version of the Anselmian theory usually called the penal theory. It starts from the ideas of

13. *Precious Blood of Christ,* 34.
14. Williams, *John Wesley's Theology Today,* 87.
15. Renshaw, "Atonement," 21.

the inviolability of law and the justice of God. God is perfectly just, and the divine law of punishment can never be set aside. Sin was seen as a breaking of law, and all such violations must be punished so that the law can be satisfied. God's justice is such that sin cannot go unpunished.

In this view Christ's death is still understood as the satisfaction rendered for sin, but whereas Anselm had made sin a violation of the divine honor and had distinguished between satisfaction and punishment, Calvin treated sin as a violation of the divine justice and satisfaction as consisting in the actual punishment of Christ.[16]

A later modification of the satisfaction theory was developed by Hugo Grotius as the governmental theory. It was an attempt to provide an Arminian version that would avoid the undesirable implication of the Calvinistic theory of a limited atonement. However, Grotius, like the others, assumed the necessity of an "antecedent satisfaction" as the condition for the remission of sins. He defined this as the punishment accepted by Christ, not in the interest of retributive justice, but for the purpose of providing a "distinguished example" of the punishment that sin deserved, and therefore acted as a deterrent to further sin in the interests of the common good. It is thus a moral influence theory in reverse. It recognizes the principle of deterrence rather than retribution as central in the concept of the Atonement.[17]

Moral Influence Theory

The third classical model is the moral influence theory, apparently first produced by Abelard in reaction to the theory of Anselm. According to this interpretation, the death of Christ is the most graphic example of God's love and, at the same time, of the heinousness of sin in putting "love personified" to death. Its purpose is to impact human consciousness with these two ultimate theological realities and thus influence human beings to respond to this incarnate love and turn away from sin or rebellion against God. The Wesleyan emphasis on fallen man's moral inability to

---

16. *Institutes*, bk. 2, chaps. 12—27.
17. The influence of Grotius upon early Methodist theology was profound, yet his doctrine was by no means received uncritically. See, e.g., Richard Watson, *Theological Institutes* (New York: Lane and Tippett, 1848), 2:87-148; William Burt Pope, *A Compendium of Christian Theology*, 3 vols. (London: Wesleyan Conference Office, 1880), 2:313.

338 □ GRACE, FAITH, AND HOLINESS

turn from sin would militate against this view being given exclusive credence. It would be more at home in the Pelagian framework.[18]

Benefits of the Atonement

We have discovered that the clue to working out a consistent and authentic Wesleyan construction of the work of Christ calls for a survey of the benefits provided by this work. Such an analysis will then provide the parameters by which to judge the adequacy of any proposal. However, this method must always be tested by the biblical revelation, since we are not proposing an inductive approach that begins with a theological premise formulated "out of whole cloth." We must, in other words, first ascertain the compatibility of the Wesleyan claim regarding the benefits of the Atonement with the New Testament claim regarding them. Thus our initial work will be to analyze the soteriological provisions stressed by Wesleyan theology as they are interpreted in the theology of the New Testament.

Prevenient Grace

Our study of Wesleyan theology up to this point has demonstrated the crucial role of prevenient grace at several decisive junctures, especially in connection with a Wesleyan understanding of revelation. These uses are all subservient to the soteriological function of this grace. It is here that one of the major distinctives of the Wesleyan perspective comes to light.

Prevenient grace is not a biblical term but a theological category developed to capture a central biblical motif. Wesley was not the first theologian to use it (he always spoke of "preventing grace," but the meaning is identical), and non-Wesleyans since his time have used it. But it seems to be more determinative for Wesley than any other teacher.[19]

Literally, it means "the grace that comes before" and refers to God's activity prior to any human movement toward God. From

---

18. Colin Williams attempts to argue that the moral influence theory is drawn into Wesley's theology in relation to his picture of the Christian life, but this writer feels that he fails to make his case. Cf. *John Wesley's Theology Today*, 77-82.

19. Thomas Aquinas argues for the term, but it has no decisive role in his theology. *Summa Theologica* 14.111.3.

the human side, its necessity is the all-pervasiveness of original sin, or total depravity, which affirms the total inability of man to initiate the divine-human relation. From the divine side, it is grounded in the nature of God as love. It is, in fact, a direct inference from the New Testament understanding of God.

Since God's character is finally revealed in the person and work of Christ, Wesley insists that prevenient grace is ultimately grounded in Christ's death on the Cross.[20]

A number of theological implications of this central doctrine must be noted. Prevenient grace must not be confused with free will. In the Fall, man completely lost his freedom for God. This did not affect his power of contrary choice in the mundane realm but did result in the loss of what Wesley called the "moral image." Thus freedom for God is not now a human possibility but is restored by the grace of God.[21] This implies that it is impossible for man to acquire merit before his Creator. Everything he has comes from God.

This doctrine centrally expresses the Wesleyan commitment to the universality of the Atonement. Unlike Calvinism's limited vision, grace for Wesley is extended to every human being but is resistible. Thus God offers himself to all men everywhere as a saving presence (see chap. 5). It creates both awareness and capacity, but neither is saving unless responded to or exercised by one's grace-endowed freedom.

Reconciliation

The New Testament provides us with a number of metaphors describing the salvation that results from the work of Christ. The term "atonement" itself is used only once in the New Testament and then only in the Authorized Version of Rom. 5:11: "And not only so, but we also joy in God through our Lord Jesus Christ, by whom we have now received the atonement" (KJV). The Greek word is *katallagē* and is elsewhere rendered as "reconciliation," which suggests that this is the basic meaning of the idea of atonement in New Testament thought.

---

20. See Arthur Skevington Wood, "The Contribution of John Wesley to the Theology of Grace," in *Grace Unlimited,* ed. Clark H. Pinnock (Minneapolis: Bethany Fellowship, 1975).

21. Cf. Chiles, *American Methodism,* where the liberalizing movement away from Wesley among his successors is referred to as "From Free Grace to Free Will."

Vincent Taylor has argued convincingly that, despite the conflation of forgiveness, justification, and reconciliation by modern theology, New Testament theology clearly separates them. Reconciliation, he insists, is the central motif of Paul's thought, with both forgiveness and justification serving as ways of removing the barriers that stand in the way of reconciliation. Failure to recognize this distinction has unhappy results in connection with the doctrine of the Atonement. "Few things," Taylor argues, "have contributed so much to the opinion that objective theories, which find a Godward aspect in the work of Christ, are obsolete and mistaken as the identification of the modern and the Biblical uses of the term forgiveness."[22]

Herman Ridderbos agrees that "one could perhaps say that reconciliation as peace with God is the consequence of justification," but does not make quite the radical distinction between them as Taylor does.[23] Nonetheless, he does support the idea that reconciliation is the primary soteriological category. Ralph P. Martin, in a monograph on reconciliation, has proposed that this motif is the "center of Paul's thought and ministry" and claims support from Peter Stuhlmacher, T. W. Manson, and Johannes Weiss, as well as Ridderbos.[24]

G. Eldon Ladd takes the same position and says:

> Justification is the divine pronouncement of acquittal upon the sinner; reconciliation is the restoration to fellowship that results from justification. Justification is the ethical condition of reconciliation, the gift to the sinner of that standing by which he can enter into fellowship with God.[25]

With these scholars we concur. Reconciliation thus provides us with an atonement metaphor that is personal in its implications and therefore less susceptible to impersonal or legalistic perversions.

---

22. *Forgiveness and Reconciliation* (New York: Macmillan Co., 1960), 27.

23. *Paul*, 182 ff. He hesitates at subordinating one of these metaphors to the other but suggests that "we are dealing here with two concepts from different spheres of thought and life."

24. *Reconciliation* (Atlanta: John Knox Press, 1981).

25. *Theology*, 455. W. D. Davies, *Paul and Rabbinic Judaism* (Philadelphia: Fortress Press, 1980), agrees that justification should not be made the quintessence of Paul's thought. Rather the essence of his thought is "in his awareness that with the coming of Christ the Age to Come had become present fact the proof of which was the advent of the Spirit; it lies in those conceptions of standing under the judgement and mercy of a New Torah, Christ, of dying and rising with that same Christ, of undergoing a New Exodus in Him and of so being incorporated into a New Israel, the community of the Spirit." 221-24.

Reconciliation implies an estrangement in personal relations that has been overcome. The idea is found both explicitly and implicitly throughout the Pauline corpus, where the apostle interprets reconciliation to have occurred (through the work of Christ) at three different levels: (1) Reconciliation between God and man (Rom. 5:1; 1 Cor. 7:15; Gal. 5:22; Phil. 4:7; Col. 3:15; 2 Thess. 3:16). (2) Reconciliation between man and man (Eph. 2:12-17; 4:3-6). (3) Reconciliation at the cosmic level (2 Cor. 5:19; Col. 1:20). This correlates with his profound consciousness of sin as personal, social, and cosmic.

In New Testament theology reconciliation is both a completed act and a yet-to-be-actualized reality. Both dimensions are present in the classic pericope of 2 Cor. 5:16-21. God in Christ has done something antecedently in history to its realization in experience. Thus it is both finished and unfinished. In the former sense, it is the work of God and in no sense the result of a human act of satisfaction offered by man to God. This is because "the rebels were obviously in no position to effect the reconciliation."[26] In the unfinished sense, its consummation awaits the response of the rebel. The message of reconciliation given the ambassador for Christ reinforces this truth. The message is "be reconciled to God" (v. 20). It is an exhortation to man to abandon his hostility to God in response to the completed work of "God . . . in Christ" (v. 19, KJV).

Rom. 5:10 also refers to a reconciliation that occurred "while we were yet sinners" (v. 8). But the reconciliation is not effective until it has removed man's enmity toward God. It is in this way that a limited atonement is avoided in the New Testament emphasis on the finished work of Christ. The death of Christ does not automatically provide salvation for the elect but makes available the possibility of salvation to all who will respond in faith. When man is reconciled to God, he then experiences the already reconciled God. Existentially, he may sing with Charles Wesley, "My God is reconciled."

Furthermore, reconciliation is both present and future. Because of the dual characteristic just noted, this is not the basis for a final universalism but implies that the reconciling work of Christ has cosmic proportions (see above) that will only be fully consummated at the eschaton.

A submetaphor of reconciliation is *Sonship* or *Adoption.* In

---

26. Alan Richardson, *Theology,* 216.

contrast to the Greek concept, man is not son of God in any kind of physical descent. Thus the term "adoption" is appropriated to describe the status of a sonship conferred in contrast to both the pagan view and the inherent Sonship of Christ himself. Adoption is the New Testament way of speaking of the sharing of Christ's Sonship as one of the benefits of His work. By virtue of his relationship to Christ, the believer is enabled, with Him, to cry, "Abba! Father!" (Rom. 8:15; Gal. 4:6).

Adoption is an unmerited gift made available by God's love through Jesus Christ. It implies a freedom in relation to the Father that is absent in the master-slave relation to which the reality of sonship is set in contrast (Eph. 1:5; Gal. 4:3-7). The outcome of adoption is inheritance, the privilege of possessions that is not a possibility with slaves.

Adoption has the same duality that is present in other salvation metaphors: It is both present and future, being realized in this present age and also containing a promise of a future consummation in the time of eschatological fulfillment (Rom. 8:23). To its present actuality, the Holy Spirit bears witness (vv. 15-16).

An additional result of reconciliation is *fellowship* with God and with other believers. While Paul refers to fellowship with God or Christ in several instances (1 Cor. 1:9; 10:16; Phil. 3:10), the idea seems to be a basic theme of the First Epistle of John. Perhaps it is this author's way of speaking about reconciliation.

In this Epistle, the motif that informs the whole book is eternal life, which is tantamount to salvation. It describes the nature of eternal life as fellowship "with God and with His Son, Jesus Christ" (cf. 1:3). The principle that informs its analysis of eternal life is that it is to be defined as fellowship with God, and this fellowship is established and maintained on the basis of the nature of God. The condition of fellowship is conformity to the divine nature as revealed in Jesus Christ. In the Epistle four characteristics of God are mentioned, around which the whole letter clusters. God is light (1:5), and thus fellowship depends upon one's "walking in the light" (cf. v. 7). God is righteous (2:29), so no fellowship with God is possible in unrighteousness. God is love (4:8), thus anyone who lives in fellowship with God loves both God and his brother. Finally, God has offered us life in the Son (5:12), and this provides the dynamic of fellowship that includes victory over the world.[27]

---

27. See H. Ray Dunning, *General Epistles*, New Testament vol. 15 in *Search the Scriptures* (Kansas City: Nazarene Publishing House, 1960).

Redemption is a third metaphor for salvation. It means being loosed from bondage or slavery, the "buying back" (literally) of something lost or sold. In the Old Testament, the person charged with the responsibility of being a redeemer (*go'el*) was usually the next of kin. This imagery plays a prominent role in Isaiah 40—55, where Yahweh is repeatedly called Israel's *go'el* (see 41:14; 43:1; 44:6; 47:4).

The pattern normally used in the Old Testament to depict redemption is the Exodus. When a future salvation is anticipated, it is usually described in terms and images derived from this original redemptive event. Isaiah, in particular, looked forward to the great day of eschatological redemption, which he describes as a new Exodus. New Testament writers also retain, at points, the Exodus imagery, but proclaim that in the work of Jesus Christ the redemption foreshadowed by that event and foretold by the prophets has come into history (Luke 1:68; Titus 2:14). It resulted in bringing into existence a new Israel in the same fashion as the first Exodus created the old Israel.

Jesus himself explicitly relates the redemptive significance of His work to the Isaianic Servant (Mark 10:45). Alan Richardson comments:

> It is surely indicative of the Master's supreme insight into the redemptive purpose of God as revealed in the Scriptures that he should have gone unerringly to the one passage in the Old Testament which clearly points to God himself as initiating the act of redemptive self-offering that is performed by the Servant-Messiah.[28]

The fourth metaphor that we shall mention is *Justification*. This metaphor is chiefly used by Paul and by him primarily in Romans and Galatians. It can be understood only in close conjunction with "righteousness," since these are correlative concepts. A further factor has created considerable confusion in attempts to understand what it implies in biblical theology. This is the ambiguity that attaches to "righteousness" due to the fact that it has multiple meanings. First, we must note its meaning as applied to God. This meaning derives chiefly from its use in Isaiah 40—55, where it refers to the character of God experienced as "faithfulness." In 43:24*d*-26, the prophet says, "You have wearied me with your iniquities. I, I am He who blots out your transgressions for my own

---

28. *Theology*, 220.

344 □ GRACE, FAITH, AND HOLINESS

sake, and I will not remember your sins. Put me in remembrance, let us argue together; set forth your case, that you may be proved right [justified]." God's faithfulness is here emphasized in contrast to Israel's unfaithfulness.

In these passages, the prophet has appropriated the conjunction of righteousness and salvation that was emphasized in the Exodus (cf. Exod. 14:13; 15:2) and adapted the same set of concepts to relate to the impending deliverance from Babylon and return from the Exile (Isa. 45:17; 46:13; 52:10). Just as God remembered His promises to Abraham and delivered the Egyptian slaves, so He will "for his own sake" (righteousness) remember and deliver the Babylonian exiles. Far from teaching that man is justified by the works of the law, the Old Testament has thus set forth a doctrine of salvation based on the righteousness of God. It is justification, not by works, but by the faithfulness (righteousness) of God alone. In a word, it is "grace," which is God acting toward man in accordance with His own nature.

It is the recovery of this Old Testament teaching that Jesus set in opposition to the works righteousness of Judaism both in precept and parable. But it is Paul, appropriating the Old Testament view, who fully develops the truth of the justifying righteousness of God as flowing from the completed work of Christ. This teaching leaves no room for the ideas of "merit" and "satisfaction," and such ideas do not occur in the New Testament. They originate from other sources.

When applied to man, "righteousness" has two possible dimensions. The first meaning is ethical and raises the question of how the righteousness of God as faithfulness relates to the righteousness of man as ethical. That question has created interpretative problems from the beginning of the Christian era for understanding the meaning of justification. To that problem we must now address ourselves.

Norman Snaith speaks of these two references of righteousness, suggesting that Paul inherited both views from the Old Testament, and comments:

> He [Paul] uses the noun in the double sense, sometimes in a truly ethical sense and sometimes practically as the equivalent of salvation. When he writes of the law of righteousness (Rom. 9:31), he is referring to the ethical demands of the Mosaic law, but when he uses the phrase "the rightousness of God," he

means that salvation which God accomplishes through Christ (Rom. 3:21).[29]

The problem of the relation between these two uses has produced two major constructions of the concept of justification in the history of Christian thought about salvation. These are usually identified as the Catholic and Protestant views. The Catholic explanation, represented classically by the teachings of Augustine and Thomas Aquinas, says that in justification, man is "made [ethically] righteous" by the infusion of divine grace. This infused righteousness then eventually became the basis of God's acceptance of man. But this position involves a confusion of justification and sanctification and makes the latter the basis of the former. If justification is a forensic term, one could simply say that it is here interpreted as God declaring a person righteous because he already is. This interpretation eventually became the basis of the whole Catholic doctrine of works righteousness and penitential system of salvation. It fails to understand the meaning of "the righteousness of God" in Romans, interpreting it as the ethical righteousness God requires and holding that we produce our own righteousness by good works.

The Protestant alternative rightly interprets the righteousness of God as faithfulness but retains the ethical meaning of righteousness in relation to man. Since it rejects the Catholic teaching that ethical righteousness is necessary for justification, it insists that justification means to "declare righteous," not to "make righteous." This led to a doctrine of imputation according to which faith is accepted by God as an equivalent for righteousness (ethically understood).[30]

While this interpretation avoids the dangers of works righteousness, it falls victim to an equally devastating criticism as being a "legal fiction." God accounts a person righteous even though he isn't. Thus God deceives himself. Man who is justified by faith is, in Luther's words, *simul justus et peccator* (at the same time sinner and justified). Neither of these classic interpretations turn out to be satisfactory.

John Wesley struggles with this dilemma. On the one hand, he

---

29. "Righteousness."
30. Vincent Taylor, *Forgiveness and Reconciliation*, 55 ff. See also Willard H. Taylor, "Justification," in *Beacon Dictionary of Theology*, ed. Richard S. Taylor (Kansas City: Beacon Hill Press of Kansas City, 1983).

attempts to distinguish justification from sanctification by denying that the former is "the being made actually just and righteous" as the Catholics said. On the other hand, he is unwilling to settle for a legal fiction as the Protestants taught. He insists that God is not deceived in those whom He justifies. He does not account "them to be otherwise than they are. It does by no means imply, that God judges concerning us contrary to the real nature of things; that he esteems us better than we really are, or believes us righteous when we are unrighteous." Yet he steadfastly steers clear of the Catholic view, not allowing any human merit to enter the picture.[31]

Most authorities agree that linguistically the verb *dikaioō* (to justify) properly means "to pronounce righteous," and that it cannot mean "to make righteous." But this does not settle the issue as to the theological significance of the term. The question is, are we left with having to decide between the two traditional interpretations discussed above? Apparently without realizing the full implications of his words, Wesley himself pointed a way out of the impasse by distinguishing between justification as a "relative change" and sanctification as a "real change." Most efforts to escape the dilemma end up confusing the two, but G. Eldon Ladd provides an explanation based on another meaning of "righteousness" that avoids both horns and is thoroughly consistent with Wesleyan theological concerns.[32]

Beginning with the premise that Paul's thought is informed by the Old Testament, he argues that righteousness in that context is not primarily an ethical quality but means "that norm in the affairs of the world to which men and things should conform, and by which they can be measured." Thus the righteous man is the one who conforms to the given norm. It is the context that determines the norm and thus the parameters of what it means to be righteous. Ladd's illustration of this is very clear as he speaks of the various contexts in which the word is used:

---

31. "Justification by Faith," *Works* 5:53-64.
32. *Theology*, 439 ff. Bernhard W. Anderson, in discussing "righteousness" in the Psalms, provides the same interpretation as Ladd. He says: "In facing this question we should divest ourselves of notions of righteousness that we have inherited from our culture, largely under Greek and Roman influence. Normally we assume that a 'righteous' person is one who conforms to some legal or moral standard. Such person is held to be righteous according to the law." The view of righteousness illustrated by Abraham in Gen. 15:1-6 is different. "The righteousness accounted to him was *being in right relationship* with God, as shown by his trust in God's promise even when there was no evidence to support it—none but the myriads of stars in the sky!" *Out of the Depths*, 100-101.

Sometimes the norm consisted of the demands imposed by family relationships. Thus Tamar, who played the harlot, was more righteous than Judah because she fulfilled these demands, which Judah did not (Gen. 38:26). David is said to be righteous because he refused to slay Saul, with whom he stood in a covenant relationship (1 Sam. 24:17; 26:23), and he condemned those who murdered Ishbosheth, Saul's son (2 Sam. 4:11). But after the downfall of Saul's house, Mephibosheth had no right to expect kindness from the new king (2 Sam. 19:28). The demands of righteousness changed with the relationship.

Thus righteousness becomes a concept of relationship. The one who fulfills the demands laid upon him by the relationship in which he stands is righteous. It does not refer to the personal ethical character of the person involved, but to faithfulness to a relationship. The conclusion is that if justification is a change of relation, as Wesley said, that new relation constitutes a real righteousness that may be distinguished from sanctification as ethical transformation of character. It does not involve a prior righteousness that in some way becomes the basis of the new relation, but it is a reality that is created in and with the forensic declaration of God that the man of faith is justified. Justification is God's proclamation that a person is righteous, and that proclamation makes it so. In this way the Catholic way of works righteousness is avoided on the one hand and the Reformation concept of a legal fiction on the other.

In Rom. 3:24—4:25 the idea of the righteousness of God as faithfulness and the relational righteousness of man based on faith is mingled with the concept of sacrifice as it comes to expression in Abraham's sacrifice of Isaac. God vindicates himself by showing himself faithful to His promise, and Abraham is vindicated or justified by his trust and obedience. It is a court setting in which both the Judge and the defendant are vindicated, or proved just, that is, justified. Thus God put forward His Son as an atoning Sacrifice, showing himself faithful to His promise; and the response of the one "who has faith in Jesus" justifies such a believer, that is, puts him in right relation to God. This should not be interpreted to mean that faith is a good work or that faith itself is the justifier. It is the acceptance of the gift of God.

The close conjunction of justification and righteousness leads us to speak further of the eschatological character of justification. The time of salvation long promised has now dawned, and therein is revealed the righteousness of God (Rom. 3:21). This interpretation reflects the basic structure of Pauline thought that the age to come has entered this present age.[33] What had previously been anticipated as a future possibility has become present reality.

> Whereas for Judaism it was an incontrovertible matter that this righteousness, as the crucial, decisive factor in the judicial declaration of God, was not to be spoken of other than in a future-eschatological sense, Paul proclaims this righteousness as a present reality already realized in Christ.[34]

The present possibility of justification is available to faith. Although it is an objective possibility in Christ, it is faith that lays hold of the justifying righteousness of God in Christ. In this sense the verdict of the final judgment has already been rendered. Yet it still is spoken of in the future. "For we through the Spirit eagerly wait for the hope of righteousness by faith" (Gal. 5:5, NKJV). It is a benefit both already attained and still to be expected. In a word, there is both present and future (final) justification.

A final salvation benefit that needs to be noted is *Sanctification*. Both "sanctification" and its cognate term, "holiness," are uniquely religious categories unlike many of the other terms that are borrowed from secular contexts. Holiness is the primary term, with sanctification being the act or process by which something or someone is made holy. Since holiness belongs primarily to God, and objects or persons are made holy only in a relative or derivative sense, the concepts have meaning only in the religious sphere.

In its earliest expression, holiness does not carry any necessary ethical content. This is seen in the Old Testament reference to "holy [i.e., temple] prostitutes" (see Genesis 38; Deuteronomy 23). They are "holy" because they belong to the deity. It is the character of the personal God of Israel that eventually informed the idea with ethical connotations. Sanctification was originally a ceremonial term in the sense that through specified rituals a person or object was dedicated to God's service or cleansed from impurity to qualify it (or him) for this task.

The cultic context of the ideas surrounding the "idea of the holy" led to perversions that were opposed by the prophets in the name of ethical righteousness. When ceremony became ceremonialism unaccompanied by justice and kindness, it called for con-

---

33. See Ladd, *Theology*, chap. 27; and Ridderbos, *Paul*, 44 ff.
34. Ridderbos, *Paul*, 164.

demnation. Thus the eighth-century prophets in particular called for an understanding of holiness in ethical terms. It is this latter emphasis that became the background for the normative New Testament interpretation.

A strand of eschatological teaching is also clearly present in the prophetic vision that anticipated a day when God would provide for real sanctification and not just ritualistic. This hope was concomitant with a recognition that sin was an inherent bent in human nature as well as lawless behavior. Both needs must be met.

Jeremiah and Ezekiel both recognized before the Exile that a new covenant with new provisions was the real need of the people of God (Jer. 31:31-34; Ezek. 36:25-27). As the prophet Zechariah described the obstacles that must be removed in order for the Messianic kingdom to come, he sees both sins and sin eliminated in two of his eight mystical visions. In the vision of the flying scroll (5:1-4) the sinner is removed from the community; and in the vision of the "woman in the barrel," it is "the very principle of sin that has to be eradicated" (5:5-11).[35]

In the apocalyptic section of the same book (chaps. 9—14), the prophet anticipated the Day of the Lord when "there shall be a fountain opened for the house of David and the inhabitants of Jerusalem to cleanse them from sin and uncleanness" (13:1). G. N. M. Collins quotes Henderson as saying that this verse "exhibits the two grand doctrines of the gospel—justification and sanctification" and adds: "The grace of the Spirit of Christ is needed for the latter, as the virtue of the blood of Christ is needed for the former."[36]

When we turn to the New Testament, an analysis of the uses of the terms "sanctify, sanctification, sanctified" yields the following picture. First, there are some nonnormative, purely ceremonial uses of the term that indicate that a person or thing is rendered sacred by its relation to God or sacred things or is fulfilling a divine purpose (note especially Matt. 23:17, 19).

The second use, which appears to be normative, is a distinctly ethical use relating specifically to the new life in Christ. The ceremonial language is still present, as is inevitable, but it is thoroughly

---

35. See J. E. McFadyen, "Zechariah," in *Abingdon Bible Commentary*, ed. F. C. Eiselen (New York: Abingdon-Cokesbury Press, 1929).

36. "Zechariah," in *New Bible Commentary*, ed. F. Davidson (Grand Rapids: Wm. B. Eerdmans Publishing Co., 1960).

informed by the ethical understanding. This second use is clearly illustrated in Romans 6; Ephesians 4; 1 Thess. 4:3; and Colossians 3. It here refers to the ethical life that follows (is subsequent to) justification and is the consequence of it. This ethical dimension is further emphasized by a unique use of the term in 1 Thess. 5:23, which is the climactic statement of a series of exhortations designed to emphasize the sanctity of the whole of life. It emphasizes the whole person's involvement in the holy life. It is the text that most clearly embodies the concept of entire sanctification meaning "through and through" (Amp., Moffatt, NBV, NIV, Phillips). Paul prays that they may be sanctified (aorist tense) "spirit and soul and body," thus encompassing all functions of the one human being, not three parts of the person. This latter is Greek rather than Hebraic.[37] Thus, in considering sanctification (in this sense), we can formulate an exegetically derived theological proposition: "Sanctification is logically subsequent to justification."

This conclusion addresses the chief issue of the Reformation debate. The Catholic position, as formulated by Thomas Aquinas, was that sanctification precedes justification. When the process of sanctification, interpreted as "faith formed by love," has reached its finis, God at that point declares a person justified, and he is ready for heaven. Luther insisted in reversing this order and argued on the basis of Scripture that sanctification is not the basis for justification, but vice versa (see discussion above on justification).

But there are other uses of the term in the New Testament. At least in the ceremonial sense, it is referred to all believers; that is, all believers belong to God (cf. 1 Cor. 1:2; 6:11). The ceremonial meaning is obviously present in the Book of Hebrews, as one would expect from its nature. In the book, most usages are connected with the blood of Christ, so the concept is that the blood of the sacrificial Lamb sanctifies that to which it is applied. This is a clear corollary of the chief emphasis of the book on Christ as the High Priest who offers himself as the eternal Sacrifice (cf. Heb. 10:10, 14, 29; 9:13-14; 13:12).

This leads us to a second theological proposition: "All believers are sanctified." As we have seen, in the New Testament, although the ceremonial language and conceptuality are retained, they are thoroughly informed by the ethical. Therefore, both in the

---

37. See W. T. Purkiser, *Exploring Christian Holiness*, vol. I, *The Biblical Foundations* (Kansas City: Beacon Hill Press of Kansas City, 1983), 188-89.

ceremonial (belonging to God) and the ethical sense, as illustrated clearly in Heb. 9:11-14 and 1 Cor. 6:11, all believers are sanctified. This is what holiness writers have traditionally referred to as initial sanctification.

This leads immediately to a third theological proposition: "Justification and sanctification are chronologically simultaneous." That is, at the moment of justification, in that same instant, the process of sanctification begins, although it is not a completed work as is justification, or regeneration. Speaking to William Law's contention that regeneration is a progressive work, Wesley replies:

> This is undeniably true of sanctification; but of regeneration, the new birth, it is not true. This is a part of sanctification, not the whole; it is the gate to it, the entrance into it. When we are born again, then our sanctification, our inward and outward holiness begins; and thenceforward we are gradually to "grow up in Him who is our Head."[38]

This is the truth to which the words of Karl Barth appropriately apply:

> What is meant by sanctification might just as well be described by the less common biblical term regeneration or renewal, or by that of conversion, or by that of penitence which plays so important a role in both the Old and New Testaments, or comprehensively by that of discipleship which is so outstanding especially in the Synoptic Gospels.[39]

Another group of scriptures relate sanctification with the Holy Spirit (cf. 2 Thess. 2:13; 1 Pet. 1:2; Rom. 15:16). Sanctification here is seen chiefly as a separating or setting apart from common use to the service of God. This is the work of the Holy Spirit. The logical conclusion to be drawn from this yields a fourth theological proposition: "All believers, being sanctified by the Holy Spirit, are recipients of the Spirit" (see also 1 Cor. 6:11; cf. Romans 8).

A general analysis of the concepts, though departing somewhat from the key terms, yields a definite development of thought: The basis of holiness in man is the holiness of God (Lev. 19:1-2; 1 Pet. 1:15-16; and possibly Matt. 5:48). This implies that the content of the holy life or holy living (ethical) is godlikeness. The New Testament clearly emphasizes that God is most fully revealed in Jesus Christ, so that we are brought to a fifth theological proposi-

---

38. *StS* 2:240.
39. *Church Dogmatics* 4.2.500.

tion: "Sanctification in the New Testament is oriented toward Jesus Christ." Crucial passages here are 2 Cor. 3:18 and Eph. 4:13.

This analysis covers the terminology and concept in a general way without taking into account specific moments within the total scope of God's sanctifying work, especially entire sanctification. This will be considered in a subsequent section.[40]

Many of these salvation metaphors explicitly imply the bringing into being of a people with whom God establishes a covenant. They are all personal but not individualistic. Receiving the benefits indicated by these various salvation images is tantamount to becoming a part of the community of faith. The implication of this New Testament truth is that salvation and thus the Atonement that makes it available must be seen in more than an individualistic way. It must have a corporate dimension.

Systematic Components

Like the reality of salvation itself, the Atonement is described in the New Testament by a profusion of figures of speech. Because of the largely metaphorical character of these references, Nathaniel Micklem has argued that they cannot become a theory of the Atonement but reflect the "deep sense of that from which by God's grace we have been delivered." The use of various terms, in other words, said something to men who apprehended their redemption in terms of their own religious experience.[41]

If this claim is true, it is not an isolated case. We have already discovered that the Bible does not give us a fully developed, explicit doctrine of the Trinity or the Incarnation but records the experiences of the realities that are incorporated in these doctrines.[42] Thus it is not altogether incongruous that we must do with the work of Christ as we have had to do with these others: take the raw materials of the personalistic message of the Scripture and seek to formulate a theory consistent with all the evidence.

We must begin with careful theological exegesis to identify as

---

40. Cf. E. C. Blackman, "Sanctification," in *Interpreter's Dictionary of the Bible*, vol. 4, ed. George A. Buttrick, 4 vols. (New York: Abingdon Press, 1962).

41. *The Doctrine of Our Redemption* (New York: Abingdon-Cokesbury Press, 1953), 41 ff.

42. See Francis M. Young, *Sacrifice and the Death of Christ* (Philadelphia: Westminster Press, 1975), 3 ff., for a similar interpretation of the relation of experience and dogma.

clearly as possible the significance of the relevant biblical material. In conjunction with this resource, a theological statement of the work of Christ logically includes the doctrine of God, the doctrine of sin, the doctrine of salvation, and an understanding of the nature of the divine-human relation. Most of these have already been addressed.

New Testament Images of Christ's Work

The authors of *God, Man, and Salvation* point out, correctly, that the elaboration of the New Testament teaching about the saving work of Christ is "rooted in the words and work of Christ. For that reason, it is necessary to examine the words of the Lord on His mission in death before venturing to a composite picture of the teaching of the entire New Testament on the Atonement."[43]

As we have already had several occasions to emphasize, the central self-understanding of Jesus about His mission focuses upon the ideal of the Suffering Servant, and He saw His death on the Cross as the climactic event in this vocation. His whole life was a living out of this Messianic pattern, and therefore it is thus possible to speak of His entire ministry as Atonement. The fact that Jesus freely forgave sins testifies to this truth. He did not need to wait until after the Cross to offer this benefit to those who sought His help.

While the picture of the Isaianic Servant informed implicitly every facet of Jesus' public and private ministry, the most explicit and sustained identification that Jesus made of the Servant's task with His own occurs in the "Supper sayings." Perhaps the most illuminating word in this setting is found in Matt. 26:28—"For this is my blood of the covenant, which is poured out for many for the forgiveness of sins." Both the setting and the words relate the impending death of Jesus to the paschal lamb slain at the Exodus, not the sacrificial system set up in Israel's later worship.[44] Both Jesus and the paschal lamb are slain as the symbol of the bringing into being of a covenant people through salvation (this term is first used at the Exodus). Both signify the culmination of a conflict between Yahweh and the powers of evil, with the latter being vanquished by the power of God. The 10 plagues were more than

---

43. P. 373.
44. See Joachim Jeremias, *The Eucharistic Words of Jesus* (Philadelphia: Fortress Press, 1966).

devices to make the Egyptians uncomfortable; they were direct challenges to the various domains controlled by Egyptian deities, showing to Pharaoh that in the contest between the nations' gods, the God of the Hebrews was greater.[45] Similarly, Jesus' death was the climactic encounter with the "powers" of the air, and in a decisive way He overcame them at the Cross, taking "captivity captive" (Col. 2:15; Eph. 4:8, KJV). One great difference between the two paradigmatic conflicts is that at the Cross the power of God was manifested in apparent weakness. The Servant in the moment of most intense suffering was the power of God in its most prevailing form (1 Cor. 1:20-31). In this difference we are seeing a transformation of the concept of power that will have crucial significance for the Christian understanding of the Holy Spirit (see chap. 13).

This ties together the motif of Suffering Servant and the function of the Servant as stated in Isa. 42:6: "I . . . will . . . give thee for a covenant of the people, for a light of the Gentiles"; and also in 49:8—"In a day of salvation have I helped thee: and I will preserve thee, and give thee for a covenant of the people" (KJV). Thus, as Alan Richardson explains,

> Isaiah interprets the whole redemption wrought by the Servant of Yahweh as a second deliverance and exodus from Egypt, in which the Servant is a new Moses, who is given for the purpose of establishing a (new) covenant with the people (of God).[46]

The fact that we refer to the literature of the Christian scriptures as the New Covenant (Testament) bears eloquent witness to the centrality of the idea in the Christian understanding of the work of Christ.

A second major source of Atonement metaphors is the idea of sacrifice. Markus Barth and many other New Testament scholars recognize and emphasize both the Servant and Sacrifice imageries as the major twofold sources of Atonement ideas.[47] In discussing Christ's death as a sacrifice, Barth writes:

> We conclude, in the New Testament and (excluding Hebrews) in the works of each of its authors the number of pas-

---

45. John James Davis, *Moses and the Gods of Egypt* (Grand Rapids: Baker Book House, 1971).

46. *Theology*, 231.

47. See Vincent Taylor, *Jesus and His Sacrifice* (London: Macmillan and Co., 1937), 131; W. D. Davies, *Paul*, 250.

sages that deal of Christ's death without using sacrificial language, motifs, doctrines, is greater than the number of texts that distinctly strike the sacrificial chord. The main competition to "sacrificial" soteriology seems to come from Old Testament quotations taken from Isaiah 53.[48]

The meaning of sacrifice is one of the most debated questions in biblical theology. Nowhere in the Old Testament is any rationale given for sacrifice, and W. D. Davies observes that "it is doubtful if there was any rationale of sacrifice in the first century."[49] He suggests that the worshiper would simply observe the ritual because God commanded it and thus not seek for an explanation of its meaning. This is difficult, but not impossible, to accept because it involves the adoption of unthinking behavior. It seems more reasonable to suggest that the absence of rationale is doubtless that the meaning was so generally accepted that no explicit articulation was needed.[50] There are also debated issues regarding the extent of the New Testament use of sacrificial images, especially in the case of the apostle Paul.[51] Scholarly literature attempting to explain the meaning of sacrifice has become so immense as to defy summary. Nevertheless, it is necessary to attempt some explanation because, as Robert Culpepper rightly notes,

> An understanding of the meaning of sacrifice in the Old Testament is essential to the interpretation of much of the New Testament material related to the atonement, to an evaluation of the historical views of the atonement, and to a constructive interpretation of the meaning of the death of Christ.[52]

---

48. *Was Christ's Death a Sacrifice?* (Edinburgh: Oliver and Boyd, 1961), 7.

49. *Paul,* 235.

50. Cf. Francis Young, *Sacrifice.*

51. See Vincent Taylor, *Atonement in New Testament Teaching* (London: Epworth Press, 1963); W. D. Davies, *Paul.*

52. *Interpreting the Atonement* (Grand Rapids: Wm. B. Eerdmans Publishing Co., 1966), 23. Markus Barth makes the perceptive suggestion that "it is factually and practically due to the 'lifting of the veil' by the New Testament, that glimpses may have been caught of what distinguishes Old Testament utterances about sacrifice from other [pagan] sacrifices. 2 Cor. 3:7-18 shows that Jesus the Lord's revelation by the Spirit is presupposition, legitimation and command to 'read Moses' otherwise than ignorance, neglect or repudiation of Jesus Christ might suggest. Only in the light of what 'now is revealed' can it be said—that 'law and prophets' give testimony to the righteousness of God that is manifested in 'the Messiah Jesus' blood' (Rom. 3:21-26). To read and treat the Bible as though there had never been a Golgotha, an Easter day, or an 'opening of the mind to understand the scriptures' (Luke 24:45, 25-27) by the risen Christ, is impossible, absurd, illogical for Paul and Matthew, for the authors of First Peter and Hebrews. Therefore, an interpreter of the New Testament has to follow the logic of the New Testament books rather than to impose a foreign scheme upon them." *Was Christ's Death a Sacrifice?* 47 n. 1.

It should be noted that the Servant images and the sacrificial images often interpenetrate, that is, they are not mutually exclusive. This is especially the case with Paul, where it is not always certain whether sacrificial atonement for sin, or vicarious representation by the Suffering Servant, or both are meant.[53] This, in part, explains the basis for the dispute over whether the apostle uses sacrificial imagery. One reason for this ambiguity is doubtless due to the fact that sacrificial motifs are incorporated into the Isaiah 53 passage, which is so crucial for the Servant image. However, these references are vague at best and involve a transformation of the whole idea of sacrifice. Culpepper clarifies this transmuted meaning:

> In the ritual of sacrifice the victim is an animal whose innocence and purity are nonmoral, but in Isa. 53 the victim is a person whose innocence and purity are moral and spiritual. The idea of sacrifice is thus spiritualized. The priest and victim are one.[54]

Sacrificial motifs, however, seem to be rather wide-ranging in their implication and, when the whole spectrum of possible implications is taken into account, appear to point to two major functions. The first use of sacrifice has to do with the establishing of covenant relations and is derived from numerous covenant-making events in the Old Testament accompanied by a sacrifice.[55] The second group of sacrificial terms is drawn from the Hebrew cult. Since the cultic sacrifice presupposes a covenant already in existence, and the offerings are specifically designed to maintain covenant relations, they cluster around the idea of sanctification (ceremonially understood). Thus a polarity is set up in the sacrificial metaphors not often noted, so that the indiscriminate use of such imagery often leads to considerable confusion.

A survey of the covenant-making ceremonies in the Old Testament reflects the presence of sacrifice in many and possibly in all, although explicit reference is not made to it in all cases (cf.

---

53. Markus Barth, *Was Christ's Death a Sacrifice?* 7; W. D. Davies, *Paul*, 230 ff.

54. *Interpreting the Atonement*, 38. H. H. Rowley also calls attention to the transformation of the idea of sacrifice occurring here: "It is the idea of a sacrifice that transcends animal sacrifice, in which instead of an animal without physical blemish, one who is without moral blemish is put to death. Morever the victim while he is cruelly maltreated and slain by others, yields himself willingly unto them." *Meaning of Sacrifice*, 106.

55. See Markus Barth, *Was Christ's Death a Sacrifice?* and W. D. Davies, *Paul*, 253 ff.; G. B. Gray, *Sacrifice in the Old Testament* (New York: Katav Publishing House, 1971), 397.

Genesis 15; Exodus 24).[56] The term *berith,* translated "covenant," may mean "to cut a covenant," implying a sacrifice. In the covenant ceremony between God and Abraham (Genesis 15) the sacrificial animal is divided into two portions, and what is called by many the "smoking lamp" passed between them. The action seems to imply the union created by the two parties similar to the ancient blood covenant, where two persons mingle their blood, thus becoming one. Ps. 50:5 makes explicit the close connection between sacrifice and covenant: "Gather My saints together to Me, those who have made a covenant with Me by sacrifice" (NKJV).

We have already noted in looking at the Eucharistic words of Jesus how the paschal lamb symbolized the institution of a covenant. W. D. Davies argues that this is also Paul's meaning in his Eucharistic passage (1 Cor. 15:23; 5:7):

> Just as in the Jewish Passover we have a memorial festival of thanksgiving for a past event that had led to the formation of the community of the old Israel so for Paul the Death of Jesus, when he thinks of the Eucharist, is primarily the means whereby the New Community is constituted. . . . It is not then as sacrificial and expiatory but as covenantal that Paul chiefly thinks of the Death of Jesus in the context of the Last Supper, although of course everything covenantal had a sacrificial basis.[57]

The second significance of sacrifice is found in the cultic context. The primary word here is *hilasmos* and related words. We are faced with a translation problem because the term can be rendered in different ways, ways that seem antithetical. In certain settings it can mean to placate or appease an angry person or god with the object of averting wrath, and is thus translated as "propitiation." In other settings it can be translated "expiation," which implies reparation made by removing the offense.

The first is clearly the view of pagan religion. If it is absent from biblical faith, it is not because the Bible does not maintain a strong sense of the wrath of God, but because, if there is propitiation at all, it is God who provides it, not man. The sacrifice of Christ is God's gift as a sacrifice for the sins of the world. So as Alan Richardson correctly says:

---

56. See Leon Morris, *The Apostolic Preaching of the Cross* (Grand Rapids: Wm. B. Eerdmans Publishing Co., 1972), 60 ff.
57. *Paul,* 252.

If we retain the word "propitiation" as a translation of *hilasmos,* we must make sure that it is understood that there is no suggestion that man can propitiate God or that God needs propitiating before he can forgive: it is God, not man, who propitiates and makes forgiveness possible. In its biblical meaning "propitiation" must be thought of as more or less synonymous with "expiation" [the performance of an act whereby guilt or defilement is removed].[58]

Culpepper, in an excellent discussion of these issues, concludes soundly:

The fact that it is God himself who covers the sin is the basic difference in the understanding of sacrifice manifested in the Old Testament as compared with that in heathen religions. It is God himself who manifests his grace to man in providing a means of covering sin so that it no longer has the power of disturbing the covenant relation between God and man.[59]

The failure to see this position is largely the result of not recognizing the context out of which these concepts arise. First, we should reiterate that these sacrifices/offerings function within the covenant; they are worship activities of the people of God. Further, in this setting we must keep in mind the nature of the covenant, which should be distinguished from a contract. The contract, as Elmer Martens demonstrates, is characteristically thing-oriented. The covenant, on the other hand, is person-oriented. This means that the covenant relation must be interpreted not legalistically but personally. As Martens says, the covenant, when speaking theologically, "arises, not with benefits as the chief barter item, but out of a desire for a measure of intimacy."[60] He concludes on this basis that while a covenant, like a contract, can be broken, "the point at which this transpires is less clear, because here the focus is not on stipulations, one, two, three, but on a quality of intimacy. Of all the differences between covenant and contract, the place in covenant of personal loyalty is the most striking."

Apparently the *hattath* (sin offering) is the most significant offering, since it seems to be the prerequisite for the others. The original meaning of the idea of atonement is probably preserved in the offering. Many scholars feel that the word *hattath* means "purify" or "purge." It makes provision for inadvertent sins that must become a matter of knowledge and acknowledged or confessed.

58. *Theology,* 224.
59. *Interpreting the Atonement,* 28; cf. also 23-30.
60. *God's Design* (Grand Rapids: Baker Book House, 1981), 73.

But, by implication, it is the sanctuary that is defiled and in need of purgation, since the blood of the offering is sprinkled there but never on a person.

This phenomenon can best be explained theologically by the corporate nature of Hebrew religion. This is reinforced by the fact that the graver the offense, "the more the resultant impurity penetrates into the sanctuary" as is reflected in the instructions about where the blood is to be sprinkled. Presumptuous sins pollute the innermost sanctuary and can be purged only by the rites of the Day of Atonement.[61]

Thus these rituals relate to the ongoing activity of sanctification as described by H. Orton Wiley, referring to the "sprinkling of the blood" mentioned in 1 Pet. 1:2 (KJV):

> Sanctification as an instantaneous act cleanses us from all sin, and brings us to a place of obedience; walking in the light of obedience we are the recipients of a progressive or continuous sanctification, which renders even our obedience acceptable to God. It is important to bear in mind, therefore, that we are cleansed by the atoning blood, only as we are (1) brought into right relation to Jesus Christ; and (2) we are continuously cleansed, or kept clean, only as these right relations are continued. We are sanctified by Christ, not separate from, but in and with Himself; not only by the blood of cleansing, but under the sprinkling of that blood (CT 2:485-86).

High-handed or deliberate sins, if not confessed and repented of, are dealt with by expulsion from the community (Num. 15:30). This type of sin implies a breach of covenant, which then needs reestablishing. Sometimes Ps. 51:16-17 is interpreted to be a repudiation of sacrifice. But it is rather a recognition that there was no sacrifice for murder and adultery (assuming it is David's prayer, as tradition understands), but that these cases could be forgiven in response to deep penitence. That such forgiveness can occur is clear from Nathan's response to David's confession.[62]

The rites of the Day of Atonement may be interpreted as providing for both types of sin. The sacrifice whose blood is sprinkled on the mercy seat is a sin offering, which according to Leviticus 4 is for unintentional sins of the whole community. In the ritual of

---

61. Rowley, *Meaning of Sacrifice*, 98-101.
62. Cf. Jacob Milgrom, "Sacrifice," in *Interpreter's Dictionary of the Bible*, suppl. vol. ed. Keith Crim (Nashville: Abingdon, 1976); Victor P. Hamilton, "Recent Studies in Leviticus and Their Contribution to a Further Understanding of Wesleyan Theology," in *A Spectrum of Thought*, ed. Michael Peterson (Wilmore, Ky.: Asbury Publishing Co., 1982).

the scapegoat, the high priest places his hands on the head of the animal, symbolically transferring the guilt of (deliberate) sin to this "sin bearer."[63] Thus instead of the expulsion of the sinner from the community, his sins are sent away into the uninhabited desert. What is of significance here is that the scapegoat is not a sacrifice to the Lord but was led away for Azazel, which according to one view was a demon residing in the desert. By this method the conditions are fulfilled for the removal of all sin, that is, both forms: actual sin and unintentional ceremonial defilement.

When sacrificial language is applied to the work of Christ from this broader background, it implies a double significance, thus enriching the concept of atonement so as to include both reconciliation and sanctification. The latter is the central theme of Hebrews. There the sacrifice of Christ provides for a real cleansing from sin, not just ceremonial as in the Jewish cultus.

This polarity in the Old Testament understanding of sacrifice, which is picked up by the New Testament teaching about the work of Christ, is reproduced in the balanced emphases of Wesleyan theology where reconciliation (justification) and sanctification are seen as the twin benefits of the Atonement. Maintaining the polar tension between these two truths is a delicate theological task as is a balanced theology in all other areas.

Doctrinal Considerations

Every doctrine of the Atonement is an expression of a particular understanding of God. Each of the classical theories sketched above reflects its own perspective. One emphasizes one attribute, and another emphasizes a different one. But as Wiley says, "A true theory of the atonement must satisfy all the attributes of the divine nature" (CT 2:258). Furthermore, the theology that informs a valid Atonement theory must build upon the biblical understanding of these attributes and not those characteristics as defined from a foreign point of view. Chapter 6, "The Nature and Attributes of God," seeks to identify the unique biblical perspective as elaborated by the best of contemporary biblical scholarship. The central focus we have opted for is that God's nature is holy love, with all other moral attributes being expressions of this decisive center.

---

63. Culpepper also interprets the scapegoat as pertaining to high-handed sins. *Interpreting the Atonement*, 25-26.

This delineation of the divine nature provides the outside parameters for a Wesleyan Atonement theory. The holiness of God stands guard against a view that either overlooks or fails to deal conclusively with the question of sin. The love of God serves as a barrier to any theory that insists upon some satisfaction of either abstract justice or personal justice before God is willing to forgive or justify the sinner.

The doctrine of sin, as we have elaborated it, is interpreted so that there must be an interpersonal dimension to the reconciliation of man and God. That is, sin cannot be conceived in an abstract way so that the Atonement deals with sin but not the sinner, for as we have seen, such a separation is impossible.

Larry Shelton correctly argues that "since all sin is essentially relational, the overcoming of the curse of sin must involve personal and relational means."[64] Salvation, in these terms, involves the overcoming of estrangement and the restoration of man to his created destiny under the conditions of existence. The result is a personal relation that transcends without abrogating legal consideration.

With these sources of wisdom in hand, we must now attempt the task of formulating a distinctive Wesleyan view of the saving work of Christ.

---

64. "A Covenant Concept of Atonement," *Wesleyan Theological Journal* 19, no. 1 (Spring 1984).

CHAPTER

12

A Wesleyan View of the Atonement

Our purpose in this chapter is to seek, in the light of the issues explored in the last chapter, to suggest a consistent formulation of how the work of Christ provides the benefits included in the broad term "salvation." By these suggestions we hope to identify those features that would characterize a systematic Wesleyan view of the Atonement.

Before looking into the possibilities of a positive contribution, we will explore in greater detail the claim made in the previous chapter that the Atonement theory that John Wesley seemed to espouse was antithetical to his central soteriological claims. This involves looking at the inadequacies of the penal satisfaction view that comes to expression in the Wesleyan corpus, at least in the language he uses.

H. Orton Wiley advances five weaknesses of this theory that we will do well to summarize:

1. Its basic premise is that sin must be punished on its own account. This is based on the view that God's primary nature is justice, which is a legal principle to which He is bound. It further involves the separation of sin from the sinner, thus reflecting at best an odd concept of sin. It involves the transfer of man's guilt to Christ as the Substitute and thus is subject to the criticism of being

immoral, since the Substitute is not really guilty but is "only an innocent victim. It is in this attempt to impute our sin to Christ as His own, that the weakness of this type of substitution appears" (CT 2:244-45).

The basic fallacy of this way of thinking is in interpreting the substitutionary work of Christ externally as "instead of" rather than "in behalf of," a distinction with a tremendous difference (CT 2:243).

2. The second weakness is in its insistence that the substitution of an innocent victim for the guilty one, the former taking the punishment that justice requires to be imposed upon sin, is the only way of conceiving a vicarious atonement. Wiley quotes approvingly an alternate explanation proposed by W. B. Pope in which Christ is interpreted as the Representative of man before God. We will attempt to give a full elaboration of this much more adequate interpretation of Christ's vicarious atonement in our constructive efforts.

3. The logical conclusion of the penal theory is either universalism or a limited atonement. If Christ suffers the penalty for sin, the justice of God is satisfied, and therefore nothing further is needed. Those for whom He died must go free from the consequences of sin. Calvin himself, as well as all his consistent successors, opts for a limited atonement in which Christ is punished for the elect. The use of the term *punishment* should be noted here. We have previously shown this to be a nonbiblical concept. The biblical language is uniformly "suffered."

4. The fourth weakness is the logical implication of the third. It leads unerringly into a view of irresistible grace. Wiley's own summary is admirably suited to express this nonbiblical conclusion:

> Christ died in the place of some, who must therefore be saved, since it would be wrong [unjust] to punish both the sinner and his substitute. Christ died for the elect, who are not only foreknown, but foreordained to this state of salvation by the decree of God. Those who are so predestinated, are unconditionally saved by the bestowal of regenerating grace, out of which arise repentance, faith, justification, adoption and sanctification (CT 2:248).

It should be noted that this quote recognizes that repentance follows regenerating grace, an accurate interpretation of the Calvinistic scheme. Given the view of grace entailed by the penal view of the Atonement, there is not only no necessity but no possibility for repentance prior to regeneration. The first movement of grace is regenerative, inevitably. Thus repentance is a Christian virtue, practiced regularly in the ongoing work of sanctification. This ignores the work of God preceding and preparatory to faith, which is reflected in the Wesleyan doctrine of prevenient grace that leads to repentance as the prerequisite of saving faith, though not a prerequisite for justification. (This distinction will be developed further on.)

5. The fifth weakness addresses a conclusion against which John Wesley manfully struggled and could only manage to avoid by artificial means. The penal satisfaction theory eliminates the practical necessity of a doctrine of sanctification, or as Wiley puts it, "it leads logically into antinomianism" (CT 2:248-49).

Wesley forcefully rejected the idea that Christ's death was substitutionary in the sense of "fulfilling all righteousness" in man's stead, on the ground that this notion was unscriptural and led to antinomianism.[1]

Gustav Aulen also provides a powerful criticism at this point:

> If God can be represented as willing to accept a satisfaction for sins committed, it appears to follow necessarily that the dilemma of laxity or satisfaction does not adequately express God's enmity against sin. The doctrine provides for the remission of the punishment due to sins, but not for the taking away of the sin itself.[2]

Even though serious efforts are made by its exponents to advocate the necessity of a holy life based on their understanding of the nature of genuine faith, it always involves arguing in a circle. If one is truly one of the elect—among those for whom Christ died—there are no logical grounds for asserting the necessity of holiness of heart and life. He will be saved without it. If such holiness does not appear, the only appeal is to invalidate the faith that is claimed by the person. There is some truth in this argument, but in the context of the penal theory it merely becomes the fallacy of circular reasoning. The real problem for a sound theology is making provision for sanctification without losing the biblical emphasis on justification by faith alone. This interpretation fails to provide an adequate solution to this problem. The proposed Wesleyan solu-

---

1. *Works* 10:332, 333.
2. *Christus Victor,* trans. A. G. Hebert (New York: Macmillan Co., 1961), 92.

tion, to be explored below, is much more adequate both biblically and logically.

In addition to these problems, we may note that the penal theory does not set well with a doctrine of prevenient grace. We have already observed one aspect of this in the discussion above on repentance. J. Glenn Gould puts his finger on this sensitive point in this manner: "Perhaps there is a basic inconsistency between Wesley's hazily defined doctrine of the atonement and his clearly stated doctrine of prevenient grace."[3]

Furthermore, the penal theory builds upon an unbiblical doctrine of God. For the Calvinistic theology, divine love is subject to the will of God, so there is no problem with God hating certain sinners whom He chooses to exclude by divine fiat from eternal bliss. For the Wesleyan (and New Testament thought) love is a manifestation of God's nature, and this will not allow the whole legal apparatus upon which the satisfaction interpretation is built.

Gould quotes a selection from William G. T. Shedd that strikingly embodies this interpretation:

> An atonement for sin, of one kind or the other, if not personal then vicarious, is necessary, not optional. The transgressor must either die himself, or someone must die for him. This arises from the nature of that divine attribute to which atonement is a correlate. Retributive justice . . . is necessary in its operation. The claim of the law upon the transgressor for punishment is absolute and indefeasible. The eternal Judge may or may not exercise mercy, but he must exercise justice. He can neither waive the claims of the law in part, nor abolish them altogether. The only possible mode, consequently, of delivering a creature who is obnoxious to the demands of retributive justice, is to satisfy them for him.[4]

In addition, Gustav Aulen has pressed the criticism that the Latin theory, as he calls it, is not wholly the work of God. Although it begins with God, it is the work of Christ "as a man" that offers satisfaction to God's justice. In this view, the legal order is uninterrupted, but the order of love is interrupted. This point implies further that in the Latin view, the Incarnation and Atonement are not organically connected. The purpose of the Incarnation is to provide a perfect manhood to offer to God as an acceptable satisfaction.[5]

---

3. *Precious Blood of Christ,* 75.
4. Ibid., 70.
5. *Christus Victor,* 87 ff., 146.

Toward a Wesleyan View

It now behooves us to seek to provide an alternate theory. Interestingly, the clue seems to be found in Wesley's own works, although it has never been developed (so far as I know) into an Atonement theology. It is well known that Wesley's Christology is built upon the threefold office of Christ as Prophet, Priest, and King. His own affinities with New Testament thought would lead us to suspect that he interpreted these functionally and therefore soteriologically. This within itself makes this structure into an Atonement motif.

This trilogy, taken either together or separately, is liberally sprinkled throughout Wesley's writings. A case can be made that this is really his most thought-out formulation of the work of Christ. Consistent with the mode of Wesleyan thought, there is both an objective grounding and a subjective grounding of these offices with their respective functions.

Objectively they are derived from the name Christ, which signifies "anointed." Among the Hebrews, prophets, priests, and kings were all inducted into office by a ceremony of anointing with oil.[6] Jesus' anointing with the Holy Spirit at His baptism, to which He bore witness in His first sermon at Nazareth (Luke 4:18), brought together in Him the prophetic, priestly, and royal functions in one Person.

Subjectively, they answer to a threefold need that we find in ourselves. First, so far as our knowledge of God is concerned, we are in darkness and ignorance, thus we need a prophet to "enlighten our minds, and teach us the whole will of God." Second, we find ourselves alienated from God and incapable of reestablishing right relations, so we stand in need of a mediator, a priest to build a bridge (literal meaning of the term "priest" is "bridge builder," from the Latin, *pontifex*) between the two estranged parties. Third, we furthermore find ourselves inwardly enslaved to appetites and passions but morally incapable of breaking free. This calls for the kingly power of Christ to reign within and "subdue all things to Himself" (cf. *Notes* on Matt. 1:16).

---

6. With the exception of Elisha (I Kings 19:16) prophets were normally not anointed in the Old Testament. This fact has been used by some to call this threefold structure into question. However, it seems feasible to think that the prophets were anointed by the Spirit of the Lord to perform their function. Alan Richardson points out that the Isaianic Prophet-figure, although a special or ideal case, is depicted as being anointed. *Theology*, 179 n. I.

Wesley distinctly relates each of these offices to both justification and sanctification. In a note on Matt. 11:28-29, apparently thinking most centrally about the Kingly function, he says: "I alone (for there is none else can) will freely give you (what ye cannot purchase) rest from the guilt of sin by justification, and from the power of sin by sanctification." All these offices are so related in a note on Phil. 3:8 where the three functions are identified as "teaching me wisdom, atoning for my sins, and reigning in my heart." Of these, he says: "To refer this to justification only is miserably to pervert the whole scope of the words. They manifestly relate to sanctification also; yea, to that chiefly." It seems improper that any one office should be interpreted as relating exclusively to either justification or sanctification.

These three functions may not be mutually exclusive, but they do point to significantly distinct characteristics of the total work of Christ, all of which focus on soteriology, conceived broadly. Since they are so interdependent, there is no fully satisfactory order in which to treat them. Each presupposes the other two. Consequently we will follow the traditional order that Wesley also uses when he is simply reciting them.[7]

One other preliminary note. Each office, as with many other aspects of Wesley's thought, has both an objective and a subjective side (not to be confused with the distinction drawn above using the same terminology). Both are necessary. Something occurs apart from my involvement, a finished work. But its value to me depends upon an existential response. In this latter sense the whole work of Christ may be conceived as unfinished.

The Prophetic Work of Christ

"Christ as a prophet is the perfect revealer of divine truth" (*CT* 2:213). This occurs both in His person and teaching and is decisive because His prophetic work is grounded in His relation to the Father. His prophetic ministry is the climax and culmination of the whole prophetic movement beginning with Moses.[8] As Prophet, Jesus proclaims and embodies both gospel and law. He is characterized by Wesley as "the great Lawgiver."

---

7. John Deschner thinks the priestly office is of greatest significance for Wesley, so he puts it last in his analysis. *Wesley's Christology.*
8. *StS* 2:316.

In order to grasp the full soteriological significance of this office, we will need to give close attention to Wesley's understanding of the law and its threefold function. A studied presentation of this is found in his two sermons on "The Law Established Through Faith" and the one on "The Original, Nature, Property, and Use of the Law." What he is here exploring is the moral law in distinction from the ceremonial law.

In substance, the law is the embodiment of the nature of God. It is "a copy of the eternal mind, a transcript of the divine nature," "divine virtue and wisdom assuming a visible form . . . the original ideas of truth and good, which were lodged in the uncreated mind from eternity, now drawn forth and clothed with such a vehicle as to appear even to human understanding." He can even speak of the law as "God manifest in the flesh."

The other side of this truth is that the law is also reflective of human nature as it was intended to be. In unfallen man, the law was really the law of his own being, "the design of their beneficent Governor . . . to make way for a continual increase of their happiness; seeing every instance of obedience to that law would . . . add to the perfection of their nature." After the Fall, this law was partially reinscribed on man's heart, assuring that he was still structurally a human being (prevenient grace), and given to Moses in a positive form to portray God's design for human destiny. Thus the law is no arbitrary imposition of rules upon man that would inhibit his happiness. In a word, it is the positive elaboration of the image of God.

It now becomes obvious how Christ as Prophet is the fulfillment of the law, in both dimensions. The incarnational language that Wesley uses of the moral law becomes actual and more realistic in the Incarnation. Christ as *homoousios* with the Father is the perfect manifestation of God's character in the flesh (John 1:14). Christ has also, as we have had occasion to note several times, embodied the essence of what it means for a human being to reflect the image of God. Paul's contrast in 2 Corinthians 3 takes on new meaning in this context as he contrasts the fading glory (image) of the law with the permanent glory (image) that shines from the face of Jesus Christ.

The weakness of the law is its limitation to prohibitions and admonishments and thus its susceptibility to being perverted into legalism that remains external and perfunctory. This weakness is overcome in Christ's prophetic function. As the embodiment of the law, He makes it unavoidable that one's being rather than just his behavior is at stake. Christ as the ideal *imago* toward which the work of sanctification moves the human spirit is more profound than asking, "What would Jesus do?" It entails "having the mind that was in Christ Jesus" (cf. Phil. 2:5, Williams margin), and that reaches to the very wellsprings of one's being and affects what he is and not just what he does.

What then is the function of the law? How does it relate to the gospel? How do both these questions relate to the prophetic office of Christ? These questions are important considerations for any theological understanding.

Along with Calvin, Wesley recognizes three functions of the law.[9] The first is to convince the world of sin by creating an awareness of shortcoming. It is like a mirror that the Holy Spirit uses to convict sinners. Similar to Luther, Wesley also characterizes the law in this role as a "hammer," "being set home on the conscience, [it] generally breaketh the rocks in pieces." In other language, the first use of the law is to "slay the sinner."

The second use is the proper consequence of the first function. It is to bring the awakened sinner to Christ as a schoolmaster. (This is different from Calvin's second use of the law. See n. 9.) The third use of the law is to keep us alive. That is, it has a sanctifying function. It sets before the believer the ideal of holiness and convicts him of his own need.

There are three uses of the law in this third category. First, it convinces us of the sin that remains within us following regeneration, driving us to faith in Christ for His perpetual cleansing of

---

9. Luther and Calvin differ on this point. Luther only recognizes two uses of the law. Its first function is to arouse the sinner to an awareness of his need or to smash the smugness of the self-righteous pharisee, while its second purpose is civil, to hold the unruly persons in check. But Luther finds no place for the law (a third use) in the Christian life as does Calvin. The consequence of this is that Luther has a much less adequate doctrine of sanctification than Calvin, whose view closely approximates that of Wesley in many ways. The practical consequence of this difference is graphically portrayed by Tillich: "In Lutheranism the emphasis on the paradoxical element in the experience of the New Being was so predominant that sanctification could not be interpreted in terms of a line moving upward toward perfection. It was seen instead as an up-and-down of ecstasy and anxiety, of being grasped by *agape* and being thrown back into estrangement and ambiguity. . . . The consequence of the absence in Lutheranism of the Calvinistic and Evangelistic valuation of discipline was that the ideal of progressive sanctification was taken less seriously and replaced by a great emphasis on the paradoxical character of the Christian life." *Systematic Theology* 3:230-31.

this remaining corruption of nature. Second, it becomes the occasion, in relation to the first use, to drive us to Christ for power to keep the law. And third, it arouses hope that God will provide the grace that His requirements implicitly promise and thus deliver us from all remaining sin.[10]

In sum, as Wesley said, "The more I look into this perfect law, the more I feel how far I come short of it; and the more I feel this, the more I feel my need of His blood to atone for all my sin, and of His Spirit to purify my heart, and make me 'perfect and entire, lacking nothing.'"[11]

But the same ideal that, when seen as demand, is experienced as law, can be experienced as gospel when it is seen as promise. And, from the Wesleyan perspective, all of God's requirements are "covered" promises. In his Sermon 5 on the Sermon on the Mount, he says:

> There is no contrariety at all between the law and the gospel; . . . there is no need for the law to pass away, in order to the establishing the gospel. Indeed neither of them supersedes the other, but they agree perfectly well together. Yea, the very same words, considered in different respects, are parts both of the law and of the gospel: If they are considered as commandments, they are parts of the law; if as promises, of the gospel.

Since Christ is the embodiment of the law and the gospel (as defined), preaching Christ substantially involves both messages, although the emphasis may be on the one or the other. This is obvious when Wesley defines what he means. "I mean by 'preaching the gospel' preaching the love of God to sinners, preaching the life, death, resurrection, and intercession of Christ, with all the blessings which in consequence thereof are freely given to these believers. By 'preaching the law' I mean explaining and enforcing the commands of Christ briefly comprised in the Sermon on the Mount."[12]

This understanding places Wesley in the classical Protestant tradition regarding his theology of evangelism. In the letter re-

---

10. *StS* 2:54. This calls attention to Wesley's common understanding of faith, which is taken from Heb. 11:1, that it is "the substance of things hoped for, the evidence of things not seen" (KJV). What God requires is a "covered" promise, and what God has promised He will do, so that faith is the earnest of the fulfilled promise. It is a basic principle with Wesley that what God requires, He will also provide. This principle becomes one of the foundation stones in his optimism of grace regarding entire sanctification.

11. Ibid., 55.

12. Letter to an unknown correspondent dated Dec. 20, 1751.

ferred to above, he fully elaborates his understanding of evangelistic preaching:

> I think the right method of preaching is this. At our first beginning to preach at any place, after a general declaration of the love of God to sinners and His willingness that they should be saved, to preach the law in the strongest, the closest, the most searching manner possible; only intermixing the gospel here and there, and showing it, as it were, afar off.

In Sermon 34 he declares, "It is the ordinary method of the Spirit of God to convict sinners by the law." And in Sermon 35 he adds that "one in a thousand may have been awakened by the gospel: But this is no general rule: The ordinary method of God is, to convict sinners by the law, and that only."

The Priestly Work of Christ

In introducing the priestly aspect of the Atonement, we encounter a complex correlation of ideas that makes this the most comprehensive title of all pertaining to the Atonement. Traditionally this function has been restricted to "sacrifice and intercession," but its implications cover a much broader range than that. In fact, taking the Old Testament priestly responsibilities seriously would even include the prophetic function (see Hag. 2:11-13). It was only gradually that the priests came to be concerned mainly with the offering of sacrifices, while the task of interpreting the law became the responsibility of the scribe.[13]

The priest is a go-between, a bridge builder who effects a bringing together of two parties. The most obvious method of so doing is through a sacrifice. The bridge building, in the case of Jesus, is much broader than just sacrifice, although this does provide a major theological category. It includes the two functions that we found in an earlier analysis to be implicit in the idea of sacrifice: (1) those that indicate the establishing of covenant relations, and (2) those that signify maintaining and developing that relation.

The primary salvation metaphor relating to the first group is reconciliation. The need for reconciliation is the estrangement caused by sin on man's side. The divine side of this estrangement is experienced by man in sin as the wrath of God. It is imperative

13. G. B. Gray, "Sacrifice," in *A Theological Word Book of the Bible*, ed. Alan Richardson (New York: Macmillan Co., 1950).

that we understand the significance of these causes of estrangement and their interrelation if we are to properly grasp the reconciling work of the Priest.

John Deschner suggests that in Wesley, "wrath" is the objective
side of the experience of fear. Wesley, himself, in his note on Rom.
5:9, says that wrath is to be taken in an analogical sense, denying
that it is the same as a human emotion. It is basically referring to
the effects of sin. Thus Deschner is doubtless correct when he
observes that "one cannot escape the impression . . . that Wesley is
more interested in describing something which sinners painfully
experience than in formulating doctrine."[14] Renshaw, in his carefully studied dissertation analysis of the Wesleys' views on the
Atonement, says substantially the same thing: "As resisted and
rejected by man, God's holy love was experienced as wrath, but the
same holy love as received, trusted, and obeyed, was the realization of divine mercy."[15] This is in full accord with the analysis of
the wrath of God developed in chapter 6, "The Nature and Attributes of God."

The logical implication of this understanding is that the sin of
man is the barrier to the reconciliation. When sin is "remedied," the
wrath of God has no more object and thus is satisfied. It is this the
New Testament unequivocally means when it recognizes that man
must be reconciled to God. That will then result in an existential
awareness of reconciliation that may validly be expressed in the
climactic words of Charles Wesley's hymn, "Arise, My Soul, Arise":
"My God is reconciled." The change in relation is simultaneous
with a change in man, the sinner, who now ceases to be a sinner.

When this estrangement is set in the context of law, the need
for reconciliation takes the form of the need for justification. The
same pattern emerges with this metaphor as in reconciliation. The
righteousness of Christ, whether seen in terms of active or passive
obedience, does not serve to satisfy God's justice as a substitute for
man's righteousness in such a way that man is excused from either
being righteous or doing righteousness. The idea that Jesus bears
the punishment for man's sins is totally foreign to the New Testament. The language it uses is "suffering," not "punishment." (It is
truly unfortunate that Wesley failed to recognize this and thus
introduced an element incongruous with his otherwise largely bib-

14. *Wesley's Christology,* 151.
15. "Atonement," 86-87.

lically sound views.) Although Wesley does use this language, there are at least two points that reflect his awareness of the inadequacy of its implications: (1) his emphasis on the continuing need for justification as well as a "final justification," which would be totally irrelevant if Christ's death satisfied the justice of God with regard to the law, and (2) the implication of this statement by Deschner:

> Wesley's main interest in justification seems to be, then, not so much God's justice, as the restored fellowship of the believer with God, which is the nerve of spiritual life and the presupposition for growth in sanctification.[16]

If this is true, justification is essentially a special case of reconciliation that occurs in a moment but must be continued, as all personal relations, by maintaining the proper conditions.

We must now turn to the question of how the work of Christ as Priest effects salvation. In attempting to develop a view that is consistent with the biblical evidence, there seems to be two crucial concepts that occur in four different relations. These are primarily developed by Paul, who provides us with the most creative material on the work of Christ found in the New Testament. As Vincent Taylor says of the apostle's teaching:

> Paulinism is not the perversion of primitive Christianity, it is the gleaming product pouring from the crucible of a gifted and consecrated mind which, with prophetic insight, has seen in the existing tradition half-guessed secrets of God's redeeming love.[17]

These two key concepts characteristic of priesthood are embodied in the terms *identification* and *representation*. In the full-orbed picture of the Atonement that informs Paul's thought, Jesus Christ identified himself with man the sinner in such an intimate way that He can represent him before God (He died for me) even to the ultimate degree in His death on the Cross. Referring to His death on the Cross, John says of Jesus in John 13:1: "Jesus knew that his hour had come and he must leave this world and go to the Father. He had always loved his own who were in the world, and now he was to show the full extent of his love" (NEB). The other side of the representative function is Christ's representation of God to man.

---

16. *Wesley's Christology*, 176.
17. *Atonement in New Testament Teaching*, 57.

The man who in faith is reconciled to God on this basis then identifies himself with his Representative ("with Him"), and it is this aspect of the correlation that provides Paul with one of his major ways of speaking about sanctification.[18]

Both of these motifs (identification and representation) are found in each of the two basic sources of Atonement metaphors isolated in our previous discussion (Servant of the Lord and Sacrifice). They are furthermore present, either explicitly or implicitly, in both dimensions of sacrifice.

In covenant making, the agreement was often made with a representative person (e.g., Noah, Abraham, Jacob).[19] Those who were identified with this representative person were considered heirs of the covenant. The Hebrew concept of corporate personality gave validity to this relation and enabled the heirs of the covenant to consider themselves as really being present in the person of their representative when the covenant was originally instituted.

This identification with the covenant representative(s) is explicitly stated in Deut. 5:2-3: "The Lord our God made a covenant with us in Horeb. Not with our fathers [alone] did the Lord make this covenant, but with us, who are all of us here alive this day."

An important qualification, which has implications for Atonement, must be noted. There were no automatic provisions of a covenant for those who were not personally present and existentially involved in the original covenant ceremony. They had to validate the agreement for themselves. Each patriarch, and each generation of their descendants, was called upon to reaffirm his own commitment to the covenant relation, in order to receive the divine commitments. This occurred as he identified himself (by faith) with his representative in the original covenant-making ceremony.

---

18. This is not to suggest that one can find a formal theological statement in Paul along this line, but rather that this is one fundamental way he perceives and elaborates the work of sanctification implicit in the Atonement. It is in this way that he addresses a critical issue raised when one begins to think about the reconciling work of God. Vincent Taylor's words reflect the character of Paul's writings about these things: "The supreme interest of St. Paul is not in the rationale of the Atonement, but in the ethical and religious problem of righteousness rendered acute by the Christian conviction that sinful men can be received into abiding fellowship by a Holy and Righteous God. A profound thinker, he is not a constructive theologian anxious to build up a comprehensive theory of the meaning of the death of Christ." Ibid., 65.

19. It should be kept in mind that a covenant is normally established with a sacrifice. We are here working with the sacrifice motif in its covenant-establishing function.

This truth is reinforced by the words of John the Baptist, who was apparently facing a perversion of it on the part of the Jews. He declares to them: "Do not presume to say to yourselves, 'We have Abraham as our father'; for I tell you, God is able from these stones to raise up children to Abraham" (Matt. 3:9). Observe the significance of this statement being recorded by Matthew, who was writing to a Jewish audience.

In the sacrificial rites within the cultus, the ideas of identification and representation also become quite explicit. A failure to understand the significance of the laying of hands on the head of the sacrificial victim has led to interpreting the animal as a substitute for the person so that the victim perishes instead of the offerer. The incident of the scapegoat is different (see above), but this ritual act in the prescribed sacrifices (Leviticus 1—7) does not signify the transference of guilt, for the offering is still regarded as holy; it is the worshiper's acknowledgment that the offering is his own, and that he identifies himself with it. It thus functions as his representative before God, but there is an even deeper identification as reflected in the words of H. H. Rowley:

> The sacrificial animal was not merely a substitute for the offerer. He laid his hands upon it and was conceived of as in some way identified with it, so that in its death he was conceived of as dying—not physically, but spiritually. The death of the victim symbolized his death to his sin, or to whatever stood between him and God, or his surrender of himself to God in thankfulness and humility.[20]

Vincent Taylor argues that one reason Jesus interpreted His sufferings and death in the light of the ideas of Isa. 52:13—53:12 was because of the concept of representative suffering that it contains and that was in turn ultimately based on this motif in the Old Testament sacrifices.[21]

Both themes are, furthermore, present in the classical Servant passage of Isaiah 53. The idea of identification is expressed explicitly in the words of verse 12 that He "was numbered with the transgressors," but it is implicit throughout. The whole movement of the song is woven around the theme of representation, especially in the dramatic phrases such as, "He was wounded for our transgressions, he was bruised for our iniquities" (v. 5). In this vi-

---

20. *Meaning of Sacrifice,* 88.
21. *Jesus and His Sacrifice,* 48.

376 ☐ GRACE, FAITH, AND HOLINESS

carious suffering, He establishes a covenant between God and wayward men.

In addition to being present in these major Atonement sources, identification is also an implied motif in the Son of Man title to which Jesus laid claim. In the original setting of this passage in Daniel 7, the Son of Man represents the saints in receiving the Kingdom from the Ancient of Days.

Christ Identifies Himself with Man

The Incarnation itself is the major act of God coming into human history in the essence of manhood by which He identifies himself with the human condition. Russell Phillip Shedd emphasizes this truth:

> The identification of Christ with the Old Aeon begins with His pre-existence and subsequent incarnation. He, being the Son of God (Gal. 4:4) and existing in the form of God, emptied Himself of the divine form to become as a man. Christ's incarnation through the medium of human birth realistically identified Him with the totality of mankind. This identification could not have been made without Christ's becoming a member of the group He represents. He, who was formerly outside the community of man, became, through the process of birth, a part of the human family.[22]

The reality of Christ's full identification with the human family is vouchsafed by the Church's insistence upon His full humanity and its resistance to any interpretation of His person that compromises that humanity. Certain specific facets of His life and work, however, emphasize the fullness of His identification with mankind.

Baptism

We have earlier noted the significance of Jesus' baptism by John for His ministry as the Suffering Servant. This supplies its primary meaning. However, subsidiary to that is His identification with sinners in this act. As Ralph Earle comments:

> He did not need a baptism for repentance, but this act was a symbol of His whole earthly career which was a baptism into the experiences and sufferings of human life. It spoke of a close identification of Christ with human need.[23]

---

22. *Man in Community* (Grand Rapids: Wm. B. Eerdmans Publishing Co., 1964), 165-66.
23. *Gospel of Mark*, note on 1:9.

Temptation

As with the Baptism, Jesus' temptation plays a significant role in the formation of His ministry. But it also is an occasion for His identification with the common places of life. Testing is the lot of all humans; and because all the possible types of temptation ("the lust of the flesh, and the lust of the eyes and the pride of life" [1 John 2:16]) are represented here, the writer of the Hebrews can say: "For we have not a high priest who is unable to sympathize with our weaknesses, but one who in every respect has been tempted as we are, yet without sin" (4:15).

Death

But the most profound dimension of His identification with the human race is in His death. In Romans 5, Paul speaks of death as the universal evidence of sinfulness (cf. 1 Cor. 15:22, "In Adam all die"). It is the most poignant symbol not only of our finitude but of our fallenness as well. This union with the human predicament at its most anguished depths identified Christ with man as sinner so intimately that He experiences the ultimate loneliness to which He gave expression in the cry of dereliction from the Cross.

We must agree with F. W. Dillistone when he says:

> Whatever his suffering means, it does not mean that God has abandoned him or even temporarily turned away from him. Never is the Son nearer to the Father's heart than in the hour of his bitterest trial; never is the Father nearer to the Son than in the moment of his deepest identification with those he had come to save.[24]

If "God was in Christ, reconciling the world unto himself" (2 Cor. 5:19, KJV), no other conclusion is possible. However, the sense of separation was real due to the intimacy of His identification with fallen humanity. As Vincent Taylor rightly puts it,

> The saying expresses a feeling of utter desolation, a sense of abandonment by the Father, an experience of defeat and despair. . . . The feeling of desolation is temporary, but it is real, and it is due, so far as it can be explained at all, to preoccupation by Jesus with the fact and burden of sin.[25]

---

24. *Jesus Christ and His Cross* (Philadelphia: Westminster Press, 1953), 27-28.
25. *Jesus and His Sacrifice*, 161. This quotation is cited with strong approval by Dale Moody, *Word of Truth*, 372. This interpretation stands against an interpretation that sees a crude substitutionary relation in which Christ actually becomes guilty in suffering the

The mystery of this reality transcends our understanding but elicits our devotion.

Representation

The identification of Christ with us then becomes the ground of the possibility of His representing us before God as well as in His encounter with evil at the Cross. The full implications of this latter truth can best be seen in relation to the Kingly office. The former pertains specifically to His priestly office. In similar fashion as Adam represented us badly in the beginning, Christ as the second Adam represented us magnificently in the middle. The solidarity of man in Adam and the possibility of the solidarity of the new race in Christ makes this understanding the most appropriate conceptualization for conceiving of the priestly, redeeming work of Christ. Wesley makes much of this representative relation of Adam and Christ to the human race.[26]

Purkiser, Taylor, and Taylor point out that this representative relationship is what constitutes the vicarious character of Christ's death. Taking the literal meaning of the Latin word *vicarius*, from which the term *vicar* is derived, carrying the denotation of "taking the place of another," they comment:

> A vicar is a deputy or substitute minister; he acts as a representative of another minister. . . . To describe Christ's death as vicarious is to declare that He in some manner endured or suffered an experience which was due us. In vicarious suffering, the effects or benefits accrue to someone other than the sufferer. It is endured on behalf of others, doing for them what they are not able to do for themselves.[27]

It should be noted here that the emphasis is on the work of Christ *for us* as meaning "on behalf of." We have already seen,

---

penalty of man's sin and thus becomes "the greatest sinner." It is this representative relation that should provide the proper explanation for the difficult phrase of Paul in 2 Cor. 5:21: "For he hath made him to be sin for us, who knew no sin" (KJV).

26. See *Works* 9:332, 333; *StS* 1:118; *Notes* on 1 Cor. 15:47. Wesley sees this to relate to the racial dimension of the Atonement.

27. *God, Man, and Salvation,* 385. While there is a slight ambiguity in their treatment of this theme, due perhaps partly to the use of a Calvinistic source (Morris, *Apostolic Preaching*) and partly to the fact that the work was produced by a committee, the weight of emphasis is clearly on the representative character of the vicarious work of Christ rather than the penal substitutionary interpretation of the concept of vicariousness. The latter, we have seen, must be rejected by the Wesleyan theologian. Hence I have followed what I perceive to be the central emphasis and have ignored the peripheral, diverging comments.

following Wiley, that it is crucial to see the difference between this interpretation and the one that sees the *for us* as "instead of." There are two Greek prefixes involved in this discussion. *Anti* suggests the notion of substitution "instead of," while *huper* implies "on behalf of." The authors of *God, Man, and Salvation* argue from lexical sources that even in the rare cases where *anti* is used, it can and does carry the meaning chiefly conveyed by *huper.* However, it is the latter term that is predominantly used and preferred by Paul. Thus the emphasis is on what Christ procured for us by His representation "on our behalf." As they say, "He acts at the Cross *on our behalf* and *for every man.*"[28]

In his rejection of the penal substitutionary theory of the Atonement, Wiley points out how the Methodist theologians (Watson, Pope) provide for the vicarious character of the work of Christ through the concept of representation. He refers to Pope's statement as a "deeper and more scriptural approach to the subject." Pope's summary reads:

> No adjective equivalent to the term Vicarious, as expressing the Redeemer's relation to mankind, is used in Scripture; nor is there any equivalent for Substitution, the noun corresponding to the adjective. But the idea of a strictly vicarious representation lies at the root of its teaching. An absolute substitution of the Saviour's obedience or sacrifice in the place of the suffering and obedience of His people is not taught in the Word of God. The substitutionary idea is in their [His people's] case qualified by that of representation on the one hand, and the mystical fellowship of His saints on the other. If unqualified at all, it is so with reference to the race at large or the world of mankind.[29]

---

28. Pp. 385-87. Vincent Taylor comments that "the meaning of the Death of Christ as vicarious in Paul's understanding is in his phrase 'for us.' In all cases except one he uses the preposition *huper* meaning 'on behalf of.' In I Thess. 5:10 (the one exception) he uses *peri*, 'on account of,' which is not appreciably different from *huper.* Nowhere does he use *anti*, 'instead of.' From this we may certainly infer that he did not look upon the death of Christ as that of a substitute. The alleged substitutionary element in his thought is rather to be discerned in his teaching about the representative work of Christ." *Atonement in New Testament Teaching*, 59.

29. *Compendium* 2:269-70. Wiley, *CT* 2:246. It is most perplexing that in a later treatment of "The Vicarious Expiation" Wiley defines "vicarious suffering or punishment" as "that which is endured by one person instead of another." 282 ff. Not only is the title of the section self-contradictory when this definition is affirmed, but also it flies in the face of his own earlier rejection of the penal satisfaction theory and apparent adoption of the Wesleyan (Methodist) theologians' reinterpretation of that view in the light of its inconsistency with Arminian presuppositions.

Historical Antecedent

The church father who most fully developed the representative function of the Savior in its soteriological significance was Irenaeus of Lyon. This Greek theologian anticipated several ideas that became distinctive of Wesleyan theology, although in his own terms. His doctrine of recapitulation is this central expression of both representation and identification.

Irenaeus's understanding of the redemptive work of Christ included a number of theological motifs that were absent from some earlier interpretations, motifs that we have indicated to be necessary to include in a Wesleyan view so as to encompass both salvific benefits of reconciliation and sanctification. He was the first father to make use of the Fall and its effects as the background for the Atonement. In this tragic event man lost "our being in the image and likeness to God" (see *Adv. Her.* 3.18.1) and came under the control of Satan. Thus the saving work of Christ involved freeing man from the bondage of sin (see below on the Christus Victor motif considered under the kingly office of Christ) and the restoring of man to the image of God. In order to accomplish these benefits, the Savior must be both truly man and truly God. Thus the incarnation and death of Christ are both essential for Irenaeus.

In his doctrine of recapitulation, Irenaeus teaches that in Christ we have restored what we lost in Adam. If we fell through our solidarity with Adam, we can be renewed through our solidarity with Christ. This is a utilization of Paul's division of humanity into the two major categories of those who are "in Adam" and those who are "in Christ."

He borrows the conception of recapitulation from Paul's description of God's purpose to "sum up all things in Christ" (Eph. 1:10, ASV). Thus as the perfect Representative of man, Christ climbs back up the ladder, step by step, down which Adam came at the Fall, living a life of perfect obedience to God. He ingeniously draws parallels between Adam and Christ and thereby shows how Christ became the Source of a new relation between God and man for those who by faith are united with Him. The Second Adam lived life through all its stages, including death, which was the crowning act of obedience. Thus "in obliterating the disobedience of man originally enacted on the tree [of the knowledge of good and evil], He became obedient unto death, even the death on the cross, healing the disobedience enacted on the tree by obedience on a tree" (*Adv. Her.* 5.16.3).

Christ the Perfect Priest and Sacrifice

The representative function of Christ in His priestly office is expressed in the imagery of sacrifice.[30] While the theme of sacrifice is applied to the work of Christ in other New Testament writings, the Book of Hebrews is the classic expression of the motif.

We have already seen that the purpose of sacrifice in the Old Testament is to expiate sin so as to make the offerer acceptable to God. Since the one who makes the offering identifies himself with the victim, he is symbolically offering himself to God. Since he is not perfect, he chooses an offering that is without blemish to represent himself before God and thus be acceptable on his behalf. Ceremonially, the divine acceptance of the holy gift implies that He also cleanses the impurity of the one who offers himself through a vicarious substitute to God. Oliver Chase Quick summarizes this understanding of the sacrificial system:

> The real intention of the old sacrifices for sin was that the blood of an unblemished victim, representing a stainless life offered to God in death, might be applied so as to remove defilements caused by sin, in order that man might draw near to God in worship, and communion between man and God be established.[31]

In the New Testament understanding as expressed by Hebrews, the superiority of the new covenant provisions lies in the greater perfection of the priest (because both sinless and fully human) and of the sacrifice (because voluntary as well as morally and spiritually perfect). The Old Testament sacrifices only provisionally, temporarily, and ritualistically took away sin. But the sacrifice of Christ by himself was final and actually efficacious to deal with the sin problem (Heb. 9:14).

One major difference between the Jewish ritual and the death of Christ is that the animal (or other offering) is given by man after he has symbolically identified himself with the gift. In the case of Jesus' death, it is a historical event with which men, by faith, subsequently identify themselves, and thus it testifies even more clearly that it is God's gracious provision. But that faith identification must

---

30. The Kingly office also embodies a representative activity as will be seen below.
31. From *Doctrine of the Creeds*, 233, quoted in Culpepper, *Interpreting the Atonement*, 151.

be made in order to appropriate the benefits of the sacrifice; it is not automatic.

Culpepper's summary admirably pulls these ideas together: "Because of the perfectness of his obedience, because Christ is the lamb without spot or blemish, his sacrifice is received by God. But because our lives are polluted by sin we dare not offer ourselves."[32]

We are now in a position to address more adequately the question of what it means for Christ to have "died for our sins according to the scriptures" (1 Cor. 15:3, KJV).

It is certainly true historically that He died for sinners. Throughout His ministry, Jesus identified himself with the off-scourings of the earth, tax collectors, prostitutes, and other sinners. Nothing incensed the "righteous" of His day more than this association. Furthermore, He virtually said that God was more interested in this class of people, and our Lord even suggested that they would precede the "chosen ones" into the Kingdom. He lived His life as the "friend of sinners." Eventually, no doubt, it was this identification that partly brought Him into disfavor with the establishment and led to His death.

But perhaps even more profoundly, it meant that God himself, in the person of His Son, was suffering for the sins of the world, that He was bearing their sins in His own bosom. It is certainly true that in order to effect a reconciliation between estranged parties, forgiveness must occur. And it is also true that the offended party who must forgive is the one who bears the cost most decisively. The deeper the love of the offended for the offender, the deeper the suffering involved in forgiveness. Forgiveness is not a glib affair; it entails inward pain. In a word, the one who has been sinned against must bear the sin. But if the one sinned against is God, how much deeper the love and how much deeper the suffering. Thus we may conclude that Jesus dying on the Cross is "God Himself . . . bearing the brunt and paying the price. . . . That is the atonement for our sins that takes place in the very heart and life of God, because He is infinite love; and it is out of that costly atonement that forgiveness and release come to us."[33]

If there must be a bearing of sin, and the holiness of God requires that there be, there are only two possibilities: Either we

---

32. *Interpreting the Atonement,* 153.
33. Donald M. Baillie, *God Was in Christ,* 177-79. The same interpretation is advanced in *God, Man, and Salvation.*

bear our own sins, or God bears them himself. Paul, both in experience and in his theological work, demonstrates indisputably the bankruptcy of the former course. Hence, if there is reconciliation between man and God at all, it must occur through the divine sin bearing. How do we know that this is indeed the significance of the Christ-event? It is the resurrection of Christ that is God's validation of this claim. By raising Jesus from the dead, God sets His seal of approval upon the mission of the Suffering Servant that the Son embodied in His total life and death. This is why Paul can say in 1 Cor. 15:17: "And if Christ be not raised, your faith is vain; ye are yet in your sins" (KJV).

The Intercession of the Great High Priest

The letter to the Hebrews lays special stress upon the once-for-all character of the sacrifice of Christ. This truth highlights the *finished* work of the Atonement. However there is also an *unfinished* or continuing aspect that Wesleyan theology has particularly perceived. This facet of the atoning work is seen in several ways. The doctrine that centrally expresses it is the so-called session of Christ at God's right hand. Wiley tells us that the intercession of Christ "teaches that His finished work of atonement was only the ground for the work of administration, which He himself was to continue through the Spirit" (CT 2:299). This implies, not that something new needs to be added, but that it is perpetually effective, covering the whole Christian life from its beginning to its final glorification.

John Wesley explicitly recognized the continuing work of cleansing that is an aspect of the ongoing priestly work of Christ. It is essential to the believer's continued acceptance with God. He speaks of this in plain terms:

> The best of men still need Christ in His priestly office, to atone for their omissions, their short-comings (as some not improperly speak), their mistakes in judgment and practice, and their defects of various kinds. . . . I believe there is no such perfection in this life as excludes these involuntary transgressions which I apprehend to be naturally consequent on the ignorance and mistakes inseparable from mortality. Therefore *sinless perfection* is a phrase I never use, lest I should seem to contradict myself. I believe, a person filled with the love of God is still liable to these involuntary transgressions.[34]

---

34. *Plain Account*, 53-54.

This ongoing work of sanctification is the New Testament appropriation of the cultic function of sacrifice, which was always for "inadvertent sin," precisely what Wesley was describing in this quotation. It is the view that informs the comforting passage in 1 John 2:1-2: "My little children, I am writing this to you so that you may not sin; but if any one does sin, we have an advocate with the Father, Jesus Christ the righteous; and he is the expiation [atoning sacrifice] for our sins, and not for ours only but also for the sins of the whole world." Furthermore, though the work is finished in the sense that the provision for reconciliation is fully and decisively consummated in the Cross/Resurrection event, it must be responded to. As Vincent Taylor puts it, "Man cannot accomplish his reconciliation with God, but he can refuse it."[35]

J. Ernest Rattenbury calls attention to this duality in the hymns of Charles Wesley. The finished work is reflected in the verse of "All Ye That Pass By":

> *What could your Redeemer do,*
> *More than He hath done for you?*
> *To procure your peace with God,*
> *Could He more than shed His blood?*

The unfinished or continuous work is implied in the words:

> *Him the true ark and mercy-seat,*
> *By faith we call to mind,*
> *Faith in the blood atoning yet*
> *For us and all mankind.*

And it breathes throughout the famous "Arise, My Soul, Arise," especially in the words "and sprinkles *now* the throne of grace."[36]

Our Identification with Him

The atoning work of Christ becomes efficacious for us only to the extent that we appropriate it by faith. It is not to be understood as a transaction between Jesus and God to which man is a spectator. He must become an active participant. This is not to suggest that he contributes something to his own salvation in such a way as to compromise the truth that salvation is the result of grace alone. This response is described by Paul and the writer of He-

---

35. *Forgiveness and Reconciliation*, 73.
36. *Charles Wesley's Hymns*, 188-203.

brews in terms of identification with Christ: We are buried with Him in baptism, we are crucified with Him, and we are risen with Him.

In His representative capacity, Christ becomes the Head of a new race of redeemed humanity, a "new Adam." To become identified with Him is to become incorporated in this new, corporate man. It involves being "in Christ." It is in this way that the Atonement becomes effective in individual life. Alan Richardson is undoubtedly correct when he observes that "the fundamental meaning of the atonement in the NT teaching is . . . incorporation into the redeemed humanity of Jesus Christ, through baptism into Christ's 'spiritual body,' the Church or Israel of God."[37]

Rattenbury finds this theme present in the Wesleyan hymnology as well. Christians are to identify themselves with the Christ who suffers, they "must share His sacrifice if they are to participate in His glory." One hymnic expression says:

Would the Savior of mankind
Without His people die?
No, to Him we all are join'd
As more than standers by.
Freely as the Victim came
To the altar of His cross,
We attend the slaughter'd Lamb,
And suffer for His cause.[38]

Since these themes involve the work of the Holy Spirit in administering the benefits of the Atonement, we will postpone treatment of them until later. They will appear in our discussion of sanctification, the Church, and the sacraments, all aspects of the work of the Holy Spirit in relation to the Christian life.

The Kingly Work of Christ

When considered in relation to His mediatorial work, the kingly office of Christ is normally restricted to His post-Resurrection administration. Thus Wiley describes it as "that activity of our ascended Lord which He exercises at the right hand of God, ruling over all things in heaven and in earth for the extension of His kingdom" (CT 2:214).

---

37. *Theology,* 205.
38. *Charles Wesley's Hymns,* 201-2.

However, for John Wesley, Christ's kingly office is an expression of His eternal Godhead, that is, it is grounded in the Trinity. But so far as His mediatorial kingdom is concerned, it has both a beginning and an ending (see *Notes* on 1 Cor. 15:24). This means that so far as His divine nature is concerned, His regal authority neither begins nor ceases. But since He rules in both natures in the Mediatorial role, His sovereign power must be bestowed on His human nature. When does this sovereignty begin?

Wesley holds that it is prefigured in David's kingship, and this relationship provides the basis for the New Testament's central claim that Jesus is the promised Son of David who fulfills the Messianic hope. Two major truths of Jesus' Kingship are foreshadowed by David's kingship. First, in David the promises of God to the patriarchs regarding the land of Canaan were realized by their descendants for the first time. By analogy, the promises of God to His people were actualized in Jesus Christ. "All the promises of God in him are yea, and in him Amen, unto the glory of God by us" (2 Cor. 1:20, KJV). The second is a corollary to this: All their enemies (especially the Philistines) were defeated and put "under their feet" by the Davidic rule. In the same way, Christ as King has triumphed over all "principalities and powers" (Col. 2:15).

But precisely when this Kingly office was actually bestowed is a bit uncertain. Clearly He demonstrated it in His miracles as He manifested sovereign power over the spiritual world as well as the world of nature. Whether this is to be interpreted as a manifestation of an office already bestowed or in a prolectic way is not clear, but since the miracles were real and not slight of hand, the former seems to have the most support. In either case the grand revelation of His Kingship clearly occurs in the Cross, Resurrection, and Ascension. It is here that He is publicly demonstrated to be Lord.

The Cross is the decisive encounter of Christ with Satan and sin. It was a battle that must be joined before the Kingdom could be established. Wesley says in his *Notes* on 1 Cor. 15:26: "Satan brought in sin, and sin brought forth death. And Christ, when He of old engaged with these enemies, first conquered Satan, then sin, in His death; and, lastly, death, in His resurrection."

Christus Victor

When Christ engaged the powers of darkness in mortal combat, it was as our Representative. Just as Adam was defeated in the garden in the first encounter, as the Second Adam, Jesus overcame the same evil force and gained the victory for us that we might recover what was lost in the Fall.

It is in this connection that the *Christus Victor* motif, so classically defended in the modern world by Gustav Aulen, comes into the picture.[39] Aulen has argued that this interpretation of the work of Christ is the truly classical view, preceding that of Anselm, which became so prominent in the medieval church. It certainly does reproduce some of the major themes of New Testament theology.

The apocalyptic dualism that provides the thought forms in which New Testament theology is cast sees the history of the world to be divided into two ages: the present age, under the dominion of demonic beings known as "powers," with Satan as the "prince of the power of the air" (Eph. 2:2); and the age to come, which is the Kingdom age. According to the teaching of the Jewish apocalypses, the age to come could only become a reality when God broke into history in a cataclysmic upheaval, bringing the present age to a close. However, the New Testament alters this pessimism with the joyful proclamation that the age to come has broken into history, not with tumult in earth and heaven, but quietly in the person and work of Jesus Christ, and the powers have been engaged and defeated at the Cross. This is Paul's meaning in Col. 2:15 as he draws upon ancient practices in warfare to depict this victory: "And having spoiled principalities and powers, he made a shew of them openly, triumphing over them in it" (KJV).

Now there are present in the world two realms, represented by these two ages. The apostle speaks of them in numerous ways. He describes those who are in these realms as either "in Adam" or "in Christ." In Col. 1:13 he gives thanks to God "who hath delivered us from the power of darkness, and hath translated us into the kingdom of his dear Son." G. Eldon Ladd rightly contends that the awareness of the coming of the powers of the new age, evidenced by the advent of the Spirit, is the center of Pauline thought.[40]

Earlier we noted that one problem for Wesley may have been the absence of an alternative to the satisfaction theory, which provided for an objective character in the Atonement. We suggested that one was not then available. This victory theme offers a viable

---

39. *Christus Victor.*
40. *Theology,* 374.

alternative that involves a truly objective dimension. It is not objective in the sense of a transaction between Christ and God, which is completely unacceptable to New Testament thought, but objective in the sense that something transpires externally, not dependent upon human response although only actualized upon such a response. On the stage of history, where the human problem of sin must be met, Jesus Christ came into mortal combat with Satan in his own sphere (this present age) and overcame him, thus making available to men the same victory over sin in the here and now and not just eschatologically.

W. M. Greathouse has contended that as an aspect of the redemptive work of Christ, the *Christus Victor* motif gives "Wesleyan theology a significant biblical and historical basis for developing a thoroughgoing Christological doctrine of sanctification."[41] Christ's victory over sin as our Representative makes possible, through faith in Him, our victory over sin. The victory in the Cross/Resurrection addresses the guilt, the power, and the consequences of sin, respectively in justification, sanctification, and glorification. Thus it is both present and future, sharing the same tension that characterizes all major experiential New Testament doctrines.

The Kingdom of God

The kingly office of Christ brings immediately into view the idea of the Kingdom. Few subjects have attracted more attention or been the object of more serious scholarship than this one, with significantly different results. It is universally agreed, however, that this was the central message of Jesus as recorded in the Synoptic Gospels. John Bright has furthermore argued convincingly that this is the unifying motif of the whole Bible.[42]

The meaning of the term "kingdom" involves the idea of "reign" or "rule" rather than a place and can be so rendered. In this it follows the usage of late Jewish thought.[43]

Although the term is absent in the Old Testament, the idea is present from the time of the Exodus, and some have argued that the idea of God as King is the central Old Testament concept of God. In the teaching of Jesus, it is depicted as coming into history

---

41. "Sanctification and the Christus Victor Motif in Wesleyan Theology," *Wesleyan Theological Journal* 7, no. 1 (Spring 1972): 47-59.
42. *Kingdom of God.*
43. Ladd, *Theology,* 63; Richardson, *Theology,* 84-85.

in His own ministry. John the Baptist announces that the Kingdom is "at hand," and in the beginning of His ministry, Jesus makes the same proclamation (Matt. 3:2; 4:17; Mark 1:15).[44]

The central question in interpreting the meaning of the Kingdom is whether it is present or future, or both. How one answers this question to a great extent determines his view of the future, since this is one of the most decisive eschatological categories.

A strong contingent of scholars have argued that the hope of the Kingdom has been fully actualized in the present. To this view, the term "realized eschatology" has been applied (C. H. Dodd). In its extreme form, it rejects any future coming of the Kingdom but sees all to be fulfilled in experience in the here and now. It is clear that there is some truth in this position. "Throughout the Synoptic Gospels, Jesus' mission is repeatedly understood as the fulfillment of the Old Testament promises."[45] However, it overlooks certain unmistakable evidences that there is a future dimension, yet to be actualized. Among other things, Jesus did teach His disciples to pray, "Thy kingdom come" (Matt. 6:10; Luke 11:2).

Other students of the Scripture have argued for a consistently future interpretation of the Kingdom. This has often occurred in radical biblical interpretation, being introduced into modern scholarship chiefly by Johannes Weiss and Albert Schweitzer. Rudolph Bultmann also held to this view. Such scholarship, notably Schweitzer, often connects this with the idea that though this was Jesus' teaching, in it He was mistaken, since the Kingdom did not come soon after His death as He expected.

Oddly enough, this view is shared by modern dispensationalism, a fundamentalist theology very popular among conservative Christians. Dispensationalism, like the popular hope rejected by the prophets of the Old Testament, equates the Kingdom with Jewish nationalism and since Jesus did not establish a political Messianic kingdom among the Jews at His first advent, they hold that this is what He will do in the eschaton (see Appendix 1).

---

44. Dispensational theologians have attempted to make a distinction between the kingdom of heaven and the kingdom of God. But a comparison of the Synoptic passages as well as an awareness of the historical situation makes this an impossible distinction. Kingdom of heaven is simply a Jewish idiom used to avoid the use of the name of God, which was held to be too sacred to pass one's lips. Doubtless, in some Jewish contexts, Jesus used the term to avoid creating unnecessary barriers. Matthew, who writes to the Jews, makes prominent use of the phrase for the same reasons.

45. Ladd, *Theology*, 65.

The soundest biblical scholarship, however, holds to a dualistic view that teaches that the reign of God is both present and future. It has entered history in the triumph of Christ over the evil forces of the spiritual realm but will be fully established at the Second Advent. The most meaningful way of describing this twofold interpretation is to speak of the Kingdom as *inaugurated* at the First and *consummated* at the Second Advent.[46]

This tension between the present and future simply reflects the basic structure of New Testament theology, which sees a present realization of the age to come but not yet a final banishment of the present age. G. Eldon Ladd, who did a Herculean task of developing the Kingdom motif of the New Testament, summarizes it this way: "There is a twofold dualism in the New Testament: God's will is done in heaven; his Kingdom brings it to earth. In the Age to Come, heaven descends to earth and lifts historical existence to a new level of redeemed life."[47]

The kingdom of God is both present reality and future hope. It is Jesus who both ushers it in at the beginning and will establish it at the end.

The Dark Side of the Atonement

Several of the themes introduced in our discussion of the Atonement have negative significance. While our major emphasis is upon the saving consequence of the work of Christ, there is also the stark reality that many persons do not avail themselves of these benefits. What are we to say concerning the result of such rejection? This raises the issue of personal destiny. If final salvation is the destiny of those who receive the gift of life, final separation is the end of those who refuse life.

In a theology of a limited atonement (Calvinism), provision is made for such persons in the plan of God. There are those who are elected to be damned as well as some elected to final salvation. This is referred to as "double predestination." But in a Wesleyan interpretation, a universal atonement is not coercive in its effectiveness but awaits faithful response. Thus greater agony should attach to the tragedy of ultimate rejection, since (unlike Calvinism)

46. Anthony A. Hoekema, *The Bible and the Future* (Grand Rapids: Wm. B. Eerdmans Publishing Co., 1979).
47. *Theology*, 69.

one cannot speak of the finally lost as somehow contributing to the glory of God. However, commitment to biblical truth prohibits the Wesleyan from succumbing to the temptation to extend the benefits of the Atonement to all regardless of their condition.

The *Manual of the Church of the Nazarene* affirms the basic options of destiny as follows:

> We believe in the resurrection of the dead, that the bodies both of the just and of the unjust shall be raised to life and united with their spirits—"they that have done good, unto the resurrection of life; and they that have done evil, unto the resurrection of damnation."
>
> We believe in future judgment in which every man shall appear before God to be judged according to his deeds in this life.
>
> We believe that glorious and everlasting life is assured to all who savingly believe in, and obediently follow, Jesus Christ our Lord; and that the finally impenitent shall suffer eternally in hell (Article XII).

It is to be noted that there is a judicious absence of speculation in these articles regarding any details of the final destiny of persons. This suggests that a theological treatment would be wise to do the same and be content with exploring certain relevant theological themes.

The first of such relevant topics is the wrath of God. We have discussed this in some detail on two occasions (see chaps. 6 and 11). However, we must extend those discussions to include the eschatological dimension of this symbolic assertion.

It is important in this connection to avoid compromising our central theological commitment to the biblical revelation of the nature of God as holy love. Many have questioned the idea of final separation on the basis of God's love. Such a misapprehension does not perceive the essential compatibility of love and justice. If justice is defined as "that side of love which affirms the independent right of object and subject within the love relationship,"[48] then it is recognized as that aspect of the divine nature that makes the divine-human relation a fully personal one, because it is the result of free choice. It does not establish a relation based on coercion or monergistic action but on attraction and invitation. Conversely, such love as justice—because it respects the subject—leaves to self-destruction that which refuses its overtures. Thus the

---

48. Tillich, *Systematic Theology* I:282.

wrath of God is the eschatological symbol for the work of love that allows its object to choose self-destruction.

The wrath of God is an eschatological concept in the New Testament in the same sense that most other themes are: There is both a present reality and a future actuality. Persons who reject the overtures of love and resist divine grace are under the wrath of God now but also will experience the "wrath to come" (1 Thess. 1:10; Matt. 3:7; Luke 3:7).

The theme that most centrally embodies this future dimension of the wrath is judgment. This teaching comes to expression extensively in the Synoptic Gospels so that, as Alan Richardson states, "There can be no doubt at all that Jesus taught the dread reality of the last judgment (e.g., Matt. 5:21f; Mark 9:43-48, etc.)."[49] But we must also be aware of the statement of Ladd that "it is impossible to construct an eschatological scheme from Jesus' teaching. He is concerned with the certainty of the future and the bearing of the future on the present, not with apocalyptic schemata."[50]

Judgment, like the wrath of God, is interpreted in the Johannine Gospel as both present and future. It is a present spiritual separation and a future separation at the last day. Both aspects are seen in relation to Christ, hence He assumes the role of Judge. Ladd's summing up of this truth is adequate:

> This future judgment has reached back into the present in the person of Christ; and the future eschatological judgment will essentially be the execution of the sentence of condemnation that has in effect been determined on the basis of man's response to the person of Christ here and now.[51]

Thus the judgment is a process that is going on wherever the Word of God is being proclaimed. By their acceptance or rejection of the gospel, men are judging themselves (cf. Heb. 4:12; John 3:18-20). By identifying themselves with the judgment suffered by Christ, men of faith have already experienced the verdict of the last day (see 1 John 4:17). Conversely, those who do not believe have sealed their doom, so that "the final judgment will in reality be the execution of the decree of judgment that already has been passed."[52]

---

49. *Theology*, 77.
50. *Theology*, 205.
51. Ibid., 307. The same dual significance attaches to the idea of "lost" in the New Testament. Men away from God are both lost now and will be eschatologically lost.
52. Ibid., 308.

In recognition of this, Wiley correctly says that "the supreme purpose of the general judgment is, therefore, not so much the discovery of character, as it is its manifestation" (CT 3:350).

Judgment then points to the reality of human accountability to God. When it is taught that followers of Christ shall "appear before the judgment seat of Christ" (2 Cor. 5:10), it may be interpreted as implying degrees of rewards in the final state. Or it may, more consistently with the truth of salvation by grace, be interpreted as a symbol indicating that all believers are accountable to God for their stewardship. For unbelievers, it stands for the truth that men's choices have eternal consequences, and destiny is directly related to present decisions and responses.

This leads us to the issue of final separation. The term used for this dread prospect is "hell." This is a rendering of the word Gehenna, which is taken from the Hebrew word for a valley south of Jerusalem identified with judgment (see Jer. 7:32; 19:6). The valley of Hinnom is thought to have later become the city's refuse dump where rubbish was continuously burning and thus became an appropriate symbol for final destruction. As Alan Richardson proclaims, "It is impossible to soften the severity of Jesus' warning against unrepented sin, and the sentimentalism which seeks to do so is a distortion of the teaching of Jesus and the NT as a whole."[53]

But we must constantly keep in mind the warning of G. Eldon Ladd that "vivid pictures of the punishments to be endured in hell, which are frequently met in apocalyptic writings, are quite lacking in the Gospels."[54] The language of Jesus (cf. Matt. 7:23; 8:12; 22:13; 25:12, 30) implies that it is separation from God that is the most appropriate way to speak of this sad truth, and that it is moreover appropriate to restrain ourselves from imaginative speculations and descriptions based upon noncanonical sources. Ladd further points out that since the imagery used to describe the fate of the lost involves both fire and darkness (cf. Matt. 10:28 with 8:12), and these are not homogeneous concepts,

> the central fact is not the form of this ultimate destruction but its religious significance. This is found in the words, "I never

53. "Hell," in A Theological Word Book of the Bible, ed. Alan Richardson (New York: Macmillan Co., 1950).
54. Theology 1:282.

knew you; depart from me, you evildoers" (Mt. 7:23; Lk. 13:27). Here is the meaning of destruction: exclusion from the joys and pleasures of the presence of God in his Kingdom. . . . Exclusion from the presence of God and the enjoyment of his blessings— this is the essence of hell.[55]

---

55. Ibid., 74, 196.

PART V

The Doctrines of God the Spirit

The Christian Experience of the Holy Spirit

The title of this chapter is intended to convey the focus of the final section of this theology. It also seeks to suggest that there is a distinctive Christian experience of the Spirit. It is our purpose to attempt to delineate the nature of this distinctiveness.

The Spirit is the doctrinal way of speaking of God's relatedness to the world, and particularly to the human spirit. It is the doctrine of the divine immanence, which is different from incarnational immanence but not unrelated to it, as we shall see. Hence, the history of Christian theology has spoken less of the doctrine of the Holy Spirit than about Christian experience. Although we refer to the Holy Spirit as the Third Person of the Trinity, this in no way is intended to suggest a third God, or that the experience of the Spirit is somehow something other than experience of God (see chap. 7, "The Trinity").

The Nature of Experience

In the famous words of William James, there are infinite "varieties of religious experience." This is no doubt the basis for the truth of

William Barclay's comment in the opening of his book on the Holy Spirit that "for the most part it remains true that our thinking about the Spirit is vaguer and more undefined than our thinking about any other part of the Christian Faith."[1] How does one account for this multiplicity and apparent fuzziness? In any case, the result is that many theologians have bypassed the task of attempting to speak of experience and restricted themselves to wrestling with more "objective" doctrines.[2] But the Wesleyan theologian cannot avoid the effort to come to terms with the bewildering plethora of experiences, even within the Bible itself, since experience is central to the Wesleyan perspective.

Is there a principle that might help us unravel this "blooming, buzzing confusion," all calling itself Christian experience? In chapter 3, in our discussion of experience, we touched on some important considerations and at other points also in discussing our knowledge of God. Now we will focus upon it more centrally in order to find guidance in discerning a normative Christian experience.

Experience has both a subjective and an objective aspect. It is always "of" something, even if only our own emotional states. There is a shaping influence that each pole has on the form or content of the experience resulting from the encounter between these poles. The more the empirical character of the object of experience prevails, the greater shaping influence it has upon the encounter. The subjective element is never entirely absent, however, even in the most mundane empirical observation.

In direct proportion as the empirical element diminishes, there is an increasing influence of the subjective pole upon the content and outcome of the encounter. It is our commitment that in religious experience, there is a real, objective counterpart to that experience, but obviously in the spiritual realm it is of a highly nonempirical nature. It is here that the incarnational principle becomes essential to Christian experience.

---

1. *The Promise of the Spirit* (Philadelphia: Westminster Press, 1960), 11.

2. It is interesting that Donald G. Bloesch, in his two-volume work titled *Essentials of Evangelical Theology*, has no chapter or section on the Holy Spirit. Dale Moody, in his massive *Word of Truth*, also excludes a special section on the Spirit, although several references are scattered throughout the book. Moody has written a monograph of the subject, however. Gustav Aulen, in his otherwise excellent systematic theology written from the Lutheran point of view *(The Faith of the Christian Church)*, has very little to say directly about the Spirit and virtually nothing about Christian experience except corporately as the church. This is a common tendency among non-Wesleyan scholars.

Herein is the danger of mysticism and various forms of the "inner light." Mysticism is here defined as the immediate, direct, and unmediated experience of the Divine (or Ultimate Reality).[3] Christian mysticism has often emerged as a reaction to institutionalism or sacramentarianism and as such has had a healthy influence. But in many of its forms it rejects the incarnational principle, whether of Christ or of Scripture, and thus opens itself to doctrinal and ethical vagaries. The tendency of this approach to religion is to set aside the intellect and even to lose one's self-identify, although this latter is chiefly stressed in non-Christian religions. Zen Buddhism is perhaps the most extreme example of an emphasis on experience as completely devoid of content.[4]

Profoundly influenced by Greek rationalistic metaphysics, mysticism tends to disparage the historical. It furthermore sees experience as the "flight of the alone to the Alone" and thus perverts the communal character of biblical faith. Hence it is true that "the NT contains a very slender showing of mysticism in the technical sense."[5] When Paul is charged with teaching a "Christ-mysticism," it must be remembered that insofar as this is a true designation, it is through and through incarnational. Consequently the New Testament experience of the Spirit (or risen Lord) is grounded in the reality of the historical Jesus.

What we are suggesting is that experience is blind. It was Immanuel Kant who helped us to see that what is presented to the mind is a "sensible manifold" that is received by categories not given in experience but brought to it. As he said in the beginning of his justly famous critique, "All knowledge begins with experience, but not all knowledge arises from experience."[6]

Whether Kant is correct that there are standard categories of the mind in terms of which all rational beings apprehend phenomena is a moot point. Certainly there are categories in terms of which all men experience spiritual realities, but these are not because of the structure of the mind but the result of education. We have previously found both psychological and theological rein-

---

3. See Rufus M. Jones, "Mysticism (Introductory)," in *Encyclopedia of Religion and Ethics*, ed. James Hastings, 13 vols. (New York: Charles Scribner's Sons, 1917).

4. Huston Smith, *Religions of Man*, 140-53.

5. Rufus M. Jones, "Mysticism (Christian, NT)," in *Encyclopedia of Religion and Ethics*, ed. James Hastings, 13 vols. (New York: Charles Scribner's Sons, 1917).

6. *Critique of Pure Reason*, trans. Norman Kemp Smith (New York: St. Martin's Press, 1965), 41.

forcement for this interpretation. Let us briefly review these insights.

In the work of Karl Rogers and Gordon Allport, it is argued that psychologically it is not the experience one has but the expectations one brings to the experience that determines expressive behavior. We also discovered that the theological analyses of John Fletcher seconds this psychological interpretation. His theory of dispensations emphasizes both cognitive and existential elements. The nature of the second is informed by the first. Daniel Steele, in his famous *Gospel of the Comforter,* recognizes the same truth in the opening observation of the preface: "This book is experimental and practical rather than theological. But since every scriptural experience must be based on the truth apprehended by the intellect, there should be a clear and scientific statement of this truth."[7]

Having identified a hermeneutical principle by which we can interpret the biblical material, let us now turn to an analysis of the experience of the Spirit as reflected in the canonical documents.

The Old Testament Experience of the Spirit

In order to gain a perspective on the understanding of the experience of the Spirit of Yahweh in the Old Testament, we must first note the significance of the term *ruach,* which is translated as "Spirit." It originally meant "air in motion" and thus could refer to either wind or breath.[8] Since the wind is often poetically referred to as the breath of God (e.g., Exod. 15:8; 2 Sam. 22:16; Ps. 18:15; Isa. 11:4), it is easy to see how the connection was made between "wind" and "Spirit," a relation that spills over into the New Testament (see Jesus' conversation with Nicodemus in John 3 and the Pentecostal narrative in Acts 2).

In particular, the mysterious, invisible, and unpredictable power or energy of the wind provided a paradigm to identify the activity of the *Ruach* of Yahweh. Hence when men (or women) were seized with a power from beyond themselves and behaved in commensurate ways, they were identified as men (or women) of

---

7. (Apollo, Pa.: West Publishing Co., n.d.), 7.

8. David Hill, *Greek Words and Hebrew Meanings* (Cambridge: Cambridge University Press, 1967), 205-6.

the Spirit. In the earliest sources, this was depicted as an unexpected, intermittent experience that energized otherwise obscure and less-than-competent persons to do mighty exploits in the interest of national freedom. This was a temporary endowment given in times of crisis and for the purpose of dealing with that crisis. In a word, it produced charismatic (Spirit-gifted) leaders (cf. Judg. 3:10; 6:34; 11:29).

Early prophecy in Israel also shared in this "Spirit seizure," which elevated the prophet's natural capacities to an intensity that caused him (or her) to behave in unusual ways. This Spirit possession was often, if not universally, precipitated by music and dancing (see 1 Sam. 10:6 ff.; 19:20 ff.).[9]

Saul of Kish, in the time of his preparation for kingship, is a classic example of this early picture of the experience of the Spirit of Yahweh (1 Sam. 10:6, 9-10). Some have suggested that the outcome of the seizure, brought on by stimulation within the group accompanied by music, was a type of glossolalia. However, one Old Testament scholar has demonstrated the uncertainty of this opinion and argued that instead of "strange utterances," the distinguishing characteristic of ecstasy was "strange actions."[10] It was this strange behavior that called forth the words of ridicule: "What has come over the son of Kish? Is Saul also among the prophets?" (v. 11).

Aside from the striking aspects of these few experiences that we classify as abnormal behavior, there is a distinctive feature of the Old Testament experiences of the Spirit that has great significance. Such charismatic (Spirit-gifted) experiences are chiefly limited to those who function as leaders in Israel. Eichrodt argues that the validation of leadership by charismatic endowment stems from Moses himself. Pointing to the difficulty of classifying Moses under any traditional category such as prophet, king, or other titles, he insists that his unusual combination of gifts enhanced by the initiating energy of the Spirit is the key to his uniqueness. In this, Moses places his stamp upon all subsequent claims to leadership. Eichrodt concludes:

---

9. Walther Eichrodt, *Theology of the Old Testament*, 3 vols. (Philadelphia: Westminster Press, 1961), 1:310 ff., discusses the role of the *sacred dance* in this phenomenon.

10. Charles D. Isbell, "The Origins of Prophetic Frenzy and Ecstatic Utterances in the Old Testament World," *Wesleyan Theological Journal* 11 (Spring 1976): 62 ff.

> At the very beginning of Israelite religion we find the charisma, the special individual endowment of a person; and to such an extent is the whole structure based upon it, that without it it would be inconceivable.[11]

This explains the central importance of judges and prophets having the power of the Spirit to demonstrate that they are sent of God. This is what Barclay's more popular treatment also suggests when he says: "The great leaders of the Old Testament are men who possess the Spirit, who have been possessed by the Spirit, and in whom the Spirit dwells."[12]

Later prophets did not generally manifest the same ecstatic traits or claims as the earlier prophets, but their authenticity was still verified by the fact that God put His Spirit within them and gave their message (cf. Num. 11:25 ff.; Mic. 3:8; Ezek. 2:2; 3:24; etc.).[13]

No doubt it was the principle of charismatic leadership that was the basis for much opposition to the institution of kingship in early Israel. The transition was bridged, thinks John Bright, by the first kings being charismatic leaders. David was the exemplar in this regard (cf. 1 Sam. 16:13-14; 2 Sam. 23:2).[14] There may be a similar significance attached to the anointing of kings at their induction into office: the hope that they would be charismatic rulers.

In addition to these more obvious endowments of the Spirit in the Old Testament understanding, there was also a less explosive and spasmodic endowment that inspired and equipped to more mundane tasks such as craftsmanship (Exod. 28:3; 31:3; 35:31). More permanent gifts of the Spirit's power are also suggested in a few exceptional cases, such as Moses and Joshua (Num. 11:17; 27:18; Deut. 34:9).

It is to be noted that these experiences that we have surveyed are task-oriented. Furthermore, there does not seem to be any necessary ethical accompaniment to the special endowments. Not all reflected the low moral tone of a Samson, but ethical stipulations are generally absent from the description of Spirit possession. One might argue that an exception to this is the classic prophets who,

---

11. *Theology,* 292.

12. *Promise of the Spirit,* 14.

13. An extensive contrast between the ecstatic and literary prophets is drawn by Abraham J. Heschel, *The Prophets* (New York: Harper and Row, Publishers, 1962), 2:131-46. Cf. also Isbell, "Origins."

14. *Kingdom of God,* 31 ff.

under the inspiration of the Spirit, decried unethical behavior among God's people and enjoined conformity to God's righteousness.

With this background, we may now note the eschatological dimension of the Old Testament understanding, which builds solidly upon these views. First, there is a chord of hope that longed for, and then predicted, a democratization of the Spirit. The distribution of the Spirit of leadership upon the 70 elders, enabling them to share Moses' burdens, was a foregleam. But its broader realization was longed for in Moses' magnanimous words in the face of jealousy over his own position as a Spirit-endowed leader: "Would that all the Lord's people were prophets, that the Lord would put his spirit upon them!" (Num. 11:29).

The prophecy of Joel explicitly envisions the sequel to the Day of the Lord being the universal outpouring upon all flesh (by which he meant "Jewish" flesh) in 2:28-29. It is important to note here that this vision relates directly to prophecy and thus stands in direct continuity with the central Old Testament understanding of the work of the Spirit as task-oriented.

In addition to these expectations there is a theme of hope that the coming of the Spirit in the eschatological age will bring moral renewal. In this regard, these passages move beyond the orbit of the usual Old Testament perception and doubtless grow out of a profound sense of need for such inner transformation for both the individual and the people.

In the Psalms, notably the 51st, there are prayers for inner renewal to provide strength to do God's will. In this psalm (v. 11), along with Isa. 63:10-11, we have the only instances of the phrase "holy Spirit." The usual Old Testament designation is "Spirit of Yahweh," but here we have not so much an anticipation of New Testament terminology as a recognition that God's Spirit is the Enabler to holiness. The phrase may literally be translated "Spirit of holiness." In Isa. 63:10, "'the grieving of the holy spirit' means the rejecting of the prophetic instruction by which God sought to guide his people towards holiness and righteousness."[15]

In Ezek. 36:26 ff., the priest-prophet implicitly recognizes the inadequacy of a restored ritual and, along with Jeremiah (31:31 ff.), anticipates an eschatological time of heart transformation. He ex-

---

15. Hill, *Greek Words*, 211.

plicitly attributes this to the operation of the Spirit: "I will put my spirit within you, and cause you to walk in my statutes" (36:27). The vision of the valley of dry bones (37:1-14) may also convey the same motif.[16]

Furthermore, there is a second strand of eschatological hope that relates the Spirit to two ideal figures: the Messianic King and the Servant of the Lord.[17] In both cases, a permanent endowment with the Spirit is a prominent feature (see Isa. 11:2; 42:1-4).

While there is a solid core of evidence in the canonical Old Testament itself regarding the Spirit-anointed character of the Messianic King (which is in accord with the validation of rulership referred to above), this theme is much more fully developed in intertestamental Judaism. Such a development is doubtless intensified by the rabbinic belief that the Spirit of Prophecy had been withdrawn from Israel, which explains the need for apocalyptic writers to attribute their visions to an ancient writer who lived during the prophetic age.[18] Hence there is, in rabbinic literature, a frequent reference to the Spirit of Prophecy.[19]

Building solidly upon Isa. 11:2, the rabbis depicted the coming Messiah as endowed with the Spirit of Prophecy. Through Him the Golden Age of the Spirit would return. Since the Spirit was withdrawn because of Israel's sin, His return would be accompanied by sanctification. "The evil impulse would be taken out of Israel's heart in the age to come, and the Spirit, as a power for moral renewal, would rest upon her."[20] The same motif is found in the "Manual of Discipline" among the Dead Sea Scrolls: "United through the holy spirit of God's truth, man shall be cleansed of all his iniquities: because of an upright and humble spirit his sin shall be atoned" (1QS 3:6-7). Hill comments: "Here we are in touch once more with the thought expressed in Psalm 51 that the powerful influence on man's life of God's truth and righteousness creates the desire for and will to achieve holiness through obedience and righteous conduct."[21]

---

16. See ibid., 213; George S. Hendry, *The Holy Spirit in Christian Theology* (Philadelphia: Westminster Press, 1965), 18.

17. We have already sufficiently addressed the issue and need not here further belabor the thesis that these two figures are not identified either in the Old Testament or post-Old Testament Judaism but are only merged in the person of Jesus Christ.

18. Cf. W. D. Davies, *Paul*, 215.

19. Hill, *Greek Words*, 227.

20. Ibid., 232-33.

21. Ibid., 240.

Thus the themes of a universal outpouring of God's Spirit, the Spirit-anointed ministry of the Ideal King, and the anticipated moral regeneration of the human heart are intertwined in Jewish expectations on the threshold of the New Testament.

Jesus and the Spirit

There are a number of issues that emerge in connection with this topic: What is Jesus' personal relation to the Spirit? What is His teaching about the Spirit? How does one relate the minimal reference to the Spirit in the Synoptics to the developed teaching in the Fourth Gospel? What are the implications of all these for the New Testament understanding of the experience of the Spirit? Obviously we cannot address in detail all these matters, since they would require a full-scale book in themselves, but we need at least to arrive at some preliminary conclusions.

The themes referred to in the previous section seem to be the focal point for the Synoptic Gospels' teaching about Jesus and the Spirit. They introduce the activity of the Spirit at crucial points in Jesus' life and ministry, apparently with the assumption that the meaning is well known and that it will readily be recognized that these incidents are evidence of the dawning of the new age. We shall look at the significance of the Spirit references at these junctures, but due to the nature of this work we shall not attempt to draw any extensive distinctions between the fuller references in Luke and the other Synoptics (Matthew and Mark).

The Conception and Birth of Jesus

We are indebted to Luke for recording the work of the Spirit in connection with the conception and birth of Jesus. Prior to the baptism of Jesus, the Spirit's work partakes, to a great extent, of the distinctly Old Testament mode. However, there is a direct relation to the eschatological hope of prophecy in that the Spirit is perceived to be initiating the new age of prophecy in these preliminary events. The Spirit is understood as the power and presence of God (Shekinah), functioning as the life-giving Agent in the birth of the One who will usher in the new age. This is emphasized by the numerous instances of the Spirit of Prophecy in the Birth narratives. These are signs that the eschatological age is dawning.

It is in this light that the central theological significance of the

Virgin Birth may be seen. It was never used by the Early Church as evidence for the Lordship of Christ. They always appealed to the Resurrection for support of this claim. It was not a part of the kerygma so far as any examples are recorded in the New Testament. But none of this provides any grounds for calling the validity of the Birth or the Gospel accounts of it into question. The Apostles' Creed, without much ado, affirms that Jesus Christ was "conceived by the Holy Ghost, born of the Virgin Mary." Hence we need not debate the facticity of it but simply inquire into its theological significance.

We may dispense, at the outset, with the proposal that the Virgin Birth was an expression of the idea that natural conception was sinful, hence the only way Jesus could be born free of original sin was by a birth excluding sexual intercourse. Such a theory, sometimes proposed, is based upon a nonbiblical view of human sexuality and, as in the Roman Catholic system, leads inevitably to the immaculate conception of the Virgin Mary and ultimately to a theory of perpetual virginity.

At a somewhat secondary level, the Virgin Birth witnesses to the truth of discontinuity in relation to the Incarnation. In the words of Isa. 53:2, he was "a root out of a dry ground" (KJV). Jesus cannot be explained as a product of natural causes, the apex of an evolutionary development, but only as the inbreaking of God into human history.

But in the scriptural context of Matthew and Luke, the primary emphasis is as an eschatological event. As perhaps the most poignant instance of the activity of the Holy Spirit, especially stressed by Luke, it reinforces that in such activity the new age was dawning. Interpreted in this setting, we may heartily concur with the scintillating apology of Alan Richardson:

> The doctrine of the Virgin Birth of Christ is an integral part of the theology of the NT. It expresses the truth that God has set in motion the train of events which will culminate in the final judgment of the world and the salvation of his elect; it is as biblical and as Jewish a doctrine as any belief that can be found in the NT. The birth of Christ is an eschatological event inhering in the New Age, and is itself a manifestation of the expected outgoing activity of the Spirit in the latter days. . . . Reluctance on the part of some modern Christians to believe in the Virgin Birth of Christ has been due to a failure to under-

stand the Bible and the nature of its testimony; ignorance of scriptural meaning always results in failure to perceive the wonderful activity of God (cf. Matt. 22:29).[22]

The Baptism of Jesus

In almost identical words, the three Synoptics describe the descent of the Spirit in the form of a dove, which had become a symbol for the Holy Spirit in late Judaism.[23] We have earlier noted the significance of the words "from heaven" as a conflation of the ordination formulas for both the Messianic King (Ps. 2:7) and the Servant of the Lord (Isa. 42:1). Thus this is an obvious fulfillment of the Old Testament hope of the coming of the Spirit as an endowment on these figures (see above). In Acts 10:38, where Peter is reciting the kerygma at the home of Cornelius, it is affirmed that at the Baptism, Jesus was "anointed . . . with the Holy Spirit and with power." There follows a brief reference to the signs of the coming of the new age embodied in Jesus' overpowering the "strong man" and "spoil[ing] his goods" (Matt. 12:29; Mark 3:27, KJV). It is of profound importance in understanding the subsequent developments in the concept of the Holy Spirit to recognize this merging of the two functions (Messiah and Servant) in the one Person; and furthermore that it is the merging of these two functions that is involved in the inauguration of the new age. From this moment on, Jesus is launched into the mission of bringing in the Kingdom.

In this connection we may note the significance of the message of John the Baptist. In announcing the Coming One, John said, "I have baptized you with water; but he will baptize you with the Holy Spirit" (Mark 1:8; Matt. 3:11; and Luke 3:16 add "and with fire"). Considerable discussion among scholars has ensued, debating whether this refers to a baptism of judgment or cleansing and precisely when it is fulfilled.[24] The words of Luke in Acts 1:5 make it quite clear that the fulfillment must be related to Pentecost unless one posits the existence of diverging traditions within the New Testament of which Luke is only one.[25] Whether it is cleansing or judgment is a much more difficult question.

---

22. *Theology,* 175-76.
23. Hill, *Greek Words,* 242 n. 4.
24. Cf. Dale Moody, *Spirit of the Living God* (Philadelphia: Westminster Press, 1968), 34-37; Hill, *Greek Words,* 244-47.
25. Cf. J. E. Yates, *The Spirit and the Kingdom* (London: Epworth Press, 1963).

First, it must be borne in mind that John's baptism was eschatological. The Baptizer was conscious of his role as a forerunner—one who prepared the way for the Greater One—and as such was also preparing the people for His coming. Hence his baptism symbolized preparation for the dawning of the new age. J. Jeremias argues that part of Israel's expectation was that, as at Sinai, she would be prepared for the day of salvation by a bath of immersion. Thus he concludes, "John the Baptist may have felt this purification of the people of God at the eschatological hour to be his task."[26]

Thus John's message with its eschatological dimension would anticipate the coming Baptism as fulfillment of an imminent hope. Such expectations are described in a fascinating manner in the Dead Sea Scrolls (1QS 4:20-21):

> Then God will cleanse by his truth all the deeds of a man
> And will refine him some of the children of men,
>   In order to abolish every wicked spirit out of the midst of
> their flesh;
>   And to cleanse them by a holy spirit from all evil deeds;
>   And he will sprinkle upon him a spirit of truth like puri-
> fying water . . .
>   Thus he will give the upright insight into the knowledge of
> the Most High and the wisdom of the sons of heaven.[27]

With regard to the question of cleansing or judgment, the best interpretation is to conclude that both are involved, but our concern here is to call attention to the element of grace or moral renewal that is clearly present in John's pronouncement.[28] From all this it may be suggested that in John's prophecy, the Holy Spirit is seen as both Agent of cleansing (moral renewal) and an endowment. Earlier we saw both of these to be united in the usage of Psalm 51. As we will have occasion to note later, both of these elements would likely be in the understanding of those who experienced the initial fulfillment of this prophecy at Pentecost, and those who interpreted subsequent "Pentecosts" (e.g., the Cornelius incident and Samaritan experience).

---

26. *New Testament Theology: The Proclamation of Jesus,* trans. John Bowden (New York: Charles Scribner's Sons, 1971), 44.

27. Quoted in Hill, *Greek Words,* 246.

28. See Willard Taylor, "The Baptism with the Holy Spirit: Promise of Grace or Judgment?" *Wesleyan Theological Journal* 12 (Spring 1977): 23.

The Temptation of Jesus

Mark says the Spirit "drove" Jesus into the wilderness to be tempted by the devil. Matthew and Luke soften this by saying the Spirit "led" him (Mark 1:12; Matt. 4:1; Luke 4:1). Luke further emphasizes that He was "full of the Holy Spirit." "Luke has a special interest in the fact that Jesus went beyond the prophetic inspiration of prophets. The prophets were 'filled' while they delivered their ecstatic utterances in the Spirit, but Jesus remained 'full.'"[29]

Here in the wilderness, as the newly anointed Servant-Messiah, Jesus encounters the demonic forces and, by the power of the Spirit, overcomes them by asserting His unqualified acceptance of the role of suffering as the nature of His mission. This is a clear affirmation that the endowment of the Spirit is to be implemented in terms of the Suffering Servant. Such spectacular displays as were often the result of the Spirit possession in the Old Testament are here being reinterpreted by another model of power.

The Ministry of Jesus

The same truth observed in the preliminary events is seen throughout Jesus' ministry, which is interpreted as being pursued "in the Spirit." Luke, in particular, emphasizes the work of the Spirit in relation to the life of Jesus. It is Luke who records how Jesus inaugurated His ministry with the claim to be a fulfillment of Isa. 61:1. He is the Spirit-anointed Prophet "whose mission is to bring in the age of salvation. . . . This important passage stands like a prologue to Luke's work: it is the charter of the ministry, the Messianic programme."[30]

A crucial encounter, recorded in all three Synoptics, is the conflict between Jesus and His opponents concerning by "what spirit" Jesus casts out demons. While there are differences among the accounts, the major thrust is clear. By inexorable logic, Jesus demonstrates the absurdity of ascribing His work to Beelzebub (Mark 3:22-26). He thus implicitly claims the power of the Holy Spirit in relation to the demonic realm. But this claim is also made explicitly in Matthew and Luke. Matthew records Him saying: "But if it is by the Spirit of God that I cast out demons, then the kingdom of God has come upon you" (12:28). Luke uses the phrase "the

---

29. Moody, *Spirit of the Living God,* 54.
30. Hill, *Greek Words,* 255.

finger of God" instead of "Spirit of God" (11:20). This critical term is derived from the Old Testament, where it is used of God's inscribing the Ten Commandments on stone (Exod. 31:18, in this setting perhaps suggesting moral renewal); and most graphically at the Exodus where the magicians attribute the third plague to the "finger of God" (8:19). In this Lukan context, it suggests that the Exodus power is being released in inaugurating the "new Exodus" through the power of the Spirit and thus illustrates the endowment theme.

Two major points need noting in this connection. (1) The Beelzebub controversy occasioned Jesus' comments about the sin of blasphemy of the Holy Spirit. Since it is by the Spirit's power that Jesus casts out demons, and it is this power that is the dynamic of His ministry, "he who attributes these exorcisms to Satan has committed blasphemy against the Holy Spirit (see Mark 3:30)."[31] Such blasphemy, Matthew records, "will not be forgiven, either in this age or in the age to come" (12:32). Note the significance of the language of the ages. This more than likely does not mean "time and eternity," but that he who does not acknowledge the power by which the new age is being inaugurated will not be able to receive the benefits of the new age when it is fully inaugurated.

(2) Second, it is of critical significance that Matthew conjoins with this account, and apparently uses it to give theological perspective to it, one of the Isaianic Servant songs. It is implied that the power of the Spirit, which is the subject of the subsequent discussion, is to be understood as having the character of the Servant.

The conclusion to this brief study of the Synoptic teaching concerning Jesus and the Spirit, is that Jesus is understood to be the recipient of the Spirit, which is the Spirit of cleansing (moral renewal)[32] and endowment whose coming is the mark of the eschatological age. Most crucially, Jesus' reception and exercise of the power of the Spirit involves a radical reinterpretation of the nature of this power. This is implicit in the union of the two anointed offices (Messiah and Servant) into one Person. Just as there was involved a reorientation of the Messianic expectation through this fusion (see above), there was likewise a similar reorientation of the

---

31. Moody, *Spirit of the Living God,* 39.
32. A variant textual reading of Luke's version of the Lord's Prayer (11:2) reads, "May the Holy Spirit come upon us and cleanse us," rather than "Thy kingdom come."

power of the Spirit that was subsequently to be bestowed upon the Messianic people. In a word, this means that in being filled with the Spirit (initially at the Baptism so far as His ministry was concerned), Jesus reshaped the experience of being filled with the Spirit—He gave it new content. This same meaning is apparent in the contexts and interpretation used by the Synoptic writers to speak of this special characteristic of Jesus' work.

When we turn to the Johannine Gospel, this somewhat veiled truth in the Synoptics becomes overt and explicit. The Fourth Gospel has an illuminating structure with regard to its teachings about the Holy Spirit.[33] There are 12 references, divided equally into two groups of 6 each. In the first 6 the reference is to the Spirit in relation to the ministry of Jesus, climaxing with the sixth (7:38-39), which emphasizes the Spirit not being bestowed until Jesus' glorification (John's shorthand term for His death, resurrection, and ascension). The second group refers to the Spirit's relation to the followers of Jesus, climaxing with 20:22, where Jesus "breathed" the Holy Spirit into His disciples following the Resurrection. In the first part Jesus is presented as the Bearer of the Spirit and in the second part as the Bestower of the Spirit. While these emphases are not hermetically separated, the distinction is generally valid.

John 1:32-33. This is the account of Jesus' baptism by John (although that fact is not explicitly made) and records some unique features. John is to recognize the fulfillment of his own work by the descent of the Holy Spirit in the form of a dove. That is, Jesus is authenticated thereby to be the Messiah. The distinctive emphasis is upon the Spirit's remaining in contrast to the temporary visitation on the Old Testament charismatic persons. Thus there is a much stronger emphasis than the Synoptics on Jesus' possession of the Spirit. This fact identifies Jesus as the One who will baptize with the Spirit. Jesus receives the Spirit in order that others may share His indwelling.

John 3:1-8. This passage is perhaps the most difficult to fit into the pattern suggested for the Johannine teaching about the Spirit. It can best be done by noting the "vertical dualism" that is characteristic of John and that is in contrast (not contradiction) with the Synoptic "horizontal dualism."[34] Hence the birth of the Spirit is

---

33. I am initially indebted to Dale Moody, *Spirit of the Living God*, for calling attention to this structure.
34. See Ladd, *Theology*.

"from above" (margin), which is to be preferred to "again" (KJV) in 3:3. Since Jesus himself is from above (8:23), it may be inferred that the Spirit "from above" effecting regeneration is from Him.

In Matthew and Luke the activity of the Spirit in relation to the conception and birth of the Messiah emphasized the creating power and activity of God bringing into being the new creation. There appears to be a parallel here to the Spirit, who is the life-giving power making man anew.

John 3:33-34. This passage quite explicitly refers to Jesus' possession of the Spirit "without measure" (NASB, Williams). While it is somewhat ambiguous as to the subject, verse 35, which reads, "The Father loves the Son, and has given all things into his hand," enables us to say with some certainty that it is upon Jesus that God bestows the Spirit completely.[35] Here is another emphasis on the work of Jesus as the Spirit-Bearer. The contrast in the passage is between the measured gift of the Spirit to John the Baptist and the unmeasured gift to the Son. This dovetails with the Johannine report of the Baptism.

John 4:14-24. In this passage Jesus is pictured as the Source of the Spirit and the Teacher of true worship in the Spirit. Jesus' description of "true worship" as being in "spirit and truth" is reflexive. Truth came through Jesus Christ (1:17), and it is in the light of this truth that Spirit-ual worship occurs. "This union of 'spirit and truth' is the most distinctive teaching about the Spirit in Johannine thought (see 1 John 5:7)."[36] One of the most characteristic Johannine titles for the Holy Spirit is "the Spirit of truth" (used three times). Hill argues that the language suggests that "'spirit and truth' are to be considered as one entity." He goes on to insist that the clue to understanding the passage is Jesus' affirmation that "God is Spirit," and that this is to be understood Hebraically rather than as a Stoic concept of spirit as a semimaterialistic substance permeating all things. He concludes: "When John says that God is 'Spirit' he is asserting his nature as creative life-giving power in relation to his people. To worship 'in spirit' is therefore to worship in the sphere of this divine activity, which was supremely manifested in Christ who is 'truth.'"[37]

---

35. Moody argues that it is Jesus who gives the Spirit, but this interpretation does not fit his own proposed structure and also erodes the distinction between Jesus' experience of the Spirit and that of His followers.

36. Moody, *Spirit of the Living God*, 159.

37. *Greek Words*, 288-89.

John 6:35-65. The life-giving power of the Spirit is stressed again in the discourse on the Bread of Life, as the explanatory section makes clear (6:63). Life is the Johannine way of speaking of the content of salvation. The Church has traditionally understood this passage to have a Eucharistic significance. Thus the flesh (Eucharistic elements) is but the vehicle of the Spirit. But by parallel, since the elements symbolize the body and blood of Christ, it is ultimately through Him that the Spirit is mediated to the believer. In this case it is His words that specifically are the source of life, thus of the Spirit.

There is no disparagement of the historical Jesus here (flesh) but the recognition that it is the earthly, physical, incarnate Christ who is the occasion for the knowledge of God in the Spirit. As G. Eldon Ladd says, "It is basic to Johannine theology that flesh becomes a vehicle of the Spirit."[38] The incarnational principle in relation to the Christian experience of the Spirit is thus explicitly affirmed while recognizing that flesh alone apart from the Spirit's activity is ineffectual.

John 7:38-39. We now come to the pivotal passage in the Johannine structure, and it must occupy more attention, since it really defines the perspective not only of the Fourth Gospel but of the entire New Testament. We are explicitly told that the bestowing of the Spirit upon Jesus' followers awaits the completion of His work.

One major interpretive problem concerning this passage needs addressing, since it bears on the theological issue at stake. There is a disputed question concerning the punctuation in verse 38. One way (Eastern form) refers "out of his inmost being shall flow rivers of living water" to the believer in Christ. The other (the Western form) relates it to Christ. The latter finds massive support among contemporary scholarship, and to interpret it this way makes the saying internally consistent with regard to the source of the outflowing Spirit. Raymond E. Brown calls attention to the difficulty of identifying the Old Testament scripture referred to in the text if the Eastern form is adopted, and he points out that there is a dogmatic prejudice involved in the Eastern hesitancy to accept the view that the Spirit "flows from" Christ. This is their rejection of the *filioque* teaching of the Western church. Brown suggests, on

---

38. *Theology,* 291.

the other hand, that it is plausible to refer the background scripture to the Exodus event when Moses struck the rock and water flowed from it (17:6). "This rock," he points out, "was seen in the early Church as a type of Christ (1 Corinthians 10:4) and therefore this background would favor the Christological interpretation of the source in John's citation."[39]

If this is a proper interpretation, we have a crowning moment in the Johannine teaching that as the Bearer of the Spirit, Jesus puts the stamp of His own person upon the content of the Spirit that is bestowed upon His followers. The remainder of the Gospel's teaching about the Spirit is developed in this light.

What is of profound and revolutionary significance is the affirmation that the bestowal of the Spirit awaits Jesus' glorification. Why is this the case? It must be said first that it is not because there is here an ontological beginning. Literally, verse 39 reads, "The Spirit was not yet." But to interpret this ontologically is to deny the biblical teaching about the Trinity. William Barclay has seen the implication clearly in these words: "It often happens that at some given point in time, and because of some action and event, men enter into a completely new experience of something which has already for long existed."[40]

E. Stanley Jones provides the best, most straightforward, and biblically soundest explanation of the issue this writer has yet found.[41] He suggests two reasons why the Spirit could not be given until Jesus was glorified. First, if the power of the Spirit was to be Christlike power, it was necessary to see that power manifested throughout the whole of His life from the carpenter's bench to the throne of the universe. It has to be seen in humiliation and triumph, on the Cross and in the Resurrection. Second, the disciples had to see that this power manifested in Jesus was the ultimate power. Such an insight would come to them in a shocking manner, challenging all their preconceived notions about the Messianic mission. They had "been nurtured in the idea that messianic power would be manifested in overwhelming display that would compel

---

39. *The Gospel According to John 1—12*, vol. 29 of the *Anchor Bible*, ed. William Foxwell Albright and David Noel Freedman (Garden City, N.Y.: Doubleday and Co., 1966).
40. *Promise of the Spirit*, 32.
41. *The Way to Power and Poise* (New York: Abingdon-Cokesbury Press, 1949), 42, 47, 55.

acceptance." But how different was Jesus' actual expression of power!

In a word, there had to be involved a total reorientation of the concept of the power of the Spirit of God. If they had been endowed with the gift of the Spirit before that gift had manifested its full range of meaning in Jesus, they would have doubtless become raging nationalists, swinging weapons like Samson of old. But they would never have recognized the power of love. "It would have been the Spirit of the Lord, but not the Holy Spirit."

The words of H. B. Swete provide an excellent transition from the first section of John to the second and thus to our discussion of the latter.

> The Fourth Gospel in its earlier chapters reveals the Holy Spirit as the author of the Spiritual life in men, and our Lord as the giver of the Spirit to those who will come to Him for the gift. In the latter part of the book, which contains the private instructions given to the disciples on the night before the Passion and after the Resurrection, the Holy Spirit is regarded in another light; the relation in which the Spirit will stand to the Christian brotherhood, the offices which it is to fulfil towards the future Church represented by the company assembled in the upper room, come here into view.[42]

This second section of the Gospel, as we have noted, contains six sayings about the Spirit. There are five *Paraclete* passages (14:15-17; 14:25-26; 15:26-27; 16:5-11; 16:12-15) and the climactic one (20:22) referring to the bestowal of the Spirit by Jesus upon the assembled disciples after His resurrection.

Rather than exegeting each passage, as in the previous section, we will here propose an overall thesis, which will then be demonstrated by a structured analysis of the teaching of these sayings as a whole. The proposed thesis would read: The Holy Spirit must be understood as inseparably related to the person of Jesus Christ. There are five truths that bear on this proposal.

The Spirit's coming is dependent on Jesus' going. This truth is initially proposed by the proclamation of Jesus at the Feast of Tabernacles (7:37-39) but is explicitly stated in 16:7—"Nevertheless I tell you the truth: it is to your advantage that I go away, for if I do not go away, the *Paraclete* will not come to you; but if I go, I will send him to you." We have already noted that the primary reason

---

42. Henry Barclay Swete, *The Holy Spirit in the New Testament* (Grand Rapids: Baker Book House, 1964), 148.

for this is so the completed work of Christ, including the Ascension, can give character to the work of the Spirit.

The meaning of the Spirit's name implies a continuation of the work of Christ. Much discussion has occurred as to the origin and meaning of the term chosen by Jesus to name the Spirit. Various translations include "Advocate," "Counselor," and "Helper." All are agreed that in today's linguistic context, "Comforter" is less than satisfactory. I would suggest that "Helper" is probably the broadest and best rendering.

The best way to see the significance of this term is to think of the situation to which Jesus spoke. The despair of the disciples over Jesus' announcement that He was leaving them was doubtless due to the dependency they felt toward Him. In their stumbling understanding and efforts to follow Him, He had always been present with words of encouragement and moral support, to say nothing of divine promises. For this support to be taken away could only produce frustration. Now Jesus is promising them to provide *another* Helper, One who would continue this work that He had been providing and in a more internal, consistent, and uninterrupted fashion. It seems safe to say that the thought involves a continuation of Jesus' ministry to His disciples.

The reception of the Spirit is dependent on a prior knowledge of Jesus. The world, Jesus said, cannot receive the promised Helper because it does not see or know Him. But "you know him, for he dwells with you, and will be in you" (14:17). It is noteworthy that this saying is introduced by identifying the Spirit as the "Spirit of truth." When this is related to verse 6 of the same chapter, we have an interesting correlation. Jesus says, "I am the truth" (NEB). In this light, "know" may carry the connotation of "recognize." The disciples will recognize the Helper when He comes because they have already become acquainted with Him by way of the Master, who models the nature of the Spirit—the Helper will be a Christlike boon.

Jesus identifies the Spirit's coming with His own personal, abiding presence. There is an illuminating interplay of pronouns in these sayings: "I," "Him," and "We." They seem to be used interchangeably, so that as A. M. Hunter says, "The Spirit comes not so much to supply Jesus' absence as to accomplish His presence."[43] The

---

43. Quoted by W. T. Purkiser, source unknown.

Spirit is not taking Jesus' place; His presence is tantamount to the presence of the risen Lord. Alan Richardson argues that this is true of the entire New Testament understanding, so that "the Risen Christ and the Holy Spirit are not differentiated, so far at least as their operations are concerned."[44]

Finally, and more generally, *The Spirit's work is decisively Christ-centered.* In 14:26, the Helper is sent by the Father in Jesus' name, and His function will be to "bring to your remembrance all that I have said to you." In 15:26, Jesus sends the Spirit and declares, "He will bear witness to me." And in 16:13-14 it is declared that the Spirit's teaching ministry is not of His own authority, but it will come from the person of Jesus: "He will glorify me, for he will take what is mine and declare it to you."

This brings us finally to the "bestowment" passage: "And when he had said this, he breathed on them, and said to them, 'Receive the Holy Spirit'" (20:22). The context is pervaded with the sense of mission. Jesus finds His disciples behind closed doors for fear of the Jews, having nothing of the boldness that He had promised them and that they would need to carry out His continuing ministry in the world. Greeting them with a Jewish *shalom,* He immediately utters a commission: "As the Father has sent me, even so I send you." Following the insufflation, He speaks again of the continuation of His own mission through them: "If you forgive the sins of any, they are forgiven; if you retain the sins of any, they are retained" (v. 23). In this setting, "the gift of the Spirit signifies power and authority to declare the gospel of redemption."[45] Ladd's words are pointed: "However this verse be interpreted, it means at the least that Jesus was bestowing on his disciples the same Spirit that had descended on him at his baptism and had filled him during his ministry."[46]

It is quite obvious that the language used here has in mind the original creation of man when God breathed into Adam the breath of life. This further parallels the initiating activity of the Spirit in Jesus' ministry as noted above.

Here we encounter a difficult problem of interpretation. How does this event relate to the Pentecostal outpouring? Many have identified this as the "Johannine Pentecost," suggesting that it is an

---

44. *Theology,* 112-24.
45. Hill, *Greek Words,* 287.
46. *Theology,* 289.

alternate account of the same happening. Ladd offers some potent arguments against this view: (1) It is difficult to believe that any Christian writing at the end of the first century did not know about Pentecost. (2) It is difficult to believe there were two impartations of the Spirit. (3) The Fourth Gospel itself teaches that the Spirit could not be given until Jesus' ascension, and so if this is the actual bestowment, then there would be two ascensions. (4) There is no evidence that the disciples began to carry out their mission until after Pentecost.

Ladd's own proposal seems to accord best with the evidence. He suggests that this "inbreathing" was "an acted parable promissory and anticipatory to the actual coming of the Spirit at Pentecost." While there are numerous parallels between the passages suggesting two reports of the same event, there is no overpowering reason why one cannot be promissory of the other.[47]

Early Christian Experience

The first accounts of Christian experience of the Holy Spirit are found in the Book of Acts, which is eminently a book of the Spirit. Twice as many references to the divine Spirit are found in Acts as occur in any other single book of the New Testament, and almost a quarter of the total number found in the whole New Testament.[48] Unfortunately, one of the most vexing questions in New Testament scholarship is the meaning of these experiences.[49] Dogmatism is therefore ill-advised. Furthermore, exegetical considerations should be given prior authority over dogmatic ones.

What clues should we look for in trying to identify the distinctive and unique features of these initial encounters? Two primary factors may be suggested. First, Luke's purpose in writing these accounts. The question of purpose suggests that theological perspective will influence the dimension of meaning that will be

---

47. Ibid.

48. J. H. E. Hull, *The Holy Spirit in the Acts of the Apostles* (Cleveland: World Publishing Co., 1968), 12.

49. Ibid.; W. F. Lofthouse, "The Holy Spirit in the Acts and the Fourth Gospel," *Expository Times* 52, no. 9 (1940-41): 334 ff.; G. W. H. Lampe, "The Holy Spirit in the Writings of St. Luke," in *Studies in the Gospels,* ed. D. E. Nineham (Oxford: Blackwell, 1955); H. B. Swete, *Holy Spirit;* Frederick Dale Bruner, *A Theology of the Holy Spirit* (Grand Rapids: Wm. B. Eerdmans Publishing Co., 1970); James D. G. Dunn, *Baptism in the Holy Spirit* (Philadelphia: Westminster Press, 1970).

overtly stressed, but that does not exclude other meanings that may be covertly present. Raising this question at the outset is an attempt to guarantee that we ask the right questions when we approach the text of Acts.[50]

Second, we should look for the understanding that informed the recipients of the Spirit. This clue is a specific application of the hermeneutical principle discussed in the first section of this chapter. This will enable us to identify such covert meanings as may be legitimately and truly present but not apparent on the surface.

Luke's Purpose

Within certain limits, there is an amazing degree of unanimity among scholars regarding the purpose of the writer of the Acts. A summary of many statements might read like this: Luke's broadest and primary intent was to demonstrate how, in the power and under the direction of the Holy Spirit, the Church, which originated as a Jerusalem-based, Judaism-oriented sect of Jewish believers, became a chiefly Gentile, worldwide phenomenon reflecting a belief in universal salvation based on grace alone.[51]

William M. Greathouse substantially restates this purpose in his commentary on Acts:

> Luke has one master purpose in mind as he writes Acts: to sketch the Spirit-empowered witness of the Church as it begins in Jerusalem, spreads into surrounding regions, and extends to the wide world. His particular concern is with the preaching of the gospel and the planting of the Church in radiating centers throughout a large part of the Roman Empire.[52]

There are secondary purposes that may also be recognized. There is an apologetic purpose to demonstrate that Christianity is not politically dangerous and that the violence that accompanied its spread was instigated by Jews and not Christians. Luke may also intend to help heal the conflict between Jewish and Gentile be-

---

50. Gordon D. Fee and Douglas Stuart, *How to Read the Bible for All Its Worth* (Grand Rapids: Zondervan Publishing House, 1982), point out the diversity of interpretations that occur when people approach the text of Acts with different expectations and/or interests, 88-89.

51. Fee and Stuart present a structural overview of the book, demonstrating how each major segment of the history is deliberately presented to reinforce the way in which this universalizing movement develops in stages. Ibid., 90-91.

52. *Acts,* New Testament vol. 5 in *Search the Scriptures* (Kansas City: Beacon Hill Press, 1954), 6.

lievers by his treatments of Peter and Paul, but the primary one is clear and unequivocal.

With this hermeneutical insight as a benchmark, we may exclude a number of proposed interpretations of Acts. It is not Luke's primary intention to provide a normative or normal pattern of individual experience. Obviously, there are implications to be drawn here, but to attempt to make this an exegetical principle will lead to mass confusion, since there is such a diversity of patterns present. Fee and Stuart point this out clearly:

> When he [Luke] records individual conversions there are usually two elements included: water baptism and the gift of the Spirit. But these can be in reverse order, with or without the laying on of hands, with or without the mention of tongues, and scarcely ever with a specific mention of repentance, even after what Peter says in 2:38-39.[53]

This understanding of Luke's purpose would immediately suggest the idea of mission, and that is precisely the theme that confronts us at the outset and overwhelms us with its pervasiveness. It is the motif that dominates Luke's thinking from the beginning to the end of his "history of early Christianity." This means that he would tend to stress the gift of the Spirit as endowment, one of the major strands of the Old Testament eschatological hope.

The opening words of the treatise provide a clear clue as to his intention: "In the first book, O Theophilus, I have dealt with all that Jesus began to do and teach." The implication is that the present writing intends to speak of what Jesus continued to do through the Spirit operative in His disciples. Jesus' last command to His disciples explicitly emphasizes this theme: "But you shall receive power when the Holy Spirit has come upon you; and you shall be my witnesses in Jerusalem and in all Judea and Samaria and to the end of the earth" (1:8).

The events of the Day of Pentecost focus on factors that highlight the universality of the message about the risen Christ (the Resurrection is what is to be witnessed to) and the power to proclaim it. The signs, especially the gift of languages, are unmistakably intended to focus on this truth. Finally, when Peter provides the explanation to the questioning crowd, he does so by quoting the Joel passage that deals with endowment for prophecy. It is illu-

---

53. *How to Read the Bible,* 92.

minating that there were other passages that could have been quoted (or reported as quoted) if other meanings were intended to be stressed.

It is this dominant theme that makes it possible for some interpreters to evaluate the early accounts of the experiences of the Spirit in Acts as little more than Old Testament phenomena. On the surface this might be a valid interpretation. However, given the situation, it is impossible to settle for this explanation as completely adequate. This moves us almost imperceptibly to the second consideration.

The Understanding That Informed the Recipients

Even the concept of mission had been transformed in the light of the fact that it was the continuation of the work of Christ. And this new understanding involved moral renewal (sanctification), because only by a radical reorientation of one's inner being, as well as his understanding of the nature of power, can the servant role be adopted. Thus we are quickly introduced to the second strand of the Old Testament eschatological hope.

As a result of this, we must now acknowledge a different meaning in Luke's use of being "filled with the Holy Spirit" in connection with the Birth narratives and his use of it here in describing the disciples' experience. Hull puts it poignantly:

> We may say for the moment that it was the same Spirit, the Holy Spirit Himself, who filled Elizabeth and Zechariah and the disciples also. But while Elizabeth and Zechariah were only able to feel that they were filled with the Spirit of One whom they had not seen, namely God, the disciples were aware that they were filled with the Spirit who had been in One they had seen, namely, in Christ Himself.[54]

This fact accounts for the ambiguity to which Alex R. G. Deasley refers as being present in the Wesleyan movement from the beginning, first emerging in a discussion between John Wesley and John Fletcher. Deasley correctly calls attention to the qualifications that Daniel Steele was called upon to make in his expositions of holiness theology. Steele explicitly recognized that the phrase "baptism or fullness of the Spirit" has multiple meanings: There is an "ecstatic fullness," involving a flood of peace, joy, and power that "may prostrate the body without cleansing the soul"; there is a

---

54. *Holy Spirit in Acts*, 68.

"charismatic fullness," in which one may be endowed with some extraordinary gift of the Spirit; and then there is an "ethical fullness," which implies entire sanctification.[55]

W. F. Lofthouse has argued that the novelty of the conception of the Spirit as it appears in Acts is not often noted because of familiarity. It is so new, he argued, that it is quite different from the Old Testament conception, nor could the Old Testament have suggested it. He proposes that it is the understanding of the Spirit that comes to expression in the Fourth Gospel, especially chapters 14—16, which provides the background for the understanding in Acts.[56]

Our survey has insisted that there is more to be said for the contributions of the Synoptic Gospels to the understanding of the Spirit in Acts than Lofthouse and other New Testament scholars allow; however, it is more implicit in these documents than explicit. Hence it is important to note the input of Jesus' last sayings, which significantly come on the threshold of His passion.

In particular we are here enabled to see the relation between Jesus' high-priestly prayer and the experience(s) of the Spirit in Acts. In John 17, the theme of mission is likewise inescapably present and can be avoided only by prior dogmatic presuppositions. The burden of Jesus' prayer for His disciples was that "the world may believe that thou hast sent me" (v. 21). In the course of the prayer He dedicated (sanctified) himself to the completion of His mission and prays that God will dedicate (sanctify) His disciples to the continuance of that mission. The carrying out of this mission involves far more than persuasive speech; it entails a unity ("That they may be one" [v. 22, cf. 21]) that can occur only through a metamorphosis of their nature. Thus the Pentecostal outpouring as well as subsequent ones have as their aim the moral renewal (sanctification) of the disciples so they may carry out this mission. The descriptions of the corporate life of the Early Church validate that Pentecost was clearly effective in accomplishing this result.

One of the crucial factors in attempting to identify the disciples' understanding of what the outpouring of the Spirit upon

55. "Entire Sanctification and the Baptism with the Holy Spirit: Perspectives on the Biblical View of the Relationship," *Wesleyan Theological Journal* 14, no. 1 (Spring 1979): 27 ff.
56. "Holy Spirit."

them meant is the charge of Jesus in Acts 1:4-5: "And while staying with them he charged them not to depart from Jerusalem, but to wait for the promise of the Father, which, he said, 'you heard from me, for John baptized with water, but before many days you shall be baptized with the Holy Spirit.'" What is the "promise of the Father"? Lofthouse has argued that since this is asserted to have been given by Jesus, it can only refer to the Johannine passages dealing with the promise of the Paraclete. Hence the promise of the Father is of the Holy Spirit, who is the Spirit of Christ. The content of Jesus has gone into it, with the result that those who received the Spirit in His fullness understood that not only were they being given a special kind of power to carry on Jesus' mission in the world, but they also were being transformed into a new existence that involved a through-and-through sanctification of their natures.

In addition to this, however, one could argue that included in the "promise of the Father" was the prophecy of John the Baptist. They were hearing this from Jesus, too. As we saw earlier, John's prediction of the "baptism with the Holy Spirit" involved both endowment and moral renewal or sanctification.

There may have been those, notably the 3,000, whose initial experience of the gift of the Spirit led them only so far as regeneration, but for those who had lived with Jesus and come through the 40-day training session about what had happened and what was about to happen, it doubtless led them to the full dispensation of the Spirit (Fletcher), and their baptism with the Spirit resulted in full or entire sanctification. We are suggesting that both the measure and character of the Spirit's work was the result of the understanding faith of those who appropriated Him at any point in their experience.[57]

Substantially the same position from much the same evidence was articulated by Alex R. G. Deasley. He concludes:

> I would suggest with great diffidence that what Luke is doing is using the phrase "baptism in the Holy Spirit" with the same breadth that the root *hagios-hagiazo* is used in the New Testament epistles. ... Luke's understanding of salvation, ex-

---

57. John Wesley, following "Macarius the Egyptian," taught that one of the prerequisites for the reality of the Spirit's sanctifying fullness was understanding of both need and provision. See Paul M. Bassett and William M. Greathouse, *Exploring Christian Holiness*, vol. 2, *The Historical Development* (Kansas City: Beacon Hill Press of Kansas City, 1985).

pressed in terms of the Holy Spirit, is in harmony with this [use]. However, that is not his prime concern in Acts. His concern is rather with the Spirit as the agent of mission . . . In keeping with this his language is correspondingly wide, and terms such as "salvation" and "fullness" can bear whatever degree of meaning is appropriate to their context.[58]

The bottom line of all this is that early Christian experience of the Spirit is interpreted Christologically whether in terms of endowment or in terms of moral renewal (sanctification); and that furthermore the result of the Spirit's filling is correlative to the recipient's understanding and appropriating faith.

Paul and the Experience of the Spirit

The mature expression of the fully developed New Testament view of normative Christian experience of the Spirit is found in Paul's Epistles. Alasdair I. C. Heron rightly observes that "in returning from the Synoptics and Acts to Paul, we find a richer conception and deeper exploration of the nature of the Spirit, of its activity, and of *its inherent connection with Jesus Christ*" (italics added).[59]

James S. Stewart's evaluation of Paul's contribution to the understanding of the Spirit is illuminating:

> In the primitive Christian community there was a tendency at the first—perhaps quite natural under the circumstances—to revert to the cruder conceptions of the Spirit, and to trace His working mainly in such phenomena as speaking with tongues. It was Paul who saved the nascent faith from that dangerous retrogression. Not in any accidental and extraneous phenomena, he insisted, not in any spasmodic emotions or intermittent ecstasies were the real tokens of God's Spirit to be found; but in the quiet, steady, normal life of faith, in power that worked on moral levels, in the soul's secret inward assurance of its sonship of God, in love and joy and peace and patience and a character like that of Jesus.[60]

One of the most discussed, as well as illuminating, features of Paul's thought is his close correlation of Christ and the Spirit.[61]

---

58. "Entire Sanctification," 39. Cf. Bassett and Greathouse, *Exploring Christian Holiness*, vol. 2, to see how baptism as understood and preached in the Early Church bore this same multiple connotation.

59. *The Holy Spirit* (Philadelphia: Westminster Press, 1983), 44.

60. *A Man in Christ* (New York: Harper and Row, Publishers, n.d.), 308.

61. See E. Earle Ellis, "Christ and Spirit in I Corinthians," in *Christ and Spirit in the New Testament*, ed. Barnabas Lindars and Stephen S. Smalley (Cambridge: Cambridge University Press, 1973).

Some have even raised the possibility that the two are identical in the apostle's mind. Passages such as 2 Cor. 3:17 seem clear: "Now the Lord is that Spirit: and where the Spirit of the Lord is, there is liberty" (KJV). But this identification is ontologically impossible in the light of the total Pauline teaching. "It would never have occurred to Paul that this personal Being, this historic Christ, and the Spirit of God were simply to be identified."[62] But this phenomenon, nonetheless, points to the close connection between Jesus and the Spirit in Paul's theology.

He can use interchangeably such terms as "Holy Spirit" and "Spirit of Christ"; and to be "in Christ" is synonymous with being "in the Spirit" (see Rom. 8:9-11). The Spirit that indwelt Christ has become the Spirit of Christ that He bestows upon all believers. A. M. Hunter puts it succinctly: "Paul does not identify Christ with the Spirit. The truth is rather that it is through the Spirit that Christ comes to Christians. Theologically, Christ and the Spirit are distinguishable; experientially, they are one."[63]

In the light of this insight into Paul's doctrine of the Spirit, it is easy to understand how his development of pneumatology, or synonymously "life in the Spirit," is ethical in nature, and the ethical dimension is defined by the person of Jesus.

We have earlier noted a dual heritage in the Old Testament hope of the Spirit: (1) endowment, especially in relation to the phenomenon of prophecy, and (2) moral renewal of the human spirit, or sanctification. Both these motifs are present in Paul, but it is the latter that becomes predominant.

The endowment theme is present in Paul's earliest writings. In the first extant letter (1 Thessalonians), he reminds the Thessalonian converts how "our gospel came to you not only in word, but also in power and in the Holy Spirit and with full conviction" (1:5). In an apparent parallelism he enjoins them to "not quench the Spirit" and "not despise prophesying" (5:19-20). But it should be noted that prophesying may not be automatically sound, even when attributed to the Spirit. The apostle's injunction to "test everything; hold fast what is good" (v. 21) undoubtedly suggests a testing of prophecy for distinctive Christian content. We are not

---

62. Stewart, *Man in Christ*, 310.
63. *The Gospel According to Paul* (Philadelphia: Westminster Press, 1966), 35-36. So also James Denney, "2 Corinthians," in *Expositor's Bible*, ed. W. Robertson Nicoll, 25 vols. (New York: A. C. Armstrong and Sons, 1903), 134.

told explicitly, however, what the criteria for such evaluation may be.

But in this early letter, he also reveals that he has brought together the concepts of the Spirit, sanctification, and the ethical dimension. In 4:3 ff. he calls his converts to holy living, which entails avoiding sexual impurity, and suggests that he who does not do so "disregards not man but God, who gives his Holy Spirit to you." Thus on the very threshold of his literary efforts, he reflects the correlation that informs his most mature thought: Sanctification is the work of the Spirit, and its goal is the production of ethical character seen in terms of Christlikeness (cf. also 2:13).

What Paul is doing in his work is elaborating the full implications of life in the new age. In the Gospels it was announced; in the Acts its dawning was celebrated; in the Epistles its implications are spelled out. Hence Paul generally speaks about the new life "in Christ" or "in the Spirit," rather than propounding theological propositions about the nature of or person of the Spirit. This is in accord with the focus that we are attempting to convey by the title of this chapter and its development. There are two realms of existence: life in the Spirit (in Christ) and life in the flesh (in Adam). These represent existence in the new age (aeon) and the old aeon respectively. As Herman Ridderbos says:

> The contrast, so constitutive for Paul's preaching, between Spirit and flesh is not to be taken as a metaphysical or anthropological, but as a redemptive-historical contrast, namely, as the two dominating principles of the two aeons marked off by the appearance of Christ.[64]

Although teachings about life in the Spirit are present in all Paul's letters with a plethora of implications, in four of them (1 and 2 Corinthians; Galatians; Romans) *pneuma* is a key term, and they provide us with bountiful material related to the question herein being explored.

The basic datum of Paul's understanding of "becoming a believer" is the gift of the Spirit. He assumes this fact in all discussions (cf. Rom. 8:9; Gal. 4:6; 1 Thess. 1:4-6; Phil. 2:1). In his theology this gift accompanies the acceptance of the preaching of the crucified Savior (see Gal. 3:1-5). It is thus that converts become *oi pneumatikoi* or have pneumatic experience. The implication, not always seen by his converts, is that the word of the gospel gives

---

64. *Paul,* 215.

content to their pneumatic encounter and subsequent life-style. Hence, in fulfillment of the Old Testament hopes, the church is a charismatic community resulting from a democratization of the Spirit. This is simply an extension of the theology of Acts.

It is furthermore clear that the gift of the Spirit is not an un-ambiguous phenomenon. Paul's two most controversial church sit-uations (Corinth and Galatia) revolved around perverted under-standings of the Spirit-filled life. In Corinth it led to "libertinism," whereas in Galatia it led to "nomism."[65]

The Corinthian problems brought Paul face-to-face with a sit-uation in which the work of the Spirit was identified with less-than-normative Christian manifestations. It interpreted the mean-ing of spirituality in terms of gifts, especially the more spectacular ones. It is altogether possible that the so-called glossolalia was a reproduction of the mantic seizures common in the pagan religions in Corinth. The Spirit-filled life was even seen to be consistent with outbroken immorality (see 1 Corinthians 5). It is noteworthy that in connection with the gifts (not the immorality), Paul does not reject the claim that the Spirit is at work, but rather calls for a more adequate understanding of what the true character of the Spirit's work should be.[66] What we see in Corinth is a confrontation be-tween normative and subnormative Christian spirituality. Corin-thian piety saw spirituality in terms of charismatic signs and gifts; Paul saw normative spirituality in terms of love (1 Corinthians 13).

At Galatia, it seems that the Christians there found life in the Spirit as they understood it to be insufficient to guard against the flesh and hence were tempted to resort to the Mosaic law as a means of avoiding libertinism. Here Paul had to argue for the ade-quacy of the Spirit as an ethical principle, so one did not have to resort to legalism. But this involved developing a Christological understanding of the Spirit-filled life.

In particular, it is to the Galatians that Paul enumerates the fruit of the Spirit and notes that "against such there is no law" (5:23). The classic words of Friedrich Schleiermacher that "the fruit of the Spirit are the virtues of Christ" capture splendidly the thrust

---

65. The issues here were greatly clarified for me by David John Lull, *The Spirit in Galatia* (Chico, Calif.: Scholar's Press, 1980).

66. For a fascinating exegetical study of I Corinthians 14 that shows how Paul seeks to eliminate the practice of glossolalia by demonstrating the superiority of the gift of prophecy over the gift of tongues, see Charles D. Isbell, "Glossolalia and Propheteialaia," *Wesleyan Theological Journal* 10 (Spring 1975): 15 ff.

of what Paul is saying. It is Christ who gives content to the fruit, and therefore life in the Spirit, rightly understood, cannot lead to either life after the flesh or life under the law.[67]

Paul's teaching about the Spirit has many ramifications for further theologizing about both personal and corporate Christian experience. We will postpone analyzing these until an appropriate context in the theological structure. We may simply conclude that for this great apostle, the Spirit is always conceived ethically, and the ethical content is the character of Christ.

The words of C. H. Dodd capture the crucial significance of Paul's virtual identification of the experience of the Spirit with the experience of the indwelling Christ:

> It saved Christian thought from falling into a non-moral, half-magical conception of the supernatural in human experience, and it brought all "spiritual" experience to the test of the historical revelation of God in Christ.[68]

In conclusion, this survey of the biblical accounts and teachings concerning the experience of the Spirit has solidly supported the thesis propounded at the outset of the chapter. The sweep of biblical revelation reflects a clear pattern of a developing understanding of experience with a pronounced emphasis emerging in the New Testament on the necessity for a distinctive revelation as prerequisite for the eschatological bestowment of the Spirit. Following this clue, all theologizing about the Holy Spirit that is informed by biblical revelation will take seriously this Christological character and insist that all facets of Christian experience be evaluated by this Christological criterion. Since the unique work of the Holy Spirit envisioned in the New Testament is *sanctification* seen in its broadest and deepest meaning, a Christian theology of sanctification will be Christological in character. Or to say the same thing differently, New Testament pneumatology is through and through Christological.

---

67. For a devotional discussion of the fruit from this perspective, see the author's *Fruit of the Spirit* (Kansas City: Beacon Hill Press of Kansas City, 1983).
68. *Romans*, 140.

The Work of the Holy Spirit

The thesis proposed in the last chapter entails an understanding of the divine-human relation that is synergistic in nature. This is in contrast to a monergistic interpretation, which sees the Spirit seizing persons and producing certain results more or less automatically, irrespective of the person's nature, understanding, or input. In such cases men become inert beings rather than rational, active partners in the encounter. In the synergistic view there is a "division of labor" between the Spirit and the human subject, so that one does not need to explain all Spirit-induced phenomena exclusively in supernatural terms (if not magical). Wesleyan theology is distinctly committed to this theological perspective and thus should be distinguished from a popular monergistic understanding. It should be carefully noted, however, that this is a "synergism of grace" and not a Pelagian denial of original sin.

Ned B. Stonehouse, a consistent Reformed scholar, recognizes this distinction and argues for a monergistic activity of the Spirit in the Book of Acts. He says:

> The baptism with the Spirit on that day [Pentecost] constituted a unilateral, eschatological action on the part of Christ, as immediate and miraculous as the resurrection of Jesus. If human cooperation or a human response had been indicated as being of the essence of what took place, the foundational sig-

nificance of Pentecost would have been obliterated or obscured.

Earlier in the same article, he had suggested that an alternate
understanding would "have a Pelagian flavor," thus reflecting the
typical Reformed misunderstanding of the synergistic view as it is
developed within a Wesleyan context.[1]

This discussion is intended to point to a fundamental commitment of Wesleyan theology in interpreting the work of the Holy
Spirit. Original sin, as stated above, is taken with great seriousness,
but the doctrine of prevenient grace, as a universal as well as a
particular gift, grants personhood to all fallen men, which includes
freedom, the capacity for genuine (not coerced) relationships, rationality, and individuality even within the divine-human encounter. This commitment gives certain distinctive characteristics to the
various works of the Holy Spirit in relation to the human spirit.

Traditionally, treatises on the work of the Spirit have included
a cosmological section. While it is true that there is a minimal reference to the Spirit's activity in the creation, it is very minimal, and
the Bible's focus is definitely on the divine Spirit-human spirit correlation. In fact, there is only one passage in the Old Testament
(Gen. 1:2) where the *Ruach* of God is clearly brought into association with cosmological activity.[2] If there are allusions to this in the
New Testament, it is only using the creation statement as an analogue for the Spirit's function in re-creating the human spirit.

Hence we shall restrict our discussion of the work of the Spirit
to those unique functions that impinge upon human persons. We
have previously discussed the function of the Spirit in relation to
inspiration and thus will forgo any additional comments.[3] We have
also fully explored the concept of prevenient grace (which is synonymous with the work of the Spirit) in relation to revelation and
shall likewise bypass further discussion. Our focus in this chapter
shall be upon the Spirit's work directly related to salvation in its
broadest meaning, and we shall divide the treatment into two ma-

---

1. "The Gift of the Spirit," *Westminster Theological Journal* 13, no. 1 (November
1950): 2, 6.
2. See Hill, *Greek Words*, 213.
3. We are referring here to the inspiration of Scripture. John Wesley used the term
inspiration to refer to the general ministry of the Holy Spirit in the Christian life. See
Starkey, *Work of the Holy Spirit*, 17.

jor sections: (1) The Spirit's Work in Preparation for Salvation, and (2) The Spirit's Work in the Process of Salvation.[4]

Preparation for Salvation

Most of the New Testament notes about the Holy Spirit refer to His work in relation to the believer.[5] However, there is also a recognition that an aspect of His executive function relates to the world of unbelievers. We have previously noted the implications of this in terms of common grace and saw the work of prevenient grace being the ground of all goodness in unregenerate persons, a restraining force. Here we are to consider the Spirit's work that is specifically intended to lead to salvation.

Awakening[6]

The first step toward salvation is self-awareness, and this is created by the Spirit. The commitment of Wesleyan theology here is that the awakening activity of the Spirit is universal in its scope. This stands in contrast to the selectivity of the Calvinistic understanding that implies that the awakening work is only directed toward the elect.[7]

Wesley is, however, in no sense a Pelagian. The natural man is totally devoid of any capacity to turn to God on his own initiative.

---

4. The term *process* used here is not intended to convey the idea that salvation is a process so as to deny decisive moments but to include the whole scope of phenomena included under the generic term *salvation*.

5. See Purkiser, Taylor, and Taylor, *God, Man, and Salvation*, 430.

6. "Awakening is a term used in theology to denote that operation of the Holy Spirit by which men's minds are quickened to a consciousness of their lost estate." *CT* 2:341.

7. This is said under the assumption that we are referring to an awakening that has salvation as its goal. There is in the Calvinistic tradition the recognition of a phenomenon known as "temporary faith," which is among the nonelect but does not lead to final salvation. This cannot be called awakening in the Wesleyan or even Calvinistic sense. Calvin has an enlightening paragraph reflecting his position clearly: "Yet this first function of the law is exercised also in the reprobate. For although they do not proceed so far with the children of God as to be renewed and bloom again in the inner man after the abasement of their flesh, but are struck dumb by the first terror and lie in despair, nevertheless, the fact that their consciences are buffeted by such waves serves to show forth the equity of the divine judgment. For the reprobate always freely desire to evade God's judgment. Now, although that judgment is not yet revealed, so routed are they by the testimony of the law and of conscience, that they betray in themselves what they have deserved." *Institutes* 2.7.9. A thorough study of the phenomenon of "temporary faith" from the Calvinistic perspective is R. T. Kendall, *Calvin and English Calvinism to 1649* (Oxford: Oxford University Press, 1979).

However, "natural man" is a logical abstraction, since "no man living is without some preventing grace, and every degree of grace is a degree of life."[8] Thus the awakening function of the Spirit is operative in the lives of all men, for

> there is no man that is in a state of mere nature; there is no man, unless he has quenched the Spirit, that is wholly void of the grace of God. No man living is entirely destitute of what is vulgarly called *natural conscience*. But this is not natural: It is more properly termed, *preventing grace*. Every man has a greater or less measure of this, which waiteth not for the call of man. Every one has, sooner or later, good desires; although the generality of men stifle them before they can strike deep root, or produce any considerable fruit. Every one has some measure of that light, some faint glimmering ray, which, sooner or later, more or less, enlightens every man that cometh into the world. And every one, unless he be one of the small number whose conscience is seared as with a hot iron, feels more or less uneasy when he acts contrary to the light of his own conscience. So that no man sins because he has not grace, but because he does not use the grace which he hath.[9]

From this quotation, it is apparent that the awakening work of the Spirit occurs at the most universal level in terms of conscience. "Conscience" Wesley defined as "that faculty whereby we are at once conscious of our own thoughts, words, and actions; and of their merit or demerit, of their being good or bad; and, consequently, deserving either praise or censure."[10] It is, in essence, an act of self-awareness in relation to our conceptions of right and wrong.

Wesley explicitly recognizes the fundamental truth about conscience: that its cognitive content is always relative to whatever sources have informed it. He argues that there are some basic universal distinctions recognized by conscience "unless blinded by the prejudices of education," but this implicitly acknowledges the informing function of education. Hence, he can admit great variety in the cognitive aspect of conscience that depends upon "education and a thousand other circumstances."[11]

Oswald Chambers, consistent with this view, rejects the idea that conscience is the voice of God because "if conscience were the

---

8. *Letters* 6:239.
9. *Works* 6:512.
10. Sermon "On Conscience," *Works* 7:187.
11. Ibid.

voice of God, it would be the same in everyone." And that is patently not the case.[12]

We may say that formally conscience is the work of the Spirit (prevenient grace), but that materially it is the result of background, experience, and education. In other words, the content is learned. It is thus in accord with the synergistic interpretation of the Spirit's activity proposed above. Consequently, through the work of the Holy Spirit, a person is awakened to the disparity between his behavior and his own recognized criteria of rightness and hence is stimulated to seek to bring the two into conformity. Here we have the correlative to the theology of general revelation, which was developed fully in chapter 5.

Beyond this preliminary work, there is a more normative work of awakening that ties this activity overtly to the work of Jesus Christ, just as the universal prevenience of grace is grounded in Christology. This is seen when we turn to the passage in John 16:8-11, which speaks explicitly of the "Helper's" work in the world of unbelievers.

Unfortunately the meaning of this passage is obscure, and there is considerable difference among interpreters as to its meaning.[13] There are two basic insights, however, that can be established: (1) the primary reference is to those who put Jesus to death; and (2) the reference is to the witnessing/preaching of those whom the Paraclete will indwell. From this we must then proceed to identify the theological significance that is universally applicable.

One problematic is the significance of the term *elenchein*, which is variously translated "convict," "convince," "expose," and similar words. Using the principle that it must make sense when applied to all three instances of its use, it seems that "convince" is much the better choice. With this brief reference, we propose the following interpretation.

Through the preaching/witnessing of the disciples (then and now) the Spirit convinces the unbeliever of his sin in relation to the

---

12. "Conscience," in *The Philosophy of Sin* (London: Simpkins and Marshall, 1949), 61.

13. Barnabas Lindars declares that "John has sacrificed clarity to gain an artificial balance of clauses." *The Gospel of John*, in *The New Century Bible Commentary*, New Testament ed. Matthew Black (Grand Rapids: Wm. B. Eerdmans Publishing Co., 1981), 500.

crucified Christ. That is, it convinces him of his need for salvation, that he is in sin, that he is lost, and that this is the direct result of the rejection of Christ. As B. F. Westcott rightly observes, "The want of belief in Christ when He is made known, lies at the root of all sin, and reveals its nature."[14] The mere proclamation of the Word is thus seen not to be in and of itself effective to awaken the sinner, but the Word enlivened and applied by the Spirit. This alone can cause the person to recognize himself as a sinner and cry out, "Woe is me!"

If the first aspect of the Spirit's convincing work concerns the need for salvation, the second points to its source: the crucified Christ. The path Jesus chose, we have noted on several occasions, was a stumbling block to the people of His own day. To claim that salvation is available through believing in a man dying as a criminal on a cross, which even the Old Testament designated as "cursed" (Deut. 21:23), was a scandal of the highest order. It was the Resurrection that was God's validation of this plan of salvation. If Jesus had remained to appear personally in His resurrected body to all men, that would doubtless have served to verify this; but He went to the Father, and it remained for His followers to proclaim the message that the Crucified One was the Source of salvation. It was this righteousness (vindication) of which the Spirit must convince the world through the preaching of the Cross.

The third work of convincing relates to the possibility of salvation and sits solidly in the theological structure of the New Testament. The present age was under the dominion of Satan, who is the "ruler of this age" (cf. 2 Cor. 4:4; Eph. 2:2, NIV). Man can be rescued from his dominion only when Satan is overpowered and judged. It is the central New Testament commitment that at the Cross, Jesus decisively bound the strong man and spoiled his goods (Matt. 12:29; Mark 3:27); and now it is possible for his subjects to go free, to avail themselves, by faith, of the judgment that has already occurred at the Cross and find deliverance from bondage. Thus they would not fear to face the judgment to come because they have already stood there proleptically and been acquitted (see John 12:31-33).

What is crucial in all this is that the awakening work of the

---

14. *The Gospel According to John* (Grand Rapids: Wm. B. Eerdmans Publishing Co., 1967).

Spirit occurs always in relation to Jesus Christ. And it occurs as He is preached by the witnesses to the Resurrection.

In an earlier discussion of gospel and law, we observed that both Wesley and the New Testament see the law as the means that the Spirit uses to accomplish this awakening. This, we argued, is a principle that simply implies that man must hear the bad news before he is ready to hear the Good News. It does not necessarily mean that there must be a proclamation of the Mosaic law (or any other set of rules) per se before a preparation can be made for the gospel. But on the premise that the law is uniquely embodied in Jesus Christ, we did see that the preaching of Christ in New Testament terms is at the same time the preaching of the law and the gospel. Hence the preaching of Christ is the vehicle through which the Spirit can most effectively and normatively accomplish His work of awakening.

Oswald Chambers sees this point in terms of conscience. He compares conscience to the eye and says:

> The eye in the body records exactly what it looks at. The eye simply records, and the record is according to the light thrown on what it looks at. Conscience is the eye of the soul which looks out on what it is taught is God, and how conscience records depends entirely upon what light is thrown upon God. Our Lord Jesus Christ is the only true light on God. When a man sees Jesus Christ he does not get a new conscience, but a totally new light is thrown upon God, and conscience records accordingly, with the result that he is absolutely upset by conviction of sin.[15]

What we are here discussing is what is traditionally spoken of in theology under the rubric of the "call." Addressing it in these terms, H. Orton Wiley distinguishes between the universal call, which is that secret influence exerted upon the consciences of man, apart from the revealed Word as found in Holy Scriptures, and the direct or immediate call, which refers to that which is made through the Word of God revealed to mankind. He further compares these to the distinction between general and special revelation.

In these terms the idea is also directly related to the concepts of election and predestination. The latter is the gracious purpose of God to save mankind from utter ruin, and election is God's universal choice of all men, which awaits their uncoerced response. "The

---

15. See n. 12 above.

elect are chosen, not by absolute decree, but by acceptance of the conditions of the call" (*CT* 2:334-40).

Repentance

When the awakening work of the Spirit is properly responded to, it results in repentance. In fact, it may even be equated with repentance (see below). To attempt to deal with this subject independently of the theme of faith is to falsify it; thus we will need to make reference to the relation between these two results of the Spirit's work within us as we explore the meaning of repentance.

The term "repent" is often used in the Old Testament of God himself and has the connotation of "changing one's mind," or "reversing one's former judgment." The Old Testament is not averse to describing God in such dynamic terms. In such a usage, it may be a morally neutral term. The distinctive idea of repentance as a moral term is expressed chiefly in the Old Testament by the words "turn" or "return." The repeated use of these terms by the prophets demonstrates that this was a fundamental theme in their preaching. They were constantly calling Israel back to God, which entailed a change of mind and behavior. It includes "a reorientation of one's whole life and personality, which includes the adoption of a new ethical line of conduct, a forsaking of sin and a turning to righteousness."[16]

John the Baptist renews the prophetic call to repentance in preparation for the dawning of the new age, and Jesus' announcement of the presence of the Kingdom echoes the same call. Repentance is a central element in the proclamation of the Early Church as it preached the message of the new age. The idea of repentance in Acts seems to particularly carry the connotation of changing one's mind. In line with the early preaching, it doubtless involves a radical reorientation of thinking about the nature of the Messiah and His kingdom. The direct corollary of this is a new understanding of the way into the Kingdom, which is faith. Hence, in the New Testament understanding, repentance and faith are inseparable corollaries.

As instruments of awakening, then, law and gospel are concomitant realities. By the law is the knowledge of sin; by the gospel is the hope of deliverance. Faith, engendered by the gospel, an-

---

16. Alan Richardson, "Repent," in *A Theological Word Book of the Bible*, ed. Alan Richardson (New York: Macmillan Co., 1950).

swers to the sense of need created by the law. This suggests two "forms" of repentance: (1) the first would lead to despair; (2) the second leads to conversion. As Hendrikus Berkhof so well puts it:

> The knowledge of grace and the knowledge of sin go together; they presuppose and reinforce each other. Without repentance all the notes of the Christian faith are off-key or fall silent. Then the gospel is changed from a marvelous message of liberation into a more or less self-evident ideology of cheap grace. If repentance falls away, the amazement and joy over God's free grace also falls away.[17]

The relationship between repentance and faith has been the subject of debate throughout Christian history. In the Middle Ages, in Catholic thought, it centered around the sacrament of penance. The original structure of this sacrament included contrition, confession, satisfaction, and absolution. Later on, it was debated that contrition (being sorry that one had sinned) was a distinctly Christian virtue, and that it was more appropriate to describe this aspect of the sacrament as attrition (feeling sorry out of fear of punishment). The Council of Trent ascribed to attrition a preparatory significance.[18] This, of course, was organically connected to a view of salvation by works.

Lutheran thought emphasized the awakening function of the law but insisted on the close relation between law and gospel, thus between repentance and faith. It certainly never conceived of repentance as a meritorious work. "This starting from the duality of repentance and faith, which corresponds respectively to the *opus alienum* of the law and the *opus proprium* of the gospel in God himself, has remained characteristic of Lutheranism."[19]

John Calvin, however, consistently developing the doctrines of election and predestination that result from his particular view of divine sovereignty, places faith/regeneration at the threshold of the Christian life and repentance as subsequent to faith. He leaves no doubt about his position:

> That repentance not only always follows faith, but is produced by it, ought to be without controversy. . . . Those who think that repentance precedes faith instead of flowing from, or being produced by it, as the fruit by the tree, have never under-

---

17. *Christian Faith*, 429. This does not imply that we agree completely with Berkhof's full understanding of repentance.
18. Ibid., 430.
19. Ibid., 431.

stood its nature, and are moved to adopt that view on very insufficient grounds.[20]

The Wesleyan doctrine of prevenient grace leads to a significantly different view from Calvin, but close to Luther in many ways. Wesley comes very close to identifying repentance with self-knowledge. In fact, it is quite clear that this is the fundamental ingredient in his thinking.[21] But it also includes ceasing from doing evil and learning to do well, and all this is necessary to salvation.

Being basically self-knowledge, repentance must be present in the sinner and also the converted but not yet fully sanctified believer. For the sinner, it involves the awareness that his sins render him unacceptable to God. This consciousness results in a sense of guilt. In the child of God, repentance is a knowledge of remaining sin but without any condemnation because it pertains to his inherited nature. Nonetheless it is the occasion for his mourning for purity.[22]

The chief question to be addressed concerns whether repentance is a meritorious work that in some way contributes to one's salvation. This is, indeed, one of the major reasons why some Reformed theologians reject it as a "preliminary state of grace." But the Wesleyan view of prevenient grace allows for it to be the work of the Holy Spirit, yet in no way a good work. Wesley addresses it this way:

> God does undoubtedly command us both to repent, and to bring forth fruits meet for repentance; which if we willingly neglect, we cannot reasonably expect to be justified at all: therefore both repentance, and fruits meet for repentance, are, in some sense, necessary to justification. But they are not necessary in the *same sense* with faith, nor in the *same degree*. Not in the *same degree*; for those fruits are only necessary *conditionally*; if there be time and opportunity for them. Otherwise a man may be justified without them, as was the *thief* upon the cross; . . . but he cannot be justified without faith; this is impossible. Likewise, let a man have ever so much repentance, or ever so many of the fruits meet for repentance, yet all this does not at all avail; he is not justified till he believes. But the moment he

---

20. *Institutes* 3.3.1. Contemporary Calvinists still insist upon this order. See G. C. Berkouwer, *Sin* (Grand Rapids: Wm. B. Eerdmans Publishing Co., 1971), chap. 7. Donald G. Bloesch, *Essentials of Evangelical Theology* 1:97, writes: "We will not truly repent and forsake our sins until our hearts are regenerated by the Holy Spirit as we hear the message of the Gospel."

21. *StS* 1:155, 212.

22. Cf. ibid. 2:361-97.

believes, with or without those fruits, yea, with more or less repentance, he is justified.—Not in the *same sense;* for repentance and its fruits are only *remotely* necessary; necessary in order to faith; whereas faith is *immediately* and *directly* necessary to justification. It remains, that faith is the only condition which is *immediately* and *proximately* necessary to justification.[23]

In this ingenious way, Wesley retains the biblical emphasis on faith as alone the condition of salvation and at the same time preserves the equally biblical emphasis upon the place of repentance.[24] Likewise, with Lutheran thought, he preserves the inseparable unity of repentance and faith, of law and gospel as we saw in our discussion earlier in chapter 12 in explicating the prophetic work of Christ. This leads us directly to the appropriating gift of the Spirit: faith.

Faith

Here we encounter one of the most ambiguous terms in the Christian vocabulary. It may convey numerous meanings. However, as it relates to salvation, there are fundamentally two possibilities: (1) belief and (2) trust. We have discussed the dynamic interplay of these two concepts of faith in our analysis of the doctrine of revelation and simply defer to that for basic distinctions. They are really inseparable, but in the saving relation, faith as trust is dominant.

In his summary of the Homilies of the Church of England on "The Doctrine of Salvation, Faith, and Good Works," Wesley approves these words:

> The right and true Christian faith is not only to believe that
> Holy Scripture and the articles of our faith are true, but also to
> have a sure trust and confidence to be saved from everlasting

---

23. Ibid., 451-52.
24. Cf. discussion by Colin Williams of this point, which is very perceptive and demonstrates how Wesley was seeking to avoid both horns of a dilemma. He argues that repentance is "preliminary faith," which is a response to prevenient grace and compares to Wesley's famous category of the "faith of a servant," whereas "justifying faith" is the "faith of a son." Williams concludes: "His increasing emphasis on fruits meet for repentance did nothing to alter his doctrine of justification by faith alone, for these works are the fruit of repentance faith and the gift of God's grace, and far from making us fit in any moral sense to receive justifying faith, they are simply the sign of our readiness to allow God to continue his work within us." *John Wesley's Theology Today,* 61-66.

damnation by Christ, whereof doth follow a loving heart to obey his commandments.[25]

Such faith has as its corollary the promise(s) of God. As Paul says in Rom. 10:17—"So faith comes from what is heard, and what is heard comes by the preaching of Christ." Hence faith is a response and not a human initiation. It is a creation of the Spirit generally and specifically in response to the Word of God. Saving faith is the response to the free offer of forgiveness.[26]

Wesley, apparently, is fully cognizant of this essential character of faith since his stock definition is Heb. 11:1—"Now faith is the assurance of things hoped for, the conviction [evidence, KJV] of things not seen." Faith is the assurance that whatever God has promised or commanded can be actualized in the here and now. This is the basis for his "optimism of grace."

It must be insisted, as Wesley does, that the faith by which one is justified is not to be understood as a good work or meritorious cause of our acceptance. The words that Wesley cites from the Homilies state that this faith by which we are justified

> is not that this our own act, to believe in Christ, or that this our faith in Christ, which is within us, doth justify us (for that were to account ourselves to be justified by some act or virtue that is within ourselves), but that although we have faith, hope and charity within us and do never so many works thereunto, yet we must renounce the merit of all, of faith, hope, charity and all other virtues and good works which we either have done, shall do, or can do, as far too weak to deserve our justification.[27]

Wiley neatly summarizes all the elements we have here addressed in this discussion of saving or justifying faith:

> We have seen that the primary element in faith is trust; hence saving faith is a personal trust in the Person of the Saviour. We may say in this connection that the efficient cause of this faith is the operation of the Holy Spirit, and the instrumental cause is the revelation of the truth concerning the need and possibility of salvation (CT 2:367-68).

One additional matter should be noted. While faith is the mode of entrance into the Christian life, it is also an element in its

25. Cited in Albert Outler, ed., John Wesley (New York: Oxford University Press, 1980), 128.
26. See ibid. "And therefore St. Paul declareth nothing on the behalf of man concerning his justification but only a true and lively faith, which itself is the gift of God." 125, italics added.
27. Ibid., 127.

continuance. One does not exercise faith as an isolated event but begins what is a walk of faith marked by continuing dependence upon the mercy and grace of God. Thus Paul says in Col. 2:6-7— "As therefore you received Christ Jesus the Lord, so live in him, rooted and built up in him and established in the faith, just as you were taught, abounding in thanksgiving."

The Process of Salvation

Since faith is the gift of God that apprehends pardon, or forgiveness, or justification, the first operation of the Spirit to which we give our attention is the witness of the Spirit to our acceptance. It is in this way that justification is related to His work. The other operations of the Spirit in connection with the Christian life may be summarized under the rubric of sanctification, defined in the distinctive Wesleyan understanding as a "real change" in contrast to justification as a "relative change." The former is what God does for us through His Son; the latter is what He works in us by His Spirit.[28]

Hence, we may speak of all those "being-transforming" works of the Holy Spirit as "sanctifying works" and recognize the distinctive Christian content of each as delineated in the last chapter. Thus in addition to the Witness of the Spirit, we will discuss Regeneration, Entire Sanctification (the distinctive emphasis of Wesleyan theology), and Growth in Grace as various facets of the broader work of sanctification.

Witness of the Spirit

This theme is commonly referred to as the doctrine of assurance. It is one of Wesleyan theology's most distinctive doctrines and at the same time one of its most difficult and controversial ones. H. B. Workman says that it is "the fundamental contribution of Methodism to the life and thought of the Church";[29] yet it was maligned and criticized, and Wesley spent much of his time defending its validity and explaining its meaning. Not a little of his effort was involved in attempting to understand it himself.

Wesley himself said that this doctrine "is one grand part of the testimony which God has given them [the Methodists] to bear to

---

28. *StS* 1:119; 2:227, 445-46.
29. *A New History of Methodism* (London: Hodder and Stoughton, 1909), 19.

all mankind. It is by His peculiar blessing upon them, in searching the Scriptures, confirmed by the experience of His children, that this great evangelical truth has been recovered, which had been for many years well-nigh lost and forgotten."[30]

What did Mr. Wesley mean by the "witness of the Spirit"? In both his sermons on the topic, preached (or written) 20 years apart, he defined it in the same way:

> The testimony of the Spirit is an inward impression on the soul, whereby the Spirit of God directly witnesses to my spirit, that I am a child of God; that Jesus Christ hath loved me, and given Himself for me; and that all my sins are blotted out, and I, even I, am reconciled to God.[31]

Both sermons were expositions of Rom. 8:16, which seemed to be the fundamental basis of his doctrine: "It is the Spirit himself bearing witness with our spirit that we are children of God." With such clear scriptural support, why did he encounter such opposition? As his statement quoted above suggests, it burst upon the English scene as a "new doctrine" that few had ever heard of. In fact, when John first encountered the idea among the Moravians, especially Peter Böhler, he had the same reaction. "I was quite amazed," he says, "and looked upon it as a new gospel."[32] Sugden briefly suggests two reasons for its demise from the religious scene: It had been both obscured by the sacramentarian teaching of the Romish church and exaggerated by the mystics.

The Council of Trent had pronounced definitely against any direct witness of the Holy Spirit to the individual believer of his present salvation and acceptance with God. Watkin-Jones concludes: "The Romanist conceptions of salvation by merit, sacramental grace, and probation could lead to no other conclusion."[33]

After surveying the evidence that there were those in England in the 16th and 17th centuries who taught that an assurance was available directly to all believers, Watkin-Jones nonetheless observes that "undoubtedly the theological attitude of the Church of England in the eighteenth century was unfavourable to this doctrine." He attributes this largely to the influence of Calvinism,

---

30. *StS* 2:343-44.
31. Ibid. 1:208; 2:345.
32. *Journal* 1:475-76.
33. Howard Watkin-Jones, *The Holy Spirit from Arminius to Wesley* (London: Epworth Press, 1929), 305.

which "had never favoured Assurance as the privilege of all believers."[34]

Wesley had to defend his faith against two major charges.
First, it was believed that such direct operations of the Spirit were
limited largely to the apostolic age and were granted to only a few
select persons. In other words, assurance was an extraordinary gift.
Against this objection, Wesley continuously insisted that it was the
privilege of ordinary Christians, available to all. In this he could
appeal to the experience of many of his contemporaries.

The second charge was doubtless more serious. He was accused of enthusiasm (fanaticism). To claim a direct and immediate
witness of the Spirit could lead to all sorts of excesses and easily
become subject to rationalization and self-deception. Developments in depth psychology since Wesley's time have given even
greater impetus to this criticism, and it must be given careful consideration. How Wesley responded to this criticism can perhaps
best be seen through a further analysis of his teaching.

It is important to note that the witness of the Spirit is directly
related to justification by faith.[35] Wesley's own experience of assurance of salvation occurs on May 24, 1738, with his Aldersgate
experience of the "strangely warmed heart." This event took place
as a climax of Wesley's encounters over a period of time with the
Moravians, especially Peter Böhler and A. G. Spangenberg.

It is instructive to compare the conversations with these men
and Wesley's own words in describing what happened to him at
Aldersgate. The interview with Spangenberg recorded in his *Journal* is clear:

> I asked Mr. Spangenberg's advice with regard to myself—
> to my own conduct. He told me he could say nothing till he had
> asked me two or three questions. "Do you know yourself? Have
> you the witness within yourself? Does the Spirit of God bear
> witness with your spirit that you are a child of God?" I was
> surprised and knew not what to answer. He observed it, and
> asked: "Do you know Jesus Christ?" I paused and said: "I know
> He is the Saviour of the world." "True," replied he, "but do you
> know He has saved you?" I answered: "I hope He has died to
> save me." He only added: "Do you know yourself?" I said: "I
> do." But I fear they were vain words.[36]

---

34. Ibid., 313.
35. Watkin-Jones says: "In the Methodist system the doctrine of the witness of the
Spirit follows naturally from the doctrine of salvation by faith." 319.
36. *Journal* 1:151.

His descriptive words of Aldersgate reflect the particularity of faith called for in Spangenberg's examination:

> In the evening I went very unwillingly to a society in Aldersgate Street, where one was reading Luther's preface to the Epistle to the Romans. About a quarter before nine, while he was describing the change which God works in the heart through faith in Christ, I felt my heart strangely warmed. I felt I did trust in Christ, Christ alone, for salvation: and an assurance was given *me*, that He had taken away *my* sins, even *mine*, and saved *me* from the law of sin and death.[37]

In his second sermon on "The Witness of the Spirit" he was probably referring to this event when he said: "The Spirit itself bore witness to my spirit that I was a child of God, gave me an evidence hereof, and I immediately cried, Abba, Father!"[38]

This makes it obvious that Wesley moved from a somewhat vague and general faith to a particular, individual appropriating one. Or one could say that it involved a change from an intellectual understanding of faith (assent) to trust. Of this transformation, Cannon says that "it is, therefore, at the point of faith, its nature and its function, that we note the radical change which took place in Wesley's thought concerning justification."[39]

There, furthermore, seems to be a shift in emphasis on the idea of justification. Before Aldersgate, Wesley's emphasis was upon works as a mode of acceptance before God. It was not that he did not know about the doctrine but that he was somewhat confused about the sole efficacy of faith. In a review of his religious life prefixed to May 24, 1738, he spoke of many sensible comforts that were short anticipations of the life of faith, yet he had not "the witness of the Spirit with my spirit, and indeed could not; for I sought it not by faith, but as it were by the works of the law."[40]

A further qualification is important. From Peter Böhler, Wesley learned of the centrality of Christ in relation to saving faith. Hence, we are introduced to what we have earlier called the incarnational principle as essential to a Christian doctrine of the Holy Spirit. It reappears here in connection with faith unto justification.

With these brief résumés in view, we can now see the validity of A. S. Yates's summary:

---

37. Ibid., 475-76.
38. *StS* 2:350.
39. *Theology of John Wesley*, 74.
40. *Journal* 1:470-71.

Assurance, as Wesley came to understand it, is an assurance of salvation; salvation based on justification by faith alone; faith, not of a vague, general kind, but a personal faith centered in Christ; a Christ who "loved me and gave Himself for me."[41]

The witness of the Spirit, then, is not some general impression from out of the blue that has no grounding in anything objective. Rather, it is directly related to the implicit promise of God observed in Jesus Christ that God loves me and sent His Son to be an atoning sacrifice for my sins. Actually, the witness is as much, or more, an assurance of God's love for me as of my subjective state. With the assurance granted as a result of this historical event, I appropriate its benefits in a moment of existential faith, and there may occur (see below), and ideally should occur, an instantaneous assurance, based on the faithfulness of God, that the universal Atonement now avails for me. This assurance, Wesley argues persistently, is more than a psychological release; it is the supernatural interaction of the divine Spirit with the human spirit, an activity that defies explanation. Here, as with other transcendental doctrines, Wesley insists on the fact but confesses an inability to explain the manner.

To finally answer the charge of enthusiasm, we must note Wesley's careful guards that he erected against this perversion. He insisted that the genuine witness could be tested by several criteria: It must be preceded by repentance, which in turn must be followed by a "vast and mighty [ethical] change." The scriptural marks of joy, love, and obedience to the law of God must follow. These may be present and the witness absent, but if these are absent, the witness cannot be present.[42]

In his sermons, Wesley really seems to distinguish three levels of witness: (1) There is an inference from empirical evidence. Where the fruit of the Spirit is present in a life, along with other observable, distinctively Christian phenomena, one may rationally infer that he is saved. (2) There is the witness of our own spirit. This refers to inward realities that are completely private but of which we are as keenly and directly aware as we are that the sun is shining. This is "a conscience void of offence toward God" (Acts 24:16, KJV). (3) There is the direct witness of the Spirit, and this is prior to the other two and the aspect of the witness that it is his

---

41. *The Doctrine of Assurance* (London: Epworth Press, 1952), 59.
42. StS 1:211-16.

concern to defend. He argues that to ground the assurance only on the fruit is to go back to justification by works.[43]

The first two of the above are commonly designated as the "indirect witness," while the third is the witness proper and is called the "direct" witness. Wesley is insistent, however, that the first two are also the work of the Spirit. "It is He that not only worketh in us every manner of thing that is good, but also shines upon His own work, and clearly shows what He has wrought."[44]

Wesley also argues for the priority of the direct witness logically:

> That this testimony of the Spirit of God must needs, in the very nature of things, be antecedent to the testimony of our own spirit, may appear from this single consideration. We must be holy of heart, and holy in life, before we can be conscious that we are so; before we can have the testimony of our spirit, that we are inwardly and outwardly holy. But we must love God, before we can be holy at all; this being the root of all holiness. Now we cannot love God, till we know He loves us. . . . And we cannot know His pardoning love to us, till His Spirit witnesses it to our spirit. Since, therefore, this testimony of His Spirit must precede the love of God and all holiness, of consequence it must precede our inward consciousness thereof, or the testimony of our spirit concerning them.[45]

One important distinction Wesley made was between the "assurance of salvation" and the "assurance of faith." In a letter to Arthur Bedford on August 4, 1738, Wesley says: "That assurance of which alone I speak, I should not choose to call an assurance of salvation, but rather (with the Scriptures) the assurance of faith. . . . I think the Scriptural words are always the best."[46]

This is far more than a semantic squabble. Both Bedford and Wesley understood that the term "assurance of salvation" meant a knowledge that we would *persevere* in a state of salvation, whereas Wesley was only willing to claim that we had the witness of the Spirit that we are *now* in a state of salvation.[47]

John Calvin maintained the position that the Christian could be certain not only of his present salvation but also of his perseverance in the faith to the very end. This is, of course, a corollary to

---

43. Lindström, *Wesley and Sanctification*, 115.
44. *StS* 1:208.
45. Ibid., 211-15.
46. *Letters* 1:255.
47. A. S. Yates, *Doctrine of Assurance*, 61, 133-34.

the belief in eternal security. As a contemporary Calvinist put it, "This is not to deny that through stubbornness and presumption they may fall time and again, but they will never fall out of the sphere of grace."[48]

Finally, we need to observe that Wesley's understanding of this scriptural teaching underwent some significant modifications in the process of time under the impact of experience. Thus his mature views were the result of an evolutionary process. Early on, he was prepared to deny saving faith, or acceptance with God, to all who did not experience the inward certainty of it. This was the basis for evaluating his own pre-Aldersgate Christianity as less than saving. But as he meditated on the experience of many believers, he came to allow exceptions. He says in a letter on March 28, 1768, "I have not for many years thought a consciousness of acceptance to be essential to justifying faith."[49]

One can see the occasion for the emergence of some of his distinctive categories as well as his deference to experience in formulating his understanding of the Christian life in his own words, which make an excellent summary of our point. He was 85 when he wrote:

> Nearly fifty years ago, when Preachers, commonly called Methodists, began to preach that grand scriptural doctrine, salvation by faith, they were not sufficiently apprized [sic] of the difference between a servant and a child of God. They did not clearly understand, that even one "who feareth God, and worketh righteousness, is accepted of him." In consequence of this, they were apt to make sad the hearts of those whom God had not made sad. For they frequently asked those who feared God, "Do you know that your sins are forgiven?" And upon their answering, "No," immediately replied, "Then you are a child of the devil." No; that does not follow. It might have been said, (and it is all that can be said with propriety,) "Hitherto you are only a *servant*, you are not a *child* of God. You have already great reason to praise God that He has called you to his honourable service."[50]

Nonetheless, he never ceased to hold that it was an experience for which all Christians should seek. He wrote in 1768, "A consciousness of being in the favour of God . . . is the common privilege of Christians fearing God and working righteousness."[51]

---

48. Bloesch, *Essentials of Evangelical Theology* I:236.
49. *Letters* 5:359.
50. *Works* 7:199.
51. *Letters* 5:235.

We have chosen to develop this topic historically, since all Wesleyans who have attempted to do it systematically have simply repeated Wesley's analyses. Also Wesley seems to have addressed most of the systematic issues. However, we will attempt a summary in conclusion.

We have noted that the witness of the Spirit, as Wesley understood it, is related to the incarnational principle that we early articulated as informative of a New Testament view of the Spirit's work. We noted the inseparable connection, indigenous to Wesleyan theology, between religion and ethics. No mystical relation to God can circumvent the ethical requirements of discipleship. The distinction between the assurance of salvation and the assurance of faith recognizes the synergistic character of Wesleyan thought. We saw the importance for Wesley of the experiential verification of dogmatic claims, and the consequent willingness to modify views in the light of experience when there was no compromise of unequivocal biblical teaching, an important methodological consideration for some of our further analyses. Furthermore (though we did not address it in the survey, since Wesley did not speak to it explicitly), since the witness of the Spirit is a common privilege open to all believers, it is obvious, as H. B. Workman points out, that "Wesley's doctrine of Assurance involved as a necessary corollary an Arminian theory of the Atonement."[52]

Regeneration

Regeneration is a metaphor taken from the field of biology to refer to the "real change" that is effected by the Holy Spirit at the threshold of the Christian life. The term occurs only twice in the New Testament. In Matt. 19:28 (KJV) the reference is to cosmic regeneration. It is used in connection with baptism as the renewing activity of the Spirit in Titus 3:5. However, the idea conveyed by the metaphor is expressed in several passages employing the imagery of being born again (cf. James 1:21; 1 Pet. 1:23; and the conversation with Nicodemus in John 3).

In his sermon "The Great Privilege of Those That Are Born of God," Wesley clearly distinguishes regeneration from justification while showing their relation:

> But though it be allowed, that justification and the new birth are, in point of time, inseparable from each other, yet they

---

52. *History of Methodism*, 34.

are easily distinguished, as being not the same, but things of a widely different nature. Justification implies only a relative, the new birth a real, change. God in justifying us does something *for* us; in begetting us again, He does the work *in* us. The former changes our outward relation to God, so that of enemies we become children; by the latter our inmost souls are changed, so that of sinners we become saints. The one restores us to the favour, the other to the image, of God. The one is the taking away the guilt, the other the taking away the power, of sin; so that, although they are joined together in point of time, yet are they of wholly distinct natures.[53]

Adequately explaining this figurative language is ultimately impossible, as Jesus implied in His comment to Nicodemus that "the wind blows where it wills, and you hear the sound of it, but you do not know whence it comes or whither it goes; so it is with every one who is born of the Spirit" (John 3:8). John Wesley, on the basis of this passage, noted that "to expect any minute, philosophical account of the manner of this," is to expect too much. Here he affirms the fact but confesses that the manner eludes him.[54]

Nonetheless, if we recognize its inadequacy, we may use a psychological definition to gain some insight into the nature of regeneration. Olin A. Curtis provides us with an excellent one: "Regeneration is the primary reorganization of a person's entire motive-life by the vital action and abiding presence of the Holy Spirit so that the ultimate motive is loyalty to Jesus Christ."[55] This correlates neatly with Alan Richardson's definition of repentance noted above as representing "a fundamental reorientation of the whole personality."[56]

When this occurs, a person becomes "a new creation . . . in Christ" (2 Cor. 5:17). He has experienced a radical reorientation of his whole being, a reversal of values, so that what he once loved, he now hates, and vice versa. The new life in regeneration involves a dying to an old way of life and the adoption of a new way. Such a transformation of one's value system is possible only through the enabling power of the Holy Spirit.

Regeneration is closely connected with the metaphor of "adoption." Wesley equates being "born of the Spirit" with having

<hr/>

53. *StS* 1:299-300.
54. Ibid. 2:231.
55. *The Christian Faith* (New York: Eaton and Mains, 1905), 365.
56. *Theology*, 31.

the "Spirit of adoption."[57] Adoption can be considered the social aspect of conversion. As Wiley says, the term refers to "the act of a man in taking into his household as his own, children which were not born to him" (CT 2:429). We can once more refer to the definition of O. A. Curtis: "Adoption is a legal term which St. Paul borrowed from the Roman law to express the social phase of conversion, namely, that a saved sinner is not only justified and regenerated, but actually incorporated into the family of God to enjoy its fellowship and to share its destiny."[58] Thus regeneration inaugurates the relationship between the believer and God called sonship.

Helmut Burkhardt refers to this resultant sonship as an ontological category.[59] It is proper to thus speak of the new life brought into being by regeneration as ontological only if one does not conceptualize it in terms of a substantival ontology. A relational ontology such as we have suggested in our discussion of the *imago Dei*, where the essence of man is identified as "man in relation to God," will allow us to legitimately consider the real change involved in the new birth as ontological in nature.

Burkhardt apparently does not hold to this stipulation; thus he falls victim to the result of thinking in terms of substantival ontology and therefore concludes that "sonship is something lasting, something which cannot be canceled, in distinction, for example from friendship. Sonship is a statement about being."[60] The fallacy of this is immediately apparent and gives rise to the popular Calvinism that affirms the perseverance of the saints in terms of "once a son, always a son," arguing that once one is born, he cannot be unborn. This conclusion is valid only if one abandons the relational understanding of the metaphors involved.

Regeneration has often been related to baptism. There is a connection of which we shall defer discussion until later, but simply observe here that the New Testament does not teach baptismal regeneration but that the rite is symbolic of the gift of the Spirit that effects the new birth. Baptism can be administered without the necessary accompaniment of regeneration, so it is therefore not an infallible sign that it has occurred.

---

57. *StS* 1:283.
58. *Christian Faith*, 367.
59. *The Biblical Doctrine of Regeneration*, trans. O. R. Johnston (Downers Grove, Ill.: InterVarsity Press, 1978).
60. Ibid., 30.

Mr. Wesley gives a great deal of attention to the marks of the new birth. The first result of this work of the Spirit is that God enables the regenerate to avoid committing sin. Even babes in Christ, he insists, "are so far perfect as not to commit sin." The sin to which he refers is a "voluntary transgression of a known law of God."[61] This is the immediate fruit of faith. The second mark is hope, which he relates to the direct and indirect witness of the Spirit. The third is the greatest of all and is that the love of God is shed abroad in the heart of him who has been converted. In a word, it is faith, hope, and love.[62]

For Wesley, regeneration is the first moment of sanctification, or what may be called initial sanctification. This is clear from several of his normative statements, including the one quoted near the beginning of this section. In his sermon by the same name, he defines the new birth as

> that great change which God works in the soul when He brings it into life; when He raises it from the death of sin to the life of righteousness. It is the change wrought in the whole soul by the almighty Spirit of God when it is "created anew in Christ Jesus"; when it is "renewed after the image of God in righteousness and true holiness"; when the love of the world is changed into the love of God; pride into humility; passion into meekness; hatred, envy, malice, into a sincere, tender, disinterested love for all mankind.[63]

Later in the same sermon, he distinguishes the new birth from sanctification, but he makes explicit that it is a distinction between an instantaneous and a progressive work. To those (e.g., William Law) who made regeneration a progressive work, he says:

> This is undeniably true of sanctification; but of regeneration, the new birth, it is not true. This is a part of sanctification, not the whole; it is the gate to it, the entrance into it. When we are born again, then our sanctification, our inward and outward holiness begins; and thenceforward we are gradually to "grow up in Him who is our Head."[64]

What Wesley consistently does is apply his generic definitions of sanctification to regeneration, showing that he understands it to be a particular expression of the work of the Spirit in restoring man to the image of God, a real change involving true holiness. There is

---

61. *Works* 11:375; 12:239.
62. *StS* 2:285-94.
63. Ibid., 234.
64. Ibid., 240.

one kind of holiness that is present in degrees at each stage of the Christian life. He makes this obvious in his sermon "On Patience" (1788). Entire sanctification, he says,

> does not imply any new *kind* of holiness: Let no man imagine this. From the moment we are justified, till we give up our spirits to God, love is the fulfilling of the law . . . Love is the sum of Christian sanctification; it is the one *kind* of holiness, which is found, only in various *degrees*, in the believers who are distinguished by St. John into "little children, young men, and fathers." The difference between one and the other properly lies in the degree of love.[65]

From these references it is unequivocal that Wesley equated regeneration with the first movement of sanctifying grace in the soul. Although it was complete in a moment, it was not qualitatively different from the subsequent working of grace. He did not use the term *initial sanctification* to refer to this aspect of conversion. This terminology arose among his successors, apparently to counter a theological teaching that equated regeneration with sanctification without remainder.[66]

It is unclear who first coined the phrase, but the identification of regeneration and the beginning of sanctification is retained among significant spokesmen for the Wesleyan movement. Richard Watson lists the components of initial redemption as "justification, adoption, regeneration, and the witness of the Holy Spirit" but does not include the term *initial sanctification* among them. He does insist that there is a distinction between a regenerate state and a state of entire and perfect holiness as he seeks to provide a place in the divine economy for entire sanctification. Wilson T. Hogue (1916) affirms that "the Holy Spirit's work of sanctification is begun and in goodly degree accomplished in regeneration. In this experience a new life is begotten in the soul, a life of holy love." He further affirms, "We cannot insist too strongly on the fact that sanctification has its beginning in the work of regeneration."[67]

In the first appearances of the idea of initial sanctification in the 19th century, it was used somewhat ambiguously as the Amer-

---

65. *Works* 6:488.
66. John L. Peters, *Christian Perfection and American Methodism* (New York: Abingdon Press, 1956), 150 ff.
67. References found in Richard S. Taylor, ed., *Leading Wesleyan Thinkers*, vol. 3 of *Great Holiness Classics*, ed. A. F. Harper (Kansas City: Beacon Hill Press of Kansas City, 1985), 25, 308, 309.

ican holiness movement sought to refine the teachings of Wesley on the doctrine of sanctification. It is without doubt this ambiguity that leads Wilber T. Dayton to observe that while it is clear that one must distinguish between "initial" and "entire" sanctification, "it is less simple to define the extent and nature" of "initial" sanctification, and he acknowledges that "not all are satisfied" with the interpretation that seems to have become standard[68] (see below).

Watson's tendencies are in the direction of emphasizing gradual sanctification. W. B. Pope made it clear that he understood entire sanctification to be "in reality the perfection of the regenerate state."[69] Thomas N. Ralston unequivocally affirms that "sanctification in its initial state, is synonymous with regeneration" and thus that Christian perfection is "regeneration grown to maturity."[70]

These references illustrate the tendencies of Wesleyan thought that, we are suggesting, led the "second blessing" advocates to develop the doctrine of initial sanctification. The work of R. S. Foster reflects the ambiguity that accompanied the transition. He differentiates between two positions, both of which see the attainability of entire sanctification in this life, but with one laying stress upon maturation, ripening, or process, holding that entire sanctification "is distinct only as a point in the process of regeneration"; and the other stressing that it is "an immediate or instantaneous work, and is almost always a distinct one; to be attained by the agency of the Holy Spirit, through faith," and is different from what precedes it (regeneration) "in kind and degree."[71]

It is not clear precisely which position Foster is espousing, but the order of arguments and manner of presentation indicate his support of the latter. If he is suggesting that the sanctified state is different in kind as well as degree from the regenerated state, he reflects a view more like Wesley's own in a later passage:

> But is not a person regenerated a perfect child, and is sanctification any thing more than development? When a soul is regenerated, all the elements of holiness are imparted to it, or the graces are implanted in it, in complete number, and the

---

68. "Initial Salvation and Its Concomitants," in *The Word and the Doctrine: Studies in Contemporary Wesleyan-Arminian Theology,* comp. Kenneth E. Geiger (Kansas City: Beacon Hill Press of Kansas City, 1965), 208-9.
69. *Compendium* 3:89.
70. *Elements of Divinity* (New York: Abingdon-Cokesbury Press, 1924), 460 ff.
71. *Christian Purity* (New York: Eaton and Mains, 1897), 56-57.

454 ☐ GRACE, FAITH, AND HOLINESS

perfection of these graces is entire sanctification; and hence, we insist that entire sanctification does not take place in regeneration, for the graces are not then perfect. And again, though in regeneration all the elements of holiness are imparted, all the rudiments of inbred sin are not destroyed, and hence, again, the absence of complete sanctification, which when it occurs, expels all sin. Regeneration is incipient sanctification in this sense—it is of the same nature of sanctification, and, so far as it extends, is sanctification.[72]

Regeneration and initial sanctification are in other sources so separated as to create a diastasis between them that results in the work of sanctification being discontinuous from the regenerating work of the Spirit. This appears in the following quotation where regeneration is defined as

> the impartation of spiritual life to the human soul, in which God imparts, organizes and calls into being the capabilities, attributes, and functions of the new nature. It is a change from death to life, from the dominion of sin to the reign of grace, and restores the spiritual life which was lost by the fall.[73]

The separation is seen even more clearly in the words of J. T. Peck that radically distinguish "life" from "holiness": "Just as natural life and the condition of the living being are distinct, spiritual life and the moral condition of the spiritually alive are distinct." They are "totally distinct from each other, as much so as a fact and a quality of a fact, a thing and an accident of a thing can be."[74]

The view that came to be considered as standard in the American holiness movement identified initial sanctification as a concomitant of justification, which cleanses the guilt and acquired depravity attaching to actual sins, for which the sinner is himself responsible. Wiley also refers to this initial moment as "partial" in

72. Ibid., 109. This could well pass for a summary of Wesley's sermon "On Patience," sec. 10, *Works* 6:488-90.

73. J. A. Wood, *Perfect Love* (Chicago: Christian Witness Co., 1880), 17.

74. Quoted in Wiley, *CT* 2:471. Wiley reflects the same ambiguity seen in Wood. He insists that regeneration should be defined as "the communication of life by the Spirit, to a soul dead in trespasses and sins," and refuses to identify regeneration with initial sanctification, being willing to grant only that the latter is a concomitant of the former. 407, 413. This, however, stands in tension with other statements, such as "Regeneration as we have seen, is the impartation of a life that is holy in its nature." 446, see also 423. He says also of regeneration, "It is an ethical change." 426. This, in Wesleyan terminology, is what sanctification is all about. The clue to this inner tension is perhaps in the fact that Wiley seems to identify sanctification not with ethical change but with cleansing, which is a ceremonial metaphor and knows of no degrees. We shall have occasion to speak of this problem with holiness terminology later.

contrast to "entire." In the latter, the believer is cleansed from inherited depravity (*CT* 2:480-81). Richard S. Taylor recognizes that both regeneration and initial sanctification are real changes, thus generically falling under the broad rubric of "sanctification," and defines the acquired depravity "cleansed" by initial sanctification in behavorial terms; for example, "old habits drop off, vocabulary changes, ways of thinking are turned inside out." These seem to embody what Wesley refers to as "outward holiness," which begins in the new birth.[75]

If one emphasizes the positive results of the new birth, as in the fruit of the Spirit, he is better able to see how the sanctifying work of the Spirit seeks to move toward the completion of the work that He began in man even in prevenient grace.[76] To place exclusive emphasis on the negative side of sanctification (e.g., cleansing from sin) tends to lose this continuity, even though one cannot exclude this aspect of the Spirit's work from a theology of the Christian life. It now appears that, in the light of these considerations, we are ready to move directly to a discussion of entire sanctification.

Entire Sanctification[77]

By *justification* we refer to that declaration of divine grace (as attitude) that restores the sinner to right relation to God by pardon and forgiveness; by *regeneration* we mean the operation of the Holy Spirit (grace as power) that makes the sinner alive unto God; by *entire sanctification* we refer to that work of the Spirit in the believer that "cuts short His work in righteousness" (Wesley, cf. Rom. 9:28, KJV), delivers from all sin, and creates a relation to God that can be referred to as perfection.

Every term and phrase in this last proposed working definition needs clarification and qualification. By entire sanctification we

---

75. Richard S. Taylor, *Exploring Christian Holiness* 3:139-41; cf. also A. Elwood Sanner, "Initial Sanctification," in *Beacon Dictionary of Theology*, ed. Richard S. Taylor (Kansas City: Beacon Hill Press of Kansas City, 1983).

76. See the author's *Fruit of the Spirit* for a demonstration of how this may be spelled out.

77. The literature on this topic is immense. There are exegetical and psychological issues that have been explored ad infinitum. Since this work is a systematic theology and not a monograph on sanctification, though it does play a major role, we cannot expect to deal with all the ramifications of the issues related to the topic of entire sanctification. One would need to refer to the many works on the subject to find many other matters explored that are not mentioned here or are merely touched on in passing.

refer to a special stage of being that is seen in continuity with the broader work of sanctification in the believer's life. By the qualification, entire, we mean the same as Paul in 1 Thess. 5:23— "May the God of peace himself sanctify you wholly; and may your spirit and soul and body be kept sound and blameless at the coming of our Lord Jesus Christ." "Wholly" means "through and through" (cf. chap. 11). In no sense does it suggest a completion that precludes further growth. As Wesley rightly insisted, "There is no perfection of degrees, . . . none which does not admit of continual increase."[78]

In this section of our discussion of entire sanctification (more later), we want to restrict ourselves to two crucial questions: (1) Is entire sanctification possible? and (2) How does one seek it?

In addressing the question of the possibility of entire sanctification in this life, we must first be aware that this question cannot be intelligently answered in isolation from a complex of other issues. In a word, it can only be adequately explored as a component of systematic theology. These relevant issues are either explored explicitly or assumed implicitly in all theological works dealing with the matter. Among the more pressing issues are included the doctrine of sin, the meaning of the Atonement, the nature of man, the meaning of grace, and the meaning attached to the concept of perfection. We have already given attention to all of these except the last two, and the student should familiarize himself with these other areas of this theological proposal in connection with the study of this topic.

There are two basic understandings of grace in the history of Christian thought. One, and perhaps the earliest, sees grace as power for healing. This early appears in the words of Ignatius of Antioch, who refers to the Eucharist as the "medicine of immortality." It is the emphasis of Augustine and becomes normative for the views of medieval Catholic piety. Grace became conceptualized as an ontological substance of a spiritual nature that was infused into the person via the sacraments. Its presence was demonstrated through its enablement to do good works.

Martin Luther, along with several of his other theological transformations, replaced this understanding with a view of grace as the attitude of God by which He was willing to accept the sinner

78. StS 2:156.

and forgive him before any worthiness. By abandoning the idea of grace as healing, and focusing upon the idea of justification in connection with it, Luther's doctrine of sanctification suffered a serious weakness. It resulted in an ambiguous vision of the Christian life marked by oscillation between victory and defeat, ecstasy and despair.

By way of anticipation, we may note that Wesley with his usual *via media* approach to theology was able to opt for both views of grace and thus produced a balance between justification (grace as attitude) and sanctification (grace as healing). In his discussion of Wesley's theological perspective, Harald Lindström takes account of these distinctions and observes:

> The basic corruption of natural man is . . . portrayed as a disease, salvation as a restoration to health [healing]. A conception of religion which accepts such a view of sin must be determined by the idea of sanctification.[79]

We propose to explore the issue of perfection by noting the various ways in which sanctification has been (or can be) interpreted and the implications of these explanations for the question of the possibility of entire sanctification. There seem to be four chief ways of interpreting sanctification, with the possibility of some interpenetration. These are (1) in terms of law, (2) in terms of love, (3) in terms of transformation of being, and (4) ceremonially or cultically.

Various interweavings of these different ways of interpreting sanctification have appeared throughout the history of Christian thought about the Christian life. There were dynamic transitions from one to the other, and it is doubtless an oversimplification to attribute a version of the Christian life exclusively in terms of any one to any particular thinker. However, to see the implication of each interpretation will enable us to sort out some important issues in grappling with the question concerning the possibility of entire sanctification in this finite existence.[80]

The earliest expositions of the doctrine of sanctification were

---

79. *Wesley and Sanctification*, 43.
80. What I am attempting to do in the following material is a systematic analysis of ideas based on the researches of Paul Bassett, whose work in *Exploring Christian Holiness*, vol. 2, is a pioneer effort, the only work of its kind in existence to my knowledge. Dr. Bassett seeks to trace the history of the idea of entire sanctification in distinction from "Christian perfection" as an ideal. The serious student may avoid the artificiality that my own inferences may suggest by reading Bassett's work in conjunction with this section.

developed in terms of a "transformation of being." This occurred largely among theologians of the Eastern church (Irenaeus, Athanasius) in terms of the realist theory of redemption. This involves a deification of human nature with a view to immortality. We have already noted the problems with this way of conceptualizing the real change when or if it is taken in the Greek sense of apotheosis, but that it is not necessary to interpret it in this way. In any case it is the formal structure of this way of seeing, rather than the content, that is of interest to us here. Irenaeus believed and taught that this transformation was the work of the Spirit received in baptism and implies that a measure of perfection is granted in this life as well as an ultimate eschatological "deification." "What we have in Irenaeus, then, is what we have in the New Testament—the exciting tension between the 'already' and the 'not yet.' . . . Even here, thanks to the Father's gift of the Spirit through the Son, we do know the Spirit in fullness and are already made perfect as part of the work of God's great earnest."[81] This healing of human nature is interpreted by Irenaeus as a restoration of man to the *imago Dei.*

The idea of a perfection in terms of love appears in the earliest fathers and is given grand expression by Clement of Alexandria. His "Christian Gnostic" is chiefly characterized as one who loves God with all his heart, soul, mind, and strength, and his neighbor as himself. Traditionally, Clement has been interpreted as also borrowing the Stoic virtue of apathy or passionlessness as a paradigm for this higher Christian life. This significantly contradicts some of his other descriptions such as the centrality of love, and thus raises a question about the appropriateness of this interpretation. It is at least a possibility that Clement is speaking of the "absence of passion" in Platonic (Socratic) terms rather than Stoic. In the *Phaedo,* Socrates claimed that the philosopher is the only truly virtuous man because he loves and pursues the virtues for their own sake and not for some secondary motive. This is almost precisely how Clement describes the ideal Christian relation to God. In the *Stromata,* he says:

> Could we, then, suppose any one proposing to the Gnostic whether he would choose the knowledge of God or everlasting salvation; and if these, which are entirely identical, were separable, he would without the least hesitation choose the knowledge of God, deeming that property of faith, which from love

---

81. Ibid., 50.

ascends to knowledge, desirable, for its own sake. This, then, is the perfect man's first form of doing good, when it is done not for any advantage in what pertains to him, but because he judges it right to do good; and the energy being vigorously exerted in all things, in the very act becomes good; not, good in some things, and not good in others; but consisting in the habit of doing good, neither for glory, nor, as the philosophers say, for reputation, nor from reward either from men or God; but so as to pass life after the image and likeness of the Lord.[82]

Hence the true Gnostic is characterized by a love for God as He is in himself and not just for His benefits. This is a love that excludes all lesser loves. Perfection in love is a present possibility.[83]

But we find some unique modifications of these ideas in the work of Augustine. He has left the Church a twofold legacy with regard to sin. Using the conceptual framework of Neoplatonism, he defined sin as "perverted love." The ontology of Plotinus provided him with an intellectual solution to the problem of evil in which he was able to identify evil with nonbeing and avoid the dualism of Manichaeism. This involved a scale of being with God, who is Being itself, as the Source of all that is with varying degrees of being mixed with nonbeing as one moves further away from the Ground of Being. Man's place on this scale is determined by his love. If one loves things or self, this is sin, because only God is the worthy object of love. Perfect love of God would then be freedom from sin, so theoretically it is possible, on this model, to be entirely sanctified.

Augustine does speak beautifully of how the Holy Spirit infuses love for God, as an act of grace, into the human heart: "We . . . affirm that the human will is so divinely aided in the pursuit of righteousness, that he receives the Holy Ghost, by whom there is formed in his mind a delight in, and a love of that supreme and unchangeable good which is God."[84]

But even on these grounds, Augustine vigorously denies that any person is free from sin in this life. He bases this on a collection of scriptures that seem to assert the universal sinfulness of man

---

82. Bk. 4, chap. 18.

83. Early on, Wesley was impressed with Clement's picture of the perfect Christian (*Journal* 5:197), but in 1774 he criticizes the "apathy" of Clement's ideal and says, "I do not admire that description as I did formerly." *Works* 12:297-98. If my interpretation has some validity, then Wesley need not have been disillusioned but would have found strong support for his own perceptions.

84. *On the Spirit and the Letter,* chap. 5.

and concludes: "Since . . . these passages cannot possibly be false, it plainly follows, to my mind, that whatever be the quality or extent of righteousness which we may definitely ascribe to the present life, there is not a man living in it who is absolutely free from sin."[85] But in the face of this disclaimer, he still affirms the possibility of perfect righteousness since it is the work of God, and who can put a limit on the power of God?

He does offer a rationale, however, why finite man cannot love God perfectly, a rationale that becomes very significant for later discussions. This argument is based upon the assumption that there is a correlation between love and knowledge or vision. The more we know God, the more we love Him; but since our present knowledge is defective ("We see through a glass, darkly" [1 Cor. 13:12, KJV]), our love is likewise. Since we will never have a flawless knowledge of God until we experience the beatific vision, perfection of love awaits this eschatological reality.

A second view of sin in Augustine's teaching poses a different kind of problem. Growing partly out of his own experience and partly out of his preoccupation with Paul's apparently seeing all the commandments summed up in the one prohibition, "Thou shalt not covet," Augustine identified sin with concupiscence, particularly sexual desire. Right off the top, it can be asserted that given this view of sin, human beings are exempt from the possibility of freedom from sin in this life.

But there are other complex factors involved in his debates with Pelagianism as it pertains to this interpretation that bear on our discussion. The Pelagian view of sin was atomistic, being identified with voluntary transgressions of particular precepts. The possibility of choosing not to sin in this way was in the power of man's will. Hence freedom from sin when the law is interpreted in this fashion is a relatively easy possibility. Augustine recognized this "easy perfection" and countered by his view of sin as concupiscence. By equating the law with concupiscence, he points out that *inward* conformity to the law is the crux of the issue. While outward conformity is possible by man alone, the inward is only possible through grace. He says:

> For whoever did even what the law commanded, without the assistance of the Spirit of grace, acted through fear of punishment, not from love of righteousness, and hence in the sight

---

85. Ibid., chap. 13.

of God that was not in the will, which in the sight of men appeared in the work; and such doers of the law were held rather guilty of that which God knew they would have preferred to commit, if only it had been possible with impunity.[86]

Before proceeding to a brief look at Thomas Aquinas and then the Reformers, we should note that early in Christian thought the ceremonial interpretation of sanctification was very prominent. As Paul Bassett points out, from the beginning the fullness of the Spirit (sanctification) was connected with baptism, especially the second moment of the ritual, which was marked by anointment with oil. The second moment was eventually separated from the initiatory rite of baptism and became known as confirmation.

At the outset the ritual was perceived as the symbol through which the reality became actualized, but in the process of time the sacramentarian view set in, and the rituals were seen as operating automatically. The ceremony, which was doubtless accompanied by the reality at first, tended to become an end in itself. Bassett suggests that one of the greatest contributions of "Macarius the Egyptian" (who was quite influential on Wesley) was his insistence that sanctification should be a living, existential work of grace and not mere liturgy.

When we turn to Aquinas, we find a fascinating analysis of sanctification in terms of *love*. We do not have the space, nor does it fit our purpose, to set a full context for Thomas's teaching. We may simply observe that he identifies three kinds of perfection: (1) There is a perfection in which we love God for all *He* is worth. This degree of love is possible for God alone, since He alone knows or comprehends himself with this degree of adequacy. (2) Agreeing with Augustine, he recognizes a degree of love in which we love God for all *we* are worth. Since our full capacity will exist only in the life beyond, this is excluded from present possibility. (3) But there is a third sort of perfection that excludes "everything 'contrary to the motive or movement *(motus)* of love for God.' This third sort of perfection 'is possible in this life in two modes': in the exclusion from the will of anything 'contradictory to love, that is, mortal sin' and in the will's rejection of anything that prevents the disposition of the soul *(mentis)* toward God from being total."[87] It is not

---

86. Ibid., chap. 14.
87. Bassett, *Exploring Christian Holiness* 2:137-38.

a perfection of performance, but a perfection of intention and/or disposition.[88]

The Reformation theologians made a subtle but significant transformation of the concept of sanctification, tending to interpret it from the problem of faith and works in terms of the law. Luther spoke much of love, but his perspective was largely informed by the controversies over justification that were always informed by law. Sanctification is doing good works and, of course, is subsequent to justification as the expression of faith.

But interpreting sanctification in this way had serious pitfalls for the question of the possibility of freedom from sin in this life. If the law and human nature are interpreted in a Pelagian fashion, there is no problem, but the Reformers followed Augustine in the doctrine of original sin and applied the law in its fullest internal requirements. Calvin's expositions of the Ten Commandments demonstrate how the law was interpreted in its profoundest spiritual demands.

In the light of this, Calvin could admonish his readers: "We ought not to be frightened away from the law or to shun its instruction merely because it requires a much stricter moral purity than we shall reach while we bear about with us the prison house of our body."[89]

Like Augustine, he vigorously denies that anyone can achieve perfect righteousness in this life in these terms. "If we search the remotest past, I say that none of the saints, clad in the body of death, has attained to that goal of love so as to love God 'with all his heart, all his mind, all his soul, and all his might.' I say furthermore, there was no one who was not plagued with concupiscence."[90]

In looking at the pre-Wesley ways of interpreting sanctification, we need to note one further point. Augustine, Luther, and Calvin all propose a full sanctification in this life in terms of imputation. While the sinner himself is not so completely changed, the perfect righteousness of Christ is accounted to him, and thus, positionally, he is considered perfect in God's sight. While no rit-

---

88. It should be kept in mind that all this is with a view to justification and thus loses its true evangelical significance.

89. *Institutes* 2.7.13. These passages may be misinterpreted as suggesting that the body, as a material substance, is evil in itself. Paul Bassett offers reasons why this is an impossible position to ascribe to Calvin. *Exploring Christian Holiness*, vol. 2.

90. *Institutes* 2.7.5.

uals are involved, we would propose that this view would fall under the rubric of ceremonial holiness in that it does not entail a real change but involves a transaction that occurs external to the person, so that no necessary moral transformation need occur. It is on this basis that Luther can affirm his classic position that the believer is at the same time sinner and justified (*simul justus et peccator*).

We can now make some very general observations that admittedly lack considerable precision but may be helpful in our transition to Wesley. Catholic thought tended to interpret sanctification in terms of love; Protestant thought tended to see it in terms of law, while Eastern thought was inclined to speak of transformation of being. With his synthesizing temperament and keen theological insights, we can now better understand how it can be said that Wesley's views were a synthesis of the Catholic ethic of holiness and the Protestant ethic of grace (Cell). But we must add to that the further observation that his synthesis reaches to the Eastern temperament as well and makes it an integral part of his understanding of the Christian life.

With this background in mind, as we read Wesley's handbook of holiness doctrine, *A Plain Account of Christian Perfection,* we can have a surer sense of where he is coming from and where he is going. To begin with, he recognizes that his position differs from his brethren in his positive answer to the question, "Should we expect to be saved from all sin before the article of death?"[91] This confidence is based upon a fourfold foundation that he discovered in scripture: (1) there are scriptures that promise this (e.g., Ps. 130:8; Ezek. 36:25, 29; 2 Cor. 7:1; Deut. 30:6; 1 John 3:8; Eph. 5:25-27; Rom. 8:3-4). (2) There are prayers for entire sanctification such as John 17:20-23; Eph. 3:14-19; 1 Thess. 5:23. (3) There are commands to perfection (Matt. 5:48; 22:37, 39). (4) Examples may be identified in Scripture who were called perfect.

Wesley's general position is not affected by the exegesis of particular passages that may not quite bear the weight he puts upon them; the tenor of his thought is still sound. The principle upon which he works relates directly to his understanding of faith as "the substance of things hoped for, the evidence of things not seen" (Heb. 11:1, KJV). We have already seen that the significance

---

91. P. 43.

of this definition is tied to the existence of a divine promise. While the promises are explicit, the commands, prayers, and examples are "covered promises." If God promises freedom from sin (perfection) either explicitly or implicitly in His Word, we may rest assured that it is a possibility within the divine power. Here is the foundation for Wesley's "optimism of grace." It is not in human ability or potentiality but in supernatural grace seen as healing and enablement.

Furthermore, if the Scripture provides for the possibility, we must come to an understanding of what such perfection involves so as not to involve the Bible in contradiction, for in Wesley's view, all biblical teaching is subject to experiential verification. It is here that he weaves his way through the thorny questions implied in the earlier survey of the various ways in which sanctification has been interpreted. If perfection entails keeping the law in its most profound requirements, it is not possible. If love can be perfect only with the beatific vision, it awaits the eschaton. Here we can see the deep significance of the discoveries he made in the devotional literature of Jeremy Taylor, Thomas à Kempis, and William Law. In brief, he discovered the centrality of "purity of intention" and the inward character of true religion. "I saw," he said, "that 'simplicity of intention, and purity of affection,' one design in all we speak or do, and one desire ruling all our tempers, are indeed 'the wings of the soul,' without which she can never ascend to the mount of God."[92]

He then set himself to the task of giving content to the ideal from the Bible. His first and foremost discovery of what sanctification meant was that it is the renewal of man in the image of God. As the only perfect embodiment of that image since the Fall is Christ, one could speak of this goal as Christlikeness. But further, from biblical input, it could also be summarized in the term "love," which is best expressed in what Jesus called the first and greatest commandment: "Thou shalt love the Lord thy God with all thy heart, . . . soul, . . . mind, and . . . strength" and the second, "Thou shalt love thy neighbour as thyself" (Mark 12:30-31, KJV). Negatively, it involved the absence of sin, by which he meant inward sin such as pride, self-will, love of the world, anger, peevishness, and

---

92. Ibid., 9-10.

other dispositions contrary to the "mind . . . which was also in Christ" (Phil. 2:5, KJV).[93]

Certain formulas may be used to illustrate the development from Catholicism through Luther to Wesley as adjustment is made between faith and love. For the Roman Catholic theology, following Thomas Aquinas, the order of the Christian life may be characterized as "faith formed by love." Luther rejected this because it made sanctification precede justification and replaced it with "faith formed by Christ." Wesley, however, with his ethical concerns adopted Paul's formula from Galatians: "faith working by love" (cf. 5:6). This, he thought, held together his stress upon faith as the foundation of the Christian life and his insistence that love is the manifestation of that life.

From his understanding of the *imago Dei* as love, Wesley interprets the Christian life as a process of developing love that moves along in part by way of definable stages. Love is instilled in the heart in regeneration. From that point on, there is a gradual development that knows no finis, not even death. But there is an instantaneous moment in the process that may be called perfect love, or entire sanctification, perfect only in the sense of being unmixed. Wesley's own description verifies John Peters' claim that the most appropriate term for Wesley's understanding of entire sanctification is "expulsion," or love expelling sin: "It is love excluding sin; love filling the heart, taking up the whole capacity of the soul. . . . For as long as love takes up the whole heart, what room is there for sin therein?"[94]

With this sketchy survey, we may clearly see that Wesley interpreted sanctification in terms of love (like Thomas) and as a transformation of being (as the Eastern fathers) but always in the context of justification by grace through faith (as the Reformers). These were all merged in a unique theological understanding that took seriously the fallenness of human nature and the power of God along with the scriptural teaching about a perfectionist ethic. With all these qualifications, Wesley could proclaim to the world that "where sin abounded, grace did much more abound" (Rom. 5:20, KJV).

We look now to the second question, "How does one seek entire sanctification?" Much of the history of the theology of the

93. Ibid., 11, 28, 41, 12, 17, 29. See also sermon on "Sin in Believers."
94. *StS* 2:448, 457; Peters, *American Methodism*, 59.

Christian life does not address this question, partly because there has been a spotty affirmation of its possibility. Often, when addressed, it is seen to be pursued by good works and/or discipline, but this approach is usually within the context of some form of works righteousness. Hence we turn directly to Mr. Wesley for his teaching concerning the way one should prepare himself for the Spirit's work of perfecting. And we must always keep in mind that sanctification is consistently seen by him in the setting of justification by faith. One's holiness, whatever the degree, is never a basis for acceptance with God.[95]

While Wesley does not provide a scheme that, if followed, will lead automatically into the experience of entire sanctification, he does speak of three factors that prepare one for the time when in His sovereign freedom, God "cuts short His work in righteousness" (cf. Rom. 9:28, KJV).

The first factor is *repentance*.[96] This repentance is different from that repentance that precedes justification. It does not entail guilt but self-knowledge concerning the existence of remaining sin of an inward, dispositional nature. It is similar to that first repentance in that self-knowledge is the central ingredient. This repentance further involves the realization of one's utter helplessness to deliver oneself from inward sin.

The second factor is *mortification*.[97] This is obviously a synergistic operation and is the gradual dimension of the work of sanctification. It is in this connection that Wesley's much-used description of how sanctification is both gradual and instantaneous is best understood:

> A man may be dying for some time: yet he does not, properly speaking, die, till the soul is separated from the body; and in that instant, he lives the life of eternity. In like manner, he may be dying to sin for some time; yet he is not dead to sin, till sin is separated from his soul; and in that instant, he lives the full life of love. And as the change undergone, when the body dies, is of a different kind, and infinitely greater than any we had known before, yea, such as till then, it is impossible to conceive; so the change wrought, when the soul dies to sin, is of a

---

95. To speak of degrees of holiness is possible in Wesley's understanding. Only ceremonial holiness disallows the idea. But ceremonial holiness does not involve a real change and therefore does not fit into Wesley's generic definition of sanctification as moral transformation.

96. See sermon "The Repentance of Believers," in *StS* 2:379 ff.

97. *Plain Account*, 42.

different kind, and infinitely greater than any before, and than any can conceive, till he experiences it. Yet he still grows in grace, in the knowledge of Christ, in the love and image of God; and will do so, not only till death, but to all eternity.[98]

It should be noted that Wesley's irreducible emphasis on sanctification as essentially ethical makes it possible for him to hold consistently to the progressive aspect of the process of coming to the moment of full salvation. When sanctification is interpreted ceremonially, there is no place for gradual sanctification. There is no such thing as degrees of ritual purity. It occurs in the moment of the ritual and is as fully actual at that moment as it will ever be.

The third factor is *faith*. This element answers to the second definition of repentance mentioned above. Faith here is confidence in the promises of God to deliver from inward sin. Knowing we cannot free ourselves from the inherent corruption of nature (which has the character of incomplete or perverted love), we wait in patience for God's action within us. It is faith that answers to the instantaneousness of entire sanctification. As Wesley said, if there be not an instantaneous deliverance from the seed of sin (self-love), there is no entire sanctification.

Faith is also the basis for his belief that one may expect the work of God to occur early in the Christian life. He had early in his experience felt that only shortly before death, after a long maturation period, could a person expect to be wholly sanctified. A change from this position is reflected in the *Plain Account*, where he says that both "my brother [Charles] and I [have] maintained . . . that we are to expect it, not at death, but every moment; that now is the accepted time, now is the day of this salvation."[99]

In the century after the Wesleyan revival, another significantly different interpretation of the way to entire sanctification emerged. This proposal is associated with the name of Mrs. Phoebe Palmer. Mrs. Palmer was the wife of a New York City physician who, with her husband, traveled widely during summer months as a lay evangelist and became a very prominent leader in holiness circles, particularly among women's groups. With the beginning of her leadership of the "Tuesday Meeting for the Promotion of Holiness," her success in leading people into the experience of entire sanctification was phenomenal and widespread until her death in 1874.

---

98. Ibid., 62.
99. P. 50.

Mrs. Palmer's unique contribution to holiness theology was in her renowned "altar phraseology." In a letter dated November 15, 1849, she explains how she arrived at this position, for which her biography claims originality:

> Her illustrations of the processes,—human and divine,— that are involved in the entire sanctification of the Christian disciple drawn from the Israelitish altar of burnt offering, and the rites and customs thereunto appertaining, are hers by right, if not of discovery, yet of distinct application, in the present century.[100]

Mrs. Palmer explains that she was seeking for scriptural support for her belief that it is one's duty to believe after having met the conditions of consecration unto sanctification. Her attention was drawn to Heb. 12:10, which she felt gave her the basis for claiming that it was a "duty to believe that the offering was *sanctified,* when laid upon the altar." This methodology became a tool in the hands of Mrs. Palmer to shorten the time span between regeneration and entire sanctification, and with it she led many people into a profession of entire sanctification early in their Christian experience. There are two simple steps: First, meet the conditions, which are in sum "presenting myself a living sacrifice to God, through Christ—laying all, whether known or unknown upon that altar which sanctifieth the gift"; and second, faith—faith that God would fulfill His promise.[101]

Wheatley sums up her activities using this method:

> In evangelistic expeditions to different places, Mrs. Palmer repeatedly witnessed . . . souls awakened, justified, and wholly sanctified within the compass of a few days or hours. In one of her works, she narrates the experience of one who was justified, wholly sanctified, and called to preach the gospel in three days.[102]

There were serious questions raised among her contemporaries to this new methodology. The chief objection had to do with the witness of the Spirit. Mrs. Palmer argued that to claim the witness before one could be certain God accepts the sacrifice is to make it "a matter of knowledge, and of course would not require faith." Her critics, however, called attention to the danger of pre-

---

100. Richard Wheatley, *The Life and Letters of Mrs. Phoebe Palmer* (New York: Palmer and Hughes, 1884), 532.

101. Ibid., 536-37.

102. Ibid., 531. See analysis by W. M. Greathouse in Bassett and Greathouse, *Exploring Christian Holiness* 2:299 ff., for the same conclusions.

sumption involved in profession without the accompanying witness of the Spirit, both internally and in terms of the ethical fruit. Perhaps the most serious problem with this interpretation is the definition of sanctification in ceremonial terms, thus laying it open to many practical dangers.[103]

In the light of the numerous distinctions noted throughout this discussion, it may be helpful to bring some things together by way of an analysis of "sanctificationist" language. We can do this with a taxonomy of terms, using a simplified version of contemporary linguistic philosophy—that is, we will seek to identify what "linguistic contexts" (we are using this term to refer to what Ludwig Wittgenstein called "language-games," having nothing to do with playing games with words but simply recognizing that the same terms have different connotations when used in different settings; for example, the term *strike* has significantly different connotations when used in a baseball game, in bowling, or in the "game" of labor relations) are involved in the use of the various terms commonly employed to refer to the experience of entire sanctification. We can identify at least four different categories. Classifying terms as *ceremonial* implies that this is the linguistic context out of which they originally arose. This does not preclude the possibility that they may be used in an adapted sense to function in other linguistic contexts. Clearly this is what Ezekiel the priest was doing when he spoke of God "cleansing" His people "from idolatry," an *ethical* concept that retains ceremonial overtones of defilement. Defilement (the contrary of purity) is either a ceremonial term or used in a completely metaphorical sense. We will use the term *dynamic* to refer to those terms that identify sanctification in terms of the Divine Agent who effects it in the person, and *structural* to refer to those terms that speak of the structure of experience without particular attention to the content.

---

103. See H. Ray Dunning, "Sanctification—Ceremony or Ethics?" *Preacher's Magazine* 55, no. 1 (September, October, November, 1979). Mildred Bangs Wynkoop makes a devastating critique of this proposed methodology: "Nothing in the Bible supports the meaning which is given it today. In an attempt to clarify a theological concept Mrs. Phoebe Palmer, one of the most brilliant lights in early American holiness history, inadvertently created a cliché which has confused and confounded sincere seekers after God ever since. She is surely not to blame, but we are to blame for making a 'biblical' (?) theology out of a phrase useful in a select situation." *A Theology of Love: The Dynamic of Wesleyanism* (Kansas City: Beacon Hill Press of Kansas City, 1972), 189.

STRUCTURAL	CEREMONIAL	ETHICAL	DYNAMIC
Second Blessing	Cleansing	Perfect Love	Baptism with the Holy Spirit
Second Work of Grace	Heart Purity	"the mind that was in Christ" "renewal in the image of God" Christian Perfection	The Fullness of the Spirit

It will be obvious from a cursory look at this that Wesley used almost exclusively ethical terminology. While in no sense did he downplay the work of the Spirit or avoid the idea of cleansing from sin, he doubtless understood that pneumatological language was always in need of definition, whereas the ethical, especially when informed by Christological concepts, was self-defining. Daniel Steele reveals an awareness of both the historical facts and the theological insight of Wesley's care with terminology. In an answer to a questioner, he said that he had counted 26 terms used by Wesley to refer to the experience of sanctification.

> But "the baptism of (or with) the Spirit," and "fullness of the Spirit," are not phrases used by him, probably because there is an emotional fullness of a temporary nature, not going down to the very roots of the moral nature.[104]

Furthermore, since the ceremonial language does not necessarily entail any ethical content, it too is constantly in need of qualification. Such language also is in danger of becoming something less than ethical because of its "nonempirical" orientation. Wesley consistently reinterpreted ceremonial language in ethical terms.[105] The conclusion to all this is that entire sanctification in the Wesleyan understanding is best spoken of in Christological terms.

Beginning with John Fletcher and Joseph Benson, Wesley's successors began to make more use of pneumatological language.

---

104. *Steele's Answers* (Chicago: Christian Witness Co., 1912), 130-31.
105. Cf. Wynkoop, *Theology of Love*, 252-53. The whole of chap. 13 in this source deals with this issue, especially the terminology of *cleansing*, which became the buzzword for the 19th-century holiness movement. See below and note Wiley's almost exclusive use of this language in his chapter on entire sanctification. *CT*, vol. 2.

While Wesley was apparently uneasy with this, he did not consider Fletcher's teaching to contradict his own.[106]

The ceremonial language seemed to become the most prominent type used by Adam Clarke and his successors in the American holiness movement, and as a result of this, this teaching took on a character quite different from that of Wesley. W. M. Greathouse says of Clarke: "The work of the sanctifying Spirit encompasses our total salvation, but its intended issue is always the purification of the heart. This is Clarke's unvarying point."[107] It was Clarke's almost total preoccupation with this linguistic context that led to the oft-quoted statement from his *Christian Theology:*

> In no part of the Scriptures are we directed to seek holiness *gradatim.* We are to come to God as well for instantaneous and complete purification from all sin, as for instantaneous pardon. Neither the *seriatim* pardon, nor the *gradatim* purification, exists in the Bible.[108]

Growth in Grace

Language, we have seen, can be bewitching. There are few places where this has been more obvious than in theological discussions about spiritual growth or maturation. Growth, when applied to the spiritual life, is a metaphor taken from the field of biology. When its metaphorical character is not recognized, and it is used as an analogy for spiritual growth, it results in the application of a completely inappropriate imagery to the issue. Natural growth is simply the result of purely natural, nonvolitional factors and does not involve real change. Paradigms from the field of personal development are far more appropriate to elucidate the idea of growth.

The result of applying nonpersonal explanations to personal life is not only less than helpful in any practical way but also creates what Mildred Bangs Wynkoop has termed a "credibility gap."[109] This is a gap between doctrine and life that ultimately causes skepticism concerning the real practicality of theological analyses.

Furthermore, as we noted in the last section, when sanctification is interpreted exclusively in terms of ceremonial concepts (pu-

---

106. See Bassett and Greathouse, *Exploring Christian Holiness* 2:240.
107. Ibid., 247.
108. (New York: T. Mason and G. Lane, 1840), 207-8.
109. *Theology of Love,* chap. 3.

rity, cleansing), it makes it extremely awkward to speak of real development, with the result that discussions carried on in this context without recognizing the metaphorical character of the language do not provide a truly viable theory of spiritual growth and leave the impression that there is no real development in the Christian life after the moment of entire sanctification. It is on this basis that it is possible to distinguish between gradual or progressive sanctification and growth in grace. But in terms of the Wesleyan definition of sanctification as a real change, real development as characterizes persons rather than things fulfills the requirements of the definition.

What we propose here is a simplified version of personal development that we believe is appropriate as a paradigm to understanding the process of growth in grace. Development that is real includes (1) intention, (2) goal, and (3) occasion.

Plants and animals normally grow toward physical maturity by the proper environment. But environment alone is insufficient to create growth of the human spirit. There must be the inward dimension of desire, commitment, or intention. Theologically, we see this drive imparted by the work of the Holy Spirit in both awakening and repentance. We have noted that awakening occurs when a person is made aware of a discrepancy between his present status and an ideal with which he has been confronted. Repentance is the human response (made possible by prevenient grace) to this awakening that precisely involves steps that reflect an intent to bring oneself into conformity with this ideal. It has both negative and positive connotations. That is, it includes a turning away from that which is inconsistent with the ideal and a turning to that which embodies or exemplifies the ideal. This is the fruit of repentance. Regeneration, following repentance, is defined psychologically as a reorientation of one's whole value structure, which implies that one's intentionality is dramatically redirected.

Gordon Allport's words provide an illuminating insight on this reorientation from a psychologist's perspective:

> It sometimes happens that the very center of organization of a personality shifts suddenly and apparently without warning. Some impetus, coming perhaps from a bereavement, an illness, or a religious conversion, even from a teacher or book, may lead to a reorientation.[110]

---

110. *Becoming*, 87.

Holiness literature has often insisted that growth in grace accelerates after the moment of entire sanctification. This has usually been explained in metaphorical language drawn from the biological realm and has led popular understanding to conclusions that cannot be rendered operational. However, it is at the point of "intention" that the truth of this contention actually comes to light. The experience of many unfortunately echoes Robert Robinson's "prone to wander" (original "Come, Thou Fount"), or as Wesley was wont to say it, one's love was mixed and not pure. But with the resolution of this double-mindedness and the expulsion of all lesser loves so that one does truly love God with all his heart, soul, mind, and strength, he has achieved purity of heart, which, as Søren Kierkegaard rightly said, is to "will one thing." Thus it is only natural that one whose intention, desire, or commitment to the ideal is so focused should more effectually achieve greater conformity to the ideal.

Indolent, lackadaisical, smug, self-satisfied believers can only stagnate into static patterns of living. Only one who like Paul does "press toward the mark" will achieve the dynamic development that ought to characterize the normal Christian. It is instructive that in the passage (Phil. 3:12-16, KJV) in which Paul with some indirectness claims perfection, or maturity (v. 15), he identifies it with being "stretched out" toward achieving the perfection or maturity that he overtly disclaims (cf. ASV).

But the greatest degree of intention is diffused and ineffective if it is devoid of direction. Hence there is the necessity of a goal or telos. Even a superficial reading of the New Testament will make the identification of such an ideal unequivocal: It is the character of Christ. The Lord Jesus is the standard of spiritual maturity, and thus Paul speaks of the adulthood of the Church as attaining to the "unity of the faith and of the knowledge of the Son of God, to mature manhood, to the measure of the stature of the fulness of Christ" (Eph. 4:13).

This passage suggests two important ingredients involved in spiritual maturation, and the larger context introduces a third. First, this picture of maturity after the pattern of Christ is corporate in nature. It is the Church of which he speaks. While growth is individual, it is not individualistic but normatively occurs in the context of the community of faith. This truth will be noted more fully in the chapter on the Church.

Second, the element of knowledge is introduced. The pervasiveness of this idea in the New Testament is remarkable and is an explicit expression of the element of the goal that we here propose (cf. 2 Pet. 3:18; Phil. 1:9; etc.). Knowledge is not the result of growth but the prerequisite of growth. It is "knowledge of our Lord and Savior Jesus Christ" that gives content to our understanding so as to provide direction. Knowledge is not itself to be equated with maturity but considered as an indispensable ingredient in its achievement.

Psychological analysis is able to identify personality disorders in terms of deviation from normal personhood. Apart from some concept of normalcy, it would be impossible to recognize such deviations or to achieve normal personhood. In the spiritual realm such normative criteria are not derived from the average but from the One who alone is fully normal. All others fall short of full humanness.

The third element in growth suggested in the larger context of the Ephesian passage is Paul's exhortation to "put off your old nature [man] which belongs to your former manner of life and is corrupt through deceitful lusts, and be renewed in the spirit of your minds, and put on the new nature [man], created after the likeness of God in true righteousness and holiness" (4:22-24).

"Old man" here refers to the preregenerate life and includes both behavior and the state of being that lies behind the behavior. All three instances of Paul's use of the metaphor (Rom. 6:6; Col. 3:9; Eph. 4:19-25) when read in context can admit of no other logical meaning.[111] Paul is exhorting his readers to put behind them all that pertained to their old life in terms of both act and being, and to put on the new life, which is given content by the character of Christ.

Spiritual maturation is both negative and positive. It is the ridding ourselves of all that is contrary to the mind of Christ and adding those virtues that are defined by the person of the Savior. The most poignant passage that embodies this truth as well as indicating the dynamic agency of this process to be the Holy Spirit is 2 Cor. 3:18: "And we all, with unveiled face, beholding the glory [image] of the Lord [in the face of Jesus Christ], are being changed

---

111. Cf. J. Kenneth Grider, "The Meaning of 'Old Man,'" *Nazarene Preacher,* February 1972, 15 ff., for a careful and, in this writer's judgment, irrefutable exegesis of these passages that argues for this interpretation.

into his likeness from one degree of glory [likeness] to another; for this comes from the Lord who is the Spirit."

These first two factors in spiritual growth may be illuminated by noting what A. H. Maslow has referred to as deficit and growth motives. Deficit motives call for the reduction of tension and restoration of equilibrium. This could correspond to the motivation that generally might inform repentance and would lead to an ethic of obligation. However, to be constantly moved by fear or guilt does not lead to a healthy spiritual life. One should move toward growth motives. These maintain tension (instead of eliminating it) in the interest of distant and often unattainable goals. This characteristic of growth motives distinguishes human becoming from animal becoming and adult becoming from infant becoming. Growth motives produce what Allport calls "oriented becoming." He comments on these two types of motivation (or intention):

> By growth motives we refer to the hold that ideals gain upon the process of development. Long-range purposes, subjective values, comprehensive systems of interest are all of this order. . . . To say that a person performs certain acts and abstains from others because he fears God's punishment would be to travesty the experience of most religious people, whose consciences have more to do with love than with fear. An inclusive path of life is adopted that requires discipline, charity, reverence, all experienced as lively obligations by a religious person. If we encounter in a personality fear of divine punishment as the sole sanction for right doing, we can be sure we are dealing with a childish conscience, with a case of arrested development.[112]

The third major element that we propose to be essential for growth in grace is occasion. Real development does not take place in a vacuum, but in encounter with situations that call for response in the light of the ideal. If one grows in faith, it is in relation to appropriating the promises of God in specific cases; if one grows in love, it is in terms of loving someone or ones and not as the increase of some abstract quantity. Real ethical transformation results from an encounter that requires a decision. If my intentionality is strong, I decide my behavior on the basis of the image of the kind of person I want to become and thus become that kind of person in a real sense. The ideal becomes more and more actualized. In the interaction between human discipline and effort and divine grace,

---

112. *Becoming*, 68, 72-73.

the interplay between these basic ingredients of growth elicits a greater conformity to the image of God as it is mirrored for us in Jesus Christ. We are being changed from one degree of likeness to another.

The Holy Spirit as Eschatological Gift

The final aspect of the work of the Spirit that we shall notice is a distinctly Pauline teaching. The Spirit that indwells all believers conveys to them the assurance of final salvation, or their resurrection. The Spirit "who raised Christ Jesus from the dead will give life to your mortal bodies also through his Spirit which dwells in you" (Rom. 8:11). Note once again the close correlation between Jesus and the Spirit. The realization that the power of the Spirit is resurrection power is derived from the knowledge that it was this same power that raised Jesus from the grave. This is one further reason for calling Him the Spirit of Christ.

Carrying this insight further, Paul speaks of the Spirit as the "first fruits" or "guarantee" or "down payment" (Amp.) of the final resurrection (Rom. 8:23; 2 Cor. 1:22; 5:5; Eph. 1:13-14). We have here another expression of the fundamental motif of New Testament theology: the tension between realized and futuristic eschatology. The future has broken into the present, but it has not yet been fully actualized. That awaits the final consummation.

The resurrection of Christ was more than an isolated event in which an individual overcame death; it was the death of the old aeon and the birth of the new aeon. Hence to be in Christ or in the Spirit (which we have seen to be synonymous) is to be in the age to come and to participate in its power.

G. Eldon Ladd correctly observes that "the death and resurrection of Christ were not merely events in past history but eschatological events." But in attempting to restrict these events to exclusively objective-historical significance, he misses one of Paul's fundamental teachings. His efforts to demonstrate that Paul does not teach that the Christian life involves "subjective experience" fails to take account of the pervasive truth that, for Paul, there is a subjective appropriation of the age to come into one's own experience. In fact, the apostle's emphasis entails an existential dimension of Christian experience that is really sanctification broadly conceived.[113]

The present experience of the Spirit is of resurrection power. This is the implication of Paul's phrase "risen with him" (Col. 2:12, KJV). James S. Stewart describes it thus:

> This life which flows from Christ into man is something totally different from anything experienced on the merely natural plane. It is different, not only in degree, but also in kind. It is *kainotas zoas,* a new quality of life, a supernatural quality. As Paul puts it elsewhere, "There is a new creation"—not just an intensification of powers already possessed, but the sudden emergence of an entirely new and original element—"whenever a man comes to be in Christ." He begins to live in the sphere of the post-resurrection life of Jesus.[114]

This leads us to observe that final salvation is seen in terms of resurrection. The future hope, within the biblical context of creation, does not anticipate a disembodied existence. In fact, this would have been less than satisfactory to the Hebrew mind. Future life to be a real hope involved full redemption of the body (Rom. 8:23) via the resurrection from the dead. Martin Luther, in a sermon during Easter season, proclaimed this faith:

> If we are, at the last day, to rise bodily, in our flesh and blood, to eternal life, we must have had a previous spiritual resurrection here on earth. Paul's words in Rom. 8:11 [mean] God having quickened, justified and saved you spiritually, he will not forget the body, the building or tabernacle of the living spirit; the spirit being in this life risen from sin and death, the tabernacle, or the corruptible flesh-and-blood garment, must also be raised; it must emerge from the dust of earth, since it is the dwelling-place of the saved and risen spirit, that the two may be reunited unto life eternal.[115]

---

113. *Theology,* chap. 34.
114. *Man in Christ,* 193.
115. *Compend,* 239.

Sanctification: Renewal in the Image of God

The New Testament and John Wesley speak with one voice in proclaiming that the great purpose of redemption is to restore man to the image of God. This is the "end of religion."[1] Salvation is defined as "the renewal of our souls after the image of God."[2] The total process of sanctification from its beginning in the new birth, its "perfection in love" at entire sanctification, and its progressive development toward final salvation has as its objective the restoring of man to his original destiny.[3] This is, as Lindström correctly observed, "the widest but also the most proper use of the word sanctification."[4]

This understanding of the meaning of sanctification did not disappear from the theological scene with the close of the New Testament only to be rediscovered by John Wesley in the 18th century. It was identified by all major interpreters of the Christian life throughout the whole period. Our brief notes on the history of

---

1. *StS* 2:223-24.
2. *Works* 8:47.
3. See *StS* 2:445 ff.; *Works* 6:509.
4. *Wesley and Sanctification*, 123.

Christian thought about sanctification have called attention to its prevalence in classical Christian teaching about sanctification. The chief issue is not whether this is a proper way of speaking about the substance of sanctification, but rather (1) what is the significance or meaning of the *imago* to which man is called, and (2) how and in what degree it is restored.[5]

At the outset we should be careful to note that there is both a positive and a negative aspect to this great goal of salvation. The positive side is the infusing of love, and the negative is the eradication of sin. W. B. Pope insists that the combination of these two elements is peculiar to Methodist theology.[6]

When the positive side is stressed, the continuity of the Christian life from its origin in the new birth to final salvation comes most clearly into view. It is when the negative side is emphasized that the instantaneous moment of entire sanctification becomes most obvious. This implies, not that there is not a definite moment in both movements, but that it is more easily recognized in one than the other. Both the nature of the sin that is expelled and support for this premise is seen in the words of Harald Lindström:

> When from this point of view [holiness as love] Wesley compares the stage of justification and new birth with that of perfect sanctification, the difference is only one of degree. The kind of life is the same in entire sanctification as in new birth.
>
> Entire sanctification is seen more clearly as a distinct stage, higher and different from that of new birth, when we turn to perfection as liberation from sin. Entire sanctification involves a love incompatible with sin. It is a love unmixed with sin, a pure love. Earlier sanctity was alloyed with sinful inclinations, which affected the soul. After the experience of perfect sanctification, however, there is "no mixture of any contrary affections: All is peace and harmony after." [From sermon "On Patience."][7]

In renewing man in His image, God's great goal of the total salvation process, one must take account of both sides, the negative and the positive. Thus we begin with the question of sin and its possible eradication from the believer's heart.

---

5. We are here deliberately reversing a trend in popular 19th-century holiness literature by giving primary consideration to the substance rather than the structure of sanctification. For elaborations of the distinction between these two and the significance of their relation, see Staples, "Sanctification and Selfhood," 3 ff.; Wynkoop, *Theology of Love*, chaps. 15 and 16. Her language is "the substance" and "the circumstance," which she claims is Wesley's.

6. *Compendium* 3:97.

7. *Wesley and Sanctification*, 142.

480 OF GRACE, FAITH, AND HOLINESS

Eliminating the Negative

Language, we noted in the last chapter in connection with sanctification linguistic contexts, may be bewitching. This is equally true with the terminology of sin. As a result much confusion has ensued, and philosophical and theological inadequacies have been propagated that have militated against proper theological understanding and further contributed to the "credibility gap" (Wynkoop).

In chapter 9 we discussed the question of sin rather thoroughly, and this should be assumed in our present discussions. There we demonstrated that sin is to be defined in terms of the image of God in the sense that it is the missing the mark of man's destiny, which is to stand in right relationship to God. This means that sin is a perversion of man's fully human existence, which in essence is the absence of holiness. As Mildred Bangs Wynkoop acutely observes, "Holiness is not the antithesis of sin (in that order), but sin is the antithesis of holiness. Holiness is prior and positive. It is not 'the absence of sin' in the same way that sin is the absence of holiness."[8]

Understanding sin as defective or perverted love provides a sound conceptual basis for theologizing about the *ordo salutis.* In the sinner, sin reigns (cf. Rom. 5:21; 6:12); that is, he gives unchecked (except by prevenient grace internally or social pressure externally) expression to this misdirected love or egocentricity. Thus he is under the power of, or enslaved by, sin. In justification the guilt of the manifestation of such sin is dealt with (pardon, forgiveness), and in regeneration the power of sin is broken.

> *He breaks the power of canceled sin;*
> *He sets the prisoner free.*
> —CHARLES WESLEY

However, there remains in the believer the being of sin.[9] Wesley finds three supports for his claim that while sin no longer reigns, it remains in the converted.

The first support he finds in Scripture. Here the struggle between flesh and Spirit is the decisive issue. "Indeed this grand point, that there are two contrary principles in believers—nature

---

8. *Theology of Love,* 152.
9. Sermon "On Sin in Believers," *StS* 2:373.

and grace, the flesh and the Spirit—runs through all the Epistles of St. Paul, through all the holy Scriptures."[10] This suggests that properly interpreting Paul's use of flesh (sarx) is crucial for understanding the nature of the sin that remains.[11]

The second support is found in experience. His research led him to affirm that it is the universal experience of believers that they were not fully delivered from all sin at the "first work of grace." Even though it may not be apparent in the early stages of the glow of a new faith, eventually its presence surfaces.

The third support is found in the creeds. Historic creeds from all traditions speak of sin remaining in believers. However, here Wesley finds less support than he supposes, since the creedal statements often identify this remaining sin as concupiscence. From our earlier study of Augustine we learned that if sin is interpreted in this way, it remains in all who are human until the end. And this is in fact what most of the creeds explicitly affirm.[12] Hence the critical question concerns the nature of the sin that remains.

First, we must observe that it is not substantival in nature, that is, a spiritual substance. Wesley has been accused, even by sympathetic interpreters, of seeing sin in this mode. Edward H. Sugden, in his editorial notes to the sermon on "Christian Perfection," says that

> both he and many of his followers have been brought into some confusion of view by the idea that the carnal mind is something in man which can be removed, like an aching tooth, or a cancerous growth; or a sort of stain or defilement which can be washed away, like an ink-blot, or a patch of filth on the body.[13]

Mildred Bangs Wynkoop, a devoted follower of Wesley's thought, also thinks he falls into this trap because he "used the language of Reformation doctrine."[14] However, it seems to this writer that these judgments do not adequately take into account the metaphorical use of language. Wesley, like Paul, makes exten-

---

10. Ibid., 367.

11. See Dennis F. Kinlaw, "Sin in Believers: The Biblical Evidence," in *The Word and the Doctrine*, comp. Kenneth E. Geiger (Kansas City: Beacon Hill Press, 1965), 119 ff., for an illuminating discussion of the biblical sources for the idea of sin in believers.

12. See Harry E. Jessop, *Foundations of Doctrine* (Chicago: Chicago Evangelistic Institute, 1944), 14-15.

13. *StS* 2:148.

14. *Theology of Love*, 153.

sive use of metaphorical language about sin; and if this is not recognized, and the figures of speech are taken literally, one would get the impression that sin is a thing. When Wesley specifies what this remaining sin is, it is always an attitude or disposition "contrary to the mind that was in Christ." If one were to ask for a connotative definition of inward sin, this would doubtless be it. But this is not substantival, as we will see below.

Second, it is also inadequate to conceptualize sin in terms of ceremonial holiness. This is the actual implication of Sugden's last statement in the quotation cited above. As we saw in the last chapter with "sanctificationist" language, so with the question of sin, ceremonial language can be quite misleading. "Cleansing," "purity," "defilement," and so on are perfectly appropriate, biblical terms, but the linguistic context from which they derive consistently provides cultic means of cleansing. Hence it is possible to see sanctification as involving ceremonial cleansing from impurity as an inner, transcendental (in the Kantian sense) experience that does not necessarily entail ethical transformation. As with his use of terms to speak of sanctification, Wesley also makes clear that his basic understanding of sin is perverted or imperfect love, and thus ceremonial language, when used, must be refocused so as to fit the context. It is here that the basic fallacy—almost universally present in contemporary popular treatments of the subject—of beginning with a dictionary definition to enlighten a theological argument comes into view. To derive a definition of holiness terms from the dictionary is an almost sure way to miss the biblical perspective. Taking the derivation of the terms seriously, the compilers of the dictionary definitions invariably interpret sanctification language from its original ceremonial source.

When we turn to Wesley's descriptions of sin in believers, it seems unequivocal that it involves attitudes or dispositions contrary to the mind that was in Christ, which means dispositions contrary to the two great commandments to love God and neighbor perfectly. Since these constitute the essence of perfect sanctification, any defection from them constitutes a missing the mark, or sin.

Representative lists of carnal traits include revengeful passion, envy, malice, wrath, unkind temper, malign affection, pride, haughtiness of spirit, self-will, love of the world, lust, idolatry, inordinate affection, evil surmisings, hatred, bitterness, resentment, desire of revenge, covetousness, uncharitable conversation, and peevishness. When unpacked as to the motive implicit in each of these, we can identify at least three basic motifs: (1) There is self-sovereignty in relation to the divine sovereignty. If one has completely abdicated the throne of his life, divested himself of his rights, and surrendered these to God, then defensiveness when one's "turf" is invaded no longer occurs, since my turf is now God's turf. Otherwise this defensiveness often emerges as anger, jealousy, or some other reaction to being invaded. (2) There is also self-gratification, the tendency to satisfy one's own appetites in such a way as to not bring glory to God, to treat other persons as things, or to puff oneself up with a sense of self-importance. (3) There are also self-centered dispositions in relation to the other person, such as lust and desire for revenge.

All this pertains to the Pauline meaning of *sarx* used in its distinctive ethical sense. Flesh does not refer to the body, or to the natural appetites in this context. Richard Howard points out that

> it will help us to better understand the term *flesh* if we realize that it has a strong *descriptive* significance, which we normally associate with an adjective. For all practical purposes it is used as an adjective—in an absolute sense. The object which it modifies is not stated but is provided by the context. Thus you need to ask first—flesh *what?*

He then concludes that "in actuality when a man lives according to the flesh *[kata sarka]* he is living *according to himself.*"[15] The clear implication here is that when "carnal" or "fleshly" is used, it is referring to attitudes, dispositions, or behaviors that are essen-

---

15. Richard E. Howard, *Newness of Life: A Study in the Thought of Paul* (Kansas City: Beacon Hill Press of Kansas City, 1975), 29, 33. John A. Knight refers to the "original" sin as "a false condition of egocentricity." *In His Likeness* (Kansas City: Beacon Hill Press of Kansas City, 1976), 64. Merne A. Harris and Richard S. Taylor likewise refer to it as "a hard core of idolatrous self-love planted deep in the self as an inherited racial fault. We might call it a predispositional set toward idolatry—with self as the substitute god. . . . The supreme threat is God; therefore He is the Object, even though more or less subconsciously, of the supreme aversion. Paul says that essentially this nature is 'enmity against God, for it is not subject to the law of God, neither indeed can be' [Rom. 8:7]. But its enmity is due to its self-idolatry—its carnal-mindedness—a *phroneo*, or disposition, which is set on the self and its interests." "The Dual Nature of Sin," in *The Word and the Doctrine,* comp. Kenneth E. Geiger (Kansas City: Beacon Hill Press, 1965), 108. Howard's comment about the adjectival characteristic of flesh highlights the fact that *carnality* is not a biblical word. This word is a noun, but it is always used adjectivally to refer to persons, behavior, or dispositions. Hence one should only speak of carnal-mindedness, not "carnality" as if it were something within one.

tially self-authoritative. One is either behaving according to, or feeling inclinations to behave under, self-sovereignty.

Carnal traits, such as anger or jealousy, need to be carefully analyzed. There is a carnal anger that may be differentiated from an anger that is sometimes termed "righteous indignation." Jesus' anger manifested toward the money changers in the Temple was a jealousy for the proper use of God's house, not a temper tantrum reflecting the absence of love. If holiness is Christlikeness, this helps us recognize that it is not a temperless, bland type of existence but may be demonstrated in rather vigorous ways. However, there are few empirical means of distinguishing between the two types of anger, or jealousy. It is a distinction that can only be known in a private way. This probably explains Wesley's answer in the *Plain Account* to the question, "What is reasonable proof? How may we certainly know one that is saved from all sin?" He answered, "We cannot infallibly know one that is thus saved (nor even one that is justified), unless it should please God to endow us with the miraculous discernment of spirits."[16]

In the light of this discussion we can see that Mildred Bangs Wynkoop is correct in defining sin as "love locked into a false center, the self," and holiness as "love locked into the True Center, Jesus Christ our Lord."[17]

We may now know more clearly what Wesley meant when he used metaphorical language such as "inbred sin," "the seed of sin," or "the root of sin." These are to be taken, not as referring to something within one, but one's condition of disordered love, focused incompletely on God. It is this condition that engenders the feeling of helplessness, which is one aspect of the repentance of believers, and leads to the conclusion, drawn explicitly by Wesley, that this problem can only be dealt with by divine grace operative in one decisive blow of instantaneous deliverance. Wesley makes it plain:

> Though we watch and pray ever so much, we cannot wholly cleanse either our hearts or hands. Most sure we cannot, till it shall please our Lord to speak to our hearts again, to speak the second time, "Be clean"; and then only the leprosy is cleansed. Then only, the evil root, the carnal mind, is destroyed; and inbred sin subsists no more. But if there be no such second change, if there be no instantaneous deliverance after justification, if there be *none but* a gradual work of God (that there is

16. P. 57.
17. *Theology of Love*, 158.

a gradual work none denies), then we must be content, as well as we can, to remain full of sin till death; and, if so, we must remain guilty till death, continually *deserving* punishment.[18]

Accentuating the Positive

We now turn to the positive side of the overall work of salvation interpreted as renewing man in the image of God. This focuses our attention upon the total Christian life in its continuity so that the stages in the Christian life become somewhat less conspicuous. Lindström makes this point well.

> What, then, from this point of view [perfection as perfect love], is the difference between new birth and perfect sanctification? Love has already been instilled into the heart of man at new birth. From then on there is a gradual development. This is thought to continue even after the stage of perfect sanctification until the very moment of death—indeed after death too. There is therefore, Wesley thinks, no perfection of degrees, i.e. no perfection of concluded development. The distinction between new birth and entire sanctification seems therefore to be nothing more than a difference of degree in a continuous development. But if so, how can they also be described as distinct stages in the Christian life?[19]

It is our purpose in this section to focus upon this larger vision of the totality of God's saving intention that is implemented in the new birth, entire sanctification, and progressive sanctification (growth in grace). It commences at the dawn of spiritual life and continues—ideally—in an uninterrupted progression throughout all finite existence. Therefore one should never ask the question, "At what point in the Christian life does this occur?" It is occurring from the beginning on.

In our discussion of the idea of sin in chapter 9 we explored the implications of the image of God for this doctrine. There we suggested that a theological exegesis of the relevant biblical passages would indicate that the *imago* could be identified as a fourfold relation: to God, to other persons, to the earth, and to self. We characterized these relations in the state of integrity as freedom for God, freedom for the other person, freedom from the earth, and

---

18. Sermon "The Repentance of Believers," in *StS* 2:390-91. Re this quotation he would have been appalled that many of his 19th- and 20th-century successors *did* deny that there was a gradual work of sanctification.

19. *Wesley and Sanctification*, 141.

freedom from self-domination. All of these relations were disrupted by the Fall, and man stands in need of having the relations restored by the redemptive process.

These four relationships constitute what the Hebrew word *shalom* (peace) signifies. It means far more than the absence of conflict. It involves the harmony of an individual with himself, with nature, with the world of people, and clearly with God. In his description of the state of integrity, Elmer Martens beautifully describes this situation: "But in Eden, as the opening chapters of Genesis describe it, that wholeness exists. Man is in tune with God. Adam and Eve are unashamed with each other; they live in harmony with themselves as well as with animals. Not only their needs but their desires are fully met. Here is the perfect state."[20]

Thus *shalom* best describes the Edenic, pre-Fall state; but even more, it is the summary term that encompasses the goal toward which all God's redemptive acts are directed. He desires to transform the present fragmented state into healing and wholeness. Holiness is wholeness and is embodied in the beautiful *shalom* of God's plan for His people.

There is obviously a hierarchical relation between these, with man's relation to God being the primary and determining one. However, each relation is known in and with the others, and therefore they cannot be artificially separated as four unrelated, discrete realities. Nonetheless they may be analyzed seriatim for discussion purposes, but there will of necessity be an interpenetration, or cumulative effect.

When repentance and faith have restored man to the favor of God, it is God's intention to bring man to his appointed destiny, which has long been thwarted by sin. That destiny, we are saying, is embodied in the image of God. This is not only what man was but also what he is intended by God to become. Thus, in the salvation process, God accepts man just as he is and at that moment begins the process of making him into the kind of person He intends him to be. This latter is the working of grace that is described in a shorthand way by the term sanctification.

What are the possibilities of grace in this regard? We have already addressed that question in an earlier discussion as we spoke of the various ways in which sanctification has been envi-

---

20. *God's Design*, 28.

sioned in the history of Christian thought. We noted that one major interpretation viewed the *imago* in legal ways, and thus the process of sanctification was seen in terms of doing good works; and these good works, which constitute sanctification, are judged in terms of their conformity to the law. When the works of redeemed man are thus measured by the law of God in its fullest expectation, there is always a deficiency. As John Calvin puts it:

> We have not a single work going forth from the saints that if it be judged in itself deserves but shame as its just reward. . . . For since no perfection can come to us so long as we are clothed in this flesh, and the law moreover announces death and judgment to all who do not maintain perfect righteousness in works, it will always have grounds for accusing and condemning us unless, on the contrary, God's mercy counters it, and by continual forgiveness of sins repeatedly acquits us.[21]

Calvin's *Institutes* contain some beautiful passages describing the progress in sanctification of the believer who is pursuing the normal Christian life. Consider this affirmation:

> We confess that while through the intercession of Christ's righteousness God reconciles us to himself, and by free remission of sins accounts us righteous, his beneficence is at the same time joined with such a mercy that through his Holy Spirit he dwells in us and by his power the lusts of our flesh are each day more and more mortified; we are indeed sanctified, that is, consecrated to the Lord in true purity of life, with our hearts formed to obedience to the law.[22]

But he is always careful to qualify these descriptions with the disclaimer that one can ever be fully sanctified short of death. Only at that point will the falling short of the perfect law of God, which is sin, be put to an end. John Wesley concurs with this judgment when it is bound to this context. In the *Plain Account* he says in answer to the question, "But do we not 'in many things offend all' . . . ?" that in one sense we do, "and shall do, more or less, as long as we remain in the body."[23]

But Wesley discovered in the Scripture and other devotional sources another way of interpreting man's relation to God other than by law. He began this process of discovery under the tutelege of Jeremy Taylor, Thomas à Kempis, and William Law. From them he learned that the essence of piety was inward and intentional.

---

21. *Institutes* 3.14.10.
22. Ibid., 9.
23. P. 82.

"Purity of intention" was the phrase he used to speak of what he learned from Taylor. This paved the way for his recognition that while man can never be restored to the image of God in any legal sense or when it is interpreted in terms of law, he can be perfectly related to Him in terms of love. He found, in a word, the truth of Paul's assertion that "love is the fulfilling of the law" (Rom. 13:10). And love is a relationship of openness.

Consequently, when he was asked what Christian perfection or entire sanctification meant, he always replied, "It is the loving God with the whole heart, soul, mind, and strength," and "our neighbor as ourselves." While in our fallen condition we can never achieve the level of perfect performance and be restored to the image of God in its untarnished splendor, we may, by grace, stand in perfect relation to Him through the "expulsive power of a new affection" (Thomas Chalmers). And from that point, man can seek ever more perfectly to reflect God's character in his character and personality until the beauty of Jesus is more and more seen in and through his life.

We are suggesting that the image of God as *Freedom for God* is restored in this relationship of love understood as complete openness to the Heavenly Father. We may note briefly three consequences of this interpretation.

First, it implies that man enjoys the presence of the Lord. While it may be a weak analogy, some intimation of this love relation may be seen in the joy persons receive by being in the presence of another person who is loved very much. There does not necessarily need to be a flood of words; just being there is adequate to satisfy a deep sense of relation. This is possibly the idea that Wesley had in mind when he appropriated the Pauline trilogy as a standard way of giving content to what it meant to be entirely sanctified, or perfected in love: one rejoices evermore, prays without ceasing, and in everything gives thanks (1 Thess. 5:16-18, KJV).

Second, love of God implies total obedience. As Jesus said to His disciples, "If you love me, you will keep my commandments" (John 14:15). Another analogy, while having some weaknesses, may help illuminate this dimension. The ideal relation between parent and child, though involving factors not present in the divine-human relation, shares some parallels. The ideal parent always seeks the good of the child, and in turn the ideal child loves and respects the parent and has confidence that his commands are not capricious or arbitrary. This may reflect the proper love relation between Creator and creature. The relation is initiated and determined from His side, but when it is seen clearly that *agapē* love is the origin of the relation from God's side, the proper response is love from man's side. As John says, "We love him, because he first loved us," and adds, "For this is the love of God, that we keep his commandments. And his commandments are not burdensome" (1 John 4:19, KJV; 5:3). Because of love, the Christian life is not like a prisoner serving a life sentence, but the joy of a son who enthusiastically carries out the will of his father.

Third, it is quite clear that the fruit of the Spirit is various manifestations of love. The unitary character of the fruit (the term is singular, not plural) is due to the fact that it flows forth, like a stream from a fountain, from a single source.[24] Joy, peace, long-suffering, gentleness, goodness, faithfulness, meekness, and self-control (Gal. 5:22-23, cf. ASV, KJV) are all present at the beginning of the Christian life because love is present from the beginning. Note Mr. Wesley's description of conversion:

> There is as great a change wrought in our souls when we are born of the Spirit, as was wrought in our bodies when we are born of a woman. There is, in that hour, a general change from inward sinfulness, to inward holiness. The love of the creature is changed to the love of the Creator; the love of the world into the love of God. Earthly desires, the desire of the flesh, the desire of the eyes, and the pride of life, are, in that instant, changed, by the mighty power of God, into heavenly desires. . . . Pride and haughtiness subside into lowliness of heart; as do anger, with all turbulent and unruly passions, into calmness, meekness, and gentleness. In a word, the earthly, sensual, devilish mind, gives place to "the mind that was in Christ Jesus."[25]

This glowing description seems to leave no room for further growth, to say nothing of need for a further work of grace. But, as we saw in an earlier section of this chapter, Wesley's experience and his observation of the experience of others revealed that the first blush of the new life in Christ, which overwhelmed the new convert with its blessing, could mislead him into thinking that no sin, that is, imperfect love, remained after initial salvation. But in time, experience revealed the following condition, which he analyzed in the same sermon just quoted:

---

24. See Wesley's *Notes*, Gal. 5:22.
25. *Works* 6:488.

He was humble, but not entirely; his humility was mixed with pride: He was meek; but his meekness was frequently interrupted by anger, or some uneasy and turbulent passion. His love of God was frequently damped, by the love of some creature; the love of his neighbour, by evil surmising, or some thought, if not temper, contrary to love.

But following the moment of entire sanctification, Wesley claims, one's love is "unmixed" (see sermon "On Patience"). It is this characteristic of being unmixed that leads him to consistently speak of perfection in terms of the first commandment.

It is not easy to describe precisely what the biblical injunction (both from Moses and Jesus) means when it enjoins undivided love of God. This is perhaps one reason why Protestant thought reflects uneasiness about direct love for God and transposes it to neighbor love.[26] Some popular Christian music has reduced love for God to sentimentality and describes the divine-human relation with almost sensual overtones, all of which is unworthy of the transcendent Creator.

We would suggest that the concept of complete openness is a fruitful way of conceptualizing the restored relationship to God, which is summarized by the ideal of perfect love. Perhaps there is also a sense in which this goal is actualized when man's love for God experiences a transition from service to God for the benefits He bestows (or even less desirable, to avoid the consequences of rejecting Him) into service and love of God for who He is in himself, because He alone is worthy.

Freedom for the Other. We now turn to the second relation, which we have suggested as constituting the *imago Dei*. It is derived from the first. In the Genesis account, we noted how the absence of clothes symbolized the radical openness marking the love relationship between the first pair. Furthermore, the loss of this openness resulted in the covering of the body with clothes. It is at least interesting that Gregory of Nyssa, who exerted considerable influence upon John Wesley, equates the skins (clothes) of Adam and Eve as symbolic of original sin.[27]

Paul Bassett's analysis of the early baptismal rites and their theological significance ties this sacrament closely with the re-

26. See Gene Outka, *Agape: An Ethical Analysis* (New Haven, Conn.: Yale University Press, 1972), 8 n. 2.
27. R. S. Brightman, "Gregory of Nyssa and John Wesley in Theological Dialogue on the Christian Life" (Ph.D. diss., Boston University, 1969).

ceiving of the Holy Spirit, thus with sanctification. He also points out that the prebaptismal liturgy included the disrobing of the candidate. While Bassett interprets this symbolic act as referring to one's coming into earthly life naked and leaving it that way and thus as disclaiming this world's goods, it could also be interpreted in connection with the idea of openness. The clean garments with which the baptizand clothed himself afterward could conceivably suggest a new relation, devoid of all subterfuge, with his fellow believer into whose fellowship he was now being ushered.[28]

With these ideas we are introduced to the corporate aspects of sanctification. Unfortunately, much teaching in the modern holiness movement has been too individualistic in its emphasis. But biblical faith is irreducibly corporate. The Old Testament provides us with a solid background for this understanding. The purposes of the sacrifices within the covenant (see discussion in the chapter on Atonement) highlight the fact that one comes into relation with God by becoming a part of the people of Israel. One enters the covenant by becoming a part of the covenant community. The other side of this truth is seen in the identification of expulsion from the community with loss of saving relation to God.

It is sometimes mistakenly thought that this sense of solidarity in Old Testament religion was abandoned with the establishment of the new covenant in Jesus Christ. While it is true that a greater emphasis upon individual responsibility and accountability was introduced by the prophets Jeremiah and Ezekiel, it is not the case that the solidarity of persons within the covenant was abandoned for a view that the community is composed of a collection of discrete individuals only externally related to each other. Rather the corporate character of the Hebrew faith informs the New Testament doctrine of the Church, as only a cursory survey of the New Testament literature unequivocally reveals.

We have seen this truth more fully by looking into the benefits of the new covenant in Jesus Christ. Here we must speak further about the role of the Holy Spirit. The people of the old covenant were constituted by blood, being a part of the people of Israel, if not by birth, then by proselyte baptism. The new people of God, the new Israel, the Church, is constituted by the Holy Spirit. One of the central truths that Luke is seeking to set forth in the Book of

---

28. *Exploring Christian Holiness* 2:41 ff.

Acts is the fact that the gift of the Spirit creates a new reality, a corporate body brought into being by the infilling of the Spirit of Christ. The gift of the Spirit is not an individualistic gift, to be received in isolation from the community. It is a personal gift that creates an organic connection with other Spirit-filled persons.

This truth further illuminates the significance of the Day of Pentecost. First, the traditional position that this day should be identified as the birthday of the Church is exegetically sound. Some holiness writers have been pressed to abandon this position because they think that it is somehow in conflict with their position that the disciples were entirely sanctified in that initial effulgence of the Spirit.[29] But if we recognize that the sanctifying work of the Spirit has this corporate dimension, that part of the meaning of sanctification is the renewal of man in the image of God as relation to the other person, there is no tension between these two positions.

What we have in Luke's picture of the Early Church is a portrayal of a sanctified church constituted by the infilling of the Holy Spirit. It is more than a group of individually sanctified persons enjoying fellowship of a more or less social nature. What is seen there is a binding together of Spirit-filled persons into an organic unity of love created by the "community-creating Spirit" who abides within. It may be further noted that we also observe there the fulfillment of Jesus' high-priestly prayer for His followers that God would sanctify them "that they may be one" (John 17:22).

A survey of the experiences of these early Christians will clearly reveal the corporate dimensions of the sanctifying work of the Spirit, actualized in the Body of Christ. There was a unity of love that was characterized by complete openness, with all that that entailed for interpersonal relations. This helps explain the dire significance of the Ananias and Sapphira incident. Here was the first breach of that openness that holiness should create when fully actualized in the Body. Perhaps the reason this incident received such drastic treatment was that this clouded the openness with lying and deceit, and the power of the Church was diminished because its Christlike character was tarnished. The words of Peter declaring that Ananias did "lie to the Holy Spirit" (Acts 5:3) show

---

29. See Charles W. Carter, *The Person and Ministry of the Holy Spirit* (Grand Rapids: Baker Book House, 1974), 20.

how closely connected are the vertical and horizontal relations in spiritual reality.

There are some implications of this aspect of the *imago* when it is renewed by the sanctifying work of the Spirit. First, the essence of holiness in personal relations is sincerity. In his prayer for the Philippian church, Paul prays "that you may be sincere and without offense till the day of Christ" (1:10, NKJV). John Wesley was almost willing to equate entire sanctification with sincerity, especially if it be given its full New Testament implication. It is no more than sincerity, he says, "if you mean by that word, love filling the heart, expelling pride, anger, desire, self-will; rejoicing evermore, praying without ceasing, and in everything giving thanks. But I doubt, few use sincerity in this sense."[30]

Second, the uninhibited activity of the Holy Spirit within a body of Christian believers is conditioned upon the presence of openness to each other. Here is the significance of Jesus' words: "So if you are offering your gift at the altar, and there remember that your brother has something against you, leave your gift there before the altar and go; first be reconciled to your brother, and then come and offer your gift" (Matt. 5:23-24).

Third, love in relation to neighbor outside the community entails service and seeking his well-being. The tension sometimes perceived between personal conversion and social involvement is a faulty tension. From the biblical point of view, the two cannot be radically dichotomized.

Paul puts it this way: "Let no one seek his own, but each one the other's well-being" (1 Cor. 10:24, NKJV). This raises the question that the lawyer addressed to Jesus, "Who is my neighbor?" (Luke 10:29). Jesus' answer has far-reaching ramifications. In the first place, He did not answer the question directly but instead told the parable of the Good Samaritan. The parable actually addressed another issue, namely: "Which . . . proved neighbor" to the man in need (v. 36)? Thus as Paul Ramsey says,

> This parable tells us something about neighbor-love, nothing about the neighbor. What the parable does is to demand that the questioner revise entirely his point of view, reformulating the question first asked so as to require neighborliness of himself rather than anything of his neighbor.[31]

---

30. *Plain Account*, 84.
31. *Christian Ethics*, 93.

The second implication is that nothing in the neighbor qualifies our love for him. Jesus' answer does not define who neighbor is because, in so doing, love would be limited to those who fit the definition. Thus love finds neighbor in every man regardless of his status or other distinguishing characteristics. In this way neighbor love takes on more the character of *agapē* than *eros*. In a word, this is the kind of disinterested love that informed Jesus' command in Matt. 5:48—"You, therefore, must be perfect, as your heavenly Father is perfect."

The third dimension of the *imago* involves *Freedom from the Earth.* In his original, created condition man was given dominion over the remainder of created reality. This dominion seems to be directly related to man's own submission to the dominion of the Creator. But with the revolt against God, the earth revolted against man, and the proper relation was lost; man was no longer free from the earth. Augustine provides a penetrating analysis of the present condition of men in this dimension when he observed that we ought to love God and use things, but instead we tend to love things and use God.

We can see the significance of sanctification as restoring the proper relation to the earth by exploring the teaching of the New Testament on the topic of possessions, riches, or wealth. All of these are the products of the earth. It is astounding how pervasive this theme is in the Bible, especially in the New Testament. Why does Scripture give so much attention to this question? Doubtless Luke T. Johnson's analysis provides us with the answer. He says, "The way we use, own, acquire, and disperse material things symbolizes and expresses our attitudes and responses to ourselves, the world around us, other people, and, most of all, God."[32] In a word, it symbolizes all the relations about which we have been speaking; that is, they all come to focus in this issue, since they are all interrelated, as we noted at the outset.

Jesus spoke extensively to the question of possessions. A large segment of the Sermon on the Mount is given over to addressing the matter of "treasures" (Matt. 6:19-34). The basic thrust of these sayings "practically requires us to free ourselves from the cares that bind us to the world."[33] Thus dependence upon wealth is the antithesis of faith.

---

32. *Sharing Possessions* (Philadelphia: Fortress Press, 1981), 40.
33. Rudolf Schnackenburg, *The Moral Teaching of the New Testament* (New York: Seabury Press, 1965), 99.

Freedom from such dependence makes possible radical freedom for God. In a penetrating analysis, Luke Johnson demonstrates how possessions intimately relate to my perception of who I am, and that to create self-identity in relation to things rather than in relation to God is not only idolatry but also self-destructive, because it involves a basic perversion of values. He says:

> The real difficulty regarding possessions lies in what they mean to us. The real mystery concerning possessions is how they relate to our sense of identity and worth as human beings. The real sin related to possessions has to do with the willful confusion of being and having.[34]

From many passages, one could conceivably draw the conclusion that Jesus condemned wealth per se and advocated poverty as somehow inherently righteous. However, this would involve Him in some interesting contradictions, for as Rudolf Schnackenburg points out, He permitted himself to be the guest of rich men (Luke 7:36; 14:1), often accepted the hospitality of the well-to-do sisters of Bethany (10:38-42; John 11:1 ff.; 12:1 ff.), and the support of women of property (Luke 8:3).[35]

Nonetheless He did require the rich young ruler to sell all of his possessions (Matt. 19:16-27; Mark 10:17-28) in order to inherit the kingdom of heaven. Commenting on this incident, Wesley notes that "he who seeth the hearts of men saw it needful to enjoin this in one peculiar case, that of the young rich ruler. But he never laid it down for a general rule, to all rich men, in all succeeding generations."[36]

That poor is equivalent to righteous, as some have suggested the Bible teaches, would be strange at best. In the passages that seem to imply this (e.g., the story of the rich man and Lazarus in Luke 16), Schnackenburg pertinently explains:

> The form of this story was clearly determined by Jewish concepts of retribution. It is certainly assumed without question that the poor who are addressed also had a moral character fitting them to enter the kingdom of God. A purely economic, materialistic outlook was alien to Judaism: a godless poor man would never have a place in the future aeon merely because of his poverty. Jesus denied it more clearly still when he made

34. See n. 32 above.
35. *Moral Teaching*, 125.
36. *Works* 5:370.

fulfillment of the will of God the condition for entering the kingdom of God.[37]

Wesley points out cogently that it would be difficult to be in total poverty and at the same time adhere to Paul's admonition to "owe no man any thing" (Rom. 13:8, KJV), nor could we provide for the needs of our own household, which to fail to do, says Paul, is "worse than an infidel" and a denial of the faith (1 Tim. 5:8, KJV).[38]

As a result of these observations, we can only conclude that it cannot be the possession of property as such that is the obstacle, but only wealth that is owned in an idolatrous way. The advocacy of poverty by Jesus would suggest that He "regarded poverty as freedom for God and as a condition for the undivided dedication to God."[39] Conversely, Wesley speaks of riches as chains that bind men to the earth.[40]

For those who have obtained riches without seeking them (such as himself), Wesley advocates a threefold policy to avoid the perversion of priorities that results from an improper preoccupation with wealth: "Having *gained*, in a right sense, *all you can*, and *saved all you can*; in spite of nature, and custom, and worldly prudence, *give all you can*."[41]

If one has the courage to follow this advice, he will demonstrate that he is indeed free from the earth, that is, earthly possessions.

Freedom from Self-domination. We have noted how each of the other three dimensions of the *imago* are actually informed by the relationship to self and are skewed when man intrudes himself into the role of sovereign of his existence. Sin, in essence, is idolatry because it elevates the finite, created self to the position rightly held only by the Creator. It is for this reason that the most decisive work of grace in human life addresses the issue of self-sovereignty. It is this that Wesley means when he speaks of the "root of sin" or the "seed of sin." He is not referring to some ontological substance, but to the perversion of authority that occurs when love of God is not the controlling intention of the human heart.

Renewing man in the image of God entails the proper relation

---

37. *Moral Teaching*, 128-29.
38. *Works* 5:366-67.
39. Schnackenburg, *Moral Teaching*, 126-27.
40. *Works* 5:370.
41. Ibid. 7:9.

to self. It is not the annihilation of self, as certain Eastern religions desire. It is the submission of self to God's authority so that the love for God and neighbor is not modified improperly by self-interest, and one does not relate to the earth solely as a means of self-gratification.

This raises the question of a proper or improper self-love. This question has exercised the minds of Christian ethicists and theologians for centuries, and it has become a subject of widespread popular discussion in the present century.[42]

The renewed relation to the self that results from the sanctifying work of the Spirit is much like the relation to the earth. Just as the ownership of possessions is not within itself to be rejected, the issue with self pertains to whether or not one seeks to be the lord of his own life. It does not imply that one hates himself or has a low self-image. In fact, the proper relation to self is the way to a psychologically sound self-image.

Self-acceptance is an important ingredient in mental health. It is our contention that the New Testament understanding of justification by faith is the soundest basis for true self-acceptance. If God accepts me "just as I am," that is the profoundest reason possible to accept myself.[43]

Bruce Narramore proposes certain hindrances to self-acceptance that support this claim. The first stumbling block is the assumption that "I must reach a certain standard of maturity, attitude, or achievement in order to be accepted."[44] This is exactly the attitude produced by a theology of works righteousness. Justifi-

---

42. See Oliver O'Donovan, *The Problem of Self-love in St. Augustine* (New Haven, Conn.: Yale University Press, 1980); Outka, *Agape*, chap. 2; Bruce Narramore, *You're Someone Special* (Grand Rapids: Zondervan Publishing House, 1978); Robert H. Schuller, *Self-esteem* (Waco, Tex.: Word Publishing Co., 1982); Paul Ramsey, *Christian Ethics*, 295-306; George F. Thomas, *Christian Ethics and Moral Philosophy* (New York: Charles Scribner's Sons, 1955), 55-58. A perceptive critique by an evangelist is found in Richard E. Howard, "Egocentric Evangelism," *Wesleyan Theological Journal* 21, no. 1 (Spring 1986).

43. In an illuminating discussion Donald M. Baillie demonstrates how the denial of the idea of sin and the failure to recognize the reality of divine forgiveness leaves modern man no way of dealing with his moral failures, whereas the belief in such truths provides a sound psychological basis for dealing with them. He summarizes his point: "I have been trying to show the 'modern' man, in his own terms, that the consciousness of sin against God and of the divine forgiveness, instead of being morbid or unpractical, is the ultimate secret of wholesome living and far more conducive to it than the moralistic substitute which belongs to a secular age." *God Was in Christ*, 160-67.

44. *You're Someone Special*, 85-86.

cation by faith rejects this approach *en toto* and insists that God's acceptance is not dependent upon my own worthiness.

But the question of self-love is more pervasive than self-acceptance. To say with Augustine that the command to love God and our neighbor includes a command to love ourselves runs the risk of elevating to a command what men do naturally and treads dangerously close to the New Testament definition of sin. Paul Ramsey may be right when he declares that "no more disastrous mistake can be made than to admit self-love onto the ground floor of Christian ethics as a basic part of Christian obligation."[45]

But is it possible to so purify love for the other person to the point that all self-regarding love is distilled away? Apparently not, and this seems to be the implication of Jesus' commandment, "Thou shalt love thy neighbour as thyself" (Matt. 19:19, KJV). However, there is a difference between seeking one's own good as a primary consideration and allowing one's love of self for one's own sake to be the paradigm for neighbor love. That there is a genuine sense of self-realization involved in the idea of the restoration of the *imago* that we are proposing is freely admitted. Yet there is a significant contrast between directly seeking one's own ends and indirectly finding fulfillment as a consequence of "seek[ing] first the kingdom of God" (Matt. 6:33), which involves undivided love of God and disinterested love of neighbor.[46]

Christian Ethics

Too often a discussion of Christian ethics is treated as almost an addendum to Christian theology. It is not integrated into the structure of the theology. But in Wesleyan theology the ethical emphasis is implicit in the total structure, since sanctification, inseparable

---

45. *Christian Ethics*, 101.
46. George F. Thomas, *Christian Ethics*, points out that "we must distinguish between *love of self* and *love of the good*. In the former, the interest of the self is centered upon itself; its desire is to have its wants satisfied and to cling to its individual life as long as possible. In the latter, the self seeks to transcend itself by devoting itself to the Kingdom of God as the highest good and is prepared to give up anything, even its life, to that end.

"This explains how it is possible for a person to be concerned for the Kingdom of God without loving himself. . . . The principle of 'life in the flesh' is love of self, aiming at the *satisfaction* of its own desires; the principle of life 'in the Spirit' is love of God and love of neighbor leading to the *transcendence* of the self." 57.

from all theological considerations, is through and through ethical.[47]

But sanctification and likewise Christian ethics are specifically for the people of God. Does this imply a limitation of universality? Not in the sense that this does not refer to God's ideal for all men. But we must recognize that God's Word clearly reveals an ideal to which only the dedicated are committed and which only the sanctified are pursuing. In our discussion of the doctrine of creation we elaborated a creation ethic that is universally applicable to all men in the sense that it reflects the structure of human nature. It is binding upon every human being in that to violate this ethical criterion is to violate one's own nature and in some measure to self-destruct.

The Christian ethic, when understood as an extrapolation of the *imago Dei*, is an extension of the creation ethic toward the achievement of full personhood. This means that in the fullest religious sense it is an ethic that enhances rather than perverts the humanity of man. Furthermore, this understanding entails the happy conclusion that God's ideals are not dehumanizing or pervertive of human nature. Holiness, as an ethical reality, does not make one less than human but more fully so.

Paul Tillich, in a transformation of categories utilized by Immanuel Kant in his classic Enlightenment attempt to reject all authority, has provided us with a brilliant insight into this truth. Kant felt that for one's personhood to be fully expressed, ethical rules must be legislated by oneself. This is autonomy. If such rules for behavior are heteronomously (by other-legislated law) imposed by either other persons or God, they take away the dignity that properly belongs to rational beings. That means that Kant also rejects a theonomous (God-legislated law) ethic.

Tillich argues that the conflict between autonomy and theonomy that Kant posited is a misunderstanding. Since God is the "depth" of one's own being, autonomy and theonomy are not in conflict. Rather, in acknowledging God's laws, one is actually affirming his own authentic personhood. Hence a theonomous ethic, while not autonomous in the Kantian sense, is designed to put a person in touch with his true self, since that relationship occurs only when he is in touch with God as the Ground of his being.

---

47. This explains why we were so insistent in earlier discussions on the thoroughly ethical character of sanctification in contrast to a ceremonial interpretation.

This, in the context of our systematic proposals, is the significance of the various relationships implied in the concept of the *imago*.

Such an interpretation of the Christian ethic suggests that it takes a particular form. This form is not something that can be detailed in a theoretical way from Scripture but only inferred. Such a conceptual model, like others that theology borrows, is derived from philosophy. In the language of philosophical ethics, it is teleological in nature or structure. This means that the life enjoined finds its validation in the goal (telos) that it seeks to achieve.[48] The telos, simply put, is the renewal in the image of God; or since the icon of the divine nature in human form is Jesus Christ, it may be termed Christlikeness. The parameters of this telos are defined by the four relationships outlined in the first part of this chapter and, when taken together, encompass all the aspects to which any ethical theory would address itself. It furthermore demonstrates how all-encompassing and adequate is the motif of love as an ethical category.

We propose now to briefly show how two other alternatives to this structure sometimes proposed as the paradigm for Christian ethics are inadequate. The first approach, usually advocated in a very unsophisticated way, is known as casuistry. Casuistry is the attempt to provide rules of thumb for every conceivable situation.[49]

Such a way of doing ethics often seeks to identify rules for conduct in the Bible and then apply these in a literalistic way to contemporary life. The inadequacies of this approach are numerous. First, it fails to recognize that while there are many specific injunctions in the New Testament that may be lifted out and used without modification, most are occasional in nature and presuppose a historical situation that may or may not be reproduced

---

48. The criticism often directed against a teleological ethic that it proposes that "the end justifies the means" is superficial and uncritical. To suggest that this critique invalidates such an approach to ethical theory is to completely ignore the implications of the telos. The fallaciousness of such an attack may be seen when we suggest that it is self-contradictory. If, hypothetically, we propose that the telos of an ethical theory is honesty, it is ridiculous to suggest that the teleological principle allows dishonest behavior as a means to the end of honesty. In the same manner, if Christlikeness is the telos of Christian ethics, the achieving of that goal excludes all unethical behavior and defines very carefully what means are useful to achieve the ideal. It is far more demanding than an approach that propagates rules as safeguards against immorality, since rules almost always admit of loopholes. The teleological approach admits of none.

49. This term has also been used to refer to any application of a general ethical principle to specific cases. All practical ethical discussion is casuistic in this sense. But we are using it in the more classical sense as defined in the text.

in the modern world. The failure to recognize this conditioned character of many biblical injunctions results in seeking to impose a rule upon a radically different situation that may in fact result in an unchristian or sub-Christian outcome.[50]

The second problem is that this way of doing ethics is extremely limited. It has no way of dealing with issues that have emerged in each new situation. The proper approach to biblical injunctions is to seek to unearth the theological principle that informs them. In some this will lie close to the surface; in others it may be deeply imbedded and require careful exegetical excavation. These principles are indeed universally applicable, and it is the contention here that one would find all of them to focus on one or more of the fourfold relations that constitute the *imago Dei*.

Others have argued that the Christian ethic is fundamentally deontological in form. This type of ethics centers in law, obligation, and duty. Its classic model in philosophical ethics is the work of Immanuel Kant. Since we are dealing with divine commands, it is claimed that the Christian ethic fits this model.

While it is indisputable that this element is present in Christian ethics, it is not clear that this is the definitive characteristic. Addressing this question raises the issues debated in the Middle Ages between the nominalists and voluntarists. The latter, making God's will primary, would support a deontological form of biblical ethics. However, in our discussion of this theological issue (see chap. 6) we saw how Wesley rejected this debate as fruitless and for all practical purposes denied the voluntarist claim. In his own understanding of the law (see chap. 12) he made it plain that the law is a replica of the divine nature. Hence if one can legitimately claim that the law is an expression of the divine nature, it thus is not arbitrary but has a purpose. One can ask why such a law is propagated, and there is an answer beyond "because God said it." If the element of purpose is present in law, it becomes teleological in nature. And we have already seen in our earlier discussion of

---

50. See the discussion in Plato's *Republic* between Socrates and Cephalus, where Cephalus proposes a simplistic definition of the good life. Socrates demonstrates that to follow this definition in all cases can lead to a morally bad act and thus invalidate goodness. Theologically, a case in point here is the preoccupation of some conservative Christians with Paul's prohibition in I Cor. 14:34 of women speaking in church. They take a historically conditioned situation and attempt to make it universally applicable and thus run afoul of more central New Testament principles.

law what the telos of the law is, and it neatly fits into this proposal regarding the structure of Christian ethics.

Historically, the holiness movement has utilized all three of these approaches, but the most adequate attempts to justify the holiness life-style used some version of the teleological approach. Consider the implications of Susanna Wesley's ethical advice to her sons: "Whatever weakens your reason, impairs the tenderness of your conscience, obscures your sense of God, or takes off the relish of spiritual things, whatever increases the authority of your body over your mind, that thing for you is sin."[51]

In the formation of his societies, John Wesley had uppermost in his mind the definition of religion as "a constant ruling habit of soul, a renewal of our minds in the image of God, a recovery of the divine likeness, a still increasing conformity of heart to the pattern of our most holy Redeemer."[52] When he articulated rules for these societies, he borrowed from William Cave's *Primitive Christianity*, which was a study of the morals of the church of the first centuries. Wesley's attraction to patristic Christianity as the paradigm for the uncorrupted faith made it natural that he would desire to take over the morals of this period for himself and his people. But the overriding consideration was that the rules and methods that he borrowed from Cave's account were seen as prudential means ordained toward achieving this "ruling habit of mind," this "complete recovery of the divine likeness." Since Wesley could and did speak meaningfully of means to holiness, such interpretation is perfectly in accord with his theological understanding.

Wesley certainly would not suggest that his rules could be used as criteria for a legalistic evaluation of one's relation to God. Rather they are continuing prods toward evermore perfect realization of the divine likeness.[53]

In seeking to justify denominational standards to their constituency, General Superintendent James B. Chapman and *Herald of Holiness* editor D. Shelby Corlett voiced a popular but soundly formulated teleologial ethical theory.[54]

---

51. See H. Ray Dunning, "Nazarene Ethics as Seen in a Historical, Theological, and Sociological Context" (Ph.D. diss., Vanderbilt University, 1969). See chap. 4.

52. See Peters, *American Methodism*, 65.

53. See H. Ray Dunning, "Ethics in a Wesleyan Context," *Wesleyan Theological Journal* 5, no. 1 (Spring 1970): 3 ff.

54. These men worked in a period when the Church of the Nazarene was going through a transition period both in terms of an influx of new church members without

As general superintendent, Chapman self-consciously saw himself standing midway between two generations, as a sort of bridge builder, justifying the ways of the founders to the new generation of Nazarenes. This was particularly true in regard to the standards of the church, and he spoke to this problem both in articles and in the "Question Box," a column he conducted sporadically from 1923 to 1948.

Chapman's concept of Christian conduct was built upon a hierarchy of values, which if rejected would cause the whole edifice to collapse. Consequently it is explicated in the context of holiness as entire devotement to God and complete commitment to realizing perfection of life. If one is not committed to the telos, his arguments would lose all their force and persuasiveness.

This scale of values is explicitly stated and is quite enlightening in evaluating the nature of the principles of conduct: First things should be kept first, and these are religious exercises such as prayer and works of mercy. Second in importance is intellectual pursuits including "attendance upon lectures." Third place is given to the body, that is, take care of it to remain healthy. Fourth is social life, where priority should be given to good friends.

Here we have an obvious ethic of self-fulfillment, the main tenor of which is in the direction of organizing the whole person around certain basic principles as to realize one's highest, sanctified aims. Chapman saw the rules of the church as prudential in guarding against anything that would militate against achieving the goal and guiding toward those activities that would actualize it.

D. Shelby Corlett, as an editorialist, attempted to speak to any situation that had relevance to the conscience of the church and strove to support the position of the church and its leaders in the event of any question. One may adequately catch a reflection of trends in the church by a study of his editorials.

His own particular approach to the ethical position of the church may be summed up in the word *expediency*, a concept that he chiefly based on 1 Cor. 6:12: "All things are lawful unto me, but all things are not expedient" (KJV). He recognized that the relation between religion and morals had more than one dimension. There are, of course, those areas where "there should exist a rigid line of

---

ecclesiastical background and the emergence of second-generation churchmen who had doubts about the validity of the General Rules of the church. See Dunning, "Nazarene Ethics."

demarcation between the white of right and the black of wrong." There are other areas that fall into the category of "unedifying."

This latter category moves into the realm of lawful matters that do not distinguish the Christian from the non-Christian but rather encompass the question of personal conscience and light. Rational reasons may not necessarily be available to support convictions of this sort, but they are not irrational. The course a Christian pursues on this basis "must be considered as being done solely because it is most satisfying to his own conscience, and for the glorifying of God in his personal life." Therefore these particular standards of conduct are not to be imposed arbitrarily upon others.

The General Rules of the Church of the Nazarene, Corlett argued, are based upon this principle. They are not a means of identifying true Christians but rather spell out what, in the opinion of the church, is the kind of life that is "more becoming to God."[55]

A further obvious implication of interpreting ethics in terms of the *imago* as elaborated here is that a social ethic is indigenous to the Wesleyan understanding. The second relationship entails consecrated effort to "do unto others as you would have them do unto you" (cf. Matt. 7:12). This transcends the brotherhood, even though this may be the central focus of the ideal of openness.[56] In the believer's relation to those outside the faith, it calls for efforts to guarantee justice, equality, and access to a quality of life that will not militate against the maintenance of personhood—not simply bodily existence.

We do not propose to have elaborated here a full Christian ethic, but to have set forth the basic contours of an ethic that follows logically from the structure and presuppositions of this systematic theology. Fully spelling out all the implications of these programmatic observations would require a separate volume.

---

55. These discussions of Chapman and Corlett taken materially from Dunning, "Nazarene Ethics."

56. See Ladd, *Theology*, 280-81.

The Communion of Saints

Few subjects have elicited the attention of contemporary theologians more than the doctrine of the Church. At least two reasons may be suggested for this. First is the ecumenical mood that pervades mainstream theological thought. As the result of the painful awareness of the splintered character of Christendom and the failure of the ideal of unity for which Jesus prayed in His high-priestly prayer (John 17), churchmen have sought for a solution to the problem by seeking to identify the nature of the Church. It is hoped that this will provide a basis for healing the Body of Christ.[1]

The second reason is more pragmatic. Many have become dis-

---

1. Cf. Colin Williams, *The Church,* vol. 4 in *New Directions in Theology Today* (Philadelphia: Westminster Press, 1968); idem, *John Wesley's Theology Today,* chap. on. the church; Paul Minear, ed., *The Nature of the Unity We Seek,* Official Report of the North American Conference on Faith and Order (St. Louis: Bethany Press, 1958); Stephen Charles Neill, *The Church and Christian Union* (New York: Oxford University Press, 1968). These concerns are clearly reflected in the words of contemporary Roman Catholic theologian Hans Kung, *The Church* (New York: Sheed and Ward, 1967): "Ecumenical efforts spring not from indifferentism, much though this might suit our modern age, but from a new awareness of God's desire that all might be one." xii. This is not to suggest that denominationalism may not have some value, as our later discussions will show.

illusioned with the institutional church, and even those who have not shared this loss of optimism have been puzzled over the failure of the church to manifest significant success in its relation to the world, either evangelistically or in influencing society toward justice and righteousness. So the church has come under careful scrutiny in an effort to diagnose the source of this weakness.[2]

The chief difficulty in formulating a theological doctrine of the Church is the intricate commingling of historical, sociological, and institutional factors with the theological. It is all but impossible to speak of the church without conjuring up elements that are accidental to the essence of "church." As John Wesley said, "A more ambiguous word than this, *the Church,* is scarce to be found in the English language."[3] Our effort here will be to attempt to identify the distinctly theological but at the same time to take account of the other elements that must be considered in the contemporary situation.

As we seek to address the topic, to follow consistently our method, we must first look at the biblical material. Following this lead, the place to begin developing the doctrine of the Church is with the corporate character of biblical faith. We have encountered this pervasive idea repeatedly in our earlier discussions. We have seen how the social character of human existence is indigenous to the creature made in the image of God. We have argued that the very structure of humanness as determined by the Word of God is cohumanity. It logically follows that the work of salvation would create community as an implementation of this created essence.

This truth is seen clearly in the Old Testament, where "salvation" means becoming a part of the people of Israel. This is the closest theological concept to what modern Christian vocabulary terms "being saved" that we find under the old dispensation. Conversely, being "lost" involves expulsion from the community. The same is true in the New Testament in the pictures we have of the Early Church both in Acts and the teachings of the Epistles. There

---

2. See Howard Snyder's series of works, all published by InterVarsity Press of Downers Grove, Ill.: *The Community of the King* (1977); *The Problem of Wineskins* (1975); *The Radical Wesley and Patterns for Church Renewal* (1980); and *Liberating the Church* (1983); Frank R. Tillapaugh, *The Church Unleashed* (Ventura, Calif.: Regal Books, 1982); D. Elton Trueblood, *The Incendiary Fellowship* (New York: Harper and Row, Publishers, 1967); Langdon B. Gilkey, *How the Church Can Minister to the World Without Losing Itself* (New York: Harper and Row, Publishers, 1964).

3. "Of the Church," in *Works* 6:392.

were no "free-lance" believers. When a person became a believer in Christ, he was therewith incorporated into the community through the rite of baptism. As we saw in an earlier discussion, the Holy Spirit created this community. It was apparently inconceivable to those early believers to speak of salvation in any other terms.

David H. C. Read calls attention to the oddity of the inclusion in the Apostles' Creed of the phrase "I believe in . . . the communion of saints." In no other statement of belief from an organization would a similar affirmation likely be found. He refers to the existence of a Flat Earth Society, which exists to affirm belief that the earth is flat; but how strange it would be for them to declare, "I believe in the Flat Earth Society." This interesting insight highlights the importance and centrality of the corporate character of Christian faith when it understands itself biblically. John Wesley revealed his thoroughly biblical mentality when he said, "Christianity is essentially a social religion; and to turn it into a solitary one is indeed to destroy it."[4]

It is important to understand what the "in" means in the creedal statement. It is misconstrued if faith in the Church is somehow understood as a means of salvation. In no way does this suggest that something other than God is the proper object of faith. It is significant that this affirmation is always set in the context of belief in the Holy Spirit; thus what belief in the Church conveys is belief in God the Spirit as the Gatherer of the people of God.

Another important aspect of biblical theology is the concept of a people of God. This goes beyond the previous point, since it conveys the idea of mission. People of God and mission are correlative and inseparable ideas in biblical faith. This leads us to speak about the concept of *election*.

The biblical doctrine of election is defined by the Old Testament. The theological understanding that comes to expression there informs the New Testament view. Its development occurs in connection with the choice of Israel as the people of God. Here we must distinguish the normative interpretation from the pervasive popular perversion of it that can be detected in the biblical material. Misunderstanding the nature and purpose of her election, Israel often thought this implied her superiority to other peoples and that she was to be the recipient of special national privilege. This

4. *The Christian Faith* (Nashville: Abingdon Press, 1956), 133. See *StS* 1:381-82.

was reinforced by the false inference that her choice was irrevocable, so that she was granted unconditional security.[5]

The election of Israel was to responsibility rather than privilege. It had in view a missionary task. As Vriezen puts it, "In Israel God seeks the world. Israel is God's point of attack on the world." In the light of this he gives an accurate statement of the biblical meaning of election: "Election means first of all that someone who is to perform a task is called upon and designated."[6]

The truth of election in the Old Testament comes most poignantly to expression in Isaiah 40—55, where it is intimately related to Israel as Yahweh's servant.[7] In 43:10, the prophet quotes God saying, "You are my witnesses." The way in which this witnessing is to be implemented is through vicarious suffering, by which many shall be brought to righteousness. Here election and mission are inseparably joined, and the nature of the mission is spelled out.

The theological implications of these passages for the New Testament understanding of the Church are far-reaching. They identify beforehand the nature of the agent who is to carry out the witness task—he is to embody the essence of servanthood. We shall later see how this truth, which was originally predicated of the chosen people, is embodied and actualized in the work of Jesus Christ and passed along to His people.

This correlation of mission and character in relation to election becomes more apparent in the New Testament. There we find further illumination of the way in which the function of the Church is to be implemented. Paul makes this clear in that concatenation of election concepts in Rom. 8:28-29. The ultimate purpose for which God chooses (predestines and elects) His people is that they "be conformed to the image of his Son."

This brief statement on the biblical doctrine of election leads

---

5. Th. C. Vriezen notes on this point that "unfortunately some Christian theologians, however strongly they combat the dangers of a mistaken idea of being elect in the Church, cannot refrain even now, in consequence of a religious romanticism, from backing up the Jews in this temptation! In particular the establishment of the State of Israel has increased this danger." *An Outline of Old Testament Theology* (Wageningen, Holland: H. Veenman and Zonen, 1958), 76 n. 2.

6. Ibid., 76, 167.

7. George A. F. Knight, *Servant Theology: A Commentary on the Book of Isaiah 40—55,* in *International Theological Commentary,* ed. George A. F. Knight and Frederick Carlson Holmgren (Nashville: Abingdon Press, 1965; rev. ed., Grand Rapids: Wm. B. Eerdmans Publishing Co., 1984).

us to infer that the scriptural understanding of the Church is functional. The people of God are chosen to carry out a task. With that preliminary finding in mind we shall now turn to the New Testament metaphors of the Church to seek to identify any further implications.

New Testament Images of the Church

Prior to looking at a few of the many images that can be identified in the New Testament,[8] we need to speak about the nature of metaphors or images in general as it relates to this issue.

There is a double difficulty involved in seeking to understand the images of the Church. The first involves the hermeneutical problem of making a transfer from the biblical "horizon" to the contemporary "horizon."[9] At the literal, or purely cognitive, level there is the necessity of entering into the thought world of the New Testament in order to avoid imposing contemporary thought patterns upon the ancient mentality. It is always an almost overwhelming temptation to force the Bible to think like us rather than putting forth the Herculean intellectual effort to think like the Bible. The second stage of the hermeneutical task then enters the picture, that of bringing the ancient perceptual perspective "to understanding" in terms comprehensible to modern man. This is the problem of what Paul Minear calls "the radical discontinuity between the mind of the New Testament and our own mind."[10]

The second difficulty lies in the nature of images or metaphors. In addition to the problem of distinguishing literal from figurative meanings, if it is even possible to do so, we have the problem posed by the nature of images. As the term implies, they are the product of the imagination. Once again the hermeneutical issue comes into play. In order to enter the world of the imagination of New Testament man, we must first recognize the "changes in the structure of the imagination" (Minear) that have occurred during the intervening 19 centuries. Minear describes the situation that arises here:

---

8. Paul Minear, *Images of the Church in the New Testament* (Philadelphia: Westminster Press, 1960), has identified 97 major and minor images within the New Testament that refer to the church.

9. Thiselton, *Two Horizons.*

10. *Images,* 17.

The images of the church are rarely the clever concoction of one person to suit his own purposes. They have been produced out of a common stock of images preserved over the generation by a living community. Their use presupposes a shared life of the mind. Produced from the collective subconscious, they speak to the collective subconscious. In them the imagination of the community is reflected and nourished. Transferred to another community where the processes of imagination are very different, they fail to speak with their initial clarity and power. The recovery of that clarity and power, therefore, often requires the conversion of the communal imagination.[11]

Furthermore, images themselves convey a vision of reality that cannot be fully articulated in conceptual terms. They have an affective as well as a cognitive dimension.[12] With regard to the images of the Church in the New Testament, M. Robert Mulholland suggests that what we have is "literary iconography—word pictures that serve as windows into a reality that is radically different from the world view in which the words usually function."[13] In other words, the images become verbal windows into reality, conveying an ontological vision.

Mulholland further argues that participation in the life of the Church, a sharing of the new order of being established by God through Jesus and actualized by the work of the Holy Spirit in the Church, is essential to perceiving the vision that is symbolically transmitted by the verbal icons. Minear's analysis supports this claim when he says that

images ... will not often arise from the acute insight or the clever tongue of one individual alone, for even the greatest poet relies upon a poetic tradition. More often will they be the possession of a community whose commerce over the centuries with the given reality has produced an extensive repertoire of effective images.[14]

11. Ibid.
12. See M. Robert Mulholland, Jr., "The Church in the Epistles," in *The Church*, ed. Melvin E. Dieter and Daniel N. Berg (Anderson, Ind.: Warner Press, 1984), for a discussion of these aspects with the claim that Wesleyan theology has a dynamic that is peculiarly adapted to coming to terms with this dual dimension.
13. Ibid., 93.
14. *Images*, 23. Mulholland's words are illuminative: "The icons are simply the cognitive lenses of human experience through which we see darkly the profound reality of that new order of being that continually intrudes into history as the Church." "Church in the Epistles," 103.

While the vision of reality must be elicited or precipitated by experience, we will here attempt to identify such cognitive theological insights as may be present in some of the major images.

The New Israel

Although not ever explicitly stated in precisely this way, the most pervasive metaphor used in the New Testament for the Church is "the new Israel."[15] The implication is that there is both continuity and discontinuity with the "old Israel." Central passages that contain this distinction are 1 Pet. 2:9-10—"But you are a chosen race, a royal priesthood, a holy nation, God's own people, that you may declare the wonderful deeds of him who called you out of darkness into his marvelous light. Once you were no people but now you are God's people; once you had not received mercy but now you have received mercy"; and Rom. 9:25-26—"As indeed he says in Hosea, 'Those who were not my people I will call "my people," and her who was not beloved I will call "my beloved." And in the very place where it was said to them, "You are not my people," they will be called "sons of the living God." ' "

These passages, along with many others, emphasize the newness of the people of God in the New Testament, and in both cases it is in relation to the "old" people of God. Hence Minear is in one sense correct and in a significant sense wrong when he says that "Paul did not fall back upon a concept of two Israels, the old and the new, or the false and the true."[16]

The distinction between the "false and the true" already appears in Isaiah 56—66. Furthermore, the distinction between the old and the new is explicit in the way the Church is constituted in contrast to the way Israel is constituted. Both are called into existence by the activity of God; but one is oriented toward a national life that provides its unifying focus, while the other is without nationalistic distinctions and is constituted by the Holy Spirit. The fact that it is election that constitutes both Israel and the Church as the people of God provides the continuity between them. It further suggests that the nature of the Church can be inferred from the

---

15. In Paul Minear's significant study of the numerous images of the church in the New Testament, while he does not mention this exact nomenclature (the term Israel is used), a preponderance of the major images are explicated in terms of this idea. We shall interact with one of his theses along this line below.

16. Ibid., 72.

meaning of Israel's election, as noted in the previous discussion of election.

Colin Williams points out how continuity is clearly intended by Paul's allegory of the olive tree in Romans 11; it is the same olive tree. However, the tree surgery is so radical in the excising of some branches and the grafting in of others that the discontinuity is also clear. "The dead branches of the old Israel are cut out of the tree and the grafting in of the Gentiles represents a major change in the look of the tree, to say the least!"[17]

The nature of both the continuity and discontinuity stands in radical opposition to the basic premise of dispensational theology that there is a dual purpose of God "expressed in the formation of two peoples who maintain their distinction throughout eternity."[18] This distinction between Israel and the Church, so widely embraced among conservative Christians, simply will not stand the test of biblical exegesis (see Appendix 1). There is one people of God, whose continuity is directly related to God's redemptive purposes.

The continuity between the old people of God and the new is theological, originating in the promise to Abraham. God's call to this patriarch involved the pledge that "in you all the families of the earth shall be blessed" (Gen. 12:3, margin). Hence mission lay at the root of God's initial choice of the father of the faithful.

In the process of carrying out this mission, there were intermingled historical and sociological factors. The people of Israel first took the shape of a theocracy, which in time developed into the monarchy, at the people's initiative rather than God's. The Lord adapted himself to these political developments, and they gave shape to the theological formulations of Israel's religion.[19] Early in the period of the monarchy the idea of a Temple arose; and even though this, like the monarchy itself, was not God's idea, it became an informing element in their theological understanding.

---

17. *The Church*, 59.
18. Daniel P. Fuller, "The Hermeneutics of Dispensationalism" (Th.D. diss., Northern Baptist Theological Seminary, 1957), 25, quoted in Hans K. LaRondelle, *The Israel of God in Prophecy* (Berrien Springs, Mich.: Andrews University Press, 1983), 10.
19. All the "Davidic theology," including the Messianic hope, could only arise out of the monarchical setting; hence this aspect of Hebrew eschatology was specifically informed by the rise of the kingdom and the transformation from a theocracy to the monarchy. Wesleyan theology is particular adapted to deal with the nature of the divine-human interaction that this truth implies.

Unfortunately these accidental features of Israel's faith, though serving a shaping influence to her theology, often became ends in themselves. Throughout much of her history, Israel tended to be more preoccupied with her national life and its political success than with the theological meaning of her existence. When these two were illegitimately joined, they served to totally pervert the purpose of her election. Amos's denunciation of the popular conception of the Day of the Lord (Amos 5:18-27) and Jeremiah's Temple sermon (Jeremiah 7; 26) serve as poignant witnesses to this perversion. Eventually the institutionalizing of the accidental features of her religion was a major factor in the destruction of first the Northern and then the Southern kingdoms and finally led to the rejection of her Messiah, who challenged their self-centered institutionalism with the principle "For whoever would save his life will lose it, and whoever loses his life for my sake will find it" (Matt. 16:25). Refusing to take the path of servanthood, they lost their place through trying to preserve it.

The same general pattern may be observed with the new Israel. The institutional elements of her life were historically and sociologically conditioned. When such structures became an end in themselves, and their preservation became the foremost consideration, the true mission fell into the background or disappeared altogether. Ecclesiastical history bears abundant evidence to this sad fact. More will need to be said later on this matter.

Concurrent with the dynamics of the interaction of sociological and theological factors is a movement of redemptive history that reflects God's efforts at accomplishing His saving purposes in the world. At the outset, there was the dream that the nation of Israel could become the kingdom of God. As the actualization of this ideal became more and more unlikely, there was a shift from the nation to the remnant within the nation. This shift took place in the Northern Kingdom with the work of Elijah and Elisha[20] and with Isaiah of Jerusalem in the Southern Kingdom during the eighth century B.C. This movement further narrowed so as to focus in one individual who carried out the mission to which Israel was originally called. Functionally Jesus of Nazareth was Israel (and the Church) in one person. From this point on the perspective broadened again to include all who responded to the call of God in Jesus

20. Cf. H. L. Ellison, *The Prophets of Israel* (Grand Rapids: Wm. B. Eerdmans Publishing Co., 1969).

Christ. His appointment of 12 men was the clear signal that He was perpetuating the Israel of God in a new dimension. The character of His ministry as the Suffering Servant was intended to give character to the new Israel who would continue that ministry in the world. Thus the Church is called to be the servant people of God. To the degree that it abandons the implication of this self-denying pattern for one marked by self-serving, it too ceases to be the people of God.

The way in which the New Testament writers take over and employ language literally appropriate to Israel demonstrate that they are thinking of the Church theologically and not as a sociological entity. In the polemical situation of the Galatian letter, Paul refers to "the Israel of God" (6:16) as those who transcend the distinction created by circumcision.

The Body of Christ

One metaphor that has occupied considerable theological attention is the Pauline reference to the Church as the Body of Christ. It has been understood in diverse ways, ways that sometimes actually perverted the nature of the Church.

One difficulty in properly interpreting the image is the problem of determining precisely what Paul means when he uses the term "body," since it can carry several connotations. Another involves a degree of ambiguity in its use in any context. It may have corporeal connotations, or it may derive from the Stoic use, as in *the body politic.* However, even with the ambiguity, it seems clear that it refers to the fact that "the risen Christ gathers his disciples to himself in such a way that they are called by him to continue in history the work of his incarnate life. They are his body for his work in the world."[21] Thus this metaphor, too, is functional and relates intimately to the concept of mission as did the previous one examined. Alan Richardson reinforces this conclusion by saying: "The Church is thus the means of Christ's work in the world; it is his hands and feet, his mouth and voice."[22]

Herein lies the significance of the common phrase that the Church is the "extension of the Incarnation." It cannot refer to the institutional church (Roman Catholic or otherwise) in some sort of

---

21. Williams, *The Church,* 62.
22. *Theology,* 256.

absolutistic way. Christ is the Head and the Church is the Body and will be in constant process of completion (Eph. 4:11-16). It cannot mean that the unbroken continuity of the institutional church with the Body of Christ can be assumed. As Williams puts it, "There is the continuity of the promises of Christ (Word) and the continuity of the symbols of his promise (Sacraments), but the life of the church as the fellowship of believers depends upon constant renewal."[23] In other words, the church is a happening directly related to the function of mission.

Ekklesia

The same truth conveyed by the two images surveyed is also implied by *ekklesia,* the central term chosen by the New Testament to refer to the new community of believers called into existence by the Holy Spirit through Christ. It is the correlative to the Old Testament term *qahal,* which was used to refer to the people of Israel, who, as we have seen, were called into being to represent the Lord to the nations.

This Greek term originally referred to a political assembly of the city-states that was called together for a particular purpose. This term, too, suggests direct continuity with the old Israel.[24]

This analysis coincides with a major development in contemporary thinking about the church that desires to speak of it as "event." The church happens in those moments when it is actualizing the purpose for which it was called into being. The words of Robert Adolphs represent this view adequately:

> Any conceptual system . . . which is static in character is essentially inadequate. The Church is to be envisaged first and foremost as *event* and not as an in essence already complete, realized entity which has, so to speak, appropriated all its assets. The Church is a continuing event that is being accomplished in history and *through* people. The being-called-together of people under Christ as the one Head (Eph. 1:9)—that in essence is the Church. But it is not something signed, sealed

---

23. *The Church,* 62.

24. J. Robert Nelson, *The Realm of Redemption* (London: Epworth Press, 1957), 6 ff. Joseph E. Coleson, "Covenant Community in the Old Testament," in *The Church,* ed. Melvin E. Dieter and Daniel N. Berg (Anderson, Ind.: Warner Press, 1984), along with others, calls attention to the fact that these terms carry the theological significance we derive from them only when the context calls for it. They are not technical terms in the strictest sense.

and delivered to us by God; rather is it—for all who belong to such a Church—*a continuing task.*[25]

We may at this point tentatively define the Church as that community of people called into being by God for the purpose of carrying out His redemptive mission in the world. In the light of the fuller implications of the images of the Church in the New Testament with their Old Testament background, we may speak of the Church as the saved and saving community. R. Newton Flew concludes the same when he says: "The Church is in the first place the object of the divine activity, and then the organ or instrument of God's saving purpose for mankind."[26] This means that the Church is envisioned as having both being and function.

The functional aspect of the Church points to its apostolic character (see below). It is to be, in H. Berkhof's words, a "bridge-event." But, as he points out, the witnessing and ministering Church can only exist as it is intensely driven by the Spirit.

> She can give only in the measure that she herself receives. She cannot be the bridge between the covenant-establishing God and his world unless she herself has a firm footing on that first shore. Her first relationship is to her Lord, and this relationship is the inspirational source and the content as well as the standard for her directedness to the world.[27]

The Kingdom and the Church

The relation of the church to the kingdom of God is an important issue in developing the doctrine of the Church. In the Middle Ages, beginning with Augustine, the two were generally equated, leading to an illegitimate triumphalism on the part of the institutional church. But while they are closely connected, they are not synonymous.

This discussion presupposes the earlier treatment of the Kingdom in the chapter on the work of Christ and should be kept in mind. Essentially the Kingdom is understood in the Synoptics as the rule or reign of God and only in a secondary or derived sense

---

25. Quoted in Williams, *The Church,* 22-23. The authors of *God, Man, and Salvation* also interpret the church as event but define it as connoting the "saved people's profound awareness of the Lord's presence at any given time." Although the idea of mission is introduced, it is not made central as do contemporary interpretations. See 562-63.

26. *Jesus and His Church,* 2nd ed. (London: Epworth Press, 1943), 24.

27. *Christian Faith,* 413-14.

as a domain.[28] Nowhere in the New Testament is the Kingdom identified with its subjects.

The reign of God has entered history in the person of Jesus Christ and is, in a sense, independent of those who subject themselves to it. The Church is composed of those who accept the rule of God. As G. Eldon Ladd says, "The Kingdom is the rule of God; the church is a society of men."[29]

Under the old dispensation, Israel was the people of the Kingdom; but having refused God's rule in Christ, the Kingdom was taken from them and given to a new people, as we saw earlier in this chapter.

It is the mission of the Church to bear witness to the Kingdom, and this involves living the Kingdom life. However, this is not to be interpreted as "building the Kingdom," since God's rule is established and is not subject to human influence. One can only submit to its authority. We may speak properly of building the Church if by this we mean seeking to lead persons to acknowledge the sovereignty of the King and share the life of the Kingdom. But even here we must acknowledge that it is not a merely human activity. Jesus said, "I will build my church" (Matt. 16:18).

As subjects of the Kingdom, the Church is amenable to the same duality that we have earlier discovered to be present in the New Testament understanding of the kingdom of God. There is both a present actuality and a future consummation. Hence we may speak of a distinction between the empirical and the eschatological Church, the Church as it now is and the Church as it is to become. Although the Church is the empirical embodiment of the age to come, it still lives in the reality that this age has not been consummated; hence it looks forward to a perfection that it has not achieved in the present. Paul's great words about the Church in Eph. 5:25-27 can only be understood in terms of this dual dimension: "Husbands, love your wives, as Christ loved the church and gave himself up for her, that he might sanctify her, having cleansed her by the washing of water with the word, that he might present the church to himself in splendor, without spot or wrinkle or any

---

28. Ladd, *Theology*, 63-64; Flew, *Jesus and His Church*, 20-21.
29. *Theology*, 111. Kung also rejects the identification of Church and Kingdom. He makes the balanced statement with which our view concurs: "The message of Jesus . . . allows for neither identification of Church and reign of God, nor dissociation between them." *The Church*, 94; cf. 88-104.

such thing." He here speaks not only of a present reality, as Wesley says in his *Notes* on this verse, but also of the final presentation. Willard Taylor summarizes it this way: "The ultimate presentation will take place at that final day of Christ's appearing, but even now it is taking place so that men might see His marvelous grace."[30]

It is this situation that justifies speaking of the Church as an "eschatological community." It lives in the middle in the time between the times. She is the recipient and beneficiary of all the promises of the new age that constituted the eschatological hope of the Old Testament. She is the new humanity envisioned in the time to come. At the same time she lives in anticipation of the consummation at the eschaton.

This latter dimension allows the language of "firstfruits" to be applied to the Church. As the resurrection of Christ is the firstfruits of those who will be raised at the last day, so the Church is the foretaste of the total people who will come from the east and the west to sit down with Abraham, Isaac, and Jacob at the final Messianic banquet (Matt. 8:11).

Recognizing the distinction between the Kingdom and the Church provides a viable alternative to the platonically inspired way of speaking of the "visible" and "invisible" church, a distinction widely called into question today. While the Kingdom calls the Church into existence, there are those within the church (a visible body of persons) who have never submitted to the rule of God and do not seek to exemplify the Kingdom life. It is the problem of the mixed character of the church as an empirical phenomenon that has exercised the minds of theologians through the centuries. As we will see in the subsequent historical survey, numerous responses have been proposed to the problem.

Historical Development of Ecclesiology

One may detect the beginnings of ecclesiology as a self-conscious undertaking in the Book of Acts. Before that point, we must more accurately speak of "the church in the thought of Jesus."[31] How-

30. "Ephesians," in *Beacon Bible Commentary*, ed. A. F. Harper, 10 vols. (Kansas City: Beacon Hill Press, 1965): 9:244.
31. Flew, *Jesus and His Church*; Joseph B. Clower, Jr., *The Church in the Thought of Jesus* (Richmond, Va.: John Knox Press, 1959).

ever, there was no fully articulated self-understanding until about the fourth century.[32] Nonetheless it seems foundational to briefly note the distinctive features of the community of Christ's people that emerged in the earliest period as well as the issues that were present in the discussions leading to a formulated ecclesiology.

The central concern in the communities described in Acts involved their distinctiveness as compared with Israel. As Alex R. G. Deasley says, "In an important measure the remainder of Acts [after Pentecost] recounts a wrestling with the definition of the term *Israel*, partly without but also partly within the Church."[33] There seems, at first, to be only the awareness that here is a sect of the Jews marked by faith that Jesus of Nazareth was the promised Messiah. But by clearly discernible stages, which Luke marks out, they came to a consciousness that the followers of the Way constituted a significantly different genre of religious community. However, as we have seen, they did not abandon the idea that they were in continuity with the Israel of the old covenant. According to J. N. D. Kelly, this is the presupposition on which the Early Church included the Hebrew scriptures in its canon. If there was a radical discontinuity, as dispensational theology claims, the logical result would have been the rejection of those scriptures.[34]

Theologically, there was first the conviction and experience that this community was constituted by the Holy Spirit and was the dwelling place of the Spirit. It may be true that in a preliminary sense the Church was in existence before Pentecost;[35] however, the distinctive feature of the New Testament Church became a reality at the Pentecostal effulgence, according to Luke's understanding. Hence it may be properly called "the birthday of the Church."[36] Each instance of the gift of the Spirit subsequent to Pentecost is corporate in nature, reinforcing the same truth.

Second, by both providential circumstances (persecution) and guidance of the Spirit (see Acts 13:2), the followers of the Way

32. Paul Bassett, "Western Ecclesiology to About 1700: Part I," in *The Church*, ed. Melvin E. Dieter and Daniel N. Berg (Anderson, Ind.: Warner Press, 1984), 128; Kelly, *Doctrines*, 190.

33. "The Church in the Book of Acts," in *The Church*, ed. Melvin E. Dieter and Daniel N. Berg (Anderson, Ind.: Warner Press, 1984), 70.

34. *Doctrines*, 190.

35. See K. N. Giles, "The Church in the Gospel of Luke," *Scottish Journal of Theology* 34 (1981): 121-46.

36. Cf. Deasley, "Church in Acts," 58.

520 □ GRACE, FAITH, AND HOLINESS

came to a full recognition that they were called to be witnesses to the resurrection of Christ and thus to the whole redemptive work to which it pointed. Furthermore, they saw that the extent of their commission was worldwide.

In the years leading up to the time of Augustine, there were two major issues that emerged in ecclesiology: the first had to do with the holiness of the church, and the other was concerned with the constitution of the church in terms of clergy and laity.

The first issue emerged out of the obvious "moral distance between earthly Christendom and the fully realized Kingdom."[37] This problem spawned several controversies as groups of rigorists insisted on the spiritual perfection of the church. First were the Montanists, who were reinforced by the conversion of Tertullian to their position. The persecutions that arose in the third century intensified the problem and gave impetus to the emergence of the interpretation of the church as a training ground for sinners instead of a community of saints.

Under the pressures of the Decian persecution, many apostatized but later, after the trials were past, desired to reenter the fold of the church. There were extremists on both sides, along with some moderates. On the one side were the Novationists, who took the position that there was no second repentance and insisted that those congregations who readmitted the *lapsi* lost their standing as the true Church of Christ. These rigorist views were partly based upon a misunderstanding of passages in Hebrews (6:4 ff.; 10:26 ff.; see H. Orton Wiley, *Epistle to the Hebrews*, for a more adequate exegesis).

Others were more moderate, such as Cyprian, but the door appeared to swing rather wide open with bishops like Callixtus, who formulated the view of the church as a mixed body. He used Jesus' parable of the tares and the wheat to support the idea and made unique use of the symbol of the ark of Noah. Like the ark, the church contains both clean and unclean inhabitants.

Such perspectives gave rise, especially in the East, to the distinction between a visible and invisible church as a way of coming to terms with the imperfect empirical church. We have already seen the Platonic presuppositions behind this, and J. N. D. Kelly also attributes it to Gnostic sources.[38]

---

37. Bassett, "Western Ecclesiology: Part I," 128.
38. *Doctrines*, 201-2.

The other issue is not unrelated to the first, since the question of the holiness of the church tended to shift from the laity to the clergy. Because the sacraments, especially baptism, were taken seriously as means of grace, and these were administered by the clergy, there was a sense of urgency over the purity of this group. The Novationists in particular called for a sanctified clergy, "so in fact, they implied that the Church is the congregation of the sanctified bishops."[39]

This development reached a significant milestone in the definitions of Cyprian, who declared that "the bishop is in the Church; the Church is in the bishop. And anyone not with the bishop is not in the Church." The basis for the unity of the church is in the bishop. It is the bishop who is the church. "The laity were adjunctive to the essence of the Church."[40]

The dichotomy between clergy and laity, with holiness attaching to the former, was formalized into a theological structure by Thomas Aquinas. This normative Catholic interpretation prevailed in Christendom until the Reformation of the 16th century.

Paul Bassett summarizes the pre-Augustinian years in ecclesiological doctrine as follows:

> In the three centuries following the first Christian Pentecost, the Church had gradually transformed itself from being a society of joyous penitents celebrating forgiveness and liberty to being a highly structured, clerically directed corps of persons confessing the same dogmae.[41]

The full flowering of the doctrine of the Church that was emerging during the first three centuries came to expression with Augustine. The views of the bishop of Hippo were hammered out in controversy with the Donatists, who were rigorist in their belief (see above). He finalized the equation of the true Church with the Catholic church of his day and insisted that there was no salvation outside this church. This conclusion was the logical outcome of his teaching that the church is Christ's mystical body. He explained the nature of the church as a "mixed body" in terms of the visible and invisible church. Not all who are in the Catholic church are part of the true Church, but all who compose the invisible Church are within the institution. He felt that "the error of the Donatists . . .

---

39. Bassett, "Western Ecclesiology: Part I," 140.
40. Ibid., 141.
41. Ibid., 144.

was to make a crude institutional division between them [the true and the apparent], whereas . . . God intended the two types of men to exist side by side in this world."[42]

These views also correlated with Augustine's interpretation of the church as the abode of the Spirit. This understanding took its roots in the New Testament and was always in the ecclesiological discussion up to his time. In the second century, Irenaeus regards the church as the unique sphere of the Spirit, and those who do not share the Spirit are not in the church. Conversely he who is not in the church does not participate in the Spirit.[43] Tertullian, likewise, before his Montanist days, insisted on the same.

Augustine held this position firmly against the Donatists. Even though they were doctrinally orthodox, they could not share the Spirit because they were schismatics if not heretics. They have rent the seamless robe of Christ. "Those who do not love God or his church . . . stand outside of it; they are strangers to the Holy Spirit."[44] These ideas, developed by later theologians, became the basis for the view of the Catholic church as the sole repository of grace and thus salvation, a view that also was dominant at the time of the Protestant Reformation.

Martin Luther's revolt against the penitential system of medieval Catholicism involved a transformation in the prevailing ecclesiology. Since the basis for his reforms was his rediscovery of the gospel, he defined the church in terms of the gospel. Since the gospel is proclaimed by preaching and sacrament, he came to define the church as where the Word is rightly preached and the sacraments rightly administered. Thus Luther sees the church as a happening. The church occurs when the proper conditions are present. The church is created by the Word, preached and enacted.[45]

The problem of the church's shortfall in terms of moral perfection still plagued the Reformation theologians. Luther's doctrine of *simul justus et peccator* eased it somewhat, and Calvin took refuge in the distinction between the visible and invisible church.

---

42. Kelly, *Doctrines*, 416. All these distinctions are called into question by Augustine's doctrine of predestination and election, but he never made any effort to reconcile the antithetical views of the church that resulted.

43. See ibid., 192.

44. Bassett, "Western Ecclesiology: Part I," 148.

45. For a brilliantly done comparison of Luther and Calvin, see Paul Bassett, "Western Ecclesiology to About 1700: Part 2," 210 ff.

However, the Anabaptists, who were Protestant rigorists, insisted that the New Testament envisioned a pure church and argued that "moral purity lay at the heart of that holiness that nearly everyone accepted as a mark of the true church." On this basis they believed that the church was an "association of believers only, separated from the world and guarding against infiltration by the world by means of strict discipline."[46]

Generally speaking, other Protestant variations worked with these three elements of Word, sacrament, and discipline with differing emphases. This leads us to the 18th century and John Wesley, whose views need special attention in a work of this nature.

As with several other theological issues, Wesley only spoke occasionally concerning ecclesiological matters. From beginning to end he was a loyal son of the Church of England, and much of what he said arose out of the tensions created by the formation of his Methodist societies and their relation to the established church.[47] Doubtless it could be argued that such views as he articulated were the result of his peculiar situation. But an equally viable case can be made that his pronouncements on the church were derived from his wide-ranging theological commitments.

In the course of his long life and ministry, his understanding obviously underwent transformation as the situation demanded. This makes it possible to appeal to the Wesleyan corpus to support divergent ecclesiologies. This has been done not only with this doctrine but with other doctrines as well. One needs to attempt to lay hold of the "whole Wesley."

Frank Baker says that the basic views to which he seemed, at times, to give support were two in number:

> One was that of a historical institution of bishops and inherited customs, served by a priestly caste who duly expounded the Bible and administered the sacraments in such a way as to preserve the ancient tradition on behalf of all those who were made members by baptism. According to the other view the church was a fellowship of believers who shared both the apostolic experience of God's living presence and also a desire to bring others into this same personal experience.[48]

However, it seems consistent with Wesley's mentality and typical approach to recognize a creative eclecticism that drew from all

---

46. Ibid., 215, 217.
47. Williams, *John Wesley's Theology Today*, appendix, 207 ff.
48. *John Wesley and the Church of England* (Nashville: Abingdon Press, 1970), 137.

the resources that were available to him. The good he incorporated, the unqualified he rejected, and all he purged and redirected
in the light of his own theological perspective, which, we have
argued in this theology, is soteriology understood as involving a
dual focus of justification and sanctification (see chap. 1). It is clear
that this same focus operates as well in Wesley's ecclesiology.[49]

Using this central motif as a prism, Wesley beams the multi-
colored tradition of ecclesiology that he inherited into a balanced,
if complex, understanding. In this way he addresses both the being
and the function of the church and does so in a fairly consistent
way.

By Wesley's day, three major ecclesiologies had emerged.
There was the Catholic view, which defines the church in terms of
ministry and which may be termed a horizontal definition. The
true church is in the apostolic succession, standing in the tradition
that extends from the beginning until the present. This approach
emphasizes the objective holiness of the church and the presence
of Christ maintained in the church through the sacraments.

There was also the classical Protestant interpretation, which
emphasized the Word and sacraments as creative of the church.
This approach may be termed an objective vertical theology that
stresses the necessity for the church to be created by the event of
the preaching of the Word. It was this interpretation by which the
Reformers distinguished the church of the Reformation from the
Catholic tradition.

Third was the free church position, which may be called the
subjective vertical view. Here the emphasis is upon the personal
experience and holiness of individual believers who then constitute the church. All of these find their appropriate place in Wesley's
thought.

Wesley also encountered four emphases that had found a
place among Protestant groups with varying degrees of importance. These are, briefly: living faith, biblical preaching, sacraments, and discipline. Usually one was given prominence, while
the others were devalued.

---

49. Clarence Bence, "Salvation and the Church," in *The Church*, ed. Melvin E. Dieter
and Daniel N. Berg (Anderson, Ind.: Warner Press, 1984), has shown decisively that this
is the case. He says: "The most striking and ever-relevant feature of Wesley's ecclesiology
is its soteriological focus, an emphasis that shaped almost every aspect of his thought and
action." 299.

Representative quotations show that all of these are present in Wesley's thought in a balanced way, thus transcending the imbalance present in many of his Protestant predecessors. He gave explicit approval to the first paragraph of the Anglican article of faith:

> The visible Church of Christ is a congregation of faithful men, in the which the pure word of God is preached, and the Sacraments be duly administered according to Christ's ordinance, in all those things that of necessity are requisite to the same.[50]

In explicating the Anglican article of faith, he points to the fact that an authorized Latin translation renders "faithful men" as "a congregation of believers," thus showing that it refers to men endued with living faith. The "one faith" of which Paul speaks in Eph. 4:1-6, the text for his sermon "Of the Church," is carefully identified as that faith "which enables every true Christian believer to testify with St. Paul, 'The life which I now live, I live by faith in the Son of God, who loved me, and gave himself for me.'"[51]

In his *Explanatory Notes upon the New Testament* he describes the Church as "a company of men, called by the gospel, grafted into Christ by baptism, animated by love, united by all kind of fellowship, and disciplined by the death of Ananias and Sapphira" (notes on Acts 5:11; cf. Jude 19).

In the text for his sermon on the church, he finds in the exhortation to "walk worthy of the vocation wherewith ye are called" (Eph. 4:1, KJV) a basis for stressing the importance of a disciplined life as essential to the church being the church.

Hence all four of the elements that are present with differing degrees of emphasis in traditional Protestant thought are incorporated by Wesley in his definitions. But they are not all of equal significance. It seems quite clear that if one is to single out the most decisive mark of the Church, it would be living faith.

This is verified further by his emphasis upon the Spirit who indwells, with different degrees of completeness, all persons who are of the Church. Thus the Church is composed of "all the persons in the universe whom God hath so called out of the world . . . to be

---

50. Quoted in Daniel N. Berg, "The Marks of the Church in the Theology of John Wesley," in *The Church*, ed. Melvin E. Dieter and Daniel N. Berg (Anderson, Ind.: Warner Press, 1984), 321. The second article of the Anglican creed is an exclusion of certain groups. Wesley abstained from this excision of others, as we shall note more carefully below.

51. *Works* 6:395.

'one body,' united by 'one Spirit;' having 'one faith, one hope, one baptism; one God and Father of all, who is above all, and through all, and in them all.'"[52]

The centrality of living faith is further highlighted by the way in which he resisted exclusive definitions in favor of inclusive ones. As Daniel Berg points out, Wesley's refusal to approve the second paragraph of the Anglican creed[53] is because of his catholic spirit. Furthermore he is unwilling to identify the preaching of the Word and the duly administered sacraments as marks of the church, thus diverging from classical Protestantism. His reasons are explicit:

> I dare not exclude from the Church catholic all those congregations in which any unscriptural doctrines, which cannot be affirmed to be the "pure word of God," are sometimes, yea, frequently preached; neither all those congregations, in which the sacraments are not "duly administered." Certainly if these things are so, the Church of Rome is not so much as a part of the catholic Church; seeing therein neither is "the pure word of God" preached, nor the sacraments "duly administered." Whoever they are that have "one Spirit, one hope, one Lord, one faith, one God and Father of all," I can easily bear with their holding wrong opinions, yea, and superstitious modes of worship: Nor would I, on these accounts, scruple still to include them within the pale of the catholic Church; neither would I have any objection to receive them, if they desired it, as members of the Church of England.[54]

Berg's comment puts this issue in focus:

> Wesley is reluctant about neither word nor sacrament in themselves. What Wesley fears is that the marks of the Church will be applied polemically to the disruption of the Church's unity. Unity, for Wesley, is a more biblical mark of the Church than either word or sacrament.[55]

And, it should be added, this unity is the product of the living faith of the believer, which knits him into a bond of love with all other believers. If the substance of living faith is love, as Wesley often avers, the result is a catholic spirit, since love sets aside minor differences of opinion, modes of worship, or forms of church government as nonessential and embraces every believer with the

---

52. Ibid., 395-96.

53. This paragraph reads: "As the Church of Jerusalem, Alexandria, and Antioch, have erred; so also the Church of Rome hath erred; not only in their living and manner of Ceremonies, but also in matters of Faith."

54. *Works* 6:397.

55. "Marks of the Church," 323.

words: "If your heart is right as my heart is right, give me your hand."[56]

It is Wesley's concern for the unity of the church that, in part, is the source of his reluctance to separate from the Church of England and the insistence that his Methodists be faithful to the means of grace provided by the establishment (see sermon "On Going to Church"). But if the established church has so far gone from vital piety, is there a theological, and not simply a historical, justification for this reticence? It may be suggested that such can be found in the doctrine of prevenient grace. The established church with its rituals and ministry and measure of continuity with the Church universal, past and present, provides a stability that guards against the splintering of the Body of Christ. Also there is a sense in which objective holiness is maintained in this connection. It is true that Wesley is never content with imputed, but insists upon imparted, holiness as a true evidence of the church.[57] But these churchly settings would provide a context within which prevenient grace could function with the possibility of renewal of the church. Schism from the church would remove the possibility of those with a living faith serving as leaven to influence the larger body.[58]

David L. Cubie proposes that the tension within the Wesleyan doctrine of holiness is the clue to the way in which Wesley was able to hold the two commitments in balance. One may interpret holiness in terms of separation or in terms of love. The former moves toward schism, while the latter seeks to maintain fellowship. Cubie argues that Wesley himself was able to hold to both without losing either, hence while he "maintained a position of both unity and separation, many of his followers were unable to do so." His conclusion is that "the difference between Wesley and many of his

---

56. Cf. 2 Kings 10:15, text for sermon "Catholic Spirit," in *Works* 5:492-504.

57. Wesley rejects Augustine's interpretation of the holiness of the church as imputed to it from the Head, who is Christ, and offers instead what he calls the "shortest and the plainest reason that can be given" why the church may be called holy: "The Church is called *holy*, because it *is* holy, because every member thereof is holy, though in different degrees, as He that called them is holy." *Works* 6:400.

58. Colin Williams thinks that Wesley reconciles the two views of the church (what he calls the "multitudinous" and the "gathered" views) that create a tension in his thinking by the concept of *ecclesiolae in ecclesia* (little church within the church), which is composed of "small voluntary groups of believers living under the Word and seeking under the life of discipline to be a leaven of holiness within the 'great congregation' of the baptized." *John Wesley's Theology Today,* 149.

followers may be that the latter failed to fully incorporate love into holiness."[59]

One final note may be made on the theological justification for Wesley's inclusion of discipline as a feature of the church. Included in his soteriological focus is the ingredient of sanctification (see below and chap. 1). As an essential emphasis, this would entail a call for the church to be a holy community.

Paul Bassett points out that a major cause of divergent ecclesiological understandings between Luther and Calvin is the latter's making place for a "third use of the law" (see section on "The Prophetic Work of Christ" in chap. 12). Thus finding no positive place for the law in the Christian life, Luther did not include discipline in his understanding of the church, whereas Calvin's view gave him a more positive doctrine of sanctification and an important place for discipline in the church.[60] Wesley agrees with Calvin against Luther here and thus consistently includes this element in his ecclesiology.

This brief discussion focuses on Wesley's complex understanding of the *being* of the church. But the *function* of the church is also perceived from the same soteriological perspective. Colin Williams affirms that for Wesley "mission is the primary mark of the church."[61] In a letter Wesley declares:

> What is the end of all ecclesiastical order? Is it not to bring souls from the power of Satan to God, and to build them up in His fear and love. Order, then, is so far valuable as it answers these ends; and if it answers them not, it is worth nothing.[62]

Thus we can conclude this survey by noting that while there are distinctive features created by his peculiar circumstances, Wesley seems to have captured the central emphasis of the New Testament, which we earlier discovered in the exegetical section of this chapter, as well as remaining true to his holistic theological commitments.

---

59. "Separation or Unity," in *The Church*, ed. Melvin E. Dieter and Daniel N. Berg (Anderson, Ind.: Warner Press, 1984), 344 ff. The same two tendencies may be noted in the early holiness movement in the United States. See Timothy L. Smith, *Called unto Holiness*, vol. 1.
60. "Western Ecclesiology: Part 2," 211 ff.
61. *Wesley's Theology Today*, 209.
62. Quoted in Bence, "Salvation and the Church," 304.

The Marks of the Church[63]

From the beginning there were threats to the distinctiveness of the Church that had to be countered. These challenges came from both inside and outside the Church. Out of this milieu came efforts to identify the characteristics of the true Church in contrast to pretenders. These proposals came to be termed *marks* or *notes* of the Church.[64] They were present informally even in the Book of Acts, but as they became formalized the number crystallized as four: Unity, Holiness, Catholicity (universality), and Apostolicity.

The Protestant Reformers accepted these creedal notes but went further and introduced the elements of the Word rightly preached and the Sacraments (reduced from seven to two) rightly administered.

We have noted several of these already as well as some others as they were present in the scriptural accounts of the Early Church and among theologians of the first three centuries. They were stated formally for the first time in the Creed of Constantinople in 381, which listed the predicates as "one," "holy," "Catholic," and "apostolic."

The attributes were first present as a reality and only gradually became a theory or dogmatic claim to be used polemically. Thus, while a historical study is important, the primary issue concerns their meaning as reality unrelated to the formal, institution-oriented significance they came to convey. This implies that Wesley's emphasis upon living faith as the crucial element in the Church is appropriate. It is the indwelling Spirit who produces the marks of the Church. They come from within and are not imposed from without. They are not the result of organization or administration but are the creation of the Spirit.

---

63. Significant contemporary discussion of this topic may be found in the following sources: Kung, *The Church*; G. C. Berkouwer, *The Church*, trans. James E. Davison (Grand Rapids: Wm. B. Eerdmans Publishing Co., 1976); Jurgen Moltmann, *The Church in the Power of the Spirit*, trans. Margaret Kohl (New York: Harper and Row, Publishers, 1977); Emil Brunner, *The Christian Doctrine of the Church, Faith, and the Consummation*, trans. David Cairns (Philadelphia: Westminster Press, 1962). Many insights from these authors are incorporated in the ensuing discussion but without specific reference.

64. H. Orton Wiley, apparently reflecting a discussion between Catholic and Protestant apologists of an earlier day, distinguishes between attributes and notes, the former being characteristic of the Church set forth in Scripture, and the latter being attributes transformed into tests by which the true Church is supposed to be known. This was the Catholic position advanced against the Protestant view. *CT* 3:111; see Berkouwer, *The Church*, 13 ff. I find no recognition of such a distinction in contemporary discussions.

In this light, most modern theologians agree that the so-called marks of the Church can no longer function in an exclusivistic sense. Although they seem to have arisen for polemical purposes, it is now recognized that they are too ambiguous to continue to be used in this way. Hence contemporary treatments tend to explore them thoroughly with serious attempts to reinterpret them in a less polemical mood and more consistently with the view of the Church that is a more accurate reflection of the New Testament.

Following in this vein, we must return to the New Testament to identify what these marks might mean, interpreted from their source. It should be understood from the start that this does not necessarily mean following the model of the Church we find in the pages of the New Testament, since most of the evidence points to a less-than-perfect community. While it may be a disturbing thought, it is nonetheless true that what was produced was a thoroughly human society, which in turn reproduced with greater or lesser completeness the qualities of the ideal.

What we shall propose is that the marks of the Church were produced by the gospel as implications of the gospel. Following this Protestant principle, we need to grasp the connection between the source and the result and in this way attempt to find our way to the essence of the Church. However, we should always be aware that preoccupation with the essence of the Church may blind us to the realities of the empirical church and thus lead to a kind of Docetism. We cannot escape to the easy evasions that have trapped so many efforts in the past. Somehow a balance must be found between idealism and realism. The Church in its concrete reality is not all it should be. But lack of conformity to the naked ideal does not invalidate the Church as it is from being the true Church. In attempting to come to terms with this dilemma, we shall need to follow our discussion of the notes of the Church with a section on the church as a sociocultural reality. This will take us to some practical conclusions regarding the present situation.

Unity

The objective ground of the unity of the Church is found in her Lord. As Paul says, "There is one Lord, one faith, one baptism" (Eph. 4:5). It is inappropriate to say that Christ founded the Church or that He was part of the Church; He *was* the Church.[65]

---

65. Cf. *God, Man, and Salvation*, 563-64; Alan Richardson, *Theology*, 310.

All who become identified by faith with Him are "in him" (Col. 2:6-7, 10-11) and share the unity of His person. Many of the images in the New Testament convey this idea, for example, Christ as the Vine with the branches abiding in Him.

The subjective ground of the unity of the Church is the work of the Spirit, which, in turn, is rooted in Christ. Hence, as James B. Chapman is quoted as saying, "The Christ in me will never be at variance with the Christ in you." This is seen in the Acts where the unimpeded activity of the Spirit is a corollary to the absence of disunity or openness within the community. The *koinonia* aspect of the Church is made a reality by the indwelling Spirit of Christ, by whom all acknowledge that "Jesus is Lord" (cf. 2 Cor. 13:14; Phil. 2:1; 1 Cor. 1:9).

From the beginning, sources of disunity appeared, and the Early Church leaders struggled manfully to maintain the ideal within the early Christian congregations and between different congregations. Few instances were as severe as at Corinth, but even in this case, Paul did not discount the churchly standing of the Corinthian congregation. He recognized their situation as unacceptable and called for renewal and repentance and correction in the light of the ideal.

As the unity of the Church became threatened by schismatics and heretics, other explanations of unity emerged in the development of ecclesiology. Appeals were made by Irenaeus to the unity of apostolic doctrine. Later, when it became apparent that schismatics could hold orthodox doctrine, the basis of unity was placed in the episcopacy. As Cyprian said, the church is founded on the bishop, it is "united and held together by the glue of the mutual cohesion of the bishops."[66] This ultimately resulted in identifying the unity with the one bishop who filled the chair of St. Peter at Rome. The move to full institutionalism was complete.

It will not do to speak of the divergences in the existing church as diversities and thus speak of unity in diversity. This is a truism that fails to touch the true situation. One must face the reality and call the church to repentance and seek to identify the sources of the rifts that so weaken the church's witness in the world (John 17). At the same time, we must affirm in optimism and faith, "I believe in the communion of saints," and mean by that the empirical church.

---

66. Kelly, *Doctrines*, 204-5.

Furthermore, the presence of division in the church should not paralyze the church into avoiding the responsibility of mission to which it is called. While dissatisfied with the present state of affairs, each congregation should press on to the task before it. We will note some significant sources of division and point to a positive answer to the problem in later sections.

Catholicity

The universality of the Church is rooted in the work of Christ as inclusive of all persons. It is not a geographical concept but refers to the all-embracing extent of the Atonement. Paul puts it succinctly: "There is neither Jew nor Greek, there is neither slave nor free, there is neither male nor female; for you are all one in Christ Jesus" (Gal. 3:28).

This is the basis for the apostle's denial in Rom. 11:1 that God has rejected the Jew. The fact that the Kingdom is taken from Israel and given to the Church is no basis whatsoever for any anti-Semitism. The salvation that God offers to the world in His Son avails also for the Jew, as Paul found out existentially, and the Church includes Jew as well as Gentile. In this sense, catholicity is another aspect of unity.

The problem with the term is its historical associations. But this need not limit our vision of its significance, which, as we have seen, is derived directly from the gospel. It need not be evidenced by the Church's presence in all places but rather is an outlook that may be present in any and all specific locations. In this way it is not an external mark of the church but an inner reality.

Holiness

We have already given considerable attention to this mark and noted several historical attempts to come to terms with the obvious unholiness of the empirical church. John Wesley, we saw, insisted that the holiness of the Church is attributable because of a real, rather than imputed, holiness. This can be sustained if we take his point that living faith is the crucial attribute of the Church. All who have such faith are holy in some measure.

Clearly there are degrees of holiness in connection with the Body of Christ, just as there are with individuals. If the Church is carrying out its mission with any success, it can be no other way, since those who are added are "babes in Christ" (1 Cor. 3:1; cf. 1

Pet. 2:2), and these are holy in one sense. Hence there would ideally be a mixture of "children, young men, and fathers" (cf. 1 John 2:12-14), as Wesley loved to characterize the stages of spiritual development.

Holiness is both an actuality and an ideal. This is the basis for communities of believers being addressed in the New Testament as "saints" and at the same time exhorted to pursue "the unity of the faith and of the knowledge of the Son of God, to mature manhood, to the measure of the stature of the fulness of Christ" (Eph. 4:13).

Perhaps the institutional dimension of the church intrudes itself into the picture here as much or more than with any of the other marks. Many are connected with the organization who give little, if any, evidence of the pursuit of holiness. One must simply recognize that the boundaries of the Church cannot be drawn synonymously with the boundaries of the institution.

It is in relation to this mark of the Church that discipline becomes an important ingredient in speaking about the Church. It is the responsibility of the Church to maintain its purity and purge itself so as to seek as untarnished a witness as is possible with earthen vessels. Given the present state of the church, each congregation or connection of congregations has both the right and the responsibility to determine the parameters of its own life-style to implement its understanding of its mission. It is this function that is appropriately termed "the conscience of the church."

In carrying out this responsibility, both biblical mandates and cultural distinctives must be taken into account. Only in this way can catholicity become a reality and cultural provincialism be avoided. Furthermore, all of this must be carried out in the context of the gospel so that discipline is clearly seen as guidance of response to God's free gift of saving grace. It is in this way that the holiness of the Church, like the other marks, is derived from the gospel.

Apostolicity

When we attempt to derive this mark of the Church from the gospel, the idea of function immediately arises. The task of the apostles was to bear witness to the resurrection of Christ (cf. Acts 1:21 ff.; 10:41). Quite obviously the apostles are dead, and their office was not perpetuated. To attempt to establish the authenticity of the truth of the gospel by tracing an apostolic succession handed down in an unbroken chain from Peter is a historically impossible task. Such simply does not exist. Furthermore, this would be external and as such inadequate.

Therefore we conclude that, as Hans Kung points out, apostolicity refers to the whole Church and not to an office within the Church.[67] This mark is present in the Church when, empowered by the Spirit, the members of the body exercise the apostolic witness to the gospel. Apostolic authority is not in historical continuity or exclusively in apostolic truth but in the truth of the gospel proclaimed in the power of the Spirit.

Word and Sacrament

When the Catholic marks of the church are interpreted according to the gospel, they merge inseparably with the Protestant marks. The church lives by the gospel, and hence the creation, maintenance, and perpetuation of her life is through the Word preached and rightly enacted.

The "rightly enacted" is of importance here. It does not indicate formal or ritual requirements but implies the nature of response. Since the gospel offers reconciliation and sanctification (see discussion of the full implications of "gospel" in chap. 5), the appropriate response is faith and obedience—in that order. It is not the hearing or performing that is crucial but the appropriation in faith of the benefits provided by Christ and the positive living out of the implicit call to discipleship.

In the beginning, the Protestant emphasis was upon the priority of the Word with sacrament as a way of proclaiming the Word through symbol. Hence preaching was the focal point of Protestant worship. This is reflected in distinctive architecture in which the pulpit (on which the Bible should be laid) is placed at the center of the building with all lines directing toward it. In more recent times many Protestant churches have modified this earlier emphasis by an architectural change, using a divided chancel with the altar at the center. This emphasizes the priority of the sacrament and is a return to the Catholic view. Evangelical churches almost universally retain the centrality of the pulpit because it implies the centrality of the gospel. But they should be warned against neglect of

---

67. *The Church*, 355.

the sacraments, which help retain the mystical elements of the gospel.

To insist on the priority of preaching has practical implications. It requires that the *keryx* or herald be qualified in terms of exegetical skills, theological understanding, and commitment to study of the Word. As the Nazarene *Manual* says of the minister, "He or she will have a thirst for knowledge, especially of the Word of God" (par. 401.4).

The sermon derives from the Scripture, is an exposition of Scripture (not personal opinion or experience, although the latter is appropriate as a verifying element per the Wesleyan quadrilateral), and an application of it to the people of the congregation. This implies that expository sermons are the most appropriate type for a church service. This lays responsibility upon the congregation, or organized group of congregations, to assure that persons who carry out this function manifest gifts and graces requisite to the task. It further requires them to demand quality preparation before one assumes the responsibilities of the pulpit.

A fuller discussion of the sacraments will be found in the following chapter.

The Church as Sociocultural Reality

Since the church is a society of men, it is inevitable that it takes on a historically conditioned form. It is important that we not confuse the essence of the Church with this historical form. Yet, as Hans Kung says,

> No form of the Church, not even that in the New Testament, embraces its essence in such a way that it is simply part and parcel of it. And no form of the Church, not even that in the New Testament, mirrors the Church's essence perfectly and exhaustively. Only when we distinguish in the changing forms of the Church its permanent but not immutable essence, do we glimpse the real Church.
> The essence of the Church is therefore always to be found in its historical form, and the historical form must always be understood in the light of and with reference to the essence.[68]

This truth is the entailment of the church as a visible, in contrast to an invisible, reality somehow existing apart from the persons who make it up.

---

68. Ibid., 6.

H. Berkhof speaks of the dominant approach to the doctrine of the Church having been "a priori-dogmatic," a way that tends to be "docetic." He encourages a sociological approach to the problem of the church, which, he says, "eventually . . . will have to be incorporated into a systematic ecclesiology."[69] We can only suggest one or two implications after noting some evidence for the validity of the claim here made.

Paul Bassett shows how even in the Book of Acts, almost every structural component of the Church's life was borrowed from its surrounding environment, whether Jewish or pagan. As it became a full-orbed institution, he says, "Whether forms were borrowed or not . . . the church was essentially an anti-type of Graeco-Roman society."[70]

This implies that all restorationist movements are misguided when they identify the essence of the Church with its forms of worship or organizational structure(s) or practices. They are seeking to recover the husk when the true spirit of restoration seeks to recover "the simplicity and spiritual power manifest in the primitive New Testament Church" (*Manual of the Church of the Nazarene*, par. 24).

In this light, the words of J. Robert Nelson are apropos when he writes: "In view of the profound difference between first-century and twentieth-century society, primitive forms can hardly be considered binding on the church today."[71]

The functional nature of the church takes priority over the form of the church and dictates the institutional characteristics. In the Early Church, practices were adopted that furthered the mission, and those that did not were abandoned. "Form was important only as it served function."[72] A case in point appears to be the practice of communal ownership. The same principle should be applied to all church organization today. There is no revealed church order, whether congregational, episcopal, or presbyterian. The principle of pragmatism may be appropriately applied in this area. Whatever system of organization best works to achieve the goals of the church is in divine order, so long as it is consistent with those goals.

---

69. *Christian Faith*, 344.
70. "Western Ecclesiology: Part I," 129-33.
71. *Realm of Redemption*, 2.
72. Bassett, "Western Ecclesiology: Part I," 129.

Throughout church history, methods of carrying out the mission have emerged from the peculiar sociocultural context in which the church carried out its ministry. The frontier situation in the early United States, for example, spawned revivalism, the camp meeting, and the mourner's bench. The American denominational form of church life, with all its weaknesses, arose in a situation where there was no effective established church. The nature of a denomination is such that it reflects most perfectly the freedom of a democratic society. Wesley's church views were certainly colored by the cultural situation of the state church, which made possible the early Methodist structure.

J. B. Chapman, in an insightful article titled "The Unchanging Message and the Changing Methods," spoke these progressive words: "The essential message of the gospel is the same in all ages, but the method of presenting it requires adaptation to times and conditions."[73]

The implication of these ideas has wide-ranging ramification for the church as an international body. Various cultural settings will legitimately be reflected in the form that the church takes in that context. Missionary efforts must seek for contextualization and avoid confusing acculturation with evangelism. There is no place for a cultural triumphalism within the Body of Christ, although it inevitably takes on cultural forms.

Conclusions

The mass of literature on the church bespeaks the difficulty of dealing adequately with all the issues, especially in so brief a compass. We would simply point out an implication of the foregoing studies. Concern for the unity of worldwide Christendom is a worthy concern and a tremendous ideal. However, at this point in history, the fragmented nature of the church with deeply entrenched divisions renders it little more than a Utopian dream. While the effort need not be abandoned, since some progress may be made, it would seem wiser to focus on those areas that would give most promise of fulfilling the New Testament vision of the people of God.

It appears to us that the local congregation is the most likely

---

73. *Herald of Holiness*, May 24, 1976, 9.

locus for the church to be the church. Pragmatically, while the body of believers in a limited situation needs connections to address the worldwide responsibilities laid upon it, it is truly possible for the marks of the church to be brought to maximum expression in this setting. Here is where spiritual renewal has its greatest impact.

If this observation has validity, the importance of the local bishop (pastor) is paramount. Connectional offices are important to facilitate the broader work of the church, but they are one step removed from the vital cells that compose the Body of Christ.

As the Spirit works in the group, unity results and vice versa. Catholicity may be realistically present as bigotry in relation to other Christian believers disappears. If, as we argued in an earlier section, catholicity is an outlook rather than a geographical concept, it can be present when the local congregation knows no barriers of race or social status but embraces all men as brothers and draws a circle around all Christians in terms of acceptance, thus eliminating an exclusivistic attitude antithetical to perfect love. Defining the boundaries of Christian fellowship by the principle of cultural homogeneity is a digression from true catholicity.

The way we sought to define both holiness and apostolicity likewise makes it feasible to find these marks in a significant degree in a body of believers. When these are present, functioning as an outgrowth of Word and sacrament, one may speak of the church at *this* place, and see the visible, empirical church in action —being the "communion of saints."

The Means of Grace

The doctrine of the Church is not complete until we examine those symbols by which the body of believers appropriates its history and the source of its life.[1] These are commonly referred to as sacraments, but the idea of means of grace is broader than the traditional understanding of that term. The questions raised here have exercised the mind of the church from the beginning and are today among the major issues in the ecumenical discussions. Even those religious traditions that reject the idea of sacraments or means still employ vehicles by or through which grace is mediated, even if it is only the silent presence of other believers or words of a sermon.

To speak of means of grace requires us to elaborate both terms. Grace is a major Christian term, but its definition is ambiguous. It may have several connotations, depending on the context, but in the setting of this chapter we may restrict it to two basic meanings. It may refer to God's attitude that is commonly spoken of as "unmerited favor." It may also mean enablement or the inner strengthening of one's spirit. These two meanings are not mutually exclusive, and in fact both may be legitimately included in the concept of means of grace.

Grace as enablement was very early conceived in quasi-materialistic terms under the influence of Stoic thought. But in

---

1. This statement makes an assumption that will be justified in the subsequent discussion. It calls for a specificity with regard to the means of grace that is much narrower than a general unspecified experience of the Divine.

Augustine's debate with Pelagius it became a central tenet as a necessary corollary to the inability of the human will to choose the good. It was generally thought to be conveyed through baptism. By the Middle Ages this aspect of grace was interpreted as providing the power to do good works in order to be pleasing to God. This grace was normally conceived as being communicated in a more or less impersonal and automatic way.

. It was in reaction to these developments that Luther rejected this meaning of grace and opted for grace as God's attitude of forgiveness toward the sinner. For him, "the grace of God signifies primarily, not a supernatural energy or quality imparted to the human soul, but the gracious dealing of God Himself, quite personally, with men."[2] For this reason also he understood the supreme means of grace to be the Word of God rather than the sacraments. And in connection with the sacraments, the different view of grace resulted in a different concept of sacrament.

Closely associated with the medieval interpretation of grace was the understanding of means. Generally, as noted above, the concept was impersonal with sacramental acts functioning *ex opere operato*. The mediation of grace furthermore occurs only in and through the church, according to official teaching. "By contrast, Luther makes the very existence of the Church dependent on the work of divine grace through the Word and sacraments of the gospel, which itself is the power of God unto salvation."[3]

In his sermon on "The Means of Grace" John Wesley recognized both meanings of grace even though the crucial passage lays heavier emphasis upon grace as mercy.

> "By grace are ye saved:" Ye are saved from your sins, from the guilt and power thereof, ye are restored to the favour and image of God, not for any works, merits, or deservings of yours, but by the free grace, the mere mercy of God, through the merits of his well-beloved Son: Ye are thus saved, not by any power, wisdom, or strength, which is in you, or in any other creature; but merely through the grace or power of the Holy Ghost, which worketh all in all.[4]

Grace as mercy is needed to address the guilt of sin, but grace as enablement is required to deliver from the power of sin. It

---

2. Philip S. Watson, *The Concept of Grace* (Philadelphia: Muhlenberg Press, 1959), 81.

3. Ibid., 95.

4. *Works* 5:189.

should also be noticed that he equated the latter with the work of the Holy Spirit within. We have discovered that the New Testament's broad understanding of the Atonement encompasses both meanings of grace (justification and sanctification), so we may therefore say that the sacraments are the means by which the Holy Spirit applies the atonement of Christ in all its ramifications.

In addressing the idea of means, we are using a term that has a long history of use. Wesley's definition will serve our purposes as adequate to delineate its significance: "By 'means of Grace,'" he said, "I understand outward signs, words, or actions, ordained of God, and appointed for this end, to be the ordinary channels whereby he might convey to men, preventing, justifying, or sanctifying grace."[5]

Two extreme positions on this topic have been adopted. The first is to deny means altogether. This is the tendency of those who lay central emphasis upon experiential religion or mysticism. Wesley himself was early influenced in this direction but soon learned the dangers of that approach. In 1736 he wrote: "I think the rock on which I had the nearest made shipwreck of the faith was the writings of the Mystics; under which term I comprehend all, and only those, who slight any of the means of grace."[6]

In his sermon on "The Nature of Enthusiasm" Wesley identifies one common sort of enthusiasm (the 18th-century term for fanaticism) as

> that of those who think to attain the end without using the means, by the immediate power of God. If, indeed, those means were providentially withheld, they would not fall under this charge. God can, and sometimes does, in cases of this nature, exert his own immediate power. But they who expect this when they have those means, and will not use them, are proper enthusiasts.[7]

Both his commitment to means and the broad way in which he understood them is reflected in a passage quoted by Albert Outler:

> One general inlet to enthusiasm is the expecting the end without the means—the expecting knowledge, for instance, without searching the Scripture and consulting the children of

---

5. Ibid., 187.
6. Quoted in Ole E. Borgen, *John Wesley on the Sacraments: A Theological Study* (Zurich: Publishing House of the United Methodist Church, 1972), 99.
7. *Works* 5:475.

God; the expecting spiritual strength without constant prayer; the expecting growth in grace without steady watchfulness and deep self-examination; the expecting any blessing without hearing the Word of God at every opportunity.[8]

On the other side is the way of making the means into an end and considering such means to function *ex opere operato*. This, when referring to the sacraments, is known as sacramentarianism. Wesley was equally as concerned over this perversion as he was with mysticism or quietism. In his sermon on "The Means of Grace" he makes this position clear:

We allow, likewise, that all outward means whatever, if separate from the Spirit of God, cannot profit at all, cannot conduce, in any degree, either to the knowledge or love of God. . . . Whosoever, therefore, imagines there is any intrinsic power in any means whatsoever, does greatly err, not knowing the Scriptures, neither the power of God. We know that there is no inherent power in the words that are spoken in prayer, in the letter of Scripture read, the sound thereof heard, or the bread and wine received in the Lord's supper; but that it is God alone who is the Giver of every good gift, the Author of all grace; that the whole power is of Him, whereby, through any of these, there is any blessing conveyed to our souls.[9]

There were two major means that Mr. Wesley seemed to identify as constitutive of the church: the pure Word of God preached, and the sacraments duly administered.[10] This puts him squarely in the Reformation tradition.

The Sacraments[11]

The previous section provides sufficient background to understand the mediating position of Wesley on the sacraments, a position that follows the Church of England. A sacrament is defined as "an outward sign of inward grace, and a means whereby we receive the same."[12] Both are essential to a true sacrament. In tradi-

8. *John Wesley*, 300.
9. *Works* 5:188.
10. See Borgen, *Wesley on Sacraments*, 95-96.
11. It is not the task of systematic theology to discuss the method of administering the sacraments; this is the work of practical theology, which should build upon the work of systematic theology and seek to operationalize the sacraments so as to most effectively implement the theological understanding. Hence the mode of baptism or the method of serving the Holy Communion are not untheological but are to be informed by proper theological interpretation.
12. *StS* 1:242.

tional terminology it includes *signum* and *res*, the sign and the thing signified.

There is a bit of ambiguity here, since there is actually a dual signification. The sign of the sacrament stands midway between the source of grace, which is the saving activity of God as manifested in Jesus Christ, and the recipient of that grace. It points in both directions at once and serves as the occasion for the communicant to experience the grace provided. That is, it symbolizes both the objective source of grace and the subjective reality of that grace that has become effective in the believer.

On the objective side, the distinctive character of a Christian sacrament is qualitatively different from the idea of a sacramental universe. It is certainly true that any finite object can mediate the ontological reality of the Ground of Being. But theologically, this would be a witness to God the Creator, whereas a sacrament is a witness to a *Heilsgeschichte* or God's redemptive work in history. This is the import of Wesley's insistence that the ordinances are established by Jesus Christ in the gospel and that the content of the "inward grace" is Jesus Christ and His benefits.

Signs are given by God as an accommodation to our weakness and inability to understand heavenly and spiritual things. But they are not chosen arbitrarily; they bear an analogical relation to the objective reality signified.[13] Perhaps what Wesley meant by signs might be more appropriately conveyed by the concept of symbol, as proposed by Paul Tillich and which we earlier discussed under the topic of religious language. There are both linguistic and nonlinguistic symbols. The latter would cover the sign that comprises a sacrament. In that terminology, the symbol both mediates and shares in the reality to which it points and thus has a sacred character within itself insofar as it is sacramentally intended.[14]

On the subjective side, the sacrament points to the existential appropriation of the saving event. Wesley refers to the inward grace signified by the water of baptism in diverse ways such as "the merits of Christ's death applied," "death to sin," or "washing away the guilt of sin," and as "regeneration" or "the new birth," all implying the beginning of sanctification. The bread and wine of the Eucharist identify figuratively the body and blood of Christ and

---

13. See Borgen, *Wesley on Sacraments*, 52; Wesley, *Works* 10:188; 7:148.
14. If this is taken seriously, it becomes an important question of how to dispose of the elements left over from a Communion service.

thus the benefits that His death provides and includes prevenient, regenerating, and sanctifying grace.

Baptism

The origins of Christian baptism are clouded in obscurity. The liturgical use of water can be traced to primitive times, but the antecedents of the early Christian practice are unclear. Many think that it finds a precedent in Jewish proselyte baptism,[15] but at least one scholar has raised a serious question that this was a prevalent custom.[16] Perhaps the most likely direct antecedent is the baptism of John.

John's administration of baptism was the visible sign that repentance had occurred as a preparation for the new age that was "at hand." It was prophetic in nature both in being rooted in the past by John's relation to the prophets of old and also to the prophecies of a general outpouring of the Spirit in the "last days." These prophecies were often associated with water (see Isa. 32:15; Ezek. 39:29). It was also proleptic in nature, experienced in anticipation of the reality that was impending in the baptism "with the Holy Spirit and with fire" (Matt. 3:11; Luke 3:16). Cullmann sheds light on this matter in these words:

> This is then the new element in Christian Baptism according to the preaching of the Baptist. This new baptismal gift of the Holy Spirit is imparted neither by Jewish proselyte baptism nor by Johannine baptism. It is bound up with the person and the work of Christ. In the course of the Gospel story, the outpouring of the Holy Spirit "on all flesh" (Acts 2:17) presupposes the resurrection of Christ and follows on Pentecost. It follows that *Christian* Baptism is only possible after the Church is constituted as the locus of the Holy Spirit.[17]

When Jesus submitted to baptism at the hands of John there was a real sense in which the new age was embodied in His person, and John's baptism was given new significance. Whereas the multitudes were baptized by John as a remnant elected to await the dawning of the age to come, Jesus received the promised descent of the Spirit, and the association of water and Spirit that had been prefigured in the metaphorical language of the prophets became

---

15. Oscar Cullmann, *Baptism in the New Testament* (London: SCM Press, 1950), 9.
16. G. R. Beasley-Murray, *Baptism in the New Testament* (Grand Rapids: Wm. B. Eerdmans Publishing Co., 1974), 18 ff.
17. Cullmann, *Baptism*, 10.

translated into reality.[18] Thus it is the baptism of Jesus in particular rather than John's baptism in general that provides the clue to the distinctive Christian use of water baptism.

Baptism in the New Testament Church involves three meanings: It symbolized (1) an identification with Christ and His baptism, (2) the believer's incorporation into the Church, and (3) the reception of the gift of the Holy Spirit by the baptizand.

Identification with Christ. John Lawson suggests that "the leading theological passage in the New Testament regarding Holy Baptism" is Rom. 6:4.[19] Here Paul speaks of being "buried . . . with him by baptism into death." How do these two matters, death and baptism, connect? It is in the fact that in his baptism, the believer shares that of Christ, and the meaning of the latter is transferred to the former.

We have seen in an earlier section that Jesus' baptism was centrally His induction into the vocation of the Suffering Servant, that in a proleptic sense He shouldered the Cross. It was indeed a rite to which He submitted with a view to death. As Ralph P. Martin puts it, "The path to Calvary runs from Jordan's River."[20]

Paul's point is that the person who says that one could "continue in sin that grace may abound" (Rom. 6:1), since good works contribute nothing to one's salvation, does not understand the nature of Christian baptism. It is actually a declaration of intent to "put to death" everything in one's life contrary to the will of God or antithetical to Christlikeness. It symbolizes the putting to death of the old life and the bringing into being a new life in Christ, "risen with him" (cf. v. 4; Col. 2:12; 3:1).

The other two meanings ascribed to baptism in the Early Church derive from this first one. To be identified with Christ is to be

Initiated into the Church. The Church is the Body of Christ, hence to be in Him is to be a part of His Body. This signified furthermore, in the light of the third meaning (see below), that

---

18. G. W. H. Lampe, *The Seal of the Spirit* (London: SCM Press, 1951), 34-35.

19. *Introduction to Christian Doctrine* (Wilmore, Ky.: Francis Asbury Publishing Co., 1980), 166; Ralph P. Martin, *Worship in the Early Church* (Grand Rapids: Wm. B. Eerdmans Publishing Co., 1974) agrees, adding to it Col. 2:12, saying, "Both texts set the sacramental significance firmly within the context of the death and resurrection." 107.

20. *Worship*, 92.

baptism marks the giving of the Spirit, and it is the Spirit who constitutes the Church.

As an initiatory rite, baptism is the Christian counterpart to circumcision, which was the sign of entry into the covenant under the old dispensation. This covenant language is employed by Wesley as he recognizes the parallel between the two ritual acts that make one a part of the covenant people. Of baptism he says, "It is the initiatory sacrament, which enters us into covenant with God."[21]

He makes the relation explicit by saying, "By baptism we are admitted into the Church, and consequently made members of Christ, its Head [note the identification motif]. The Jews were admitted into the Church by circumcision, so are the Christians by baptism."[22] The covenant language does not exhaust the meaning of the relationship established, however. It is legal, whereas the primary character is personal and points to the next dimension.

This further dimension is an explicit implication of the believer's baptism when interpreted as sharing Christ's baptism. At the Jordan there was the descent of the Holy Spirit symbolized by the dove. This points to the third meaning.

Reception of the Spirit. In several instances in the New Testament, the gift of the Spirit accompanies the administration of the rite of baptism (Acts 2:38; 10:44-48). It furthermore is significant that Christian baptism is practiced only after Pentecost. However, there is sufficient variety of pattern found in the instances recorded in Acts to prohibit any formalization of the rite. As Ralph P. Martin correctly deduces: "There is no automatic process or magical formula which guarantees the bestowal of the Spirit, or which necessarily implies that all who were baptized in water received the spiritual counterpart in the gift of the Spirit."[23] (Cf. Acts 8:12-24; 9:17-18; 19:5-6 for variation in the pattern.)

In later times, as Paul Bassett has shown,[24] separate rites of Christian initiation began to be practiced in conjunction with the gift of the Spirit so that baptism was no longer perceived as the distinctive event marking the bestowing of the Spirit.[25]

21. *Works* 10:188. Cf. also 191, 192, 193, 194-95.
22. Ibid., 191.
23. *Worship*, 99-100.
24. *Exploring Christian Holiness*, vol. 2.
25. So also Kelly, *Doctrines*, 207.

John Wesley lays special stress upon this latter aspect of the New Testament emphasis in terms of the "new birth," or "regenerating grace." Since this is the peculiar work of the Spirit, it is the Spirit's activity in renewing the spirit of man that is signified by the rite. As Wesley himself puts it, "The terms of being regenerated, of being born again, of being born of God . . . always express an inward work of the Spirit, whereof baptism is the outward sign."[26]

If we recall that Wesley defines a sacrament in terms of both an outward sign and an inward grace, it will be clear that both must be present for the rite to be efficacious or valid as a sacrament. While the outward sign is not automatic, he insists that it is God's ordained and ordinary means by which the birth of the Spirit occurs and should not be hastily or carelessly dismissed. That, however, he did not make it essential is seen in his observation that not "even baptism," to say nothing of a particular mode, "is 'necessary to salvation.' . . . If it were, every Quaker must be damned, which I can in no wise believe."[27]

It now becomes obvious from the way in which Wesley adumbrates the New Testament understanding that he encompasses in baptism both justification and sanctification. Cullmann argues that both (described as "forgiveness of sins" and "transmission of the Spirit") were in a significant relation to each other in the New Testament view of baptism.[28] The latter is experienced in terms of the new birth as the beginning of sanctification, or the initial moment of a continuous process that is maintained and perpetuated by other means of grace, including the Lord's Supper.

Infant Baptism

There is no clear-cut reference to the practice of infant baptism in the New Testament.[29] However, the ritual appears very

---

26. *Letters* 4:38; *StS* 1:300, 303. Borgen summarizes Wesley's position clearly: "The only grounds upon which any means of grace attain any importance is that God is actively at work in and through the means he has ordained." *Wesley on Sacraments,* 134.

27. *Letters* 3:36; see *StS* 2:242.

28. *Baptism,* 13-15.

29. Nelson, *Realm of Redemption,* says, "That the New Testament says nothing explicitly about the baptizing of little children is incontestable." Cullmann argues, however, that this is not decisive, since there is even less evidence that children of Christian parents who grew to adulthood were ever baptized. *Baptism.* Wesley argues in a similar vein, almost curiously, that if no reference in the New Testament to women being baptized had been made, the same reasoning would have refused the rite to females. *Works* 10:196-97.

early in Christian liturgy and had become common practice by the third century.[30] Few issues have been more hotly debated.

If one takes Wesley's definition of a sacrament as implying an inward grace mediated by the ritual, it would seem to be excluded. However, Wesley unequivocally affirms his commitment to the practice and proposes to support it from "Scripture, reason, and primitive, universal practice."[31]

His chief argument seems to be based on the covenant concept. The basic presupposition here is the continuity of the "evangelical" covenant made with Abraham and the new covenant in Christ. Just as infants were circumcised and thereby brought into the covenant with its benefits, privileges, and duties, so does baptism effect the same result. "When the old seal of circumcision was taken off, this of baptism was added in its room [place]; our Lord appointing one positive institution to succeed another."[32]

He includes all the benefits surveyed above as being bestowed in infant baptism, including "the washing away the guilt of original sin, the engrafting us into Christ, by making us members of his Church."[33] In a word, he actually believed that an infant was "born again" through the means of baptism.[34]

Wesley rejects the objection to this on the basis that there must be a conscious awareness of the appropriation of the work of Christ. This is a position articulated by Calvin and employed by Karl Barth in this century to vigorously—and consistently—reject infant baptism.[35] But in Wesley's view, just as infants were really within the covenant relation by circumcision, so are they in baptism.

This may be interpreted as saying that baptism is the *ordinary* (a term Wesley insisted on) means by which the child appropriates prevenient grace, which would nonetheless be efficacious apart from baptism even as adults may be born again without the administering of water. That, however, is not the ordinary way. This places great responsibility upon sponsors to nurture the grace that

---

30. Kelly, *Doctrines,* 207.
31. *Works* 10:193.
32. Ibid., 194.
33. Ibid., 198.
34. See *StS* 2:238. He says: "Nor is it an objection of any weight against this, that we cannot comprehend how this work can be wrought in infants. For neither can we comprehend how it is wrought in a person of riper years."
35. Cullmann, *Baptism,* 23 ff.

is imparted to the child, since the grace of baptism may be lost.[36] This can be the only conclusion of Wesley's Arminianism in contrast to the Roman Catholic teaching that infant baptism carries an "indelible mark" or a Calvinistic doctrine of perseverance. Thus early education is an important ingredient in the stewardship of life granted to the parents. In regard to the inherent corruption that Wesley does not believe is remedied by infant baptism, he says of the value of education:

> Scripture, reason, and experience jointly testify that, inasmuch as the corruption of nature is earlier than our instructions can be, we should take all pains and care to counteract this corruption as early as possible. The bias of nature is set the wrong way: Education is designed to set it right. This, by the grace of God, is to turn the bias from self-will, pride, anger, revenge, and the love of the world, to resignation, lowliness, meekness, and the love of God.[37]

At the risk of an oversimplified ad hominem, we would suggest that the difficulty of many of Wesley's more evangelical successors to relate to these teachings about baptism derives in part from a different cultural milieu that has been influenced by several factors. Whereas Wesley worked in the context of an established church, the present situation in most areas of the world reflects a denominational form of church structure with the loss of the sense of unity that follows from such a fragmented situation. There is furthermore the influence of the Enlightenment and American frontier individualism, which has exalted the lone individual as the locus of meaning, so the corporate dimensions of human existence seem unreal. This has contributed largely to a loss of the awareness of the significance of the church in constituting the Christian life, an awareness that Wesley keenly felt.

An additional influence that rather radically altered the understanding prevalent in Wesley's day regarding religious conversion was the emergence of American revivalism. The emphasis on dramatic, emotion-laden, will-oriented experience that resulted in a marked and sudden transformation has resulted in a depreciation of the sacraments. Stress on sacramental religion is often looked upon in such a milieu with disapproval as being less than genuine. The reality of radical conversion cannot be questioned,

---

36. See "Serious Thoughts Concerning Godfathers and Godmothers," in *Works* 10:506-9.

37. *Works* 13:476.

but it must be recognized that the shape and expression of it is culturally influenced.

All of this raises the question of the possibility of recovering the New Testament understanding of baptism or of Wesley's views insofar as they are validly biblical. First, we can recall a principle that we enunciated and elaborated in the early part of this section on the work of the Holy Spirit. This is the idea that experience is given form by understanding. We saw this supported by John Fletcher's theological work as well as contemporary psychological views. On this basis it appears possible to move, in certain limited ways, toward a more New Testament view of baptism. With instruction and guidance, people may come to see the significance of experiencing the benefits of Christ through the God-appointed sacraments.

Furthermore, a genuine validity can be attached to infant baptism if it is seen as the induction of the child into the covenant community with a concomitant commitment of the community to help guide the child "in the nurture and admonition of the Lord" (Eph. 6:4, KJV). It might, in fact, militate against the loss of children from the church by guarding against the church becoming spectators until the child experiences an adult conversion. But more theologically, there is solid basis for infant baptism as a ritual that bears witness to the reality of prevenient grace. The grace that flows from the Cross to all men is appropriated by the community for that child. Not that it is not efficacious before, but here would be expressed the ordinary means by which that universal grace is manifested. Even if adult baptism is interpreted as a subsequent testimony to inward grace previously received, the pattern for infant baptism would be still appropriate: It is the witness to an already existing "covering of the Blood" and covenant provisions for salvation.[38]

The Lord's Supper[39]

If baptism is that sacrament that initiates one into the church and signifies the identifying of oneself with Christ, the Lord's Sup-

---

38. The presently existing article of faith on baptism in the *Manual of the Church of the Nazarene*, while not explicitly reconciled so as to have internal consistency, does allow for this interpretation, as does the twofold ritual pertaining to the "dedication" or "baptism" of infants.

39. As at no other place in this work, we are primarily seeking to provide a fair presentation of the views of John Wesley as a more or less historical study. This seems to

per is the sacrament that celebrates the continuance of this relationship as well as serving to perpetuate it. It is variously termed Eucharist (meaning thanksgiving), Holy Communion, and the Lord's Supper.

Like baptism, it is not a vague, undefined mediation of the Divine to human consciousness but a means of bringing to presence the historical events that constitute the *Heilsgeschichte* of the Christian faith and reinforcing its significance. It is generally agreed that historically it derives from the last supper that Jesus ate with His disciples, a meal commonly identified as the Passover meal.[40] The Lord's Supper thus becomes the Christian counterpart to the Jewish Passover.

The significance of the Supper derives from this event. Jesus identifies the bread and the cup with His own body and blood and announces that thereby He is inaugurating the new covenant with all the provisions included therein. Thus the Lord's Supper is one of the means by which the benefits of Christ's work are mediated to the communicants,[41] as well as mediating the presence of Christ himself. With these summary observations, we need to now explore the relation of "sign" to "signified."

---

be the best approach as, at least, a starting point for the developing of a Eucharistic theology from the Wesleyan perspective, a task to which we are unable at this time to give the time and energy. We are relying considerably on the work of Borgen, *Wesley on Sacraments.* Frank Baker, one, if not the leading, contemporary Wesley scholar, recommends this work as surpassing others in this area. "Unfolding John Wesley," *Quarterly Review* I, no. I (Fall 1980). One major point needs to be noted, a point reflected in Albert Outler's statement that "in the area of sacramental theology proper Wesley was prepared simply to borrow—from his father, his brother Charles, Daniel Brevint and others." *John Wesley,* 307. Borgen makes extensive use of the Brevint source, which was a tract titled *The Christian Sacrament and Sacrifice,* which Wesley included as a preface to his *Hymns on the Lord's Supper,* and which he argues is an expression of Wesley's own views. Borgen's main contention is that Wesley's sacramental legacy has largely been replaced with a preference for the Word and nonbaptismal regeneration. Works on the subject, he contends, have generally (1) failed to take into account the whole Wesley, (2) tended to use him to support preconceived ideas, or (3) not sufficiently understood the significance of Wesley's understanding of the *ordo salutis* for his sacramental theology.

40. There is significant debate over this issue among biblical scholars. The chronology of the four Gospels cannot be easily conflated, and therefore there is a serious problem as to whether or not this was the actual Passover meal (see Jeremias, *Eucharistic Words of Jesus,* et al.). However, it is still generally accepted that there is a typical relation between the Passover and the Lord's Supper. See Paul's statement in 1 Cor. 5:7.

41. Wesley said, "I showed at large: (1) That the Lord's Supper was ordained by God to be a means of conveying to men either preventing, or justifying, or sanctifying grace, according to their several necessities." *Journal* 2:361.

Relation of "sign" to "signified." There are four classic interpretations of this relationship: transubstantiation (Roman Catholic), consubstantiation (Lutheran), spiritual presence (Calvin/Reformed), and memorialist (Zwinglian).

In *transubstantiation,* the roots of which may be traced back to earliest times, the words of institution ("this is my body") are taken literally. On this basis Catholic thought sees all Protestant views as weakening the reality of the sacrament, and all were rejected by the Council of Trent.

On this interpretation, through the priest's words of consecration there is a substantial change of the bread and wine into the body and blood of Christ. The proclamation has a mysterious power that effects this transformation of the host (bread and wine).

The crudity of this is somewhat obviated when it is understood that a metaphysical subtlety is at work. The doctrine is based on a distinction between substance and attributes, the latter being the empirical qualities experienced, whereas the underlying substratum transcends the empirical. The teaching is that whereas the attributes retain all the properties of bread and wine, it is the substance that is transformed. The defense of this position is an appeal to the word "is," and the insistence that it is the decisive matter in guaranteeing the "real presence," the coincidence of the "sign" and the "signified."

Along with the Protestant Reformers, Wesley rejects this interpretation vigorously. His Article 17 taken over from the Thirty-nine Articles of the Anglican church says: "Transubstantiation, as the change of the substance of bread and wine in the supper of the Lord, cannot be proved by holy writ; but is repugnant to the plain words of Scripture; overthroweth the nature of a sacrament, and hath given occasion to many superstitions."[42]

In his essay "Popery Calmly Considered" he responds to the doctrine:

> We answer: No such change of the bread into the body of Christ can be inferred from his words, "This is my body." For it is not said, "This is *changed* into my body," but, "This *is* my body;" which, if it were to be taken literally, would rather prove the substance of the bread to be his body. But that they are not to be taken literally is manifest from the words of St. Paul, who calls it bread, not only before, but likewise after, the consecra-

---

42. Quoted in Borgen, *Wesley on Sacraments,* 58.

tion. (1 Cor. x.17; xi.26—28.) Here we see, that what was called his body, was bread at the same time. And accordingly these elements are called by the Fathers, "the images, the symbols, the figure, of Christ's body and blood."[43]

Luther rejected the Roman teaching, but desiring to take seriously the words of institution, he formulated an alternate theory of "real presence" referred to as *consubstantiation*. He rejects the Aristotelian (via Thomas) distinction between substance and accident and affirms, even though transcending reason, that Christ's body and blood are really present in the bread and wine. Luther's own words make quite clear his position on this matter:

When I fail to understand how bread can be the body of Christ, I, for one, will take my understanding prisoner and bring it into obedience to Christ; and, holding fast with a simple mind to His words, I will firmly believe, not only that the body of Christ is in the bread, but that bread is the body of Christ. . . . What if the philosophers do not grasp it? The Holy Spirit is greater than Aristotle. . . . Thus what is true in regard to Christ is also true in regard to the sacrament. It is not necessary for human nature to be transubstantiated before it can be the corporeal habitation of the divine, and before the divine can be contained under the accidents of human nature. Both natures are present in their entirety, and one can appropriately say: "This man is God"; or "This God is man."[44]

Luther finds the rationale for this view in the Christological doctrine of ubiquity or "communication of properties." This is reflected in the words of the preceding quote: "This man is God" and "this God is man." Hence we may speak ubiquitously of the body and blood and the bread and wine.

Luther thus maintained, as the doctrine of transubstantiation intended, a real corporeal presence of the body of Christ in the bread. However, there is a significant reorientation. For the Catholic view, the Presence is objectively in the sacrament, conferring grace upon the communicant. Luther rejects this and replaces the *ex opere operato* function with an evangelical one. His definition of a sacrament reflects this change. It is composed of an outward sign and a promise from God. The sign was a pictorial proclamation of the word of the gospel, which is received in faith. Thus the Pres-

43. *Works* 10:151.
44. Quoted in Alasdair I. C. Heron, *Table and Tradition* (Philadelphia: Westminster Press, 1983), 111-12.

ence is not automatic but is actualized by the communicant's laying hold of the promises of God by faith.

While Wesley is most vocal regarding his rejection of transubstantiation, he recognizes that consubstantiation is little different and rejects both any "corporal" or "local" presence and the doctrine of ubiquity.[45] He is much closer to the Reformed (Calvinistic) position, which speaks of *spiritual presence.*

Alasdair Heron's words provide a clue to Calvin's departure from the arena in which the debate between Luther and Rome had taken place:

> Judicious scholarship accompanied by a lively sense for the heart of the matter set him free alike from the trap of simple literalism and from the temptations of a superficial rationalism, and gave him the freedom to tackle the questions afresh in their theological and practical bearing.[46]

Calvin rejects the idea of "carnal presence" on the basis of a rejection of the "communication of properties." The body or human nature of Christ is localized in heaven and hence cannot be held to be corporeally present in the elements of the sacrament. To teach this is to turn the humanity of Jesus into "something other than he is witnessed to in the New Testament, the Word of God made flesh in the specific, human individual Jesus Christ, incarnate, crucifed, risen and ascended."[47]

In essence, for Calvin, the issue is how the blessings that God has made available to us through His Son are to be appropriated. This is not through a physical presence in the sacrament but by the energy of the Spirit of God who is active in the situation of faith, creating union with Christ. He says: "The sacraments duly perform their office only when accompanied by the Spirit, the internal master, whose energy alone penetrates the heart, stirs up the affections, and procures access for the sacraments into our souls." This coincides with his definition of a sacrament: "It seems to me, then, a simple and appropriate definition to say, that it is an external sign, by which the Lord seals on our consciences his promises of good-will towards us, in order to sustain the weakness of our faith, and we in our turn testify our piety towards him."[48]

45. Ibid., 124.
46. Ibid., 126.
47. *Institutes* 4.14.9.
48. Ibid., 1.

In a word, when the sacrament is properly received, the sign involves the reality signified when it is apprehended in faith. Borgen argues that while there are affinities between Calvin and Wesley, the latter does not quite fit into Calvin's formulations. Calvin, he says,

> will stress the importance of the presence of Christ's body, in terms of "power and strength" mediated through the Holy Spirit, while Wesley will emphasize the presence of Christ in his divinity; in fact the whole Trinity is present and acting, bestowing upon men the benefits of the incarnation, crucifixion, and resurrection. The emphasis is upon unity rather than distinction.[49]

It must be granted that this is a very subtle distinction, but it is a critical one as we shall see. It is a watershed that enables Wesley to avoid the problems of interpreting real presence in some corporeal sense.

Quite different from any of these first views surveyed is the position attributed to Huldreich Zwingli and referred to as the *memorialist* theory. The Reformer of Zurich had "absorbed much more of the spirit of humanist learning and much less of that of medieval piety and scholastic theology than had Luther,"[50] and thus was more radical in his departure from traditional views.

Zwingli picked up on the motif of "remembrance." In contrast to the Catholic Mass, which was conceived as a "sacrifice," he held that the finality of Christ's historical death precluded the validity of a repeated sacrifice. Thus he felt it was more appropriate to engage in an act of *remembering* that event. He found scriptural support in the words of institution, "This do in remembrance of me" (Luke 22:19; 1 Cor. 11:24-25, KJV). The sacrament became thus a subjective occurrence.

The "eating and drinking" of the flesh and blood of Christ was stripped of any realistic significance and was interpreted as the spiritual function of faith. Zwingli replaces Luther's emphasis on the "is" of the words of institution with the idea of "signifies." The bread is a symbol of the body, the wine a symbol of the blood, and the entire activity symbolizes our faith in Jesus Christ, who was sacrificed for us. Hence it is a memorial to a past event. This view has been sometimes referred to as the doctrine of "real absence."

---

49. Borgen, *Wesley on Sacraments*, 67-68.
50. Heron, *Table and Tradition*, 115.

556 □ GRACE, FAITH, AND HOLINESS

Although Wesley's vocabulary includes the term "memorial," it cannot be seen as an empty ceremony that may wear thin through repeated occurrence.

It should now be clear that the divergences between these views hangs largely on the interpretation of the words of institution: "This is my body." How does Wesley exegete this crucial passage? His note on Matt. 26:26, 28 is instructive:

> *This* bread *is*, that is, signifies or represents, *my body*, according to the style of the sacred writers. Thus, Gen. xl. 12, "The three branches are three days." Thus, Gal. iv. 24, St. Paul, speaking of Sarah and Hagar, says, "These are the two covenants." Thus, in the grand type of our Lord, Exod. xii. 11, God says of the paschal lamb, "This is the Lord's passover." Now Christ, substituting the Holy Communion for the Passover, follows the style of the Old Testament, and uses the same expressions the Jews were wont to use in celebrating the Passover. . . . *This is* the sign of *my blood*, whereby the new testament, or covenant, is confirmed.

Hence Wesley clearly rejects any kind of literal interpretation of the words of institution. Thus he sides with the Reformed and Zwinglian views on this point. He speaks of receiving "those signs of Christ's body and blood"[51] instead of receiving the "body and blood" of Christ.

When asked why he does not hold to the literal sense of the words, he replies: "(1.) Because it is grossly absurd, to suppose that Christ speaks of what he then held in his hands, as his real, natural body. . . . (2.) The sense of, 'This is my body,' may be clearly explained by other scriptures, where the like forms of speech are used."[52]

He understands the "forms of speech [that] are used" to refer to the function rather than the nature of the sacrament. In correspondence with his mother, his views become clear. She writes, in response to his explanation of a friend's views on the sacrament:

> The young gentleman you mention seems to me to be in the right concerning the real presence of Christ in the sacrament. I own I never understood by the "real presence," more than what he has elegantly expressed, that the "divine nature of Christ is then eminently present, to impart, by the operation of his Holy Spirit, the benefits of his death to worthy receivers." And surely the divine presence of our Lord, thus applying the

---

51. *Works* 7:147.
52. Ibid. 9:278.

virtue and merits of the great atonement to each true believer, makes the consecrated bread more than a sign of Christ's body; since by his so doing, we receive not only the sign, but with it the thing signified, all the benefits of his incarnation and passion! But still, however this divine institution may seem to others, to me it is full of mystery. Who can account for the operation of God's Holy Spirit, or define the manner of his working upon the spirit in man, either when he enlightens the understanding, or excites and confirms the will, and regulates and calms the passions, without impairing man's liberty?

John responds to this letter about a week later:

One consideration is enough to make me assent to his and your judgment concerning the Holy Sacrament; which is, that we cannot allow Christ's human nature to be present in it, without allowing either con- or transubstantiation. But that His divinity is so united to us then, as He never is but to worthy believers, I firmly believe, though the manner of that union is utterly a mystery to me.[53]

Although the language is absent, the same sentiment is present that we have found in other paradoxical Christian beliefs. Wesley affirms the fact but confesses that the manner eludes his understanding.

Function of the Lord's Supper

In a passage from Daniel Brevint that Wesley incorporated as his own, three aspects of the Lord's Supper as a sacrament are clearly set forth:

THE LORD'S Supper was chiefly ordained for a *Sacrament*, 1. To *represent* the Sufferings of CHRIST, which are *past*, whereof it is a *Memorial*; 2. To *convey* the first Fruits of these Sufferings, in *Present Graces*, whereof it is a *Means*; and 3. To assure us of *Glory to come*, whereof it is an infallible *Pledge.*[54]

The Atonement Remembered. This aspect, as Zwingli saw, is given validity by the words of Jesus in instituting the sacrament, "This do in remembrance of me." But Wesley goes beyond the level of mere memory and interprets it as involving a "dynamic drama of worship in which both the believer and the Holy Spirit are actively involved."[55]

This makes it a true act of worship in which the worshiper enters vicariously into the sufferings of Christ and leads to the

53. Quoted in Borgen, *Wesley on Sacraments*, 63.
54. Quoted ibid., 86.
55. Ibid., 88.

awareness of the love of God, which is the fountainhead of it all. At the same time it makes it a present reality. As Augustine said, "This Sacrament duly received, makes the thing which it represents, as really present for our Use, as if it were newly done."[56] Much of Wesley's Eucharistic theology is contained in the hymns, one of which conveys this motif:

> PRINCE of Life, for Sinners slain,
>> Grant us Fellowship with Thee,
> Fain we would partake thy Pain
>> Share thy mortal Agony,
> Give us now the dreadful Power,
> Now bring back thy Dying Hour.

> Surely now the Prayer He hears:
> Faith presents the Crucified!
> Lo! the wounded Lamb appears
>> Pierc'd his Feet, his Hands, his Side,
> Hangs our Hope on yonder Tree,
> Hangs, and bleeds to Death for me!

This understanding is solidly grounded in the Old Testament understanding of sacrament. Remembrance was not merely a mental recollection but the restoration of a past situation that has for the moment disappeared. To remember is to make present and actual. This was the basis for the celebrating of the Paschal feast, which, according to Exod. 12:14, was instituted "for a memorial" (KJV). This means that each participant, by remembering the deliverance from Egypt, became aware that he was himself the object of the redemptive action, regardless of how many years he was removed from the historical event. When it is a question of redemptive history, the past is contemporaneous.[57]

The Atonement Applied. Wesley's understanding of "memorial" prepares the heart of the worshiper for the second function of the sacraments, to convey what it shows. It may become the instrument by which the benefits of Christ are bestowed upon men according to their needs.

---

56. Found in Brevint source, quoted by Borgen, *Wesley on Sacraments,* 89-90.

57. See Oscar Cullmann and F. J. Leenhardt, *Essays on the Lord's Supper,* trans. J. G. Davies (Atlanta: John Knox Press, 1972), 61-62; also William M. Greathouse and H. Ray Dunning, *Introduction to Wesleyan Theology* (Kansas City: Beacon Hill Press of Kansas City, 1982), 109-10.

For Wesley, the term "communion" goes beyond some mystical sense of fellowship but is understood in its active sense of "communicate." In his sermon on "The Means of Grace" he says:

> And that this is also an ordinary, stated means of receiving the grace of God, is evident from those words of the Apostle which occur in the preceding chapter: "The cup of blessing which we bless, is it not the communion," or *communication*, "of the blood of Christ? The bread which we break, is it not the communion of the body of Christ?" (1 Cor. x. 16). Is not the eating of that bread, and the drinking of that cup, the outward, visible means whereby God conveys into our souls all that spiritual grace, that righteousness, and peace, and joy in the Holy Ghost, which were purchased by the body of Christ once broken, and the blood of Christ once shed for us?[58]

Here seems to be the heart of Wesley's theology of Eucharist. He does not profess to explain the mystery but acknowledges the testimony of experience. There is neither static presence nor automatic communication but the appropriation of the benefits of Christ's atoning work both in its finished aspect and its continuing aspect. On the latter, Wesley's note on Heb. 7:25 applies: "He died once; He intercedes perpetually"; and on 1 Thess. 1:10—"He redeemed us once; He delivers us continually; and will deliver all that believe *from the wrath*, the eternal vengeance, which will then *come* upon the ungodly."

The Lord's Supper in this light has a possible dual significance. (1) It may function as a converting ordinance. Wesley rejected the "stillness" that refuses to partake of the means of grace until the fullness of faith. They are rather avenues into this faith. The following words from his *Journal* make this clear:

> What is to be inferred from this undeniable matter of fact—one that had not faith received it in the Lord's Supper? Why: (1) that there are means of grace—that is, outward ordinances—whereby the inward grace of God is ordinarily conveyed to man, whereby the faith that brings salvation is conveyed to them who before had it not; (2) that one of these means is the Lord's Supper; and (3) that he who has not this faith ought to wait for it in the use of both this and of the other means which God hath ordained.[59]

Furthermore, (2) the attendance at the ordinances are vehicles of the continuing growth in holiness of which Wesley speaks so

---

58. *StS* I:252-53.
59. Vol. 2, p. 315.

often. Salvation is not a once-for-all experience but a dynamic
relation needing moment-by-moment cultivation. The Lord's Supper is thus both a converting ordinance and a confirming one.
Hence it functions in terms of the main branches of God's grace
that operate within the soteriological focus of Wesleyan theology:
preventing, justifying, and sanctifying grace, "thus emphasizing
the dynamic and continuous bestowal of God's grace in all its
branches and pointing to the 'thing signified' rather than the outward sign."[60]

The Eucharist is both an aid to faith and a means to holiness.
In relation to the latter, Wesley's words about an awakened person
form a fitting summary:

> And as he was deeply sensible of the truth of that word,
> "Without Me ye can do nothing," and, consequently, of the
> need he had to be watered of God every moment; so he con-
> tinued daily in all the ordinances of God, the stated channels of
> His grace to man: "in the Apostles' doctrine," or teaching, re-
> ceiving that food of the soul with all readiness of heart; in "the
> breaking of bread," which he found to be the communion of
> the body of Christ; and "in the prayers" and praises offered up
> by the great congregation. And thus, he daily "grew in grace,"
> increasing in strength, in the knowledge and love of God.[61]

Interpreting Communion as communication does not invalidate the idea of communion, however. In fact, communion
with Christ is an essential aspect of the sacrament. But beyond
that, it involves also a communion among the members of the
church. Although the gift of salvation symbolized by the elements
is given to each one individually, it does not signify an isolating
individualism. The words of the ritual portray this characteristic:
"Let us not forget that we are one, at one table with the Lord"
(*Manual of the Church of the Nazarene,* par. 802).

This unity or oneness extends across both space and time. It
includes believers of all communions and from every age. It is not
so difficult to acknowledge the unity with Abraham, Isaac, Jacob,
and Paul that the image of the vine and branches implies, but it is
much more difficult to experience the unifying significance of the
Eucharist in our own time and world. Nonetheless that is what the
celebration of the sacrament calls us to do.

---

60. Borgen, *Wesley on Sacraments,* 198.
61. *StS* 1:97.

Aulen's paragraph presents the salient implications of this biblical truth:

> The Lord's Supper is, therefore, the sacrament of Christian unity, even though differences in theories and practices have caused divisions within the church. The unity is present because the Lord's Supper is communion with Christ. However men think, speak, and act, the Lord's Supper remains the sacrament of Christian fellowship and unity. But this character of the Lord's Supper involves at the same time the most compelling obligation on the church to manifest this unity in its life.[62]

As Pledge of Glory to Come. This is the third aspect of the Lord's Supper, which reveals that the sacrament has a past, a present, and now a future dimension.[63] This aspect is also validated by the Pauline version of the words of institution: "For as often as you eat this bread and drink the cup, you proclaim the Lord's death until he comes" (1 Cor. 11:26).

Just as the sacrament *points to* (signifies) the ground of our acceptance with God and assures us of our present relationship, it warrants our title to the inheritance with the saints. It is the pledge of our hope of heaven.

The Eucharist is a proleptic event, eaten in anticipation of the eschatological feast, the marriage supper of the Lamb. A Wesley hymn highlights this truth:

> *And will He not his Purchase take*
> *Who died to make us all His own,*
> *One Spirit with Himself to make*
> *Flesh of his Flesh, Bone of his Bone?*

> *He will, our Hearts reply, He will;*
> *He hath ev'n here a Token given,*
> *And bids us meet Him on the Hill,*
> *And keep the Marriage-Feast in Heaven.*

Both baptism and the Lord's Supper are described as a "pledge" that God will fulfill His promise.[64] However, in Wesley's Arminian context, this must be seen as a covenantal contract that involves a synergistic outcome. There is the possibility of falling

---

62. *Faith of the Christian Church*, 352.
63. For a full development of the eschatological dimension of the Eucharist in the light of recent developments in eschatology in biblical and systematic theology, see Geoffrey Wainwright, *Eucharist and Eschatology* (New York: Oxford University Press, 1981).
64. See *Works* 10:188.

from grace, but the sacrament is God's pledge that He will keep His word. It is a seal of the covenant, marking its authenticity. "Baptism is the entering seal, as was circumcision before. The Lord's Supper, on the other hand, is a confirming seal."[65]

The Lord's Supper as Sacrifice

We have seen how the Eucharist, as a sacrament, has a three-fold function. It is a "memorial," a "means of grace," and a "pledge of heaven." But in the sources Wesley appropriates as his own, it is also described as a sacrifice.

This immediately raises the specter of the Mass, which, in Catholic theology, is understood as a real sacrifice, the same as that offered by Jesus Christ on Calvary. This was vigorously rejected by Luther because of its implicit denial of the finality of the work of Christ and the addition of some further prerequisites to salvation beyond faith alone. There is no doubt that Wesley also uncon-ditionally rejects this view of sacrifice and for the same reasons. In his note on Heb. 10:15 he refers to the author as "describing the new covenant as now completely ratified, and all the blessings of it secured to us by the one offering of Christ, which renders all other expiatory sacrifices, and any repetition of His own, utterly needless." Only the once-for-all sacrifice of Christ can take away sin. What then is meant by seeing the Supper as a sacrifice?

We saw in our discussion of the priestly work of Christ that in Wesleyan theology there is a twofold significance. There is the completed aspect embodied in the historical Cross, and there is the continuing or unfinished aspect represented by Christ's inter-cessory role at the right hand of the Father. In this way Christ's atoning work is continual and ongoing. There is a sense in which, through this work, the great High Priest continually presents him-self as sacrifice to the Father, not as a repetition but as symbolizing the ongoing efficacy of the Atonement. A Wesleyan hymn em-bodies this truth:

> *He dies, as now for us He dies,*
> *That All-sufficient Sacrifice.*
> *Subsists Eternal as the Lamb,*
> *In every Time and Place the same,*
> *To all alike it co-extends,*
> *Its Saving Virtue never ends.*

---

65. Borgen, *Wesley on Sacraments,* 220.

What is involved here is a "showing forth" of the death of Christ and not an "offering up" of the elements of bread and wine. It occurs in the actual partaking of the elements by eating and drinking. This is reflected in his words from the sermon on "The Means of Grace":

> "For as often as ye eat this bread and drink this cup, ye do show forth the Lord's death till He come" (I Cor. xi. 23&c.): ye openly exhibit the same, by these visible signs, before God, and angels, and men; ye manifest your solemn remembrance of His death, till He cometh in the clouds of heaven.[66]

Words from Brevint that Wesley appropriates makes the relation between the final Atonement and its continuing significance quite lucid:

> Nevertheless this Sacrifice, which by a *real* Oblation was not to be offered more than once, is by a Devout and Thankful Commemoration, to be offered up every Day. This is what the Apostle calls, To set forth the Death of the LORD; To set it forth as well before the Eyes of GOD his Father, as before the Eyes of Men.[67]

This intends the showing forth of the oblation of the Son as the grounds of our continuous acceptance with God. The eating and drinking enters the communicant into the sufferings of Christ and thus enables him to share in the graces that are offered to man through His atoning sacrifice, including sharing access to God's throne. Thus the Supper as sacrifice is closely associated with its function as a means of grace.

This understanding emphasizes the present efficacy of the Atonement and thus reflects Wesley's repeated emphasis upon the importance of a moment-by-moment sustained relation to God based upon present grace, which of course flows from the expiatory sacrifice of Christ on the Cross. It is powerful in the "now" of one's existence. There is thus a decisive difference between Christ's sacrifice as *procuring* salvation and the continual intercessory sacrifice as the foundation and fountain of the Atonement applied and appropriated by men here and now.

Unlike the Catholic view, where the priest offers up the propitiatory sacrifice to God in the Eucharist, for Wesley it is Christ who offers up himself. As the words of Brevint say, "Our LORD, by

---

66. *StS* 1:251-52.
67. Quoted in Borgen, *Wesley on Sacraments*, 241.

that everlasting Sacrifice of himself, offers himself for us at the Holy Communion, in a peculiar manner."[68]

All of this draws upon the rich imagery of the Old Testament. Just as Aaron, being identified with Israel, bore his people with him into the presence of God, so does the Greater Aaron, the eternal High Priest. "And what a comfort it is to us, in all our addresses to God, that the great High Priest of our profession has the names of all his Israel upon his breast, before the Lord, for a memorial, presenting them to God."[69]

In our discussion of sacrifice in the section on the priestly work of Christ, we noted how the laying of hands upon the head of the sacrificial victim, when rightly understood, symbolizes the worshiper's offering himself to God. It is here that the Wesleyan doctrine of sanctification specifically comes into the picture. In referring to his own experience in the *Plain Account,* he says:

> Instantly I resolved to dedicate all my life to God, all my thoughts, and words, and actions; being thoroughly convinced, there was no medium; but that every part of my life (not some only) must either be a sacrifice to God, or myself, that is, in effect, to the devil.[70]

This was the beginning of his pursuit of holiness. The same truth is embodied in his sermon on "Christian Perfection":

> They were "sanctified throughout" . . . they "loved the Lord their God with all their heart, and mind, and soul, and strength;" . . . they continually "presented" their souls and bodies "a living sacrifice, holy, acceptable to God;" in consequence of which, they "rejoiced evermore, prayed without ceasing, and in every thing gave thanks." And this, and no other, is what we believe to be true, scriptural sanctification.[71]

We have shown earlier that the positive content of sanctification is love of God and men; the converse side of this is the sacrifice of oneself, dying to sin, being crucified with Christ. These stand in correlative relation to each other as positive and negative. As one grows in grace, he more and more dies to sin. Love is conveyed through the sacrament functioning as a means of grace, enabling the believer to present himself to God. Hence, as we noted in the

68. Quoted ibid., 266.
69. Wesley's *Notes on the Old Testament* on Exod. 28:15.
70. *Works* 11:366.
71. Ibid. 6:526.

opening of this chapter, grace as mercy and grace as enablement interplay throughout Wesley's sacramental theology.

There is thus a twofold character to the Supper as sacrifice. It symbolizes Christ presenting himself before God and us with Him (note the representational motif), and it is the church presenting Christ's sacrifice here below as a memorial of the saving death by which we live.

> *His Body torn and rent*
> *He doth to GOD present;*
> *In that dear Memorial shews*
>   *Israel's chosen Tribes imprest:*
> *All our names the Father knows,*
>   *Reads them on our Aaron's Breast.*
>
> *He reads, while we beneath*
> *Present our Saviour's Death,*
> *Do as JESUS bids us do,*
>   *Signify his Flesh and Blood*
> *Him in a Memorial shew*
>   *Offer up the Lamb to GOD.*

SOLI DEO GLORIA!

Appendixes

Appendix 1

Speculative Eschatology

In the body of this work we have noted that virtually every doctrine has an eschatological facet. This reflects the fact discovered
by more recent theological studies that eschatology is not an em-
barrassed addendum to theological work but is in the very warp
and woof of the biblical message. The careful reader will have
noticed, however, that in none of these discussions have we gone
beyond the affirmation of faith in this dimension but rather have
self-consciously exercised great reserve. It is so easy to pass over
the boundary of "what is written" into the realm of speculation.
The incredible curiosity of the human mind almost irresistibly
drives us in that direction. However, in a Wesleyan theology, addressing speculative questions beyond issues that have soteriological implications is inappropriate. Furthermore, writing a systematic theology in the context of the Church of the Nazarene as
this writer is doing dictates the same reserve. The article of faith
that speaks about eschatological issues of set purpose refuses to
venture beyond the central affirmations of eschatological reality.
Historically the Church of the Nazarene has refused to commit its
members to any particular opinion on this issue. For these reasons,
we have chosen to deal with this topic in an appendix to emphasize its status as secondary to soteriological concerns and ancillary
to essential matters of biblical faith. Nothing in this area can be
made a test of orthodoxy. As Mr. Wesley himself put it in a letter to
Christopher Hopper:

> My dear Brother, I said nothing, less or more, in Bradford
> church, concerning the end of the world, neither concerning
> my own opinion, but what follows:—That Bengelius had given
> it as his opinion, not that the world would then end, but that
> the millennial reign of Christ would begin in the year 1836. I

have no opinion at all upon the head: I can determine nothing at all about it. These calculations are far above, out of my sight. I have only one thing to do,—to save my soul, and those that hear me.[1]

The early stages of the holiness movement also shared this same kind of determination to avoid secondary topics that create divisions. A. M. Hills prefaces his chapter on "Eschatology" with the words "The Millennial Doctrine has been a veritable 'troubler in Israel.'"[2] The National Holiness Association at the turn of the century "banned those who made ... premillennialism ... their 'hobby,'" and "for years ... had forbidden the discussion of 'divisive' themes like divine healing or the Second Coming, on its camp meeting platforms or in the columns of the *Christian Witness.*"[3]

The points of this appendix are: to explore some of the issues relating to the topic that has become such a major preoccupation of contemporary conservative Christians; to survey the history of speculative eschatology in order to emphasize the ultimate futility of dogmatism about such matters; and to call attention to the un-Wesleyan assumptions of the most prevalent eschatological schema among present-day evangelicals—so that as Wesleyans, we may at least avoid self-contradictory positions, even in our speculations about the future.

Interpreting Eschatological Scripture

In our discussion of biblical authority we argued that it is not one's theory about Scripture that is crucial, but rather how one interprets it. This same principle is even more true—if possible—when it comes to biblical passages that refer to the end of the age. In a word, the question of hermeneutics is fundamental to the study of eschatology. Even Hal Lindsey, "high priest" of contemporary pop prophecy, concurs. He recognizes that "the real issue between the amillennial and the premillennial viewpoints is whether prophecy should be interpreted literally or allegorically."[4] The problem with this statement is that it oversimplifies the options, since the two

---

1. *Works* 12:319.
2. *Fundamental Christian Theology* 2:339.
3. Timothy L. Smith, *Called unto Holiness* 1:35, 127.
4. *The Late Great Planet Earth* (Grand Rapids: Zondervan Publishing House, 1970), 165.

ways mentioned are not exhaustive and in fact may not even include the most important ones.

Furthermore, in our lengthy survey of the relation between the Testaments in search of a clue for the best method of biblical interpretation, we discovered that the New Testament claims for fulfillment demonstrated conclusively that most prophetic passages could not be taken literally, else the claim of fulfillment was devoid of validity. We discovered that with one voice the church has insisted from the beginning that if the Old Testament be taken literally, it cannot be included in the Christian Bible; it is not then a Christian book. That is why biblical interpreters from the second century on have sought for a more adequate hermeneutic. William J. Dalton expresses the significance of this in a clear way:

> The prophets of the Old Testament did not have a sort of mental photograph of the future when they warned their hearers of God's coming judgment and of his salvation. If this were the case, then over and over again, they could be convicted of falsehood. . . . Prophecies made in the name of God are fulfilled in God's own way: He is not bound to the letter of the prophet's word. It is the event itself which reveals the meaning of the word.

The point is the same when transferred to the New Testament: "The event which is still hidden, will reveal the full meaning of the words of the New Testament."[5]

This implies that "fulfillment" is an a posteriori category that is extremely complex and rich. It is impoverished when it is interpreted in terms of some sort of wooden relation between prediction and fulfillment. Jesus himself expanded it far beyond this in His conversation with the despairing disciples on the Emmaus road, as recorded in Luke 24. There the Risen One pointed out how He was spoken of in the Law, the Prophets, and the Psalms (the Writings), thus including the total Old Testament canon in its threefold fullness.

Hence "fulfillment" actually conveys the idea of "filling full," with more profound significance than the original idea. It involves pouring new wine into old wineskins so that often they burst, that is, far transcend the original literal meaning. One cannot say beforehand what precise contours the fulfillment will take.

---

5. *Aspects of New Testament Eschatology* (Perth, Australia: University of Western Australia Press, 1968), 3.

Augustine long ago articulated this understanding of eschatology. He lays down a principle with regard to the future spoken of in the Word of God: "All these things, we believe, shall come to pass; but how, or in what order, human understanding cannot perfectly teach us, but only the experience of the events themselves" (*City of God* 20.30). In speaking of Paul's eschatological pronouncements in 2 Thess. 2:1-11, he says, "Why they are called signs and lying wonders, we shall then be more likely to know when the time itself arrives" (ibid., 19). And concerning the final resurrection, he observes that "the manner in which this shall take place we can now only feebly conjecture, and shall understand it only when it comes to pass" (ibid., 20).

In his note on Matt. 2:17-18, which suggests that Herod's slaughter of the children was a fulfillment of Jer. 31:15 (which refers to Rachel weeping in her tomb for the Judeans deported in the Babylonian Captivity and so has no literal relation to the incident of Herod's atrocity), Wesley says, "A passage of Scripture, whether prophetic, historical, or poetical, is in the language of the New Testament fulfilled when an event happens to which it may with great propriety be accommodated." This clearly acknowledges the a posteriori character of the category of "fulfillment."

H. Orton Wiley substantially supports this same position, speaking of what he calls "the law of prophetical reserve": "There is enough given us in the Scriptures to furnish the Church with a glorious hope; but the events can never be untangled until prophecy passes into history, and we view them as standing out clearly in their historical relations" (*CT* 3:307).

These hermeneutical principles grow out of the nature of eschatological passages in the Scripture. When the future is envisioned, including anticipations of the end of the age, it is always firmly rooted in the historical present. This is even true of apocalyptic writings that are self-consciously seeking to predict the consummation of history.[6] We are not reading history written in advance in a reportorial way as if the writer (or speaker) were an eyewitness to times and events unrelated to his own day. Rather he is projecting the end as the culmination of events in which both he and his audience are fully immersed. No matter how enigmatic his

---

6. See discussion of the characteristic of pseudonymity in relation to apocalyptic writings in Leon Morris, *Apocalyptic.*

references may be, a thorough knowledge of his times can identify them as deriving from historical experience.

Thus the author of the Book of Daniel describes the great anti-God in terms of Antiochus IV (Epiphanes), although in a veiled form; the author of Revelation describes the Antichrist in terms of Nero. When the end did not materialize as they described it, these descriptions pass into the repertoire of prophecy as yet-to-be-fulfilled realities and become paradigms for the actual end of the age. This is why it will always be futile to take these descriptions as reportorial accounts and attempt to use them to identify in advance precisely what they predict in terms of actual persons or countries or whatever. In a word, there may be many penultimate fulfillments that are anticlimactic to the ultimate fulfillment.

C. E. B. Cranfield expresses this position classically in his comments on Jesus' predictions of the fall of Jerusalem in Mark 13. He suggests that in Jesus' own view the historical and the eschatological are mingled and that the final eschatological event is seen through the "transparency" of the immediate historical. This way of viewing the future expresses the view that "in the crises of history the eschatological is foreshadowed. The divine judgments in history are, so to speak, rehearsals of the last judgment and the successive incarnations of antichrist are foreshadowings of the last supreme concentration of the rebelliousness of the devil before the End."[7]

Paul had some very definite things to say about the end in his earliest letters, especially 2 Thessalonians. Interestingly he identifies three things that must take place before the end will come (a great apostasy, the removal of a restraining force, and the appearance of the Antichrist), all of which *have not yet* occurred despite the claims of some that no prophecies remain unfulfilled. Yet the statement of Gunther Bornkamm about Paul's eschatological teachings is to the point and demonstrates how even the apostle's most explicit teachings do not provide the basis for reportorial knowledge of the end:

> The language and concepts of apocalyptic deeply influenced the Pauline theology as well as that of the primitive church, but were radically changed there. Apocalyptic speculations, panoramas, and concepts fall away or are even ex-

---

7. "St. Mark 13," *Scottish Journal of Theology* 6 (1953): 297-300. See also Ladd, *Theology*, 198-99.

pressly rejected (1 Thess. 5:1ff), and as a rule occur in fragmentation and with no coherence. The most fundamentally new thing in Paul's eschatology is his insight that the sending, death on the cross and resurrection of Jesus constitute the turning point in history.[8]

The most decisive argument against the possibility of determining fulfillment a priori is the words of Jesus himself. In Mark 13:32 and Matt. 24:36 He declared that no one knows the day or the hour of His return, not even the Son. Someone has observed that this statement of Jesus has been ignored more than any other one. Many still persist in seeking to identify what they call "signs of the times." It should be noted that only once in the Bible is this phrase used (Matt. 16:3), and there it refers not to something that is about to happen but to something that has already come to pass, namely the Kingdom has entered history in the person of Jesus Christ.[9]

An excellent essay on the hermeneutics of eschatological scripture is one by prominent Catholic theologian Karl Rahner.[10] In this insightful essay Rahner sets forth several theses. We will summarize the crucial five with which, I perceive, the preponderance of Protestant biblical and theological scholars will agree (excepting, of course, those committed to the presuppositions of dispensational theology to be noted later).

The underlying assumption is that since assertions about the *eschata* deal with a reality quite unlike other objects of knowledge, a special way of knowing is needed and hence a special hermeneutic of interpretation. It is not merely that the worldview of the biblical period is different from that of today, so that one only needs to correlate the two. We are dealing with a unique situation. These theses attempt to come to terms with the need to explain how such distinctive affirmations should be interpreted.

Thesis 1. The Christian understanding of the faith and its expression must contain an eschatology that really bears on the *future*, that which is still to come, in a very ordinary, empirical sense of the word *time*. This affirms what has been sometimes termed a realistic eschatology. It explicitly rejects such an exis-

---

8. *Paul*, trans. D. M. G. Stalker (New York: Harper and Row, Publishers, 1971), 199.
9. See Anthony A. Hoekema, *Bible and the Future*, chap. 11, for an extended excellent discussion of this point.
10. "The Hermeneutics of Eschatological Assertions," in *Theological Investigations* 4:323-46.

tential view as that advocated by Rudolf Bultmann. In Bultmann's interpretation the meaning of eschatology is transformed from "last things" to "ultimate things" and refers to the present moment in which decision is made that determines one's existence. Hence Bultmann's work is titled *The Presence of Eternity* and removes all timeful dimensions from eschatological assertions.

Thesis 2. The Christian understanding of God affirms His omniscience as including His knowledge of future events and the corollary that since such are human events, they do not, in principle, preclude the possibility of being communicated in an understandable way. This thesis raises a question we mentioned in an early discussion, namely, that the foreknowledge of God must involve a paradoxical relation between such foreknowledge and human freedom, a paradoxical relation that transcends the human capacity to formulate a rational explanation without losing one truth or the other. What Rahner is affirming is that one cannot lay it down as an a priori principle that the future is unknowable. However, in doing so, he is leaving open the nature and limitations of this potential knowledge. We must speak, not about what God *can* do, but about what He in fact does. It is from the latter that hermeneutical principles must be derived.

Thesis 3. The sphere of eschatological assertions and hence of their hermeneutics is constituted by the dialectical unity of two limiting statements. The first says, "It is certain from Scripture that God has *not* revealed to man the day of the end." This implies that genuine eschatological assertions bring the *eschata* into the present without losing the character of mystery that is essential to them. Rahner's words are adequate to state this simply:

> It may therefore be said that wherever we have a prediction which presents its contents as the anticipated report of a spectator of the future event—a report of an event in human history which of itself excludes the character of *absolute* mystery and hence deprives the eschatological event of its hiddenness—then a false apocalyptic is at work, or a genuine eschatological assertion has been misunderstood as a piece of apocalyptic because of its apocalyptic style and form. We have therefore to investigate *how* it is possible that an assertion can bring the future into the present in such a way that it retains a very specific character of hiddenness when it comes with threat or promise into our existence.

The second principle that defines the sphere of eschatological assertions is the essential historicity of man. He lives out of the past and toward the future, both of which are real. This leads to the next thesis.

Thesis 4. Knowledge of the future will be knowledge of the futurity of the present; otherwise the fulfillment would remain alien and unintelligible. Put somewhat more theologically,

> The end which brings the individual, man and the world in general to a close is precisely the completion of the beginning which came about with (the risen) Christ, and it is no more than this. This final consummation, as the end of all history, does not derive from another event which is still to come: the beginning, which is Christ, is the sole and adequate law of the end, and hence the fulfillment bears in all things the traits of this beginning.

While Rahner does not discuss this point, it is this truth that makes the claim that the Book of Revelation is an apocalyptic writing invalid. It shares certain literary features with this genre, but theologically it departs from it. Apocalyptic lives from the end, but the movement toward the end described symbolically in Revelation involves the consummation of a victory that had already been won at the midpoint of history as depicted in chapter 4. Only the Lamb slain could open the seven-sealed book to inaugurate the process of world judgment.

Thesis 5. Based on the previous theses, especially the twofold claim of No. 3, "We may at least presume that man's knowledge of the future still to come, even his revealed knowledge, is confined to such prospects as can be derived from the reading of his present eschatological experience." "Eschatology is not a pre-view of events to come later—which was the basic view of false apocalyptic in contrast to genuine prophecy. . . . It looks forward to the definitive fulfilment of an existence already in an eschatological situation." As a summary statement, Rahner says that "to extrapolate from the present into the future is eschatology, to interpolate from the future into the present is apocalyptic."

This final thesis has been very simply set forth in a popularly written article by J. R. McQuilkin, titled "This I Know."[11] After passing through a deep valley of doubt, he came to a position radically different from his previous approach, which he describes: "I had

---

11. *Action*, Nov. 1, 1956, 3 ff.

gone about delving into the future and attempting to write history ahead of time in great detail, like any good prophetic student or teacher." But he came to see that what the Bible tells us about prophecy is "not for the use commonly made of it." After a thorough study of prophetic passages in the New Testament he came to the conclusion that "the study of Bible prophecy should be, then, primarily for two purposes: the study of fulfilled prophecy to confirm our faith, the study of unfulfilled prophecy to influence our conduct."

Chasing the Millennium

It could be argued that the central eschatological category is the kingdom of God. How one conceives the Kingdom determines to a great extent his view of eschatology. Otto Weber declares that "the Kingdom of God stands at the center of all Christian expectation and it comprehends everything which must be said about it in detail."[12]

If the Kingdom is conceived as exclusively a present reality, the result is a "realized eschatology" (C. H. Dodd). If it is conceived as exclusively future, it results in "consistent eschatology" (J. Weiss). As we have noted in the body of this work, the most adequate view sees the Kingdom as both present and future. Even though the reign of God has entered history in a unique way in the person and work of Jesus Christ, its consummation awaits a future intervention. The concept of a millennium is normally developed as an offshoot of Kingdom theology and hence becomes a central issue in speculative eschatology. This is the rationale for tracing in some detail the development of millenarianism as a speculative teaching.

Millenarianism in the Second Century

It appears that from the beginning there was a twofold emphasis in the Christian doctrine of last things. While stressing the reality and completeness of present salvation, it has further pointed believers to certain eschatological events located in the future. Thus the Christian hope, as presented by the biblical writers, was a consciousness of blessedness here and now in this time

---

12. *Foundations of Dogmatics*, trans. Darrell L. Gruder (Grand Rapids: Wm. B. Eerdmans Publishing Co., 1983), 2:675.

and also blessedness yet to come; and the final wrap-up was conceived realistically as a series of events to be carried out by God on the plane of history. This double emphasis could be dissolved in either direction.

There were four chief moments in the eschatological expectation of early Christian theology in the second century: the return of Christ (known as the Parousia), the resurrection, the judgment, and the catastrophic ending of the present world order. But there were a number of developments during the course of the century.

Against the attacks of Jewish critics, the apologists argue that Old Testament prophecy anticipates a twofold coming of Christ. They insist that in addition to His coming in lowliness at His incarnation, Christ will come again in glory with the angelic host when the dead, both just and unjust, will be raised (cf. Justin Martyr's *First Apology*, 50-52).

In the process of time there was the emergence of a schematized understanding of history much like apocalypticism, claiming to provide a key to the time of the Parousia. "Barnabas" thinks that the creation story gives the clue. The six days of creation represent 6,000 years (from the words of 2 Pet. 3:8). This time has about expired. When it is stated that God rested on the seventh day, the meaning is that Christ will appear at the beginning of the seventh millennium in order to dethrone the lawless one, judge the ungodly, and transform the sun, moon, and stars (cf. *Letters*, 15).

Out of this milieu arose the millennial teachings of the second century. Millenarianism, or chiliasm, is the doctrine of two resurrections derived from Revelation 20. The first, that of the righteous dead, which will take place at the time of the second advent of Christ; and the second, that of the righteous and the wicked at the end of the world. Between these two resurrections there is to be a personal, corporal reign of Christ for 1,000 years to take place upon the renovated earth.

William Barclay argues that this doctrine was especially prevalent in those parts of the Church that had received their Christianity from Jewish sources, and this is the key to its origin, namely, certain Jewish beliefs about the Messianic age common in the time after 100 B.C. Before this time the general belief was that the Kingdom would be eternal when it was established. From 100 B.C. onward, however, there was a change produced by an increasing pessimism about the world. There emerged the concept that the

Messiah would have a limited reign upon this earth, and that after the reign of the Messiah the final consummation would come. His point is that this is the source of the passage in Revelation 20, and the basis for the interpretation of it that arose in the second century.[13] This would suggest that it is of a piece with Jewish earthly expectations.

Millenarianism first appeared in the system of Cerinthus, the Gnostic who was a contemporary and opponent of John and whom John attacked in his First Epistle. It appears only in the apostolic fathers in the writings of Barnabas, the Shepherd of Hermas, and Papias, the latter teaching it in a gross form. William Burt Pope argues that the teaching was not the received faith of the church, as is evidenced by its absence from the creeds.[14] The period between the year 150 and 250 is the blooming age of millenarianism.

So general had the tenet become in the last half of the second century that Justin Martyr declared it was the belief of all but the Gnostics (Dialogue with Trypho, chaps. 80—81). However, Irenaeus speaks of good Catholics who opposed it. The difference between the two groups seems to be hermeneutical, since those who adopted it followed the literal interpretation of the Old Testament prophecies and often gave them a very sensuous exegesis. Eusebius refers to a bishop who taught "a millennium of bodily luxury upon the earth."[15] Scholars of the Alexandrian School (see Appendix 2) who were inclined toward an allegorical exegesis, such as Clement and Origen, rejected the idea as unworthy.

Augustine's Reconstruction

It was Augustine who effected a change in the situation and provided an alternative that became the classical position of the mainline church from then until now.

First, he repudiated all efforts to set a date for the end of the world and to connect the coming of that event with concrete developments and with definite historical incidents. Several attempts to do this had been made. One was to number the persecutions. This theory took its clue from the 10 plagues in Egypt, with the event of the Red Sea being the type of the final or 11th persecution in

---

13. *Revelation of John* 2:238 ff.
14. *Compendium* 3:396.
15. Quoted in Barclay, *Revelation of John* 2:243.

which the Antichrist shall pursue the church and finally perish. Augustine says, "I do not think persecutions were prophetically signified by what was done in Egypt, however nicely and ingeniously those who think so may seem to have compared the two in detail, not by the prophetic Spirit, but by the conjecture of the human mind, which sometimes hits the truth, and sometimes is deceived." Furthermore, there is difficulty in determining which persecutions shall be included among the 10, and all efforts at specifying which ones to count do not take account of all persecutions; that is, such a scheme does not fit history (*City of God* 18.52). It is amazing how history repeats itself, as for instance the way in which prophetic teachers attempt to fit history into a sevenfold pattern to match the seven churches in Revelation, which they say represents seven ages leading to the end. The problem is, church history will not fit any of the patterns.

A second, and more pervasive, attempt had been made, based on the idea that there would be a series of monarchies followed by the end of the world. The Jewish source for this idea may be found in the Book of Daniel, where the images and visions of Daniel depict a fourth monarchy overthrown and replaced by the kingdom of God (the stone hewn out of the mountain). A similar belief prevailed in other cultures as well. There was a widespread belief that Rome was the fourth and last of these monarchies and that when it fell, the end of the world would occur. Thus there was great consternation when Rome fell to a Visigothic army under King Alaric in 410.

In reply to those who attempted to determine the exact date of the end of the world and connect it with concrete developments and historical events such as "the fall of Rome," Augustine declared that such a question is improper. He points out that Christ himself told His disciples: "It is not for you to know the times or the seasons, which the Father hath put in his own power" (Acts 1:7, KJV). "In vain then," Augustine went on, "do we attempt to compute definitely the years that may remain to this world, when we may hear from the mouth of the Truth that it is not for us to know this" (*City of God* 18.53).

Strangely enough, however, Augustine seems to accept the seven millennia concept based on the seven creation days, but he radically modified the concept of the millennium, as we shall now see.

His second major reconstruction of eschatology occurred in his reinterpretation of millennialism or chiliasm in a spiritual way, which included also a reinterpretation of the kingdom of God as spiritual and present rather than earthly and future. The locus classicus for this transformation is found in Book 20 of the *City of God.*

His starting point is a rejection of a "carnal" millennialism. The idea of a literal 1,000 years, he says, would not be too objectionable if it were held that the joys of the saints in that "Sabbath" were spiritual and consequent on the presence of God. He admits that he once held that view. However, he proposes a significantly different understanding of the "thousand years" (Rev. 20:2-7).

The entrée into his view is his interpretation of the "first resurrection" referred to in Rev. 20:5-6. This resurrection pertains to the soul, he argues, and not to the body. Souls of men are "dead in trespasses and sins" (Eph. 2:1, KJV) and in need of life. Hence in the first resurrection they are renewed in a spiritual resurrection. "As, then, there are two regenerations . . . —the one according to faith, and which takes place in the present life by means of baptism; the other according to the flesh, and which shall be accomplished in its incorruption and immortality by means of the great and final judgment—so there are two resurrections." The first is spiritual, and the second is of the body.

This opens the door to his interpretation of Rev. 20:1-10. In the light of the fact that Scripture uses the idea of "thousand" symbolically in other places, there is no reason to suspect that it is not so used in this place. Hence, the author "used the thousand years as an equivalent for the whole duration of this world, employing the number of perfection to mark the fullness of time." Following this spiritualizing of the text, the casting of the devil into the abyss is interpreted to mean the restricting him to the hearts of the wicked "whose hearts are unfathomably deep in malignity against the Church of God; not that the devil was not there before, but he is said to be cast in thither, because, when prevented from harming believers, he takes more complete possession of the ungodly."

It is here that he provides his definition of the Kingdom as being equated with the church, where during this millennium (the whole church age) the saints reign with Christ. As he says, "Therefore the Church even now is the kingdom of Christ, and the kingdom of heaven. Accordingly, even now His saints reign with Him, though otherwise than as they shall reign hereafter."

The releasing of the devil after this present age is for his final destruction both "bound" and "loosed." Contrary to his own principles, Augustine believed that during this period of being loosed, there is to be a three-and-one-half-year period of intense persecution preceding the "eternal reign of the saints."

As G. Eldon Ladd says, "Augustine's doctrine of the City of God banished the millennial interpretations of the kingdom from the realm of dogmatic Catholic theology."[16] Throughout the Middle Ages this identification of the church with the Kingdom precluded millennial speculation. The Protestant Reformers did not radically alter this idea, identifying the Kingdom with the "invisible Church," the reign of God in the hearts of believers and so a present reality.

Modern Millenarianism

The modern period of millenarian speculation apparently began with the work of Johann Albrecht Bengel (1687-1752). He has been called the "father of modern premillennialism" because of his prediction of the Parousia in 1836 (see reference in Wesley's letter quoted earlier).

Three general types of millenarianism arose in the 18th century: (1) There was the premillennial view of the Adventist type, whose distinctive feature is that the Church is complete at the Second Advent. (2) The second is the premillennial view of the Keswick type, represented by Joseph A. Seiss. The distinctive aspect of this view is that the Church is incomplete at the time of the Second Advent, that is, the work of salvation continues during the millennium. This view seems to be a forerunner of contemporary dispensationalism. (3) There was the rise of postmillennialism, which was an extension of Augustinianism. The person associated with the origin of this view is Daniel Whitby (1638-1726). On this theory, the preaching of the gospel will usher in the Golden Age, which will be followed by the Second Advent. Hence this teaching agrees with the first form, that the Church is complete at the Second Advent.

---

16. *Crucial Questions About the Kingdom of God* (Grand Rapids: Wm. B. Eerdmans Publishing Co., 1952), 24-25.

Many of the early leaders of the holiness movement in the 19th and early 20th centuries subscribed to this third position. A. M. Hills was an open proponent, as apparently was P. F. Bresee. Daniel Steele was a strong advocate of it. There was considerable optimism that the preaching of holiness could turn "the cities of America into a garden of the Lord." The change in climate caused by the Great Depression and two world wars resulting in the demise of liberalism likewise turned the sympathies of conservatives from postmillennialism to premillennialism. Virtually all who believe in millennialism at all hold to some version of premillennialism.

The Achilles Heel of Millennialism

It was during the 17th and 18th centuries that the "soft underbelly" of millennialism began to expose itself. Put simply, how does one explain the emergence of the wicked who are deceived and summoned by the devil at the close of a 1,000-year reign of Christ?

During the 17th century several fantastic solutions were proposed. Nathaniel Homes, in a work titled *Revelation Revealed* (1653), proposed that those who survived the conflagration (destruction of the earth by fire) would be made like Adam, including being susceptible to falling. They would actualize this potentiality and become those deceived. Thomas Burnet (*Sacred Theory of the Earth,* 1681) provided the most bizarre solution. In his own words:

> It seems probable that there will be a double race of mankind in the future earth, very different from one another. . . . The one born from heaven, sons of God and of the resurrection, who are the true saints and heirs of the millennium: the others born of the earth, sons of the earth, generated from the slime of the ground and heat of the sun, as brute creatures were at the first. This second progeny, or generation of men, in the future earth, I understand to be signified by the prophet under these borrowed or feigned names of Gog and Magog. (Quoted by Wiley, CT 3:275.)

Another view was that Gog and Magog (the wicked) will be composed of the resurrected wicked who will be raised for the purposes of this judgment.

In contemporary times a small booklet by Arthur H. Lewis, titled *The Dark Side of the Millennium,* has renewed the charge that this question is really the weakness that invalidates all attempts to interpret Rev. 20:1-10 as implying an earthly, physical reign of Christ.

Unlike 17th-century millenarianism, modern proponents picture this period of earthly rule as a society containing a mixture of saints and sinners. This view precludes the necessity for such weird explanations as that movement required and provides a relatively easy explanation for the rise of Gog and Magog, since it is the wicked ones who are already living who respond to the deception of Satan. Lewis, operating within the presuppositions of the hermeneutic that produces millenarian speculation in the first place, proceeds to call into question the prevailing idea that the millennium is the age to come. An analysis of the so-called Kingdom texts in both Old and New Testaments reveals, Lewis argues, that there is no support whatsoever for the idea of a mixed society in the millennium. Incidentally, the idea of a mixed society has some interesting implications, at least one of which is that the world is an armed camp with only Christians bearing arms to guard the remainder and keep them in check with a "rod of iron." This is bizarre to say the least.

The position to which Lewis feels one is driven by the exegetical evidence is traditional *amillennialism*. But this is a misnomer, he says, since it implies *no* millennium. He prefers the phrase *present-day millennium*, to convey the idea that there is a real millennium stretching from Christ's first coming to His second. Thus, he insists, he is retaining the literal meaning. This is, of course, a semantic squabble, since this defines precisely what classic amillennialism taught and teaches. What one encounters in this noble effort is an attempt to come to terms with the inadequacy of a theory without rejecting the presuppositions that inform the theory. The only legitimate way to avoid the unsatisfactory conclusions of such theorizing is to abandon the starting point and search for a more adequate exegetical method as addressed in the first section of this appendix.

At least we should keep in mind the words of J. B. Chapman. In his presentation of the position of premillennialism he said: "Millenarianism cannot be said to be the 'touch-stone' of orthodoxy as is truthfully said regarding the deity of Christ and of spiritual regeneration."[17]

---

17. Quoted in Hills, *Fundamental Christian Theology* 2:340.

Dispensational Eschatology[18]

During the 19th century a system of theology known as dispensationalism arose, which included a completely new eschatology with many strange features.[19] For some reason it has become so pervasive among conservative Christians, especially among the rank and file, that it has assumed the status of orthodoxy among large groups of both laymen and ministers. There is not a Wesleyan scholar known by this writer, however, who would subscribe to it. Furthermore some literature written by Wesleyan scholars speaks explicitly against it.[20] But it still remains entrenched. For this reason it needs some special attention in a work committed to Wesleyan theology because all the basic theological presuppositions that inform dispensationalism are antithetical to Wesleyan theology as well as sound biblical exegesis.

The key to the system of eschatology that is the most public aspect of the teaching may be the idea of the Kingdom.[21] Here a distinction is made between the kingdom of God, which expresses God's authority over all the universe, and the kingdom of heaven, which refers to the divine government when considered as limited or earthly.[22] The latter is understood as Jewish and physical or earthly. It is this Kingdom that Jesus offered to the Jews, not a spiritual kingdom but an actual restoration of the throne of David.

When the Jews rejected the Kingdom, its establishment had to be postponed until a future time, since the Old Testament prophecies must be literally fulfilled. During the interim period of the

---

18. Analytic studies of dispensationalism are almost innumerable. The spate of literature by persons who once espoused its teachings but through careful study have found it fallacious is astounding. Solid studies rejecting its basic premises include: George Eldon Ladd, *The Blessed Hope* (Grand Rapids: Wm. B. Eerdmans Publishing Co., 1956), and many other of his subsequent works; Clarence Bass, *The Backgrounds to Dispensationalism* (Grand Rapids: Wm. B. Eerdmans Publishing Co., 1960); George L. Murray, *Millennial Studies* (Grand Rapids: Baker Book House, 1948); sound critiques are included in Hoekema, *Bible and the Future;* see also H. Ray Dunning, "Biblical Interpretation and Wesleyan Theology," *Wesleyan Theological Journal* 9 (Spring 1974).

19. See H. Ray Dunning, "Dispensationalism," in *Beacon Dictionary of Theology*, ed. Richard S. Taylor (Kansas City: Beacon Hill Press of Kansas City, 1983).

20. Purkiser, *Exploring Our Christian Faith*, 424-25.

21. This being a systematic theology, one could actually begin at any point, but we choose this one because of the relation to eschatology.

22. There is absolutely no exegetical justification for this distinction. Parallel passages in the Synoptic Gospels where Kingdom language appears show they are used synonymously. Matthew, writing to a Jewish context, avoids the use of the divine name, since to use it often would offend sensitive Jews.

postponed Kingdom there is the Church age, which is not God's Kingdom intention but a "second order" situation.

At the close of the Church age, the Christian believers will be taken out of the world by way of a secret rapture so that God can resume His original intention to establish a Jewish earthly kingdom. After this Rapture occurs, a seven-year tribulation period follows, the "time of Jacob's trouble" (Jer. 30:7, KJV). Then comes the millennial reign in which the prophecies of the Old Testament of a Golden Age will be literally fulfilled.

The idea of the Rapture is a biblical concept. When Paul says in 1 Thess. 4:17, "then we who are alive, who are left, shall be *caught up* together with them in the clouds to meet the Lord in the air" (italics added), he is expressing the idea. The Vulgate translation of "caught up" uses the Latin term *rapio,* from which the term *rapture* is taken. But the idea of a *secret* rapture is another matter, and even alert dispensationalists admit that it is an assumption brought to Scripture and not one derived from exegesis.[23]

The idea of a secret rapture originated in the 19th century (1830) as a result of a vision of a teenage Scottish girl named Margaret MacDonald.[24] From this auspicious beginning it became a standard teaching of J. N. Darby and the Plymouth Brethren and from there became a very widespread doctrine.

Charles C. Ryrie, a leading contemporary spokesman for this theological system, identified three premises that constitute the sine qua non of dispensationalism: (1) A dispensationalist keeps Israel and the Church distinct. (2) This distinction between Israel and the Church is born out of a system of hermeneutics that is usually called literal interpretation. Therefore, the second aspect of the sine qua non of dispensationalism is the matter of plain hermeneutics. (3) A third aspect concerns the underlying purpose of God in the world. It is broader than salvation, namely the glory of God.[25]

From this brief and incomplete survey we may detect a num-

---

23. See Walter Scott, *Exposition of the Revelation of Jesus Christ* (London: Pickering and Inglis, n.d.), 117.

24. Dave MacPherson, *The Great Rapture Hoax* (Fletcher, N.C.: New Puritan Library, 1983), 47 ff. See also Ladd, *Blessed Hope.*

25. *Dispensationalism Today.*

ber of basic theological flaws that lead to the fantastic type of eschatological schema.

First, it is based upon a Calvinistic view of covenant with Israel that is unconditional and cannot be broken. This leads to an eternal distinction between Israel and the Church that is so crucial to the pattern of end-time events that includes the salvation of the Jews and their restoration to the land and the rebuilding of the Temple. All of this completely overlooks both the teachings of the prophets from the eighth century on and the clear-cut statements of the New Testament that such distinctions are done away in Christ, as well as the way in which these nationalistic prophecies are seen as being fulfilled. To speak about the salvation of a people as a whole is to make an assumption congenial to Calvinism, one that ignores human freedom in favor of determinism. What assurance does one have that the response will be any different from the First Advent? This is in no sense of the word to be taken as anti-Semitism but rather as a recognition that Paul explicitly affirmed in Romans 9—11 that Jews will be saved on the same basis as all other persons, without distinction and unrelated to national origin.

Second, it adopts and perpetuates the popular concept of the Kingdom that preoccupied the mind of the rank and file of the Old Testament people and that the prophets of the eighth century and their successors worked manfully to demolish. It might be added, they had little success (see the Book of Jonah). In the first centuries Christianity carried on a running debate with Judaism concerning whether spiritual Israel (the Church) or physical Israel (the Jews) stood in the line of succession to Moses and prophets. In these circumstances it would have been surrender without battle to say, as contemporary dispensationalism does, that the Church was a parenthesis in God's plans for Israel.

Third, it adopts a hermeneutic that the Christian Church has rejected from the beginning, insisting that it invalidates the Old Testament as a Christian book. This would be immaterial, however, to dispensationalists, since their contention is (with Marcion of the 2nd century, Rudolf Bultmann of the 20th century, and all other Gnostics in between) that the Old Testament is *not* a Christian book but speaks of the promises to Jews that shall be fulfilled literally and physically. Donald Bloesch is certainly correct when he says that this view is "entirely untenable in the light of the New Testament identification of the church as the true Israel."[26]

Fourth, it assumes that the Church is condemned to failure from the beginning, and instead of the Church age climaxing with a shout of glory, it will go out with a whimper; and that this failure implies that its evangelistic work is misguided, since it, by God's design, cannot succeed. Lewis Sperry Chafer, early systematic theologian of the movement, said, "Many tasks which Christians undertake would not be assumed if God's program and its future aspects were better known. He has given no commission to convert the world and enterprises based on that sort of idealism are without His authority."[27] On this point, L. L. Loetscher says, "It is chiefly by its unusual philosophy of history that dispensationalism so effectively seals the Church off from the world."[28]

It is little wonder that Christian scholars have made harsh, negative judgments of this whole system. Speaking of the system of dispensationalism as embodied in the notes of the famous and influential Scofield Bible, John Wick Bowman says, "This book represents perhaps the most dangerous heresy currently to be found within Christian circles."[29]

James Barr, in a scathing criticism, expresses appreciation for the creativity of dispensationalism, referring to it as a "remarkable achievement of the mythopoeic fantasy." Then he adds:

> But whatever may be said about its creativity, when it is considered as a statement of Christian theological truth . . . it can scarcely be doubted that dispensational doctrine is heretical and should count as such, if the term "heresy" is to have any meaning. If dispensationalism is not heresy, then nothing is heresy.[30]

The ultimate lesson from all of this is that speculative eschatology can only create divisions in the Body of Christ. The reality of Christ's second advent, the consummation of the Kingdom, and the eternal abode of the saints are precious truths of the faith, firmly grounded in the Word of God; but the real significance of these doctrines is aborted when they are made the object of such

---

26. *Essentials of Evangelical Theology* 2:195.
27. *Systematic Theology* (Dallas: Dallas Seminary Press, 1947-48), 4:261.
28. Source unknown.
29. "Dispensationalism," *Interpretation* 10, no. 2 (April 1956). This was, interestingly, in a series titled The Bible and Modern Religions.
30. *Fundamentalism* (Philadelphia: Westminster Press, 1978), 195, 196.

theorizing as seeks to pry into mysteries that transcend our present state of knowledge, or construct systems that depict history in advance. One is doubtless free to engage in speculation *consistent with his theological commitments and the best grammatico-historical biblical exegesis;* but it should never become a preoccupation that will divert from the preaching of the gospel that God has *already* decisively won a victory over sin and Satan in this present age so that He can deliver from all sin here and now, or cater to a morbid curiosity that does not make eschatological realities a stimulus to holiness, or be so dogmatic on such speculative matters as to threaten the unity of the Church.

Appendix 2

Hermeneutics

This biblical, historical, and systematic study of hermeneutics provides a background and rationale for the claim in the text that a theological hermeneutic is the proper way to come to terms with biblical authority, and also is the indispensable step in the exegetical process.

The hypothesis upon which we are proceeding is that the New Testament's use of the Old Testament provides the most productive clue to an adequate hermeneutical theory. Thus we are focusing on this issue in the survey that follows with the intention of extrapolating a general hermeneutic from the evidence.

In the light of this thesis, we are suggesting that the best approach to the issue is to begin with the central question of the New Testament, which is "Who is Jesus?" This question was raised for His followers by His death and resurrection. These events had climaxed a series of occurrences that were contrary to all their preconceived expectations, and now they had to begin a process of theological reorientation. In answering this question, the earliest of Jesus' followers, being chiefly Jewish in background, sought their answers in their Scriptures, that is, the Old Testament.

This immediately placed the Scriptures at the heart of the New Testament faith, and the way in which the Early Church understood their meaning is embodied in the kerygma or proclamation of their message. This is the point where one should begin the study of the faith of the New Testament Church, according to C. H. Dodd, who has done definitive work in isolating this central declaration of what God has done through His Son.

From the sermons in the Book of Acts and the preaching of Paul, Dodd has discovered several ingredients that consistently occur and thus make up the kerygma. One essential element of this message was the claim that all that had occurred was "according to the scriptures." Compare, for example, the words of Peter in Acts 3:24: "And all the prophets who have spoken, from Samuel and those who came afterwards, also proclaimed these days"; and Rom. 1:1-2: ". . . the gospel of God which he promised beforehand through his prophets in the holy scriptures." In a word, "the death and resurrection of Christ are the crucial fulfillment of prophecy."[1]

Where did this conviction originate? Recently, modern critics of a school of biblical study known as form criticism *(formgeschichte)* have proposed that the Gospels were products of the Early Church's theologizing for its own situation *(sitz im leben)*. The Jesus we see pictured there is a construction of these theologians for purposes of expressing their own Christian self-understanding. This suggests a great deal of historical unreliability. But without taking the time to refer to the numerous critiques of this position, we simply take our stand with those scholars who hold that "Jesus himself was for the earliest Christians both the source of their basic convictions and the paradigm in their interpretation of the Old Testament."[2] This position takes the Gospels as historically reliable and the word placed in the mouth of Jesus as truly representative of His actual teaching even if not necessarily a stenographic report. Thus the starting point for our study must be the teachings of Jesus.

It is instructive to notice that Jesus' appeal to the Scripture (Old Testament) is quite often in the face of a kind of spiritual blindness that is unable to correctly interpret the evidence at hand, and the references are almost exclusively in reference to His passion. These two items are integrally related.

The disciples of Jesus, like most of the Jews of their day, had read the Messianic passages of the prophets in a nationalistic vein. It was almost inevitable that this would be the case if the strictly Messianic texts were taken in isolation from the total pattern of prophetic teaching, since they did, in fact, depict a Davidic king

---

1. C. H. Dodd, *Apostolic Preaching;* idem, *According to the Scripture* (New York: Charles Scribner's Sons, 1963).

2. Longenecker, *Christology,* 9. D. M. Baillie, *God Was in Christ,* chaps. 1—2; Alan Richardson, *Theology,* 125; Dodd, *According to the Scripture;* Bright, *Kingdom of God,* 209.

who would rule over a restored kingdom.[3] Consequently, when the course of Jesus' life began to take on the contours of the Suffering Servant of the Lord (cf. Isa. 42:1-7; 49:1-6; 50:4-9; 52:13—53:12), the disciples were mystified. This inability to understand the significance of what was happening comes vividly to expression in Matt. 16:21-23 (cf. Mark 8:31-33). Jesus had come to the crisis time in His ministry when, following the heightened enthusiasm of the crowd for a national kingdom stimulated by the feeding of the 5,000,[4] He had rejected the desires of the multitude for a political Messiah and offered them His spiritual benefits in the discourse on the Bread of Life (John 6). At this juncture the large following melted away, and He turned to those close to Him in an attempt to prepare their minds for the trials that were to follow. He now spoke openly: "He must go unto Jerusalem, and suffer . . . and be killed, and be raised again the third day" (Matt. 16:21, KJV). In Peter's protestations Jesus heard the same voice that He had heard in the wilderness, trying to divert Him from His God-chosen vocation, and He responded in the same way: "Get thee behind me, Satan" (v. 23, KJV). Peter's inability to comprehend symbolizes the blindness to the true mission of Jesus that continued like a pall over the minds of all His disciples until the Resurrection cast a new light upon their understanding (cf. John 2:22).

It is against this backdrop that Jesus sought to appeal to the Scriptures, to verify that the course He had actually followed was the true one. Perhaps we can consider Luke 24:25-27 as the pivotal passage. The two travelers to Emmaus were in despair because of their unrealized expectation. Pathetically they say to the "stranger": "But we had hoped that he was the one to redeem Israel" (v. 21). Now, they infer, their hopes were unfulfilled and so still empty.[5]

But their blindness was expelled when Jesus, "beginning at Moses and all the prophets . . . expounded unto them in all the scriptures the things concerning himself" (v. 27, KJV). The same

---

3. During the intertestamental period there was an intensification of the Messianic expectation, and the Messiah came more and more to be regarded as a military and political figure. Cf. D. S. Russell, *Between the Testaments* (Philadelphia: Muhlenberg Press, 1960).

4. This is the only miracle recorded in all four Gospels, showing its pivotal role in Jesus' career.

5. The significance of the terms "empty" and "filled" in relation to "hope" should be carefully noted.

pattern recurs further on in the same chapter during Jesus' encounter with a group of the gathered disciples. He specifically reminds them of His teachings while He was "yet with" them (KJV) and then refers to the Scriptures in terms of the threefold division of the Hebrew canon—the Law, the Prophets, and the Psalms (Writings)—as all being fulfilled in himself (v. 44). The result: "Then opened he their understanding, that they might understand the scriptures" (v. 45, KJV).

At the Last Supper, in anticipation of His impending betrayal and death, Jesus speaks of the Scriptures being fulfilled (Matt. 26:24); and again at the actual betrayal scene in the garden He rebukes Peter's attempt to defend Him with these words: "How then shall the scriptures be fulfilled, that thus it must be?" (Matt. 26:54, KJV; cf. v. 56). Even his reference to Ps. 118:22-23 is in connection with the parable of rejection, which necessarily has in view His passion (cf. Matt. 21:42 and Mark 12:10-11).

The Fourth Gospel contains numerous references to the Scriptures as being a witness to Jesus' divine origin, but they still maintain the same pattern as noticed in the Synoptic passages. Only here, in some cases, it is the blindness of the Jews through unbelief that hinders them from recognizing Jesus for who He is. This situation is epitomized by John 5:39-40: "You search the scriptures, because you think that in them you have eternal life; and it is they that bear witness to me; yet you refuse to come to me that you may have life" (note the indicative, which is a better translation than the KJV imperative). The material in these accounts may be structured to accomplish the writer's purpose, but it is certainly "grounded in Jesus' own arguments."[6]

We must emphasize and later elaborate the idea that all these passages focus on the suffering aspects of Jesus' work. If there had been a literal fulfillment of prophecy in terms of contemporary (to Jesus) exegesis, there would have been no problem. But the blindness to the true intent of Scripture that prevailed among both friend and foe implies rather conclusively that there needed to be a reorientation of understanding. This could not occur with a better translation but only in taking a totally different stance when looking for the sense in which this drama was the unfolding of God's redemptive purpose.

---

6. Raymond E. Brown, *Gospel According to John 1—12*, 228.

This point is precisely what Paul is working toward in his contrast between the old covenant and the new in 2 Corinthians 3. Like the veil that hid the fading glory on Moses' face from the people at the time of the giving of the law, a veil still remains on the face (mind) of the Hebrew who reads his scripture in the synagogue; "to this day, when they read the old covenant, that same veil remains unlifted, because only through Christ is it taken away. Yes, to this day whenever Moses is read a veil lies over their minds; but when a man turns to the Lord the veil is removed" (2 Cor. 3:14-16). In modern technical language, Christ becomes a "new hermeneutic" in terms of which the Christian must read his Old Testament.

Such a reorientation of exegesis is what characterized the New Testament preachers, and in the light of it they declared unequivocally that God's work in Christ was "according to the scriptures."

We must now seek to elaborate on the implication of the fact that Jesus' appeal to the Scriptures was almost exclusively in relation to His passion. The importance of this truth lies in the necessity of Jesus to show, in the face of the popular expectation, that it was precisely this facet of His ministry that constituted the fulfillment of Scripture. The following pages seek to delineate in outline form how Jesus' own ministry self-consciously embodied this reinterpretation.

Without going into detail, since this is one of the most exercised points in New Testament studies, we should simply note to begin with that the popular expectations of a coming Redeemer (whether called Messiah or some other title) was chiefly nationalistic and militaristic. Jesus' own life self-consciously avoided these connotations and assumed rather the vocation of the Servant of the Lord, a figure that appears in the last half of the Book of Isaiah. John Bright has written classically of the Servant in Isaiah:

> There steps before us the strangest figure, a figure almost without ancestry or progeny in Israel, a figure so laden with offense that neither Israel nor we know what to do with him; the Suffering Servant of Yahweh. It is perhaps fair to say that thus far, for all the nobility of his concepts, the prophet has advanced nothing essentially new. ... But the Suffering Servant is something totally unique.[7]

---

7. *Kingdom of God*, 146.

As modern scholarship fairly well agrees, "The figure of the servant gives a unity to all that Jesus said and did from the moment of his baptism to the moment of his death upon the cross."[8] To the analysis of His ministry in this light we now turn.

Baptism and Temptation. Jesus' baptism has been explained in many different ways. The primary meaning, however, must be derived from the role that it played in the pattern of His whole ministry. From this perspective we see it as the ordination service in which He was inducted into the office of the Servant. The words from heaven as recorded in Mark 1:11 are "Thou art my beloved Son; with thee I am well pleased." They are a combination of two Old Testament passages (Ps. 2:7 and Isa. 42:1) that together constitute the ordination formula of the Servant Messiah.

Later in His ministry Jesus referred to His work in terms of baptism: "I have a baptism to be baptized with; and how I am constrained until it is accomplished!" (Luke 12:50). Obviously His reference is to His passion, and the use of the symbol of baptism further supports the interpretation that His baptism by John was a proleptic event that anticipated the Cross. In this light Jesus' temptation in the wilderness becomes an integral part of the acceptance of the Servant vocation. Each temptation, in its own peculiar way, was an attempt to divert Jesus from the role that He had accepted, or to which He had been appointed, at the Jordan.[9]

Feeding of 5,000 and Transfiguration. We have already suggested that the turning point of Jesus' ministry was the feeding of the 5,000 and the discourse on the Bread of Life. Now we can see even more clearly how this event involved conflict between His ordained mission and the popular hopes. It is significant that two intimately related events follow closely on the heels of this crisis. Having turned to His immediate disciples, He takes them away from the scenes of His mighty works to an isolated place in the country near Caesarea Philippi. Here He tests their conclusions and finds that they have arrived at the belief that He is the Messiah (Christ) (Matt. 16:13-20). It now becomes His task to attempt to relate their faith to a proper understanding of His Messiahship in terms of the Suffering Servant.

---

8. Wright and Fuller, *Acts of God*, 277.
9. Cf. James S. Stewart, *The Life and Teaching of Jesus Christ* (New York: Abingdon Press, n.d.), 40-45.

Here the second of these two events come into play: the Transfiguration. Jesus, transformed before Peter, James, and John, appears with Moses and Elijah. The former stands for the Law and
the latter for the Prophets. The whole scene symbolizes the truth
that both Law and Prophets approve this unexpected turn of
events surrounding the Messianic hope. Looking back upon the
experience from a later perspective, Peter announces its significance in their lives: "We heard this voice borne from heaven, for we
were with him on the holy mountain. And we have the prophetic
word made more sure" (2 Pet. 1:18-19). The voice that had ordained Jesus into this mission was now voicing further approval of
His actions and teachings, and the spiritual encounter assured the
disciples of the divine sanction.

In a word, as John Bright so well put it, "Christ took up and
arrogated to himself the concepts of Messiahship. But all of them
he transfused (and transformed) with the concept of suffering."[10]
Thus with this understanding we may see in general terms the
significance of the claim, both by Jesus and the Early Church, that
He was the fulfillment of prophecy.

The issue for the early Christians, however, was: "If Jesus fulfilled that prophecy (of the Servant), was it as the Christ (Messiah)
that He suffered?" The opponents of Christianity denied that this
was the case, and therefore the Christian theologians had to mount
a scriptural apologetic for this central tenet of their faith, that is,
that the Messiah should suffer. To do so, they were "probably dependent on the use of Isaiah 53 for this purpose, though there are
few actual verbal links."[11]

Lindars suggests that there may be present in the biblical material three stages of development, showing theological interest at
three levels. There is first the primary theological interest "to formulate a doctrine of the atonement," that is, to explain the work of
Jesus as "giving his life a ransom for many" (Mark 10:45). In this
way, the early Christians answer for themselves the question of the
purpose of Jesus' death. Then "there is secondly the apologetic
issue of the Passion in relation to theoretical messianism" where
they defend their position against criticism that denied Jesus the
title of Messiah on the basis of His death, the enigma that we have
just explored. It is in connection with these first two aims that

10. *Kingdom of God*, 207.
11. Barnabas Lindars, *New Testament Apologetics* (London: SCM Press, 1961), 81.

Isaiah 53 becomes so central. But the nature of their appeal to this scripture is unique. As F. F. Bruce puts it:

> It is not so much a matter of direct quotation or of verbal echoes of the Servant Songs (more particularly of the fourth) among the words of Jesus: it is more the fact that His conception of His life-mission, crowned by suffering and death, is anticipated more clearly than any others in the Old Testament.[12]

However, the New Testament writers go beyond this generalized hermeneutic and specify, in numerous instances, where specific fulfillments occur; or as Lindars puts it, "There is a tendency to use the prophecy for subsidiary purposes."[13] That is to say, definite aspects of the Christ-event have also been in some fashion foretold by definable passages of scripture as well as the general tenor of certain great passages. Here is where some of the most difficult problems arise for explaining how the New Testament used the Old Testament scriptures.

This procedure is quite prominent, for example, in the Gospel of Matthew. This Gospel apparently originated in a Greek-speaking Jewish-Christian branch of the Early Church and therefore dictates that the writer show a close correlation of Jesus and the sacred writings of the Jews. This explains why it emphasizes so persistently the note of fulfillment. The characteristic formula that recurs some 10 times is "That it might be fulfilled."[14]

A number of the Old Testament quotations are apparently wrested from their original contexts and applied in a way quite foreign to their historical origin. Let us note a few examples for emphasis.

Matt. 1:23 is a quotation from the Septuagint rendering of Isa.

---

12. *New Testament Development of Old Testament Themes* (Grand Rapids: Wm. B. Eerdmans Publishing Co., 1968), 30. Cf. also Lindars, *Apologetics,* 77: "Although actual quotations from this famous chapter are not specially numerous in the New Testament, allusions to it are embedded so deeply in the work of all the principal writers that it is certain that it belongs to the earliest thought of the primitive church."

13. While there may be grounds for questioning this threefold historical development, at least it calls attention to various types of Scripture usage in the New Testament materials.

14. Numerous studies have been made of these quotations from different perspectives. One popular approach explores the problem of the text from which they are derived, whether Masoretic Text, Septuagint, or whatever, since there are certain problems of verbal correlation. Cf. Krister Stendahl, *The School of St. Matthew* (Philadelphia: Fortress Press, 1968); Robert Horton Gundry, *The Use of the Old Testament in St. Matthew's Gospel* (Leiden, Netherlands: E. J. Brill, 1967).

7:14.[15] In its setting in the original context, we are dealing with Isaiah's attempt to convince King Ahaz not to appeal to Assyria for help against the coalition of Syria and Israel. This verse is a threat to Ahaz, in the face of his refusal, that if he persists in his chosen course of action it will result in destruction and that right soon. In fact, it will occur before a child, already conceived, will reach the age to be weaned. Even if it is true, as George Adam Smith persuasively argues, that this is a Messianic prophecy,[16] it identifies a child born at that time and therefore has a specific historical reference that no one can possibly deny who has any sense of the meaning of language. At this point in our discussion, we will make no effort to explain how this problem may be solved. Here we are only indicating the need for coming to terms with it and the form that the problem takes.

The second citation (2:15) is taken from Hos. 11:1. Matthew applies these words to the flight into Egypt by Joseph and Mary to escape the sword of Herod. In Hosea, the reference is to God's action in the deliverance of Israel from Egyptian slavery at the time of the Exodus.

In the case of Herod's slaughter of the infants, Matt. 2:17-18 cites Jer. 31:15 as in some way being fulfilled in these tragic events. However, the Jeremiah passage is poetically depicting Rachel in her tomb near Ramah, weeping over the deportation of the Israelites into exile in Babylon.

The lines of correspondence are even farther apart in the fourth instance (2:23), where there is even an absence of verbal coincidence. The basis of comparison seems to be the similarity of the Hebrew word for branch (netzer) to the name Nazarene. The original in Isa. 11:1, however, is a clear Messianic passage of the first order.

While not all the instances used by Matthew create crucial issues of interpretation, most of them are in need of some justification for a nonliteral application. The problem is seen in its most radical form when one takes account of the possible approach to it represented by Rudolf Bultmann. After analyzing many of the passages in the New Testament where claim is made for the fulfillment

15. For a sound, informed, and conservative discussion of the significance of the term "virgin" in the translations, see *Beacon Bible Commentary*, vol. 4 (Kansas City: Beacon Hill Press of Kansas City, 1966), 57, note by W. T. Purkiser.

16. *Expositor's Bible*, 25 vols. (New York: A. C. Armstrong and Son, 1903), 115-18.

of prophecy, including the ones we have just examined, he remarks: "To talk of this kind of prophecy and fulfillment has become impossible in an age in which the Old Testament is conceived of as a historical document and interpreted according to the method of historical science."[17]

If, in fact, the New Testament claim is not in the main based upon some kind of literal "word fulfillment," or is not the carrying out of a prediction of the type that makes the predicted events a kind of "prearranged puppet show" (C. H. Dodd), how are we to deal with it? This is the issue that is our primary concern. Then we will be able to see that it has ramifications in the areas of the inspiration and authority of Scripture.

We propose to discuss the issue by first tracing the history of the "argument from prophecy," giving special attention to the 2nd, 16th, and 18th centuries. It will be significant to see the way in which the rise of historical criticism affected the way the problem was handled and the form of the solutions offered. Finally we will make an attempt to set forth the best of contemporary solutions as well as propose one of our own.

The Apologetic from Prophecy

In this section we propose to survey the various ways in which the church has attempted to provide an interpretation of the Old Testament in relation to the Christian faith. This will involve focusing on, as noted in the preceding paragraph, the 2nd, 16th, and 18th centuries. The first and last of these pivotal periods are generally regarded as "apologetic" centuries of Christian theology. The Protestant Reformation occurred during the 16th, and this event is crucial for the history of hermeneutics. The purpose of this historical approach is to show how the church wrestled with the problem posed in the previous section and ran into several hermeneutical dead-end streets. This should set the stage for the positive suggestions in the following section of the chapter. One of the great values of the study of tradition is surely to let us know which wells are dry.

---

17. "Prophecy and Fulfillment," in *Essays on Old Testament Hermeneutics,* ed. Claus Westermann (Richmond, Va.: John Knox Press, 1963), 52.

The 2nd Century

As we look at the second century, there are two things that must be borne in mind in order to properly evaluate the exegetical work of the Christians of this time. First, as is commonly known, when one moves from the canonical writings into the discourses of those men known as Apostolic Fathers,[18] it is like moving from a brilliantly lighted room into the twilight shadows. F. W. Farrar's evaluation of them is fair: "Their glory is for the most part the glory, not of intellect, but of righteousness and faith."[19] Such an insight serves the dual purpose of highlighting the inspired character of the New Testament documents as well as calling our attention to the inadequacy of these otherwise great men as competent teachers of hermeneutical method.

The second feature, which is often overlooked, has to do with their sources. Their Bible was the Old Testament in Greek translation (Septuagint); but particularly important, they did not have access to the New Testament, and that for a good reason—it had not yet been compiled. Many mistakenly believe that there was suddenly a complete New Testament that dropped like a bombshell out of the sky in full dress immediately upon the close of the so-called Age of the Apostles. Whereas in fact, not only was it composed over a period of time, but the finalization of the canon did not occur until the fourth century.[20] While the fathers had access to some of the New Testament documents, many of them showed awareness of only a limited number of our present list.[21]

At least one significance of the latter point—and that a major one—is that they did not have extended examples of New Testament hermeneutics as practiced in the canonical writings and therefore were left with the option of employing exegetical methods that were prevalent in the world of that day. They utilized methods of interpretation that were "to a great extent those of the Jewish schools," including a Jewish tradition of allegorical exegesis

---

18. Clement of Rome, Ignatius, *The Didache, Epistle of Barnabas, Shepherd of Hermas, Letter to Diognetus,* and Polycarp.

19. *History,* 164.

20. The final step seems to have been taken with the Easter letter of Athanasius in A.D. 367. Cf. E. J. Goodspeed, "Canon," in *Encyclopedia of Religion,* ed. Vergilius Ferm (New York: Philosophical Library, 1945).

21. Farrar, *History,* 171 ff.

that had developed in Alexandria, Egypt, and was classically represented by Philo of Alexandria.[22]

Living as Philo did in the cosmopolitan environment of Alexandria, he sought to bridge the chasm between his own Jewish heritage and the Hellenistic philosophy that flourished in this great intellectual center. In carrying out this task, Philo attempted to show that already the insights of Greek philosophy had been present in the writings of Moses. He demonstrated this claim by allegorical exegesis of the Old Testament text. This involved both removing from the biblical text any element that seemed repugnant to the Hellenistic mind by interpreting it as symbolizing some deeper truth and positively attributing philosophical ideas to Moses. Thus he looked for hidden meanings beneath the literal sense, the latter being "but the gateway or starting point for the true meaning which is to be sought at a deeper level."[23]

Largely by making use of the same allegorical method, the Apostolic Fathers read Christ and the Church into the whole Old Testament. As Farrar sums it up:

> Allegory was already a familiar method among the Jews, and just as the Alexandrians had adopted it in order to find in Moses an anticipation of Greek philosophy, so the Apostolic Fathers, before the full formation of the New Testament Canon, were driven to it in order to make the Old Testament an immediate witness for Christian truth.[24]

The problem faced by these early Christians in using the Old Testament as their Source Book of sacred writings, however, was that its documents were Jewish in nature; and "as its promises were quite plainly made to them, many uninstructed Christians were at a loss to understand their own relation to it."[25] One approach would be to take the Scriptures literally, as did the Ebionites, and maintain the eternal validity of Mosaism.[26] Another way, adopted

---

22. Ibid., 164-65; Sydney G. Sowers, *The Hermeneutics of Philo and Hebrews* (Zurich: Eva-Verlag, 1965), 18.
23. E. C. Blackman, *Biblical Interpretation* (Philadelphia: Westminster Press, 1957), 83.
24. *History*, 166-67.
25. "Introduction," in *The Apostolic Fathers*, vol. 1 of *The Fathers of the Church*, ed. Ludwig Schoff, 72 vols. (Washington, D.C.: Catholic University of America Press, 1962), 188. It has been claimed that "the real battle in the second century centered around the position of the Old Testament." F. C. Burkett, *Church and Gnosis*, quoted in Kelly, *Doctrines*, 68.
26. Farrar, *History*, 164. The Ebionites were Jewish Christians noted primarily for their Christology that denied Jesus' essential deity on the basis of their Jewish pre-

by Marcion, was to reject the Old Testament entirely as being unworthy of the Christian faith. But the mainline Christian tradition insisted on the unity of the Hebrew-Christian faith and sought to make use of the Jewish Bible for its purposes.

Among the Apostolic Fathers, the *Epistle of Barnabas* is a signal example of this struggle to Christianize the Old Testament. The writer argues that the covenant with Israel was broken forever when the people turned to idols and Moses cast down the tablets of stone, shattering them. "Their covenant was broken," he says, "in order that the covenant of Jesus, the Beloved, should be sealed in our hearts by the hope which faith in Him gives."[27]

He suggests that part of the Old Testament refers to Israel and part to "us," by which he means the New Testament Church.[28] However, he does not set forth any principle by which these two meanings can be distinguished.[29] All in all, his basic approach is to allegorize on the basis of a claim to special insight (gnosis) that he calls an "innate gift of teaching."[30] Farrar remarks: "The only glimmer of an exegetical principle which he discloses is to find throughout the Old Testament something which can be referred to Christ or to Christianity."[31]

As in all allegorizing, the literal and historical sense of the text plays a relatively minor role, giving way to spiritual truths. According to Kelly, Barnabas felt that "the fatal error of the Jews was to let themselves be beguiled by the literal sense of scripture."[32]

The argument for the validity of Christianity on the basis of prophecy reaches its highest pinnacle in Justin Martyr, whose writings were chiefly apologetic. Justin had two audiences in view: the civil authorities and the Jews. His two *Apologies* are addressed to the former, while his *Dialogue with Trypho* has the second in mind. The aim of the *Dialogue* was to show from Hebrew prophecy that

---

suppositions. Cf. Kelly, *Doctrines,* 139-40. Their position on the eternal validity of Mosaism based on a literal interpretation is virtually identical to contemporary dispensationalism (see Appendix 1).

27. 5.2.
28. Ibid.
29. There is some affinity here with the dispensationalist "dividing the word" hermeneutic (2 Tim. 2:15, KJV), except it is applied to the New Testament, whereas Barnabas is speaking of the Old Testament.
30. *Epistle of Barnabas* 9.17.
31. *History,* 168.
32. Kelly, *Doctrines,* 661.

Christianity according to God's purpose has taken the place of Judaism and that Jews as well as Gentiles can be saved only if they become Christians.[33] However, even in his *First Apology*, which is addressed to the secular community, he partly bases his case on an appeal to prophecy, this argument occupying about one-third of the treatise. His point was not primarily to establish the inspiration of the Old Testament but rather to demonstrate that Jesus, His work, and His Church had been spoken of beforehand in certain writings and therefore must have a divine origin. However, his chief use of prophecy is naturally in the appeal to the religious (Jewish) audience.

Like Barnabas, Justin holds that the Old Testament was meant mainly for Christians and makes his case by the abundant use of unbridled allegory; thus, as Farrar puts it, "following in the steps of the Rabbis he denies the plainest historical facts."[34] Also, like Barnabas, such exegesis is esoteric, that is, the result of gnosis derived from a spiritual grace. Justin further substantiates his interpretations by calling attention to the absurdities that result from a strictly literal exegesis.[35]

An almost unbelievable example of the application of the allegorical method appears in chapters 89—90 of the *Dialogue with Trypho*. Trypho admits that the Jews look forward to the coming of Christ but insists that Justin prove to him that He was to suffer on the Cross, a death that would place Him under a curse, according to Deut. 21:23. Justin answers that "Moses was the first to make known this apparent curse of Christ by the symbolic acts which He performed." He refers, as anyone with insight should plainly see, to that incident during Israel's battle with the Amalekites when Moses stretched out his hand in the figure of the Cross. "In truth," he says, "it was not because Moses prayed that his people were victorious, but because, while the name of Jesus was at the battle front, Moses formed the sign of the Cross."

Irenaeus was a much more biblical theologian than Justin, but his hermeneutics still leaves much to be desired. For our purposes we only need to note a comment by J. N. D. Kelly in which he cites Irenaeus as saying in effect that "prophecy by its very nature was

---

33. A. C. McGiffert, Jr., *History of Christian Thought*, 2 vols. (New York: Charles Scribner's Sons, 1950), 1:97.

34. *History*, 173.

35. *Dialogue with Trypho*, 112.

obscure and enigmatic" and "divinely points to events which could only be accurately delineated after their historical realization."[36] Here is an insight of no mean proportion. (See Appendix 1.)

At the close of the second century, or early part of the third, the allegorical hermeneutic was given scientific formulation by Origen, the first real biblical exegete.[37] Origen's "three levels of meaning" that he detected in Scripture[38] became established in the church as the standard position until the Reformation. He too affirms the Old Testament as a book of prophecy fulfilled in Christ but revealingly points out how both Jews and heretics have been prevented from true understanding of the Old Testament because they took it literally. Another revealing insight of Origen bearing on the issue under discussion is that the prophets' mode of knowledge was different from that of the apostles, for they contemplated the mysteries of the Incarnation before their accomplishment.[39]

With this very cursory survey, we may make some observations about the hermeneutics of the second-century fathers. First, and very importantly, they never hesitated in affirming the continuity of the Old Testament and the new movement originating with Jesus of Nazareth. They claimed themselves to be the successors of Israel in the purposes of God; and that the new covenant had superseded the old in a relationship of organic unity. The theological premise that gave validity to these claims was the unity of God—thus the continuity of the two Testaments, or, as J. N. D. Kelly puts it: they were "grounded in the fact, pointed out by Theophilus of Antioch ... that both the prophets and evangelists were inspired by one and the same spirit."[40]

Furthermore, it is only with considerable interpretation that the fathers could think of a "literal fulfillment of prophecy." Their practice was such to indicate that it would be better to say, "Prophecies are literally fulfilled when allegorically interpreted." We have noted their repeated emphasis on the shortcomings of a literal reading of the Old Testament. Their most obvious answer to this problem was the allegorical hermeneutic.

Allegory is somewhat difficult to define precisely, but the ge-

---

36. *Doctrines,* 68.
37. Blackman, *Interpretation,* 95
38. The historical or literal sense, the moral sense, and the mystical or spiritual sense.
39. Kelly, *Doctrines,* 69.
40. Ibid.

neric characteristic that seems present in every case is a disregard for history. It is

> always unhistorical and usually antihistorical. It approaches its Scriptures not for the purpose of discerning in them a pattern of historical revelation, but rather as a source of absolutely normative words that can be fitted to any present requirements.[41]

The corollary to this nonhistorical view of the text is a mechanical view of inspiration that can give no serious consideration to the factor of the human authorship of Scripture. "To the allegorist the human personalities through which the word was presumably delivered become anonymous cyphers [sic], relevant only as tools employed by a divine oracle-giver."[42] This means that the exegetical method required by such an understanding is totally subjective, "renouncing as it does every access to the minds through which the scripture words passed and in which they were formulated."[43] While one can admire the concerns of the allegorists, namely to make the ancient texts contemporary, he must deplore the disparagement of the literal, historical sense of the sacred text.

Even in this early period, opposition to allegorical exegesis was prominent in the School of Antioch in Syria. In this school, in contrast to the Alexandrian School, emphasis was laid on a literalist interpretation, and its leading representatives were "united in believing that allegory was an unreliable, indeed illegitimate, instrument for interpreting scripture."[44]

The result of this reaction was a drastic limitation of the strictly prophetic element in the Old Testament. The following analysis of the position of Theodore of Mopsuestia by J. N. D. Kelly is instructive:

> Theodore, for example, refused to recognize such traditionally accepted texts as Hos. 11:1f; Mic. 4:1-3; 5:1f; Hag. 2:9; Zech. 11:12-14; 12:10; Mal. 1:11; 4:5f as directly Messianic; they did not conform to his rigourous criteria, and their contexts provided (he thought) a fully satisfying historical explanation. Similarly, he reduced the number of Psalms which he allowed to be directly prophetic of the Incarnation and the Church to four (2; 8; 45; 110). In the case of other Psalms (e.g.

---

41. Vawter, *Biblical Inspiration*, 32.
42. Ibid.
43. Ibid.
44. Kelly, *Doctrines*, 76; Blackman, *Interpretation*, 103-6; leading figures here were Chrysostom, Diodore, and Theodore of Mopsuestia.

21; 2; 69; 22) which had been applied to the Savior either by
the apostolic writers or by Himself, he explained that they lent
themselves to this use, not because they were predictive, but
because the Psalmist had been in an analogous spiritual predicament. Yet he was prepared to concede that some Psalms (e.g.
16; 55; 89) and prophecies (e.g. Joel 2:28f; Amos 9:11; Zech. 9:9;
Mal. 3:1), although not Messianic if taken literally, could legitimately be interpreted as such insofar as they were types which
reached their true fulfillment in the Christian revelation.[45]

This passage introduces another pattern of hermeneutics that
in modern times has received much emphasis—the typological.
Many contemporary scholars insist that the fathers were using this
kind of hermeneutic, if not instead of allegory, at least in addition
to it.[46] However, we will defer a discussion of this approach for a
later section where we will need to give it very serious consideration. Our purpose of demonstrating the hermeneutical problems of substantiating the prophetic claim in the second century
has been accomplished.

The 16th Century

The Reformation of the 16th century provided two significant
developments in the Christian use of the Old Testament. The first
had to do with the canon. The Jewish list of authoritative writings
had been finalized at the Council of Jamnia about A.D. 90. However, the Christian Church in the West had continued to accept
certain other writings known as the Apocrypha as part of the Old
Testament canon. Martin Luther and the other Reformers called
these writings into question, partly because certain Roman doctrines were based upon them, and therefore rejected them as noncanonical, that is, as not authoritative for doctrine.

Although the Roman Catholic Council of Trent (1545-63) declared most of the Apocrypha to be canonical and pronounced
anathema upon all who denied their status, Protestant Christianity
continued to affirm its acceptance of the ancient Jewish canon of
24 books (39 in the English Bible). Thus when a Protestant theologian refers to the scriptures of the old covenant, he has a narrower
field than the Roman theologian.[47]

---

45. Kelly, *Doctrines*, 77-78. Cf. also Blackman, *Interpretation*, 103.

46. Jean Danielou, *Origen* (New York: Sheed and Ward, 1955); Hanson, *Allegory
and Event*; G. W. H. Lampe and K. S. Woollcombe, *Essays on Typology* (Naperville, Ill.:
Alec R. Allenson, 1957).

47. Gerald A. Larue, *Old Testament Life and Literature* (Boston: Allyn and Bacon,
1968).

More important for our studies are the hermeneutical insights of Martin Luther. First, he vehemently rejected the allegorical method of the fathers. "Origen's allegories are not worth so much dirt," and "Allegories are empty speculations, and as it were the scum of Holy Scriptures" are quotations that represent his typical reaction. His awareness of the excesses to which this method may lead is seen in his famous analogy that Allegory is a sort of beautiful harlot, who proves herself specially seductive to idle men.[48] A more moderate statement giving some positive evaluation comes from his lectures on Isaiah (1527-30):

> One should think much, and magnificently, about history, but little about allegory. You should use allegory like a flower, for it illustrates the sermon rather than strengthens it. . . . Allegory does not establish doctrine, but like color, can only add to it.

Also Luther repudiates the fourfold meaning of scripture that had come to be the accepted exegetical premise by this time: (1) the literal; (2) the allegorical; (3) the tropological or moral sense; and (4) the analogical or eschatological sense. In contrast to this multiple meaning, Luther declares that "the literal sense of Scripture alone is the whole essence of faith and of Christian theology" and notes, "I have observed that all the heresies and errors have arisen not from Scripture's own plain statements, but when that plainness of statement is ignored, and men follow the Scholastic arguments of their own brains."[49]

This position was a corollary to his basic premise that each man is his own priest and therefore may read the Bible for himself without the necessity for elaborate exegetical "monkey tricks," as he called them. The Scripture, he insisted, is to be understood by all, and the common believers should have access to it and were capable of receiving the Word through it.[50]

Luther's stress upon the literal sense, which he preferred to call the grammatical sense, implied more than simply "historical-

---

48. Quotes from Farrar, *History*, 328.

49. Heinrich Bornkamm, *Luther and the Old Testament*, trans. Erich W. and Ruth C. Gritsch (Philadelphia: Fortress Press, 1969), 89; Farrar, *History*, 327 ff.; Blackman, *Interpretation*, 118-19; Alan Richardson, *Apologetics*, 183-84.

50. Cf. Blackman, *Interpretation*, 118. Farrar comments: "There was nothing which Luther found it more difficult to maintain with unflinching faithfulness than this indefeasible right to private judgment. He was sorely tried by the excesses of individual opinion." *History*, 330.

factual interpretation." He understood it as "literal, prophetic sense," which seems to mean that the literal sense is to be taken seriously but that it mediates the "spiritual" sense. The implications of this are seen in Blackman's statement:

> In opposition to Scholasticism, Luther gave up the notion that Scripture has a multiple sense. And yet he did not entirely reject the spiritual meaning, nor the allegorical method. What he does, with a really new emphasis, is to relate the literal and spiritual senses much more intimately to one another.[51]

What Luther was really opposed to in Scholastic allegorizing was the reading of church dogma *into* the Scripture through this method of exegesis. Therefore he proposed a principle by which allegory can be controlled, involving an objective criterion that could be applied in order to avoid unbridled subjectivism. Luther clearly saw that if one strictly adhered to the grammatical-historical interpretation, it would be very difficult to regard the Old Testament as Christian scriptures. Out of this complex of problems Luther introduced the "analogy of faith," a phrase found in Rom. 12:6 (Gk., *analogia*), by which he meant simply that the whole Bible, including the Old Testament, is to be interpreted by the analogy of saving faith in Christ.[52]

This is essentially a theological hermeneutic and judgment. It involves discovering, *within Scripture itself*, the principles or truths by which the whole canon may be interpreted. It is really more than comparing text to text. That way of applying it is actually, as Farrar puts it, the rule of the analogy of Scripture rather than the analogy of faith.[53] It is even in its best expression, more than interpreting obscure passages by plain ones, although this is involved.

While not a Reformation figure, John Wesley's explanation of this rule is helpful:

> St. Peter expresses it, "as the oracles of God"; according to the general tenor of them; according to that grand scheme of doctrine which is delivered therein, touching original sin, justification by faith, and present, inward salvation. There is a wonderful analogy between all these; and a close and intimate connection between the chief heads of that faith "which was once delivered to the saints." Every article, therefore, concerning which there is any question should be determined by this rule;

---

51. *Interpretation*, 120.
52. Alan Richardson, *Apologetics*, 184.
53. *History*, 337.

every doubtful scripture interpreted according to the grand truths which run through the whole. (Note on Rom. 12:6.)

For Luther the overall purpose of Scripture is to reveal Christ. This is the meaning of his formula, *Christus regnum Scriptura* (Christ is King of Scripture). Consequently, Christ may be found anywhere in Scripture, and any interpretation, including allegorical, is legitimate if Christological. Other allegorizing is illegitimate.

Alan Richardson's analysis sums up both Luther's purpose and the chief weaknesses of this new approach:

> Luther doubtless held that, by providing a fully Christian and biblical category of interpretation for the elucidation of spiritual meanings in the historical record, he was doing away with all subjectivity and wishful-thinking in the theological exegesis of the Bible. We have here a nice illustration of the paradoxical nature of all categories of interpretation, which, while they appear to provide an utterly valid or objective way of looking at things from the standpoint of those who see through them, nevertheless appear to other men, who make use of other categories, to be quite subjective and arbitrary. Thus, it is often objected that Luther's method of biblical interpretation and exegesis is wholly subjective, being based upon his own intense experience of salvation and justification.[54]

The real significance of Luther's contribution is his point that there must be a hermeneutical norm in the light of which the total Scripture is read. It is the task of biblical theology to determine what this key principle may be.

The 18th Century

The apologetic situation of the 18th century has different contours from preceding eras. The chief opponent of revealed religion at this time was natural religion. This was the age of rationalism with its chief premise that nothing is to be accepted as valid that does not conform to the canons of reason. This eliminates all elements of supernaturalism from religion including revelation, especially if it claims truth that goes beyond reason. Natural religion, in a word, "means simply those religious tenets justified by reason and found in religions generally."[55] While many churchmen sub-

---

54. *Apologetics,* 184-85.
55. Dillenberger and Welch, *Protestant Christianity,* 128. Cf. also Edward Carpenter, "The Bible in the Eighteenth Century," in *The Church's Use of the Bible,* ed. by D. E. Nineham (London: SPCK, 1963).

scribed to this position, one form of natural religion—deism—was in open opposition to Christianity.

Against these attacks, Christian apologists brought to bear objective supports to the faith in the form of miracle and prophecy. There was a flurry of activity in this controversy, which once again highlights the problem of a literal fulfillment of prophecy that we have observed in each period analyzed. In 1722 a book was published by William Whiston in which he argued for the evidential value of Old Testament prophecy in proving Jesus' Messiahship and the divine origin of Christianity. But he observed in certain cases a lack of correspondence between prophecy and alleged fulfillment. His solution to the problem was to accuse the Jews of intentionally corrupting the text of the Old Testament, and so he attempted to restore the true text of the original. This was a gambit employed earlier by Justin Martyr also. Whiston's book was titled *An Essay Toward Restoring the True Text of the Old Testament, and for Vindicating the Citations Made Thence in the New Testament.*

Whiston's work occasioned a reply by Anthony Collins in two different works that gave appearance of support but were in reality designed to destroy the argument from prophecy. In his *Discourse on the Grounds and Reasons of the Christian Religion,* published in 1724, he argued that the single most decisive proof of Christianity is the prophetic one. However, he went on to note that the "lack of correspondence between prophecy and fulfillment which Whiston had noticed in some cases is true of every case when the prophecies are *literally interpreted,*" and therefore Whiston's proposed restoration does not adequately deal with the problem.[56] Collins wrote:

> It seems therefore most destructive of Christianity to suppose; that typical or allegorical arguing is in any respect weak and enthusiastical, and that the apostles always argued in the matter of prophesies [sic], and the way of reasoning used in the schools: since it is most apparent; that the whole gospel is in every respect founded on type and allegory; that the apostles in most, if not in all cases, reasoned typically and allegorically; and that if the apostles be supposed to reason always after the rules used in the Schools, and if their writings be brought to the test of those rules, the books of the Old and New Testaments will be in an irreconcilable state, and the difficulties against

---

56. A. C. McGiffert, Jr., *Protestant Thought Before Kant* (London: Duckworth and Co., 1919), 216-17, italics added.

Christianity will be incapable of being solved. Any that call themselves Christians, says Dr. Allix, should take heed how they deny the force and authority of that way of traditional interpretation, which has been anciently received in the Jewish Church.[57]

Here, as may be seen, he denied that the fulfillment of prophecy could legitimately be regarded as in any way literal or historical; rather it must be understood in an allegorical way. As A. C. McGiffert comments: "The book amounted to a very severe attack upon the evidence from prophecy, since the allegorical method could not be taken seriously and was not meant to be."[58] In a later work (1727) titled *The Scheme of Literal Prophecy Considered*, Collins openly attacked the prophecy appeal.

The debate evidently stirred up widespread interest. Collins himself refers to more than 30 replies to his first work. One of the most powerful replies was from Thomas Sherlock (1678-1761) in *The Use and Intent of Prophecy in the Several Ages of the World* (1725). He makes a significant modification of the form in which the argument had been stated. It was rather easy to find weaknesses, as Collins had done, in the argument if it is interpreted to mean that "all the ancient prophecies have expressly pointed out and characterized Christ Jesus." Rather it should be stated as follows: "All the Notices which God gave to the Fathers of his intended Salvation are perfectly answered by the Coming of Christ." As Carpenter rightly comments, "The distinction is a subtle but no less important one."[59] Whether or not John Wesley was influenced by Sherlock's statement is impossible to say, but he did espouse the same position in the same period. In his notes on Matt. 2:17-18, commenting on the phrase "Then was fulfilled," he says, "A passage of Scripture, whether prophetic, historical, or poetical, is in the language of the New Testament fulfilled when an event happens to which it may with great propriety be accommodated."

Once again it becomes obvious that a literal reading of the scripture in this context leads down a dead-end street. The other viable option seemed to be allegory with its many weaknesses. But there was a development afoot even in this century that was to

---

57. Quoted by Carpenter, "Bible in Eighteenth Century," 107-8. Unfortunately, only one of these original sources was available to me. I have had to depend on secondary works.

58. *Protestant Thought*, 217.

59. Carpenter, "Bible in Eighteenth Century."

eventually lead to a more fruitful way of looking at the issues, a way that is far more in accord with the facts in the case and to the true biblical point of view.

Heretofore the stress had been upon the literal fulfillment of the words of Scripture, and this inevitably led to allegory. The new insight suggested that the Bible focuses on events rather than words, and that it is the fulfillment of *history* that is at stake. The man who seems to be the father of this development was the renowned biblical scholar, Johann Albrecht Bengel, tutor of John Wesley in scriptural exegesis.[60] This new understanding is so revolutionary, so apropos to the facts as we find them in Scripture, and so influential in contemporary hermeneutics that we must devote the next section to the development of these ideas.

Emergence of the Historical Perspective

The basic criticism that we have noted of allegorical exegesis is its disregard for history. But if the presuppositions underlying its emergence are noted, the approach may be better understood and even appreciated. As James N. S. Alexander says, "Allegorists often have the most honest and honorable motives even when, as frequently, they produce and deduce nonsense."[61]

Allegory originally arose out of the conviction that certain ancient documents were inspired and therefore had relevance to the present. But since these writings were conditioned by the situations of their origin, they were susceptible of critical rejection unless they could be reinterpreted. Thus allegory is called forth to find hidden meanings, beneath the letter, which are applicable to the present situation.[62]

Another premise behind the impulse to allegorize is the idea of literal inspiration. If the very words of Scripture are divinely dictated, they all must have significance. Still, while these concerns may be appreciated, we must pronounce a word of disapproval for the reasons that are implicit in our discussion. To read contem-

---

60. Otto A. Piper, "Heilsgeschichte," in *Encyclopedia of Religion*, ed. Vergilius Ferm (New York: Philosophical Library, 1945), 330.

61. "The Interpretation of Scripture in the Ante-Nicene Period," *Interpretation* 12 (1958): 272 ff.

62. Sowers, *Hermeneutics*, 11-14.

porary ideas indiscriminately back into these ancient writings is to commit what Peter Berger graphically calls "the rape of the historical materials."[63]

Even in the Early Church, it was soon discovered that allegory was just as effective a tool in the hands of the heretic as the orthodox. Therefore the early fathers, notably Irenaeus and Tertullian, required that Scripture must be interpreted in terms of the "rule of faith," that is, the authoritative teaching of the Catholic faith. It was actually out of the dilemma arising from the problems of biblical interpretation that the Roman teaching concerning the priority of the church over Scripture arose.

In addition to this practical concern just noted, there also appeared in these times a hermeneutical objection to the allegorical method. This opposition centered in the theological School of Antioch with such men as Diodore, John Chrysostom, and especially Theodore of Mopsuestia. These men are not widely known today, but they had significant and helpful insights into the hermeneutical problem. Theodore, who is the purest example of non-allegorical exegesis, insisted on treating the text of the Old Testament in such a way as not to deny its historical reality.

> The Old Testament is to be read primarily as the account of God's gracious acts embodied in Israel's history. And the ultimate importance of that history is that it was designed in the purposes of God to provide the setting for God's supremely gracious act in Christ, by which the new age was realized as God's salvation made available universally.[64]

In line with his principles, emphasizing a literal and historical exegesis, Theodore broke most radically with ecclesiastical tradition at the point of interpreting the Old Testament. "He did not read the New Testament into the Old. He did not find the Old Testament permeated with predictions of Christ and the Church as did Origen, for example, or Augustine."[65] He maintained that his view secured for prophecy a historical basis, and magnified the

---

63. *A Rumor of Angels* (Garden City, N.Y.: Doubleday and Co., 1970), 83.

64. M. F. Wiles, "Theodore of Mopsuestia," in *Cambridge History of the Bible*, ed. P. R. Ackroyd and C. F. Evans (Cambridge: Cambridge University Press, 1970), 1:508. Cf. G. H. Gilbert, *Interpretation of the Bible* (New York: Macmillan Co., 1908), 132-45, who says, "In Theodore I have found no single instance of allegorizing." 138.

65. Gilbert, *Interpretation*, 138. Gilbert says that this point "marks his affinity with modern scientific exegesis" and furthermore that "his position approximated that of Jesus though apparently without his knowledge of the fact."

Christian economy as that which converted into sober fact the highest imagery of the ancient Scriptures.[66]

The Alexandrian School had partially defended its use of allegory by an appeal to Pauline practice, particularly in Gal. 4:21-31. Although the apostle does use the word *allēgoreō* in the text ("allegorically speaking," NASB), the Antiochians insist that there is a significant difference between what Paul *did* and what the Alexandrians do. "The Apostle believes in the reality of the events which he describes and uses them for examples. The Alexandrians, on the other hand, deprive the whole Biblical record of its reality."[67] The proper principle of interpretation, they say, is *theoria* (theory) rather than *allegoria* (allegory), by which they mean a sense of Scripture higher or deeper than the literal or historical meaning, *but firmly based on the letter.*[68]

So as Gilbert says, "Exegesis has at last come down out of the clouds, and has planted its feet firmly on the earth. For the first time there is here a wholly serious and determined effort to find out what the sacred authors meant."[69] Unfortunately, however, the old traditional method soon overcame this promising new development, and it became lost to the memory of the church.

But despite its continual widespread use in the church as a means to establish some sense of unity between the Old Testament and the New Testament, allegory is totally inadequate as a sound exegetical principle. James D. Smart has driven the final nail in its coffin when he says:

> Allegory is a means of discovering meaning that is not actually present. Therefore, if the Christian Gospel cannot be found in the Old Testament without allegory, this is tantamount to a confession that it is not there but has to be inserted from without.[70]

It was not until the 18th century that a real breakthrough in achieving a historical perspective occurred. This came about, as we noted in the last section, partly through the influence of J. A. Bengel.[71] The man who took Bengel's suggestions and developed them,

---

66. James D. Smart, *The Interpretation of Scripture* (Philadelphia: Westminster Press, 1961); quoted in Swete, *Dictionary of Christian Biography.*
67. Quoted in Alexander, "Interpretation," 276.
68. Ibid.
69. *Interpretation,* 135.
70. *Interpretation,* 132.
71. It should be kept in mind for the underlying purpose of this study that Wesley virtually translated Bengel's *Gnomon* into his own *Notes,* preface, par. 7.

and first used the term *Heilsgeschichte,* now common coin in contemporary scholarship, was J. C. K. von Hofmann.

Bengel suggests in his preface to the *Gnomon* that it is the chief
task of the commentary to recover the historical situation of the
text and then let the text speak to the reader out of that setting as
it did to the original reader who did not need a mass of commentary aids. The text, in the situation of the first reader, was self-
evident or apparent to him. Here is embodied the suggestion that
began to flower with von Hofmann's work.

Von Hofmann is one of those figures who has been buried in
history and did not become well known either to his contemporaries or subsequent scholars. One major reason for this was his
position, which was midway between rationalism on the one hand
and extreme orthodoxy on the other. Thus he was regarded with
suspicion from both sides.

It was his concept of "holy history" that was von Hofmann's
unique contribution. He maintained that there was an organic
unity in the Scriptures with an "intrinsic connection between
prophecy and history." That means that there must be an *organic*
connection between the sphere in which prophecy was made and
the circumstances of its fulfillment. This was a significant departure from the existing traditional views, which laid stress upon
the words of prophecy as oracular with merely incidental contemporary relevance. In contrast, von Hofmann sought to find prophecy "primarily in historical events, and only secondarily in the interpretive words of the prophets."

Thus, like Bengel before him, von Hofmann "entirely abandoned the notion of mechanical inspiration." If revelation occurs
primarily in events and these are understood in a dynamic way, the
necessity of allegorizing is bypassed. Every stage of biblical history
carries in it the germ of a future development and therefore points
beyond itself to the subsequent stage of the purpose of God and
ultimately to its fulfillment in Jesus Christ's first and second coming.[72] Rather than the fulfillment of words, we are speaking about
the fulfillment of events. Rudolf Bultmann's criticism serves the
purpose of setting forth the true implications of von Hofmann's
thesis on these lines:

---

72. Otto A. Piper, "J. C. K. von Hofmann," *Encyclopedia of Religion,* ed. Vergilius
Ferm (New York: Philosophical Library, 1945).

This is naturally something quite different from when, in accordance with the traditional view, prophecy becomes understandable from fulfillment, in the sudden coming to light of a secret meaning of words which in their context had originally meant something quite different.[73]

Christian Preus's analysis provides an illuminating summary:

In developing [his] thesis, Hofmann shows how the pivotal events of Old Testament history fit into the process of Holy History in a vital way, and at the same time, because of their incomplete character, portend a complete fulfillment in the future. An examination of Old Testament history on this basis reveals the intrinsic necessity of prophecy in the work of redemption, and restores prophecy and fulfillment to the central place which they enjoyed in the Apostolic Church. It was the first time in the history of biblical interpretation that an organic view of history was applied to the problems of exegesis in a systematic way.[74]

Von Hofmann's work stands in contrast to two other interpretations of his time, both of which fail to take history seriously. On the right was the work of Ernst Wilhelm Hengstenberg (1802-69), a very conservative German Lutheran theologian; and on the left was the explanation of Friedrich Schleiermacher (1768-1834), the father of modern (liberal) theology and teacher of von Hofmann.

Schleiermacher operated under the influence of philosophical idealism, which tended to emphasize the reality of a nonhistorical realm of ideas (universals) in which absolutes reside and correspondingly the relative unreality of the historical realm (particulars) in which contingency prevails. Utilizing these distinctions, Schleiermacher distinguishes two kinds of prophetic predictions. The one is "special prediction," which refers to individual events and is therefore "hypothetical" or contingent. The other kind is an "exposition of the universal" and so has absolute value. This latter is the basic category into which Messianic predictions fall. They have both an accidental and an essential dimension. The former is the shell, while the latter is the kernel. "The individual assertions, more or less, are nothing but an external vesture, so that it often remains uncertain whether this point is that which does or does

---

73. "Prophecy and Fulfillment," 56. Bultmann's criticism, which follows this quote, is so superficial as to be ludicrous.
74. "The Contemporary Relevance of von Hofmann's Hermeneutical Principles," *Interpretation* 4 (1950): 311 ff.

not really belong to the prediction itself." The claim of Jesus to be the fulfillment of prophecy then has a twofold significance. He is the "end" of prophecy of the first type through His perfect fore-telling of the end of existing Jewish institutions and the "end" of the second type in the sense that "essential prophecy has now been completely fulfilled."[75] This view has been very influential.

Hengstenberg, at the opposite pole theologically from Schlei-ermacher, developed a similar thesis. He distinguished between "general truths" that were the prophets' major concern, and acci-dental particulars used "in order that the glory of the idea itself would be accentuated."[76] But rather than making Christ the goal of Old Testament history, Hengstenberg tended to make Him the con-tent of the Old Testament, which is most unhistorical, and there-fore resorted to allegorical interpretation.

One of the major gains of the development represented by von Hofmann is its recognition of the historical context of the bib-lical material. The prophets are now recognized to be men whose chief function was the proclamation of the Word of God *to their own times,* rather than seers who describe future events that had no relation to their own day. Virtually all of modern scholarship agrees with the writers of *Exploring the Old Testament* when they say:

> The term prophet is derived from a Greek word *prophetes,* which means "one who speaks on behalf of another." . . . The modern concept of a prophet as "one who predicts" or "fore-casts the future" is based upon the fact that the ancient prophet did occasionally predict future events through divine inspira-tion. But this represented only one aspect of his ministry. *Forth-*telling, rather than *fore*telling, was his primary function.[77]

Even the occasional foretelling that is referred to in this quota-tion is integrally related to the prophet's own audience, since it is their future about which he speaks. Also, their predictions are al-most invariably moral in nature, therefore contingent. That is to say, the coming to pass of the predicted judgment or blessing, as the case may be, is dependent upon the moral response of the people. Therefore, forecasting the future so as to put a determin-istic bias upon the course of history is not really involved. Gurdon

---

75. *The Christian Faith* (Edinburgh: T. and T. Clark, 1960), par. 103.3, 446-48.

76. Brevard Childs, "Prophecy and Fulfillment," *Interpretation* 12 (1958): 260-61.

77. W. T. Purkiser, ed., *Exploring the Old Testament* (Kansas City: Beacon Hill Press, 1955), 287-88.

C. Oxtoby speaks of this phenomenon as "conditional prediction."[78]

Unfortunately, among the rank and file of lay Christians the earlier, and inaccurate, concept of the biblical prophet generally holds sway.[79] This, coupled with the inundation of dispensationalistic literature posited largely upon the unhistorical premise, provides an effective bulwark against a proper understanding of the biblical position.

Typology

In the wake of this new historical understanding of the Scriptures, hermeneutical scholars have begun to talk about a new method of interpretation that is called *typology*. While the employment of types in exegesis is not new, this particular approach is. The older typology, so called, is as unhistorical as allegory, of which it is only a species.[80] The correspondence that it seeks to establish is not so much a relation between the past and the future, the foreshadowing and the fulfillment, as between the earthly and the heavenly, the shadow and the reality.[81]

Briefly stated, the distinction between allegory and typology is that in the former the text is treated as a mere symbol of spiritual truths. The literal, historical sense, if it is regarded at all, plays a relatively minor role.[82] Typology, on the other hand, takes as its guiding principle the idea that the events and personages of the Old Testament were types of, that is, prefigured and anticipated,

---

78. *Prediction and Fulfillment in the Bible* (Philadelphia: Westminster Press, 1966), 77-78.

79. Cf. Lampe and Woollcombe, *Typology*, 9-14.

80. Note, e.g., the allegorical typology practiced in the notes of the Scofield Bible. Scofield defines a type as "a divinely purposed illustration of some truth." Cf. notes on Gen. 1:16, where the "greater light," meaning the sun, is declared to be a type of Christ. This is a signal example of the standard criticism that dispensationalism literalizes prophecy and allegorizes history.

81. Lampe and Woollcombe, "Reasonableness of Typology," in *Typology*, 33: "To this sort of typology belongs the supposed correspondence which was popular in the Church of the Fathers between the Scarlet Cord of Rahab at Jericho, which served as a token of salvation and the blood of Christ, the sign of the salvation of mankind. Here the parallel between the type and its supposed fulfillment is plainly unreal and artificial."

82. The basis of allegorical exegesis is a "conception of the Scripture as a single vast volume of oracles and riddles, a huge book of secret puzzles to which the reader has to find clues." Lampe and Woollcombe, *Typology*, 31.

the events and personages of the New. The typologists take history seriously.[83]

This neo-typology, as we shall call it to distinguish it from the older unhistorical typology, arose as a response to the emergence of the widespread modern concern for the unity of the Bible. The rise of historical criticism, with its stress upon the historical character, and therefore the diversity, of the various biblical documents, had weakened the older views of the unity of the Scriptures based upon allegory and unhistorical typology. But as Lampe and Woollcombe assert, with the renewed emphasis on the continuity of the Scriptures as a whole, "Typology has again come into its own."[84]

Neo-typology is firmly grounded in the prophetic view of history. In a word, that view involves the prophetic conviction that God is in control of history, working His will especially in relation to the history of the chosen people. The inspiration of the prophets gives them insight into the inner meaning of occurrences in the life of these people so that they are able to interpret those events and declare their outcome. Such prophetic pronouncements, of course, have an eschatological dimension, but they are essentially related to their own times.

As seen through prophetic vision, then, biblical history falls into a pattern, or a recurrent rhythm, so that earlier interpreted events become a type of later events; and the forces that were at work in the former come to a kind of culmination in the latter, so that there is an analogical relation between the two, and the second may be referred to as the fulfillment of the earlier typical event.

When this view is applied to the New Testament, the situation seems to be that there is just such a relationship seen between certain Old Testament events and those that constitute the gospel. As Alan Richardson puts it:

> The fulfillment of prophecy is thus seen to involve more than the fulfillment of words and predictions; it involves the fulfillment of history, the validation of the prophetic understanding of history in the events of which the New Testament records and interprets for us.[85]

---

83. Kelly, *Doctrines*, 70-71.
84. *Typology*, 18; Alan Richardson, *Apologetics*, 192. For a brief summary of some of the factors that stimulated this renewal of interest in the unity of the Bible, cf. Smart, *Interpretation*, chap. 3.
85. *Apologetics*, 188.

Such fulfillment involves making explicit what was implicit in the pattern of the earlier historical events. There is a real correspondence in historical events that have been brought about by the recurring rhythm of the divine activity.

It should be noted in this connection that the neo-typologists are careful to deny that their interpretation involves a cyclical view of history. Such an understanding was prevalent in the ancient Greek and Oriental world as well as in the Canaanite culture that Israel encountered in Palestine. But the biblical view of history is linear in nature and does not allow for the cosmic repetition of events.[86] According to the view of history as cosmic cycles, all events will reoccur in a continuously repeating circle so that the actual event is reenacted. It is on these grounds that Gerhard von Rad suggests that we must see the basic ideas of typology less in the notion of repetition than in that of correspondence. "In the one case, the earthly gains its legitimacy through its correspondence with the heavenly, in the other, the relation of correspondence is a typical one: the primeval event is a type of the final event."[87]

Consequently, as Lampe and Woollcombe conclude, typology is

> grounded in a particular view of history which the New Testament writers undoubtedly held themselves and which Christians for whom the Bible is authoritative can scarcely repudiate. On this view a type may be called in the language of the Fathers a "mystery," but it is a "mystery" in the normal New Testament sense of the word. It is a secret in the counsel of God which is being made known in Christ; an element in the hidden purpose of God which has been made manifest in being fulfilled.[88]

The neo-typologists find this sort of interpretive activity already present within the Old Testament as the prophets look forward to the future when there shall be a repetition or recapitulation of previous significant events of holy history. For example, Isaiah and Amos speak of the return of paradise (Isa. 11:6-8; Amos 9:13); Hosea expects a repetition of the wilderness period (Hos. 2:16-20); Isaiah looks for a return of the old David in Jerusalem

---

86. It appears to this writer that Ecclesiastes is an apologetic for the biblical view of history against the cyclical view based upon cycles of nature with its deadening pessimism about human life.

87. "Typology," in *Essays on Old Testament Hermeneutics,* ed. Claus Westermann (Richmond, Va.: John Knox Press, 1963), 20.

88. *Typology,* 29.

(Isa. 1:21-26); and often we sense the longing for a new Exodus. "It is the pattern of divine action which the prophet discerns, rather than the recurrence of the outward historical event; that for him, as for Israelite thought as a whole, divine action is indicated in the actual events of history."[89]

But it is more than isolated events that provide types; the Old Testament as a whole displays the pattern of the divine salvation in the recurring themes of death and resurrection, annihilation (or at least peril and disaster) followed by restoration. This pattern typologically anticipates the salvation that was accomplished through the coming of God's Messiah of whom the prophets had spoken. So, in the words of Alan Richardson, "The prophets were able to discern the inner significance of the events of their own days in such a manner that they apprehended, however dimly, the very pattern of the process of salvation in history."[90]

This view has much to commend it. The seriousness with which it takes history in contrast to allegory is sound. In fact, it provides us with some tremendous insights into present-day interpretation of eschatological writings, including the much-abused Book of Revelation.

Like all other prophecies of the Bible, this last book is also firmly grounded in the events of its own day. The apostle, through the insight of the Spirit, is able to penetrate into their cosmic meaning and see that there are forces at work that must ultimately precipitate the consummation of this age. The intensity of the interaction of these forces gives him a sense of urgency, so that the age-ending conflict is seen to be near at hand. The struggle, the cataclysmic events, and the outcome are all described in symbolic language that has reference to the writer's own circumstances and those of his readers. Consequently, it is not possible to use these scriptures to find a blueprint of future events in any kind of detailed specification. But it *is* possible to project an analogical relation between God's action in the crises of the latter first century and the final end of world history, when God's purposes shall at last be completely accomplished.[91]

It is this situation that makes possible the identification of

89. Ibid., 26-27; cf. von Rad, "Typology," 19-20.
90. *Apologetics*, 190-91; cf. Lampe and Woollcombe, *Typology*, 27-28.
91. Cf. Alan Richardson, *Apologetics*, 199. This view is soundly developed in Hoekema, *Bible and the Future*.

every age with the last day, as prophetic preachers unfailingly do. The same structure of forces, analogically understood, are present with varying degrees of intensity and therefore recognizable. The tragedy is that these latter-day prophets make positive identification and consequently discredit themselves (and oftentimes the biblical message) as history moves on and their identifications fail.

But to return to our main question: Is typology as reinterpreted here sufficient as a hermeneutical principle, or does it too have shortcomings that need correction? Lampe and Woollcombe, two of the leading exponents, seem to be showing some uneasiness when they wonder if such an approach may be legitimately employed in a "postcritical" age. They question if any criterion can be discovered for making a distinction between legitimate and exegetically justifiable typology, on the one hand, and the unwarrantable exercise of private and uncontrolled ingenuity on the other.

Actually, the method is susceptible to several criticisms. Lampe and Woollcombe's typology has been criticized for their theory that there is a "recurring rhythm in past history." This suggests an impersonal rhythm in the events themselves and therefore may be interpreted as little more than the logos of Heraclitus. Smart rightly argues that it is much better to talk about the faithfulness of God manifesting itself in a personal direction of history. He says:

> It is this which produces a pattern of correspondence throughout the Old Testament. The story of the exodus was retold in each new age to remind Israelites that their God is a God who delivers his people in a marvelous way in spite of every obstacle, and to create the expectation of a new deliverance. . . . The correspondence, therefore, between the events of the past and the anticipated events of the future is no mystic foreshadowing of the future but is simply an expression of the confidence of the prophet that God's faithfulness to his own nature must be vindicated in the events of history, since he is Lord of the world and its history.[92]

While this criticism has an element of quibbling in it, it does call attention to a more dynamic view of history while retaining the biblical stress upon the personal activity of God in the history of His people. The interaction of God and Israel may in truth reflect certain patterns, based upon the nature of God rather than

---

92. *Interpretation*, 102.

blind forces of nature, that recur again and again and that find their highest expression in the Christ-event and those influences that flow from it.

On the basis of this understanding, Smart further criticized the whole typological approach as being too artificial. He really seems to be saying that the typologists do not take the biblical concept of fulfillment seriously enough, but rather are positing their method as a hermeneutical device by which the early Christians discovered parallels between their new faith and the Old Testament so as to derive some authority from the Jewish Scriptures. Rather, "fulfillment means the completion in him [Christ] of the work of God to which the Old Testament bore witness." When Jesus spoke of the new covenant in relation to the Passover,

> He was not concerned about interpreting the old or establishing parallels, but with establishing a new relation between God and man in which all the hopes of those who had served God before him would be joyfully fulfilled. It is sufficent, therefore, to recognize that the saving work of Christ in his lifetime and in his church is the completion of a redemption begun in the Old Testament.[93]

While it is true that the neo-typology takes very seriously the historical setting of typical scripture, it does seem to *add* the typological meaning to the historical. If it is remembered that the historical meaning of any text is determined by its context, and the context is not necessarily limited to the immediate setting, then it can be seen that the total context of Old Testament scripture that is needed to establish its full historical meaning includes the life, death, and resurrection of Jesus Christ and the birth of the Church. In this way, to read an Old Testament text in the light of the New Testament is to see it in its *full* historical setting. "There is not historical *and* typological meaning but only different levels of a meaning that is both historical and theological."[94]

With this background, we may now propose what we believe to be an adequate hermeneutical principle by which to do justice to the New Testament claim and provide us with a proper and sound method of interpreting the biblical source so as to make legitimate use of it in the task of theologizing.

---

93. Ibid., 112.
94. Ibid., 117.

Toward a Theological Hermeneutic

Our survey has revealed the necessity for an adequate hermeneutic if one is to handle the question of the relation between the Testaments in such a way as not to sabotage the Christian faith. We have noted the continued rejection by the church of a literalistic reading of the Old Testament, since doing so inevitably produces this undesirable result.[95] Several attempts have been made to provide alternative methodologies. Some are patently inadequate, others have intermingled strengths and weaknesses. In this section we propose to set forth a hermeneutical principle that we believe validly represents the biblical point of view and provides a solution to the chief difficulties resident in the issue under discussion. It will furthermore demonstrate the nature of biblical authority for theological work.

The major problem that we have noted arises from the occasional lack of correspondence between the New Testament use of certain Old Testament scriptures alleged to have been fulfilled in Christ and their original meaning, a problem that cannot be ignored. One of the influential attempts to handle this problem was a proposal by Rendel Harris titled "Testimonies."

It was the contention of this study that the early Christians used collections of texts that had been compiled in handbooks. This proposal enjoyed considerable popularity for many years. However, no evidence was ever found to support the idea, that is, there were none of these testimonials that survived if they ever existed. Eventually it was generally abandoned by scholars, but the discovery of the Dead Sea Scrolls revived interest in Harris's theory, because it was found that such testimonials were actually in use by Jews of that age.

Commenting upon the Qumran discoveries, J. N. Allegro says:

> There can be little doubt that we have in this document a group of testimonia of the type not long ago proposed by Bur-

---

95. Cf. a statement made by Thomas Woolston, one of John Wesley's contemporaries, who was engaged in the debate during the 1700s: At the conclusion of his argument he says, "I can't but think from what has been said there is Encouragement enough to search after the Allegorical and Spiritual sense of the Law and the Prophets, and to lay aside our literal interpretations, which are the death of those witnesses of Christ; for not only St. Paul saith that the Letter killeth, but the ancient Fathers often caution us against the Literal sense of the Scriptures least [lest] we be the death of them." *The Old Apology for the Truth of the Christian Religion, Against the Jew and Gentiles Revived* (London: John Torbuck, 1732), 302-82.

kitt, Rendel Harris, and others to have existed in the early Church. Our collection has the added interest of including two testimonies used by the early Christians concerning Jesus. Furthermore, the first testimony quoted has a particular importance in that it demonstrates the type of composite quotation well represented in the New Testament.[96]

But even if this proposal be accepted as valid, we do not have a genuine solution but merely a way of pushing the problem one step farther back. It may account for the way in which the biblical apologists located their texts, but it does not explain the basis for their inclusion in the handbooks in the first place. Of course, if there is merely a verbal connection between the Old Testament text and its alleged New Testament fulfillment, this solution would be satisfactory, but not satisfying.[97]

A much more reasonable and acceptable answer was proposed by C. H. Dodd. As a matter of fact, Dodd's thesis is built upon and is an extension of Harris's proposals and speaks precisely to the problem that we have raised.

Through an analysis of the Old Testament scriptures used by New Testament writers, he discovered that there were certain sections of the Old Testament ("Testimonia") that were employed by at least two different authors. This use by different men indicated, Dodd contends, a precanonical tradition from which each drew. This tradition was not written, as Harris had suggested, but oral in nature.

It will be worthwhile to quote Dodd's own summary of his findings as they relate to the hermeneutical method of the early Christian writers:

> The method included, first, the *selection* of certain large sections of the Old Testament scriptures, especially from Isaiah, Jeremiah and certain minor prophets, and from the Psalms. These sections were understood as *wholes,* and particular verses or sentences were quoted from them rather as pointers to the whole context than as constituting testimonies in and for themselves. At the same time, detached sentences from other parts of the Old Testament could be adduced to illustrate or elucidate the meaning of the main section under consideration. But in the

---

96. Quoted in E. F. Osborn, *Word and History* (Melbourne, Australia: Jonker Printing Pty., 1971), 8.

97. One might see a parallel to this sort of relationship in most center-margin references of contemporary Bibles or so-called chain-reference Bibles, which are based largely on verbal correspondence rather than content or contextual relation.

fundamental passages it is the *total context* that is in view, and is the basis of the argument.[98]

Each of these units of Scripture represented a particular pattern of thought or a plot, though they may be referring to various and sundry situations. This pattern is that the victory of God comes through, and is subsequent to, suffering or judgment. Since this idea was applied consistently to Israel by the prophets and not to the Messiah, it came as a distinct shock to discover that He, too, must follow this pattern in carrying out His work.

Certain specific passages having this pattern became standard references for early Christian preachers.[99] Within these large passages, there were individual statements that had special significance because there was a striking literal correspondence between them and events connected with the life of Christ.[100] The fact that their context pointed in a different direction *literally* was not important because they were simply representative verses of a pattern of thought that *was* directly and literally applicable to Jesus and His Church. Thus the fulfillment was neither literal and mechanical, nor allegorical, but *theological*, that is, the theology taught by the Prophets (and the other divisions of the Hebrew canon) was fulfilled by Christ.

We may find this theological hermeneutic at work, with added dimensions, throughout the Old Testament. Isaiah of Jerusalem analyzed the situation of the people of his beloved Judah and saw that their way of life could only bring the judgment of God. He declared the outcome in 7:17-20: " 'The Lord will bring upon you and upon your people and upon your father's house such days as have not come since the day that Ephraim departed from Judah—the king of Assyria.' In that day the Lord will whistle for the fly which is at the sources of the streams of Egypt, and for the bee which is in the land of Assyria. And they will all come and settle in the steep ravines, and in the clefts of the rocks, and on all the thornbushes, and on all the pastures. In that day the Lord will shave with a razor which is hired beyond the River—with the king

---

98. *According to the Scripture*, 126.

99. This phenomenon could also account for the vagueness that some biblical writers show in referring to the passages they quote. Cf., e.g., Heb. 2:6.

100. This, in Dodd's explanation, accounts for the use of Jer. 31:15 in Matt. 2:17-18, a problem that we have already noted. This verse comes from a larger context (Jer. 31:10-34), which manifests the plot that was fulfilled, in this case, by the new Israel.

of Assyria—the head and the hair of the feet, and it will sweep away the beard also."

Note that the impending judgment is seen to be at the hands of the then-dominant world empire—Assyria. Years later when the end actually came, it was not Assyria but Babylon that was the instrument of God. Did that in some way invalidate Isaiah's proclamation? Certainly not! He was proclaiming a theological vision that was grounded in his understanding of the nature of God and human sin, and there was a theological fulfillment that differed in certain details from Isaiah's own specifications but was just as truly the fulfillment of his words.

Furthermore, each revelation-event became a source of theological interpretation or reinterpretation of previous events in such a way that the former event is said to be fulfilled in the latter. J. A. Bewer has some years ago called attention to this fact in declaring that a corollary of "progressive revelation" is "progressive interpretation":

> The record remained, as it was written down, even after the revelation had progressed, but the same words were read and understood in a new way. The deeper insight into the truth vouchsafed through the higher revelation saw much more in them than their original authors and their first hearers or readers had seen.[101]

The clearest illustration of this point is the interpretation of the patriarchal narratives in the light of the Exodus. Quite obviously the lives of the fathers are written from the perspective of the great deliverance, and therefore their experiences are presented as preparatory for that event. Their careers were fulfilled in the Exodus.

By analogy, the Christ-event becomes the point of focus in the light of which the earlier events and their interpretations are seen and reinterpreted. What happens is not a falsification but rather a new understanding derived from the Christian revelatory-event by

---

101. "Progressive Interpretation," *Anglican Theological Review* 24 (1942) : 89. This reference does not imply a tacit acceptance of progressive revelation, since that position has some serious difficulties with it. If progressive revelation is interpreted to imply that early sections of Scripture are preliminary and preparatory and therefore retain only historical value when superseded by a "higher" revelation, this is to make parts of the Bible of only antiquarian interest and deprived of any real authority. We are proposing a position in this appendix that gives the *whole* Bible authority and is a much more conservative view than that of progressive revelation as defined above. This position, however, does not fail to recognize the superiority—the fulfilling character—of the revelation of Christ.

which the Messianic hope was reinterpreted. Likewise the Israel of the old covenant is radically reinterpreted by the new Israel of the new covenant. It came to light that it was not simply the message of God being conveyed to non-Israelites by Jews as Old Testament universalism had envisioned it, but that the true Israel is made up of Gentiles as well as Jews, with the latter not having any priority.

The utilization of this understanding provides us with a theological hermeneutic with which we are able to say that the theology of the Old Testament is fulfilled in the theology of the New Testament. This is not merely the theology of the Prophets, but that of the whole Hebrew canon.

By taking the view that we are advocating, and emphasizing the theological dimension, we make the whole Old Testament authoritative for Christian preaching[102] and provide a rationale for understanding the central claim of the Early Church that God's act in Christ was "according to the Scriptures."

When this position is extrapolated to a general principle applicable to the whole Bible, as was suggested in the beginning, we have a criterion by which to identify the authoritative cognitive element in the Scripture—it is the theological.

---

102. This is the thesis of Bright's great *Authority of the Old Testament,* upon which this whole discussion is heavily dependent.

Works Cited

Articles

Aalen, S. "Glory, Honor." In *The New International Dictionary of New Testament Theology,* vol. 2. Edited by Colin Brown. Translated from *Theologisches Begriffslexikon zum Neuen Testament.* 3 vols. Grand Rapids: Zondervan Publishing House, 1975.

Alexander, James N. S. "The Interpretation of Scripture in the Ante-Nicene Period." *Interpretation* 12 (1958).

Baker, Frank. "Unfolding John Wesley." *Quarterly Review* 1, no. 1 (Fall 1980).

Barr, James. "Revelation." In *Hastings Dictionary of the Bible,* edited by James Hastings. Rev. ed. by Frederick C. Grant and H. H. Rowley. New York: Charles Scribner's Sons, 1963.

Bassett, Paul M. "The Holiness Movement and the Protestant Principle." *Wesleyan Theological Journal* 18, no. 1 (Spring 1983).

————. "Western Ecclesiology to About 1700: Part 1." In *The Church,* edited by Melvin E. Dieter and Daniel N. Berg. Wesleyan Theological Perspectives Series, vol. 4. Anderson, Ind.: Warner Press, 1984.

————. "Western Ecclesiology to About 1700: Part 2." In *The Church. See* above.

Bence, Clarence. "Salvation and the Church." In *The Church. See* Bassett.

Berg, Daniel N. "The Marks of the Church in the Theology of John Wesley." In *The Church. See* Bassett.

Betteridge, Walter. "Glory." In *International Standard Bible Encyclopedia,* vol. 2. Edited by James Orr. 6 vols. Grand Rapids: Wm. B. Eerdmans Publishing Co., 1949.

Bewer, J. A. "Progressive Interpretation." *Anglican Theological Review* 24 (1942).

Blackman, E. C. "Sanctification." In *Interpreter's Dictionary of the Bible,* vol. 4. Edited by George Buttrick. 4 vols. New York: Abingdon Press, 1962.

Bowman, John Wick. "Dispensationalism." *Interpretation* 10, no. 2 (April 1956).

Brockington, L. H. "Presence." In *A Theological Word Book of the Bible,* edited by Alan Richardson. New York: Macmillan Co., 1950.

Bultmann, Rudolf. "Prophecy and Fulfillment." In *Essays on Old Testament Hermeneutics,* edited by Claus Westermann. Richmond, Va.: John Knox Press, 1963.

Carpenter, Edward. "The Bible in the Eighteenth Century." In *The Church's Use of the Bible,* edited by D. E. Nineham. London: SPCK, 1963.

Childs, Brevard. "Prophecy and Fulfillment." *Interpretation* 12 (1958).

Coleson, Joseph E. "Covenant Community in the Old Testament." In *The Church. See* Bassett.

Cranfield, C. E. B. "St. Mark 13." *Scottish Journal of Theology* 6 (1953).
Cubie, David L. "Separation or Unity." In *The Church. See* Bassett.
Cushman, Robert. "Faith and Reason." In *A Companion to the Study of St. Augustine,* edited by Roy W. Battenhouse. New York: Oxford University Press, 1956.
Davies, G. Horton. "Glory." In *Interpreter's Dictionary of the Bible,* vol. 2. *See* Blackman.
Dayton, Wilber T. "Initial Sanctification and Its Concomitants." In *The Word and the Doctrine: Studies in Contemporary Wesleyan-Arminian Theology,* compiled by Kenneth E. Geiger. Kansas City: Beacon Hill Press, 1965.
Deasley, Alex R. G. "Entire Sanctification and the Baptism with the Holy Spirit: Perspectives on the Biblical View of the Relationship." *Wesleyan Theological Journal* 14, no. 1 (Spring 1979).
———. "The Church in the Book of Acts." In *The Church. See* Bassett.
Denney, James. "2 Corinthians." In *Expositor's Bible,* edited by W. Robertson Nicoll. 25 vols. New York: A. C. Armstrong and Sons, 1903.
Dinkler, Eric. "Myth." In *Handbook of Christian Theology,* edited by Marvin Halverson and Arthur A. Cohen. Meridian Books. Cleveland: World Publishing Co., 1958.
Dunning, H. Ray. "Biblical Interpretation and Wesleyan Theology." *Wesleyan Theological Journal* 9 (Spring 1974).
———. "Dispensationalism." In *Beacon Dictionary of Theology,* edited by Richard S. Taylor. Kansas City: Beacon Hill Press of Kansas City, 1983.
———. "Ethics in a Wesleyan Context." *Wesleyan Theological Journal* 5, no. 1 (Spring 1970).
———. "Sanctification—Ceremony or Ethics?" *Preacher's Magazine* 55, no. 1 (September, October, November, 1979).
Ellis, E. Earle. "Christ and Spirit in 1 Corinthians." In *Christ and Spirit in the New Testament,* edited by Barnabas Lindars and Stephen S. Smalley. Cambridge: Cambridge University Press, 1973.
Ferm, Vergilius. "Philosophy of Religion." In *Encyclopedia of Religion,* edited by Vergilius Ferm. New York: Philosophical Library, 1945.
"Genesis and the Babylonian Inscriptions." In *A Commentary on the Holy Bible,* edited by J. R. Dummelow. New York: Macmillan Co., 1936.
Gibson, A. Boyce. "The Two Ideas of God." In *Philosophy of Religion,* edited by John E. Smith. New York: Macmillan Co., 1965.
Giles, K. N. "The Church in the Gospel of Luke." *Scottish Journal of Theology* 34 (1981).
Gilkey, Langdon B. "Cosmology, Ontology, and the Travail of Biblical Language." *Journal of Religion* (July 1961).
Goodspeed, E. J. "Canon." In *Encyclopedia of Religion. See* Ferm.
Grave, S. A. "Reid, Thomas." *Encyclopedia of Philosophy,* vol. 7. Edited by Paul Edwards. New York: Macmillan Co. and Free Press, 1967.
Gray, G. B. "Sacrifice." In *A Theological Word Book of the Bible. See* Brockington.

Greathouse, W. M. "Sanctification and the Christus Victor Motif in Wesleyan Theology." *Wesleyan Theological Journal* 7, no. 1 (Spring 1972).

Grider, J. Kenneth. "The Meaning of 'Old Man.'" *Nazarene Preacher,* February 1972.

Hamilton, Victor P. "Recent Studies in Leviticus and Their Contribution to a Further Understanding of Wesleyan Theology." In *A Spectrum of Thought,* edited by Michael Peterson. Wilmore, Ky.: Asbury Publishing Co., 1982.

Harris, Merne A., and Taylor, Richard S. "The Dual Nature of Sin." In *The Word and the Doctrine. See* Dayton.

Harvey, Van A. "Myth." In *A Handbook of Theological Terms.* New York: Macmillan Co., 1964.

Howard, Richard E. "Egocentric Evangelism." *Wesleyan Theological Journal* 21, no. 1 (Spring 1986).

"Introduction," in *The Apostolic Fathers.* Vol. 1 of *The Fathers of the Church.* Edited by Ludwig Schoff. 72 vols. Washington, D.C.: Catholic University Press, 1962.

Isbell, Charles D. "Glossolalia and Propheteialaia." *Wesleyan Theological Journal* 10 (Spring 1975).

————. "The Origins of Prophetic Frenzy and Ecstatic Utterances in the Old Testament World." *Wesleyan Theological Journal* 11 (Spring 1976).

Jones, Rufus M. "Mysticism (Christian, NT)." *Encyclopedia of Religion and Ethics.* Edited by James Hastings. 13 vols. New York: Charles Scribner's Sons, 1917.

————. "Mysticism (Introductory)." *Encyclopedia of Religion and Ethics. See* above.

Kevan, E. F. "Genesis." In *The New Bible Commentary,* edited by F. Davidson. 2nd ed. Grand Rapids: Wm. B. Eerdmans Publishing Co., 1960.

Kinlaw, Dennis F. "Sin in Believers: The Biblical Evidence." In *The Word and the Doctrine. See* Dayton.

Lampe, G. W. H. "The Holy Spirit in the Writings of St. Luke." In *Studies in the Gospels,* edited by D. E. Nineham. Oxford: Blackwell, 1955.

Lane, A. N. S. "Christology Beyond Chalcedon." In *Christ the Lord,* edited by H. H. Rowdon. Downers Grove, Ill.: InterVarsity Press, 1982.

Lewis, C. S. "On Obstinacy in Belief." In *The World's Last Night.* New York: Harcourt, Brace, Jovanovich, n.d.

Line, John. "Systematic Theology." In *Encyclopedia of Religion. See* Ferm.

Lofthouse, W. F. "The Holy Spirit in the Acts and the Fourth Gospel." *Expository Times* 52, no. 9 (1940-41).

Luther, Martin. "On the Bondage of the Will." In *Library of Christian Classics,* vol. 17. Edited by E. Gordon Rupp. Philadelphia: Westminster Press, 1957.

McFadyen, J. E. "Zechariah." In *Abingdon Bible Commentary,* edited by F. C. Eiselen. New York: Abingdon-Cokesbury Press, 1929.

McQuilkin, J. R. "This I Know." *Action,* Nov. 1, 1956.

Milgrom, Jacob. "Sacrifice." In *Interpreter's Dictionary of the Bible,* suppl. vol. Edited by Keith Crim. Nashville: Abingdon, 1976.

Mulholland, M. Robert, Jr. "The Church in the Epistles." In *The Church. See* Bassett.

Outler, Albert. "The Place of Wesley in the Christian Tradition." In *The Place of Wesley in the Christian Tradition,* edited by Kenneth E. Rowe. Metuchen, N.J.: Scarecrow Press, 1976.

Piper, Otto A. "Heilsgeschichte." In *Encyclopedia of Religion. See* Ferm.

———. "J. C. K. von Hofmann." In *Encyclopedia of Religion. See* Ferm.

———. "Knowledge." In *Interpreter's Dictionary of the Bible,* vol. 3. *See* Blackman.

Preus, Christian. "The Contemporary Relevance of von Hofmann's Hermeneutical Principles." *Interpretation* 4 (1950).

Richardson, Alan. "Repent." In *A Theological Word Book of the Bible. See* Brockington.

Rorty, Richard. "Relation, Internal and External." In *Encyclopedia of Philosophy,* vols. 7 and 8. *See* Grave.

Sanner, A. Elwood. "Initial Sanctification." In *Beacon Dictionary of Theology. See* Dunning.

Schmitz, E. D. "Knowledge." *The New International Dictionary of New Testament Theology,* vol. 3. *See* Aalen.

Shelton, R. Larry. "A Covenant Concept of Atonement." *Wesleyan Theological Journal* 19, no. 1 (Spring 1984).

———. "John Wesley's Approach to Scripture in Historical Perspective." *Wesleyan Theological Journal* 16, no. 1 (Spring 1981).

Snaith, Norman H. "Righteousness." In *A Theological Word Book of the Bible. See* Brockington.

Sproul, R. C. "Right Now Counts Forever." In *The Necessity of Systematic Theology,* edited by John Jefferson Davis. Grand Rapids: Baker Book House, 1980.

Staples, Rob L. "Sanctification and Selfhood." *Wesleyan Theological Journal* 7, no. 1 (Spring 1972).

Stendahl, Krister. "Biblical Theology." In *Interpreter's Dictionary of the Bible,* vol. 1. *See* Blackman.

———. "Method in the Study of Biblical Theology." *The Bible in Modern Scholarship.* Edited by J. Philip Hyatt. Nashville: Abingdon Press, 1965.

Stonehouse, Ned B. "The Gift of the Spirit." *Westminster Theological Journal* 13, no. 1 (November 1950).

Taylor, Richard S. "A Theology of Missions." In *Ministering to the Millions.* Kansas City: Nazarene Publishing House, 1971.

Taylor, Willard H. "The Baptism with the Holy Spirit: Promise of Grace or Judgment?" *Wesleyan Theological Journal* 12 (Spring 1977).

———. "Justification." In *Beacon Dictionary of Theology. See* Dunning.

Thomas, George F. "The Method and Structure of Tillich's Theology." In *The Theology of Paul Tillich,* edited by Charles W. Kegley and Robert W. Bretall. New York: Macmillan Co., 1964.

Thompson, W. Ralph. "Facing Objections Raised Against Biblical Inerrancy." *Wesleyan Theological Journal* 3, no. 1 (Spring 1968).

Tillich, Paul. "The Meaning and Justification of Religious Belief." In *Religious Experience and Truth,* edited by Sidney Hook. New York: New York University Press, 1961.

———. "Reply to Interpretation and Criticism." In *The Theology of Paul Tillich. See* Thomas.

von Rad, Gerhard. "Doxa." In *Theological Dictionary of the New Testament,* vol. 2. Edited by Gerhard Kittel. Translated and edited by Geoffrey W. Bromiley. 10 vols. Grand Rapids: Wm. B. Eerdmans Publishing Co., 1964.

———. "Typology." In *Essays on Old Testament Hermeneutics. See* Bultmann.

Wiles, M. F. "Theodore of Mopsuestia." In *Cambridge History of the Bible,* vol. 1. Edited by P. R. Ackroyd and C. F. Evans. Cambridge: Cambridge University Press, 1970.

Wood, Arthur Skevington. "The Contribution of John Wesley to the Theology of Grace." In *Grace Unlimited,* edited by Clark H. Pinnock. Minneapolis: Bethany Fellowship, 1975.

Books

Achtemeier, Paul J. *The Inspiration of Scripture.* Philadelphia: Westminster Press, 1980.

Allport, Gordon. *Becoming.* New Haven, Conn.: Yale University Press, 1955.

Althaus, Paul. *The Theology of Martin Luther.* Translated by Robert C. Schultz. Philadelphia: Fortress Press, 1966.

Anderson, Bernhard W. *Creation Versus Chaos.* New York: Association Press, 1967; Philadelphia Fortress Press, 1987.

———. *Out of the Depths.* Philadelphia: Westminster Press, 1983.

Anderson, Ray S. *On Being Human.* Grand Rapids: Wm. B. Eerdmans Publishing Co., 1982.

Athanasius. *De incarnatione Verbi Dei* (The incarnation of the Word of God). London: Religious Tract Society, n.d.

Aulen, Gustav. *Christus Victor.* Translated by A. G. Hebert. New York: Macmillan Co., 1961.

———. *The Faith of the Christian Church.* Translated by Eric H. Wahlstrom. Philadelphia: Fortress Press, 1960.

Ayer, A. J. *Language, Truth, and Logic.* New York: Dover Publications, n.d.

Baab, Otto J. *The Theology of the Old Testament.* New York: Abingdon Press, 1949.

Baillie, Donald M. *God Was in Christ.* London: Faber and Faber, 1961.

———. *The Theology of the Sacraments.* New York: Charles Scribner's Sons, 1957.

Baillie, John. *The Idea of Revelation in Recent Thought.* New York: Columbia University Press, 1965.

———. *Our Knowledge of God.* New York: Charles Scribner's Sons, 1959.

———. *The Sense of the Presence of God.* New York: Charles Scribner's Sons, 1962.

Baker, Frank. *John Wesley and the Church of England.* Nashville: Abingdon Press, 1970.

Barclay, William. *Daily Study Bible: Gospel of John,* vol. 1. Philadelphia: Westminster Press, 1956.

———. *Daily Study Bible: The Revelation of John.* 2 vols. Philadelphia: Westminster Press, 1960.

———. *The Promise of the Spirit.* Philadelphia: Westminster Press, 1960.

Barr, James. *Fundamentalism.* Philadelphia: Westminster Press, 1978.

———. *Old and New in Interpretation.* New York: Harper and Row, Publishers, 1966.

Barth, Karl. *Church Dogmatics.* Edited by G. W. Bromiley and T. F. Torrance. Edinburgh: T. and T. Clark, 1957.

———. *Dogmatics in Outline.* Translated by G. T. Thomson. London: SCM Press, 1960.

Barth, Markus. *Was Christ's Death a Sacrifice?* Edinburgh: Oliver and Boyd, 1961.

Basic Writings of St. Augustine. Edited by Whitney J. Oates. 2 vols. New York: Random House Publishers, 1948.

Basic Writings of St. Thomas Aquinas. Edited by Anton C. Pegis. 2 vols. New York: Random House Publishers, 1945.

Bass, Clarence. *The Backgrounds to Dispensationalism.* Grand Rapids: Wm. B. Eerdmans Publishing Co., 1960.

Bassett, Paul M., and Greathouse, William M. *Exploring Christian Holiness.* Vol. 2, *The Historical Development.* Kansas City: Beacon Hill Press of Kansas City, 1985.

Beasley-Murray, G. R. *Baptism in the New Testament.* Grand Rapids: Wm. B. Eerdmans Publishing Co., 1974.

Berger, Peter. *A Rumor of Angels.* Garden City, N.Y.: Doubleday and Co., 1970.

Berkhof, Hendrikus. *The Christian Faith.* Translated by Sierd Woudstra. Grand Rapids: Wm. B. Eerdmans Publishing Co., 1980.

Berkhof, Louis. *The History of Christian Doctrines.* Grand Rapids: Baker Book House, 1976.

Berkouwer, G. C. *The Church.* Translated by James E. Davison. Grand Rapids: Wm. B. Eerdmans Publishing Co., 1976.

———. *Man: The Image of God.* Grand Rapids: Wm. B. Eerdmans Publishing Co., 1962.

———. *Sin.* Grand Rapids: Wm. B. Eerdmans Publishing Co., 1971.

Bicknell, E. J. *The Christian Idea of Sin and Original Sin.* New York: Longmans, Green, and Co., 1923.

Blackman, E. C. *Biblical Interpretation.* Philadelphia: Westminster Press, 1957.

Bloesch, Donald G. *Essentials of Evangelical Theology.* 2 vols. San Francisco: Harper and Row, Publishers, 1978.

Bonhoeffer, Dietrich. *Creation and Fall.* New York: Macmillan Co., 1967.

Borgen, Ole E. *John Wesley on the Sacraments: A Theological Study.* Zurich: Publishing House of the United Methodist Church, 1972.

Bornkamm, Gunther. *Paul.* Translated by D. M. G. Stalker. New York: Harper and Row, Publishers, 1971.

Bornkamm, Heinrich. *Luther and the Old Testament.* Translated by Erich W. and Ruth C. Gritsch. Philadelphia: Fortress Press, 1969.

Bowman, John Wick. *The Intention of Jesus.* Philadelphia: Westminster Press, 1943.

Bretall, Robert, ed. *A Kierkegaard Anthology.* New York: Modern Library, 1946.

Bright, John. *The Authority of the Old Testament.* Grand Rapids: Baker Book House, 1975.

———. *The Kingdom of God.* New York: Abingdon Press, 1953.

Brown, Raymond E. *The Gospel According to John 1—12.* Vol. 29 of the *Anchor Bible,* edited by William Foxwell Albright and David Noel Freedman. 38 vols. Garden City, N.Y.: Doubleday and Co., 1966.

Brown, William Adams. *Christian Theology in Outline.* Edinburgh: T. and T. Clark, 1912.

Bruce, F. F. *New Testament Development of Old Testament Themes.* Grand Rapids: Wm. B. Eerdmans Publishing Co., 1968.

Brueggemann, Walter. *Tradition for Crisis: A Study in Hosea.* Atlanta: John Knox Press, 1968.

Bruner, Frederick Dale. *A Theology of the Holy Spirit.* Grand Rapids: Wm. B. Eerdmans Publishing Co., 1970.

Brunner, Emil. *The Christian Doctrine of Creation and Redemption.* Translated by Olive Wyon. Philadelphia: Westminster Press, 1952.

———. *The Christian Doctrine of the Church, Faith, and the Consummation.* Translated by David Cairns. Philadelphia: Westminster Press, 1962.

———. *Man in Revolt: A Christian Anthropology.* Translated by Olive Wyon. New York: Charles Scribner's Sons, 1939.

———. *Revelation and Reason.* Translated by Olive Wyon. Philadelphia: Westminster Press, 1946.

———. *Truth as Encounter.* Philadelphia: Westminster Press, 1964.

Brunner, Emil, and Barth, Karl. *Natural Theology.* Edited by John Baillie. London: Geoffrey Bles; Centenary Press, 1946.

Bultmann, Rudolf et al. *Kerygma and Myth.* Edited by Hans Werner Bartsch. New York: Harper and Bros., Publishers, 1961.

Burkhardt, Helmut. *The Biblical Doctrine of Regeneration.* Translated by O. R. Johnston. Downers Grove, Ill.: InterVarsity Press, 1978.

Burnaby, John. *Is the Bible Inspired?* London: Duckworth and Co., 1949.

Burrows, Millar. *Outline of Biblical Theology.* Philadelphia: Westminster Press, 1956.

Cairns, David. *The Image of God in Man.* New York: Philosophical Library, Xerox copied in 1978.

Calvin, John. *A Compend of the Institutes of the Christian Religion.* Edited by Hugh T. Kerr. Philadelphia: Westminster Press, 1964.

———. *Institutes of the Christian Religion.* Translated by Henry Beveridge. London: James Clarke and Co., 1949.

Cannon, William Ragsdale. *The Theology of John Wesley.* New York: Abingdon Press, 1946.

Carter, Charles W. *The Person and Ministry of the Holy Spirit.* Grand Rapids: Baker Book House, 1974.

Cell, George Croft. *The Rediscovery of John Wesley.* New York: Henry Holt and Co., 1935.

Chafer, Lewis Sperry. *Systematic Theology.* Vol. 4, of 4 vols. Dallas: Dallas Seminary Press; 1947-48.

Chambers, Oswald. *The Philosophy of Sin.* London: Simpkins and Marshall, 1949.

Chapman, James B. *A Christian: What it Means to be One.* Rev. ed. Kansas City: Beacon Hill Press of Kansas City, 1967.

Chiles, Robert. *Theological Transition in American Methodism: 1790-1925.* New York: Abingdon Press, 1965.

Clark, Gordon H., ed. *Selections from Hellenistic Philosophy.* New York: Appleton-Century-Crofts, 1940.

Clarke, Adam. *Christian Theology.* New York: T. Mason and G. Lane, 1840.

Clarke, William Newton. *An Outline of Christian Theology.* New York: Charles Scribner's Sons, 1922.

Clower, Joseph P., Jr. *The Church in the Thought of Jesus.* Richmond, Va.: John Knox Press, 1959.

Cole, R. Alan. *Exodus.* In *The Tyndale Old Testament Commentary.* Downers Grove, Ill.: InterVarsity Press, 1973.

Copleston, Frederick. *A History of Philosophy.* Vol. 1, pt. 2; vol. 2, pt. 1. Garden City, N.Y.: Doubleday and Co., Image Books, 1962.

Craigie, Peter C. *The Problem of War in the Old Testament.* Grand Rapids: Wm. B. Eerdmans Publishing Co., 1978.

Cullmann, Oscar. *Baptism in the New Testament.* London: SCM Press, 1950.

————. *The Christology of the New Testament.* Philadelphia: Westminster Press, 1959.

Cullmann, Oscar and Leenhardt, F. J. *Essays on the Lord's Supper.* Translated by J. G. Davies. Atlanta: John Knox Press, 1972.

Culpepper, Robert. *Interpreting the Atonement.* Grand Rapids: Wm. B. Eerdmans Publishing Co., 1966.

Cunliffe-Jones, H. *The Authority of the Biblical Revelation.* London: James Clarke and Co., 1945.

Curtis, Olin A. *The Christian Faith.* New York: Eaton and Mains, 1905.

Dalton, William J. *Aspects of New Testament Eschatology.* Perth, Australia: University of Western Australia Press, 1968.

Danielou, Jean. *Origen.* New York: Sheed and Ward, 1955.

Davies, W. D. *Paul and Rabbinic Judaism.* Philadelphia: Fortress Press, 1980.

Davis, John James. *Moses and the Gods of Egypt.* Grand Rapids: Baker Book House, 1971.

Dentan, R. C. *Preface to Old Testament Theology.* New York: Seabury Press, 1963.

Deschner, John. *Wesley's Christology: An Interpretation.* Dallas: Southern Methodist University Press, 1960.

Dillenberger, John. *God Hidden and Revealed.* Philadelphia: Muhlenberg Press, 1953.

———. ed. *Martin Luther.* Garden City, N.Y.: Doubleday and Co., 1961.

Dillenberger, John, and Welch, Claude. *Protestant Christianity.* New York: Charles Scribner's Sons, 1954.

Dillistone, F. W. *Jesus Christ and His Cross.* Philadelphia: Westminster Press, 1953.

Dodd, C. H. *According to the Scripture.* New York: Charles Scribner's Sons, 1963.

———. *The Apostolic Preaching.* New York: Harper and Bros., Publishers, 1962.

———. *The Epistle of Paul to the Romans.* London: Collier, 1959.

———. *Gospel and Law.* New York: Columbia University Press, 1951.

Dowey, Edward A., Jr. *The Knowledge of God in Calvin's Theology.* New York: Columbia University Press, n.d.

Downing, F. Gerald. *Has Christianity a Revelation?* Philadelphia: Westminster Press, 1964.

Dunn, James D. G. *Baptism in the Holy Spirit.* Philadelphia: Westminster Press, 1970.

Dunning, H. Ray. *Fruit of the Spirit.* Kansas City: Beacon Hill Press of Kansas City, 1983.

———. *Search the Scriptures.* New Testament vol. 15, *General Epistles.* Kansas City: Nazarene Publishing House, 1960.

Earle, Ralph. *The Gospel of Mark.* In *The Evangelical Commentary.* Grand Rapids: Zondervan Publishing House, 1957.

Ebeling, Gerhard. *Word and Faith.* Philadelphia: Fortress Press, 1963.

Eichrodt, Walther. *Theology of the Old Testament.* 3 vols. Philadelphia: Westminster Press, 1961.

Ellison, H. L. *The Prophets of Israel.* Grand Rapids: Wm. B. Eerdmans Publishing Co., 1969.

Farley, Edward. *The Transcendence of God.* Philadelphia: Westminster Press, 1960.

Farmer, H. H. *The World and God.* London: Fontana Library, 1963.

Farrar, F. W. *History of Interpretation.* Grand Rapids: Baker Book House, 1961.

Fee, Gordon D., and Stuart, Douglas. *How to Read the Bible for All Its Worth.* Grand Rapids: Zondervan Publishing House, 1982.

Ferré, Nels F. S. *The Christian Understanding of God.* Westport, Conn.: Greenwood Press, 1979.

Feuerbach, Ludwig. *The Essence of Christianity.* Translated by George Eliot. Torchbooks/Cloister Library. New York: Harper and Bros., Publishers, 1957.

Fletcher, John. *The Works of John Fletcher.* 4 vols. Salem, Ohio: Schmul Publishers, 1974.

Flew, R. Newton. *The Idea of Perfection in Christian Theology.* London: Oxford University Press, 1934.

———. *Jesus and His Church.* 2nd ed. London: Epworth Press, 1943.

Fortman, Edmund J. *The Triune God.* Philadelphia: Westminster Press, 1972.

Foster, R. S. *Christian Purity.* New York: Eaton and Mains, 1897.

Frank, Eric. *Philosophical Understanding and Religious Truth.* London: Oxford University Press, 1963.

George, Alfred Raymond. *Communion with God.* London: Epworth Press, 1953.

Gilbert, G. H. *Interpretation of the Bible.* New York: Macmillan Co., 1908.

Gilkey, Langdon B. *How the Church Can Minister to the World Without Losing Itself.* New York: Harper and Row, Publishers, 1964.

————. *Maker of Heaven and Earth.* Garden City, N.Y.: Doubleday and Co., 1959.

Gould, J. Glenn. *The Precious Blood of Christ.* Kansas City: Beacon Hill Press, 1959.

Grave, S. A. *The Scottish Philosophy of Common Sense.* Oxford: Clarendon Press, 1960.

Gray, George Buchanan. *Sacrifice in the Old Testament.* New York: Katav Publishing House, 1971.

Greathouse, William M. *From the Apostles to Wesley: Christian Perfection in Historical Perspective.* Kansas City: Beacon Hill Press of Kansas City, 1979.

————. *Search the Scriptures.* New Testament Vol. 5, *Acts.* Kansas City: Beacon Hill Press, 1954.

Greathouse, William M., and Dunning, H. Ray. *An Introduction to Wesleyan Theology.* Kansas City: Beacon Hill Press of Kansas City, 1982.

Gundry, Robert Horton. *The Use of the Old Testament in St. Matthew's Gospel.* Leiden, Netherlands: E. J. Brill, 1967.

Hall, Douglas John. *Imaging God.* Grand Rapids: Wm. B. Eerdmans Publishing Co., 1986.

Hampshire, Stuart. *Thought and Action.* New York: Viking Press, 1960.

Hanson, R. P. C. *Allegory and Event.* Richmond, Va.: John Knox Press, 1959.

Hasel, Gerhard. *Old Testament Theology: Basic Issues in the Current Debate.* Grand Rapids: Wm. B. Eerdmans Publishing Co., 1972.

Hatt, Harold E. *Encountering Truth.* Nashville: Abingdon Press, 1966.

Heidel, Alexander. *The Babylonian Genesis.* Chicago: University of Chicago Press, 1951.

Hendry, George S. *The Holy Spirit in Christian Theology.* Philadelphia: Westminster Press, 1965.

Hepburn, Ronald. *Christianity and Paradox.* New York: Pegasus Press, 1968.

Heron, Alasdair I. C. *A Century of Protestant Theology.* Philadelphia: Westminster Press, 1980.

————. *The Holy Spirit.* Philadelphia: Westminster Press, 1983.

————. *Table and Tradition.* Philadelphia: Westminster Press, 1983.

Heschel, Abraham J. *The Prophets.* New York: Harper and Row, Publishers, 1962.

Hick, John. *Evil and the God of Love.* New York: Harper and Row, Publishers, 1966.

Hill, David. *Greek Words and Hebrew Meanings.* Cambridge: Cambridge University Press, 1967.

Hills, A. M. *Fundamental Christian Theology.* 2 vols. Pasadena, Calif.: C. J. Kinne, 1931.

Hirsch, Samuel Raphael. *The Pentateuch.* London: L. Honig and Sons, 1967.

Hoekema, Anthony A. *The Bible and the Future.* Grand Rapids: Wm. B. Eerdmans Publishing Co., 1979.

Holmes, Arthur F. *The Contours of a World View.* Grand Rapids: Wm. B. Eerdmans Publishing Co., 1983.

————. *The Idea of a Christian College.* Grand Rapids: Wm. B. Eerdmans Publishing Co., 1975.

Hook, Sidney, ed., *Religious Experience and Truth.* New York: New York University Press, 1961.

Howard, Richard E. *Newness of Life: A Study in the Thought of Paul.* Kansas City: Beacon Hill Press of Kansas City, 1975.

Hull, J. H. E. *The Holy Spirit in the Acts of the Apostles.* Cleveland: World Publishing Co., 1968.

Hunter, A. M. *The Gospel According to Paul.* Philadelphia: Westminster Press, 1966.

Hyatt, J. Philip. *Exodus.* In *The New Century Bible Commentary,* Old Testament edited by Ronald E. Clements. Grand Rapids: Wm. B. Eerdmans Publishing Co., 1971.

————. *The Heritage of Biblical Faith.* St. Louis: Bethany Press, 1964.

Jacob, Edmund. *Theology of the Old Testament.* New York: Harper and Row, Publishers, 1958.

Jeremias, Joachim. *The Eucharistic Words of Jesus.* Philadelphia: Fortress Press, 1966.

————. *New Testament Theology: The Proclamation of Jesus.* Translated by John Bowden. New York: Charles Scribner's Sons, 1971.

Jessop, Harry E. *Foundations of Doctrine.* Chicago: Chicago Evangelistic Institute, 1944.

Johnson, Luke T. *Sharing Possessions.* Philadelphia: Fortress Press, 1981.

Johnson, Robert K. *Evangelicals at an Impasse.* Atlanta: John Knox Press, 1979.

Jones, E. Stanley. *The Way to Power and Poise.* New York: Abingdon-Cokesbury Press, 1949.

Jones, W. T. *Kant and the 19th Century.* New York: Harcourt Brace Jovanovich, 1975.

————. *The 20th Century to Wittgenstein and Sartre.* New York: Harcourt Brace Jovanovich, 1975.

Kant, Immanuel. *Critique of Pure Reason.* Translated by Norman Kemp Smith. New York: St. Martin's Press, 1965.

Kantonen, T. A. *The Theology of Evangelism.* Philadelphia: Muhlenberg Press, 1954.

Kaufman, Gordon. *Systematic Theology.* New York: Charles Scribner's Sons, 1968.

Kelly, J. N. D. *Early Christian Doctrines.* San Francisco: Harper and Row, Publishers, 1978.

———. *The Athanasian Creed.* New York: Harper and Row, Publishers, 1964.

Kendall, R. T. *Calvin and English Calvinism to 1649.* Oxford: Oxford University Press, 1979.

Kerr, Hugh T., ed. *A Compend of Luther's Theology.* Philadelphia: Westminster Press, 1974.

Kierkegaard, Søren. *Philosophical Fragments.* Translated by David F. Swenson. Oxford and New York: Oxford University Press, 1936.

Knight, George A. F. *Servant Theology: A Commentary on the Book of Isaiah 40—55,* in *International Theological Commentary.* Edited by George A. F. Knight and Frederick Carlson Holmgren. Nashville: Abingdon Press, 1965. Rev. ed.: Grand Rapids: Wm. B. Eerdmans Publishing Co., 1984.

———. *Theology as Narration.* Grand Rapids: Wm. B. Eerdmans Publishing Co., 1976.

Knight, John A. *In His Likeness.* Kansas City: Beacon Hill Press of Kansas City, 1976.

Kohler, Ludwig. *Old Testament Theology.* Translated by A. S. Todd. Philadelphia: Westminster Press, 1953.

Kung, Hans. *The Church.* New York: Sheed and Ward, 1977.

Ladd, G. Eldon. *The Blessed Hope.* Grand Rapids: Wm. B. Eerdmans Publishing Co., 1956.

———. *Crucial Questions About the Kingdom of God.* Grand Rapids: Wm. B. Eerdmans Publishing Co., 1952.

———. *A Theology of the New Testament.* Grand Rapids: Wm. B. Eerdmans Publishing Co., 1974.

Lampe, G. W. H. *The Seal of the Spirit.* London: SCM Press, 1951.

Lampe, G. W. H., and Woollcombe, K. S. *Essays on Typology.* Naperville, Ill.: Alec R. Allenson, 1957.

LaRondelle, Hans K. *The Israel of God in Prophecy.* Berrien Springs, Mich.: Andrews University Press, 1983.

Larue, Gerald A. *Old Testament Life and Literature.* Boston: Allyn and Bacon, 1968.

Lawson, John. *Introduction to Christian Doctrine.* Wilmore, Ky.: Francis Asbury Publishing Co., 1980.

Leff, Gordon. *Medieval Thought.* Chicago: Quadrangle Books, 1959.

Lewis, C. S. *Miracles.* New York: Macmillan Co., 1947.

Lindars, Barnabas. *The Gospel of John.* In *The New Century Bible Commentary.* New Testament edited by Matthew Black. Grand Rapids: Wm. B. Eerdmans Publishing Co., 1981.

———. *New Testament Apologetics.* London: SCM Press, 1961.

Lindsell, Harold. *The Battle for the Bible.* Grand Rapids: Zondervan Publishing House, 1976.

Lindsey, Hal. *The Late Great Planet Earth.* Grand Rapids: Zondervan Publishing House, 1973.

Lindström, Harald. *Wesley and Sanctification: A Study in the Doctrine of . Salvation.* Wilmore, Ky.: Francis Asbury Publishing Co., n.d.

Lonergan, Bernard. *The Way to Nicea.* Translated by Conn O'Donovan. Philadelphia: Westminster Press, 1976.

Longenecker, Richard. *The Christology of Early Jewish Christianity.* Naperville, Ill.: Alec R. Allenson, 1970.

Lull, David John. *The Spirit in Galatia.* Chico, Calif.: Scholar's Press, 1980.

McDonald, H. D. *Theories of Revelation: An Historical Study, 1700-1960.* Grand Rapids: Baker Book House, 1979.

McGiffert, A. C., Jr. *The God of the Early Christians.* New York: Charles Scribner's Sons, 1924.

———. *History of Christian Thought.* 2 vols. New York: Charles Scribner's Sons, 1950.

———. *Protestant Thought Before Kant.* London: Duckworth and Co., 1919.

———. *The Rise of Modern Religious Ideas.* New York: Macmillan Co., 1915.

MacGregor, Geddes. *He Who Lets Us Be.* New York: Seabury Press, 1975.

McIntyre, John. *The Christian Doctrine of History.* Grand Rapids: Wm. B. Eerdmans Publishing Co., 1957.

McKinley, O. Glenn. *Where Two Creeds Meet.* Kansas City: Beacon Hill Press, 1959.

Mackintosh, Hugh Ross. *The Doctrine of the Person of Christ.* New York: Charles Scribner's Sons, 1915.

Macmurray, John. *Persons in Relation.* London: Faber and Faber, 1961.

———. *The Self as Agent.* London: Faber and Faber, 1966.

MacPherson, Dave. *The Great Rapture Hoax.* Fletcher, N.C.: New Puritan Library, 1983.

Macquarrie, John. *God and Secularity.* Vol. 3 of *New Directions in Theology Today.* Philadelphia: Westminster Press, 1967.

———. *Principles of Christian Theology.* New York: Charles Scribner's Sons, 1966.

Manson, T. W. *The Servant-Messiah.* Grand Rapids: Baker Book House, 1977.

Marsden, George M. *Fundamentalism and American Culture.* New York: Oxford University Press, 1980.

Marshall, I. Howard. *Biblical Inspiration.* Grand Rapids: Wm. B. Eerdmans Publishing Co., 1982.

Martens, Elmer. *God's Design.* Grand Rapids: Baker Book House, 1981.

Martin, Ralph P. *Reconciliation.* Atlanta: John Knox Press, 1981.

———. *Worship in the Early Church.* Grand Rapids: Wm. B. Eerdmans Publishing Co., 1974.

Micklem, Nathaniel. *The Doctrine of Our Redemption.* New York: Abingdon-Cokesbury Press, 1953.

Micks, Marianne H. *Introduction to Theology.* New York: Seabury Press, 1967.

Miley, John. *Systematic Theology.* New York: Eaton and Mains, 1894.

Minear, Paul. *Images of the Church in the New Testament.* Philadelphia: Westminster Press, 1960.

————, ed. *The Nature of the Unity We Seek.* St. Louis: Bethany Press, 1958.

Moltmann, Jurgen. *The Church in the Power of the Spirit.* Translated by Margaret Kohl. New York: Harper and Row, Publishers, 1977.

Moody, Dale. *Spirit of the Living God.* Philadelphia: Westminster Press, 1968.

————. *The Word of Truth: A Summary of Christian Doctrine Based on Biblical Revelation.* Grand Rapids: Wm. B. Eerdmans Publishing Co., 1981.

Morgan, G. Campbell. *The Practice of Prayer.* Westwood, N.J.: Fleming H. Revell Co., 1960.

Morris, Leon. *Apocalyptic.* Grand Rapids: Wm. B. Eerdmans Publishing Co., 1972.

————. *The Apostolic Preaching of the Cross.* Grand Rapids: Wm. B. Eerdmans Publishing Co., 1972.

Moule, C. F. D. *The Origin of Christology.* Cambridge: Cambridge University Press, 1977.

Mowinckel, Sigmund. *He That Cometh.* New York: Abingdon Press, n.d.

Murray, George L. *Millennial Studies.* Grand Rapids: Baker Book House, 1948.

Narramore, Bruce. *You're Someone Special.* Grand Rapids: Zondervan Publishing House, 1978.

Neill, Stephen Charles. *The Church and Christian Union.* New York: Oxford University Press, 1968.

Nelson, J. Robert. *The Realm of Redemption.* London: Epworth Press, 1957.

Neve, J. L. *History of Christian Thought.* 2 vols. Philadelphia: Muhlenberg Press, 1946.

Niebuhr, H. Richard. *The Meaning of Revelation.* New York: Macmillan Co., 1962.

Niebuhr, Reinhold. *The Nature and Destiny of Man.* 2 vols. London: Nisbet and Co., 1946.

Niesel, Wilhelm. *The Theology of Calvin.* Translated by Harold Knight. Philadelphia: Westminster Press, 1956.

Norris, R. A., Jr. *God and World in Early Christian Theology.* New York: Seabury Press, 1965.

O'Donovan, Oliver. *The Problem of Self-love in St. Augustine.* New Haven, Conn.: Yale University Press, 1980.

Osborn, E. F. *Word and History.* Melbourne, Australia: Jonker Printing Pty., 1971.

Outka, Gene. *Agape: An Ethical Analysis.* New Haven, Conn.: Yale University Press, 1972.

Outler, Albert C., trans. "Creed of Chalcedon." In *Creeds of the Churches,* edited by John H. Leith. Rev. ed. Atlanta: John Knox Press, 1977.

————, ed. *John Wesley.* New York: Oxford University Press, 1980.

Oxtoby, Gurdon C. *Prediction and Fulfillment in the Bible.* Philadelphia: Westminster Press, 1966.

Pannenberg, Wolfhart. *Jesus—God and Man.* Translated by Lewis L. Wilkins and Duane A. Priebe. Philadelphia: Westminster Press, 1977.

Pelikan, Jaroslav. *The Emergence of the Catholic Tradition.* Chicago: University of Chicago Press, 1973.

Peters, John L. *Christian Perfection and American Methodism.* New York: Abingdon Press, 1956.

Pittenger, Norman. *The Divine Triunity.* Philadelphia: United Church Press, 1977.

Polman, A. D. R. *The Word of God According to St. Augustine.* Grand Rapids: Wm. B. Eerdmans Publishing Co., 1961.

Polyani, Michael. *Personal Knowledge.* Chicago: University of Chicago Press, 1962.

Pope, William Burt. *A Compendium of Christian Theology.* 3 vols. London: Wesleyan Conference Office, 1880.

Purkiser, W. T. *Exploring Christian Holiness.* Vol. 1, *The Biblical Foundations.* Kansas City: Beacon Hill Press of Kansas City, 1983.

————, ed. *Exploring Our Christian Faith.* Rev. ed. Kansas City: Beacon Hill Press of Kansas City, 1978.

————, ed. *Exploring the Old Testament.* Kansas City: Beacon Hill Press, 1955.

Purkiser, W. T.; Taylor, Richard S.; and Taylor, Willard H. *God, Man, and Salvation.* Kansas City: Beacon Hill Press of Kansas City, 1977.

Rahner, Karl. *Theological Investigations.* Vols. 2 and 4. Baltimore: Helicon Press, 1966.

Rall, H. F. *The Meaning of God.* Nashville: Abingdon-Cokesbury Press, 1925.

Ralston, Thomas N. *Elements of Divinity.* New York: Abingdon-Cokesbury Press, 1924.

Ramsdell, Edward T. *The Christian Perspective.* New York: Abingdon-Cokesbury Press, 1950.

Ramsey, A. M. *The Glory of God and the Transfiguration of Christ.* London: Longmans, Green, and Co., 1949.

————. *The Resurrection of Christ.* Philadelphia: Westminster Press, 1946.

Ramsey, Paul. *Basic Christian Ethics.* New York: Charles Scribner's Sons, 1950.

Rattenbury, J. Ernest. *The Evangelical Doctrines of Charles Wesley's Hymns.* London: Epworth Press, 1941.

Read, David H. C. *The Christian Faith.* Nashville: Abingdon Press, 1956.

Richardson, Alan. *The Bible in the Age of Science.* Philadelphia: Westminster Press, 1961.

————. *Christian Apologetics.* New York: Harper and Bros., Publishers, 1944.

————. *Creeds in the Making.* London: Macmillan and Co., 1969.

————. *An Introduction to the Theology of the New Testament.* New York: Harper and Bros., Publishers, 1958.

Richardson, Cyril. *The Doctrine of the Trinity.* New York: Abingdon Press, 1958.

Ridderbos, Herman N. *Paul: An Outline of His Theology.* Translated by John Richard de Witt. Grand Rapids: Wm. B. Eerdmans Publishing Co., 1975.

Robinson, William. *The Devil and God.* Nashville: Abingdon-Cokesbury Press, 1945.

Rogers, Jack. *Confessions of a Conservative Evangelical.* Philadelphia: Westminster Press, 1974.

———, ed. *Biblical Authority.* Waco, Tex.: Word Books, Publisher, 1977.

Rogers, Jack, and McKim, Donald K. *The Authority and Interpretation of the Bible.* San Francisco: Harper and Row, Publishers, 1979.

Rowe, Kenneth E., ed. *The Place of Wesley in the Christian Tradition.* Metuchen, N.J.: Scarecrow Press, 1976.

Rowley, H. H. *The Meaning of Sacrifice in the Old Testament.* John Rylands Library Bulletin, vol. 33, no. 1 (September 1950).

Rusch, William G., ed. and trans. *The Trinitarian Controversy.* Philadelphia: Fortress Press, 1980.

Russell, Bertrand. *A History of Western Philosophy.* New York: Simon and Schuster, a Clarion Book, 1967.

Russell, D. S. *Between the Testaments.* Philadelphia: Muhlenberg Press, 1960.

Ryrie, Charles C. *Dispensationalism Today.* Chicago: Moody Press, 1965.

Sandeen, Ernest R. *The Roots of Fundamentalism.* Chicago: University of Chicago Press, 1970.

Schleiermacher, Friedrich. *The Christian Faith.* Edinburgh: T. and T. Clark, 1960.

———. *On Religion: Speeches to Its Cultured Despisers.* Translated by John Oman. New York: Harper and Row, Publishers, 1958.

Schnackenburg, Rudolf. *The Moral Teaching of the New Testament.* New York: Seabury Press, 1965.

Schuller, Robert H. *Self-esteem.* Waco, Tex.: Word Publishing Co., 1982.

Scott, R. B. Y. *Proverbs, Ecclesiastes.* Vol. 18 in *The Anchor Bible,* edited by William Foxwell Albright and David Noel Freedman. Garden City, N.Y.: Doubleday and Co., 1965.

Scott, Walter. *Exposition of the Revelation of Jesus Christ.* London: Pickering and Inglis, n.d.

Seeburg, Reinhold. *Textbook of the History of Doctrines.* Translated by Charles E. Hay. 2 vols. in 1. Grand Rapids: Baker Book House, 1964.

Sellers, R. V. *The Council of Chalcedon.* London: SPCK, 1961.

———. *Two Ancient Christologies.* London: SPCK, 1954.

Shedd, Russell Phillip. *Man in Community.* Grand Rapids: Wm. B. Eerdmans Publishing Co., 1964.

Smart, James D. *The Interpretation of Scripture.* Philadelphia: Westminster Press, 1961.

Smith, C. Ryder. *The Bible Doctrine of Man.* London: Epworth Press, 1951.

———. *The Bible Doctrine of Sin.* London: Epworth Press, 1953.

Smith, Huston. *The Religions of Man.* New York: Harper and Row, Publishers, 1965.

Smith, John E. *The Analogy of Experience.* New York: Harper and Row, Publishers, 1973.

Smith, Timothy L. *Called Unto Holiness.* Vol. 1, *The Story of the Nazarenes: The Formative Years.* Kansas City: Nazarene Publishing House, 1962.

Snaith, Norman H. *The Distinctive Ideas of the Old Testament.* London: Epworth Press, 1944.

Snyder, Howard. *The Community of the King.* Downers Grove, Ill.: InterVarsity Press, 1977.

————. *Liberating the Church.* Downers Grove, Ill.: InterVarsity Press, 1983.

————. *The Problem of Wineskins.* Downers Grove, Ill.: InterVarsity Press, 1975.

————. *The Radical Wesley and Patterns for Church Renewal.* Downers Grove, Ill.: InterVarsity Press, 1980.

Sowers, Sydney G. *The Hermeneutics of Philo and Hebrews.* Zurich: Eva-Verlag, 1965.

Spurrier, William A. *Guide to the Christian Faith.* New York: Charles Scribner's Sons, 1952.

Starkey, Lycurgus M., Jr. *The Work of the Holy Spirit.* Nashville: Abingdon Press, 1962.

Steele, Daniel. *The Gospel of the Comforter.* Apollo, Pa.: West Publishing Co., n.d.

————. *Steele's Answers.* Chicago: Christian Witness Co., 1912.

Stendahl, Krister. *The School of St. Matthew.* Philadelphia: Fortress Press, 1968.

Stewart, James S. *The Life and Teaching of Jesus Christ.* New York: Abingdon Press, n.d.

————. *A Man in Christ.* New York: Harper and Row, Publishers, n.d.

Swete, Henry Barclay. *The Holy Spirit in the New Testament.* Grand Rapids: Baker Book House, 1964.

Taylor, A. E. *Plato: The Man and His Work.* Cleveland and New York: World Publishing Co., 1964.

Taylor, Richard S. *Biblical Authority and Christian Faith.* Kansas City: Beacon Hill Press of Kansas City, 1980.

————. *Exploring Christian Holiness.* Vol. 3, *The Theological Formulation.* Kansas City: Beacon Hill Press of Kansas City, 1985.

————. *A Right Conception of Sin.* Kansas City: Nazarene Publishing House, 1939.

————, ed. *Leading Wesleyan Thinkers.* Vol. 3 of *Great Holiness Classics.* Edited by A. F. Harper. 6 vols. Kansas City: Beacon Hill Press of Kansas City, 1985.

Taylor, Vincent. *Atonement in New Testament Teaching.* London: Epworth Press, 1963.

————. *Forgiveness and Reconciliation.* New York: Macmillan Co., 1960.

————. *Jesus and His Sacrifice.* London: Macmillan and Co., 1937.

Taylor, Willard. "Ephesians." In *Beacon Bible Commentary,* vol. 9. Edited by A. F. Harper. 10 vols. Kansas City: Beacon Hill Press, 1965.

Temple, William. *Nature, Man, and God.* London: Macmillan and Co., 1935.

Thielicke, Helmut. *The Evangelical Faith.* Vol. 1. Grand Rapids: Wm. B. Eerdmans Publishing Co., 1974.

Thiselton, Anthony C. *The Two Horizons.* Grand Rapids: Wm. B. Eerdmans Publishing Co., 1980.

Thomas, George F. *Christian Ethics and Moral Philosophy.* New York: Charles Scribner's Sons, 1955.

Tillapaugh, Frank R. *The Church Unleashed.* Ventura, Calif.: Regal Books, 1982.

Tillich, Paul. *Biblical Religion and the Search for Ultimate Reality.* Chicago: University of Chicago Press, 1963.

————. *Dynamics of Faith.* New York: Harper and Row, Publishers, 1957.

————. *Systematic Theology.* 3 vols. in 1. Chicago: University of Chicago Press, 1967.

————. *Theology of Culture.* London: Oxford University Press, 1968.

Torrance, T. F. *Calvin's Doctrine of Man.* London: Lutterworth Press, 1952.

————. *Reality and Evangelical Theology.* Philadelphia: Westminster Press, 1982.

Travis, Stephen H. *Christian Hope and the Future.* Downers Grove, Ill.: InterVarsity Press, 1980.

Trueblood, D. Elton. *The Incendiary Fellowship.* New York: Harper and Row, Publishers, 1967.

————. *Philosophy of Religion.* New York: Harper and Bros., Publishers, 1957.

Vawter, Bruce. *Biblical Inspiration.* Philadelphia: Westminster Press, 1972.

von Balthasar, Hans Urs. *A Theological Anthropology.* New York: Sheed and Ward, 1967.

von Rad, Gerhard. *Genesis.* Philadelphia: Westminster Press, 1961.

Vriezen, Th. C. *An Outline of Old Testament Theology.* Wageningen, Holland: H. Veenman and Zonen, 1958.

Wainwright, Geoffrey. *Eucharist and Eschatology.* New York: Oxford University Press, 1981.

Watkin-Jones, Howard. *The Holy Spirit from Arminius to Wesley.* London: Epworth Press, 1929.

Watson, Philip S. *The Concept of Grace.* Philadelphia: Muhlenberg Press, 1959.

Watson, Richard. *Theological Institutes.* New York: Lane and Tippett, 1848.

Webber, Robert E. *The Secular Saint.* Grand Rapids: Zondervan Publishing House, 1974.

Weber, Otto. *Foundations of Dogmatics.* Translated by Darrell L. Gruder. Vol. 2. Grand Rapids: Wm. B. Eerdmans Publishing Co., 1983.

Wesley, John. *Explanatory Notes upon the New Testament.* London: Epworth Press, 1954.

————. *The Journal of John Wesley, A.M.* Edited by Nehemiah Curnock. 8 vols. London: Epworth Press, 1949.

————. *Letters of the Reverend John Wesley.* Edited by John Telford. 8 vols. London: Epworth Press, 1931.

————. *A Plain Account of Christian Perfection.* Kansas City: Beacon Hill Press of Kansas City, 1966.

————. *Standard Sermons.* Edited by E. H. Sugden. 2 vols. London: Epworth Press, 1961.

————. *Works of John Wesley.* 3rd ed. 14 vols. London: Wesleyan Methodist Book Room, 1872. Reprint, Kansas City: Beacon Hill Press of Kansas City, 1978.

Westcott, B. F. *The Gospel According to John.* Grand Rapids: Wm. B. Eerdmans Publishing Co., 1967.

Westermann, Claus. *Blessing in the Bible and the Church.* Philadelphia: Fortress Press, 1978.

Whale, J. S. *Christian Doctrine.* London: Cambridge University Press, 1960.

Wheatley, Richard. *The Life and Letters of Mrs. Phoebe Palmer.* New York: Palmer and Hughes, 1884.

White, Stephen S. *Essential Christian Beliefs.* Kansas City: Beacon Hill Press, n.d.

Wiles, Maurice F. *What Is Theology?* New York: Oxford University Press, 1976.

Wiley, H. Orton. *Christian Theology.* 3 vols. Kansas City: Beacon Hill Press, 1940-43.

————. *God Has the Answer.* Kansas City: Beacon Hill Press, 1956.

Wiley, H. Orton, and Culbertson, Paul T. *Introduction to Christian Theology.* Kansas City: Beacon Hill Press, 1946.

Williams, Colin W. *The Church.* Vol. 4 in *New Directions in Theology Today.* Philadelphia: Westminster Press, 1968.

————. *John Wesley's Theology Today.* New York: Abingdon Press, 1960.

Wilson, John Cook. *Statement and Inference.* Edited by A. S. L. Farquharson. 2 vols. Oxford: Clarendon Press, 1969.

Windelband, Wilhelm. *A History of Philosophy.* 2 vols. Torchbook ed. New York: Harper and Bros., Publishers, 1958.

Winward, Stephen. *A Guide to the Prophets.* Atlanta: John Knox Press, 1976.

Wolfson, H. A. *The Philosophy of the Church Fathers.* Vol. 1. Cambridge: Harvard University Press, 1964.

Wood, J. A. *Perfect Love.* Chicago: Christian Witness Co., 1880.

Wood, Laurence W. *Pentecostal Grace.* Wilmore, Ky.: Francis Asbury Publishing Co., 1980.

Woolston, Thomas. *The Old Apology for the Truth of the Christian Religion, Against the Jew and Gentiles Revived.* London: John Torbuck, 1732.

Workman, H. B. *A New History of Methodism.* London: Hodder and Stoughton, 1909.

Wright, G. Ernest. *The Old Testament Against Its Environment.* Chicago: Henry Regnery Co., 1950.

Wright, G. Ernest, and Fuller, Reginald H. *The Book of the Acts of God.* Anchor Books. Garden City, N.Y.: Doubleday and Co., 1960.

Wynkoop, Mildred Bangs. *The Foundations of Wesleyan-Arminian Theology.* Kansas City: Beacon Hill Press of Kansas City, 1967.

————. *A Theology of Love: The Dynamic of Wesleyanism.* Kansas City: Beacon Hill Press of Kansas City, 1972.

Yates, A. S. *The Doctrine of Assurance.* London: Epworth Press, 1952.

Yates, J. E. *The Spirit and the Kingdom.* London: Epworth Press, 1963.

Yoder, Perry B. *Toward Understanding the Bible.* Newton, Kans.: Faith and Life Press, 1978.

Young, Francis M. *Sacrifice and the Death of Christ.* Philadelphia: Westminster Press, 1975.

Young, Norman. *Creator, Creation, and Faith.* Philadelphia: Westminster Press, 1976.

Unpublished Material

Brightman, R. S. "Gregory of Nyssa and John Wesley in Theological Dialogue on the Christian Life." Ph.D. diss., Boston University, 1969.

Dunning, H. Ray. "Nazarene Ethics as Seen in a Historical, Theological, and Sociological Context." Ph.D. diss., Vanderbilt University, 1969.

Knight, John Allan. "The Theology of John Fletcher." Ph.D. diss., Vanderbilt University, 1966.

Renshaw, John Rutherford. "The Atonement in the Theology of John and Charles Wesley." Ph.D. diss., Boston University, 1965.

Rogers, Charles Allen. "The Concept of Prevenient Grace in the Theology of John Wesley." Ph.D. diss., Duke University, 1967.

Subject Index

Abraham
and justification, 347
Accommodation (Calvin), 112, 135
Actual sin, 283, 296-301
Adequacy, 98 n
Adoption, 341-42, 450
Adoptionism (see Dynamic
    Monarchianism)
Agapē, 195
contrasted with eros, 294
Age to come, 174
Age of Immanence, 114
Aldersgate, 443-44
Alexandrian School, 614
Christology, 325
Allegorical exegesis, 71, 601
Allegory, 612
definition of, 604-5
Altar phraseology, 468
Amillennialism, 584
Analogia entis, 120-21
Analogia fides, 121
Analogy of faith, 608
Anglican view of the Church, 525
Anhypostasia, 328
Anthropopathism, 188
Antinomy, 117
Antiochian School, 613
Christology, 325
Anxiety, 245
Apocalyptic dualism, 387
Apologists
on the Logos, 215-17
Apostles' Creed, 190, 200, 406, 507
Apostolic Fathers, 49 n, 600, 601,
    602
Apostolic tradition, 78
Apotheosis, 458
Arianism, 215, 217-19
and Apollinarianism, 325
Aristotelian anthropology, 325
Asah, 240
Aseity, 200-201
Assurance (see witness of the
    Spirit)
Astrology, 243

Athanasian Creed, 209, 224-33
Atonement
benefits of, 333, 338-52
corporate nature of, 352
Day of, 359-60
governmental theory, 337
limited, 390
moral influence theory, 337-38
penal theory, 336-37
ransom theory, 335-36
satisfaction theories, 336-37
Attributes of God
biblical, 204-7
classification of, 198-207
Authority
cognitive, 64-65
existential, 59-60
nature of, 56, 58-59
Awakening, 431-36, 431 n
Babylonian creation epic, 237
Baptism, 544-50
as identification with Christ, 545
infant, 298, 547-50
as initiation into the Church,
    545-46
of John as antecedent to
    Christian baptism, 544-45
as reception of the Spirit, 546
Bara, 240
Barnabas, Epistle of, 578, 602-3
Bible
authority, 58-65
and history, 57
inerrancy, 60-62
as revelation, 176
theological interpretation, 74
as theological norm, 45
Biblical language
as historically conditioned, 71
Brahman, 129
British empiricism, 88, 90
Call, 435
Calvinism
and God's will, 196
Camp meeting, 537

Canon
  NT, 600
Canonicity, 78 n
Cappadocian fathers
  on the Trinity, 221-23
Carnal-mindedness (carnality),
  483 n, 484
Casuistry, 500, 500 n
Catholicity, 532
Ceremonial holiness, 466 n, 469
Chalcedon, Creed of, 329
Chaos
  and evil, 253-54
  as sea, 253-54
Charismatic leadership, 401
Chesed (hesed), 206-7
Chiliasm, 578
Christian ethics, 498-504
Christian Science, 246
Christological problem, 308, 322-23
Christology, 322-31
  in the NT, 307-22
  paradox, 330
  as soteriology, 302-3
  as theological norm, 50
Christotokos, 326
Christus regnum Scriptura, 609
Christus Victor, 386-88
Church
  in Acts, 518-19
  Anglican view of, 525
  as Body of Christ, 514-15
  catholicity of, 532
  conscience of, 533
  constitution of, 521
  defined by the gospel, 522
  empirical and eschatological,
    517-18
  as eschatological community, 518
  essence and form, 535
  as event, 515
  as extension of the Incarnation,
    514-15
  as firstfruits, 518
  as functional, 508-9
  holiness of, 520, 532
  and the kingdom of God, 516-18
  marks of, 529-35
  mission of, 517
  as a mixed body, 521-22
  as New Israel, 511-14
  NT images, 509-16
  and the OT, 519
  organization as pragmatic, 536

(Church, continued)
  Protestant view of, 524
  as sociocultural reality, 535-37
  and the Spirit, 522
  unity of, 530-32
  visible and invisible, 518, 520
Church of England
  Thirty-nine Articles, 334
Church of the Nazarene
  on eschatology, 569
Circumincession, 232
Cleansing, 470 n
Common grace, 296
Communicable attributes, 204
Communication of properties, 324
  applied to sacraments, 553
Confirmation, 461
Conscience, 167 n, 432-36
  of the Church, 533
Constantinople, Council (Creed) of,
  212, 529
Consubstantiation, 553
Coram Deo, 192
Corinthian church, 427
Corporate personality, 300, 374
Cosmological argument, 246-47
Covenant
  and contract, 358
  meaning of, 356-57
Creation
  creatio ex nihilo, 240-47
  as eschatological, 266-69
  ethics, 269-71
  and evil, 250-55
  existential meaning, 248
  goodness of, 238-40
  as historical, 237
  and Incarnation, 245-46
  narratives
    contrasted with Babylonian
      epic, 237
    monotheistic, 237
    theological meaning, 237
  not mythical, 236
  and purpose, 246-47
  and salvation, 245
  and the Trinity, 234 n
Credo ut intelligam, 84-85
Creed
  as biblical interpretation, 80-81
Cross
  as conflict with Satan, 386
  and evil, 254-55
Culture, 283

David
  prefigures Christ's Kingship, 386
Davidic theology, 512 n
Day of the Lord, 513
Dead Sea Scrolls, 314, 404, 408,
  624-25
Death of God theology, 184
Deism, 113
Deontological ethics, 501
Deus velatus, 111-12
Development
  elements in, 472
Didache, 175
Dispensationalism, 389, 389 n,
  585-89
  on Israel and the Church, 512
Docetism, 323
Double predestination, 390-91
Doxa, 101
Dualism, 240
  in Hellenistic philosophy, 107
Dynamic Monarchianism, 215
Eastern Christianity
  on sanctification, 306-7
Eastern religions, 245
Ebionite heresy, 323
  on biblical interpretation, 601-2
Ecclesiolae in ecclesia, 527 n
Economic Trinity, 228-33
Ekklesia, 515-16
Election, 435-36, 507
Enlightenment, 85
Entire sanctification, 455-71
  as love, 452
  possibility of, 456
  as unmixed love, 490
Ephesus, Council of, 328
Epistemological subjectivity, 131
Eros, 166, 166 n
Eschatology
  consistent, 577
  realistic, 574-75
  realized, 389, 577
  and theological method, 13
Essence, 140 n
Eternal Generation of the Son, 217
Eternity, 201
Eucharist (see Lord's Supper)
Eutychianism, 328
Evil
  definition of, 250
  and finitude, 252
  natural and moral, 252

(Evil, continued)
  nature of, 243
  as pedagogical, 251
  problem of, 199
Existential
  meaning of, 30 n
Existential truth, 126 n
Existentialism
  atheistic, 248
Exodus, the
  and Jesus' death, 353-54
  paradigm of redemption, 343
Ex opere operato, 540, 542
Experience
  communal, 91-92
  as confirming source, 90-93
  meaning of, 88-89
  as a medium, 89-90
  nature of, 397-400
  source of Christian doctrine, 89
  as subjective and objective, 398
Extramarital sex
  as sin, 293-94
Faith, 439-41
  for entire sanctification, 467
  as existential, 52 n
  formed by Christ (Luther), 465
  formed by love (Aquinas), 465
  and promise, 440
  and revelation, 134
  working by love (Wesley), 465
Fall, the, 283-86, 300
  and revelation, 132-33
Fallenness
  and reason, 132-39
  and revelation, 132-39
Feeding of 5,000, 595
Fellowship with God, 342
Filioque, 233, 413-14
Final salvation and resurrection,
  477
Flesh (sarx), 483
Flood, the, 253
Form criticism, 591
Fulfillment, 571
Fundamentalism
  defined, 27 n
Galatian church, 427-28
Gehenna, 393
General revelation
  nature of, 166
  and non-Christian religions, 166
  and prevenient grace, 161-70
  and salvation, 168

Glory of God, 101
  as eschatological, 105
  as image, 276
Glossolalia, 427 n
Gnosticism, 40, 79-80, 126, 241,
    289
God
  arguments for His existence, 84
  attributes of, 192-207
  central importance in theology,
    183-84
  as Creator, 234-71
  Fatherhood of, 190-91
  fellowship with, 342
  freedom of, 246
  holiness of, 187-89
  image of, 150-57
  jealousy of, 188
  kingdom of (see kingdom of
    God)
  as living, 186-87
  as love, 190
  love, nature, and will, 365
  natural and moral attributes, 198
  nature of in 1 John, 342
  passivity, 195
  as personal, 203
  prayer, implication for, 264
  as social reality, 281
  sovereignty and free will, 257-58
  as unfathomable, 115 n
  unity of, 189
  as wholeness, 486
  wrath of, 191-92, 291, 371-72,
    391-92
Gog and Magog, 584
Gospel, 171
  and law, 435, 436-37
Governmental theory of
    Atonement, 337
Grace
  growth in, 471-76
  meaning of, 456, 539
  means of, 540
  Pelagian view, 299-300
Grammatico-historical
    interpretation, 71
Heilsgeschichte, 34, 174
Hell, 393
Hellenistic philosophy, 106-11
Heresies, 184
Hermeneutics
  and eschatology, 570-71
  typological, 606

Hinduism, 129
History
  cyclical, 249
  dual meaning, 57
  knowledge of, 57
  as revelatory, 56-57, 247
Holiness
  and attribution, 192-93
  as Christlikeness, 464-65
  of God and Atonement, 361
  and idolatry, 194
  meaning of, 187, 193
  religious significance, 193
  as sincerity, 493
Holy Spirit
  and convincing, 433-35
  democratization of, 403, 426-27
  as eschatological gift, 476-77
  eschatological in OT, 403
  indwells all believers, 426
  and Jesus, 405-18
  and Messianic King, 404
  and ministry of Jesus, 409-18
  Pauline teaching, 425-28
  and sanctification, 428
  Spirit of Yahweh, 400
  and Suffering Servant, 404
  witness of, 441-48
Homoousia, 219
Hypostasis, 213, 221-22
I-Thou and I-it, 127-29
Identification and representation,
    Atonement motifs, 373
Idolatry, 243-44
Illusionistic critiques of religion,
    135
Image of God (imago Dei), 150-57,
    490
  and the body, 281-83
  goal of sanctification, 478
  as legal righteousness, 278
  as love, 465
  moral and natural, 152
  and prevenient grace, 157-61
  as relation, 155
  as relic, 297
Immanence, 101
  in relation to revelation, 105-6
Immutability, 202
Incarnation, 376
  and revelation, 304-6
  theological significance, 303-7
Incarnational principle, 129

Infant baptism, 298, 547-50
  and prevenient grace, 550
Initial sanctification, 351, 451,
    452-55
Inspiration
  dynamical theory, 69-70
  extent, 71
  the fact, 65-67
  and historicity, 70-71
  the meaning, 65
  mode of, 67-71
Intellectualism and voluntarism,
    196
Israel and the Kingdom, 517
Jamnia, Council of, 606
Jesus Christ
  baptism of, 376-77, 407-8
  baptism and temptation, 595
  Catholicity, 532
  as Creator, 234, 234 n, 239-40,
    247
  death as identification, 377-78
  deity of, 212
  as goal of maturity, 473
  and the gospel, 172
  kingly work, 385-90
  as locus of revelation, 130
  as Lord, 318-20
  as Messiah, 309-12
  on possessions, 494-95
  as Priest, 381-83
  priestly work, 371-85
  as Prophet, Priest, and King, 366
  prophetic work, 367-71
  resurrection of, 434, 476
  as Sacrifice, 381-83
  as Second Adam, 378, 385-86
  self-understanding, 309
  as Son of Man, 316-18
  and the Spirit, 405-18
    in Paul's teaching, 424-28
  temptation of, 326, 377, 409
  and unity of the Church, 530-32
  work of
    for us, meaning, 378-79
Johannine Pentecost, 417-18
John the Baptist, 407, 436
Judgment, 392
Justice
  and righteousness, 205
Justification, 342, 455
  Catholic view, 345
  defined, 441
  as eschatological, 347-48
  Protestant view, 345

(Justification, continued)
  relation to sanctification, 47 n
  Wesleyan view, 347
Kabod, 101-2
Kerygma, 174-75, 590
Kingdom of God, 388-90
  dispensational view, 585
  as eschatological category, 577
  meaning of, 388, 516-17
Knowledge
  biblical view, 123-26
  existential, 125-32
  of God, 123
  and revelation, 123-32
  scientific, 126-32
Knowledge of God, 123
  and knowledge of other minds,
    164
Language-games, 469
Lapsi, 520
Law
  and gospel, 435, 436-37
  as gospel, 370
  as incarnational, 368
  third use of, 369, 528
Leo's Tome, 329
Linguistic idolatry, 122
Living faith
  as a mark of the Church, 525
Logos, 110-11, 216
  in Philo, 108
  two-stage theory, 110 n
Lord's Supper, 543-44, 550-65
  as Atonement applied, 558-61
  as Atonement remembered,
    557-58
  as confirming ordinance, 560
  as converting ordinance, 559
  and eschatology, 561 n
  as means of grace, 550 n
  as means to holiness, 560, 564
  as pledge of glory to come,
    561-62
  as sacrifice, 562-65
  as spiritual presence, 554
Lost, the
  dual meaning, 392 n
Love
  of God, 192-201
  as holy, 194
  and passivity, 195
  and sovereignty, 199-204
  and will, 196-97
Macarius the Egyptian, 423 n, 461

Man, doctrine of (see theological anthropology)
Manual, Church of the Nazarene
on baptism, 550 n
on the Church, 536
on eternal destiny, 391
on inspiration of Scripture, 72
on the minister, 535
on prayer and faith, 265
ritual on the Lord's Supper, 560
on the Trinity, 211, 228
Marcion, 601-2
Marks of the Church, 529-35
produced by the gospel, 530
Protestant, 524-25
Marriage
monogamous, 238, 269
Memorialist theory, 555
Mercy
as attribute of God, 206-7
Messianic age
Messianic hope, 512 n
Messianic secret, 312
Metaphysical objectivity, 131
Millennium, millenarianism, 577-84
as mixed society, 584
modern views, 582-83
problem of the wicked, 583-84
Miracle, 259-62
definition of, 259
and natural law, 259, 260
and revelation, 261
Modalism, 213, 214
Modalistic Monarchianism, 214
Monergism, 429
Monotheism, 212
in OT, 189
Montanists, 520
Moral influence theory of Atonement, 337-38
Mortification, 466-67
Moses, 401-2
and glory, 103-4
Mourner's bench, 537
Mystery, 116
Mysticism, 399, 541
Myth, 120 n, 236, 236 n
National Holiness Association, 570
Natural man, 432
Natural religion, 609-10
Natural theology
Thomas Aquinas on, 149-50

Nature
and revelation, 56 n
as theological source, 55-56
Nature and grace
Wesleyan view, 159
Nature, human (see theological anthropology)
Negative theology, 107
Neoplatonism, 107-11
Nestorian controversy, 327-28
New birth
distinguished from sanctification, 451
New covenant, 175
New Testament theology, 174
Nicea, Council of, 212-20
Nihilism, 248
Novationists, 520
Old covenant, 175
Old man, 474
Old Testament
as gospel, 173
Omnipotence, 201
Omnipresence, 201-2
Omniscience, 202
Opera Trinitatis ad extra sunt indivisa, 232
Ordo cognoscendi, 163
Ordo essendi, 163
Ordo salutis, 480
Original righteousness
as freedom, 278
as image of God, 277-78
Original sin, 290-301, 483 n
as corruption of nature, 294-96
as loss of relation, 290-94, 297
Ousia, 221-23
Pantheism, 244
Papal infallibility, 81
Paradox, 43, 117, 330-31
Patripassianism, 195, 214
Pelagianism, 289, 299-300, 460
Penal theory of Atonement, 336-37
Penance, sacrament of, 437
Pentecost, 407, 408, 420, 422, 429-30
as the birthday of the Church, 492, 519
People of God, 507
Perfection as love, 458
Perichoresis, 232
Person, 226-27
meaning of, 203

Philosophy
  relation to theology, 29-30 n
  source of theology, 86-87
Philosophy of religion, 28-31
Plain Account of Christian Perfection,
  463, 467, 484, 487
Platonic anthropology, 325
Plenary inspiration, 72-73
Plymouth Brethren, 586
Pneuma, 426
Possessions, 494
Prayer, 262-66
  and faith, 265
  and fasting, 265-66
  types of, 262
Preaching
  centrality for Protestant worship,
  534-35
Predestination, 435-36
Prevenient grace, 197, 296, 333,
  338-39, 430, 432, 433
  as epistemological principle, 161
  and free will, 339
  and general revelation, 161-70
  and image of God, 157-61
  and infant baptism, 550
  and original sin, 290-96
  and repentance, 438
  and satisfaction theory, 365
  as theological norm, 49-50
  and universal atonement, 339
Primitive religions, 166
Princeton theology, 60 n
Prophecy
  ecstatic, 401
  as forthtelling, 617
Prophets
  eighth-century, 204, 349
  as forthtellers, 617
Protestant
  architecture, 534-35
  principle, 36, 209, 530
  Reformers
    on transcendence, 111-13
  scholasticism, 113-14
Providence, 256-58
  general, 256
  meaning of, 256
  special, 256-57
Psalms of Solomon, 311
Purity of intention, 464, 487-88
Quicunque Vult, 224
Ransom theory of Atonement,
  335-36

Rapture, 586
  secret, 586
Realistic theory of redemption,
  218-19, 307
Reason
  and fallenness, 132-39
  limitations of, 84-85
  preparation for faith, 84-85
  and revelation, 85, 132-39
Reconciliation, 339-52
  finished and unfinished, 341
  and justification, 372-73
  present and future, 341
Redeemer *(go'el),* 343
Redemption, 306-7, 343
Regeneration, 448-55 (see new
  birth)
  and adoption, 449-50
Relation
  and biblical language, 15-16
  internal and external, 15
  and substance, 14
Religion and opinion, 31
Religionsgeschichte, 35
Religious experience, 88-89
Religious language, 26, 92, 117-19
Repentance, 436-39, 472
  in the believer, 438, 466
  Calvinistic view, 363-64, 438 n
  and faith, 436-37
  and self-knowledge, 438
Representation and identification,
  Atonement motifs, 373
Resurrection
  bodily, 246
  of Jesus, 434, 476
Revelation
  and doctrine of God, 99-101
  as eschatological, 178-79
  and fallenness, 132-39
  history of, 98-99
  mode of, 173-74
  and reason, 132-39
  and salvation, 100, 131
Revivalism, 537, 549
Righteousness
  as attribute of God, 205-6
  ethical, 344
  God's, as faithfulness, 344
  multiple meanings, 343-47
  in the Psalms, 346 n
  as relational, 346
Ruach, 400, 430
Sabbath principle, 237

Sabellianism, 213
Sacrament
  as symbol, 543
  Wesley's definition, 542
  as witness to God's work, 543
Sacramentarianism, 542
Sacred dance, 401 n
Sacrifice
  and Atonement, 354-55
  and covenant making, 356
  as expiatory, 357
  meaning of, 355
  twofold meaning, 356
Saga, 236
Salvation, 245
  corporate character, 506
  process of, 441-76
Samaritan Pentateuch, 313-14
Sanctification
  ceremonial sense, 350, 469
  as corporate, 491
  defined, 441
  as discipleship, 351
  as doing the law, 462
  entire, 455-71
    as love, 452
    possibility of, 456
    as unmixed love, 490
  gradual, 467
  and Holy Spirit, 351, 428
  how to seek, 465-69
  imputed, 462-63
  initial, 351, 451, 452-55
  as instantaneous, 484-85
  interpreting, ways of, 457
  and Jesus Christ, 351-52
  and justification, relation to,
    47 n, 350
  linguistic analysis, 469-71
  as love expelling sin, 465
  NT use, 349-52
  OT hope, 349
  pneumatological language,
    470-71
  positive and negative aspects,
    479
  and possessions, 494
  prophetic or ethical, 348-49
  in the Reformers, 462
  as religious term, 348
  as renewal in the image of God,
    464-65
  as transformation of being,
    457-58

Satan (devil), 242
  origin of, 243
  and the serpent, 285 n
Satisfaction theories of Atonement,
  336-37
Satori, 24, 129
Scapegoat, 359-60
Scofield Bible, 588
Secret tradition, 81
Secularism, 184
Self-love, 497, 498 n
Septuagint, 600
Servant, Servant songs, 594-99
Session of Christ, 383
Sexuality
  as sin, 289-90
Shalom (peace), 486
Signs of the times, 574
Simul justus et peccator, 345, 463,
  522
Sin, 480
  actual, 283
  in believers, 480-81, 489
  as a covenant term, 276
  deliberate, 359
  as disobedience, 288-89
  dual in nature, 296-97
  as egocentricity or pride, 287-88
  as environmental exploitation,
    294
  essence of, 286-90
  as idolatry, 288, 496
  inadvertent, 358-59, 384
  inbred, indwelling, 298-301
  man in, 283-90
  offering, 358-59
  in OT, 349
  as ontological, 284-85
  original, 290-301, 483 n
    and actual sin, 296-301
    and guilt, 298
    and prevenient grace, 290-96
  as perversion, 246
  as a religious concept, 284
  as sensuality, 289-90
  as sexuality, 289-90
  as substance, 481
  transmission of, 300
  as unbelief, 286-87
  as universal, 299-301
Social ethics, 504
Sola scriptura, 81, 82, 86

Son of God
  and Messiah, 321-22
Son of Man, 316-18
  and Suffering Servant, 318
Sonship, 341-42
Special revelation, 175-77
  as gospel, 171
  in relation to general revelation, 178
Spirit (see Holy Spirit)
Spiritual maturation, 474-75
Subordinationism, 213, 214
Substance, 226
  and attributes of God, 198
Suffering Servant, 314, 353, 545
  and meaning of suffering, 255
  and sacrifice, 356
Supper sayings, 353
Symbol
  nonauthentic, 122
  as religious language, 121-22
Synergism, 429-30
Systematic theology, 33, 176
  definition of, 36-43
  and historical theology, 35-36
  norm of, 43-52
  organization, 12-13
  and philosophy, 13-14
  a rational discipline, 42
  and theological exegesis, 76
Teleological ethics, 500, 500 n
Temporary faith, 431 n
Temptation
  of Jesus, 326, 377, 409
Tetragrammaton, 105
Theologia crucis, 111, 112
Theologia gloria, 111
Theological anthropology, 140, 160
  man's essential goodness, 160-61
Theological exegesis, 75-76
Theological method, 94
Theology
  and the Church, 6, 9
  definition of, 9, 23
  and faith, 31-32
  and falsification, 26-27
  nature of, 10
  and ontology, 40
  and philosophy of religion, 28-30
  relation to philosophy, 29-30 n
  and religion, 30-31
  and the Scripture, 6

Theology, biblical
  definition of, 33
  history of, 33
Theology of history, 169 n
Theotokos, 327
Third use of the law, 369, 528
Time and eternity, 186, 201
Total depravity, 300-301
Tower of Babel, 292
Tradition
  as biblical interpretation, 79
  as creed, 80-81
  in Gnosticism, 81
  importance of, 81-83
  secret, 81
  subordinate to Scripture, 83
Transcendence, 101-22
  and God's knowability, 100
  in relation to revelation, 105
Transcendental ideas, 117-18
Transfiguration, 596-99
Transubstantiation, 552
Trent, Council of, 437, 606
  on witness of the Spirit, 442
Trinity
  derived from experience, 90
  contra pantheism and deism, 231-32
  and vital religious experience, 210-11
  and salvation, 226
Tritheism, 213
Truth
  as attribute of God, 204-5
  Greek view, 205
  and prevenient grace, 163
Tuesday Meeting for the Promotion of Holiness, 467-68
Typology, 618-23
Ultimate concern, 203
Vatican Council, First, 81
Via media, 47-48 n
Via negativa, 119-20
Vicarious Atonement, 376, 378, 379
Vicarious death, 378
Vicarious suffering, 376
Virgin Birth, 405-7
  as eschatological, 406-7
Voluntarism and intellectualism, 196
Wesleyan norm, 47-48
Wesleyan quadrilateral, 77

Western Church
  as legal-minded, 306, 324
Wisdom literature, 269
Witness of the Spirit, 441-48
  and assurance of salvation, 446
  criteria of genuineness, 445
  and the Cross, 445
  direct witness, 446
  and incarnational principle, 448
  indirect witness, 446
  and Phoebe Palmer, 468-69

Word
  and sacrament, 534-35
  and Spirit, 93
Word-flesh Christology, 325
Word-man Christology, 325
Wrath of God, 191-92, 291, 371-72,
  391-92
Yahweh, 105, 319, 400
Zen Buddhism, 24, 129, 399
Zwickau prophets, 93

Index of Persons

Abelard, 337-38
Adolphs, Robert, 515-16
Albright, W. F., 189
Alexander, James N. S., 612
Allegro, J. N., 624-25
Allport, Gordon, 472, 475
  experience, 400
Anderson, Bernhard W.
  eschatology, 268
Anselm
  satisfaction theory, 336
Aquinas, Thomas, 84
  knowledge of God, 117
  knowledge of self, 164
  natural theology, 149-50
  nature and grace, 149
  religious language, 120
  sanctification as love, 461-62
Athanasius, 279
  contra Arianism, 218
  Incarnation and *imago Dei,* 305
Augustine
  the Church, 521-22
  contra cyclical view of history,
    249-50
  denies freedom from sin, 459
  doctrine of illumination, 144
  the Eucharist, 558
  fallen reason, 133-34
  general and special revelation,
    148
  grace, 456
  the incarnate Logos, 134
  knowledge of God, 143-46
  love of things, 494
  memory, 143-46
  millenarianism, 579-82
  miracle, 261
  paradox, 190
  prophecy, 572
  reason, 84-85
  righteousness, 206
  Scripture, 68 n
  self-love, 498
  sin as concupiscence, 290, 460

(Augustine, *continued*)
  sin as perverted love, 459
  sin as pride, 287-88
  Son and Spirit, 224
  total depravity, 301
  trinitarian imago in man, 281-82
  the Trinity, 210, 221, 223-24
  volitional epistemology, 146-48
Aulen, Gustav, 561
  Christology, 330
  Christus Victor, 387
  creation, 247
  faith, 132
  image of God, 276-77, 286
  Incarnation as revelation, 305
  knowledge of God, 112
  natural and moral attributes, 198
  original sin, 301
  person, 227
  power and love, 200
  prayer, 264-65
  satisfaction, 364
  sin, 284
  systematic theology, 39, 42
  contra tritheism, 233
Ayer, A. J., 51
Baab, Otto, 186-87
Baillie, Donald
  anhypostasia, 328
  religious language, 119
Baillie, John, 128
  human nature, 160
Baker, Frank, 523
Barclay, William, 414, 578-79
  charismatic leadership, 402
  the Holy Spirit, 398
Barr, James
  dispensationalism, 588
Barth, Karl, 10-11
  vs. Emil Brunner, 152-54
  creation, 236
  the creation, 159
  essential Trinity, 230
  God's power, 200

(Barth, Karl, *continued*)
  image of God as male and
    female, 280
  image of God as relation, 156-57,
    279
  natural theology, 152
  religious language, 121
  revelation, 97-98
  sanctification, 351
  systematic theology, 52-53
  theological anthropology, 160
  transcendence, 184-85
Barth, Markus, 354-55
  sacrifice, 355 n
Bassett, Paul, 461, 490-91, 521,
    528, 536, 546
Bengel, Johann Albrecht, 582, 612,
    614-15
Berg, Daniel N., 526 (twice)
Berger, Peter, 613
Berkhof, Hendrikus, 78, 437, 516,
    536
  persistent prayer, 264
Berkouwer, G. C.
  image of God, 154, 155
Bewer, J. A., 627
Blackman, E. C., 608
Bloesch, Donald G.
  common grace, 296
  dispensationalism, 587-88
  imago as relic, 297
  wrath and love, 191
Böhler, Peter, 443, 444
Bonhoeffer, Dietrich
  image of God, 278
  loss of dominion, 292
Borgen, Ole, 555
Bornkamm, Gunther, 573-74
Bowman, John Wick, 311
  dispensationalism, 588
  prophetic Messiah, 315-16
Bresee, P. F., 583
Brevint, Daniel, 557, 563-64
Bright, John, 189
  kingdom of God, 388
  Suffering Servant, 594, 596
Brown, Raymond E., 413-14
Bruce, F. F., 597
Brunner, Emil
  vs. Karl Barth, 152-54
  creation, 240
  explanation, 235-36
  I-Thou knowledge, 128

(Brunner, Emil, *continued*)
  image of God as relation, 156
  natural theology, 152
Bultmann, Rudolf, 575, 598-99, 615
Buber, Martin, 127
Burkhardt, Helmut
  regeneration, 450
Burnaby, John, 161
Burnet, Thomas, 583
Burney, C. F., 315
Cairns, David
  body as imago, 282
  realistic theory of redemption,
    307
Callixtus
  the Church, 520
Calvin, John, 487
  accommodation, 135
  assurance, 446-47
  biblical authority, 62
  the Church, 528
  common grace, 296
  Eucharist, 554
  fallen reason, 134-35
  image of God, 156
  knowledge of God, 112-13
  law, function of, 369, 369 n
  Luther, contrast with, 369 n
  penal satisfaction theory, 336-37
  repentance and faith, 437-38
  speculation, 113
Cannon, William R., 444
Carpenter, Edward, 611
Carrel, Dr. Alexis
  prayer, 263
Cell, George Croft, 48
  Atonement in Wesley, 332
Cerinthus, 579
Chafer, Lewis Sperry, 588
Chalmers, Thomas, 488
Chambers, Oswald, 301
  conscience, 432-33, 435
Chapman, James B., 31, 537
  ethics, 502-3
  millenarianism, 584
Clarke, Adam, 471
Clement of Alexandria, 108-9,
    458-59
  adornment, 282
Collins, Anthony, 610-11
Confucius, 138
Corlett, D. Shelby
  ethics, 502-3

Craigie, Peter C.
  transcendence and immanence,
    185-86
Cranfield, C. E. B., 573
Cubie, Davie L., 527
Cullmann, Oscar, 544, 547
  Mark 14:61-62, 313
Culpepper, Robert, 382
  propitiation, 358
  sacrifice, 355
Cunliffe-Jones, H., 73-74
Curtis, Olin A.
  adoption, 450
  regeneration, 449
Cushman, Robert
  Augustine, 148
Cyprian, 214, 531
  the Church, 520
Cyril of Alexandria, 327-28
Dalton, William J., 571
Darby, J. N., 586
Davies, W. D.
  justification in Paul, 340 n
  Passover, 357
  sacrifice, 355
Dayton, Wilbur T., 453
Deasley, Alex R. G., 421, 519
  baptism in the Holy Spirit,
    423-24
Delitzsch, Franz, 291
Dentan, R. C., 35
Deschner, John, 50, 302
  justification in Wesley, 373
  wrath of God in Wesley, 372
Dillistone, F. W.
  cry of dereliction, 377
Dodd, C. H., 174, 428, 577, 590,
    599, 625
  wrath of God, 191-92
Downing, F. Gerald, 99-100
Earle, Ralph
  Jesus' baptism, 376
Eichrodt, Walther
  charismatic leadership, 401-2
Engels, Friedrich, 136-37
Farmer, H. H., 252
  personal God, 203
  prayer and miracle, 262
  providence, 257
Farrar, F. W., 600, 601, 602, 603
Ferm, Vergilius, 28-29
Ferré, Nels F. S.
  love and power, 199-200, 200
Feuerbach, Ludwig, 135-37

Fletcher, John
  doctrine of dispensations, 64,
    168-69, 400
  non-Christian religions, 170
  systematic theology, 50
Fortman, Edmund J., 226
Foster, R. S., 453
Freud, Sigmund, 137-38
Gabler, Johann Philipp, 34
Gilkey, Langdon, 247
  creation and metaphysics, 40 n
  doctrine of creation, 235
  holiness of God, 193
  meaning, 248
  religious language, 119
Gould, J. Glenn, 365
Greathouse, W. M., 471
  Acts, 419
  Christus Victor motif, 388
Gregory of Nazianzus, 326
Gregory of Nyssa, 490
Grotius, Hugo, 337
Harris, Rendel, 624
Hengstenberg, E. W., 34, 616
  prophecy, 617
Hepburn, Ronald, 128-29
Heron, Alasdair I. C., 554
  Paul and the Spirit, 424
Hill, David, 404
Hills, A. M., 61, 570, 583
Hobbes, Thomas, 295-96
Hodge, Charles, 53
von Hofmann, J. C. K., 615
Hogue, Wilson T., 452
Holmes, Arthur F., 131
  personal relation, 294
Homes, Nathaniel, 583
Howard, Richard E., 483
Hull, J. H. E.
  "filled with the Spirit," 421
Hume, David
  cosmological argument, 246-47
Hunter, A. M., 416-17, 425
Hyatt, J. Philip, 46
Ignatius of Antioch, 456
  Christology, 323-24
Irenaeus, 109-10, 531
  apostolic tradition, 79-80
  church as sphere of the Spirit,
    522
  image of God, 151
  the Logos, 111
  prophecy, 603-4

(Irenaeus, *continued*)
  recapitulation, theory of, 307,
    380-81
  sanctification, 458
  the Trinity, 228
Jacob, Edmund
  eschatology, 268
James, William, 397-98
Jeremias, J.
  John's baptism, 408
Johnson, Luke T., 494, 495
Jones, E. Stanley, 414
Kant, Immanuel, 117, 229, 499
  experience, 399
  teleological argument, 133
  universal moral consciousness,
    167
Kaufmann, Gordon, 41
  Incarnation, 304
  miracle, 262
Kelly, J. N. D., 80, 519, 520, 602,
    603-4, 604, 605
  Apollinarianism, 325
  relation, 223-24
Kierkegaard, Søren, 64, 114-15, 473
  learning truth, 141-43
Knight, John A., 169
Kung, Hans, 535
  apostolicity, 534
Ladd, G. Eldon, 387, 392, 417,
    476-77, 582
  flesh and Spirit, 413
  hell, 393-94
  Johannine Pentecost, 418
  Kingdom and Church, 517
  kingdom of God, 390
  Pauline view of sin, 288
  reconciliation, 340
  righteousness, 346
  wrath of God, 192
Law, William, 451
Lawson, John, 545
Lessing, G., 85, 142
Lewis, Arthur H., 583-84
Lewis, C. S., 259
Lindars, Barnabas, 596-97, 597
Lindsey, Hal, 570
Lindström, Harald, 457, 478, 479,
    485
Loetscher, L. L., 588
Lofthouse, W. F.
  Spirit in Acts, 422
Lonergan, Bernard, 220

Longenecker, Richard, 309, 311-12
  1 Enoch 37—71, 317
  Jesus' Sonship, 321-22
  Messianic claims, 314
Luther, Martin
  against allegory, 607
  Calvin, contrast with, 369 n
  the canon, 606
  consubstantiation, 553
  ecclesiology, 522
  general revelation, 167
  God's righteousness, 206
  the gospel, 172-73
  grace, 456-57, 540
  image of God, 152
  law, function of, 369
  resurrection, 477
  sin, 287
    as self-love, 290
  the Trinity, 299
  wrath of God, 191
MacDonald, Margaret, 586
McGiffert, A. C., 114, 611
MacGregor, Geddes, 195, 230
  divine self-limitation, 258
  evil, 251
Mackintosh, H. R., 323, 330-31
Macmurray, John, 130
Macquarrie, John, 232
  Karl Barth, 184-85
  the Cross and divine attributes,
    207
  immanent Trinity, 230-31
McQuilkin, J. R., 576-77
Manson, T. W.
  Messianic hope, 310
Martens, Elmer
  covenant, 358
  shalom, 486
Martin, Ralph P., 545, 546
  reconciliation, 340
Martyr, Justin, 108, 215-17, 602-3
  Second Coming, 578
Marx, Karl, 136-37
Maslow, A. H., 475
Melanchthon, Philipp, 333
Micklem, Nathaniel
  Atonement, 352
Micks, Marianne, 23-24
Minear, Paul, 509, 510, 511
Moody, Dale, 190
Morgan, G. Campbell
  prayer, 262

Moule, C. F. D., 317-18
Mowinckel, Sigmund
  Messianic hope, 310-11
Mulholland, M. Robert, 510
Narramore, Bruce, 497-98
Nelson, J. Robert, 536
Niebuhr, H. Richard, 172
Niebuhr, Reinhold
  pride as sin, 287
  sin as sensuality, 289, 290
Origen
  biblical interpretation, 604
  Eternal Generation of the Son,
    217
  God, 109
  Scripture, 68 n
  the Trinity, 213
Outler, Albert, 541-42
Oxtoby, Gurdon C., 617-18
Paley, William, 247
Palmer, Phoebe, 467-69
Pannenberg, Wolfhart, 302
Paul of Samosata, 215
Peck, J. T., 454
Peters, John
  Wesley on entire sanctification,
    465
Philo, 107-8, 601
Pinnock, Clark H., 61-62
Plato
  anthropology, 325
  cosmology, 241
Polyani, Michael, 127
Pope, William Burt, 453, 479
  millenarianism, 579
  vicarious Atonement, 379
Preus, Christian, 616
Purkiser, W. T., 11, 16, 240
  knowledge of God, 131
  sin, 275
Quick, Oliver Chase, 381
von Rad, Gerhard
  chaos, 253
  typology, 620
Rahner, Karl
  eschatological hermeneutics,
    574-77
  mystery, 116
Rall, H. F., 184
Ralston, T. N., 453
Ramsey, A. M., 102
Ramsey, Paul, 156, 493, 498
Rattenbury, J. Ernest, 384, 385
  Wesley and Atonement, 333 n
Read, David H. C., 507

Renshaw, John Rutherford, 334-35
  wrath of God in Wesley, 372
Richardson, Alan, 90, 105, 220,
    343, 417
  adoptionism, 215
  baptism, 385
  Church as Body of Christ, 514
  general revelation, 178
  hell, 393
  knowledge of God, 125
  the last judgment, 392
  Luther's exegesis, 609
  propitiation, 357-58
  repentance, 449
  revelation as miraculous, 261
  Servant of the Lord, 354
  Son of God, 321
  special revelation, 178
  typology, 619, 621
  Virgin Birth, 406-7
Richardson, Cyril
  the Trinity, 227
Ridderbos, Herman, 426
  reconciliation, 340
Robinson, H. Wheeler, 300
Robinson, John A. T., 184
Robinson, William
  evil, 242
  providence, 258
  suffering and the Cross, 255
Rogers, Jack, 10, 31-32, 52
Rogers, Karl, 400
Rowley, H. H.
  identification, 375
  sacrifice, 356 n
Ryle, Gilbert, 259
Ryrie, Charles C., 586
Sabellius, 214
Sanday, William, 69-70
Sartre, Jean-Paul, 248
Schleiermacher, Friedrich, 87-88,
    616
  fruit of the Spirit, 427-28
  miracle, 261
  prophecy, 616-17
  religion, 243-44
Schnackenburg, Rudolf, 495 (twice)
Schweitzer, Albert
  kingdom of God, 389
Seiss, Joseph A., 582
Sellers, R. V.
  realistic theory of redemption,
    307

Shedd, Russell Phillip
  Incarnation, 376
Shelton, R. Larry, 62-63
  sin as relation, 361
Sherlock, Thomas, 611
Smart, James D.
  allegory, 614
  typology, 622
Smith, George Adam, 598
Snaith, Norman, 187
  righteousness, 344-45
Socrates
  as intellectual midwife, 142
Spangenberg, A. G., 443-44
Sproul, R. C., 10
Spurrier, William
  Atonement, 335
Steele, Daniel, 470, 583
  experience, 400
Stewart, James S., 477
  Paul and the Spirit, 424
Stonehouse, Ned B., 429-30
Sugden, E. H., 442
Taylor, Richard S.
  biblical authority, 63
  initial sanctification, 455
Taylor, Vincent, 373, 377, 384
  reconciliation, 340
  representation, 375
Taylor, Willard H., 518
Temple, William, 128, 176, 245
Tertullian, 110
  influence of Atonement theory,
    336
  Christology, 324
  church as sphere of the Spirit,
    522
  corporeal nature of God, 110 n
Theodore of Mopsuestia, 605-6,
  613
  Christology, 326
Thielicke, Helmut, 37-38, 45
Tillich, Paul
  denominational tradition, 83
  experience, 89
  immanent Trinity, 230-31
  knowledge of God, 143
  Lutheran view of sanctification,
    369 n
  mystery, 116
  personal God, 203
  Protestant principle, 209-10
  sin as ontological, 284-85
  symbol, 121

(Tillich, Paul, continued)
  systematic theology, 42
  theistic arguments, 163
  theological norm, 43-44
  theonomous ethics, 499
  tradition, 82
Torrance, T. F.
  Calvin, 156
  essential Trinity, 230
  knowledge of God, 185
Trueblood, D. Elton
  Feuerbach, 136
  illusionistic critiques, 138
Vriezen, Th. C., 508, 508 n
Watkin-Jones, Howard, 442
Watson, Richard, 452
Weber, Otto, 577
Weiss, Johannes, 577
Wellhausen, Julius, 35
Wesley, Charles, 341, 480
Wesley, John
  analogy of faith, 608-9
  Anglican ecclesiology, 526
  Athanasian Creed, 226
  Atonement, 332-33, 333 n
  baptism and regeneration, 547
  biblical authority, 61
  Christ and the law, 305-6
  the Church, 523-28
  Clement's Christian Gnostic,
    459 n
  conscience, 167
  consubstantiation, 554
  conversion, 489
  direct witness, 446
  eschatology, 569-70
  ethical language, use of, 470
  evangelism, 370-71
  experience, 90-91, 92
  faith, 370 n, 439-40
  faith not a good work, 440
  fulfillment, 611
  fundamental doctrines, 12
  general revelation, 168
  image of God, 277
  Incarnation theories, 302-3
  infant baptism, 548-50
  inspiration, use of term, 430 n
  inspiration of Scripture, 66
  intellect and will, 196
  justification, 345-46
  justification and regeneration,
    448-49

(Wesley, John, *continued*)
  justification and sanctification,
    48 n
  kingly office, 386
  knowledge of God, 128
  the law, 368-70
  logic, 86
  marks of the new birth, 451
  means of grace, 540-42
  metaphorical language for sin,
    484-85
  natural man, 157-58, 431-32
  natural senses, 84
  natural theology, 133
  ongoing work of Christ, 383
  ontological dependence, 245
  optimism of grace, 464
  original sin and guilt, 298
  poverty and riches, 496
  preparation for entire
    sanctification, 466
  prophetic fulfillment, 572
  purity of intention, 487-88
  reason, 43, 83
  regeneration, 351
  religion, 31
  repentance, 438, 439 n
  representation, 378
  rich young ruler, 495
  rules, 502
  sanctification as love, 465
  satisfaction theory of the
    Atonement, 334
  sin defined, 288
  sin as unbelief, 287
  sincerity, 493
  social religion, 507
  theoretical explanations, 68
  transubstantiation, 552-53
  Trinitarian significance, 232
  the Trinity, 209
  witness of the Spirit, 441-42
  Word and Spirit, 93
Wesley, Susanna, 502
  the Eucharist, 556-57
Westcott, B. F., 434
Whale, J. S., 183, 211, 218
Whiston, William, 610
Whitby, Daniel, 582
Wiles, Maurice F., 45-46
Wiley, H. Orton, 11, 520
  adoption, 450
  Arianism, 218

(Wiley, H. Orton, *continued*)
  biblical authority, 57, 62
  the call, 435
  Christ, 56
    as prophet, 367
  continuous sanctification, 359
  creation as historical, 284
  creation narratives, 236
  the Cross and divine attributes,
    207
  defining God, 186
  divine attributes, 197
  dynamical theory of inspiration,
    69
  election and predestination,
    435-36
  essential Trinity, 228
  experience, 88
  faith as trust, 440
  glory, 102-3
  God as holy love, 197
  inspiration, 72-73
  intercession of, 383-84
  the judgment, 393
  knowledge of God, 128
  miracle, 261
  natural attributes, 198-99
  Origen, 217
  original sin and guilt, 298
  person, 227
  philosophy, 42
  prophecy, 572
  reason, 85
  regeneration and initial
    sanctification, 454 n
  representative theory of
    Atonement, 379
  contra satisfaction theory, 362-65
  sin and human nature, 300
  systematic theology, 54
  theology as a science, 51-52
  transcendence of God, 105
  tree of life, 279
  the Trinity, 213, 219
    as soteriological, 232
  truth, 54
  wrath of God, 192
Williams, Colin, 73, 85, 89, 333,
    512, 515, 528
Wilson, John Cook
  intuitive knowledge, 164-65
Wittgenstein, Ludwig, 469
Wolfson, H. A., 226
Workman, H. B., 441, 448

Wrede, William, 312
Wright, G. Ernest, 189
Wynkoop, Mildred Bangs, 471, 480,
    481, 484

Yates, A. S.
    assurance, 444-45
Zachariae, B. T., 33-34
Zwingli, Huldreich, 555

Scripture References

Genesis
1—11 276, 279,
 290-91, 294-95
1:1 26, 279
1:1-2 253
1:1—2:4a 235-40,
 279
1:2 234, 430
1:26 149, 151, 279,
 282
1:27 279
1:28 283
1:31 239
2:7 65
2:25 281
3:5 287
3:8 279
3:9 291
3:10 291
3:18 292
3:22 293
3:24 291
4:9 295
6:1-8 295
6:2 321
9:6 151
11:1-9 292
12:3 512
15 357 (twice)
38 348
38:26 347
40:12 556
45:7-8b 257
Exodus
3:2 112
4:22 321
6:7 124
8:19 410
9:27 205
10:1-2 124
12:11 556
12:14 558
14:13 344
14:17-18 102
14:30 171
15:2 344
15:8 400
16:7 102

16:10 102
17:6 413-14
18:8-11 124
20:2 186
20:3 188
24 357
24:7 321
24:10 104 n
28:3 402
31:3 402
31:18 410
33:18 102
33:18-23 103
35:31 402
40:34 104
Leviticus
1—7 375
19:1-2 351
Numbers
11:17 402
11:25 ff. 402
11:29 174, 188, 403
27:18 402
Deuteronomy
1:27 206
4:32-39 124
5:2-3 374
5:24 102
6:4 189
14:29 205
16:11, 14 206
18 314
21:23 434, 603
23 348
30:6 463
34:9 402
Joshua
24 188
24:19, 23 188-89
Judges
3:10 401
6:34 401
8:19 187
11:29 401
Ruth
3:13 187
1 Samuel
10:6 ff. 401

10:6, 9-10 401
16:13-14 402
16:14 ff. 242
18:10 242
19:6 187
19:9 242
19:20 ff. 401
20:21 187
24:17 347
26:23 347
2 Samuel
4:11 347
6 189
7:14 321
19:28 347
21:2 188
22:16 400
23:2 402
1 Kings
19:16 366 n
22:20-23 242
Job
1:6 321
38:7 321
42:1-5 254-55
Psalms
2 605, 606
2:7 316, 321, 407,
 595
8 605
8:4-5 317
16 606
18:15 400
19:1 102
21 606
22 606
24 189
25:4, 12 125
34:8 90
45 605
49:16-20 101-2
50:5 357
51 403, 408
51:3 124
51:4 284
51:11 403
51:16-17 359
55 606

667

69   606
74   254
77   254
85:10   207
89   606
89:26 ff.   321
96:3   102
102:25-27   320
104:30   234
110   605
112:19   205
118:22-23   593
119   125
130:8   463
139:7-10   202
148:1-6   239
148:13   102
Proverbs
25:3   125
Ecclesiastes
1:2, 9   249
1:5-7   249
8:14   270
Isaiah
1:21-26   620-21
6   187-88
6:1   104 n
6:3   102
7:14   597-98
7:17-20   626
11:1   598
11:2   404 (twice)
11:4   400
11:6-8   620
24—27   268
27:1   268
31:1, 3   193
32:15   544
33:14-16   189
35:10   267
40—55   255, 267,
   343 (twice), 508
40:5   102
40:21-23, 25-26   267
41:14   343
42:1   316, 407, 595
42:1-4   404
42:1-7   592
42:6   354
43:1   343
43:10   508
43:24d-26   343-44
44:6   344
44:24-28   267
45:17   344
45:23   320
46:13   344

47:4   334
48:6b-7   267
49:1-6   592
49:8   354
50:4-9   592
51:9-11   254
52:10   344
52:13—53:12   375,
   592
53   356, 596-97
53:2   406
54:9-10   267
56—66   511
60:1   102
60:1-3   104
61:1   409
61:1-2   171
63:10   403
63:10-11   403
65:17   268
66:11-12   102
66:22   268
Jeremiah
2   175
7   513
7:32   393
10:10   187
17:5-8   293
17:9   299
19:6   393
26   513
30:7   586
31:15   572, 598
31:31-34   175, 349
Ezekiel
2:2   402
3:24   402
31:31 ff.   403
36:25-27   349
36:25, 29   463
36:26 ff.   403
36:27   175, 404
37:1-14   404
37:21 ff.   310
39:29   544
Daniel
4:27   205
7:13   317
9:25-26   310
Hosea
2:16-20   620
4:1-2   125
6:6   125
11:1   321, 598
11:1 f.   605
Joel
2:28-29   403, 606

2:28-32   174
Amos
1—2   270, 295
5:18-27   513
9:11   606
9:13   620
Micah
3:8   402
4:1-3   605
5:1-2   605
6:8   169
Haggai
2:9   605
2:11-13   371
Zechariah
5:1-4   349
5:5-11   349
9—14   349
9:9   311, 606
11:12-14   605
12:10   605
13:1   349
Malachi
1:11   605
3:1   606
3:6   202
4:5-6   605
Matthew
1:23   597-98
2:15   598
2:17-18   572, 598,
   611
2:23   598
3:2   389
3:7   392
3:9   375
3:11   407, 544
4:1   409
4:3, 6   321
4:17   389
5:21-22   392
5:23-24   493
5:37   279
5:48   351, 463, 494
6:10   389
6:19-34   494
6:33   498
7:12   504
7:21-23   319
7:23   393, 394
8:11   518
8:12   393, 394
10:28   393
11:25-27   321
11:28-29   367
12:28   409
12:29   407, 434
12:32   410

16:3 574
16:13-20 595
16:16 74
16:17 313
16:18 6, 517
16:21 592
16:21-23 592
16:23 592
16:25 118, 513
19:16-27 495
19:28 448
20:28 335
21:42 593
22:13 393
22:29 407
22:37, 39 463
23:17, 19 349
24:36 574
25:12, 30 393
25:31-46 318
25:40 318
26:24 593
26:26, 28 556
26:28 353
26:54, 56 593
Mark
1:8 407
1:11 595
1:12 409
1:15 389
1:23-25, 34 312
1:43-44 312
2:10, 28 318
3:11-12 312
3:22-26 409
3:27 407, 434
3:30 410
4:41 254
5:43 312
6:51 254
7:20-23 299
7:36 312
8:27 ff. 313
8:31 318
8:31-33 592
8:35 118
9:7 104
9:9 312
9:12 318
9:43-48 392
10:17-28 495
10:45 318, 335, 596
12:10-11 593
12:30-31 464
13 573
13:32 574
14:41 318

14:61-62 312-13, 318
15:2 ff. 313
15:39 320
Luke
1:68 334
2:38-39 420
3:7 392
3:16 407, 544
4:1 409
4:3, 9 321
4:18 366
4:18, 21 171
7:36 495
8:3 495
9:24 118
10:29 493
10:36 493
10:38-42 495
10:45 343
11:2 389, 410 n
11:20 410
12:50 595
13:27 394
14:1 495
16:29, 31 260
17:24-25 318
22:19 555
23:47 320
24 571
24:21 592
24:25-27 592
24:27 592
24:44 593
24:45 593
John
1 239
1:3 234
1:9 158, 162, 333
1:14 85, 104, 116, 304, 368
1:17 412
1:18 305
1:32-33 411
2:22 592
3 400, 448
3:1-8 411-12
3:3 412
3:8 449
3:18-20 392
3:33-34 412
4 313-14, 319
4:14-24 412
5:39-40 593
6 592
6:15 314
6:35-65 413

6:63 412
7:37-39 415
7:38 413
7:38-39 411, 413-16
8:23 412
8:44 243
11:1 ff. 495
12:1 ff. 495
12:31-33 434
13:1 373
14—16 422
14:6 12
14:9 305
14:15 488
14:15-17 415
14:17 416
14:25-26 415
14:26 417
15:26 417
15:26-27 415
16:5-11 415
16:7 415-16
16:8-11 433
16:12-15 415
16:13-14 417
17 422, 531
17:20-23 463
17:21, 22 422
17:22 492
20:22 411, 415, 417
20:23 417
20:31 318
Acts
1:4-5 423
1:5 407
1:7 580
1:8 420
1:21 ff. 533
2 400
2:17 544
2:36 319
2:38 546
3:24 591
4:12 162
5:3 492
5:11 525
7:56 316
8:10 320
8:12-24 546
9:17-18 546
10:34-35 169
10:38 407
10:41 533
10:44-48 546
12:22 320, 321
13:2 519
14:11 ff. 320

14:17 162
17:26-27 168
17:28 245-320
19:5-6 546
24:16 445
28:6 320
Romans
1 168
1—3 133, 276
1:1-2 591
1:3-4 319
1:5 289
1:16 172
1:18 288
1:20 150
2:14 168
3:21 345, 348
3:23 276, 300
3:24—4:25 347
5 298
5:1 341
5:2 105
5:8 195
5:9 372
5:10 341
5:11 339
5:13 298
5:20 465
5:21 480
6 350
6:1 545
6:4 545
6:6 474
6:12 480
7:7-8 289
8 351
8:3-4 463
8:7 483 n
8:9 426
8:9-11 425
8:11 476, 477
8:15 342
8:15-16 342
8:16 442
8:18 105
8:23 342, 476, 477
8:28-29 257, 508
9—11 587
9:4 104
9:13 196
9:23 105
9:25-26 511
9:28 455, 466
9:31 344
10:9 318
10:17 265, 440
11 512

11:1 532
12:6 608
13:8 496
13:10 488
14:23 286-87
15:16 351
16:26 289
1 Corinthians
1:2 350
1:9 192, 342, 531
1:18-25 178
1:20-31 354
2:2 172
2:7 112
3:1 532
3:18-19 139
5 427
5:7 357
6:11 350, 351 (twice)
6:12 503
7 79
7:15 341
8 239
8:3 125
8:5 ff. 319
8:6 234
10:4 414
10:13 192
10:16 342, 559
10:24 493
11:7 276
11:23 ff. 563
11:24-25 555
11:26 561
13 427
13:12 100, 178, 460
14 427 n
14:34 501 n
15:1-3 78-79
15:3 382
15:17 383
15:22 377
15:23 357
15:26 386
2 Corinthians
1:20 386
1:22 476
3 306, 368, 594
3:14-16 594
3:17 425
3:18 105, 151, 276, 352, 474-75
4:4 434
4:6 104, 179
4:7 246
4:17 105
5:1-18 179

5:5 476
5:10 393
5:16-21 341
5:17 153, 449
5:19 177, 341, 377
5:21 378 n
7:1 463
13:14 531
Galatians
3:1-5 426
3:28 532
4:3-7 342
4:6 342, 426
4:9 125
4:21-31 614
4:24 556
5:5 348
5:6 49, 465
5:22 341
5:22-23 489
5:23 427-28
6:16 513
Ephesians
1 239
1:5 342
1:10 380
1:13-14 476
2:1 581
2:2 387, 434
2:4 192
2:12-17 341
3:14-19 463
4 350
4:1 525
4:1-6 525
4:3-6 341
4:5 530
4:8 354
4:11-16 515
4:13 352, 473, 533
4:19-25 474
4:22-24 474
5:25-27 463, 517-18
6:4 550
Philippians
1:9 463
1:10 493
1:27 175
2:1 426, 531
2:5 369, 465
2:6-11 79
2:9 320
2:10-11 320
3:8 367
3:10 342
3:12-16 473
4:7 341
4:19 104

Colossians
1 239
1:13 387
1:15 306
1:16-17 234
1:20 341
2:6-7 441, 531
2:10-11 531
2:12 477, 545, 545 n
2:15 354, 386, 387
3 350
3:1 545
3:4 105
3:9 474
3:15 341
1 Thessalonians
1:4-6 426
1:5 425
1:10 392, 559
2:13 426
4:3 350
4:3 ff. 426
4:17 586
5:1 ff. 574
5:16-18 488
5:19-20 425
5:21 425-26
5:23 350, 456, 463
5:24 192
2 Thessalonians
2:1-11 572
2:13 351
2:14 105
2:16 192
3:16 341
1 Timothy
2:9-10 282
3:16 79
4:10 168
5:8 496

2 Timothy
2:13 201
3:16 65
3:16-17 65, 66
Titus
1:2 201
2:11 168
2:14 343
3:5 448
Hebrews
1:1-3 319
1:3 104, 306
1:10-12 320
2:6 316
4:12 392
6:4 ff. 520
6:18 201
7:25 559
9:11-14 351
9:13-14 350
9:14 381
10:10, 14, 29 350
10:15 562
10:26 ff. 520
11:1 370 n, 440, 463
11:6 169
12:10 468
13:12 350
James
1:17 263
1:21 448
5:12 279
1 Peter
1:2 351, 359
1:14 289
1:15-16 351
1:23 448
2:2 532-33
2:9-10 511
3:3-5 282

2 Peter
1:16-19 179
1:18-19 596
1:20-21 65, 67
2:4 243
3:8 66, 578
3:13 268
3:18 64, 473
1 John
1:3 342
1:5 342
1:7 342
2:1-2 384
2:12-14 533
2:16 377
2:29 342
3:4 288
3:8 243, 463
4:8 342
4:15 377
4:17 392
4:19 195, 489
5:3 489
5:7 412
5:12 342
Jude
6 243
19 525
Revelation
1:13 316
14:14 316
17:14 268-69
20 578, 579
20:1-10 581, 584
20:2-7 581
20:5-6 581
21:1 254, 268
21:4 254